"The Most Dangerous Communist in the United States"

"The Most Dangerous Communist in the United States"

A BIOGRAPHY OF HERBERT APTHEKER

Gary Murrell

With an afterword by Bettina Aptheker

University of Massachusetts Press   AMHERST AND BOSTON

ISBN 978-1-62534-154-9 (paperback); 153-2 (hardcover)

Designed by Dennis Anderson
Set in Garamond Premier Pro by House of Equations, Inc.
Printed and bound by Sheridan Books, Inc.

Library of Congress Cataloging-in-Publication Data

Murrell, Gary, 1947–
"The most dangerous communist in the United States" : a biography of Herbert Aptheker /
Gary Murrell.
     pages cm
Includes bibliographical references and index.
ISBN 978-1-62534-154-9 (paperback : alkaline paper) —
ISBN 978-1-62534-153-2 (hardcover : alkaline paper)
1. Aptheker, Herbert, 1915–2003.   2. Historians—United States—Biography.
3. African Americans—Historiography.   4. Du Bois, W. E. B. (William Edward Burghardt),
1868–1963—Friends and associates.   5. Communists—United States—Biography.
6. Communist Party of the United States of America—Biography.
7. Political activists—United States—Biography.   8. Radicals—United States—Biography.
9. Intellectuals—United States—Biography.   I. Title.
CT275.A7935M87   2015
973.07202—dc23
                              2015009738

British Library Cataloguing in Publication Data
A catalogue record for this book is available from the British Library.

Publication of this volume and other titles in the series In the Spirit of
W. E. B. Du Bois, edited by John H. Bracey Jr., is supported by the
Office of the Dean, College of Humanities and Fine Arts, University of
Massachusetts Amherst.

Frontispiece: photograph of Herbert Aptheker, date unknown, no. 0174,
The Daily Worker and the *Daily World* Photographs Collection (Photos 223),
box no. 4, folder no. 589, Tamiment Library and Robert F. Wagner Labor Archives,
New York University.

To Nelle Brady, Linda Orgel, Arthur (R. D.) Grunbaum, Fred Rakevich, and good people throughout the world who carry on the struggle for political, social, and economic justice.

The evil that men do lives after them;
The good is oft interrèd with their bones.

—Shakespeare, *The Tragedy of Julius Caesar*

Contents

Preface

THE RECENT deaths of Eric Hobsbawm and Eugene Genovese remind us that few members of the first generation of eminent Marxist historians remain. Herbert Aptheker was a charter member of that generation. After reading his three-volume *History of the American People,* I was intrigued and went for the first time to hear him speak at a Marxist Scholars Conference at the University of Washington in the late 1980s. A few years later Herbert, accompanied by his wife, Fay, spent a week as a scholar in residence at my alma mater, Southern Oregon State College (as it was known then). That week I heard several of Herbert's presentations and had the opportunity to have dinner with him and Fay and to engage in lively conversation with them in people's homes. Herbert and Fay both were delightful, warm, open, often funny, and enormously considerate.

In the early 1990s, while working on my doctoral degree at the University of Oregon, I suggested to my adviser that perhaps I should write a biography of Herbert for my dissertation. "Absolutely not," he said. "Aptheker's work can't be trusted." Much more acceptable to him was a biography of a reactionary, anti–New Deal former governor of Oregon. Washington State University published my biography of that governor in 2000: *Iron Pants: Oregon's Anti–New Deal Governor, Charles Henry Martin.*

I began research for a biography of Herbert in 1999 after turning in the manuscript for the Martin book. That summer I contacted Herbert to propose the project, and he agreed to meet with me for a series of interviews, which we completed over a ten-day period in August, two months after Fay's death. We talked for a total of about thirty-five hours. Herbert was eighty-four years old at the time and in ill health after a decade-long series of strokes. He lost track of his thoughts at times and tended to repeat himself. He had difficulty remembering names and confused dates. He broke down in tears, understandably, when talking about Fay, whose death he still felt as a raw wound. He spoke warmly and with a father's pride about his daughter, Bettina. For the most part, though, he was animated, especially when talking about the Second World War, a topic to which he returned often. When the subject of his major publications came up, his legendary arrogance and sense of self-importance at times overwhelmed our conversations. If he wanted to emphasize what he was saying, he would point-edly stop the discussion to ask if I understood the importance of what he had said. "I don't think you do," he declared several times and then repeated more emphatically the point he had just made.

He responded fully to all of my questions except when it came to the Com-munist Party, about which he was evasive and talked about by resorting to plati-tudes. When I asked about specific people he told me that this or that person was quite a person, wonderful, brilliant, remarkable: "I admired him . . ." or "I loved him . . ." or "I was very close to him." About other people, almost all of whom had quit the Communist Party, he said they were "limited, emotional, remote." His responses when discussing the party, except when it came to Henry Winston, Elizabeth Gurley Flynn, and Gus Hall, were flat: his words had no depth, no emotion, little analysis. When I asked about the specific actions the party took or how or why decisions were made within the leadership, his stan-dard answer was that he had not been in the leadership, and then he quickly moved on. At some points he simply refused to answer my questions. "You don't need it," he said very forcefully in response to questions dealing with personali-ties within the party leadership: "It's not necessary. . . . I don't want to do it. It's a question of families." More often than not he became defensive and turned the conversation to the actions taken against him by a vindictive capitalist system that failed to give him his due because he was a communist.

I realized later, after viewing earlier recorded interviews he had given and reading interview transcripts as well as his unpublished autobiography, that many of his responses to my questions were verbatim reiterations of statements he had previously made to others, either verbally or in writing. He told the same stories, emphasized the same points, used exactly the same words: he had created a script for his life, and he resisted deviating from it.

I corresponded with Herbert for the next three years and, at his insistence, twice returned to talk with him again. He was now fragile and repeated many of the points he had made in our original interviews. After his death on 17 March 2003, I attended the memorial at Saint Peter's Church in Manhattan in October that celebrated the lives of both Fay and Herbert. Bettina gave a moving and often funny tribute to her mother and father. Toward the end of her eulogy she interjected a disturbing anecdote that, in the course of the event, went almost unnoticed: "Ten days after my mother died," she began, "dad asked me if he had ever hurt me as a child. 'Yes,' I said finally, he had. And so we talked. For someone who never expressed personal emotion, who never processed anything, he was amazing. He stayed with this conversation with me for over an hour. He was filled with remorse and anguish. He asked me to forgive him. Of course I did. And then I wanted so much to help him to heal. . . . And, of course, I loved him," she said, "with a great lump in my throat the size of the century, I loved him."

I made a note on a piece of paper: "Ask Bettina how Herbert had hurt her." I didn't. I forgot.

I knew Bettina slightly at the time. I met her in August 1999 when I interviewed Herbert, two months after the remarkable conversation that she recounted at the memorial service and developed more fully in her memoir. Our interactions since that first meeting have been conducted through correspondence. She has been, throughout that time, even through flashes of irritation over one point or another, a warm, caring, encouraging confidant and enormously helpful to me while I was writing this biography. She read early drafts of the manuscript and made probing comments and useful suggestions.

In 2005 Bettina had her publisher send me a bound galley of her memoir, *Intimate Politics: How I Grew Up Red, Fought for Free Speech, and Became a Feminist Rebel.* In the memoir Bettina revealed that over the course of the eight years it took her to write the book, memories she had repressed suddenly "erupted . . . often unbidden." She remembered that Herbert had sexually molested her from the age of three until she was thirteen. I read and reread that paragraph in the introduction to *Intimate Politics* in which she introduced the "choo choo train" game she and Herbert played on the living room Persian rug. I kept telling myself, "No, I didn't read that right. That's not what she is saying. For ten years? 1947 to 1957?" After an interview, the historian Chris Phelps quoted me in an article he wrote about Bettina's revelations for the *Nation* as saying my "jaw dropped." I guess that's right. I recall feeling numb, stunned, and sick at heart and having a tremendous feeling of sadness: for Bettina, for Fay, for Herbert, for Bettina's children, for Herbert's comrades. I put the manuscript for the biography aside for two years while I attempted to process Bettina's charge of incestuous molestation.

I did, however, observe the firestorm that developed after Phelps published a review of the memoir in the *Chronicle of Higher Education* a month before its official publication. "He focused entirely on the revelations about childhood sexual abuse as a way to reconcile his understanding of the historian Herbert Aptheker," Bettina wrote later. "From a feminist perspective," she said, "it was as though I had had no life at all." As Phelps wrote in another piece in the *Nation* in 2007, "Its greatest reverberations . . . have been among radicals, historians, and African-Americans, particularly those who knew and respected Herbert Aptheker." Some critics, apparently without reading the book, denounced Bettina from the perspective of their years of friendship with Herbert. The historian Herbert Shapiro, who knew Herbert for four decades, rejected Bettina's accusation in a letter to the *Chronicle of Higher Education:* "My wife and I find the accusations quite unbelievable, both in terms of Herbert's moral character and the unlikelihood that Fay, a most perceptive woman, would have seen nothing grievously amiss in the relationship between father and daughter."

Others, as Phelps pointed out, took to the H-Net discussion list of the History of American Communism, where they "homed in on her admission that she had failed to remember the abuse for decades." Her "recovered memories are less than convincing evidence," wrote the historian Melvyn Dubofsky. David Horowitz, no friend of Herbert or Bettina, said he suspected that "the incest story is probably made up." The historian John Bracey, who knew both Bettina and her father, found himself in a quandary: "If somebody had come to me and said that Herbert had done that, I wouldn't have believed it," he told Phelps, "but I also know that Bettina wouldn't make up something like that."

Then the tone of the discussion changed. The historian Jesse Lemisch, Herbert's comrade in the battle against C. Vann Woodward and Yale University to defend Herbert's academic freedom, staunchly defended Bettina in an article on the History News Network titled "Shhh! Don't Talk about Herbert Aptheker." "All this leads me to the conclusion that a general public silence by Old Leftists in response to the report of Herbert Aptheker's sexual molestation of his daughter Bettina may be writing another chapter in the strange history of American Communism," Lemisch wrote. "Fellow Red Diaper Babies and many former Communists seem to want to sweep this under the rug—or, may I say, airbrush it—as if there had never been a Women's Liberation Movement, and it had never occurred to anybody that there might be a connection between the personal and the political, or as Bettina puts it in her memoir . . . 'The personal reveals the political . . . relations of power are often enacted in moments of intimacy.'" Ruth Rosen, in a very favorable review in the *San Francisco Chronicle,* called the memoir "a political, intellectual and emotional story of one woman's redemption. . . . Her revelation is not an act of vengeance. . . . Bettina Aptheker's life and intellectual biography make no sense without understanding what she suffered and repressed."

Although I can't claim to have been close to Herbert or to have been privy to his personal life except as it was revealed in his papers, ten years of incestuous pedophilia just seems so inconsistent, so beyond the realm of possibility, for the man I interviewed and came to know through the research. Herbert sent anguished letters to Fay from Europe during the war, many of them centered on the plight of starving, abused children. To think of him as having molested his daughter almost from the time he left the army through the decade of McCarthyism is incongruous with the real anguish displayed in his letters.

Bettina suggested to me and told Phelps that she thinks Herbert "was abused as a child in some manner, shape or form, he may well have had his own memories of that but never talked about it. We don't know . . . that's entirely speculative." If Bettina is right, then perhaps the idyllic childhood he always claimed to have had was somehow not so idyllic, and some childhood experience led him to abuse her. It is possible that post-traumatic stress disorder (PTSD) resulting from his war experiences could have been a factor. Bettina said in her eulogy, "Memories of atrocity and suffering haunted him."

Like Bracey, I am conflicted. I too do not believe Bettina would invent a tale of abuse at the hands of her father. I know she believes her repressed memories are real and therefore that her accusations deserve credence. And yet, as a classically trained historian who employs the usual tools of the trade, emphasizing primary sources, I have reservations about the validity of memory, my own included. Memory is a mystery. Speaking personally, I have a vivid memory of an adventure from forty-five years ago, when I was twenty years old. I recently mentioned that adventure to one of the participants, and much to my amazement he told me I wasn't even present, that I had heard the story from him. Granted, my memory has nothing to do with incest or sexual abuse, but it tells me I was there. How could that memory be so clear if I wasn't there? "Malignant memory, cruel, taunting, deceiving," Bill Ayres wrote in his memoir, *Fugitive Days*, "—it twists and turns, flatters and begs, often torments. But everything gets garbled in the end, everything burns to ash, and I can't remember the half of it."

"The scientific and psychological literature on memory and abuse is contested," Phelps wrote in the *Nation*, "but a number of studies have concluded that it is not rare for those abused in childhood to lose memory of it for long stretches." There is abundant criticism in the literature about repressed memory as well. "Most peak psychological and psychiatric professional bodies in the English-speaking world have issued memoranda to their members outlining the lack of scientific evidence for the concept of repressed memory," Brent Waters, a child psychiatrist, told the Public Defenders Annual Criminal Law Conference in 2007. My confusion should in no way be taken as a denial that the occurrence of father–daughter incest is real and far more widespread than we knew only thirty years ago. "To be sexually exploited by a known and trusted adult is a central and formative experience in the lives of countless women," Judith Lewis Herman, a professor of clinical psychiatry at Harvard University Medical School, wrote in her pathbreaking study of the subject, *Father/Daughter Incest* (1981).

Should Bettina's revelations have any bearing on Herbert's writing and his place as a scholar of African American history? Phelps raised that possibility and then, rightly, I think, backed away from it. "To what extent," he asked, "should disheartening revelations about a scholar's conduct be held against his oeuvre?" Lemisch at first favored exploring that question further, but, when misquoted, drew a sharp distinction between discussing the question and believing in the validity of the proposition: "I CAN'T SEE IT," he wrote at the History News Network, "but discussion may bring out some continuity. . . . I CAN'T SEE HOW THESE REVELATIONS of despicable sexual behavior make *American Negro Slave Revolts* or the horrifying *Truth about Hungary* any more true or false. But I am interested in what connections people might be able to sketch in. There might be some."

If there are connections, they have not been sketched in as far as I'm concerned. I don't see them. Bettina has written about her life as a radical, a woman, a lesbian, and her repressed memories play a central role in that story. I bring up the subject of her memoir here because this biography would not be complete without some acknowledgment of what she wrote. But I can't see how discussing her revelations further in the biography would bring any more clarity to the question of the truth or fallacy of the accusations nor do I see any need to attempt to show how they relate to Herbert's oeuvre: I'll leave that to the psychohistorians.

I suspect that Herbert's fiercest critics and his most ardent supporters will probably have the same reaction to what they read in the biography: you didn't go far enough. You didn't criticize enough here. You didn't praise enough there. So be it. They will see the work through the prisms of their own lives. I have tried to tell Herbert's story as it was, with its triumphs and its tragedies, and, like many biographers, I suppose that goal is unattainable. I have attempted to maintain objectivity, at which Herbert probably would have scoffed: "It is intense partisanship," he wrote, "on the side of the exploited and therefore on the side of justice that makes possible the grasping of the truth." That philosophy of history led to the propounding of great errors in some of Herbert's works, among them, as Lemisch pointed out, the "horrible *Truth about Hungary*" and a similar book defending the Soviet invasion of Czechoslovakia. Is objectivity attainable in any historical study? I don't think so. I constructed Herbert's biography through the prism of my life, which by definition will mean there is distortion in this work. I selected the evidence to be used, and I imposed an artificial logic on the story in order to create a coherent picture. "Biographies are but the clothes of the man," Mark Twain wrote. "His real life is led in his head, and is known to none but himself. These are his life, and they are not written. . . . [T]he biography of the man himself cannot be written."

Acknowledgments

RESEARCH AND writing are often solitary processes, but without the generous help and encouragement of dozens of people along the way this book would never have been possible.

I am deeply indebted to the many people who shared their wisdom, scholarship, and insights in interviews in person, by phone, through letters and e-mails, or who opened their personal files to me along the way: Jesse Lemisch, Harris Wofford, John Hope Franklin, Gerald Meyer, William Mandel, Laura Hilton, Tim Patrick McCarthy, Jason W. Moore, Anthony Flood, Danny Rubin, Pete Daniel, Eric Foner, Ramsay MacMullen, Peter Filardo, Marvin Gettleman, Barry Cohen, Charlene Mitchell, Arthur Schlesinger Jr., Eugene Genovese, Lloyd Brown, Julie Kailen, John Cammett, Brick Mohr, Irene Hull, Paul Chevigny, Otto Olsen, Robert Paguette, Gwendolyn Patton, Leone Stein, David Du Bois, Sidney Gluck, Richard S. Kirkendall, Jonathan Jackson, Nik Mills, Mark Solomon, Erwin Marquit, Staughton Lynd, Ernest Allen, David Laibman, Stanley N. Katz, Ken Margolis, Jeffrey Weiss, James W. Loewen, John Herbert Roper, Robert Cohen, Melvyn Dubofsky, Chris Phelps.

I was ably assisted, sometimes beyond the call of duty, by a host of librarians and library staff, especially at the following institutions: Timberland Library, Aberdeen, Washington; Grays Harbor College; Stanford University Special Collections; Tamiment Library, New York University; Portland State University; University of Washington; New York Public Library and the Schomburg Center; Columbia University; Communist Party Reference Center for Marxist Studies; University of North Carolina, Chapel Hill; Hastings College of Law; Library of Congress; Temple University Paley Library; Yale University; University at Albany, SUNY; University of Louisville Law Library; University of Oregon; National Archives; Erasmus Hall High School; Allegheny County Historical Society.

The debt of gratitude I owe to those who read and commented on drafts of chapters and the entire manuscript is difficult to express. They all made this a better book than it would have been without them. Bettina Aptheker has been enormously supportive and at critical moments, for more than a dozen years, provided insight and criticism without which I would have gone seriously astray.

John Bracey's generous and careful reading of the manuscript helped me see the way through the trees to confront the forest. An anonymous referee and Maurice Isserman, who read the manuscript for the University of Massachusetts Press, offered encouragement and incisive observations at just the right moment. Karen Christine Jorgensen exceeded the bonds of friendship to contribute her expertise with care and precision.

I thank the Board of Trustees at Grays Harbor College for twice providing sabbatical leave from my teaching duties so that I could concentrate on scholarship. A Littleton–Griswold Grant from the American Historical Association and Excellence Awards from Grays Harbor College brought much-needed financial assistance during the research process.

Bruce Wilcox at the University of Massachusetts Press proved to be an early champion of the book. He and my supervising editor, Clark Dougan, not only made suggestions that improved the book, but also, with their enthusiastic support, made the process of seeing the book through to publication easy and pleasurable. The staff at the Press, true professionals, have been wonderful to work with, especially Carol Betsch, Mary Bellino, Jack Harrison, and Karen Fisk. The careful attention to detail of the copyeditor Lawrence Kenney provided needed clarity and sharpened language.

Melinda Tanner and David Cromwell, old friends indeed, graciously provided for my housing needs in New York City, hospitality without which I could not have accomplished my research. Bruce Haines did the same in Oakland, Jim D'Entremont and Bob Chatelle in Boston, and Pat Roche in Blackpool, England. Other friends, who over the years must have grown weary of hearing about my research but had the generosity of spirit never to let on, gave me the sustenance without which life is not worth living: Linda Orgel, Arthur (R. D.) Grunbaum, Anneka and Wolter Van Doorninck, Tracey Rizzo, Fran Voss, Karen Christine Jorgensen, Helen Libonati.

And always my beloved Michael, partner of thirty-four years and spouse for two, whose love, infinite patience, and unequivocal support, standing beside me the whole way, afforded me the luxury to pursue this quest.

"The Most Dangerous Communist in the United States"

1   An Immigrant Family's New York

For most of the twentieth century in the United States, especially during the seven decades after the Bolshevik Revolution in 1917, holding beliefs and advocating positions associated with the radical Left, and most assuredly acknowledging membership in the Communist Party of the United States (CPUSA), meant that politically and often socially one was unacceptable, outside agreed-upon standards of decency, beyond the pale. For radicals the message was clear: there is an accepted ideological boundary, and decent people stay inside it.

Herbert Aptheker was beyond the pale in the figurative meaning of the phrase as people used it in Cold War America. But for Aptheker the characterization was a double entendre: while his political affiliations and philosophical foundations certainly qualified him as a member of the radical Left—he was, after all, a card-carrying member of the CPUSA for fifty-two years—he was also literally beyond the Pale, one generation removed from the Pale of Settlement that Catherine the Great created in Russia in 1791 as a Jewish ghetto to restrict trade between Jews and native Russians. By the late 1880s more Jews lived within the Pale of Settlement than anywhere else in the world.[1]

Although most Jews in the Pale of Settlement lived in abject poverty, often forbidden from owning land, the Aptheker family was "fairly prosperous," although the distinction, as one writer put it, seemed to have been between "being poor and being hopelessly poor." The patriarch of the family, Abraham Aptheker, controlled enough land to enable him to farm profitably, and he held some position of authority in the Ukrainian shtetl Gorodishche, outside Kiev, where the family lived. Abraham and Hannah, his wife, brought thirteen children into the world, eight of whom survived to adulthood. Their children did not have to help with household chores, according to family legend, because Abraham could afford "plenty of servants." While the male Aptheker children attended school, "the girls were tutored at home in Yiddish, Russian and perhaps in Hebrew as well."[2]

The assassination of Czar Alexander II in March 1881 by the nihilist People's Will organization brought the reactionary, anti-Semitic czar Alexander III to power. Czar Alexander inaugurated a quarter century of arrests, trials, executions, and, for the Jews of the Pale, violent pogroms.

Born in 1868, Philip Aptheker, Hannah's and Abraham's second son, came to adulthood within the Jewish tradition of respect for scholarship, a tradition in which "a man's prestige, authority, and position depended to a considerable extent on his learning." By the time he became associated with a nihilist group in the late 1880s he was educated and very well read. When Czar Alexander ordered increases in the conscription of Jews into the Russian army in 1888, Philip evidently faced stark choices: he could become a committed revolutionary, which meant he would probably join others, including Alexander Ulianov, Vladimir Lenin's brother, whom the czar's government executed, or he could emigrate to the United States. "America was in everybody's mouth," one emigré later wrote. "All talked of it, but scarcely anyone knew one true fact about this magic land." Philip, deciding his prospects were better in the United States, chose to emigrate. He joined the millions of debilitated, pauperized Jews who fled eastern Europe for the United States between 1881 and 1915, the first Aptheker to put himself beyond the Pale. He was one of the eighty thousand mostly young Jews who arrived in New York City between 1885 and 1889.[3]

Like an overwhelming number of immigrant Jews who worked in New York during the 1890s, Philip found employment in the needle trades. He entered the long line of exploited workers who toiled in the garment industry, carried his sewing machine to work on his back, saved his money, and eventually opened his own garment business, manufacturing "ladies' underwear." In 1898, at the age of thirty, Philip married the twenty-one-year-old Sarah Rosenthal, an immigrant from Grudna Gibernia in Poland. Sarah's mother opposed the marriage because she felt Philip "was too radical and also a little too old for her daughter," but nonetheless Philip and Sarah lived with Sarah's mother on the Lower East Side. While Sarah helped Philip with his underwear business, Grandmother Rosenthal took care of the Apthekers' two daughters, Anne and Tillie. Sarah was expecting another baby when Philip, after a series of asthmatic attacks, died suddenly on 4 December 1904.[4]

Two months after Philip's death, in February 1905, Sarah gave birth to another daughter, Fannie, who later changed her name to Fay. With her mother's help, Sarah, suffering from tuberculosis, attempted to assume the duties of both family and business. Her younger brother Nathan worked with her, but after he stole a payroll and gambled it away Sarah succumbed to despair and sold the business to Philip's younger brother Benjamin, who also had immigrated. Sarah, increasingly incapacitated by tuberculosis, died at the age of thirty-two, five years after Phillip, on 9 January 1909.

Family members recalled that Benjamin Aptheker, or BA as they called him, was short in stature but strong. The third son of Abraham and Hannah, Benjamin had served in the czar's army, where "he won medals and a gold watch as a wrestler." Like his brother Philip, Benjamin, when he immigrated to the United States, initially found work in the garment industry. There he met, fell in love with, and married another Ukrainian immigrant, Rebecca Komar. Benjamin and Rebecca also settled on the Lower East Side and began to raise a family. Their firstborn, Moses, died in infancy, but then in quick succession they had three daughters, Leona, Minna, and Augusta, and a son, Abraham, who later changed his name to Alvin because he didn't like being called Abe. Benjamin's ladies' underwear business became so successful under his guidance that he moved his burgeoning family from the Lower East Side to the semirural Borough Park in Brooklyn, where he bought a stately three-story, seventeen-room house sitting on a parklike lot the size of a square block. In that house, on 31 July 1915, Rebecca gave birth to her sixth and last child, another son, Herbert.[5]

While Benjamin spent his days building his business, B. Aptheker and Sons, and adding to his considerable fortune, which by the time of Herbert's birth had reached at least a million dollars, Herbert spent his childhood being pampered and protected by his three older sisters, his mother, and Angelina Corbin, the live-in servant whom Benjamin hired to assist Rebecca. In her early twenties, Angelina, or Annie as she was known in the Aptheker household, had a decisive effect on young Herbert. She "was a rather large, heavy black woman from Trinidad," Aptheker recalled. "I loved her as much as Mama, or almost as much as Mama," Aptheker said in an interview in 1994. "I knew mother loved her, which was very important to me."[6]

The Aptheker home often resembled a community center, as it was always packed with children from the neighborhood. Recently arrived relatives from abroad found refuge at the Aptheker home while they adapted to life in the United States. Benjamin's niece, Fay, whom he had assisted financially after the death of her father, Philip, married her first husband in the Apthekers' living room in 1926. Throughout the years, Fay and Herbert's sisters often gathered around the Steinway grand piano to entertain themselves and other members of the family with music and song.[7]

Aptheker resolutely maintained that happiness permeated his parents' bourgeois household and that he had a perfect childhood. "It was a glorious childhood for me," he asserted.[8] In that insistence there was always an implication of adoration for his mother and of a hasty, fixed, mechanical reference to his father. "My . . . childhood was very happy. Mother was marvelous, Papa was very hard working and so he left at dawn," Aptheker told the journalist Jack Fischer in 1993.[9] He said once, near the end of his life, that his father was "too much," words that Bettina, his daughter, to whom he made the remark, took to mean that his father was "overbearing, or overpowering."[10] In his interview with Fischer, Aptheker mentioned that he didn't recall ever hearing a word about politics from his father, and certainly the radicalism of his brother Philip had not rubbed off on Benjamin. "By the way," Aptheker told Fischer, "I don't remember poppa talking very much in general. . . . I cannot remember any talk with father."[11]

Happiness, however, apparently did not envelop everyone in the Apthekers' home, especially Herbert's older brother, Alvin. The two boys often spent Saturday afternoons together at the movies, but Herbert said Alvin was always quiet and withdrawn. "I loved him," Aptheker recalled, "but I wasn't close. He wasn't jovial. He was always . . . serious . . . and self-centered. . . . He always gave me the impression he had problems."[12]

Alvin married Jeannette Zevin, the daughter of the famous Yiddish writer Israel Joseph Zevin, who used the pen name Tashrak. Neither the marriage nor the birth of their daughter, Isadora, brought Alvin much happiness. He worked for his father at B. Aptheker and Sons through the early years of the Great Depression. For reasons unknown to his family, he committed suicide in 1937 in the Packard automobile his father had bought for him to use on his business trips.[13] In the 1960s, contrary to the claim he made thirty years later in his interview with Fischer, Herbert told Bettina that he and Alvin "were very close." He called Alvin's suicide "one of my wounds."[14] Exhibiting his penchant for glossing over difficult emotional issues, he didn't elaborate on this assertion, and what he meant by the statement is uncertain.

The Depression diminished Benjamin's fortune considerably. He sold the family's house in Borough Park and with Rebecca, Augusta, and Herbert moved in with his daughter Leona and her husband, George, in another house he had purchased in Borough Park as a wedding present for Leona. He fired Annie Corbin sometime in the late 1920s because he could no longer afford to keep live-in help, although Herbert recalled that she did occasionally visit Rebecca.

Benjamin, assisted by his son-in-law George, the company accountant, struggled to keep his business going during the Depression. In 1931, when Herbert was sixteen, Benjamin and George invited him to accompany them on a business trip to Alabama. The trip had a searing effect on the young Aptheker: it "changed my life," he said in his unpublished autobiography.[15] When they reached Maryland, Herbert recalled, he began noticing signs on restrooms and drinking fountains that read Colored and White. The crude racism they represented shocked him. That was the first time, he said, that he had encountered overt racism, Jim Crow, the southern variety of racism, "raw and legal and open."[16]

As Benjamin, George, and Herbert moved further south, the stark realities of the Great Depression closed in on them. While the economic stagnation of the time was hard on most people in the United States, it was even harder on black people, especially black people in the South. "One could feel despair, and sense hunger," Aptheker later wrote. When his father stopped the car for some reason along an open stretch of road in Alabama, Herbert, looking across the open fields, saw a young black boy, younger than he, standing not far off in the field. Beyond was a shack. In the doorway, which had no door, he remembered, stood "a rather heavy women, about Annie's age, not as heavy as Annie and not as dark as Annie, but who might have been Annie's sister." Herbert alighted from the car to go talk to the black youngster in the field. The boy's clothes were ragged, he wore no shoes, and his emaciated condition spoke to the deplorable conditions of black people in the rural South during the Depression. When Herbert spoke, the black boy did not respond. Undeterred, Herbert took one of the cookies his mother had supplied for the trip out of his pocket and held it out as a gift. The boy did not take the cookie, Aptheker said, in a story he told again and again in interviews. "He came to it and bit it as though he were a dog, as though I were giving the cookie to a dog!" That black boy, the ubiquitous racism, and the desperate poverty he observed during the trip left an indelible image on Herbert's consciousness and set him on a course he pursued for the remainder of his life.[17]

That fall, during his last year at Erasmus Hall High School, Aptheker began conducting research on the current and historical conditions in the South. He simply could not believe that anyone else in the country, especially people in positions of power with the ability to remedy the dreadful conditions, knew about what he had seen. "Were the conditions known?" he asked himself. What he found in his research disturbed him deeply: yes, the conditions were well known. Why then, he asked himself, had he not been taught about them? What else was not being taught? As his knowledge and understanding developed, Herbert began to write a weekly column in his high school newspaper titled "The Dark Side of the South," revealing what he had seen and documenting his observations with verifiable sources.[18]

By the time Herbert graduated from high school in the spring of 1933, Columbia University, adhering to a policy established by its president, Nicholas Murray Butler, had filled its strict quota for Jews for that year. Although his father could afford the tuition, the officials at the university, instead of assigning Aptheker to Columbia College, the elite undergraduate college at the Morningside Heights campus in Manhattan, enrolled him at Seth Low Junior College, established by Butler to pacify his critics, where they assigned many Jewish students: "Columbia's ghetto," Aptheker called it.[19] Seth Low, located in Brooklyn Heights, was an "undergraduate college of the university, . . . about half Jewish and half Italian-American." After two years there, Aptheker transferred to the Morningside Heights campus, where officials classified him not as a member of Columbia College but as a "university undergraduate." Graduates of Columbia College received a bachelor of arts degree, "the Gentleman's degree," whereas university undergraduates were awarded the "less prestigious" bachelor of science degree. Aptheker received a BS degree and never knew, even late in his life, that Columbia automatically awarded the less distinguished degree to university undergraduates. His fellow Seth Low classmate, the future celebrated science fiction writer Isaac Asimov, also earned a BS degree, which he later called "a gesture of second-class citizenship." Columbia closed the Seth Low campus in the late 1930s.[20]

Aptheker's direct experience in the South and his research and writing about the experiences of black people propelled him down the path of radicalization while he was in college. "I know in my own case, it was knowledge of injustice," Aptheker said in an interview in answer to a question about the process of his radicalization. "And knowledge that the injustice was lied about. Falsified. And particularly in terms of racism . . . the horror of Jim Crow and the horror of the living standard and the horror of the children. That was basic in my development."[21]

Aptheker began his college career just as the first mass student protest movement in American history was developing in the 1930s, led by Communist and Socialist undergraduates through the National Student League (NSL) and the Student League for Industrial Democracy (SLID). He immersed himself in radical student politics. During his two years at Seth Low he wrote about, organized for, and spoke at antiwar rallies and arranged for speakers to come to campus. The NSL manifesto drew his sympathy and affected the development of his radical philosophy. "We propose to expose the sham of 'democracy' and the failure of 'representative government' to represent the working class under capitalism," the document began. Further, "the Soviet Union stands out as an inspiration and guide to us in other parts of the world experiencing and witnessing the social and economic evils which accompany capitalism." Aptheker became an avid reader of the Communist Party newspaper the *Daily Worker* and the Marxist magazine the *New Masses,* and by the end of his time at Seth Low thought of himself as a Socialist.[22]

Aptheker moved to the Morningside Heights campus in 1935, where his activism earned him the respect of his fellow students. "I'm proud to know a guy who could be 'very, very liberal,'" a classmate wrote several years later, "and yet not offend the conservatives; who could march in anti-war parades and not seem silly; who could gather an 'A' average and still pitch a smooth game of ball—and not seem out of place doing either." As he organized and marched, Aptheker's antiwar efforts, which until then had focused on a generalized opposition to American involvement in any European war, took on new meaning and attracted new allies when Italy invaded Ethiopia in October 1935. He opposed the Italian invasion and protested the war alongside Communist activists from the NSL and the American League Against War and Fascism, organized in New York in 1933.[23]

In 1935 personal tragedy intruded on Aptheker's studies and political activism. Herbert still lived with his parents at his sister's house in Brooklyn and while he commuted to Morningside Heights every day, his father commuted to Sag

Harbor, Long Island, to the B. Aptheker and Sons factory. When a fast-moving fire broke out in the factory Benjamin called the fire department, then tried to put the fire out himself. By the time the firemen arrived Benjamin lay dead on the factory floor, felled by a heart attack brought on by his exertion in fighting the fire. A year later in a religious ceremony at which family members unveiled his father's gravestone at the cemetery, Herbert saw his cousin Fay Aptheker for the first time in many years. "For some reason," Fay told an interviewer, "when we spoke to each other [at the ceremony] there was some sort of a click." The couple parted that day, Herbert leaving on a research trip to Virginia and Fay to Mexico—but the "click" never unclicked.[24]

Fay, who as noted had changed her name from Fannie and declared her own middle name, Philippa, never knew her father, Herbert's Uncle Philip, who died before her birth. Her mother, Sarah, debilitated by tuberculosis, died when Fay was four. Sarah's mother, whom Fay called Bubie, convinced the authorities that "she could take care of the children" rather than send them to the orphan asylum, as required by New York law. Benjamin, whom the girls occasionally visited in Borough Park, supplemented the small monthly stipend provided by the Hebrew Orphan Asylum for the girls' upbringing. During Fay's last year at P.S. 12, Bubie Rosenthal moved with the girls to Williams Avenue in the Brownsville section of Brooklyn, where Fay recalled taking her first bath in a bathtub rather than "weekly baths in the wash-tubs that were in the kitchen."[25]

Fay aspired to an artist's career in the theater. She studied the piano and took singing lessons throughout her childhood, practicing on her teacher's piano in the Lower East Side tenement in which she lived. After Fay graduated from high school, Herbert's mother encouraged her to attend business school, which she did, thanks to her Uncle Benjamin, who paid her tuition. After graduating, Fay worked as a secretary by day and continued her piano and singing lessons in the evenings at the East 3rd St. Settlement House. She began studying dance also, with Bertha Uhr at the Henry Street Settlement House, and later enrolled in the Wigman School, studied with Charles Weidman at the Humphrey–Weidman School, and for a time studied at the Martha Graham School of Dance. She opened her own studio on 14th Street between 5th and 6th Avenues in Manhattan, and there, with others, she founded the New Dance Group.[26]

Fay was a beautiful woman. "Her dark brown hair, almost black in its lushness," extended "below her hips." She wore "smart tailored blouses and skirts, suits and dresses, picked with exquisite care from the racks of Lord & Taylor or Abraham & Straus," Bettina recalled. "I remember the smell of her freshness, like a spring morning, the breadth of her smile, the expanse of her laughter, the optimism of her energetic thrust out into the world as she left for work."[27]

While studying at the East 3rd St. Settlement House Fay met Alfred L. Steiner, a pharmacist and frustrated journalist whom she married in 1926. The couple, it turned out, were not suited for each other. In 1931, while working as "secretary to the head of the Training School for Social Work at the Jewish Family Welfare Society in Brooklyn," Fay was "recruited into the Communist Party." Then, "after nine long years of an unhappy marriage," Fay divorced Steiner in 1935, the year Benjamin Aptheker died, and moved to a small apartment on Montague Street in Brooklyn Heights across the street from the Brooklyn public library.[28]

Meanwhile, Herbert, once he began work on a master's degree at Columbia in 1936, often conducted research at the Brooklyn public library. As he recalled the story of meeting Fay again after the event for his father at the cemetery, he ran out of paper while working at the library and went in search of a store to buy some. But they were all closed, so out of desperation he rang the bell at Fay's house, hoping to borrow some paper. Fay contested that account. "This is the God's honest truth," Herbert claimed. "She says I'm making it up. It's true." Fay contended, as they talked about their meeting in an interview, that the search for paper was a ruse Herbert used to see her again. "I figured she had paper. And I was an innocent youngster," Aptheker playfully asserted. Fay laughed. "I decided to go to Fay and ask for paper. That's the last I heard of anything. She opened the door and that was the end of everything. . . . I must have gone back to the library, or she may have doped me." Fay explained, "He says I had a net and threw it over him. He can't remember anything else." But Fay, too, was struck: "I don't remember anything after that and neither does he. . . . And I don't remember whether he got the paper and left or whether he stayed." Whatever the truth, for the next six years the cousins met clandestinely, keeping their romance a secret from the rest of the family, especially Herbert's mother. "He keeps on saying that I wouldn't marry him. It's ridiculous. I was very fond of my aunt, his mother. I would not hurt her in any way. And I knew that it would be a blow to her to know that I, a divorced woman, would marry her son, and I was so much older than he. So we just did not think of marriage."[29]

The two lovers saw each other often. She attended his lectures, which throughout this period grew more numerous. They took walks together and went to concerts, Fay introducing Herbert to music, about which he knew little to nothing. They went to plays. Fay began to take Herbert to CPUSA affairs, where members of the party knew of his work on behalf of black liberation, but she never attempted to draft Herbert into the party.[30]

2   The Red Decade

APTHEKER'S MOVE to the Morningside Heights campus in 1935 co-incided with a qualitative shift in his scholarship and activism. At Seth Low, Aptheker easily mastered the required survey courses in world history, European history, and the history of ancient Greece and Rome. At the main Columbia campus he began to focus on the history of the United States and more specifi-cally that of African Americans. But he was isolated in that pursuit: very few of his contemporaries or the faculty members with whom he worked had the slightest interest in the history of Negro people, as they were referred to then. Aptheker filled that void upon coming into contact with Elizabeth Lawson, whom he met when he began teaching U.S. and black history at night classes held at the CPUSA New York Workers School.[1]

Lawson developed black history courses that pointed to an authentic and usable past, "intended both to appeal to black workers and to combat prejudice among whites." A writer and teacher, she had been politically active for years. When the first editor of the *Southern Worker,* the paper of the CPUSA, left the South in the fall of 1931, Lawson, "using the by-line Jim Mallory," took over the running of the paper for a year when it campaigned for the release of Angelo Herndon, an African American labor organizer whose arrest and conviction for insurrection in Georgia the Communist Party promoted into a cause célèbre.[2] Aptheker described Lawson as "one of these selfless Party people.... She was one of the very few people with whom I could discuss what we call Negro history."[3]

Lawson recognized the value of Aptheker's research into the condition of black people in the South and put him in touch with Robert F. Dunn, Grace Hutchins, and Anna Rochester at the Labor Research Association (LRA). Dunn, Hutchins, Rochester, and Alexander Trachtenberg, the president of the party's press, International Publishers, founded the LRA in 1927, the same year Hutchins and Rochester joined the CPUSA. Dunn, whose membership in the party remained secret, and Hutchins impressed Aptheker by treating him as a peer and a valuable resource.[4]

Eager to put his abilities to a useful purpose, Aptheker agreed to write for *Labor Notes* and *Economic Notes,* two LRA publications. He completed at least two research projects in 1935: a study of the federal income tax system and an examination "of the wage system in the textile industry, observing especially the differential in wages paid workers for similar work in the North and in the South." Party organizers in the South found the latter, titled "The Southern Differential," "of tremendous interest" when it appeared, without attribution, in *Labor Notes* in December 1935. "I have in mind a real campaign against the differentials to be carried in the S. W. [*Southern Worker*]," an organizer wrote to Dunn. "I think the widest possible circulation should be given this document. . . . Copies should also be sent to each of the Southern DO's [district organizers] in my opinion." His wide-ranging research drew Aptheker further into the study of blacks in the South and helped him to recognize a class connection between southern workers and farmers, black and white. "Division of the working class by ceaseless stimulation of race antagonism, particularly between black and white workers, has long been one of the strongest weapons of capitalists throughout the country and especially in the South," he wrote. "In other words, every wage scale that permits discrimination against Negro workers, supplies a lower level toward which the wages of so-called 'subnormal' white workers may be driven."[5]

A beneficiary of the Columbia University system that rewarded students with high grades additional points toward graduation, Aptheker earned his BS degree in spring 1936, only three years after matriculating. He immediately began work on a master of arts degree in history under the tutelage of Allan Nevins, whom Aptheker recalled as being "learned in a conventional sense," a teacher who did not do "anything to hurt me so far as I know—nor did [he] help."[6] Aptheker read the standard U.S. history texts, in which, to his outrage, he found black people referred to as "coon" and "Sambo."[7] He was appalled when he read Samuel E. Morison's and Henry Steele Commager's book *The Growth of the American Republic,* in which the authors wrote, "If we overlook the original sin of the slave trade, there was much to be said for slavery as a transitional status between barbarism and civilization."[8] Aptheker found that when the standard texts made reference to the rebellion of the slave Nat Turner in 1831, which many did not, "it was presented as an isolated erratic event, not characteristic of the slave system, due to this lone religious fanatical maniac." His experiences led him to question those assumptions. He saw black people in Harlem rise up in 1935; he saw black people aided by Communist allies picketing department stores in Harlem; he saw black and white people, forty thousand of them, in Harlem at a march in August 1935 demonstrating against the Italian invasion of Ethiopia; he read about the mass movements organized to defend Angelo Herndon and the Scottsboro Boys, nine black teenagers falsely accused of the rape of two white women in Alabama in 1931.; he had seen, researched, and written about the condition of black people in the Depression South; and most of all, as he often declared throughout the rest of his life, he knew and loved Angelina Corbin as a second mother.[9]

   Aptheker's experiences, his instincts, and his training as a historian caused him to formulate questions. If black people fought for their rights in the 1930s, did they not also fight for their rights under the brutal system of slavery? If slaves resisted the slave system, why was that not broadly known? Why did people only know, if they knew at all, about one instance of a slave uprising, Nat Turner's rebellion in Virginia? What was the reality of that event? "I put to myself the question," Aptheker said, "how is it that it came about, what was the environment, why in Virginia in 1831 did this happen, why did it have the impact it had? Why did the ruling class react in such a furious way?" Thus fortified, Aptheker set out to research Nat Turner's uprising and to use the results as the subject of his master's thesis. He received little guidance from Nevins, his thesis adviser, although he found the professor William L. Westermann, an expert in the study of ancient slavery, particularly helpful. There was no subdiscipline in the History Department centered on African American history and no scholarly books devoted to the Turner uprising. Aptheker developed his sources and his intellectual sustenance outside of the department. He studied the writings of W. E. B. Du Bois, whose monumental work *Black Reconstruction* appeared that year. Aptheker contacted Carter G. Woodson, "the father of Negro history" and the founder, in 1915, of the Association for the Study of Negro Life and History. They corresponded and met several times in Washington, D.C., where Woodson lived. Woodson evidently liked Aptheker, encouraged his study, and attempted to keep him on the right track. "You ask my opinion also about what Virginia would have done if the Civil War had not happened," Woodson wrote in his first communication with Aptheker. "This would be invading the field of prophecy which I do not care to do. My field is history. I have no desire to depart for this sphere."[10]

   During the summer of 1936, financed by his mother, Aptheker rented a room in Richmond, Virginia, where he immersed himself in the Virginia state archives. Engrossed in the work, he spent every day combing through "newspapers, journals, diaries, military and naval records, police reports, court cases," and legislative records. Piece by piece he reconstructed the Turner revolt and added evidence to his growing research files documenting other slave uprisings. He unearthed "petitions, appeals, pamphlets, and letters attesting to the black quest for freedom. Without benefit of duplicating facilities as we know them today, he copied the documents he found—totaling some two million words—by hand." He discovered in Virginia one of three extant copies of a practically unknown pamphlet, "the so-called confessions of Nat Turner which consisted of his being interrogated while he was in prison facing execution the next day." The Virginia government had sequestered and destroyed most copies of the pamphlet, fearing the incendiary character of Turner's revelations about the nature of slavery. Since then, the pamphlet had never been republished, but it was the basis for the only published source about the Turner uprising, *The Southampton*

Insurrection by William S. Drewry, a popular "racist book . . . almost completely falsified." Drewry referred time and again to blacks generally as inferior people and concluded that only the "deluded, the cowardly, and the stupid among the slaves ever took part in a revolt." One of the book's main points "was . . . that [the Turner uprising] was exceptional, isolated in terms of the normal equanimity and placidity which characterized the slave institution in this country." "For the truth of the Turner event," Aptheker wrote of the Drewry book, "it would have been better if Drewry had never published."[11]

Aptheker's master's thesis was the first full-length scholarly study of the Turner episode. The research he did for the thesis, while significant in and of itself, led Aptheker to more important discoveries. When embarking on his investigation, he asked himself, Was the Turner uprising an isolated event? Aptheker discovered that, "at that time in the summer of [18]31," it was "the culmination of manifestations throughout the South of significant slave unrest." He found records from Louisiana, Mississippi, Alabama, North and South Carolina, and elsewhere indicating that alarmed state governments in the South reinforced state militias during the late 1820s, increased slave patrols, and promoted more restrictive legislation, all prior to the Turner insurrection. And he "showed that there were . . . conspiracies and minor uprisings in other places prior to Turner. All this was unknown. The whole business was unknown." He concluded that "the whole depiction of the institution and the response of the slaves to the institution was erroneous."[12]

In February 1937 Aptheker presented to Nevins his 120-page thesis, "Nat Turner's Revolt: The Environment, the Event, the Effects." That month Columbia conferred on Aptheker a master of arts degree, and his study of Turner joined thousands of other resources on the shelves of Columbia's library. Three decades later, in 1966, Humanities Press, under the auspices of the American Institute for Marxist Studies, published the manuscript.

As Aptheker, still an unaffiliated radical, began work toward his doctoral degree in 1937, he continued to participate in the antiwar movement as it shifted its focus to the Spanish Civil War and the growing threat of Adolf Hitler. He taught nights at the Workers School and began delivering an extensive series of public lectures on black history around New York City and as far away as Atlanta, mostly for black audiences at black colleges, churches, and civic organizations. The first of his articles documenting slave uprisings appeared in two parts, in the summer of 1937 and the summer of 1938, in the new journal *Science & Society: A Marxist Quarterly,* founded in 1936. Aptheker entitled his articles "American Negro Slave Revolts" as a direct and purposeful rebuke to Ulrich B. Phillips's *American Negro Slavery.*[13]

Through his activism, publications, and personal relationships during the latter part of the 1930s, Aptheker became more involved with the CPUSA.

His work began to appear in the *Daily Worker.* One of his first articles attacked Theodore Bilbo, a U.S. senator from Mississippi who proposed sending black people back to Africa. Aptheker also began writing and working as a volunteer editor for the weekly *New Masses,* the "dynamic center of the literary-political Left in the 1930s." During this time the political overlapped with the personal. Fay was a member of the party, and he and Fay, sometimes with his older sister Augusta, also a member, attended party functions. Lawson helped promote Aptheker's speaking engagements and introduced him to leading black activists. Dunn and Hutchins had introduced him to Trachtenberg, who agreed to publish a series of short books by Aptheker dealing with black history. Between 1938 and 1941, International published *The Negro in the Civil War, Negro Slave Revolts in the United States, 1526–1860, The Negro in the American Revolution,* and *The Negro in the Abolitionist Movement.* Although some reviewers of *The Negro in the Civil War* complained about his "polemical . . . tone . . . [and] inflated rhetoric," Aptheker's works helped to lay the groundwork for the revisionist historiography that by the 1970s supported the class hypothesis he presented. Forty-eight pages long, *The Negro in the Civil War* sold for ten cents. The party distributed thousands of copies and advertised its availability in *Crisis,* the magazine of the National Association for the Advancement of Colored People (NAACP).[14]

Aptheker continued his research in the South whenever he had the opportunity to travel there. At the invitation of Louis Burnham, whom he met at the Workers School, Aptheker went south again during the spring and summer of 1939. Burnham was a seasoned organizer and party member who had helped organize the American Student Union at City College of New York, where he was president of the Frederick Douglass Society, and later, with his wife, Dorothy, and other members of the party, helped steer the civil rights work of the Southern Negro Youth Congress (SNYC). That summer Burnham focused on an effort by the CPUSA to organize field hands for the Tobacco Workers International Union. Aptheker knew nothing about union organizing, but Burnham had plans for Aptheker's other talents. The two men loaded hundreds of copies of Aptheker's first two booklets into the rumble seat of Burnham's car and headed south, with Burnham at the wheel. They traveled through Virginia, North Carolina, Georgia, and Tennessee, visiting tobacco fields, talking to workers, and attending meetings. In Memphis, where Burnham had arranged for Aptheker to speak on black history at LeMoyne Junior College, two thousand students jammed the lecture hall. Aptheker presented the results of his research into black resistance to slavery, exposing those in attendance, some for the first time, to the rich history of black Americans' defiance of and insurgency against slavery and oppression. After the lecture, he and Burnham sold every copy of the books they had brought with them.[15]

When Aptheker returned to New York in late August 1939, he and V. J. Jerome, the editor of the *Communist,* met for lunch to arrange for further publication of Aptheker's work. After their meeting Jerome invited Aptheker to the party's headquarters. While ascending to Jerome's office in the building's elevator, Aptheker asked Jerome, "How does one join the Party?" Astonished, Jerome replied incredulously, "You're not in the Party?" When Aptheker's responded that no, he wasn't, Jerome asked, "Do you have fifty cents?" Aptheker dug into his pockets and handed two quarters to Jerome, who declared, "Now you're in the Party." "That's how I joined this secret organization," Aptheker recalled.[16] Bettina remembered her father telling a slightly different version of that story that offered some insight into Jerome's disbelief. "What Herbert told me," Bettina wrote, "was that Jerome said to him, 'you want to join the Party? Everyone's leaving it!' "[17]

Aptheker's decision to join the CPUSA flowed from his work and experience throughout the 1930s. His commitment to the destruction of racism and to the liberation of black people led to his being readily accepted by his Communist acquaintances and by the party. Then, too, he found that the Communist Party provided the model for the black–white unity through which he sought to fight discrimination: there simply was no other group that put its antiracism into practice via a militant agenda. At the insistence of the Sixth Communist International Congress in 1928, the CPUSA, which until then had paid little attention to "*specific* Negro problems," began to devote considerable resources to recruiting blacks into the party. Party leaders "drove the party into Negro work" during the Depression, the historians Irving Howe and Lewis Coser wrote in their history of the CPUSA. "All through these bitters years the Communists stood almost alone in systematically wooing the American Negroes."[18] The party emerged, according to the historian Mark Naison, "as a major center of social and cultural interaction between blacks and whites during the Thirties and Forties." Aptheker had just returned from his summer of organizing among tobacco workers in the South. When he reflected on the experience he marveled at the brave organizers he had encountered. They were all Communists. "It was only comrades who would do this kind of work," Aptheker said later, "put your life at stake."[19] His older sister was a member of the party. The woman he loved was a member. He taught at the Workers School, a CP school. The CP opposed Nazism and Fascism and had been in the forefront of international opposition to the destruction of Ethiopia and the Spanish republican government. The party thought Aptheker's intellectual abilities and his focus on black history would be useful in carrying out its agenda, so Aptheker encountered, in party-controlled publications, the place where his intellectual work had been most readily accepted. What is odd is that no one in the party recruited him for membership before 1939.[20]

Aptheker could not have chosen a more unpropitious moment to join the Communist Party. Just days before he gave Jerome his fifty-cent membership fee in the elevator at headquarters, Joseph Stalin had signed a nonaggression pact with Hitler.

Throughout the 1930s, the "Red Decade" and the "Heyday of American Communism," according to one historian, the CPUSA, while never enjoying "full political acceptance . . . had won . . . a kind of grudging tolerance," especially after the adoption of the Popular Front or People's Front in 1935. The Popular Front moved Communist parties throughout the world away from confrontation with other leftist groups toward a policy of unity in the fight against Fascism and for collective security. Anti-Fascist unity rather than proletarian revolution became the main goal. The Popular Front allowed Communists to forge links with bourgeois parties and liberals as well. "Overnight," the party organizer George Charney recalled, "we adjusted our evaluation of [President Franklin D.] Roosevelt and the New Deal." The general secretary of the CPUSA, Earl Browder, who led the party throughout the 1930s, "proposed to support the Roosevelt administration directly, working to make the Communists a small but vociferous part of the New Deal coalition."[21]

The announcement of the new CPUSA Popular Front position, most notably by means of the flamboyant slogan Communism Is Twentieth-Century Americanism, won almost immediate acceptance "among many union members, liberals, educators, and others who had been attracted philosophically to Marxism." The party retreated from a strict reading of Marxist–Leninist revolutionary doctrine and "even from the notion of a vanguard Party" to play what the editor of the *Daily Worker,* Clarence Hathaway, described as "a junior and somewhat hidden role in the coalitions it was helping to build." Most Communists breathed a sigh of relief. Party membership expanded. The CPUSA grew from twenty-five thousand members in 1934 to seventy-five thousand by 1938. The shift in policy allowed the party to move back into the mainstream of the labor movement, and it played an "important and commanding role in the rise and development of the CIO [Congress of Industrial Organizations]."[22]

While the policies of the Popular Front allowed the CPUSA to form successful alliances for carrying out a domestic agenda, the Communist International's broader agenda, the adoption of a collective security agreement with the United States, England, and France to thwart Hitler's designs, failed utterly. Stalin hoped the policies of the Popular Front would bring the West to adopt a more favorable opinion of the Soviet Union. They didn't.[23]

Stalin's anxiety grew when Gen. Francisco Franco led an audacious assault on the newly elected democratic Spanish government in 1936, an onslaught against the Spanish republic that had a profound influence on Aptheker. While never taking his eye off his studies at Columbia, he wrote about and spoke against the rise of Fascism. "I was a part of . . . the student movement where there was a great attraction to the strength of Marxism and the Soviet Union," he said in one interview. "I became a leader of the student body in the struggle against [Spanish fascists]," he said in another interview. "I became known."[24]

England and France rejected Stalin's overtures to improve relations between the countries and thereby "greatly increased Soviet mistrust and cynicism." Soviet anxiety reached its peak in September 1938, when the British Tory prime minister Neville Chamberlain signed the Munich Pact in appeasement of Hitler, an act which Chamberlain said would bring "peace for our time." In actuality it led to the dismemberment of Czechoslovakia by the Nazis. The Soviet Union saw the Munich Pact as "an abdication and a betrayal." In essence, "the West left the Soviet government little choice but to conclude the nonaggression pact with Hitler." The Hitler–Stalin Pact was "poor statesmanship, . . . but then, in the extreme tension of the last weeks of peace, it seemed like the only way to assure at least the short-term security of the Soviet Union."[25]

These developments were occurring at precisely the time that Aptheker decided to join the CPUSA. Is there any connection? If Aptheker provided a rationale contemporaneous with the events, it has not survived, but later, in interviews and in the manuscript for an autobiography, he held fast to an explanation. The Hitler–Stalin Pact "seemed to me at the time to be a logical step of self-defense." "If I had been in charge of the Soviet Union," Aptheker told the historian Tim McCarthy, "I would have sought some way to have postponed the [anticipated Nazi] attack and prepared, especially since the so-called Western Allies had betrayed and signed the Munich Pact." Elsewhere, he elaborated by asking, "What was the USSR to do?"

> Were they to fall into the trap that Chamberlain had set? No! I saw no alternative. What was the USSR to do except wait to be attacked? And this way to gain a year to a year and a half? Why not? Was only the USSR to be hostile to Hitler and Chamberlain and France could make alliances with him and meet him and come back and hail peace and so on? . . . I thought it was perfectly logical. And I said so. And I was one of the very few people to say so. I not only said so, but I joined the Party at that moment. What were they to do? What was the alternative to that? The alternative was war at the moment. They weren't prepared were they? No![26]

The signing of the Hitler–Stalin Pact catapulted the CPUSA into crisis. The party members reacted with shock. Throughout the period of the Popular Front "we had been the most consistent advocates of collective security against the spread of fascism," Dorothy Healey, the party leader in California, wrote in her autobiography, *California Red*. Is it possible? party members asked of the decision. Browder appealed to the members' loyalty to the Soviet Union and to their solidarity to hold the party's ranks together. The majority of CP members did stay, but there were some losses outside of major cities.[27]

The primary consequence of the pact with regard to the party was a loss of credibility. As the historian Maurice Isserman remarked, there were occasions in the fall of 1939 when official party pronouncements "left listeners with the impression that the Nazis were in some ways preferable to the Allies. Hitler, after all, had made his peace with the Soviet Union, while British and French intentions remained unclear and seemed to hold more sinister potential." "It is still difficult," Charney wrote many years later, "to measure the moral setback suffered by the Communist movement in the West as a result of the pact." Stalin's decision forced the CPUSA "to endorse not just any change of line but an alliance with Nazism, after years of boasting that there were no more determined and resolute foes of fascism than the Soviet Union and the Comintern."[28]

Aptheker exhibited little sympathy for people who abandoned the movement because of the pact. "Everybody was fleeing," he recalled. "Ridiculous! What do they think the movement is, some sort of a game? It's not a game. It's a question of life and death." Yet disaffected party members and liberals, as it turned out, were the least of the party's worries. Reactionary anticommunists and their liberal allies "began demanding the suppression of the party as Stalin's 'fifth column' in America," inaugurating a Red Scare that ushered in the anticommunist Smith Act in 1941 and culminated, a decade later, in the rise of Sen. Joe McCarthy.[29]

When the war began in earnest in Europe with the German and Soviet invasions of Poland during September, the party once again altered its position toward President Roosevelt and began attacking him, which it did consistently until June 1941. The party's two major slogans for those twenty-two months captured the new position: The Yanks Are Not Coming and Hands Off. Aptheker spent considerable time writing and speaking publicly against the war and against any involvement in the European conflict by the United States. "It was clear to me," he wrote, "that the ensuing war of 1939–40 was a 'phoney one.'" Characteristically, Aptheker's criticism of a "phoney war" centered on concepts of democracy and racism. Black people "see democracy and equality *preached*," he wrote in the *New Masses,* "segregation and Jim Crow *practiced*. They hear their worst enemies, the Dixie demagogues, the Negro-hating, labor-hating, freedom-hating poll-tax congressmen, leading the cry for a war to defend 'democracy.' They know that a war conducted by such individuals, by the class which those individuals represent, can bring them only further misery and pain."[30]

That position adhered to the party's position, which, by early September 1939 had solidified as the party recovered its equilibrium and received instructions from Moscow on the correct line to follow. Essentially, the Soviet Union expected all Communist parties to emphasize the imperialist nature of the war and draw parallels to the "Wall Street–Downing Street axis and the Rome–Berlin–Tokyo axis, and called for a denunciation of the attempt of the Allies to repeat the fraudulent moral claims of World War I."[31] Henceforth, catastrophically in terms of its credibility, the party, during the entire period in which the pact was in force, downplayed its previous uncompromising opposition to the Nazis, arguing that there was no essential difference between Nazi Germany and British imperialism. Sixty years later Aptheker continued to hold to his and the party's position of 1939, notwithstanding evidence to the contrary vis-à-vis some aspects of that analysis.

By means of the pact the Soviet Union jettisoned its commitment to the international proletariat, including that in Poland, Finland, Latvia, Estonia, and Lithuania, in favor of nationalist concerns. Decades later Aptheker still maintained there was a justification for the actions of the Soviet Union. "Hitler had said he was going to attack the Soviet Union," Aptheker recalled during the course of two interviews in the 1990s. "He had more or less finished with Western Europe, which gave up, and I knew he would attack the Soviet Union, so the Soviet Union was preparing to defend itself. I felt that was the reason for taking over a part of Finland, where it was directly threatening Leningrad. . . . They had a hell of a time, after a year and a half of feverish preparation, where they took . . . part of Finland back . . . to get the borders solid, and feverishly prepared for war. . . . That didn't bother me. . . . The Soviet Union wanted as much time as possible to prepare, and got an extra year and eliminated a threat from the north, so that Leningrad never was captured."

Contrary to Aptheker's half-century-long, passionately held belief, the evidence suggests that Stalin did not "feverishly prepare" for war. In fact, Stalin seemed to have put some faith in the pact and used the treaty's protocols to justify his invasion of Poland and the annexation of Latvia, Lithuania, and Estonia. Even though the Allies repeatedly warned Stalin of Hitler's intention to invade the Soviet Union, when the attack eventually began in June 1941 Stalin was caught off guard because he had failed to mobilize the country and suffered acutely for having purged and executed his most experienced military leaders. The German invasion caught the Soviet Union desperately unprepared. That Stalin "eliminated a threat from the north," as Aptheker put it, is also true, but not quite in the sense that Aptheker meant. The Red Army fabricated a border incident on 30 November 1939, then invaded Finland. "Herbert Hoover became the chairman of 'Defend Finland,' or something," Aptheker wrote flippantly, "and if Herbert Hoover was for Finland, I was against it." The *Daily Worker* and *New Masses* supported the Soviet invasion as well. Claiming that the Red Army severed "the encircling noose" created by the Allied governments during the period since the First World War, A. B. Magil, the editor of *New Masses,* argued that the "Red Army's advance into Finland" completed that process.[33]

The party managed to hold on to most of its sixty-five thousand members during the period of the Hitler–Stalin Pact. Browder's first inclination—and Aptheker's subsequent position—to present the pact, a diplomatic document, as an indispensable means of survival for the Soviet Union would have fared better among both party members and fellow travelers if, as Healey pointed out, the party had not translated the pact into a political directive. "Communists mercilessly attacked those who held to the anti-Hitler front," wrote the historians Paul Buhl and Dan Georgakas, "alienating themselves from the very groups with whom they had been most intimate."[34]

The same year Europe erupted in all-out war, four black men in Oglethorp County, Georgia, declared their own kind of war on the system of debt slavery under which they lived. The men lived and worked on cotton plantations owned by William T. Cunningham, but one day they fled because he held them as virtual prisoners through threats, "beatings, bloodhounds and other brutalities." One escapee described what awaited anyone caught escaping from the Cunningham plantations: "Cunningham beat him over the head with his pistol and then . . . made him pull off his clothes and laid down cross a sack of syrup cane seed and beat him with a bugger trace [a buggy trace is a piece of leather approximately six feet long, two inches wide and a quarter inch thick] and let him up and . . . beat him again." The four escapees eventually made their way to Chicago. The planter Cunningham pursued his peons to Chicago, where he "persuaded the Chicago police to aid in rounding them up." He attempted to push through extradition proceedings, but William Henry Huff, an Oglethorpe County native and Chicago lawyer who grew up under the same brutal system, intervened. Huff exposed Cunningham as a modern-day slaver, and when he appealed for aid to Gov. Henry Horner of Illinois, Cunningham "fled to neighboring Indiana to await the outcome of the case." Huff, who hated peonage "with all [his] heart, soul, and mind," decided that something had to be done to end the odious practice. It's not exactly clear how he found Herbert Aptheker in Brooklyn—perhaps he had read Aptheker's books, which were advertised near Huff's own advertisement in *The Crisis*—but one day in late 1939 Huff knocked on Aptheker's apartment door.[35]

The term *peon* had its origins in a Spanish word that "originally meant foot soldier but that came through popular usage to mean a man indebted to an employer." As the historian Thomas R. Frazier pointed out, "Peonage [was] the system in which a debtor must work out what he [or she] owes in compulsory service to his creditor. In the South, this was the condition of the sharecropper, who went deeper and deeper into debt to the planter on whose farm he worked.

Since the planter furnished the goods the cropper needed and kept the account books himself, it was virtually impossible for the black cropper to free himself from debt and thus escape the system." Congress enacted a law in 1867 prohibiting forced labor, debt slavery, "and, by name, the system of peonage." In 1905 the Supreme Court, in *Clyatt v. United States,* definitively upheld the constitutionality of the law of 1867. But, as Aptheker pointed out in 1940 in an article that appeared in *New Masses,* "there is a very wide margin between illegalization and abolition of an evil—between *saying* that something is wrong, and *doing* something about wiping out that wrong." While most southerners approved of the peonage system, or at least "quietly accepted" it, as the historian Pete Daniel wrote, southern plantation owners ruthlessly enforced the system. The few federal prosecutors who even contemplated prosecutions under the Peonage Statute demurred because, as one prosecutor explained, "he feared that his case would have failed before a sympathetic jury." Southern white people of all classes "united to coerce black laborers . . . even as they had since the days of slavery."[36]

After hearing Huff's story, Aptheker took him to the home of Louise Thompson in Harlem to see the Communist leader and attorney William L. Patterson. Aptheker first met Thompson in 1937 when he attended a meeting at her apartment, often a center of radical organizing, to plan educational events for the International Workers Order. Prominent as a central figure in black cultural circles during the Harlem Renaissance, she founded a salon called Vanguard that "attracted Harlem artists with concerts, dances and discussions of Marxist theory" during the early 1930s. She had worked with such influential figures as Paul Robeson, Langston Hughes, and Zora Neal Hurston, and by the later part of the decade, as she moved deeper into the Communist Party's inner circle, she "was a critical liaison linking black popular culture and Harlem's literati with Communist Popular Front politics." In fact, according to the historian Martin Duberman in his magisterial biography of Robeson, "The Party threw itself into pronounced support for black arts, helping to sponsor a variety of efforts to encourage black theater, history, and music."[37]

Patterson, "one of the most prominent African-American Left leaders," gained his stature through his defense work for Nicola Sacco and Bartolomeo Vanzetti, Italian-born anarchists convicted of murder and executed by the State of Massachusetts in the 1920s. He, like Thompson, whom he married in 1940, was a leading figure in Harlem's black cultural circles. Robeson and Du Bois were two of his closest friends and associates. Patterson became the national secretary of the International Labor Defense (ILD) in 1932, and under his leadership the organization strenuously defended the Scottsboro Boys in the infamous case of their false accusation of rape. By the late 1930s Patterson became the party organizer in Harlem, then, in 1938, moved to Chicago to organize blacks on the South Side.[38]

After his conversation with Aptheker and Huff, Patterson at once took charge. "Well, we have to organize," Patterson said. "We have to have a committee." Patterson proposed forming an organization, "a black–white organization," that would shed light on the system of peonage and get the facts out to a wide audience, an organization that "could institute suits against people like Cunningham." Patterson wanted to create "as much commotion as possible, get big names to support us." He suggested a name, the Abolish Peonage Committee (APC). Huff would be "a guiding light in this effort," Patterson said, adding "[Aptheker,] you will be secretary." The ILD, Patterson avowed, "would support this to the hilt." Thus, in that moment the three men formed "the first public organization to combat peonage." The committee eventually set up its headquarters in Chicago, with Alderman Benjamin A. Grant as chair, Patterson as executive secretary, the ILD secretary Bob Wirtz as secretary, and Huff as chief counsel. Aptheker concentrated on writing, speaking, and fund-raising.[39]

Among others, Aptheker contacted the novelist, journalist, and civil rights advocate Henrietta Buckmaster, who had sought Aptheker out for help on her novel *Let My People Go*. The novel, published in 1941, brought Buckmaster international recognition for its approach to slavery and the abolitionist movement from a black perspective. Buckmaster credited Aptheker for his assistance in her research, for his "scholarship [and] generosity . . . whose special domain is that vast and obscure region of court records, buried items in newspapers—the whole, unembellished picture of Southern internal struggle." She opened her home in Greenwich Village for APC fund-raising events. The folk singers Woody Guthrie and Pete Seeger, the folk and blues man Huddie Ledbetter ("Lead Belly"), and the jazz composer and musician W. C. Handy all performed at fund-raising events. Aptheker outlined the facts about peonage for those gathered and also wrote articles that appeared in *New Masses* and the radical alternative to *Life* magazine, *Friday*. As other publications responded to the appeal of APC, articles appeared in the *Nation,* the *New Republic, Christian Century,* and black newspapers like the *Chicago Defender,* the *Afro-American* in Baltimore, and the *Amsterdam News* in New York City. In this and other ways the APC raised funds to carry on its work.[40]

Huff, as the APC legal council, wrote to the FBI director, J. Edgar Hoover, requesting that the situation in Oglethorpe County be investigated and Cunningham indicted. On 10 February 1940 Hoover responded coolly to Huff's entreaty: "I wish to advise the matter concerning which you wrote has been presented to Assistant Attorney General [O. John] Rogge and he has advised that no further investigation should be made in the matter. The case, therefore, is being carried as closed in our files." Further rebuffs from Hoover and the Department of Justice that dismissed sworn affidavits "evoked greater action on the part of the committee." In Popular Front fashion, APC, ILD, and the party joined with the National Negro Congress, the NAACP, the Elks, the National Baptist Convention, and the CIO Cannery, Agricultural, Packing, and Allied Workers of America to press the federal government to take action.[41]

While Huff worked through the legal system, others in APC created a modern underground railroad by spiriting captive black farmers, both men and women, out of peonage. At first, the committee purchased bus tickets in Chicago and mailed them to black people working on Cunningham's plantations. But Cunningham intercepted the tickets with help from the local postmaster. The APC decided to send someone secretly to Oglethorp County to give bus tickets to anyone who wanted to escape. Aptheker eagerly volunteered for the dangerous assignment. Early in 1940, adopting the nom de guerre H. Biel, Aptheker, posing as a traveling insurance salesman, made his way by bus to Lexington, Georgia, the seat of Oglethorpe County.

Aptheker timed his arrival so that he could spend Saturday night in Lexington, the one night on which Cunningham allowed black farmworkers to leave his plantations. Huff, through relatives of his and friends in Oglethorpe County, made arrangements from Chicago, notifying workers that a white man holding bus tickets would be in Lexington on a certain day at a certain rooming house. Aptheker let it be known in the various rooming houses where he stayed (he evidently registered in a different house each trip) that he was interested in purchasing the services of a black prostitute, a not-uncommon practice among white men. When a black woman escapee appeared at his rooming house on Saturday night no one took notice. The escapees, two at a time, went first to New Orleans, a circuitous route to Chicago made necessary by the suspicion that would have been aroused had two black farmworkers shown up with expensive tickets in hand for a trip north. Aptheker had arranged for some comrades who owned a bookstore to meet the escapees at the end of the first leg of the journey. From New Orleans the escapees passed to comrades in Memphis or Nashville and then traveled on to Chicago, where Huff met the bus and arranged for necessities. Aptheker made three trips to Lexington, assisting perhaps a dozen workers to escape their enforced servitude. On his last trip, as he was shaving on Sunday morning with the door to his room open, a black man cleaning the hall of the rooming house said to him softly as he passed the door, "Go home." Aptheker, unsure he had heard what the man said, asked, "What did you say?" Without raising his face and still sweeping the floor, the man said again, softly, "Go home. Now!" Aptheker took the man's words as a warning that his identity was known. "I got the hell out of there," he said, fearing that should he be detained by Cunningham or his agents the body of a New York Jewish Communist would likely wash up somewhere on a riverbank or never be seen again.[42]

Daniel concluded that the "energetic backing of the Cunningham case by the Abolish Peonage Committee probably spurred the lethargic Justice Department into acting more vigorously on civil rights." The Justice Department did eventually indict Cunningham on a conspiracy charge, but a Georgia federal judge "refused to approve extradition of the principals. . . . Why the Department of Justice did not indict Cunningham on a peonage or slave-kidnapping charge remains a mystery." When the Justice Department did begin to pursue peonage cases more vigorously in 1942, "the prod came not from their concern with those held in peonage" but from a foreign propaganda threat. Nazi and Japanese propagandists claimed that "the democracies are insincere," so President Roosevelt, to counter the propaganda, "ordered that 'lynching complaints shall be investigated as soon as possible,' and that the investigations be fully publicized."[43]

International Publishers issued two more booklets by Aptheker: in 1940, "The Negro in the American Revolution" and in 1941, "The Negro in the Abolitionist Movement." Aptheker's essays on black history also appeared in the National Urban League's *Opportunity*—among these were "Negroes Who Served in Our First Navy," in April 1940; "They Bought Their Way To Freedom," in June 1940; and "Negro History—A Cause for Optimism," in August 1941. In addition to his writing on peonage in *New Masses,* Aptheker published numerous book reviews. In November 1939 he reviewed Du Bois's *Black Folk, Then and Now.* The twenty-four-year-old reviewer found the book to be "fine" and "definitely salutary," although he criticized Du Bois for "calling the post–Civil War southern governments proletarian dictatorships." When Du Bois published *Dusk of Dawn* in 1940, Aptheker praised the work as "beautifully and brilliantly written" but lamented what he called Du Bois's "vulgarization and falsification of Marxism." That tendency, Aptheker noted, "was most apparent . . . in Du Bois' identifying Marxism with economic determinism and in placing the onus for violence, should it appear, in the revolutionary process, upon advocates of fundamental change, rather than upon defenders of a senile social order," themes to which Aptheker would have reason to return during the Cold War Red Scare. Aptheker's review turned out to be the most critical of any published about *Dusk of Dawn,* but Du Bois contacted Aptheker and told him to keep writing, as his work was "thought-provoking."[44]

As an unpaid contributing editor at *New Masses* in 1941, Aptheker, in addition to writing book reviews, assisted in the office, read galleys, and solicited articles from other writers. He suggested the periodical put out a series of articles on black history, including Franz Boas on anthropology and racism, Samuel Putnam on Latin America, Ralph Ellison on black people in literature, and Aptheker on Afro-American historiography, but there is no evidence that any of these articles were written or published. His attempt to include an essay on the oppression of black women gave rise to problems Aptheker did not fully understand. After corresponding several times with Mary Inman, "a long-time Marxist from Long Beach, California," and reading her book *In Woman's*

Defense, Aptheker asked her to write "an article on the problems of Negro women." Inman had just returned to California from New York after a contentious meeting with the CPUSA National Committee at which she had failed to persuade the party leaders Elizabeth Gurley Flynn, Ella Reeve ("Mother") Bloor, Avram Landy, and Johnny Williamson of the validity of her assertions that "housework, like factory work, is productive labor . . . [with] economic value" and that "progressives could organize housewives as workers." Bloor and Flynn expressed some sympathy for Inman's views, but after three days of intense argument with Inman both Bloor and Gurley Flynn felt Inman was intransigent, argumentative to the point of making ad hominem attacks, and "a real danger to Party unity." Aptheker apparently knew nothing about the controversy surrounding Inman or about her meeting with the leaders. In late August Inman at first accepted Aptheker's invitation to write an article, but by 17 September she had begged off. "Owing to factors beyond my control, I shall not be able to send to you an article on the Negro Woman Question," she wrote. "It is not that I couldn't have made the time schedule, but there is a great deal of confusion in certain quarters on basic theory relating to woman in capitalist society, which has any . . . analysis of the Negro Woman's problems stymied," Inman continued and then, with a veiled reference to the leaders, concluded, "when done under the direction of those who are confused." In a letter a few days later she went further: "Responsible people are endorsing theories which they are going to be ashamed of later, when they know more about what they are doing." Aptheker told Inman that "confusion will be eliminated only by discussion & study. It is precisely because of the confusion on the subject that I've asked you to write about it. If it were perfectly clear & universally understood discussing it would be pointless." But he did not understand Inman's indirect references to the party leaders. "The 'direction' you speak of is not too clear to me. This series is my responsibility. And my judgement about an article is then either confirmed or rejected by the editorial board. That's all the 'directive' there is here. At any rate, controversy is healthy. You write the article, please, as you understand the problem. Then let us decide as to its importance and value. I feel confident you will not have wasted your time or labored in vain." Aptheker's "spirit" convinced Inman to change her mind, she said, although their correspondence breaks off in late October, and there is no evidence that she did, in fact, complete the article. The party expelled Inman in 1942 because her ideas on women's oppression and the exploitation of women's reproductive labors in the family did not conform to the views of the party. Inman spent the next four decades, until her death in 1985, seeking vindication for her theories, an effort that eventually met with some success "when feminists," among them Selma James, a coauthor with Mariarosa Dalla Costa of the women's movement classic *The Power of Women and the Subversion of the Community,* and Bettina Aptheker, "inspired by the women's liberation movement . . . rediscovered her work."[45]

Aptheker meanwhile kept up his teaching and lecturing. Howard Selsam, a former philosophy professor at Brooklyn College and then-director of the School for Democracy, a party institution that bridged the Workers School and the Jefferson School of Social Science established in 1944, asked Aptheker to teach a course to be called the "History of the Negro in America." Aptheker accepted. He also developed a six-part lecture series that he sold for twenty-five dollars to groups as varied as the Waterfront Research Committee of the National Maritime Union, the Brooklyn chapter of the Association for the Study of Negro Life and History, and the Bedford Professional Forum. In addition, during the latter half of 1941 he spoke one Sunday a month at the black YWCA in Philadelphia. His lecture there on 7 December ended in commotion when a soldier in uniform burst in to announce that the Japanese had attacked Pearl Harbor.[46]

3   "Double V"

EVEN THOUGH publicly he held to the party position throughout the twenty-two-month period of the Nazi–Soviet Pact, Aptheker and other members of the party continued in private to press antifascist policies. This was particularly true in Aptheker's case with regard to the inherent racist and anti-Semitic character of Nazism. In the outlets available to him he continued to use his scholarly research on the condition of black people to propel an antiracist agenda.

The uneasy ambivalence between private doubts and public acceptance of party policy ended with the Nazi attack on the Soviet Union on 21 June 1941. "The treaty came as a megaton shock, stunning, sudden, wrenching," the long-time party activist Al Richmond wrote. "Hitler's invasion of the Soviet Union, among all its complex facets . . . was an enormous sense of release. . . . [T]he anti-Nazi passion had not been extinguished [by the treaty], it had smoldered, and now it burst forth . . . for crushing this supreme evil." "It was now a battle to the death," Aptheker stated in his unpublished autobiography, "that is, either the defeat of fascism or its conquest of all Europe and probably much of the rest of the globe."[1]

The attack on the United States by Japan on 7 December 1941 unleashed another torrent of passion among American Communists. Aptheker decided, even before his train reached New York after his lecture in Philadelphia was disrupted on 7 December, that he must enlist in the armed forces of the United States. After consulting with Fay and his mother, then notifying his teaching colleagues and his coworkers at the *New Masses,* he chose Lincoln's birthday, 12 February, to report for induction into the U.S. Army. Aptheker was one of fifteen thousand Communists who served in the military during the war: "By January 1943 nearly one-fifth of all male Communists, including hundreds of veterans of the Abraham Lincoln Brigade, were serving in the armed forces." At twenty-six, Aptheker could easily navigate the intricacies of major research libraries, write complicated, detailed examinations of historical topics, analyze census records, and convey his thoughts in the press, but he was not prepared for the absurdities he encountered in the army.[2]

At Fort Dix, New Jersey, Aptheker lined up with hundreds of other enlistees for medical and intelligence tests. The army described him as being "five-feet nine-inches tall, weighing 188 pounds (overweight, muscular, not obese) with poor posture, brown hair, hazel eyes, ruddy complexion, almost perfect vision and hearing." Aptheker was issued a new set of clothes that, except for the shoes, which fit perfectly, should have gone to a soldier considerably larger than he was. After declaring Aptheker's intelligence to be suitable, a noncommissioned officer assigned him for training to the field artillery at Fort Bragg, North Carolina.[3]

The grueling physical demands of basic training tested Aptheker's confidence in himself. "I cannot write of myself," he wrote to Fay in one of his daily letters. "I am not physically ill—but were it not for you, [my] mother, and the aim of the war, I could not go on." Service in the military put a severe strain on his emotional well-being too. Early on he encouraged Fay to remain upbeat in the letters she wrote to him every day: "Darling, make your letters happier, or I shall go berserk," he wrote late in February. Promoted to corporal after basic training, he mastered the nuances and capabilities of antitank weapons so well that he found himself instructing the recruits who followed him into training. Much of the artillery training was difficult for him and the way of thinking foreign, but his superiors recognized his potential and recommended him for Officer Candidate School (OCS). While waiting for an OCS position to open up at Fort Sill in Lawton, Oklahoma, he received some preliminary training. He had taken few math courses at college, but now he needed math proficiency for OCS. Fay arranged for a friend who taught high school math, Sarah Malkin, to send him daily lessons that enabled him to pass the math test for entry into OCS. One aspect of the preliminary training prompted an especially enthusiastic response from Aptheker. "Have I told you," he wrote to Fay on 11 April, "that Negroes are in our classes? No discrimination is present there & this is N.C.—What a sight it is, here, to see Negroes giving orders to white men—for we, at school, get practice in issuing commands and orders of all sorts." Aptheker threw himself into his responsibilities but found much that distressed him. He learned to give orders and to yell at recruits, although he found that job difficult in some cases. When one of the young soldiers appeared "slow . . . in his responses," Aptheker didn't have the "heart to yell at him & so I'm afraid to look at him—for, as sure as Hitler will die, he is wrong . . . [but] trying so God Damn Hard." Late in May Aptheker transferred to OCS at Fort Sill.[4]

In October 1940 President Roosevelt had issued a statement that outlined U.S. military policy with regard to African Americans. Blacks, the statement declared, would "be enrolled in the American armed forces on the basis of their 10% population ratio to that of the nation; they would be used in all branches of the services; that they would receive the same facilities and training as white soldiers but that 'the policy of the War Department is not to integrate colored and white enlisted personnel in the same regimental organizations.'" As the historian Stephen Ambrose pointed out, "The world's greatest democracy fought the world's greatest racist with a segregated Army." When Aptheker arrived at Fort Sill he immediately understood the revolutionary potential of the integrated school. Indeed, the sociologist E. Franklin Frazier stated that "World War II marked the point where 'the Negro was no longer willing to accept discrimination,'" an alteration in American race relations that laid the groundwork for the protest movements of the 1950s and 1960s. "You know, schnitzy [his pet name for Fay]," Aptheker wrote during his first week at Fort Sill, "there is no jim-crow here—absolutely none—Negro and white sleeping in the same tent—shaving at the same mirror, showering together . . . side by side." Some "racial 'experts'" had "predicted that the program would fail," but as the integration experiment progressed throughout the war, at least in the officer candidate schools, experience proved the experts wrong. "No life, but such a life as we have had could be more intimate than army life," Aptheker wrote, "so you understand what a social revolution is occurring right here around me. And I hear and see & sense no objections. The men are great—& from everywhere." When some white officer candidates complained about the absence of segregation "they were told to live with it and behave themselves or get out."[5]

Herbert's mother died in late July while he was at OCS. He took a leave of absence to attend her funeral, and while on leave again in September, prior to completing OCS, he and Fay married. The news came as a shock to his family. "I write to give you great news," he said to his sister Minna on 5 October 1942. "I have been married—to the one I've loved for several years—our own Fay. The times are mighty and strange—and for reasons you'll understand—we postponed this for a long, long time . . . but now things are as they should be. I keenly regret the fact that you were not present, and that news of this comes to you in so abrupt and detached a way as a letter. Do not be too angry with me because of that."[6]

Returning to Fort Sill, he completed his training and received his commission as a second lieutenant in the U.S. Army. The army allowed new officers to request their assignment, and Aptheker asked to serve with the 350th Field Artillery Battalion, one of the army's nine "Negro field artillery battalions," at Camp Livingston, twenty miles from Alexandria, Louisiana. He purposely chose the camp because of its troubled history.

Black people in the United States reacted to the Second World War much as they had to the Civil War, the Spanish–American and Philippine Wars, and the First World War, that is, they responded "not simply as Americans, but as Black Americans." They realized that the war would be fought on two fronts, at home and abroad. That realization had its most prominent manifestation in the "Double V," or Double Victory, campaign, "Fighting on Two Fronts," a "grassroots civil rights movement that called for 'Victory at Home, Victory Abroad'" and was led by the NAACP and black newspapers: "Some of its supporters were so passionate that they burned or carved a 'Double V' on their chests." Adherents of Double V wanted nothing less than the defeat of Hitler in Germany and the destruction of racism in the United States. The movement battled discrimination within the military, spurred on by racist outbursts that developed almost simultaneously with the induction of the first black soldiers in April 1941.

Leaders of the Communist Party "harshly denounced" the Double V campaign, according to Irving Howe and Lewis Coser, who were critics of the party. But even a somewhat more sympathetic writer, the historian Wilson Record, noted that "party spokesmen, who were in commanding positions," objected that such a campaign was disruptive. Some white politicians in Washington unwittingly showed the need for Double V as they stirred up racial hatred toward black citizens. Typical of that practice was a speech delivered in the House of Representatives on 28 May 1942 by a notorious racist from Mississippi, Rep. John Rankin. "Mr. Speaker," he began, "one of the most vicious movements that has yet been instituted by the crackpots, the Communists, and parlor pinks of this country is that of trying to browbeat the American Red Cross into taking the labels off the blood bank they are building up for our wounded boys in the service so that it will not show whether it is Negro blood or white blood. That seems to be one of the schemes . . . to try to mongrelize this nation."[7]

In the segregated military training camps, most of them in the South, black soldiers understood full well the hypocrisy involved in a Jim Crow military supposedly dedicated to the destruction of an enemy that proclaimed a master race ideology. Black soldiers also were acutely aware that "the life of the Negro soldier was one of constant fear and danger while his unit was still in training." Incidents of racial violence involving white mobs and city, state, and military police agents erupted as early as 1941. The black press carried accounts of the incidents, and the most serious, like the one that happened in Alexandria, Louisiana, found their way even into mainstream newspapers.

In January 1942, one month after the attack on Pearl Harbor, military police in Alexandria, in the heart of the so-called Negro district, attacked a black soldier from the 367th Infantry Regiment whom a white woman accused of accosting her, setting off what became known as the Lee Street Riot. As other black soldiers came to the aid of their comrade, city police reinforced the military police. Hundreds of black troops carrying loaded weapons poured into Alexandria, released prisoners from the local jail, burned cars, overturned trolley cars, and eventually engaged in fierce gun battles with the town's civilians. How many soldiers and civilians died is not clear, but the army "characterized the situation as a police riot." Accounts of the number of black soldiers shot during the uprising varied. One story claimed that four soldiers were shot, while another listed "twelve black soldiers hit by gun-fire." The press explained that white military police enforced "discrimination against Negro soldiers, all of whom were from Northern states."[8]

Aptheker arrived at Camp Livingston in September. The group commander, a colonel named Oliphant, cautioned the dozen new white officers: "We are officers in an artillery battalion," he told them at the first assembly, "and our men are Negroes. These are men, not boys and no one is to refer to them as boys. We will make them artillery men." No one responded when the colonel offered to transfer any officer who was unhappy commanding black soldiers. Oliphant assigned Aptheker to the headquarters battery, one of the five batteries of the battalion, and for the first few months Aptheker had multiple duties: handling supplies, drilling and training, and field exercises. By the time the battalion reached full strength he had been promoted to first lieutenant and placed in command of the headquarters battery, where his duties included surveying, communications, and intelligence.[9]

After a racial incident in the officers mess involving two black officers and a lieutenant colonel named McEwen, the battalion commander, Aptheker decided to eat permanently with the enlisted men under his command. The morning after the incident, having informed the mess sergeant of his plans the previous evening, Aptheker arrived for breakfast to find a separate table set up for him. The rest of the tables in the enlisted men's mess had been rearranged into two V shapes, a Double V. Aptheker understood the meaning and backed the Double V campaign despite the party's reservations, but he ordered that the tables be put back in their regular position, fearing McEwen would make life even more difficult for his battery and the battalion as a whole.[10]

A continuing complaint by black soldiers at Camp Livingston, one that engendered deep racial animosity, had to do with Jim Crow transportation. When black soldiers on pass were ready to return the twenty miles to camp from Alexandria late in the evening, they consistently had to step aside to let white soldiers get on the army bus first. Often the bus filled up before black soldiers could get on, leaving them stranded, which caused them to be late and led to their being listed as AWOL. Aptheker arrived at a novel solution to the problem. He arranged to have one of the enlisted men assigned for a driving lesson in a large truck anytime members of his battery had passes. The men with passes rode into Alexandria with the driver trainee, who waited for them until curfew and then drove them back to the camp. White soldiers made such a ruckus about the arrangement, the supposed special treatment for black soldiers, that within weeks all Fort Livingston soldiers with passes rode to town and back with driver trainees.[11]

After months of intensive training Aptheker's battery readied itself for the Ground Forces Test mandated by the army for all troops prior to their being shipped overseas. Part of the test required the whole battery, 110 men, including officers, to complete a twenty-five-mile march within eight hours. Aptheker and his first sergeant designed the route for the march to pass through the town of Pollock, Louisiana, a town "notorious to all of us," Aptheker recalled, because of a sign at the city limits that read, "Nigger, don't show yourself in Pollock." Most rural Louisiana towns had sundown customs or ordinances that forced black people to leave town after sundown, but Pollock was unique in that it threatened any black person who showed up in town at any time. On the day the march was scheduled, the battery, to avoid the heat of midday, set off in late evening. About midnight 110 black soldiers carrying rifles, with Aptheker out front, reached Pollock. As they entered the town the battery broke into song: "John Brown's Body lies a-mouldering in the grave, but his soul goes marching on." Aptheker recalled that "lights appeared throughout lily-white Pollock. . . . People there looking on, seeing this mass of armed Black men with a maniac at the head of it. Another John Brown, you see. God knows how they felt. It must have been reported. Anyway we did that. That was something not to be forgotten."[12]

In September 1943, not long after that incident and apparently unrelated to it, Aptheker began an odyssey of short stints with various all-white field artillery units around the country. In Texas, at Camp Moxey with the 758th Field Artillery Battalion, his commanding officer, Lt. Col. Theodore Parker, the namesake and a relative of the prominent abolitionist leader, nominated Aptheker for the Army Command and Staff School, which would have resulted in Aptheker's being promoted to major. Col. Buell Smith, the battalion commander, countermanded the appointment. When Aptheker inquired into the situation, Colonel Parker wrote to Aptheker that Smith's "unfortunate bias," his anti-Semitism, was the reason for the denial.[13]

In addition to revoking the nomination, Colonel Smith transferred Aptheker to another unit. Before the move took place, one morning a bedraggled and earnest private from another battery approached Aptheker, as Aptheker remembered, "an enlisted man carrying himself and uniform clumsily." The soldier identified himself as Nelson Algren. He had recognized Aptheker from an encounter they had had at the *New Masses* office. Algren, a writer who went on to win the first National Book Award for fiction in 1950 for *The Man with the Golden Arm,* pleaded with Aptheker to help him get out of the artillery to "maintain sanity." Algren hated guns, "especially the formidable howitzers . . . those dumb and eyeless mammoths," according to his biographer. Aptheker, who by then had been promoted to captain, said that at his relatively low rank he had little influence but promised he would do his best. He did not see Algren again but did relay the request to Colonel Parker. Whether Parker played a role or not,

Algren spent the remainder of the war in the army medical corp and credited Aptheker for the transfer. Years later in Chicago Algren approached Aptheker after one of his speeches: "Nelson Algren comes up to me," Aptheker recalled, "and he says something like 'You know, Aptheker, you saved my life.' And then he repeated it."[14]

After only a few months the army again transferred Aptheker, first to Blacksburg, Virginia, then back to Fort Bragg, where he joined the 940th Field Artillery Battalion, an unattached unit not part of a division and able to be assigned wherever and whenever needed. According to the military records that itemize his duties during that period, Aptheker "served as Assistant S-2 . . . [and] functioned as the Survey Officer for the battalion . . . to locate the target area . . . collected, evaluated and disseminated information relative to enemy strength, disposition and capabilities. Established and coordinated observation for the battalion." Aptheker recounted that he also had "charge of the morale of the men, including . . . (somewhat ironically in my case) questions of loyalty to our country."[15]

Aptheker did not hide his membership in the CPUSA, but he didn't advertise it either. He understood party policy for soldiers to be one of hands off while in the military. Yet many Communists had a difficult time while serving their country. Regulations adopted by the War Department in 1942 specified procedures whereby unit commanders could identify "potentially subversive persons," including Communists, fascists, and enemy aliens. Once identified prior to the unit's departure for the European war, such potential subversives could be "transferred to specially organized service and labor battalions slated to remain in the United States." Military Intelligence (G-2) carried out this policy until the party and the liberal press raised the question of discrimination against Communists. Eventually the War Department issued orders that prohibited discrimination against party members "unless there is a specific finding that the individual involved has a loyalty to the Communist Party as an organization which overrides his loyalty to the United States." Nonetheless, agents "rifled their lockers, read their mail, and questioned their barracks-mates to uncover evidence of disloyal utterances or behavior." Although he thought several times when a commanding officer summoned him that he had been identified as a party member, Aptheker never ran afoul of the regulations. At one meeting with Military Intelligence, after his arrival at Fort Bragg in May 1944, Aptheker suspected that someone had exposed his party membership. "Again, I thought, now my past has caught up with me," Aptheker wrote. However, the G-2 officer instructed Aptheker to be on the lookout for Communists in his unit. How should Aptheker identify a Communist? Be on the alert, the G-2 officer said, for "possibly some effort at indoctrination of other soldiers, of excessive worry about treatment of Negroes in general and Negro soldiers in particular, of constant agitation about the horrendous evils of fascism, of the remarkable resistance of the Soviets." On one occasion someone informed Aptheker that one of his men was a party member, so Aptheker talked to the younger man. If he was a Communist, Aptheker told him, he could apply for a service battalion position that would keep him from being sent to Europe. The suggestion of a transfer outraged his comrade, the enlisted man. He remained with his unit.[16]

At each of Aptheker's duty stations along the way, Fay had moved and set up a new household to be with him. They packed up their few possessions, loaded them into a car, and drove to each new army camp. At Fort Bragg, as the training became more intense in obvious preparation for deployment overseas, Fay progressed through the last few months of pregnancy. Fay's and Herbert's only child, Bettina, was born on 2 September 1944. Not long after Bettina's birth, the 940th made final preparations for departure in December, and Fay closed up the small apartment the couple had been renting and moved back to Brooklyn with Bettina. Like all young lovers separated by war, Herbert and Fay constantly pledged their devotion and love. "Today," Herbert had written to Fay during a previous separation, "you are not part of me—at least not a distinguishable part. You and I have become, to me, indissoluble. I know not where one or the other begins, or ends. This is absolutely tangible, physical with me, and I think you understand, though re-reading the sentence, the words, as such, seem to make poor sense."[17]

Other letters written in December 1944 and January 1945 by other figures carried a sinister message. In December 1944 J. Edgar Hoover issued written instructions to FBI agents to check into the background of Capt. Herbert Aptheker, then on his way to Europe to join the war. A witness had mentioned Aptheker's name in connection with a probe by the House Military Affairs Committee to ascertain the truth about "alleged Communist 'infiltration' of the army's officer corps." On 4 January 1945, as Aptheker's unit in France was poised for battle, New York Special Agent in Charge E. E. Conroy reported to Hoover that Aptheker had connections to the *Daily Worker,* Columbia University, the *Journal of Negro History,* the *New Masses, Science & Society,* and the *Journal of Negro Life.* Conroy's letter explained that Aptheker's work centered on the history of black people, listed his publications, and detailed the content of his writing. The agent quoted Aptheker without comment: "This government's treatment of . . . the negro people . . . is a deliberate expression and important component of American Imperialism."[18]

Aptheker's writing evidently did not sit well with Hoover, who, after receiving Conroy's report, did not waste any time in pursuing the matter. On 16 January 1945 he wrote to the assistant chief of staff, G-2, War Department. He submitted for "your information" the gist of Conroy's report and noted that "*New Masses* and *Science and Society,* [were] both Communist-dominated publications." From that modest beginning Aptheker's FBI file would grow by about one thousand pages per year for the next thirty years.[19]

In December 1944 the 940th sailed on the *SS Ericson* for La Havre, France. After docking there, the battalion moved a few miles to a staging area near Lillebonne and began hasty training procedures in anticipation of being used as reinforcements in the Ardennes in the Battle of the Bulge, the last great German counteroffensive, launched on 16 December 1944. The battalion passed quickly from training exercises to the battlefield when the supreme allied commander, Gen. Dwight Eisenhower, launched his own counterattack on the retreating Germans in what turned out to be the final offensive of the war in Europe.[20]

As Aptheker's artillery battalion rolled across France, Belgium, Holland, and eventually into Germany, he snatched moments every day to write to Fay. The letters ranged from philosophical discourse and observations on the brutality of war to thoughts on what Ambrose has called "the most ordinary day-to-day activities of civilian life." "Took about 25 men back with me to a fairly large city and saw that they got a bath, and ate a meal inside four walls," Aptheker wrote on 30 January 1945. "And then I did the same," he continued. "You've never seen your schnitzy so anxious for a bath in real warm water inside a building. What luxury! . . . and the toilet, or W.C. as it is labeled here—again inside, & dry and warm." On another day he wrote, "Oh to get the killing over with so that we can get to the rebuilding—to love and to heat—kindness and food—certainty and creative effort." With a new baby at home to worry about, he constantly cast an eye on the children in Europe ravaged by war: "Had I but ten thousand chocolate bars I would but begin to meet their clamors. This, too, is an experience—being *unable* to give a hungry kid something to eat. . . . There is so much suffering. The children eat me up. They wander about ragged and hungry, scared and tired, and above all, without security or love." The children's deprivation brought out the killer instinct in Aptheker: "What is to be done with the children—little girls and boys and the lame and halt (so many). The pig tails tied & the faces dirty. The eyes young and so old. The quivering mouth. . . . And I have seen and see the children & I've fondled them. Some are afraid of everything. Some respond unlike any kids I ever saw before—they respond like a dog that has been beaten often. They withdraw like the head of a frightened turtle. . . . The Nazis force cruelty upon all—how good it is to be killing them! The opportunity elates me."[21]

By the time of the Battle of the Bulge the Allied forces experienced a shortage of infantry troops, especially experienced ones. In the Ardennes the Germans attacked "eighteen- and nineteen-year-old barely trained Americans. Both sides had been forced to turn to their children to fight the war to its end. In the last winter of World War II, neither army could be said to be a veteran army." The manpower shortage was apparent to army commanders as early as 1943. As had happened in earlier wars, necessity led the War Department to contemplate the use of black combat units rather than employing black soldiers exclusively as noncombatant, service battalions driving trucks and burying corpses. After the Battle of the Bulge, Eisenhower, while confirming the need to maintain a Jim Crow army in Europe, "declared that Negro volunteers would be trained as platoons and put into the line on that basis." On 1 March 1945, a day when Aptheker wrote optimistically, "Things are going well with us. . . . They cannot stand many more weeks like the past one—God damn their souls!," the first 2,253 of the 4,562 black volunteers completed infantry retraining. Each of them "relinquished any ratings they might have had and accepted the grade of private." Organized into all-black infantry platoons commanded by white platoon leaders and sergeants, many found themselves at the front fighting Nazis for the first time. They also found themselves assigned as individuals to white units. "The 'experiment' was a sensational success," according to the historian L. D. Reddick. To Aptheker, who eventually welcomed black troops into the all-white battery under his command, the event was life affirming. "Has the press acclaimed the colossal event," he asked Fay, "namely, the placing of front-line Negro soldiers within *same* units as whites fighting side by side? Has the press made clear the fact that this act was performed because of necessity not as a gift—because such action was needed on that front in the struggle against Fascism? It is this necessity that gives the act its ultimate significance. Has that been made clear?" He raised the matter again the next day: "The declared and announced policy of no racial discrimination, which has reached its culmination in the recent order allowing Negroes & whites to fight together within the same units, is truly a colossal event." He continued,

> It has penetrated the minds and sharply challenged the shibboleths and taboos of millions. One sees a Negro soldier and a white female civilian together very frequently. What is the bigoted one to do? Basic to his rationalization of his prejudice is the belief that the aversion which he feels is instinctive, is natural. Rarely will he admit it is artificial and conditioned, that it is nurtured in and by environment. But here, time after time, he sees waking, living refutations of this basic conviction. He sees whites—and women—who obviously do not possess this prejudice. Not that they have conquered it—this he would understand and it would not disturb him so very much. No, they haven't conquered prejudice, they simply do not have it. So, it is not natural. And he sees that a dozen times. Normally he is enraged and bitter, for what is so hopeless as a bigoted mind which has lost its rationalizations and retains but its taboos? And officially, expressions of his basically challenged prejudices are illegal, are forbidden. This . . . is a time for a being to be alive.[22]

Through Belgium and Holland the 940th had no direct contact with the retreating Germans. They fired their artillery from five, ten, or sometimes fifteen miles from enemy positions. As he and his unit pressed on east into Germany, refugees, fleeing west, clogged the road. As much as he wanted to kill German soldiers Aptheker would not allow the men under his command to murder fleeing civilians. When his driver, a corporal named Alman, saying he wanted "to kill every one of the bastards," one day nearly ran down a group of refugees while Aptheker was in the jeep, only Aptheker's stern warning, he asserted, narrowly averted a potential calamity.[23]

The shooting war ended for Aptheker and his men when the 940th helped secure the western third of Dusseldorf, from which his unit battered the SS in the other part of the city across the Rhine River, killing thousands. Their howitzers demolished apartment buildings where they thought German soldiers were hiding. Headquarters ordered the 940th to dig in and consolidate its position while at the same time reassigning Aptheker, possibly because of his language skills—he read German and he spoke German and Yiddish—to a job he relished: "Counter-Intelligence Activity locating and arresting Nazis." "A good day—quite a haul," he wrote to Fay on 17 April. His unit had captured the Gestapo chief of the Dusseldorf area, and Aptheker interrogated the young Nazi: "Plenty of interesting and useful records taken & vicious people dispatched . . . records of the slave laborers, including children as young as 12! One dreams of such opportunities." After questioning the Gestapo leader, Aptheker turned him over to headquarters. "I still see him and his cockiness," Aptheker wrote decades later, "and now and then regret turning him over, alive. Perhaps a few years later he became Mayor of Dusseldorf!" When a German woman, "tall, about 35, handsome, well dressed," recently returned to Dusseldorf, asked for a pass to look for buried dishes in a restricted area where her house had been, Aptheker asked her what had happened to the sixty thousand Jews who had lived in the city before the war. "I have nothing," the woman said. "Not even my piano. That is all that interested me. I never mixed in politics. I do not know what went on in the cellars of the Gestapo & the SS. . . . And one could not look, it was not allowed. One could say nothing. It was not allowed. . . . I know nothing of such things." The woman told him, "I teach piano and that is all I do. I teach the piano. Now, all is gone." Aptheker gave her the pass. Not long after his encounter with the piano teacher Aptheker came into contact with a refugee Frenchman. "Very thin. A little gray. 42 years old. Stutters badly," he told Fay. The man had wounded, infected, misshapen hands and torn, lacerated legs, so Aptheker had a medic examine him. The medic discovered that the bones of the man's hands and legs, "from his knees to his ankles," had been broken by the Gestapo nine months previously and had never been set. "They had used a hammer on his hands and legs. He, too, had played the piano."[24]

Captain Aptheker took satisfaction in having Nazi district leaders and Gestapo agents snap to attention when brought into his office for questioning.

When he spoke to captured Nazis he knew his German was mixed with Yiddish, and he knew that they knew it, which "increases the delight twenty-fold," he wrote in one letter on the stationery of "Kurt Liebeneiner, Oberleutnant." When he found and arrested the secretary of the Criminal Investigation Department of the Gestapo of Dusseldorf, Fritz Drees—a "pig-eyed bastard" Aptheker called him—he took special delight in playing cat and mouse. He let Drees stand at attention for several minutes while he rifled through his dossier, which contained a photograph. "What is your name . . . and what do you do?" Aptheker began in his mixed German-Yiddish. "Carl Lehrer: I am a chemist," came the response. "So you are Carl Lehrer? Write the name Fritz Drees. You can spell it— D R E E S? You are Fritz Drees?" Aptheker demanded. "He holds the pen but has not written. He does not write—he says yes, I am Fritz Drees. . . . He identified the papers [in his dossier]. The Gestapo?—yes, yes, even the Gestapo. He's in a hurry now. Get it over with. We oblige, and he is sent, under arrest . . . to await his trial."[25]

Finding and arresting Nazis had its dark side for Aptheker too. "I have seen with mine eyes the Gestapo chambers," he wrote to Fay:

> I have seen the broken hands, crushed ribs, mutilated genitals—I have seen these things & smelled Fascism—and so have many of us. Let the Ku Klux Klan remember that & we have learned how to fight—have we not? . . . after seeing these things they are still unbelievable. Wholesale, organized, institutionalized lynchings—a taste of the South with a predominant, uncontrolled KKK. This racialism can produce the end of everything, even mercy—even the essence of humanity . . . and suffering, pain, deprivation can become so common, so wide-spread that it appears to be normal and correct. (Like Negro slavery appeared to most Americans a hundred years ago.) . . . Sometimes I wish the Nazis did not surrender quite so readily these days for when they do one must not kill them.[26]

With the German army in full retreat and society in chaos, millions of people displaced by the war wandered the countryside: "Trudging on foot, hitching rides on bicycles, motorcycles, looted German cars, trucks and hay wagons, this stumbling mass of humanity moves steadily on, urged by one fixed idea: to get home." Military planners assigned by President Roosevelt as early as November 1943 to restore civil society in Germany after the war, "to plan and execute civilian relief," realized that providing food and "controlling the spread of disease" would be key elements for securing "a strong and orderly occupation." To accomplish twin goals, first, to care for displaced persons and then to repatriate persons to their home countries, military planners "divided the responsibility for the repatriation process and the provision of material aid . . . among several institutions . . . with final authority resting with military commanders. It assigned responsibility for the location, care and control of DPs [displaced persons], for submitting regular reports as to their numbers and locations, for providing safe living conditions and adequate medical care, and for arranging their repatriation to military commanders." As part of this process the army assigned Aptheker additional duties as a "Military Government Officer in charge of 8 Displaced Person Camps harboring from 5000–7000 people," who had to be "fed, clothed, housed and ministered to," according to Aptheker's military record. Aptheker estimated, when writing to Fay about his additional duties, that "there are in Germany some 9 million people to be relocated, in Europe some 25 million." He added, with special emphasis, "And ragged, rickety children with wide eyes everywhere." But he remained optimistic: "Working hard & generally getting a kick out of it. One now has an opportunity to help rebuild lives directly as well as destroying what is left of the enemy. . . . Sometimes I am tired & my heart hurts so that I look for you—I look for you. . . . And I find you & the kid in the pictures & see also the lit faces of the people we have freed & see them hug & kiss each other and it's all right again."[27]

Most of the people passing through the camps under Aptheker's control, freed slave laborers from Poland and Russia, were women, some were children and infants, and a few were wounded or disabled men. To house the thousands of displaced persons Aptheker took over a village, located abandoned houses, and had them repaired. He commandeered Gestapo headquarters, a monastery, at Klaus Knechsteden that had escaped artillery bombardment. The monastery had a large kitchen and room for about a thousand people who eagerly made themselves at home. When a priest approached Aptheker to complain about the shameful spectacle of men and women living together under the same roof, Aptheker thought, right, the Gestapo is okay but freed slaves, no. When Aptheker "told the priest to tell the monsignor to write out his complaint and I would see that his Holiness the Pope was informed of this awful situation," the priest disappeared, never to be seen again.[28]

The Allied forces had freed the foreign slave laborers on whom Germany had come to depend to till the fields at bayonet point, but as early as May food shortages wracked the already desperate refugees. "There may well be a food scarcity in parts of Europe (is already, of course) that will become quite serious," Aptheker wrote in May. He predicted there would be frequent public demonstrations. He lamented the cause of the protests but felt that if they erupted that would be a good thing. "Let the people demonstrate, demand, and speechify, unite and act in a united open fashion," he wrote. "They've got to learn how to do this once more and they've got to get the feel of masses out again at their own initiative, hearing their own speakers and their own words & their own demands. Do democrats envisage anything else or want anything else? Certainly not. To some people, masses creating a new order represent disorder—but not to me." He was not as sanguine about resistance to demands for cooperation from local Germans. As military planners had predicted in their "Outline Plan of June 1944" for handling displaced persons, which forecast that "foreign displaced persons would be treated with hostility," the German officials in Aptheker's area did not readily cooperate. At Aptheker's request, the local mayor reluctantly supplied milk for the uprooted crowds, but at a subsequent meeting, exasperated by the mayor's intransigence, Aptheker cocked his pistol, pointed it at the mayor's head, thought better of killing him, regretted not doing it, he said, then, pounding his pistol on the mayor's desk, ordered him to obtain "sanitary napkins" for the thousands of women in his care.[29]

Throughout April anticipation built among U.S. forces that an end to the war was imminent. Aptheker too felt victory in the air. "The shell has cracked, absolutely and without question," he wrote late in April. "Perhaps this May Day will indeed be memorable." He lamented the death of Roosevelt ("sure it was an awful blow"), yet he realized that "no one is indispensable" because even at that late date "a lot of good men get it regularly—even now though it's all but over they're still getting it." But he felt sure Allied victory was near: "We go on—nothing can stop us now. . . . And we will have lived to see the war against Fascism concluded successfully. This is a rich life. And we shall be together. Be of good cheer my comrade," he wrote to Fay.[30]

At the end of April the army sent Aptheker to Paris temporarily to study a new piece of artillery. From there he wrote of a memorable May Day indeed: "Most beloved—Well, darling, a happy May Day—The Soviet flag flies over the Reichstag, Munich is ours, Mussolini is on exhibit in Milan. This is the day for which millions have waited, labored, suffered, died. Let the People rejoice! Let tyrants tremble! Let future would-be despoilers of humanity heed well this lesson written in blood, tears, stench, and immortal courage." He joined the throngs in the streets, "people on crutches, babies in carriages, men and women dancing and singing and hysterical with joy and overhead everywhere waved the Red Flag of the Communist Party of France, of the Party of Liberation." Groups of excited Parisians hoisted Americans in uniform onto their shoulders, including Aptheker. They carried him aloft, kissed him, hugged him, hailed "the American! Vive America! Vive France! Vive Liberty! Vive, vive, vive God Almighty," he wrote, "surely once in a lifetime."[31]

Finally, on 8 May 1945, Victory in Europe Day began: "The excitement in Paris on VE-Day echoed that of the city when it had been liberated eight and a half months earlier." "Millions were out last night, . . . all of France," Aptheker wrote to Fay, "unconditional surrender, beloved one! . . . We have crushed them . . . the people are so happy. . . . I watched 2 million people in the process of exhibiting their ecstasy at the termination of 5 years of hell, slavery, anxiety, terror. It was a marvelous sight. . . . Flowers, tears, smiles, shouts, shining eyes, mouths open so that overflowing hearts might not burst. . . . [T]he very pavements shed tears."[32]

Back at the displaced persons' camps Aptheker oversaw a steady stream of former slaves repatriated, ten or twelve thousand by mid-May, he estimated. In mid-June, as Aptheker felt life returning to some kind of normality, he strolled the banks of the river Kocher reading a book he had rescued from a destroyed house, the love letters of Elizabeth Barrett Browning and Robert Browning. He felt refreshed, "better than I have felt for some months." His sense of accomplishment in a job well done was shared by his commanding officers. They wrote that Aptheker was "exceptionally well informed . . . intelligent . . . loyal . . . quiet in manner but is resourceful and dependable . . . enthusiastic, ingenious, and circumspect. He is very methodical and meticulous . . . is friendly and tactful." Both Lt. Col. James V. Sanden and Lt. Col. C. W. Wilmore recommended that Aptheker be promoted and that, if at all possible, the army keep him in service when the war was over.[33]

Then, abruptly, it was over. His unit began breaking up. "The worst part of Army life is now here," he lamented in a letter home, "the breaking up of units, the separation of friends—brothers. . . . Those I loved most . . . move elsewhere, and my own men—who worked in closest proximity to me—we've dug into the same trembling earth and looked into each other's eyes when those eyes were clear windows rather than drawn shades, as eyes so often are in ordinary contacts among people. How close humans become sharing common adversities and working together for a common goal! Yet, how resistant is man's spirit." Through June and most of July he waited for his orders to leave Europe. In early August, as the troopship in which he rode steamed across the Atlantic toward what he felt sure would be a brief leave before continuing on to war in the Pacific, word came that the atom bombs dropped on Hiroshima and Nagasaki had ended the war with Japan.[34]

Aptheker certainly hated Hitler and the Nazi regime and no doubt held equal enmity for the Japanese military machine. But he never succumbed to the overpowering racism toward the Japanese that gripped much of the United States during and after the war. In February 1944, in fact, he openly criticized such racism in a letter to the *Field Artillery Journal*. Responding to an article by Lt. Col. Earl W. Hunting titled "The Hymn of Hate," Aptheker granted a degree of truth to Hunting's statement that "the American soldier frequently lacks hatred for his Nazi and Japanese enemies" but strongly disagreed when Hunting opined that the Japanese "should be cursed as a 'Yellow son [of a bitch].'" "Our hatred of the enemy must be rational," Aptheker wrote, "must be based not only on hatred for him who challenges our lives in a physical sense, but also, and at least as strongly, for him who challenges our way of life, and the possibility of enhancing the dignity and creative value of humanity." What he found most disturbing in Hunting's article, he said, was that "a hatred based upon illusionary 'racialistic' presumptions is positively dangerous for us if we are to achieve one of our prime war aims—the destruction of fascism." Besides, Aptheker wrote, from a purely practical viewpoint one should keep in mind that "we are allied with some 450,000,000 people whose complexions happen to approximate that color." He later criticized the use of atomic weapons against Japanese cities. "It is an ironic and tragic thing," he wrote, "that the culminating horror in this catalogue of atrocities [the bombing of civilian populations during the Second World War] fell upon the American Republic which, in visiting two Japanese cities with portable crematoria, consumed in their flames thousands of men, women and children."[35]

In September the U.S. government diverted several troopships carrying U.S. soldiers home from Europe "to transport US-armed French soldiers and Foreign Legionaries from France to re-colonize Vietnam." The troopship crews organized protests, "condemning the US government for using American ships to transport an invasion army 'to subjugate the native population' of Vietnam." The Second World War had ended, but the fight to end the threat of nuclear war and to stop what became an American war against Vietnam would occupy decades of Aptheker's life. But then, in August 1945, the hot war was over and although the Cold War had already begun in the spring of 1945 when the United States and the Soviet Union found themselves unable to agree on the political future of Poland, Aptheker's thoughts centered on Brooklyn, on home, on Fay and Bettina.[36]

4   The Aptheker Thesis

WHEN APTHEKER took up the intensive study of African American history in order to complete his master's degree in 1936, few white historians were interested in the subject—"very few, if any, mainstream white historians read, cited, or reviewed African American scholarship"—and fewer still chose to work exclusively in the field. In fact, not until the 1970s did the greater part of white historians recognize African American history "as anything more than a marginal specialty." Black people had written about their experiences, but the books and pamphlets that blacks had produced, even before the Civil War, "came from the pens of popularizers" and polemicists "rather than scholars" trained in the study of history. In 1915, the year Carter G. Woodson founded the Association for the Study of Negro Life and History (ASNLH), there were only two black PhDs trained in history, W. E. B. Du Bois, who in 1895 was the first black to receive a Harvard doctorate, and Woodson himself, who received his doctoral degree from Harvard in 1912. Over the next two decades, Woodson, whose parents had been slaves, molded the ASNLH and the *Journal of Negro History* (*JNH*), which he also founded in 1916, into the premier institutions championing the study of black history. ASNLH and the *JNH* "were the preeminent outlets for scholarly expressions and institutionally personified the field" of black historical study. Aptheker constantly reiterated how indebted he was to Woodson's pioneering work. "He was a prodigious worker, a remarkable organizer and an extraordinary scholar," Aptheker recalled not long after Woodson's death in 1950, "a Negro with a consuming love for his people and pride in them and a contempt for the 'barbarians'—as he used to refer to the chauvinists—who oppressed the Negro."[1]

Even Woodson's dogged determination to advance "the race through the promotion of Negro history" couldn't overcome the virulent racism that characterized the United States through the first five decades of the twentieth century. In the forty-five years after Du Bois received his doctorate, universities awarded only twelve additional PhDs in history and the history of education to black scholars. Nonetheless, as the historians August Meier and Elliott Rudwick pointed out in 1986 in their study of the historical profession, those fourteen black scholars were the "first generation of professionally trained black doctorates associated with Woodson who were chiefly responsible for laying the foundation for the study of Afro-American history as a genuine scholarly specialty."[2]

Up to the mid to late 1930s few of the white historians who studied black history, with some notable exceptions, wrote sympathetically about blacks. Herbert Baxter Adams, who believed that blacks and whites would find it difficult to "live peaceably together with equal civil rights," encouraged early studies of slavery at Johns Hopkins University. At Columbia University the historians John W. Burgess and William Archibald Dunning focused on studies of Reconstruction from a decidedly racist perspective. One of Dunning's students, Ulrich B. Phillips, who received his doctoral degree in 1902, published *American Negro Slavery* in 1918, a book that made his name "virtually synonymous with slavery historiography." Phillips, whom Aptheker acknowledged in 1943 as being "generally considered the outstanding authority of the institution of American Negro slavery," described blacks as "suffering from 'inherited ineptitude,' and as being stupid, negligent, docile, inconstant, dilatory and 'by racial quality submissive.'" Aptheker thought that the social consequences for black people affected by Phillips's interpretation involved more than simple academic debate. Phillips's historical construct, Aptheker later wrote, "was fundamental to the racism in idea and in practice, that characterizes the United States from its colonial past to its Reaganomic present. It characterized as it bulwarked the status quo; it excused a barbarous past as it rationalized a putrid present." "Let there be no mistake about it," the historian Eugene Genovese wrote in his foreword to the reissue of *American Negro Slavery* in 1966, "Phillips was a racist, however benign and paternalistic." Looking at the weaknesses of *American Negro Slavery,* Genovese claimed that Phillips's "racism cost him dearly and alone accounts for his lapse from greatness as a historian. It blinded him; it inhibited him from developing fully his own extraordinary insights; it prevented him from knowing many things he in fact knew very well."[3]

Because Aptheker did take black people seriously as men and women, as actors in the historical process, he was able to arrive at many of the extraordinary insights to which Phillips's racism blinded him. That breakthrough is apparent in Aptheker's early pamphlets and articles, but his work on the Nat Turner rebellion shows an especially crucial turning point. Aptheker located the Turner uprising in a broader global setting "which placed Turner's rebellion within the context of falling cotton prices, rising abolitionist sentiment in Great Britain and Mexico, and fear generated by slave revolts in Antigua and Martinique." He found that "no data exist to show the innate inferiority of the Negro (or any other peoples) but that, on the contrary, what data exist tend to confirm the opposite conclusion." The evidence about Turner, gleaned from the contemporary observations of white southerners, revealed, said Aptheker, "a highly intelligent man who finds it impossible to accept the status quo and discovers his rationalization for his rebellious feelings in religion." Aptheker wrote of Turner's followers that one should consider them "not as deluded wretches and monsters (unless all revolutionists may thus be described) but rather as further examples of the woefully long, and indeed veritably endless, roll of human beings willing to resort to open struggle in order to get something precious to them—peace, prosperity, liberty, or, in a word"—here Aptheker alluded to Thomas Jefferson's phrase in his manifesto for revolution—"a greater amount of happiness."[4]

Aptheker asserted that "when I looked into Nat Turner I found he was not alone, that the Nat Turner insurrection was only the high point of a volcanic, seething force that had manifested itself in Louisiana and in Mississippi, etc., and that suppression preceded Nat Turner—none of the books made that point—that the laws came in the 1820s, not the 1830s." That conclusion, accepted as it currently is in the historiography of slavery in the United States, ran counter to the conventional reading of the slave experience, for example, that of Phillips, who wrote that "slave revolts and plots very seldom occurred in the United States." "Nothing in American historiography has been more neglected," Aptheker wrote in the introduction to his article in *Science & Society* (1937) on slave uprisings, titled "American Negro Slave Revolts," "nor, when treated, more distorted, than the story of these revolts." While confining himself to sketching numerous slave revolts in the *Science & Society* article, he saw revolts and rebellions as only one manifestation of a broad resistance to slavery among black people: "He carefully itemized [other instances of resistance]—the purchasing of freedom, strikes, sabotage, suicide, flight, enlistment in the armed services, and anti-slavery agitation." Aptheker advanced some tentative conclusions in his master's thesis and in the article of 1937 that he continued to explore in publications and research for his doctoral dissertation, conclusions that would occupy other historians of the slave experience for decades.[5]

He concluded that "the fear of slave revolts and the panic that ensued upon the discovery, or supposed discovery of plots, or the suppression of revolts, were factors of prime importance in the social, political and economic life of the United States. This panic was no rare phenomenon." The black struggle for freedom, he asserted, played a central role in the larger political, social, and economic history of the United States. He found evidence to substantiate the notion that the fear of revolts drove the establishment of laws and customs in the South that reinforced the "instruments of class rule in America's slave system," class rule that not only fixed relations with slaves but also had often to address a large measure of black–white unity in slave unrest and the nineteenth-century antislavery struggle.[6]

Aptheker explored these class issues in publications over the next few years as he uncovered more evidence while working on his dissertation. He sought to elucidate a dynamic among masters, slaves, and poor whites. In his article of April 1939 about fugitive slaves, or Maroons, in the *JNH,* called "Maroons Within the Present Limits of the United States," he established the existence of "at least fifty" Maroon communities "in various places and at various times, from 1672 to 1864." In the "Dismal Swamp between Virginia and North Carolina" in the seventeenth century, in North and South Carolina, Georgia, and Virginia during the eighteenth century, and in the mountainous, forested, or swampy regions in most of the South during the nineteenth century. Maroon communities "offered havens for fugitives, served as bases for marauding expeditions against nearby plantations and, at times, supplied the nucleus of leadership for planned uprisings." Maroons established relations with nonslaveholding white people who lived on the frontier and carried on "regular, if illegal, trade." Aptheker's research showed that in many Maroon communities blacks and whites and Indians lived and worked together and were a constant source of "perpetual anxiety and apprehension" among nearby whites. When the government decided to evict Indians from Florida and catch runaway slaves for the citizens of Georgia in the Second Seminole War of 1835, a war that "cost the American military 1,600 lives, with many more wounded, as well as a staggering thirty to forty million dollars," army officers complained that "the maroon allies of the Indians were 'their best soldiers.'" During the Civil War poor whites avoiding the draft and Confederate Army deserters joined up with Maroon communities. "Many deserters . . . are collected in the swamps . . . and have organized, with runaway negroes, bands for the purpose of committing depredations upon the plantations and crops of loyal citizens and running off their slaves," one Confederate officer declared. Not until 2014, aside from brief digressions in some books and articles, was a study of Maroons published in the United States. For almost seventy-five years Aptheker's examination of these communities remained the most complete analysis of the phenomenon.[7]

Appearing almost simultaneously with the *JNH* article, Aptheker's two-part essay "Class Conflicts in the South—1850–1860," published in the *Communist* for February 1939, dwelled neither on the international scene, which he often included in his analysis, making reference to such events as the Haitian Revolution and the fluctuation in world cotton prices, nor on the national scene, the "spectacular political struggles between the North and the South," but on the "equally important contests which went on . . . within the South itself." Here Aptheker asked why the southern ruling class had turned to bullets. The Civil War, he had written a year earlier in his pamphlet *The Negro in the Civil War,* "will be better understood when it is remembered that they [the slaveholders] had become desperate not only because they had seen their external, or national power almost completely overthrown by an emerging industrial, free-labor society, but also because they were seeing their local, internal, power being seriously threatened by revolutionary stirrings among the slaves and poor whites."

In the *Communist* essays, which buttressed his previous analysis, while showing cognizance of the "growing conflict between an agrarian, slave-labor society and an increasingly industrial, free-labor society," he found a "growing internal disaffection . . . among the exploited classes—the non-slaveholding whites and the slaves," manifest in slave uprisings and instances of poor whites overcoming the "divide-and-rule policies established by slaveowners." Indeed, "independent political action of the non-slaveholding whites aimed at the destruction of the slavocracy's control of the state governments" explained "the desperation of the slaveholding class which drove it to the expedient of civil war." "This struggle," Aptheker concluded, "manifested itself in serious slave disaffection, in frequent cooperation between poor whites and Negro slaves, and in the rapid maturing of the political consciousness of the non-slaveholding whites." Here also, as in all of his writing prior to the publication of his dissertation, one finds an underpinning for Aptheker's contention that "American life as a whole cannot be understood without knowing" the history of African Americans and comprehending the centrality of the black struggle to the larger political history of the United States: he mentions the influence of racism on, among other things, the Declaration of Independence, the Constitution, the abolitionist movement, the Compromise of 1850, the publication of *Uncle Tom's Cabin,* the bloody war in Kansas, the Dred Scott decision, John Brown's raid, the battles fought in state constitutional conventions, censorship of the mails, the Fugitive Slave Law, and the election of 1860.[8]

"Aptheker's . . . work on black history presents a number of theses and suggestions that illuminate American history as a whole," Genovese wrote in 1995, "and have yet to receive the attention they deserve." Genovese acknowledged that not all of Aptheker's theses had "panned out as he would have liked, but all have proved fruitful, and many in fact have panned out." He continued, "Let me settle for a few of particular importance: the thesis of continuity, cumulative effect, and mutual reinforcement in the slave revolts; the thesis of interracial unity and the relation of the struggle of the slaves for freedom to the struggle of the southern yeomen and poor whites for material advancement and democratic rights; and the thesis of the centrality of the slaves' contribution to the struggle for political democracy in the United States as a whole."[9]

Genovese saw the first two theses as being useful to a point but not as fruitful as Aptheker might have hoped. Of the third, he wrote, "Aptheker's larger argument about class struggle in the South . . . is being proved right by the new work on antebellum political history. . . . The Confederate war effort collapsed in no small part because of the parallel struggles of slaves and yeomen against the slavocracy."[10]

Although Aptheker's early publications built on the pioneering efforts of Woodson and Du Bois, his conclusions came as a revelation to some black scholars. The historian John Hope Franklin recalled that when he first heard Aptheker read a paper based on his booklet *The Negro in the Civil War* (1938) at a conference of the ASNLH, he "was appalled not only by his graphic account of the carnage, caused in part by the lack of training of the black soldiers, but also by the fact that earlier historians of the Civil War scarcely recognized blacks as a fighting force in 'their war for freedom.'" The revelatory nature of Aptheker's work arrived in a somewhat variant form for other historians. Charles S. Sydnor of Duke University wrote acidly that *The Negro in the Civil War* "may be of some interest to students of current propaganda techniques, [but] its obvious deficiency in research and its one-sidedness of interpretation render it value-less to the historian, especially since Bill I. Wiley's *Southern Negroes, 1861–1865,* is now available." And Wiley himself wrote, in an ad hominem attack in the *American Historical Review,* that Aptheker's work "would make an excellent Emancipation Day oration before an audience composed of Negroes, Marx-ists, and descendants of William Lloyd Garrison." As the historian Julie Kailin pointed out, "Wiley had acknowledged in his own work the participation of Blacks in the Union Army," but Aptheker's conclusions about Reconstruction evidently festered in Wiley's psyche: "Working through the reactionary wing of the Republican Party," Aptheker had written, "the Northern big bourgeoisie sold out the Revolution by giving the old slave oligarchy a free hand ('home rule') in the Southern states. . . . The heroic fight of the Negro people and their allies for democracy, land and civil rights in the South was defeated chiefly as a result of the shameful betrayal by the industrial and financial bourgeoisie of the North. . . . This 'gentlemen's agreement' meant disenfranchisement for the Negro, sharecropping peonage, lynch terrorism, and the loss of civil liberties and educational opportunities."[11]

Red-baiting of Aptheker's work became de rigueur for some critics. Meier and Rudwick, writing in 1966, asserted with disapprobation and no specific evidence that Aptheker interpreted his sources "in the framework of his Communist ide-ology," although twenty years later, again without examples, they claimed that in *American Negro Slave Revolts* Aptheker "only hinted at the Marxist outlook." They would have been on surer footing, not to say accurate, had they claimed that Aptheker interpreted his sources by employing a Marxist dialectical method, "an insistence upon the objective nature and causal relatedness of historical facts."[12] Indeed, Aptheker employed the strongest element and the most indispensable part of Marxist theory, the use of the dialectic, as a historical method. To Ap-theker, the dialectical method was the only basis for deriving an adequate theory of history. He examined interconnections and treated each historical aspect as being implicated in the whole. He understood that the fight for slave libera-tion and, more broadly, for democracy could be defined and understood only by identifying what suppressed and excluded slaves: the slavocracy and racism.

Aptheker continued to collect research materials for his dissertation while serving in the army. At each new posting he gathered more documentation. In addition to hundreds of secondary sources, he examined letters, diaries, memoirs, and personal papers of the famous and humble, colonial, state, and national government documents, law digests, dozens of periodicals, newspapers, and pamphlets, travel accounts, and contemporary histories at universities, libraries, and archives in seven states—Massachusetts, New York, Virginia, Mississippi, North Carolina, Maryland, and South Carolina—and the Library of Congress. In Alexandria, Louisiana, while he worked on writing his manuscript in longhand, Fay furiously typed the document on their portable typewriter, a collaboration that lasted the rest of their lives together. "I typed five copies with carbons," Fay recalled, "[and] I had a time with the footnotes. I had to be sure that I was able to get all the footnotes in on the page," a tedious and exacting process in those days. "It was quite a chore," Fay said of typing the four-hundred-plus-page manuscript. Aptheker sent drafts of the dissertation to his graduate advisers at Columbia. Frank Tannenbaum, the eminent professor of Latin American history, cautioned Aptheker on the length of the work: "The real question is this: your thesis seems . . . entirely too long. We . . . wonder whether you wouldn't want to cut the manuscript before you have the five copies made, to save expense. . . . I really think you have entirely too many details for your basic point." But the dissertation challenged Phillips, the leading authority on the slave experience, and he did not want anyone to charge that he had not advanced sufficient evidence for his heretical thesis.[13]

Some faculty members were reluctant to award a doctorate to Aptheker because doing so meant that, following the usual protocol, Columbia University would be required to publish his dissertation. After his oral exams, "a rather grueling 5 hour" process, the conservative economic historian Joseph Dorfman, who had sat in on the exam, confided to Aptheker that "there had been resistance to giving a Communist a doctorate from Columbia, but he thought this would be overcome." In the end Columbia did award Aptheker a PhD degree in history, and Columbia University Press did publish his dissertation, *American Negro Slave Revolts,* in 1943 as part of its prestigious series History, Economics, and Public Law.[14]

In the book Aptheker brought together all the themes that had characterized his writing up to that point. He began with an extended discussion of his argument that there were "few phases of ante-bellum Southern life and history that were not in some way influenced by the fear of, or the actual outbreak of, militant concerted slave action." "One finds," he wrote, "very nearly unanimous agreement concerning the widespread fear of servile rebellion." To maintain their social order, to "prevent or . . . efficiently to suppress mass Negro rebelliousness," the "legal, social, and theological aspects of pre–Civil War Southern life" revolved around a system constructed to protect slaveholder interests. He examined that system, illuminating the "machinery of control" set up by slaveholders to extinguish slave rebellion. "They called into play every trick, rule, regulation, and device that the human mind could invent to aid them; the attempted psychological, intellectual, and physical debasement of an entire people," Aptheker wrote of the slavocracy, "the inculcating and glorifying of the most outrageous racial animosities . . . in short, of a social order within which the institution of Negro slavery became so deeply imbedded that it was true that to touch one was to move the other." Cruelty was "an innate, inextricable part of American Negro slavery, for [slaves] had to be maltreated, had to be made to suffer physical cruelty, had to be chained and lashed and beaten into producing for a profit. . . . Instead of a slave's value preventing cruelty, it was exactly because of that value, and that greater value he could produce—when forced—that cruelty existed." He explored the dialectical nature of the relationship between masters and slaves, which showed that the essential element underlying revolt and rebellion was the social system itself: "It may be declared that many factors appear to have been of consequence in bringing on slave rebellions," such as "the prevalence of slogans and propaganda about liberty and equality . . . a disproportionate growth of the Negro population as compared with white . . . industrialization and urbanization . . . economic depression. Yet, the fundamental factor provoking rebellion against slavery was that social system itself, the degradation, exploitation, oppression, and brutality which it created and with which, indeed, it was synonymous." The cause of slave revolts, he declared, was slavery.[15]

After examining individual acts of resistance carried out by slaves, including flight, sabotage, pretending illness, stealing, suicide, self-mutilation, and strikes, among others, Aptheker turned to extensive presentation of the plots and rebellions he had uncovered in his research. He carefully defined his terms so readers would make no mistake. Whereas Texas law defined a slave insurrection as "an assemblage of three or more, with arms, with intent to obtain their liberty by force," Aptheker's definition was more demanding: "The elements of the definition . . . are: a minimum of ten slaves involved; freedom as the apparent aim of the disaffected slaves; contemporary references labeling the event as an uprising, plot, insurrection, or the equivalent of these terms. The study, moreover, excludes, with a few exceptions, the scores of outbreaks and plots that occurred upon domestic or foreign slave-traders." Using those criteria as a foundation, Aptheker had found "records of approximately two hundred and fifty revolts and conspiracies in the history of American Negro slavery." He noted that "occasionally the plans or aspiration of the rebels were actually *reported* as going beyond a desire for personal freedom and envisioning, in addition, a property redistribution; and, . . . that, white people were frequently implicated—or believed to be implicated—with the slaves in the plans or efforts to overthrow the master class by force." In temperate, considered language Aptheker ended the study by observing that "the generally accepted notion that [the slave] response was one of passivity and docility" needed revision, which his evidence had presented. "The evidence," he wrote in the last sentence of the book, "points to the conclusion that discontent and rebelliousness were not only exceedingly common, but, indeed, characteristic of American Negro slaves." Decades later, when asked about the significance of his book, Aptheker responded with somewhat less restraint: "I challenged the whole goddamn thing, . . . U. B. Phillips, there was nothing else . . . and I lived long enough to say, with modesty, that Aptheker destroyed Phillips. Which is one good thing in terms of a life. That's something I did. Nobody can read U. B. Phillips's *American Negro Slavery* and take it seriously. And I called my book *American Negro Slave Revolts.* His is called *American Negro Slavery.* Very few people notice that, but I noticed it. It's one of my points."[16]

Black scholars and the leftist press, with a few exceptions, received the book with markedly favorable reviews. E. Franklin Frazier, writing in the *American Journal of Sociology,* maintained that Aptheker's conclusions were "at variance with the generally accepted opinions concerning the contentedness of the slaves. . . . [T]hat these slave rebellions were more frequent than our inadequate sources of information have led us to believe is proved by the documentation of the numerous cases of rebellions described by the author. . . . The information contained in this book will provide a corrective for the tendency on the part of sociologists to overemphasize the accommodation of the Negro to slavery." Frazier found the book to be "an important contribution to the literature on the Negro" and went on to note that the new information, while illuminating the period of slavery, could be useful as a corrective to ending Jim Crow: "It contains much information which might aid our thinking today concerning the so-called 'adjustment' of the Negro to his subordinate status in the South." In the *Journal of Negro Education,* Ellis O. Knox pointed to the "irrefutable evidence" with which "the author has showed that plans for slave control were neither effective nor practicable. . . . It is readily realized," he went on, "that such documentary evidence is a contribution to Southern, American and World history. Future historians must depict the American slave as a human being who possessed a will to resist oppression and a brain with which he hoped, and even helped to plan its demise." Knox justifiably called attention to the "stilted and somewhat difficult" style of the book found in Aptheker's "relating of series after series of events establishing the prevalence of slave revolts." Yet he excused the defect "for an authoritative presentation of a quantity of copiously documented data [as] necessary to expurgate a racial phantom which infected the minds of Southerners prior to emancipation, and continues to infect the minds of many competent historians, even today." Malcolm Cowley criticized the style more harshly when he called the book "an iceberg nine-tenths submerged in footnotes and inhospitable to landing parties, since it is written in a ruggedly academic style." Nonetheless, he wrote that the book contained "a mass of neglected information."[17]

The views emanating from the mainstream historical profession were decidedly less friendly. Writing for the *American Historical Review* (*AHR*), J. G. de Roulhac Hamilton, of the University of North Carolina, acknowledged that Aptheker's book was "clearly the result of tireless industry and tremendous research" but "fails completely to prove his thesis." Hamilton judged that Aptheker exaggerated "the rebellious character of the slaves quite as much as most writers have magnified their docility" and charged that the book relied too heavily on unverified rumor, "much of it of doubtful origin." He dismissed Aptheker's contention regarding the unremitting cruelty of slavery. "It is quite evident that the author does not know the South of the period of slavery, nor yet does he know slavery as it was," Hamilton wrote. "That cases of cruelty were not infrequent is of course true . . . but the whole body of authentic sources proves fairly conclusively that cruelty was the exception rather than the rule." The problem resided, said Hamilton, in Aptheker's choice of sources. If Aptheker had consulted planters' sources rather than those of "antislavery orators and abolitionist writers," *American Negro Slave Revolts* might not have been such an absurd piece of work with "several serious defects of arrangement, treatment, and interpretation."[18]

When he read Hamilton's review Aptheker quickly sent off a response to Guy Stanton Ford, the editor of *AHR*. Ford wrote back to say he would publish Aptheker's rejoinder to the Hamilton review but informed Aptheker that "I have [another response], from a professor who is equally outraged, and I think it would be better if we published his letter." Aptheker thought the advice sound, and Kenneth W. Porter's "communication" appeared in the *AHR* for October 1944. Porter, then a professor at Vassar College, "charged Hamilton with having attempted 'a brisk brush-off' and with providing no evidence to support his critical evaluation. . . . Porter added that citing a single specific and demonstrated error 'would have at least possessed more value than the last four-fifths of the alleged review.'" Porter, whom Aptheker had not yet met, later became a good friend, a relationship cut short by Porter's untimely death at a young age. As a professor at the University of Oregon, Porter often sponsored Aptheker's appearances there during the 1960s.[19]

AMERICAN NEGRO SLAVE REVOLTS was the culmination of the first of what the historians Meier and Rudwick called "three distinct bursts of slavery scholarship." Its effect was largely confined to scholars associated with the ASNLH and the *JNH*, Rayford Logan, Franklin, Woodson, and others who engaged Aptheker's thesis. But, as the historian Eric Foner pointed out in an interview,

Logan, Franklin, Woodson, and even Du Bois "were marginalized in the historical profession . . . in the late fifties, early sixties, nobody assigned articles in the *Journal of Negro History*. They *knew* it was there, but it wasn't considered part of the mainstream." In the mainstream white history profession the Phillipsian view still prevailed. The historian David Brion Davis acknowledged that perhaps a "few graduate students had at that time encountered Herbert Aptheker's *American Negro Slave Revolts*," but Davis "remained totally ignorant of the work of such black historians as W. E. B. Du Bois, Carter Woodson, Charles H. Wesley, Benjamin Quarles, Eric Williams, C. L. R. James, and John Hope Franklin" in 1954 when preparing for his doctoral oral exams. Aptheker's work, like that of Du Bois, was "dismissed because [it] didn't fit," Foner claimed, "partly because it was easy to dismiss someone who was a Communist in the middle of the Cold War; but partly because they [Aptheker and Du Bois] didn't fit with the general trend of American historical interpretation in the 1950s. . . . *American Negro Slave Revolts* and [Du Bois's book from 1935] *Black Reconstruction*, . . . essential building blocks of the American historical consciousness . . . classics, were twins in that sense, in that they were simply outside the dominant paradigm of American history, the consensus school, the vision of slavery and race relations which was dominant at that time." Foner asserted that Aptheker and Du Bois articulated essential challenges to the consensus interpretation: they both "took on the existing historiography forthrightly," but in general white historians did not criticize the work of Du Bois and Aptheker. "Any work should be criticized," Foner said, "but they were not even engaged."[20] The historian Robin D. G. Kelly recalled having the "mainstream profession's attitude toward Aptheker's work really hit home during the written portion of [his] Ph.D. qualifying examination." Asked to write a "critical essay on a major historian," Kelly had decided to write on Aptheker. Before beginning the essay he approached one of the faculty proctors and asked if Aptheker "fell under the category of 'major.' 'Absolutely not,' was the answer, delivered so abruptly [he] felt embarrassed for even asking the question."[21]

Sixteen years elapsed between the appearance of *American Negro Slave Revolts* and the opening of the second "burst of slavery scholarship" with the appearance of Kenneth Stampp's *The Peculiar Institution* in 1956 and Stanley Elkins's *Slavery: A Problem in American Institutional and Intellectual Life* three years later. During those years the United States and the Soviet Union plunged into the Cold War, the McCarthy witch hunts sought out enemies within, a travesty that included a purge of faculty at the nation's colleges and universities, and black people's demands for freedom and equality could no longer be ignored. An open Communist, Aptheker challenged the blacklist that kept him from being appointed to a university position and excoriated the profession as "a closed, intensely conservative, lily-white, anti-Semitic bulwark and reflection of the . . .

ruling class." He asked a basic question of academia: Should an avowed Communist be allowed to teach in an American university? The universities said no, and so did most liberals. "There were liberals or others, non-liberals, who were willing to defend the notion of academic freedom . . . but the question of Aptheker posed the issue of academic freedom in a more stark way." Academic freedom could be defended "for people who didn't turn in other people, or who didn't answer questions, or refused to cooperate, or who took the Fifth Amendment. . . . But they were not willing to defend an actual, bona fide, up-front Communist." Aptheker was, according to the activist and historian Staughton Lynd, "beyond question the American historian most discriminated against because of political belief." Historians who dominated the profession wrote him out of the canon of American history and created a "wall of silence around Aptheker."[22]

Stampp did engage Aptheker's thesis early on but echoed the charge that he had exaggerated the number of slave revolts. "If the significance of these cases has been overstated by Herbert Aptheker," he wrote in 1952 in an article in the *AHR*, "it has been understated by many of his predecessors." But then, in his *The Peculiar Institution,* Stampp made good use of Aptheker's groundbreaking work without any mention of exaggeration. "Aptheker," Stampp wrote in a footnote, "presents evidence of many conspiracies and a few rebellions, each involving ten or more slaves, from the colonial period to the end of the Civil War." Elkins's book ignored Aptheker's conclusions because rebellion and revolt did not fit in with the "Sambo" model he constructed for slavery, a victimization model that employed the analogy of the German concentration camps that harkened back to the Phillipsian image of the slave as a dependent, docile being. Elkins recognized only three revolts of any note.[23]

When International Publishers reissued *American Negro Slave Revolts* in 1963, the novelist William Styron, who oddly claimed the mantle of historian in his essay, chastised Aptheker in the *New York Review of Books.* Styron praised Elkins's "brilliant analysis" but pilloried Aptheker's work as "extremist revisionism" and "badly misleading." He did, however, albeit grudgingly, acknowledge the depth of documentation in Aptheker's book and contended that it made "a good case against the theory of universal content and docility among the slaves." Styron ignored his own conclusions however: "There was only one sustained, effective revolt in the entire annals of slavery," he wrote, referring to that of Nat Turner. Aptheker failed "almost completely in his attempt to prove the universality of slave rebelliousness . . . [and] in his eagerness to prove the actuality of what was practically non-existent . . . [indulged] in distortion. . . . The slave in revolt is a product of the white man's ever-accommodating fantasy, and only the dim suggestion of the truth." Styron accepted Aptheker's evidence but dismissed his analysis. Aptheker and Styron entered into fierce polemics several years later over Styron's novel *The Confessions of Nat Turner* (see chapter 16). Aptheker, on whose work Styron based much of his novel without crediting him, and many black intellectuals decried Styron's portrait of Turner for being a continuation of racist stereotypes.[24]

Even more exasperating to Aptheker than red-baiting criticism was the profession's determination to ignore his work. In his preface to the 50th Anniversary edition of *American Negro Slave Revolts* Aptheker made note of "the careful avoidance of my name" in the new material appearing on slave revolts. Nonetheless, historians continued to erase Aptheker's name right up to the end of the century. The historian Edmund S. Morgan surveyed several new books dealing with slavery in an article for the *New York Review of Books* for 3 December 1998. Morgan, who surely knew better, excised a whole generation of white and black scholars from the study of slavery when he observed that it was "not until the late Sixties and early Seventies that studies in depth of slave life began to appear." Aptheker's themes are apparent in Morgan's article, but there is no mention of Aptheker. "The history of slavery," Morgan wrote, "could be understood only as an interchange between two parties, the one not as wholly subdued to the other as had been generally supposed. . . . Slaves mistreated could easily take to the woods. Swamps deep in the interior harbored 'maroon' settlements of successful runaways. . . . The effect, and surely in some measure the intention, of all these studies must be to induce a greater respect by whites for the 'Negro Past' and a greater pride in it on the part of blacks." Six months later Morgan was back in the same publication with a new essay, "Plantation Blues," in which he wrote about dispelling the supposed myths surrounding slavery: "A large number of . . . studies . . . have explored the slave culture of resistance," he remarked, then named only John Blassingame's *The Slave Community: Plantation Life in the Ante-Bellum South* (1972) and Herbert G. Gutman's *The Black Family in Slavery and Freedom, 1750–1925* (1976). Morgan declared that "violent rebellion was never a possible option for Afro-American slaves because they were outnumbered everywhere in the United States," but he also argued, erroneously, that the book under review was "the first comprehensive analysis of slave resistance during the seventy years prior to emancipation." Here again Aptheker's themes, but not his name, are present.[25] George M. Fredrickson, also writing in the *New York Review of Books,* dated the interest in slavery among historians to the publication of the Stampp and Elkins books. Fredrickson labeled as "neo-abolitionists" the unnamed scholars who, before Stampp and Elkin, had focused on the brutality of the slave system and the discontent of blacks enmeshed in the system.

Writing in the *New Yorker* for 13 December 1999, Tony Horwitz maintained that "Nat Turner's insurrection was one of very few slave revolts in American history . . . yet the true story of what happened during those two hot days and nights in 1831 remains largely untold." Horwitz credited Styron with resurrecting the memory of Nat Turner but quoted the historian Kenneth Greenberg, who blamed the scholarly neglect of Nat Turner on frightened academics who "didn't want to throw themselves on the flames" generated by the controversy surrounding Styron's novel. The most egregious evasion of Aptheker appeared at the end of Horwitz's article when the historian Nell Irvin Painter averred that new work on the Turner uprising opened up "a whole range of possibilities— *that there was widespread organized resistance to slavery,* which runs against the myth of a solid south." Painter, like Morgan, certainly knew, or should have known, better.[26]

When scholars began to take the notion of slave resistance more seriously in the late sixties and seventies and to acknowledge that "slavery was really a battleground between master and slave," they "rediscovered" *American Negro Slave Revolts* and "began to turn to it for evidence of slave resistance of one kind and another." In looking back at the book's impact, Genovese, who over the years severely criticized Aptheker's work, wrote that when one reviewed the "way in which historians have discussed the theme of slave resistance in the United States . . . the seminal character of Aptheker's *American Negro Slave Revolts*" becomes apparent. "The literature falls easily into categories of 'before' and 'after.' " Aptheker's theses, he went on, "notwithstanding ritual disclaimers and signs of acute discomfiture at being associated with a real live Communist," had influenced all writing on the history of slavery and had "prepared the ground for such subsequent works as Kenneth Stampp's *Peculiar Institution.*" "We confront an astonishing fact," Genovese asserted:

> For fifty years, marked by the Cold War and the criminal exclusion of Aptheker and other Communists from the universities by especially fierce red-baiting and by attempts to denigrate the work of Communist Party historians, no one has even tried to replace Aptheker's book with a fresh synthesis and reinterpretation. The book has stood up as the indispensable introduction to its subject and no broad challenge is in sight. All subsequent work on the subject, no matter how critical of Aptheker on particulars, has had to build on it. . . . There is no hint that a new synthesis will challenge its fundamental viewpoint and principal conclusions. Few books have exercised such dominion over a subject of prime importance. That fact speaks for itself. It provides the context for, and defines the limits of, all criticism worthy of respect.[27]

In the foreword to the 40th Anniversary Edition of *American Negro Slave Revolts,* the historian John Bracey wrote, "From personal experience I can testify that *American Negro Slave Revolts* made a tremendous impact on those of us in the civil rights and Black liberation movements. . . . It was the single most effective antidote to the poisonous ideas that Blacks had not a history of struggle or that such struggle always took the forms of legal action and non-violent protest.

It provided Black youth with that link to our past that few even thought existed or were willing to help us find. For this reason we could develop our nationalist feelings yet reject Harold Cruse's talk of 'the sentimental slave hero worship of the Aptheker cult.' "[28]

"As long as scholars don't accept the legitimacy of the slave system," Foner said, *American Negro Slave Revolts* will be a central text for them to turn to.[29]

5   Into the Fires

THE TROOP ship bringing Aptheker back from Europe landed in Hoboken, New Jersey, in August 1945. As he disembarked, he saw his older sister Minna on the dock in her Red Cross uniform greeting the victorious soldiers. After a warm reunion with her and a brief sojourn with Fay and Bettina at the apartment Fay had rented near Prospect Park in Brooklyn, Aptheker had to leave again to complete his military service. He reported to Fort Jackson, South Carolina, where he turned down an offer from the army for a permanent position as a lieutenant colonel in the intelligence corps. Not "if they wanted me as a Lt. Gen.," he wrote Fay, "I'd turn it down—and be free, and creative."[1]

At the end of the year the army moved Aptheker to Washington, D.C., where he began work as an army historian. Evidently unaware of or perhaps ignoring his identification by the House Military Affairs Committee as one of thirteen army officers "possessing communist background[s]," Aptheker began preparing for the army a history of Army Ground Forces within the United States during the Second World War. "Glorious news!" he wrote to Fay. "I have been appointed as an historian." The army provided Aptheker with living quarters at the Army War College and an office with a secretary at the Pentagon, where, for the first few days, until he learned the directions to his office, he required a guide to show him around that labyrinthine maze. Working there Monday to Friday from 9 a.m. to 5 p.m., Aptheker could call on messengers to fill his requests for documents and records: "orders, units, personnel, activity, particular events, chronological developments." Every evening he wrote, in longhand, instructions for his secretary to follow the next day, but she worked so speedily that he found it difficult to keep up with her. Aptheker ignored his supervisor, a colonel who questioned the report's "excessive attention to the Negro troops," and finished the study, a document of about 450 pages, he recalled, just before Christmas. Then he returned to Brooklyn on leave.[2]

Before he left he met with Carter Woodson at Union Station, where they lingered over dinner and talked until late in the evening. Woodson told Aptheker that the *Journal of Negro History* would soon publish several of his essays. "He liked them," Aptheker wrote to Fay about Woodson's comments, "but said they were too *short*!" When he returned from leave after Christmas, the commanding officer, Maj. Gen. Clarence Huebner, who never once looked at Aptheker during their one brief meeting, approved the study. "Is it finished?" Major General Huebner asked Aptheker's supervisor, Col. James Lay, ignoring Aptheker. "Very well, you may go." "And that," Aptheker said of his work in the Pentagon and his career in the U.S. Army, "finished that . . . with that my active army service ended."[3]

Aptheker took pains to note in his unpublished autobiography, "An Unrepentant [sic] Rebel," that he returned from the war a much more belligerent, pugnacious person than the student scholar who entered military service. As a private he followed orders.[4] But the young man who left to go to war was now filled with a seething rage he was barely able to control. He had grown used to giving orders. Brandishing a pistol, he had faced down Nazis and had obliterated the enemy with howitzers. He knew victims of the concentration camps. "I have seen with mine eyes the Gestapo chambers," he told Fay.[5] He had killed human beings, perhaps thousands, and had watched his comrades in arms die. He had done all that to rid the world of fascism, he said.[6]

His combativeness and propensity to threaten violence erupted almost immediately after he moved into the apartment in Brooklyn. "He was a flaming torch," Bettina recalled, "and he could be set off in explosive, violent ways."[7] When told by the building superintendent that the rent on their apartment, kept relatively low for a woman and child alone, would have to be raised, he "blew up and told him to leave on his own two feet while he could still walk." On another occasion, in Brooklyn, while still wearing his army uniform, he threatened to tear apart a delicatessen brick by brick unless the owner sold him a pound of corned beef rather than a sandwich that was more expensive. "I exploded," Aptheker wrote. "I'll destroy your store. I'll shatter your windows. I'll destroy everything, do you understand?"[8]

Aptheker claimed that in time he overcame the rage, but for years he displayed all three types of disturbances that the Mayo Clinic now identifies as symptoms of post-traumatic stress disorder: "intrusive memories, avoidance and numbing, and increased anxiety or emotional arousal (hyper-arousal)." The manifestations of PTSD include troubled dreams, trouble sleeping, relationship difficulties, irritability or anger, trying to avoid thinking or talking about the traumatic event, and guilt or shame, among others.[9] Aptheker may not have recognized the fierce temper he often displayed for decades after the war as being related to his wartime service or understood, perhaps in a state of denial, the memories that haunted his dreams: war assaults memories and minds as well as bodies. For years Fay and Bettina "were often awakened by the screams from his nightmares." He became terribly shaken once after running over a cat with his car in the driveway. He told Bettina he was upset "because, he said, 'I have never killed anything.'"[10] In his last years "he spoke of the war incessantly," haunted by the memories of atrocity and suffering he had witnessed and in which he had participated; these were "the most intense experiences of his life."[11] When his adult grandson, Joshua, asked him once if he had ever killed anyone, "he became terribly agitated . . . and shouted . . . and didn't sleep for days."[12]

The victory over the Nazis confirmed Aptheker's faith in the Soviet Union and the CPUSA. He knew that the Soviet Union under Stalin's leadership had won the war against Germany. To him, the nine-hundred-day German siege of Leningrad exemplified the heroic struggle of the world's first Socialist state. "There's never been anything like it in history," he said in an interview. "I can't point to another example of it. Nine hundred days. And no suggestion of surrender. . . . [P]eople dropping dead from not having food . . . but never surrendering."[13] He considered the Soviet victory over fascism only the first step in a worldwide Socialist victory, a struggle that would again be led by the Soviet Union, to bring an end to racism and anti-Semitism and the rule of capitalism. At the end of the war the CPUSA was, he said, "the force opposed to fascism, to anti-Semitism, to Hitlerism, to chauvinism (I'd been in the South), and that it was a progressive instrument, which it was. It was the only really progressive force, the party, there was nothing else."[14] The victory of Socialism would usher in a golden era of human fulfillment and human liberation. As a Communist he believed he would be a leading player in the vanguard of that victory in the United States.[15]

If that eventuality was his dream, reality intruded almost immediately. He convinced himself, not without some justification, that his doctoral degree from Columbia guaranteed him a teaching position at a major university. But the history profession, the white mainstream history profession of the forties and fifties, was a relatively small, exclusive club, a tight-knit group, "an old boys network basically . . . they all knew each other." Most university history professors had earned their degrees at a few elite universities, for example, Columbia, Harvard, and Michigan. When a history professor wanted to find a teaching position for one of his graduate students and one was not open in his own department, he called up a colleague at another institution and said, " 'I've got a man here'—it was 'man' always," Foner asserted. " 'I've got a man here who needs a job.' And that's how you got a job." Aptheker knew how the system worked, and he also was aware that the system was rife with anticommunism and anti-Semitism. "Though they could get Ph.D.s from the first-rate schools," Ellen Schrecker wrote of Jewish graduates, "they could rarely teach there."[16] When he arrived home from Europe in August 1945 he made an appointment with one of his dissertation advisers, William L. Westermann, for whom he had worked briefly as a research assistant, to discuss his employment prospects at Columbia. Aptheker admired, trusted, and respected Westermann even though he had terminated Aptheker's research work when William Martin Canning, an English instructor at City College, testified at the Rapp–Coudert Hearings (hearings sponsored by the New York state legislature to examine the extent of communist infiltration of the public education system) that "Henry Apotheker" was a communist who had been ordered by a Soviet agent to write books and pamphlets on "Negro history." According to a document prepared by *Counterattack,* a right-wing journal published by an anticommunist organization of the same name founded by ex-FBI agents, Canning said he had been present at a meeting of the supposed historians of the party, Philip and Moe Foner, Anna Rochester, and Henry Apotheker, convened by Alexander Trachtenberg. At the meeting, Canning said, the group laid plans to issue "pamphlets and brochures about American history and to prove in these publications the thesis of the COMMUNIST PARTY that Communism was the Americanism of the Twentieth Century." Nonetheless, Westermann cited Aptheker's dissertation in two articles that, Aptheker wrote to Fay, "touch my fearful vanity." Westermann, the president of the American Historical Association that year and a distinguished authority on ancient slavery, greeted Aptheker warmly at their meeting and seemed genuinely happy to see that he had survived the war. But when Aptheker put the question to him about a teaching position, Westermann told him that "Columbia would never hire a person with your political views. . . . No, Herbert, Columbia would never hire a Communist."[17]

By 1945, even before the start of the Cold War, the history profession and universities in general "drew a very rigid line around what was acceptable and what was not acceptable." Communist professors were categorically not acceptable. The blacklisting of Aptheker was certainly not unique: many controversial academics suffered, beginning with the purges in New York initiated by the Rapp–Coudert hearings. The academic blacklist was "at least as comprehensive and far less well known than the one in the entertainment industry," Schrecker wrote in her study *No Ivory Tower: McCarthyism and the Universities.* Most administrators and academic department chairs denied that a blacklist existed. But Aptheker never did secure a permanent faculty appointment, despite the provenance of his degree, and not until 1969 did he begin to receive offers for temporary positions. It was only because of the demands of black students that he was even considered later at Bryn Mawr, Yale, the University of California at Berkeley, and the University of Massachusetts.[18]

When Aptheker left military service in February 1946, he was not without financial resources. His mother had left him six thousand dollars in her estate, and Fay had saved a sizable amount of his officer's pay, which was augmented by extra pay for his combat duty abroad. But he needed a job. Fortunately, help arrived from an unlikely source: capitalist philanthropy. Prior to leaving the military Aptheker had applied for a fellowship at the Guggenheim Foundation, and in April 1946 he learned that he had been awarded one. Aptheker's grant, which ran from 15 April 1946 to 15 April 1947, required him, during the term of his appointment, "to devote himself . . . to a study of the American Negro in the Second World War," for which he would be paid the sum of twenty-five hundred dollars. Among others receiving fellowships that year were Aptheker's friend the artist Jacob Lawrence, the sociologist C. Wright Mills, with whom Aptheker would in time collaborate, and the historian C. Vann Woodward, whom Aptheker would later engage in fierce controversies.[19]

By accepting the award Aptheker agreed he would not take any other kind of employment. Fay, the family's financial planner, observed that his stipend for completing the study was barely enough to keep the family going for a year: perhaps the foundation could be persuaded to increase it? Aptheker approached Henry Allen Moe, the secretary general of the foundation, about the matter and found that he was amenable to increasing the amount of the award. How much did Aptheker have in mind? Aptheker hesitated: Fay had not coached him on how much to ask for, and he didn't know what to say. When he suggested five hundred dollars, Moe readily agreed. When he returned home feeling triumphant, Fay expressed her pleasure, then, "in her practical way," wondered why he had asked for so little.[20]

Between the time he applied for the fellowship and the time he began work as a fellow, Aptheker completed his study of blacks in the ground forces of the army during the war. He knew from his work on that piece that much of the documentation about black troops in the Second World War that he needed for the task he had proposed to the Guggenheim Foundation would not be available during the tenure of his fellowship. He decided to change the topic of his research and approached his friend Phillip Foner, who, with Morris Sorkin and Allan Wilson, had founded Citadel Press. Aptheker suggested to the three men that he write a documentary history of black people in the United States. They agreed to publish the book at Citadel, and as an advance they promised to pay Aptheker twenty-five dollars a month to meet his research expenses.

Once he had settled on the new topic for his research and had the approval of the Guggenheim Foundation, Aptheker made an appointment to meet with Du Bois. At the end of the Second World War Du Bois was seventy-seven years old. Among the Left and in the black community in the United States and around the world he held legendary status. A cofounder of the NAACP in 1910, he edited that organization's official magazine, *Crisis,* from its founding until 1934, when he was forced out of his position over philosophical and personal differences with other NAACP staff and board members. In the summer of 1944 Du Bois returned to the NAACP, where he became "a sort of minister of foreign affairs, while bearing the title 'Director of Special Research.'"[21]

In the ten years he was away from the NAACP, the organization became a center of power for black Americans' challenge to Jim Crow. "The results astonished me," Du Bois wrote in his autobiography. The group's executive secretary, Walter White, who micromanaged a rigidly top-down organization, clashed almost immediately with Du Bois and his politics. By mid-1946, when Aptheker met with Du Bois, the personal animosity between Du Bois and White had grown to open hostility.[22]

Aptheker laid out for Du Bois his plans for a documentary history of black people. At the end of the presentation, Du Bois, to Aptheker's astonishment, asked, "Herbert, would you like to share my office?," an offer Aptheker immediately accepted. Du Bois, the "most distinguished representative . . . of the history of Black people, . . . whose astonishing memory went back to the 1880s," told Aptheker to "feel free to ask me questions whenever you wish!" For more than a year Du Bois and Aptheker worked side by side in Du Bois's small office at the NAACP.[23]

As the bond between the two men strengthened through their work on projects that overlapped, Aptheker agreed, at Du Bois's insistence, to edit for publication a collection of Du Bois's correspondence and articles. Anson Phelps Stokes, the director of the Phelps–Stokes Fund, had urged Du Bois to seriously consider writing and publishing an autobiography and contemplate "leaving your papers to some institution or individual" for future use. "Surely . . . there are some very competent Negro scholars such as Charles H. Thompson, or Alain Locke, or Dr. Logan, or others who could do the work admirably," Stokes wrote. Du Bois responded that Shirley Graham intended to write a biography and that "Herbert Aptheker, a Columbia doctor in philosophy, is going over my letters and articles with view to publication."[24]

Aptheker began to systematically pore over the tens of thousands of documents in Du Bois's files. He placed requests for correspondence to and from Du Bois in several leftist and black publications as well as in the *New York Times Book Review* and then, wasting no time, began to seek a publisher. Du Bois warned him that the proposed project would likely be met with something less than real cooperation, but Aptheker carried on. He corresponded with and sometimes met editors from Little, Brown, Houghton Mifflin, Harper, Harcourt, Brace, Lippincott, the presses of Columbia and Harvard universities and others: "All rejected the proposal, some quickly and some belatedly, but all firmly." After a discouraging meeting with a representative of Columbia University Press, Aptheker intimated that perhaps his difficulty in finding a publisher might be owing to the person whom Du Bois had chosen to be editor. "How much deterring effect . . . is my association with it having?" Aptheker asked Du Bois in January 1948. "This troubles me very much," the letter continued. "If you feel for a moment that a somewhat more respectable—and perhaps, more capable—person engaged in this effort might have better luck in accomplishing the main job, please be good enough to indicate that to me." Du Bois dismissed the suggestion out of hand, responding, "I think you are by far the best fitted person to edit my letters, and I hope you will not consider giving up the job, although, as I said before, it is going to be difficult." Just how difficult did not dawn on Aptheker at that moment: in fact, intermittently over the next twenty-five years, even after Du Bois's death, Aptheker sought in vain to find a publisher for Du Bois's correspondence. He did not succeed until the University of Massachusetts Press reached a publishing agreement with him in 1973.[25]

Aptheker began his work with the party coincident with his fellowship year and his research on the documentary history. He spoke widely throughout the country on black history and Marxism during 1946. Several times each month, a pattern that continued at least through the late sixties, he spoke at various colleges around the city or was on the road, combining speaking engagements with his search for documents. In March he spoke to the Karl Marx Society of Brooklyn College, delivering a lecture titled "The Roots of Negro Oppression." In October he spoke at Cornell, where he was sponsored by the Marxist Discussion Group, on the topic "What Marxism Offers the Student," and in April he had several engagements over a period of a week in Chicago. That same month he was in Philadelphia, where he addressed an audience at the formal opening of the Franklin D. Roosevelt Memorial Library, and during November he spoke to groups in Madison, Champaign, Minneapolis–St. Paul, and again in Chicago, where he wrote lightheartedly to Fay and Bettina—he wrote to them every day he was away from home—"the . . . engagements were splendid—your husband & father was nothing short of (indeed, somewhat in excess of) stupendous; seriously, the quiet confidence (& not so quiet pride) that I know you have in me, accompanies & sustains me wherever I go."[26]

IN JUNE the National Negro Congress (NNC), on whose board Aptheker sat in the thirties, held its Tenth Anniversary Convention in Detroit under the banner "Death Blow to Jim Crow." Delegates to the convention heard speeches by Paul Robeson, Rep. Adam Clayton Powell Jr. of New York, Hugh DeLacy of Washington, and the New York City Council members Benjamin J. Davis Jr., one of the national leaders of the CPUSA, and Michael Quill, a union leader. Prior to the convention the NNC president, Max Yergan, and the executive secretary, Revels Cayton, approached Aptheker about writing a section of the petition they would present to the convention, a "Petition to the United Nations on Behalf of Thirteen Million Oppressed Negro Citizens of the United States of America." The petition, offered, the NNC said, "with an expression of profound regret," called on the new United Nations to investigate the racist conditions under which blacks lived in the United States. "Ironic, indeed, is our 'reward,'" the petition stated, in view of the fact that blacks had "joined hands with our countrymen . . . and peoples of other lands to crush the fascist monster." The dire circumstances in which they lived drove blacks to appeal to the world body: "Barred from most industrial and business employment on the spurious grounds of 'race,' bound to the soil in semi-feudal serfdom on the cotton plantations of the Deep South, forced to live in overcrowded slum ghettos in our great cities, denied any substantial education for millions of our children, lynched and terrorized, kept from effective use of the ballot in many states, segregated like pariahs, the more than 13,000,000 Negro Americans still suffer an oppression which is revolting to all the canons of the civilized world." In the statement of evidence to support the petition, "The Oppression of the American Negro: The Facts," Aptheker proffered statistical documentation outlining population, occupations, income, health, and education of blacks in the United States. The statement concluded with examinations of the denial of civil and political rights and institutionalized peonage and violence. "The cancer of racism," Aptheker wrote, "has spread its poison throughout the life of America. Its throttling and killing effect upon the people of the entire nation—North and South, Negro and white—grows more fearful and more anachronistic with the passing of each hour. The Negro people, for themselves, and for the benefit of all other inhabitants of America, demand full freedom and absolute equality. Nothing short of this will satisfy them. Where one is enslaved, all are in chains."[27]

The NNC printed one hundred thousand copies of the petition and distributed them around the United States at five cents each. The black press gave the document wide and favorable coverage, as did "much of the media elsewhere in the world." Cayton, Yergan, Robeson, and Aptheker presented the petition to an assistant to Secretary-General Trygve Lie of the United Nations on 6 June 1946. Lie passed it on to the UN Economic and Social Council, where it quietly passed into oblivion, prevented by the U.S. delegates to the body from coming under serious discussion. Across town, furnished a copy of the petition by an informant, FBI agents made note of Aptheker's contribution to it in his growing dossier at the bureau and quoted from it extensively and accurately.[28]

Du Bois did not accept the burying of the petition with equanimity. He sought and received the unanimous endorsement of the NAACP board to begin fashioning a similar document for the NAACP. He assembled a team of five scholars who worked "at breakneck speed" to complete the study for presentation to the United Nations. The second petition to the United Nations by black Americans, *An Appeal to the World: A Statement on the Denial of Human Rights to Minorities in the Case of Citizens of Negro Descent in the United States of America and an Appeal to the United Nations for Redress,* met a fate similar to that of the first. The United States delegation to the first round of UN talks in Geneva focused on human rights initially maneuvered and then applied direct pressure on a number of other delegations to stop any official acceptance of the *Appeal.*

Eleanor Roosevelt threatened to resign from the NAACP board in December 1947, saying that the *Appeal* had "embarrassed her in her capacity as a member of the United Nations Economic and Social Council and embarrassed the nation." Through his worldwide network of contacts, Du Bois made arrangements to have the *Appeal* presented for debate at a full UN General Assembly meeting in Paris that he planned to attend as an NAACP observer. The discussion did not take place. The NAACP board replaced Du Bois with White on the NAACP Paris delegation and then, at the board meeting in September 1948, fired him.[29]

Throughout this period Aptheker carried on with his speaking schedule. Invited to speak at the University of North Carolina, Chapel Hill, by the historian Howard K. Beale, Aptheker delivered a scathing attack on Gunnar Myrdal's *An American Dilemma: The Negro Question in the United States.* In his concluding remarks Aptheker chastised the all-white audience and criticized the segregationist policies of the university. "I gave them hell," he recalled, ". . . told them . . . you ought to be ashamed of yourselves." Aptheker had an appointment to speak after the lecture at a downtown leftist bookstore sponsored by the North Carolina CP organizer Junius Scales. When Scales didn't show up to walk to the bookstore with him, Aptheker set off by himself and, on the way, to save time, he crossed an empty field. Hurrying because he was late, he did not notice the men who crept up behind him and assaulted him. He staggered under the first blow that struck the back of his head, then attempted to defend himself, but it was too late. The men were on him and beat him until he was unconscious. When he recovered consciousness, the men were gone. He was lucky, as they certainly could have killed him, but evidently that was not the object of the attack. Aptheker spent several days in the hospital and then recuperated at Scales's home. To keep from worrying her, he informed Fay that he had pneumonia, not telling her about the beating until years later.[30]

Simultaneous with his scholarly work during the period of the Guggenheim Fellowship and his numerous speaking engagements, Aptheker's writing appeared regularly in the *Journal of Negro History* and the monthly *Negro History Bulletin.* But more often his polemical essays and book reviews appeared in the *People's Voice,* the *Negro Digest,* and especially in the weekly *New Masses,* which he had joined again soon after leaving the military in his old capacity as an unpaid staffer doing editorial duties. The influence of *New Masses* on the Left had diminished noticeably following its support for the Nazi–Soviet Pact in 1939, but it managed to survive through the war. Aptheker joined others in a vain attempt to keep it going, in February 1946 publishing an article that examined the successful integration of black troops in the U.S. Army at the end of the war. In the issue of 14 May he wrote a long article critical of Myrdal's *An American Dilemma,* then fully developed his challenge to the philosophical content of Myrdal's book in his extended, eighty-page polemic *The Negro People in America: A Critique of Gunnar Myrdal's "An American Dilemma,"* released by International Publishers in November 1946.[31]

Aptheker found little in Myrdal's book to praise, and the qualified compliments he gave it dripped with sarcasm, something against which Fay continually warned him. The work, he wrote, contained "keen insights into the minds of—significantly—middle and upper class whites and Negroes, and apt material on the vested interests in segregation that lead some of the latter to adopt reactionary attitudes generally and even specifically towards the aspirations of their own people." He called the study a summarization of other work best read in the original, marred by "too frequent errors," which Aptheker pointed out in the most extensive portion of his book, and "ensconced in the midst of weak and dubious interpretation."[32]

Aptheker's critique began with the title of the study itself and the word *dilemma.* What is a dilemma, he wondered, but a situation involving choice, especially in actions, between equally unsatisfactory alternatives. "The philosophy motivating the study," he wrote, "leads inevitably to the conclusion that the Negro question is an insoluble problem, and does, indeed, represent a dilemma." To Aptheker, Myrdal's fundamental, underlying error lay in the fact that "[he] explicitly repudiates a materialist concept of society and adopts that of an idealist. For him, therefore, the status of the American Negro represents a moral problem." He called Myrdal's conclusions circumlocutions: "If the status of the Negro is a problem, and if it is a problem in the heart and the mind of every American, and if it is moral in origin, then there can be no solution. And, obviously, there is none, for has it not been labeled a dilemma?" Aptheker found "Myrdal's philosophy to be superficial and erroneous, his historiography demonstrably false, his ethics vicious and, therefore, his analysis weak, mystical, and dangerous." Aptheker saw the "Negro question" not as a moral matter but a material one: "The oppression and super-exploitation of the American Negro— and the prejudice based thereon—exist and are maintained because they were and are profitable and useful to America's propertied interests." Ironically, "as it turned out," wrote the historian Maurice Isserman, "Myrdal's framing of the question of black inequality as a moral rather than a material question, would be the foundation of the emergence of the mass civil rights movement of the 60s, both in its church and student wings. And *An American Dilemma* would continue to be read widely in those circles into the early 60s, while nobody read or recalled Aptheker's critique. For all his genuine commitment to the struggle against racism, Aptheker's sectarianism blinded him, as this episode suggests, to important truths."[33]

For people who believed in "democracy and full rights for all people," Aptheker concluded in his critique of Myrdal, there was no dilemma. He acknowledged that people in the United States found themselves in a situation that involved choice, but to Aptheker "the alternatives are not equally unsatis-factory." The choice, he wrote, "lies between the attempted preservation of our existing exploiting system, which nurtures the oppression of minority peoples, or the introduction of fundamental and vital changes now, and the consequent hastening of the transformation of our society into a pattern of socialism." The end of oppression was to be found not in the "reformist, liberal bourgeois school of moderation pleaders" represented by Myrdal but in direct confrontation and radical action: the development of a "mass movement for the immediate out-lawry of Jim-Crowism and all other manifestations of bigotry." In the unity of black and white "in the fires" of that struggle would be "forged a comradeship . . . whose drive towards a peaceful, fruitful, and creative life for humanity [would] be irresistible."[34]

6   Prelude to McCarthyism

AMERICAN COMMUNISTS entered the final year of the Second World War with high expectations, bolstered by the alliance between the United States and the Soviet Union. In 1944 General Secretary of the CPUSA Earl Browder misread what he thought was a signal from Stalin the previous year and dissolved the U.S. party, seduced by the political promise he found in the Teheran Declaration, the wartime agreement among Roosevelt, Churchill, and Stalin, who "pledged that their nations would 'work together in the war and the peace that will follow' and would seek to make a peace which would 'banish the scourge and terror of war for many generations.' "[1] The party then immediately reconstituted itself as the Communist Political Association (CPA). Browder envisioned a postwar Popular Front that would extend its actions into the indeterminate future, in which, he said, "we have to help the capitalists to learn how to run their own system. . . . We will not raise any socialist proposals for the United States, in any form that can disturb this national unity."[2] Distancing the organization markedly from its traditional philosophy of Marxism–Leninism, Browder essentially steered the CPA on a course back to Popular Front class collaboration rather than class struggle. By the time Soviet forces surrounded Hitler in his Berlin bunker in late April, the leading members of the party were calling Browder's leadership into question, catapulting the organization once again into a series of crises that would last for a dozen years.

Browder's independent thinking caught up with him early in May 1945, as Aptheker was celebrating with Parisians the announcement of Hitler's death. The April issue of *Cahiers du Communisme,* the theoretical journal of the French Communist Party (PCF), arrived in New York, signaling Browder's demise. In an article called "On the Dissolution of the American Communist Party," the PCF second in command, Jacques Duclos, apparently speaking for Stalin, criticized Browder's "notorious revision of Marxism." He argued that Browder had "deformed" the Teheran agreement by crafting a collaborationist political program from a purely diplomatic document and lionized the former CPUSA general secretary William Z. Foster as "Leninism's heroic American defender." Both Foster and Browder recognized that, at the least, U.S. communists would have to reverse course in order to revive Lenin's prophecy that had sustained the party after the Nazi–Soviet Pact: "When the locomotive of history takes a sharp turn, only the steadfast cling to the train."[3]

At an emergency national convention held on July 26–29, 1945, the delegates (who did not include Browder among their number) voted unanimously to reestablish the CPUSA, elected Foster chairman, and established a four-man secretariat to run the day-to-day operations: Foster, Eugene Dennis, who became general secretary in 1946, John Williamson, and Robert Thompson. Browder spurned an offer from the party's new National Board of a research position at his full regular salary, deciding instead to publish a weekly newsletter pushing his Teheran thesis. After the first issue appeared, in January 1946, presenting views opposed to the party's adopted policies, the CPUSA expelled him. Browderism, as his policies became derisively known, could best be described, Browder's biographer explained, "as a mutant strain of mid-twentieth-century Communism. Pragmatic and ideologically vague, it attempted to blend Great Plains radicalism with loyalty to Joseph Stalin." Browderism, Maurice Isserman wrote, "[held] the potential for leading to something other than itself—sheltering and lending legitimacy to the efforts of those American Communists who had the capacity for and commitment to finding . . . the 'American Road to Socialism' . . . [but] his political vision was limited by his craving for respectability, his penchant for behind-the-scenes maneuvering, his attachment to the chimeras of Teheran. But something else might have been built on the foundations he provided."[4]

What Aptheker knew of the events that transpired within the party while he served in the military is not clear. His letters home contain no mention of the struggle (and he evidently did not keep Fay's letters to him), but they do reflect an optimism inherent in Browder's Teheran thesis regarding postwar cooperation. Bettina nevertheless recalled that "Herbert often told me that William Z. Foster had 'saved the Party,' and he expressed only reverence for him."[5]

Unlike some returning veterans, such as George Charney, John Gates, and Al Richmond, Aptheker did not assume a paid position in the party or join the leadership. He neither attended regular meetings nor belonged at that point, like most members, to a specific party club. His work for the party was his work as an intellectual coupled with teaching U.S. and African American history at the Jefferson School for Social Science, the school founded by the party in 1944. When he spoke on college campuses, which he did regularly from 1946 to 1949, he invariably spoke at some kind of party function as well. He couldn't have been unaware of the controversy that continued to roil the party even after Foster's ascension to power. Under Foster's leadership, as the Cold War deepened and domestic repression intensified, the party began a disastrous series of purges directed both at "right opportunists," which referred to, according to Gates, party members who sacrificed "principle for the sake of mass popularity," and at "left sectarians," members even further to the left of Foster who advocated policies that isolated the party from the masses. The expulsions, numbering "as many as several thousand Communists . . . in the first years after the war," reached down into the writers at the *New Masses,* where Aptheker was working as an associate editor when the party expelled at least two editors, the wife and husband duo Ruth McKinney and Bruce Minton, as left sectarians.[6]

New Masses, begun in 1926 as a direct heir to *Masses* (1911–17) and the *Liberator* (1918–24), was, during the period of the Popular Front, at the center of the radical Left but had lost much of its appeal by 1946. The various associate and contributing editors attempted, as noted above, to keep the weekly running, but to no avail, as it ceased publication in 1947. Then, after merging with the quarterly *Mainstream,* it reappeared in February 1948 as the monthly *Masses & Mainstream* (*M&M*), with Samuel Sillen as editor in chief and Aptheker, Lloyd Brown, and Charles Humbolt (aka Clarence Weinstock) as assistant editors. Operating out of a cramped three-room office, *M&M* achieved, wrote the former contributing editor Annette Rubenstein, "an extraordinary level of literary sophistication, imaginative breadth, and cosmopolitan interests" but relatively few readers.[7]

Nineteen forty-eight was not a propitious year for the appearance of a new party-dominated publication, and *M&M* struggled to find readers, subscribers, space at newsstands, and writers. Aptheker constantly urged his friends and acquaintances to submit articles. One letter, typical of the responses to his solicitations, came from his old friend Henrietta Buckmaster in March 1948. "Alas," Buckmaster wrote, "I cannot, as I have tried to explain so often, identify myself at this time with publications as politically marked as *Mainstream.* It is a disgusting business, but there you are, and many have to show their desire for a peaceful world in other ways which perhaps are just as effective, but more discreet. . . . I feel sure you understand my reluctance to say NO." Aptheker earned sixty dollars a week, money that was frequently unavailable, to write essays directed at historical and political issues and to review nonfiction books. Given the "bitterly reactionary" Republican-dominated 80th Congress, the Truman Doctrine, virulent Dixiecrat anticommunism and its counterpart even within the liberal wing of the Democratic Party, the advent of the Cold War, and the persecution of the CPUSA, Aptheker didn't lack for topics about which to write.[8]

The midterm elections of 1946, in which Republicans won a majority in the House, made President Harry Truman's life decidedly more difficult in the face of continual cries that he was soft on Communism. Truman met the charges in March with his announcement of the Truman Doctrine: containment of communism, essentially "the economic, political, and military encirclement of the Soviet Union" and intervention "wherever 'aggression' threatened peace or 'freedom.'" Later that month Truman launched a domestic war against communism when he signed Executive Order 9835, which instituted loyalty boards in every branch of government and commenced, wrote the historian David Caute, "a purge of the federal civil service and inspired imitative purges at every level of American working life." The loyalty boards—in conjunction with a provision of the executive order that authorized the U.S. attorney general to create a list of allegedly subversive organizations, "membership in which was grounds for dismissal from, or denial to employment in, federal office"—linked "dissent with disloyalty and legitimized guilt by association."[9]

When a faction of liberals formed the Progressive Citizens of America (PCA) and coalesced with their supporters, including the CPUSA, around the third-party presidential campaign of former vice president Henry Wallace, liberals found themselves in one of two warring camps: the PCA, which supported Wallace, or Americans for Democratic Action (ADA), formed from the ashes of the old Union for Democratic Action by the historian Arthur Schlesinger Jr., the journalist James Wechsler, and the attorney Joseph Rauh, who, somewhat reluctantly, supported Truman. In his monthly *M&M* column Aptheker scorned the adherents of the ADA. The ultimate purpose of the ADA, Aptheker wrote, "is to prolong the life of an obsolete social order; the function is to hide its decay with euphonious lies." Quoting William Harlan Hale's *The March of Freedom*, Aptheker chided Schlesinger for viewing history "as 'a pendulum [swinging] from reform to reaction' and back again, full of movement, yet motionless." In another article reflecting the party's position as crafted by Foster, Aptheker held out high hopes for Wallace's Progressive Party: "*This third-party movement is,*" he wrote with characteristic finality and quite in error, "*a permanent one.*" It had the potential to break "the two-party front for capital that has characterized American history from Ulysses Grant to Harry Truman."[10]

As early as 1945 the FBI began working toward a prosecution of the CPUSA under the Smith Act of 1940, which mandated criminal penalties for persons advocating overthrow of the government. By 1947 the bureau had completed a study that ran to 1,850 pages and included 846 exhibits that represented, the historian Michal Belknap wrote, "the most complete summary of the activities and aims of American communism ever assembled." Attorney General Tom Clark decided to move against the party, but in late 1947 a former attorney in the Justice Department, O. John Rogge, leaked information to the press that brought the proposed prosecution to a halt. Eager to show that he was taking some kind of action, Clark used deportation laws to expel the top leaders of the party Alexander Bittleman, Claudia Jones, John Williamson, and Irving Potash. As pressure built on Clark from the House Committee On Un-American Activities (HCUA) to prosecute the party under the Smith Act, he asked John F. X. McGohey, the U.S. attorney for the Southern District of New York, to examine the massive FBI report and then present an indictment to an espionage grand jury sitting in New York City. Pressed for the next two months by Clark,

McGohey and another lawyer from the Justice Department drafted an indictment on a Smith Act conspiracy charge that targeted the leaders of the party and
"those members responsible for the Party's publications."[11]

The grand jury unsealed the indictments on 20 July 1948, five days after the
Democratic National Convention and three days before the Progressive Party
Convention. The criminal indictment charged that twelve members of the
party's National Board "had conspired with one another and with unknown
persons to . . . organize as the Communist Party of the United States, a society,
group, and assembly of persons who teach and advocate the overthrow and destruction of the Government of the United States by force and violence, and
knowingly and willfully to advocate and teach the duty and necessity of overthrowing and destroying the Government of the United States by force, which
said acts are prohibited by . . . the Smith Act."[12]

Late in the afternoon on the twentieth, FBI agents burst into party headquarters, where they found Foster, Dennis, Williamson, Henry Winston, and
Jack Stachel, who, having been alerted, were waiting calmly to be arrested. Later
that night FBI agents picked up Carl Winter and the New York City council-
man and National Board member Benjamin Davis. The next morning Gates,
the editor of *Daily Worker,* turned himself in at the federal courthouse in Foley
Square. Later that same day Aptheker scribbled a hasty, short note to Fay, who
was at River Styx, Lake Hopatcong, New Jersey, with Bettina. "All is well," he
wrote, "it did feel a little strange this morning, though, when in starting for work
it occurred to me to wonder for a moment—am I going to my desk or am I going
to jail, this bright and fine morning?"[13]

Agents of the FBI did not arrest Aptheker in 1948—or ever for that matter.
In fact, until late 1949, when Aptheker acknowledged his party affiliation on the
witness stand in the Foley Square trial of the leadership of the party, FBI agents
in New York were not even sure he was a member. "[He] has been active as a
lecturer and writer on negro history," an agent reported in 1949. "There is no
evidence to the effect that he is actually a member of the Communist Party." The
ten-page report showed evidence of considerable research on the part of agents
into Aptheker's writing and his connection to suspect organizations. Agents
referred to articles by and about Aptheker from as early as 1941 in the *Daily
Worker, New Masses, Mainstream, New York Age,* and *People's Voice* as well as to
his association with the Jefferson School and the National Negro Congress. Two
unidentified informants, who admitted having only superficial knowledge about
Aptheker, agreed to "testify . . . that Aptheker's political views were definitely
Communistic . . . [and his] articles are well received by the negro people."[14]

Aptheker's polemical essays in *M&M* directed at government leaders, anti-
communist liberals, "certain misinformed Communists," and even Henry
Wallace intensified after the arrest of the leaders of the party. He chastised

Wallace's suggestion that "needed reforms . . . against scarcity, racial discrimination, and exploitation . . . [represent] the only effective antiseptic against Communism" by equating it with President Truman's charge that "the Communists . . . are counting on economic collapse in this country." "How is one to explain this deliberately assumed insanity of the Little Foxes?" Aptheker wrote in September 1948. "It is the madness of desperation. It is the intellectual smokescreen covering the assault of the fascist phalanx. It is the result, as it is the proof, of utter corruption and total bankruptcy." He ridiculed the suggestion that Communists would resort to violence, as the government had charged in the indictment of the party's leaders. In language very like that he used numerous times in years to come he proclaimed, "Always and everywhere the reactionaries who despise life and have played the role of leeches turn to violence; it is never the revolutionists who first resort to violence for they cherish life and exist to ennoble it." To Communists, who had earned it through "militant, organized mass struggle . . . against the onslaught of reaction," he wrote, the hatred of the bourgeoisie "is a crown of glory."[15] Some anticommunists demonstrated the hatred and violence Aptheker claimed they would use. In September three men stabbed and beat the indicted party leader Robert Thompson on the street near his home in Queens. His injuries required doctors to put a metal plate in his head to repair the damage to his skull. In reporting the assault, the *New York Times* included Thompson's street address in the story, as it did when writing about other communists.[16]

At the NAACP in 1947 and 1948 White fired suspected Reds who were on the staff. When he learned that Du Bois had lent his name to the Wallace campaign, White warned Du Bois, in February 1948, that "association officers were 'prohibited from any partisan activity' and 'they may not speak at meetings called by partisan political groups.'" Du Bois ignored him. White then threw the association's support to Truman, which turned "the 1948 NAACP national convention . . . into a Truman campaign rally." In September the NAACP board used a technicality to oust Du Bois for the second time from the organization he had cofounded.[17]

Like Du Bois, Aptheker had friends and comrades who encompassed circles within circles and often overlapped with Du Bois. When reading the names of officers of organizations, courses taught at the Jefferson School, writers and contributors at the *New Masses, Mainstream,* and *M&M,* board members and sponsors of organizations, the National Negro Congress, the Jefferson School of Social Science, the Council on African Affairs, the National Council of Arts, Sciences and Professions, some formally linked to the party, others not, but all of which concentrated on similar causes, one finds familiar names appearing again and again. Within Aptheker's circles one encountered Du Bois and Shirley Graham, Lloyd Brown, William L. Patterson, Paul Robeson, Doxey Wilkerson,

Max Yergan, and Henry Winston, among others. As Du Bois's troubles at the NAACP mounted, Aptheker, Wilkerson, and Robeson devised a plan to bring Du Bois to the Council on African Affairs (CAA) as honorary vice chairman, for which he would receive an office and a secretary but no salary. Wilkerson and Du Bois had known each other for fifteen years, and, like Du Bois and Aptheker, Wilkerson combined scholarship with activism. Uncomfortable with Howard University's "authoritarian president," Wilkerson quit his position there to work full-time for the party, which installed him as director of the Jefferson School, where he interacted closely with Aptheker and Du Bois, both of whom taught there. "Tall, courtly, with an easy manner, a distinctly cultured voice, and super-lative analytical powers," Wilkerson had written the introduction to Aptheker's Myrdal critique. All four men, Aptheker, Wilkerson, Du Bois, and Robeson, served as members of the executive committee of the CAA, which Robeson had founded together with Yergan in the late thirties. Earlier that year, in February 1948, Yergan, for reasons that are still not clear, walked into the office of the FBI in New York to inform on the party and his former comrades. At the same time he publicly accused Communists of attempting to take over the CAA. "This action," Aptheker wrote, "led to a fierce inner struggle and Yergan was ousted from his positions." When the NAACP fired Du Bois, Aptheker and Wilkerson approached Du Bois with Robeson's offer, which Du Bois readily accepted. Having a place and a position from which to work and seeing his fi-nances somewhat stabilized through the assistance of the philanthropist Anita McCormick Blaine, Du Bois seemed secure. Within three years, as his biog-rapher David Levering Lewis pointed out, Du Bois's "reputation would lie in ruins and his freedom to work and walk among his compatriots would hang in the balance of Cold War justice. . . . yet the humiliation to be visited upon him, as with his friend Paul Robeson, was meant as an express warning to his people and their leaders—a message that their long struggle for equality must continue to exemplify commendable patience, conventional patriotism, and indifference to radical economic ideas."[18]

Robeson and Aptheker grew closer in 1948 through their mutual association with Du Bois's and Aptheker's colleague at M&M, Lloyd Brown. An unlikely pair, Brown and Aptheker "couldn't have been more dissimilar," Brown, both a novelist and a biographer of Robeson, recalled. A radical organizer during the 1930s, Brown decided after the Second World War to take up a career as a journalist. When Aptheker returned to New Masses after the war, Brown was the managing editor there. Brown, the "under-privileged" young black man, worked in cramped quarters every day with the "middle-class, educated, comfortable," Jewish Aptheker, yet the two men formed a lifelong bond. Their mutual admi-ration and respect cushioned the minor disagreements they had. "Lloyd was a man of vast experience—despite his youth," Aptheker wrote lightheartedly of his friend. "He had served . . . in a Pittsburgh prison where conditions were . . . fiendish for Black inmates. He was a fine editor and sensitive writer."[19]

Brown measured Aptheker during those years prior to 1952, when Brown left M&M to work full-time with Robeson, in relation to Robeson and Du Bois. Like Du Bois, Aptheker was a "highly organized person," Brown recalled in an interview. "He could work on two books at one time. Didn't let things distract him. Stuck to business like Du Bois." But, he added ruefully, "[he] didn't smell the flowers or go to a ball game. [He was] programed to work like a demon." He remembered that Aptheker, like Robeson, believed that to criticize the Soviet Union "would give aid and comfort to war: to the genocidal policy of a United States ready to commit genocidal action at any time." Brown, who described himself in 2001 as a retired Communist rather than a former Communist, which would have implied "a change of mind," saw Aptheker as "single-minded and driven." But that led to "narrowness about Aptheker's singular focus," Brown observed. He cautioned Aptheker, unsuccessfully, as Fay had some years earlier, about his lack of moderation in language and tone, especially when Aptheker's polemics grew more "abrasive or sarcastic" after the indictment of the party's leaders. "He put people off," Brown said regretfully, "rather than drawing them into his world."[20]

Brown and Aptheker worked and socialized together. At the Browns' apartment the lives of the Aptheker, Brown, and Robeson families often intersected. Aptheker's relationship with Robeson was never as intimate as that with Brown and Du Bois, yet Robeson obviously relied on Aptheker's expertise. In the battle for control of the CAA, Aptheker staunchly supported Robeson. During the period of that crisis in early 1948, Robeson brought Aptheker the script of a new play by Du Bose Hayward called Let My People Go. The play dramatized the slave conspiracy in South Carolina in 1822 led by Denmark Vesey. Before he accepted the role of Vesey, Robeson wanted Aptheker to assess the historical accuracy of the play. When he read the play Aptheker "found the version of the conspiracy poorly presented . . . seriously inadequate." The play did eventually reach Broadway, without Robeson, where it had a short run.[21]

Aptheker looked on Du Bois as a father figure, and by 1948, according to Levering Lewis, "Herbert Aptheker had become indispensable to Du Bois." That intimacy comforted Du Bois, who during this period felt a sense of isolation and loneliness. He had outlived many of his friends, and his wife, Nina, an invalid since 1945, died on 1 July 1950. He had, he said, "a certain illogical reticence" that discouraged the formation of intimate friendships, but that reserve broke down in the company of his many women friends and of Aptheker and his family. Du Bois and his now-constant companion, Shirley Graham, on whom he came to rely more and more and whom he eventually married, entertained the Apthekers at Du Bois's home in Brooklyn Heights. Du Bois often cooked

Sunday breakfast for the two families, while Graham made elaborate dinners. Du Bois sought out Aptheker's advice on numerous issues. When his eighteen-year-old granddaughter requested that he "send her some Marxist literature," which he thought "would be unwise," Du Bois wondered if Aptheker could recommend some reading "the possession of which at Fisk [University] would not involve her summary expulsion." Aptheker cited two books by the founder of *Monthly Review,* Leo Huberman: *America Incorporated* and *Man's Worldly Goods.* Later, Aptheker guided Du Bois and Graham through the process of purchasing the printing plates of Du Bois's classic from 1903, *The Souls of Black Folk.* Using those plates, Howard Fast published a new edition of the book in 1953 at his Blue Heron Press.[22]

When the attacks against him intensified in the late forties and early fifties, Du Bois grew wary of requests, especially from strangers, for the use of his personal files for research. "It's rather a nuisance having anyone work here and also a certain risk in opening my personal files freely to a stranger," he wrote to Graham and Aptheker in June 1950 when C. F. Kellogg asked if he could examine Du Bois's files for his doctoral dissertation research into the history of the NAACP. Du Bois asked Aptheker and Graham to "decide just what should be done" in response. Graham, suspicious of the young white student, adamantly opposed opening Du Bois's papers to Kellogg. "My answer to his query in NO. I do not know this young man. . . . This is no time for naive acceptance of a cultured accent," she wrote to Aptheker. Graham allowed that a "frantic" effort was under way "to gain access to every plane and corner of Negro life . . . to perfect the machinery of control and to continue the enslavement" of black people. She saw a struggle coming. Even though the white racist "enemy is aware that he has blundered badly in the past," she wrote, she did not want Du Bois's files to "yield up invaluable information" that would advance the racist cause in the future. "Perhaps the young man will be another casualty of the cold war. He will not, however, go to jail for it." In Graham's mind there was no alternative. "In the final analysis I trust only *one white American,*" she wrote, referring to Aptheker. "White America has forced me to this position. White America will have to change before I change that decision." Aptheker evidently interceded with Graham on Kellogg's behalf, for Kellogg assured Aptheker he would abide by any restrictions "you and Miss Graham . . . care to impose. Likewise," Kellogg wrote, "I would like to assure you & Miss Graham that I will do nothing whatso-ever to injure the cause of the Negro."[23]

Aptheker sought out Du Bois for assistance also. With the leadership of the party on trial early in 1949, Aptheker already knew the party would call him as a defense witness. Together with Harry Sacher, one of the defense attorneys, Aptheker approached Du Bois to request that he testify on behalf of the party. Aptheker spoke to Du Bois "at some length" about testimony Du Bois could give linking the black struggle with the persecution of the Communists. Du Bois "expressed great sympathy for the defendants" but deferred his answer while he attempted to reconcile his reservations, and ultimately decided not to testify. "As I have assured you before," Du Bois wrote to Aptheker on 11 April 1949, "anything that I can do in reason to help the accused martyrs, I will do. But again in this case, I think the analogy between the American Negro, whose position I know fairly well, and the Marxists is not good." Besides ruling out testimony based on a faulty analogy, Du Bois had a real fear that "a good attorney might easily elicit from me a confession that force and violence have been used by Communists and certainly may be used just as in the case of Negro slaves."[24]

The actual or contemplated use of force and violence by Communists was, however, tangential to the government's case. The government did not charge the party's leaders with attempting to overthrow the government or of using force and violence or of executing any overt act; it did not accuse them of *practicing* force and violence or of *advocating* force and violence; it did not accuse them of forming a party to practice or advocate. Rather, the government charged that the leaders *conspired* "to organize a party ... which would so advocate *at some time in the future.*" Government prosecutors employed a conspiracy charge based on the Smith Act because it did not require the establishment of "actual advocacy of armed revolt." The charge required only that prosecutors establish a conspiracy "to advocate or organize." The prosecutors were not prepared to argue nor could they have substantiated charges of revolutionary plots or deeds. The government prosecuted the party's leaders simply because they were Communists, and, as Caute correctly stated, "only one potential stumbling block presented itself: the First Amendment, which protected beliefs, speech, assembly and advocacy" in unambiguous language, prohibiting congressional enactment of any law in these areas.[25]

The trial of the leaders began in New York City at Foley Square Courthouse in January 1949, "with four hundred uniformed and plainclothes policemen ringing" the building. Public opinion had been so aroused by newspapers around the nation that the outcome was all but inevitable. It would have been impossible for the defense to select an unbiased jury anywhere in the country: "Newspapers ranging from the reactionary *Chicago Tribune,* through the moderate *San Francisco Chronicle,* to the liberal *New York Times* all gave the idea of a Communist trial their editorial endorsement." In addition, the defendants faced an ambitious, unscrupulous federal prosecutor in McGohey and an anticommunist judge, Harold Medina, who, as the trial wore on, "managed to create a distinct impression of bias" and "for all practical purposes, aligned himself with the prosecution." Throughout the proceedings Judge Medina made his anticommunism clear to the jury and infused racism into the proceedings when he called one of the two black defendants, the Harvard graduate Winston, boy.[26]

Once the prosecution began its case it became obvious it was not the defendants who were on trial but the books they used in party schools and clubs: Marx's and Engels's *The Communist Manifesto* (1848), Lenin's *State and Revolution* (1917), Stalin's *Fundamentals of Leninism* (1929), *The History of the Communist Party of the Soviet Union (Bolsheviks)* (1925), and *The Program of the Communist International* (1928). "This dated literary evidence was the guts of McGohey's case," argued Belknap. "From these snippings and cuttings," Aptheker wrote, "fall out, drop by drop, like one's heart-blood, the words and phrases that are to make prison cells for men and women—and a whole nation." To prove the case, McGohey called a string of former party members, professional witnesses, and paid informants to the stand, most notably a former prominent member, Louis Francis Budenz, to introduce and interpret the books and pamphlets and explain how the party used them in its activities. Hour after hour the prosecutor read to the jury passages out of the suspect books that seemed to call for "force and violence," then asked Budenz to offer an interpretation. When asked about passages in the CPUSA constitution that provided for the expulsion of any member advocating violence, Budenz, as the Smith Act defendant Dorothy Healey recounted, "charged that the Communists habitually made use of 'Aesopian language'—which meant that whenever we talked about peaceful change, it was intended as a kind of code or double-talk to confuse outsiders." "This was a very convenient concept for the prosecution," she continued, "because it meant that if the defendants openly advocated violence they were guilty, and if they openly opposed violence, they were still guilty—and deceitful hypocrites to boot. All of this made the Foley Square trial into an Alice-in-Wonderland trial." Healey ridiculed the process further: "This kind of trial could not have been conducted in any other advanced capitalist country—France or England or Italy—because the basic concepts of Marxism were so well known, studied in every university, and familiar to every active trade unionist, . . . people would have laughed at the outrageous simplifications offered up so solemnly at our trial. That was a peculiarly American phenomenon."[27] The trial may have been a farce, but a guilty verdict carried real consequences.

The party rejected a defense based "on such artifacts of the bourgeois legal system as the First Amendment" and decided instead to "take their case to the people." They convinced themselves with an assurance that in retrospect seems delusional that through proper organization the party could arouse the masses and incite them to pressure the government to end the persecution. They launched "a prosecution of their own . . . to present a comprehensive exposition of the philosophy and program of the CPUSA." The defendants attempted to introduce evidence that outlined what they actually did teach and advocate, evidence that Judge Medina continually refused to allow. In the process, as the historian Ellen Schrecker wrote, "they came across as wooden, doctrinaire ideologues instead of as the victims of government repression that they also were," in this most blatant political trial in U.S. history.[28]

How the party chose Aptheker to be the defense witness who would counter Budenz's false characterizations of Marxism–Leninism is not known with certainty. Aptheker knew all of the men on trial but had met privately with few of them: V. J. Jerome in the 1930s and, in 1947, Jack Stachel, the CPUSA national education director and national organizational director, and Winston to discuss teaching classes at the Jefferson School. Yet Jerome, Alexander Trachtenberg, Wilkerson, and others with whom Aptheker closely worked surely must have been in favor of the decision. The defense called Aptheker to the witness stand on the morning of 19 August 1949. He spent most of the day there, although Judge Medina did not allow him to testify to much more than his name, address, occupation, and party affiliation. More specifically, Medina did not let him testify about the meaning of Marxism–Leninism, repeatedly sustaining prosecution objections to the defense lawyers' questions. Typical was an extended exchange over the meaning of sentences from the preamble to the party's constitution. The prosecutors had read a sentence from the document and then asked Budenz for an interpretation: "The Communist Party upholds the achievements of American democracy," McGohey read, "and defends the United States Constitution and its Bill of Rights against its reactionary enemies who would destroy democracy and popular liberties." The defense attorney Richard Gladstein objected to the question. He pointed out "that Budenz was being asked to interpret the C. P. Constitution and claimed that it was not his function and that he was not qualified to do so and, further, that no foundation had been laid. Gladstein had said that Budenz was called to testify concerning a written document and that any opinion expressed was immaterial and invaded the province of the Jury." Judge Medina overruled the objection. When Sacher asked Aptheker the same question, McGohey objected, and Medina sustained the objection. Sacher then read aloud to the court from the trial transcript the results prompted by the same question to Budenz. Medina stopped him in midsentence, saying, "he thought he got Sacher's point, that Sacher wanted to show that the same question was asked by the prosecution and was attempting to read all the objections in order that it might appear that the defense was not given equal latitude." Nonetheless, Medina said that "many questions and testimony that had been permitted at length earlier in the trial would no longer be permitted." Further "argument," the judge remonstrated, "was not desired." So it went through the morning and afternoon. Finally Sacher gave up: "Under such circumstances," he said, "[he] found it impossible to proceed with further examination of the witness." McGohey had no questions for Aptheker, and the judge dismissed him.[29]

Judge Medina turned the case over to the jury on 12 October 1948. After seven hours of deliberation the jury found all of the defendants guilty as charged. Newspapers of every political stance around the country and local, state, and national politicians hailed the verdict. Medina "became a popular hero," wrote Schrecker, "the recipient of thousands of fan letters lauding him for defending American liberty," and the president appointed McGohey to a federal judgeship. Alone among the major newspapers, the *St. Louis Post-Dispatch* raised a cautionary note, warning that "the verdict . . . had altered the First Amendment, establishing a new and repressive limitation on freedom of speech."[30]

Aptheker made the same point but carried it further in a two-cent pamphlet he wrote, "Why Defend the Rights of Communists?," published in a run of one hundred thousand copies the same month the jury reached its verdict. He recounted his being "gagged" on the witness stand, likening this treatment to a scene in the Congress when former president John Quincy Adams, then a representative from Massachusetts, was prevented from reading the Declaration of Independence as a petition from his constituents by "shouts resound[ing] through the [hall], 'Gag!' 'Gag!'" because the "gag rule" of 1836 prevented Congress from hearing antislavery petitions. Freedom was at risk, Aptheker declared: "We tell you that liberty is indivisible. We tell you that when one man is unjustly dealt with, justice for all is in danger. . . . We tell you that if the defense of Communists can be gagged, then the defense of no man is free." Reflecting Foster's pessimism that "domestic policies raised the danger of fascism" in the United States, Aptheker predicted that dire consequences for the country as a whole lay in the political persecution of Communists. "They're plotting fascism," Aptheker warned, "and fascists are not finicky when it comes to persecution and to torture. Every decent human being will have his turn; every decent human being did in every fascist country that has ever existed. . . . But the beasts are at work, here and now. . . . Fascism is being brewed in our land. . . . If the liberties of Communists are forfeited, the liberties of no person are safe." Two years later, when a citizen in Detroit mailed a copy of Aptheker's pamphlet to J. Edgar Hoover with the recommendation that the pamphlet's author "be dismissed from the public school system," Hoover thanked the person for his courtesy, then had his agents investigate the letter writer.[31]

The convicted leaders immediately appealed the case to the U.S. Court of Appeals for the Second Circuit and, after losing there, to the U.S. Supreme Court. They argued that the government could not make the exercise of First Amendment rights a crime. The appeal warranted that even if they had advocated policies that could be defined as a substantive evil, in the absence of "a clear and present danger" such advocacy fell under the protection of the First Amendment. The appeal also attacked "the conspiracy section of the Smith Act," which, they argued, "was independently unconstitutional because, by making it a crime to agree to exercise civil rights at some unspecified time in the future, that provision imposed prior restraint on speech, press, and assembly."[32]

In 1951 Chief Justice of the Supreme Court Frederick Vinson wrote the majority opinion in *Dennis v. United States* upholding the convictions of the party's leaders by a six to two majority. Vinson asserted that the leaders "intended to overthrow the Government of the United States as speedily as the circumstances would permit . . . [which] created a 'clear and present danger' of an attempt to overthrow the Government by force and [violence]."[33] Vinson saw the Cold War as another of those extraordinary times when Congress had the right and the duty to limit speech.

The majority's decision did not sway the two dissenters, Justices Hugo Black and William O. Douglas. Douglas wrote a lengthy dissent expressing his fear that the Court's decision would lead to the destruction of the First Amendment. The majority opinion "waters down the First Amendment," Douglas wrote, to a point where it "is not likely to protect any but those 'safe' or orthodox views which rarely need its protection." He took note of the anticommunist crusade sweeping the country and the Cold War attitudes prevailing in government. "There is hope," he wrote optimistically, "that in calmer times, when present pressures, passions and fears subside, this or some later Court will restore the First Amendment liberties to the high preferred place where they belong in a free society."[34]

The Supreme Court decision in *Dennis* measurably eroded the rights guaranteed in the First Amendment and altered the three-decade-long interpretation of the clear-and-present-danger test as it had been applied to determine limits on protected speech. Until the Supreme Court began to modify the decision several years after *Dennis,* in which the First Amendment went down to defeat, free speech rights in the United States were dependent "on the identity of the person attempting to exercise them."[35]

Aptheker demonstrated his determination to uphold free speech rights throughout the period of the Red Scare, what the blacklisted screenwriter Dalton Trumbo called "the time of the toad." He traveled across the United States, spoke at dozens of colleges and universities to thousands of students, energizing local Communist clubs with a message to return the First Amendment to its place as the first among rights. He had, according to Brown, who chuckled when quoting Sender Garland, "an inoperable ego," yet during the 1950s, when leftists "were scared to death," Aptheker "stepped forward to speak out."[36]

7   The Time of the Toad

WITH A determination bordering at times on recklessness Aptheker
charged over the anticommunist barricades erected by domestic Cold War
policy. He published polemical broadsides against U.S. foreign policy, racism,
the McCarthy witch hunt, and what he viewed as a corrupted intellectual and
academic establishment. He testified at inquisitorial hearings constituted to
destroy the party as an organization held by the Subversive Activities Control
Board and at the trials of comrades prosecuted under the Smith Act in Maryland, Connecticut, and Pennsylvania. He confronted Sen. Joseph McCarthy in
the lion's den and walked away unscathed.

Aptheker's polemical howitzers zeroed in on anticommunist liberal intellectuals, especially historians, to whom he referred as "Laureates of Imperialism."
"In an economy dominated by the bourgeoisie," Aptheker wrote, "its scribes
dominate the writing of the country's history. . . . He who controls the past," he
continued, "thereby may better dominate the present and shape the future. Thus,
history-writing is central to the ideological battle of our time." During the 1950s
Arthur Schlesinger Jr., because of his visibility, was one of Aptheker's prime targets. Schlesinger, Aptheker wrote, "epitomized the N. C. L. [non-Communist
left] intellectual," and when Schlesinger published his anticommunist polemic
The Vital Center in 1949, Aptheker struck back. His essay, which he later recalled, "was entitled, with a marked lack of subtlety, 'The Schlesinger Fraud,'"
appeared in October 1949. This attack exemplified Aptheker's penchant for
"abrasive and sarcastic" prose.[1]

Schlesinger contended that by 1949 liberalism and conservatism were emerging from a crisis of confidence. "Sentimentality, tragedy, the depravity of human nature, man's inability to control history: these were the central themes of
Schlesinger's political writings at the time," the historian Jesse Lemisch wrote.
In *The Vital Center* Schlesinger called for a left-liberalism expunged of Communists and "sentimental . . . Doughface" progressives who did not repudiate Communists. He urged "the revival of responsibility on the right—the development
of a non-fascist right to work with the non-Communist left in the expansion
of free society. . . . The non-Communist left and the non-fascist right must,"
he contended, "collaborate to keep free society truly free." Thus the coming

together from right and left of the vital center, those who would attack Communists in a responsible, principled way as opposed to the "promiscuous and unprincipled attack" carried out by HCUA. That attack, Schlesinger thought, interfered with the work carried out by legitimate government agencies like the FBI. Schlesinger found that "there is surely no alternative to paying exact and unfaltering attention to the communists in our midst." He asserted that "the national Communist parties play an important role in Soviet espionage. . . . [T]here can be no serious question that the USSR, through . . . the American Communist Party," had penetrated " 'sensitive' branches of the Government."[2]

In his no-holds-barred response, Aptheker boldly questioned Schlesinger's integrity as a historian. Schlesinger claimed the mantle of truth, Aptheker wrote, "to persuade the people that . . . 'cooperation with Communists is impossible.' " He consistently omitted portions of quotations, Aptheker charged, in a way that distorted the meaning of passages from Lenin and the speeches of Eugene Dennis. Further, Schlesinger "shoveled up . . . quotations made out of whole cloth by fellow-mythologists." His *general technique,* Aptheker wrote, ". . . consists largely of slipping the maximum number of falsifications into the minimum number of words." Aptheker denounced Schlesinger's "insufferable arrogance," which "becomes positively laughable. Thus, this bourgeois begotten,—nurtured and—bound intellectual describes Karl Marx as 'so characteristically a bourgeois intellectual'!" Aptheker brought his onslaught against Schlesinger to a close by saying he offered a program "groomed to the needs of a ruling class seeking war and fascism. . . . The meretriciousness of Schlesinger's method befits the iniquitousness of his ideology."[3]

At Harvard University, where an active John Reed Club (JRC), one of a federation of local organizations established by the CPUSA in 1929, still existed, the student Albert Feuerwerker, later a longtime professor in the History Department at the University of Michigan, read Aptheker's attack on Schlesinger. "Your recent article 'The Schlesinger Fraud' leaves Arthur, Jr. without even his fig leaf," Feuerwerker wrote to Aptheker on 13 October 1949. Feuerwerker, writing on behalf of the JRC executive committee, invited Aptheker to speak at Harvard "on the role of Mr. Schlesinger's 'vital center,' " which, the JRC felt, "is too good an opportunity to expose social-democracy to let slip by." Aptheker eagerly accepted the invitation. Feuerwerker then convinced Schlesinger to participate in a debate with Aptheker. "He [Schlesinger] refused to speak on 'The Role of the Center,' " Feuerwerker told Aptheker in a letter written late in November 1949. "However, he will speak if the notice reads that he and you will present opposing views on 'the Center and the Left.' We are going ahead on that basis. . . . Undoubtedly he will stress the above point, but that should give you plenty of ammunition as he is speaking first! Of course, it would not be good if the meeting stuck on the liberal-communist issue without getting to the main point,

Schlesinger's role as ideological salesman for the bourgeoisie." Aptheker couldn't have agreed more. "You will be interested to know," Aptheker wrote to Howard Fast, "that I am going to Harvard this Friday to debate with Mr. Schlesinger, Jr. himself, under the auspices of the John Reed Club. The challenge came from us, of course, and after about ten days the lad said yes."[4]

In his unpublished autobiography "An Unrepentent Rebel," Aptheker wrote that the hall where the event was to be held "was jammed to the rafters." In the debate, he said, he repeated his charges that Schlesinger was an "apologist for an expansionist and repressive ruling class" and emphasized his "sloppy scholarship (including mis-quoting Lenin in a way important to his argument)." Interviewed by the journalist Jack Fischer, Aptheker said, "I slashed into him, murdered him. Towards the end of it he said to me quietly, 'This is something I won't do again.' And I said to him, 'I don't wonder.' Anyway this was quite a moment."[5]

Whether or not Aptheker's description of the debate is accurate—there is no contemporaneous account to refute his memory—what stands out are the violent images he used in his insistence that he "murdered" Schlesinger in debate or, as he said in another interview, "I slaughtered him, without mercy, . . . mercilessly." For Aptheker the words uttered became shells fired, bombs exploded. His goal in debate was to annihilate "the enemy." Peter Filardo, a former archivist at Tamiment Library at New York University (NYU), recalled being present at a debate some years later between Aptheker and the NYU law professor and director of the New York ACLU Police Practices Project, Paul Chevigny. Aptheker and Chevigny debated the concept of hate speech, and Aptheker took the position, weakening his defense of free speech, that certain words and writing should be proscribed. He believed, for instance, that the Ku Klux Klan and Nazis would not have free speech rights in a Socialist United States, that racist speech presented "a clear and present danger." Aptheker likened racist ideas "to pollution such as might be at the bottom of a body of water, and would need to be cleaned up." That analogy inspired approval among Aptheker's supporters in the audience, whom Filardo called "Blue-hair Reds . . . Aptheker's senior citizen fan club." Filardo worked for Aptheker at the time in the offices of the American Institute for Marxist Studies in New York. He grew up a "Red diaper baby" in a family that looked up to Aptheker, and Filardo arrived at the institute, he said in an interview, "revering Aptheker as a hero figure." As the debate with Chevigny played out, Filardo recalled, Aptheker "grew more and more agitated and polemic in his presentation, attacking Chevigny unnecessarily and agitating the Reds in the audience to belittle the ACLU representative." Filardo was so nonplussed that as he left the debate he began questioning his admiration for Aptheker. In an interview decades later Chevigny remembered the event vividly. He "went out of the meeting sobered," he said. "I was frankly surprised and disappointed, naively I suppose, that Aptheker and his supporters did not accept the ideal of content neutrality." Chevigny pointed out that "the analogy to physical filth was misleading, and that . . . those present would be the most injured by such analysis." "I thought," Chevigny wrote, "that those like Communists who had been hounded for their ideas would hug the position that one can't be punished for content. I was wrong."[6]

In responding to a question about the debate in 1949, Schlesinger replied bluntly, "I know of Herbert Aptheker primarily as a Communist hitman. . . . I never thought that Aptheker's party-line fidelity was a clear and present danger to anything and always welcomed the opportunity to debate him, which I think we did twice. Neither of us convinced the other of anything."[7]

As government agencies and academic institutions introduced ever more draconian measures to stifle deviation from the anticommunist consensus, Aptheker perceived necessity driving his actions. The debates and the polemical broadsides constituted skirmishes in—the military imagery seems apt—the war Aptheker waged to win legitimacy and acceptance: of his scholarly work, of the party, of Communists to teach, of a Marxist school to exist, of the right to study Marx.

The most heretical ideas were those of Marx. The hegemonic, anticommunist ideology's prohibition on teaching Marx was almost absolute, a blackout, as Aptheker pointed out in 1954, that had incalculable effects. "To speak of serious instruction," Aptheker wrote in *M&M*, "to talk about 'the search for truth'—not to mention academic freedom—and to keep from students the ideas of a Galileo in the social sciences, of a mind which ranks among the three or four greatest, of one who was a great pioneer blazing new and promising paths in the wilderness of human thought . . . to do this, is to deceive and not to enlighten." That deception occurred, Aptheker pointed out, "in the sacred names of freedom and loyalty and patriotism, while corrupt ignoramuses in state legislatures, on Congressional committees, in Boards of Education, fire teachers and terrorize school systems so that students may not heed Veblen's advice, 'Study Marx,'—to be a party to this is not to be an educator but rather to be a betrayer of that high calling and an accomplice in the assault upon reason."[8]

Sidney Hook, a professor of philosophy and the chairman of the Philosophy Department at NYU, became, along with Schlesinger, a leading academic identified with a redefinition of academic freedom. Hook asserted that he was *defending* academic freedom by urging a ban on communist teachers. Hook wrote several long magazine articles on the topic, claiming in one of them that "no one can contend that any individual bound by . . . [Communist Party] instructions can do an honest job of teaching wherever the interests of the Communist Party and the Soviet Union are involved. . . . It cannot therefore be too strongly emphasized that the Communist Party teacher has rendered himself unfit for his task by unprofessional conduct. . . . [His] conclusions are not reached by a free inquiry into the evidence. . . . [Because] once he joins and remains a member, he is not a free mind." When Hook made the same arguments in a student newspaper, a group of students at NYU invited Aptheker "to challenge Hook to a public debate on the issues raised." Aptheker wrote to him, but Hook rejected the offer, not by communicating directly with Aptheker but in a two-thousand-word reply published in the student newspaper. Aptheker had no opportunity to reply in the same issue of the paper, a circumstance he pointed out in an *M&M* essay responding to Hook's charges. Hook had accused Aptheker, quite erroneously, of writing black history at the behest and under the control of the Kremlin and offered for proof the records of the Rapp–Coudert hearings of 1940. "You say that because I am a Communist I must think in such and such a manner," Aptheker wrote, "and if I think in such a manner, I cannot be an objective scholar. In exactly the same way teachers are accused as Communists and fired. You say that they must violate the ethics of their profession because as Communists they must think and act in a certain way. But you distort and falsify the position and practices of Communists [examples of which, such as a distorted Lenin quotation found in Hook's letter that Aptheker had previously pointed out], and on the basis of such distortion come to conclusions which you insist are inevitable. . . . It was only on the basis of a syllogism with a false foundation that the persecution is conducted, because the purpose is not the protection of free education but rather its vitiation."[9]

With radicals and radicalism eliminated or silenced and as professors altered their teaching and writing, "the university was purged of audible radical criticism, and academic thought grew slovenly and stultified in its one-sidedness." Some historians responded eagerly to a call Conyers Read, the president of the American Historical Association, made in his Presidential Address of 1949 for a revised history. Aptheker's master's thesis adviser, Allan Nevins, "stepped forward," Aptheker wrote, "as the leading advocate of the re-writing of American history in the image of monopoly capitalism." Aptheker wrote in *Laureates of Imperialism,* his assault on the mainstream historical profession, that Wall Street regarded it as "vital that the people's past, the history of their country, be reshaped completely in the image of Big Business. . . . Of course, in an economy dominated by the bourgeoisie, its scribes dominate the writing of the country's history."[10]

Nevins called for revision of the history of the industrial revolution to put right the injustice done to "the Rockefellers, Carnegies, Hills and Morgans . . . the heroes of our material growth," not robber barons. Nevins "explicitly related his revisionism to the Cold War," Lemisch wrote. "The era in which the United States, summoning all its strength," Nevins asserted, "led democracy in winning the First World War, the Second World War, and the ensuing struggle against Communist tyranny, was one of the imposing eras of history."[11]

Aptheker dissected Nevins's work to show that ideology was not dead, that contemporary historians wrote not as ideological neutrals but as Cold War historians in the service of bourgeois ideology. After Nevins published a two-volume biography of John D. Rockefeller in 1940 and a revised edition of it in 1953 Aptheker examined the differences between the two editions. In the early book Aptheker "found interpretations that reflected the liberalism of the time." But he noted, as Foner remarked, "that when Nevins put out the new edition in 1953, the sentences had been rewritten so that what in 1940 looked to Nevins like evidence of dissatisfaction by employees now became converted into a feat of industrial statesmanship by Rockefeller." Aptheker pointed out that in both editions Nevins devoted "precious little" space in "two thousand pages" to laboring men and women. Nevins, he said, and other Big Business historians wrote "as though Rockefeller drilled wells, or Gould built railroads or Guggenheim mined copper, and an amorphous mass, called the poor or the under-privileged or the unfortunates, lived in slums and afforded objects for the heroes' philanthropy . . . still, even for them [Big Business historians] . . . labor does exist, if only as a necessary evil!" When Aptheker compared the account of the Ludlow Massacre of 1914 in Colorado in the two editions of Nevins's biography, the transformation of the 1940 Nevins into the 1953 version stood out conspicuously. In a six-page account in the first edition Nevins described the massacre as "a heart-rending incident," the responsibility for which "is still open" but "that 'the strikers were in the right.'" Not much of a discussion of "a strike and its murderous suppression," Aptheker wrote, "which showed monopoly capitalism as its naked, characteristic, unrestrained self." Thirteen years later in the revised edition, in a chapter titled "The Well-Being of Mankind," Nevins dismissed the Ludlow Massacre in two sentences: "In 1914 Rockefeller and his son became involved in the labor troubles of the Colorado Fuel and Iron Company, an unprofitable company in which they held a 40% interest. Since Rockefeller, then almost 75, had no active concern with the company, this story belongs to the biography of his son." Aptheker, pointing out that Rockefeller lived another twenty-three years and kept "all his faculties to the end," observed that Nevins had stated in the first edition that Rockefeller's son did not take "charge of the Rockefeller empire until 1920." Aptheker ended by saying, "The past history-writing was not sufficiently strident and arrogant in its defense of monopoly capitalism: not sufficiently slashing. Nothing namby-pamby now." Big Business wanted a history that "identified their needs, their deeds, their schemes and dreams with the needs and deeds and schemes and dreams of America. Make *us* America!" he declared sarcastically in the voice of Big Business.[12]

Throughout the period of the Red Scare, the academy purged itself of ideas the way it purged itself of radicals. The dominant ideas prospered, those that propagandized for the state. Dissent found scant sanctuary within the university structure, and the universities attempted to mitigate the influence from outside through such actions as banning radical speakers. No wonder, Lemisch pointed out, "that the students of the fifties were called a silent generation." "The academy's enforcement of McCarthyism had silenced an entire generation of radical intellectuals," Schrecker summarized in *No Ivory Tower,* her book examining academia during McCarthyism. When the campus finally awoke from the nightmare, it was students, not faculty, who led the way, demanding that the pretentious rhetorical slogans be abandoned for real democracy and freedom. Aptheker played a role in bringing that process to pass.[13]

As consensus historians worked to rehabilitate capitalist heroes, they steered clear of black history. In 1950 students, black and white alike, were still reading in Samuel Eliot Morison's and Henry Steele Commager's *Growth of the American Republic,* a required text at many colleges, that "there was much to be said for slavery." Students found black people referred to as "n——rs, Topsy, Sambo, mammy, pickaninnies, and darkies," while slaves were "childlike, improvident, humorous, prevaricating and superstitious." When students at City College in New York boycotted classes twice in 1949 to force the book's removal from the required reading lists, Commager "defended the slanders by asserting that these were terms used by Mark Twain and even by some slaves themselves." Commager "labeled the growing protests against the book as the work 'of a few troublemakers' and 'oversensitive Negroes.'" Aptheker had already confronted Morison personally some years earlier with regard to *Growth of the American Republic,* but that was prior to the publication of his *American Negro Slave Revolts.* By the 1950s he expected his scholarly work to have had some influence on the writing of mainstream historians, but they ignored his work or labeled it, as Hook had done, Communist-hack-history. That Nevins's work in Civil War and Reconstruction history continued to reflect a "white chauvinist" perspective drew the caustic criticism of Aptheker. He ridiculed Nevins's contention that "slaves, the Negroes had been cared for, in health and sickness, by their masters." "The masters 'cared for' the slaves!" Aptheker shouted from the pages of *Laureates of Imperialism.* "The masters produced nothing but misery and agony," he proclaimed, "the slaves produced everything. . . . Yes, if the Rockefellers, Carnegies, Fords and Morgans were 'the heroes of our material growth,' then Calhoun, Davis, Stephens and Lee 'cared for the slaves!'"[14]

As he continued producing polemics critical of the work of consensus historians and government racism, Aptheker, after two delays—one occasioned by lack of funds to continue research and the other by a lack of time to devote exclusively to the work—published in 1951 the massive one-thousand-page first volume he had edited, *A Documentary History of the Negro People in the United States.* Covering the period from the early American colonies to the founding of the NAACP in 1910, the book was the culmination of the work he began while sharing an office with Du Bois at the NAACP. The genesis of the *Documentary History* occurred, as the historian Sterling Stuckey remarked, "before he [Aptheker] realized it, materials for it falling into certain categories as they were filed away in memory." Aptheker located the conception of the work in his reading of the statement-of-purpose editorial in the first black newspaper, *Freedom's Journal,* which appeared in New York City on 16 March 1827. "We wish to plead our own cause," wrote the owner and the editors Samuel Cornish and John B. Russwurm. "Too long have others spoken for us." Aptheker wondered, "How can I make them speak for themselves? Slaves mostly. Illiterate, by law." But he had unearthed the evidence: the documents, speeches, letters, diaries, court records, and newspapers he had copied by hand by the thousands. He had collected the primary sources; he had sought out collections in public and academic libraries, state and national archives, historical societies, and historical commissions; he had consulted friends, comrades, and acquaintances; he had scoured every document. "I had enormous energy," he recalled in an interview. "I was healthy, and I was tremendously motivated. Quite frankly, I knew that what I was doing was history-making and it was new.... [It] was a thrilling thing to do, this research, especially knowing I was the first one and that no one had done this." He recalled finding what became the first entry in the *Documentary History,* a faded, yellow document archived at the New York State Library in Albany: it was a petition for freedom filed in 1661 by a black woman. But he couldn't read it because it was written in Dutch. Applying his knowledge of German, he stumbled through the document, understanding enough to know he needed a complete translation. Only after Margaret Schlauch of NYU and Adriaan Barnouw of Columbia furnished a translation did Aptheker grasp the full significance of the document to his research. "It's the first thing I have written by a Black person," Aptheker said in the 1990s. "I don't know any other here. So it's precious and it is significant that it is an appeal for freedom."[15]

That petition from a female slave was history to Aptheker. "What are the obligations of the Marxist historian?" he asked in an essay in 1947, "particularly so far as the United States is concerned?" He responded to his question by quoting Engels: "All history must be studied afresh." The inherent responsibilities Aptheker found in Engels's words carried him to other questions: "Do we mean what we say when we speak of the dignity, maturity, wisdom bestowed upon a people and a class who are in possession of their heritage, who understand from whence they derived in order to know where they are going and in order to get there?" Since American history "almost in toto, is the work of non-Marxists," he wrote, "*we* must re-write it, at first hand. We must search out new meanings from established facts and from newly-uncovered facts. Our eyes must search for *sources,* and we must search out meanings from those sources." To root out and replace the dominant interpretation of history, Marxist historians needed to "uncover and use sources never touched by [mainstream bourgeois historians] because of distaste, disinterest or ignorance."[16]

In the *Documentary History* Aptheker offered new sources and thereby provided a vantage point from which ordinary black people could see the distant shore "from whence they derived" and, armed with that knowledge, chart a course for the journey ahead. "Here the Negro speaks for himself," he wrote in the introduction. "These are the words of participants, of eye-witnesses. These are the words of the very great and the very obscure; these are the words of the mass. This is how they felt; this is what they saw; this is what they wanted. *And that is history.*"[17]

In a preface he wrote for the first volume, Du Bois hailed the appearance of Aptheker's work for its lucidity and the presentation of evidence that refuted the hegemonic racist assumptions that dominated most historical scholarship in the United States:

> It is a dream come true to have the history of the Negro in America pursued in scientific documentary form. . . . Historians were not prepared to believe that Africans even in America had any record of thought or deed worth attention. . . . Then came the long hammering of Carter Woodson, the series of researches by a continuous line of students, black and white; and especially the painstaking and thorough scholarship of Herbert Aptheker. At long last we have this work which rescues from oblivion and loss the very words and thoughts of scores of American Negroes. . . . I hasten to greet the day of the appearance of this volume, as a milestone on the road to Truth.[18]

Reviews of the *Documentary History* were mixed. L. D. Reddick, writing in *Phylon,* and Harvey Wish in the *Mississippi Valley Historical Review* greeted the publication of the book warmly, although both, inexplicably, criticized Aptheker for not including documents created by white people. Wish characterized as unfortunate what he viewed as Aptheker's "partisan distortions and dubious principles of selection," flowing from what he called a Marxist interpretation of events. John Hope Franklin praised Aptheker's admirable success in "making the point that not only have Negroes left a written record that extends back into the seventeenth century, but also that the record is voluminous." Franklin thought Aptheker's judgments in the later sections of the book "somewhat more obtrusive" because of "the very language that he uses." Franklin wanted different words: "industrial leaders" instead of "the industrial bourgeoisie," "the growth of trusts" rather than "the rise of 'monopoly capitalism.'" He thought Aptheker's injection of class into the introductory remarks inappropriate, for instance, the description of a black insurance man as "an early representative of the Negro bourgeoisie, and in 1895 the 'masters' of South Carolina had 'class brothers in Mississippi.'" Franklin speculated that perhaps Aptheker's judgments helped explain what appeared to be the editor's becoming "increasingly impatient with certain practices and institutions in American life." Still, almost fifty years later in an interview Franklin averred that the book was and "should be used by an historian or anyone who wants to get at that kind of documentation." He acknowledged that by the 1990s other useful sources had appeared as well, but, he said, "this is a pioneer work and extremely important." Aptheker's contribution was "a courageous stand for justice, and equality, a fearless commitment to the ideals of justice and a willingness to take on any and all comers who challenged or questioned that position."[19]

The white mainstream press ignored the *Documentary History,* as it had *American Negro Slave Revolts.* But reviews in the black press agreed that the work was a prodigious achievement. Saunders Redding, the author of *They Came in Chains,* wrote in the *Afro-American* chain of newspapers that "the *Documentary* is a definitive work of historical scholarship. 'Nothing important is left out' . . . its 'assiduous research will solve certain research problems for a generation of students. . . . Here are the Negro people.'" The *New Orleans Christian Advocate* hailed the book as "a monumental work" and said that "no person should attempt a treatise on the Negro in America without perusing its pages." J. A. Rogers wrote in the *Pittsburgh Courier* that the book had done "an immense service not only to Negro history, but to documentation in a generally neglected phase of American life."[20]

Du Bois's review of the *Documentary History* in the *National Guardian* predicted that "it will not be reviewed in the commercial press. Why? Because Herbert Aptheker is an editor of *Masses & Mainstream* and has ideas about democracy and justice which some folk do not like. His ideas do not interfere with his scientific accuracy or breadth of research, but they may interfere with American business and war. To this depth has the Land of the Free sunk."[21]

Lloyd Brown asserted that the silence of the mainstream press could be traced to racism, "for this is a book in which the Negro people speak for themselves (without the aid of Those Who Know Best)," coupled with red-baiting, "for its editor is a Marxist." Brown urged readers of *M&M* to recommend the book to others. "Those of us who know the truth in this case have a responsibility," he wrote, "to foster the reading and study of the *Documentary History of the Negro People in the United States.* Never to cease in the struggle against the oppressors of the Negro people."[22]

Aptheker's work on black history found a wide audience, especially among the burgeoning generation of radical black students. His scholarship was a link for those young activists involved in the struggle in the 1950s and 1960s "to our past that few even thought existed or were willing to help us find." The revelations they found in Aptheker bolstered their search "for our nationalist feelings." Stuckey recalled that the *Documentary History* gave sustenance to other radical black student activists and in fact assigned the book to his Chicago high school students in 1962. "There was such intellectual excitement about the book," Stuckey wrote, that a number of his students, "many of them from the projects that still line State Street, . . . had me order copies for their parents." In the fall of 1964 "over two hundred thousand African American students, answering the call for 'quality education,' boycotted the schools." "Freedom Schools" sprang up in black churches on Chicago's South Side, where a group of students, among whom were twenty of Stuckey's students who belonged to the Student Advocates of Negro History, used the *Documentary History* as the principal text in their classes. Stuckey wrote that "these students were among the first anywhere to be exposed to history from the bottom up."[23]

Manning Marable, a historian at Columbia University, related a similar story: "For an entire generation of young African-Americans, our entry into learning about our own people's experience in this country was Herbert's *Documentary History of the Negro People in the United States*." Aptheker's book "was a constant reference work," Marable said. "There is no way that I can describe the extraordinary impact it had for young African Americans growing up in this country in the fifties and sixties. . . . It gave us a concrete sense of the voices of Black protest throughout history." Marable credited Aptheker with building the foundation for his understanding that "history could be a profession where the critical rethinking of the past might shape possibilities for the future. . . . Aptheker's work symbolized that effort to combine a scholarly pursuit with a political vision, based on understanding how people create their own history through struggle."[24]

In the mid-1960s the head of the student government association at the historically black Tuskegee Institute, Gwen Patton, responded to fellow students' pleas that she find a historian "who can really present Black history from an activist's perspective." One student suggested "this Black guy named Herbert Aptheker—let's bring him here."[25] They wrote to Aptheker, who agreed to speak. "I recall the incident vividly," Patton said in response to questions about Aptheker's speech.[26] On the appointed day she went to the bus station to meet "this Black guy" Aptheker. She waited until everyone but him had left the station and only then, feeling "shocked," did she realize that they had mistaken Aptheker's race. "Aptheker delivers a stirring address before the students and he's accepted as part of the Black liberation struggle," Marable recalled of the event. "So, I suppose white academia's loss was the Black community's gain."[27]

Stuckey remembered the fifties and early sixties as "a time when African American self-hatred was such that Negro history was not generally appreciated in public school, to say nothing of universities and colleges." Aptheker built on that same point when he recalled in an interview that black people "had been raised in [an] educational system [where they were told] that [their] past was nothing but servility. And in that way [they] were unique and they were ashamed of themselves, and ashamed of their parents." That Aptheker's work helped diminish that self-hatred by opening the way to "create their own history through struggle," as Marable put it, struck Aptheker as a singular accomplishment. "It's an interesting example of how history actually changed someone's consciousness, their self-awareness, their self-image," he said. "In this sense those books of mine and the work I did and the lectures I gave were of historic consequence in the history of this country."[28]

Aptheker understood his duty as a radical, as a Marxist, was to combat the ideology of the ruling class. "The ruling ideas in each age," Marx and Engels wrote in *The Communist Manifesto,* "have ever been the ideas of its ruling class." Aptheker sought to expose the falsification of history as written by "the scribes of the ruling class" in order to vigorously contest the received interpretations of history, to bring into being new, universal ideas for a new ruling class: a united black and white proletariat. "Each new class which puts itself in the place of the one ruling before it," Marx wrote, "is compelled merely in order to carry through its aim, to represent its interest as the common interest of all the members of society, that is . . . it has to give its ideas the form of universality, and represent them as the only rational, universally valid ones." Human consciousness changed, Marx said, "with every change in the conditions of his material existence, in his social relations and in his social life." That a Marxist intellectual and scholar like Aptheker succeeded in changing the consciousness, self-awareness, and self-image of others through the writing of history epitomized one of Marx's most famous dictums: "The philosophers have only interpreted the world, in various ways; the point, however, is to change it."[29]

8   Are You Now or Have You Ever Been?

FAY FOUND a silver lining in Herbert's academic blacklisting: it held a dialectical opportunity for his polemical and activist work, she thought. Even though he regretted the loss of the opportunity to teach and supervise graduate students in a formal setting, Fay insisted that "he would not have accomplished what he [had] accomplished if he taught at any particular college. . . . He wouldn't have written as much as he [had]," she said. "Once you are a professor you are tied down to the students and you have so many things to do that you have no time to do all the research that he did and to write as many books as he did." Being tied down would also have reduced the hundreds of speaking engagements he could accept during the 1950s. He crisscrossed the country from New York to South Carolina to Michigan, Illinois, and California during the late 1940s and through the 1950s. He encouraged organizers at each venue to schedule as many engagements as possible. "Anything that you are able to arrange will be satisfactory to me," he wrote to one organizer, "and in your plans do not spare me in terms of the number of engagements you arrange. I have in the past lectured 3 times a day and will be happy to do this again on this visit." The reactions of the audiences, though, sometimes baffled him. From San Francisco he wrote home early in February 1949 of his astonishment that a member of the California Labor School's choir, after hearing him speak, performed an original song in his honor, "Lift That Burden from My Shoulder." "Imagine me inspiring a song!" he wrote to Fay.[1]

In "traditional Black colleges and universities," especially after the onset of the civil rights movement, Aptheker's "voice was heard and was a familiar voice interpreting the African American past," the historian Manning Marable recalled. At times the ubiquity of his presence at those institutions led to confusion among black students because, like the students at Tuskegee Institute, they thought they had invited a black man to speak.[2]

Unlike the black seaman who extolled Aptheker's virtues in song and the black students who, according to Marable, found his presentations stirring, FBI agents in California detected ominous portents in Aptheker's effectiveness. An FBI informant within the California Labor School reported that his speeches in Los Angeles during 1949 had "stirred . . . Negroes in the Watts area of Los Angeles . . .

into action. This action resulted in the Bank of America hiring a Negro for the first time.... The Negro hired by the bank talked to him [Aptheker] following [a] lecture ... at which time he remarked that for the first time in his life he was proud to be a Negro." Aptheker, agents warned, "attempted to cause agitation among the Negroes by publicly protesting acts of Negro discrimination."[3]

It is not surprising that the FBI targeted Aptheker, especially after his bold admission during the Foley Square trial that he was a member of the CPUSA. As Aptheker moved to a position of more prominence as a party spokesperson during the fifties, particularly after the Supreme Court upheld the convictions of the leadership, FBI surveillance and documentation increased exponentially. Ominously, however, by August 1950, six months after Senator McCarthy, in Wheeling, West Virginia, brandished his list of supposed Communist infiltrators in the State Department, Aptheker had joined nearly twelve thousand other citizens in the FBI's Security Index. Labeled one of the "most potentially dangerous" among those listed in the index, Aptheker was "scheduled to be arrested within one hour after the order is given . . . [under] the custodial detention plan [designed by] the FBI and authorized by Congress with the passage of the McCarran Act."[4]

Three months later the U.S. Army, which in 1945 had urged him to make a career of military service, instituted proceedings to strip Aptheker of his officer's commission. He left the army in 1946 a captain but, as was usual practice, he retired as a major, one grade above active duty rank. In November 1950 Adj. Gen. C. A. Beall Jr. sent Aptheker a list of twenty-six allegations to which he had thirty days to respond if he wanted to maintain his commission in the Army Reserve. The charges, going back to events that occurred as early as 1941, linked Aptheker to Communist publications, advertisements placed in Communist publications, meetings he attended, and his advocacy of black civil rights. Aptheker's attorney advised him that short of demanding a court-martial, "whose verdict, given McCarthyism, might be more onerous than dismissal as an officer in the Army's Reserve," there was little he could do to halt the proceedings. One month later General Beall wrote again, bluntly: "By direction of the President, you are hereby discharged from your commission as Major, Army of the United States, effective this date." In a letter to the *New York Post* in 1959, responding to an article about the American Nazi Party, Aptheker pointed out the irony in his dismissal from the officer corps while George Lincoln Rockwell, an acknowledged Nazi, remained a commander in the U.S. Naval Reserve. The navy "finds it can do nothing about that," Aptheker wrote, "because Mr. Rockwell is granted free speech and non-interference in political matters. . . . Is one to understand from this that the Navy is more concerned about 'free speech' than the Army? Or is the real question one of what is said, by whom, and on whose behalf?"[5]

In June 1950 Communist North Korea invaded American-backed South Korea, igniting war on the Korean peninsula. In July and August the U.S. government arrested Julius and Ethel Rosenberg, charging them with conspiracy to commit espionage. Congress reacted with the passage of the Internal Security Act of 1950, or the McCarran Act, as it was more widely known because of its author, Sen. Pat McCarran of Nevada. Title Two of the McCarran Act established the detention camps to which the government would consign those persons on the Security Index in a time of national emergency. Title One was the Subversive Activities Control Act, "a straight out law which [outlawed] the Communist Party, made it illegal to be a member of the Communist Party," the general counsel of the party, John Abt, declared. Introduced in Congress as the Mundt–Nixon bill in 1948, which failed to pass, the Internal Security Act survived President Truman's veto with overwhelming congressional support. The passage of the act compounded the assault on and intimidation of the Communist Party, its leadership, and individual members.[6]

The McCarran Act established a five-member board appointed by the president, the Subversive Activities Control Board (SACB), which would hold hearings to determine whether any organization that the attorney general had identified was guilty as charged. The act required organizations found guilty by the SACB to register with the attorney general. The SACB could also declare that if individuals were members of certain groups they were likewise required to register. The act mandated as well that the organizations' officers and members had to register, provide lists of its members, account for its finances, and acknowledge its status as action, front, or infiltrated, "to brand itself, to quote the Act," wrote the historian David Caute, "as dedicated to 'treachery, deceit . . . espionage, terrorism'; as having the objective of setting up a totalitarian dictatorship subservient to a foreign power; and as consisting of members who 'repudiate their allegiance to the United States, and in effect transfer their allegiance' to a foreign power." Failure to register carried a fine of ten thousand dollars for each day the organization refused to register. Individual members and officers who did not register faced five years in jail for each day that their refusal to register continued: that is, thirty-five years for the first week, seventy for the second week, "and after that," Abt remarked, "who could care less?"[7]

With the CPUSA leaders' appeal pending before the Supreme Court, the party leaders John Gates and Betty Gannett approached Abt to inquire if he would join Rep. Vito Marcantonio in representing the party at SACB hearings. The attorney general had already announced his intention to have the SACB determine whether the party was or was not a Communist action organization. Abt agreed to represent the party.[8]

A debate arose within the party over what tactics should be used at the SACB hearings. Some in the leadership felt that the party should boycott the hearings altogether "because to do otherwise would create the illusion that we could get a fair hearing before this board, which obviously we couldn't get and wouldn't get, that the terms of the Act itself prohibited us from getting." William Z. Foster insisted that the party raise a defense of the Communist International, an idea "which everybody else thought would be a mistake and not necessary." Abt and Marcantonio, who waged a lonely opposition to the McCarran Act in Congress, argued against Foster's notion and insisted that the party "should take every opportunity and use every legal tactic . . . to expose the nature of this act, and to prolong the proceedings." That argument prevailed. "It was decided," Abt remembered, "that we would appear before the board and fight every inch of the way."[9]

After Abt and Marcantonio tried and failed to convince a three-judge federal court that "the Act from beginning to end was . . . patently unconstitutional," the SACB hearings began in April 1951. The first day of the hearings, Abt recalled, "the hearing room was like an armed camp, police all over the place," but soon settled down to a monotonous routine. For fourteen months, in New York and Washington, the government paraded before the SACB its stable of paid FBI informers and ex-communists—Louis Budenz, Benjamin Gitlow, and twenty others—to demonize the party. In presenting their affirmative defense beginning on 9 June 1952, Abt and Marcantonio, who had been joined by the attorney Joseph Forer, called only three witnesses: the convicted Smith Act defendant John Gates, who by then had spent a year in the Atlanta federal penitentiary after the Supreme Court upheld his conviction; Elizabeth Gurley Flynn, who testified during a recess in her own Smith Act trial; and Herbert Aptheker.[10]

Gates testified first. For about a week he "was transported to and from the city jail [in Washington], forced to submit to being stripped naked and to having all [his] bodily openings searched twice a day." According to Abt, "[Gates] did a very very fine job as a witness for the party and under these very trying circumstances." Aptheker conferred with Gates and heard him testify. "[He] looks all right and feels o.k.," Aptheker wrote to Fay from Washington. "A terribly sweet person. . . . John has been splendid on the witness stand—direct, plain."[11]

"Both Elizabeth and Herbert did very fine jobs in their testimony," Abt recalled, "all of which of course did us no good." But their testimony was not without its moments of levity. Reading from the official record of her testimony when questioned by Abt, the control board counsel, William Paisley, asked Gurley Flynn to "give more details concerning the many street fights in which she had participated." Gurley Flynn insisted that she had never been in any street fights. " 'So,' said Paisley, sensing a significant victory, 'did you not testify at page so-and-so of the transcript to your participation in many street fights?' " He showed Gurley Flynn the transcript. "And, sure enough, so it was recorded," Aptheker wrote in *M&M,* "and so it was understood and so it was argued—

until finally the veteran battler for civil rights persuaded all and sundry that she had testified to taking part in *free speech fights,* not in *street* fights!" The hearing record misquoted Aptheker as well. When he "said 'the ancient poet, Terence' this appears in those records as 'the ancient proletariat;' when [he] referred to Lenin's mastery of Marxism, the record had [him] saying 'Lenin's massacre of Marxism;' when [he] defined imperialism as the stage of moribund capitalism, this became 'the age of more abundant capitalism;' Lord Bryce, who seventy years ago characterized the Republican and Democratic parties as Tweedledee and Tweedledum, became 'Lord Christ;' dialectical materialism was, according to the government, 'direct imperialism.'"[12]

When asked "whether the Soviet Union did not have a dictatorship of the Communist Party," Aptheker responded, according to his *M&M* article, "in the negative." The question, Aptheker wrote, "was and is important to the Government, for the McCarran Act 'finds' the U.S.S.R. to be a 'dictatorship' of the Communist Party. It is important for the Government to maintain the fabrication because its refutation shows the profoundly democratic content of the dictatorship of the proletariat, the Communist Party's organic ties to the masses, and the Marxist–Leninist concept of leadership as springing from, tied to and nourished by those masses."[13]

Toward the end of his testimony on 1 July, in the closing session of the SACB hearings, which had moved to the Foley Square Courthouse in New York City, Paisley asked Aptheker "if he really [believed he could] ever end man's inhumanity to man? Ever end greed, envy, jealousy?" "What irony!" Aptheker wrote. "Because we did believe this we were traitors!" "Really," he wrote in August 1952, "it was obscene to see a Paisley question the integrity and patriotism of a John Gates and an Elizabeth Gurley Flynn, whose lives are poems of dedication to the noblest aspirations of humanity." "The government had called twenty-two witnesses," the *New York Times* reported the day after the hearings ended, "and the hearing record filled approximately 15,000 pages."[14]

THE PRELIMINARY decision of the SACB issued on 20 October "ruled that the CP was both foreign-dominated and dedicated to violent overthrow" of the government of the United States. Then, on 20 April 1953, the board "issued a 138-page report finding that the Party was a 'Communist-action organization' and [ordered] it to register, with full disclosure of its rolls and finances." For the next thirteen years Abt and the party maneuvered through the legal system challenging the SACB decision, filing lawsuits that reached the Supreme Court three times. As the consensus that supported the McCarran Act began to break apart, cracks developed also in the Supreme Court itself. The State Department, during the administration of President John F. Kennedy, acted under a provision of the McCarran Act that denied passports to Communists by canceling those of Gurley Flynn and Aptheker. Abt appealed the decision. He argued before a federal Court of Appeals that at least one component of the congressional finding—the one that labeled the worldwide Communist movement as monolithic—was, given the friction occurring in the late fifties and early sixties between and among Communist parties in the Soviet Union, Yugoslavia, and China, "obviously false." The three-judge panel upheld the cancellation of Gurley Flynn's and Aptheker's passports, leading Abt to appeal to the Supreme Court. Justice Arthur Goldberg, writing for the majority in the case *Aptheker v. Rusk,* "held that the passport provision of the Act was unconstitutional," Abt recalled, "as a denial of due process of law, . . . that this kind of presumption of disloyalty from the mere fact that the person is a member of the Communist Party is a violation of due process of law." In 1965 the Supreme Court finally "ruled that the [Internal Security] Act violated the Fifth Amendment, and in 1967 the Justice Department gave up the ghost," Caute wrote, "thus terminating a curious episode in political pathology apparently sustained by a fanatical determination to humiliate a heresy into branding itself as infamous." While the party managed to survive, albeit barely, the Justice Department and SACB assailment of the Jefferson School proved fatal. Faced with overwhelming debts when it attempted to fight the SACB order that it register as a "Communist-controlled organization," harassed by the FBI, and under the continual assault on both its students and the building itself by Catholic anticommunist thugs, the school shuttered its doors in 1956. The SACB, despite the Supreme Court's ruling in 1965, lingered on into the administration of President Richard Nixon until March 1973, "when Congress dropped it from the budget."[15]

On 4 June 1951 the Supreme Court announced its decision upholding the convictions of the party's leaders in the first Smith Act case. Sixteen days later the federal government launched what the historian Michal Belknap called "a nationwide assault . . . the all-out attack on the CPUSA." FBI agents fanned out across New York at dawn on 20 June to arrest the leaders who had not already been prosecuted, including Gurley Flynn, the only woman on the National Committee. Agents took the publisher Alexander Trachtenberg and the editor of *Political Affairs,* V. J. Jerome, into custody. Across the country over the next few years, until 1957, the government prosecuted more than 125 party members under the Smith Act.[16]

Foster and other party leaders "took the Supreme Court decision and the political repression resulting from it as signs that the United States had reached 'five minutes to midnight' and was now on the verge of war and fascism," Foster's biographer, James Barrett, observed. Foster believed that the government would outlaw the party completely. With the concurrence of others on the National Board, Foster urged that all the Smith Act defendants jump bail and go underground. Those opposed to that idea, led by Gurley Flynn, reached a compromise with their fellow board members by agreeing that most of those convicted would report to jail. Five of the eight Smith Act victims who eventually fled succeeded in eluding the FBI. Robert Thompson and Sidney Steinberg managed to evade capture for more than a year until the FBI caught up with them at a remote mountain cabin in California. Gus Hall, "ignoring a warning from the California Party that Mexico was unsafe for Yankee radicals," attempted, at the party's direction, to hide out "south of the border." The party sent George Watt, a veteran of the Abraham Lincoln Brigade in the Spanish Civil War, and three or four of his young American comrades ahead of Hall to Mexico to join Mexican party comrades "to help Gus get settled and to see that comrades in Mexico . . . would help him and would keep him alive." Unbeknownst to them, the man the Mexican party assigned to assist the American comrades was a police agent. Within a month of his flight FBI agents detained Hall and spirited him back across the border clandestinely. After Hall's disappearance, Watt and his companions were stranded in Mexico with "very little money," according to Aptheker. General Secretary Eugene Dennis asked Aptheker to go to Mexico to help arrange their return to the United States, giving him money to pay for their transportation. Dennis's wife, Peggy, warned Aptheker to be cautious. Hall's disappearance had shaken the party's leaders. Gurley Flynn and others thought that whoever had kidnapped Hall—they presumed the FBI had some hand in the affair—might kill Aptheker and anyone assisting him. Undaunted, Aptheker flew to Mexico City, where he met an old friend and comrade from *New Masses,* Abe Magil, who was living in Mexico City and working as a correspondent for a newspaper in Prague. With Magil's help, Aptheker, Watt, and the others made it back to the United States without incident.[17]

The party's "self-isolating policies" and the decision to send some members into hiding made it immeasurably more difficult to carry on the campaigns that the party organized to mobilize moral and financial support in order to gain amnesty for the Smith Act defendants. Through 1951, 1952, 1953 Aptheker spoke at innumerable rallies to raise money and win pardons for his comrades. He signed petitions, wrote essays, and sent letters to prosecutors, judges, and governors. He twice put up over a thousand dollars as a share of Jerome's bail. He chaired the Committee of Neighbors and Friends of Si Gerson, for which he wrote "an eight page illustrated brochure entitled, 'The Story of our Neighbor, SIMON W. GERSON.'" Aptheker acted on his own: the party did not direct him to write or act and in fact did not contact him at all about the campaigns. He wrote to Gurley Flynn in October 1953,

> I'm not a member of the National Amnesty Committee. I'd like to be, but I've never been approached about joining. In fact, and I suppose this is typical of work in this field, I've never been approached officially or organizationally by

anyone on the amnesty question—though about 18 of my articles ran regularly in the press. What speaking I've done on the subject—in Boston, Philadelphia, Connecticut, upstate and locally—has been as the result of requests to me for speaking engagements and my suggesting the subject of amnesty. I must add that this suggestion is rarely greeted with enthusiasm; on the other hand the people who attend listen with great interest and invariably ask really dozens of questions. There is a real hunger for information and for activity in this field.[18]

The leaders of the party fantasized that defense campaigns organized around an amnesty theme would garner broad public support, but with the party under attack and the leadership in jail or under indictment, the campaigns didn't garner the backing even of the leadership. Gurley Flynn, though on trial herself, worked to the point of exhaustion on the amnesty campaigns, but in October 1953 she fled the city in despair. "It will not be possible for me to write the promised article on amnesty," she wrote to Aptheker, who was editing *Political Affairs* in Jerome's absence. "I am still not well," she said, "but it is not entirely due to this which I could overcome if there were anything new to write about. No use repeating the same platitudes," she lamented, "[since] the committee has so far issued no new material or plans; . . . and I confess I am quite disheartened and discouraged about the outlook. . . . I feel like a voice crying in the wilderness, carrying on a one-woman campaign." No longer willing to assume the burden alone, she demanded that the priority for amnesty become "the concern of all in the organization." She acknowledged Aptheker's role in pursuing the demand for amnesty: "You certainly did your share," she wrote, but "I wish others did as much."[19]

Aptheker quickly responded with an enthusiasm for the amnesty campaign that Belknap ascribed only to Gurley Flynn and a few others in the party. "Dear Elizabeth," he wrote,

> In the New York Public Library I found, bound in three volumes, the letters written from prison by Kate Richards O'Hare to her husband. And, searching further, I found, what did not at all surprise me, that the Secretary of the Committee leading the fight to secure the release of this militant Socialist battler against imperialist war was—Elizabeth Gurley Flynn.
>
> Almost all the letters of Mrs. O'Hare expressed a vibrancy and a realistic optimism, but once in a while notes of great despondency and near-bitterness crept in. . . . And it was the day-to-day work of Committees such as you led— the people they reached, the sentiment this aroused, that got her and thousands of other prisoners out.
>
> It's tougher today—we don't have to spell out the reasons here—but it can be done, and when it is done this time it will have even more importance than it did last time. In a way that's why it's harder.
>
> The way to do it is to do it—and no one is doing enough yet.[20]

Despite the pervasive anticommunist sentiment in the country, Aptheker held on to his enormously optimistic belief that the masses would rise to the defense of the Communist Party if only the members worked hard enough. Neither the masses nor even the party rose to the occasion. The lack of action by the leadership soured even the veteran Communist Steve Nelson. "Many of us now believe that had there been a real mass campaign, what is now the opinion of the minority [in a Circuit Court ruling] might have been the decision itself," Nelson wrote to Aptheker in June 1955. "Without a mass campaign, what right have we to expect anything of the U.S. Supreme Court?"[21]

As the amnesty campaigns stalled, going nowhere, juries throughout the nation regularly convicted Communists on trial. Aptheker testified as an expert witness at Smith Act trials in Philadelphia, Baltimore, and New Haven as well as at Nelson's second state sedition trial in Pittsburgh. This trial, one of the earliest in which the court actually allowed Aptheker to respond to questions, furnished the blueprint for his subsequent testimony at other trials.

A longtime Communist activist who went from the anthracite coalfields of eastern Pennsylvania to the Spanish Civil War and on to "the upper reaches of Party leadership in New York City," Nelson, wrote the historians James Barrett and Rob Ruck, led a life that was "virtually a chronicle of class conflict in the twentieth century." During the early 1950s he endured "two state sedition trials, one federal Smith Act trial, and appeals all the way to the Supreme Court." Severed from the other defendants in his first state sedition trial because of injuries he had sustained in an automobile accident, Nelson's second state trial began in December 1951. Seeking an attorney to represent him, Nelson contacted more than 150 lawyers, most of whom "simply refused." Nevertheless, Judge Harry Montgomery demanded that the trial proceed, forcing Nelson to represent himself. Calling paid witnesses, informers, and former party members in the mold favored by the federal government in the Smith Act trials, the prosecutors spent about six weeks introducing evidence to prove the indictment, evidence which consisted, wrote Nelson, "of thirty-three distorted quotations from the Marxist classics." Still suffering from the effects of his accident and having little time to prepare for the next day's court session, Nelson relied on Aptheker and other friends to coordinate plans for his defense.[22]

Aptheker stayed in Pittsburgh during most of the trial, sharing a "shabby two room apartment, a walk-up, in a run down part of the city" with the *Daily Worker* correspondent Jim Dolsen. During the day Aptheker sat unobtrusively in the courtroom watching the proceedings. He and Nelson did not speak or acknowledge each other, as they wanted Aptheker's appearance on the witness stand to be a surprise to the prosecution. When the day arrived, 16 January 1952, Nelson wrote, "This time the prosecution was anxious. They searched the corridors and had FBI agents trail me and my friends. They wanted to find out who my witnesses would be." That was the last time the FBI was caught off guard when Aptheker appeared at a Smith Act trial. Prior to each of his subsequent appearances the bureau sent messages containing detailed biographies of Aptheker and copies of his previous testimony to prosecutors in cities around the country.[23]

When Aptheker and Nelson met the night before Aptheker took the witness stand, they pored over "the large amount of material he [Aptheker] had prepared. I was sure," Nelson wrote, "that even if all the questions were not written out, we could present our case effectively." The next morning, Nelson wrote in his memoir of the trial, "a stocky man of medium height, with square jaw, gray smiling eyes, and brown hair, walked into the courtroom with us [Nelson and his wife, Margaret] and sat down beside me." They planned to read the quotations offered in the indictment, "discuss what book each was extracted from, and then explain its real meaning when considered in that context," or, as Nelson said elsewhere, expose "the distortions." Aptheker pointed out those distortions several times. In his four days of testimony he showed how the prosecution had used passages plucked out of context to "give an exactly opposite meaning to that intended by the authors." "You could prove, for example, by this method" he told the jury at one point, "that Christ said, 'Go and Sin;' he did say, 'Go and sin;' but he said, 'Go and sin no more.' " Nelson recreated the courtroom scene in a contemporary memoir of the trial, *The 13th Juror,* in which he wrote that Aptheker "tackled the answers in the most elementary way, giving American examples to explain the statement in the Marxist volumes cited" to jurors, most of whom had been "hand-picked stooges of the prosecution [who] couldn't follow a high, complicated discussion." Later, decades after leaving the party, Nelson tempered that view somewhat. "If most of the jurors had been well-versed in these matters," he wrote, together with Barrett and Ruck, "we might have gone into greater detail, but it became evident right off that they couldn't follow a complicated discussion of Marxism."[24]

Aptheker did get bogged down in his testimony when he attempted to explain Marxist theory to the jury. Given the nature of the terms he attempted to explain—*class struggle, bourgeois property, bourgeois democracy, bourgeois family, Aesopian language, Marxism–Leninism,* Marxist concepts of the use of force and violence—the task was probably insurmountable from the beginning. Added to his difficulties, as Nelson later wrote, "Herb was not a guy who could explain things in workingman's language for he had too many years in academia behind him." Aptheker, too, recognized the difficulty when he wrote, years after the trial, that "the jury seemed to lose interest in my remarks." But, as Nelson also acknowledged, Aptheker "was wonderful when it came to discussing the history of the United States and really conducted a mini-course in the courtroom. His explanations of American history," most of which centered on some aspect of black history, "captivated jurors and audience alike in a way his theoretical presentations simply did not."[25]

In one exchange during which Judge Montgomery broke into Aptheker's testimony, as he often did in an attempt to discredit the veracity of the witness, Aptheker captured the discussion. He attempted to answer a question Nelson posed about majority rule and the overthrow of the government by force and violence.

Mr. Nelson:
Q. How is it [Marxism] applicable to our system of government where theo-
retically say the government is in charge of the majority?
A. [The] whole idea of Marxism–Leninism, [Aptheker said], and the whole
idea of Communism is to peacefully persuade the majority of the American
people that Socialism is to their interest, to their immediate interest, and
their long range interest; to convince them of this and to get them to vote
in favor of this, to think in favor of it and to want it and to feasibly bring
about this in our country.

Mr. Nelson:
Q. You mean by that, don't you, Doctor, to elect officials to the Assembly and
to Congress who favor such an idea?
A. Exactly. I mean the normal democratic process with which we are familiar
. . .

The Court:
Q. How does this apply in the Civil War that you were talking about yesterday?
A. I applied it this way, sir. There was a minority. There wasn't—
Q. The thing that troubles me, Doctor, is that it was a minority, the Southern
Slave Owners that took up arms, it wasn't the majority.
A. No sir. That was why it was not a revolution.
Q. That was a secession.
A. Not only was that a secession, sir, but it was also a counter-revolution.
Q. Well, where was the first revolution if it was a counter-revolution? If you
have a counter-revolution you must have a primary revolution.
A. The primary one was the establishment of a democratic republic based
upon the Declaration of Independence. The counter-revolutionists were
the slave holders who were seeking to destroy that Republic and cut it in
half and deny the truth of the Declaration of Independence and it is precisely this anti-progressive, anti-human and people content to this force
and violence which made it a minority movement, a conspiratorial one and
one against the will of the majority of the people and that is why they took
up arms and fired upon Fort Sumter. That is exactly my point, sir.[26]

The jury returned a verdict of guilty on all counts, for which Judge Montgomery sentenced Nelson to twenty years in prison and a ten-thousand-dollar fine, the maximum sentence.[27]

Inquisitions proliferated. By 1953 McCarthy stood at the pinnacle of his power. He dominated the Senate and intimidated presidents of both political parties. Emboldened by the accolades heaped upon him, absorbed in the deference shown him by government officials, and consumed by his power as chairman of the Permanent Subcommittee on Investigation of the Senate Committee on Governmental Operations, McCarthy injected a steady dose of fear into the nation that served as the basis for a growing public enthusiasm in favor of ever more authoritarian measures, especially against Communists and those so accused.

McCarthy targeted the State Department that year, aiming to "weed out the subversive elements that he suspected still remained from the tainted Truman–Acheson reign," Schrecker wrote. After first targeting the Voice of America, the State Department's overseas broadcast operation, where he uncovered no Communists, he moved on to the State Department's overseas libraries, where, he claimed, subversives found a home for their treasonous literature. In anticipation of committee hearings McCarthy sent his top aide, the twenty-six-year-old former U.S. attorney and the committee's chief counsel, Roy Cohn, to Europe to inspect and purge U.S. Information Libraries of suspect books. Cohn and his companion, G. David Schine, made stops in Paris, Munich, Bonn, Berlin, Rome, Athens, Vienna, Belgrade, and London to inspect libraries. The two McCarthy lieutenants carried out a figurative and, in at least a few places, literal book burnings, spectacles that received wide press coverage. Secretary of State John Foster Dulles "said that eleven books literally had been burned," Milton Bracker wrote in the *New York Times*, "without specifying where the fires had been set." Among the authors whose works went up in smoke were Howard Fast, Earl Browder, Philip Foner, Dashiell Hammett, and Herbert Aptheker. Years later Cohn struggled to rationalize what he and Schine had done: "David Schine and I unwittingly handed Joe McCarthy's enemies a perfect opportunity to spread the tale that a couple of young, inexperienced clowns were hustling about Europe, ordering State Department officials around, burning books, creating chaos wherever they went, and disrupting foreign relations."[28]

During the McCarthy committee's televised hearings, which lasted from April to July, the FBI lent the committee its top informer, Budenz, the former editor of the *Daily Worker*. The ex-Communists Freda Utley and Harvey Matusow, then a McCarthy aide who had previously named names for a living, joined Budenz. (Two years later Matusow again made headlines when he recanted his testimony in a widely publicized book, *False Witness*, in which he claimed that the FBI, Mc-Carthy, and Cohn had coached him in his perjured testimony.) After weeding out almost "anybody who stood up to him in closed-door hearings," McCarthy called two sets of witnesses before the committee: first, the ex-Communist informers, then the Communists or fellow travelers whose books Cohn and Schine had found on the shelves of the libraries. Budenz identified seventy-five Communist authors, and Matusow added the names of Foner and Aptheker. None of the authors worked for the government. Most had no idea why the United States Information Agency had purchased their books. Some of the writers called before the committee grasped at their opportunity for redemption. Witnesses who recanted their Communist pasts and named names, such as the historian Daniel Boorstin, received absolution from the committee. Other historians refused to cooperate, which prompted a congressional investigation of the American Historical Association (AHA). R. R. Palmer, the president of the AHA, said in his Presidential Address in 1970, "The presence of . . . W. E. B. Du Bois, Herbert Aptheker and Howard Fast . . . and others on our membership list, in the days of Senator Joseph McCarthy, caused trouble for the Association, which in 1953 was denounced as the 'second most subversive' scholarly group in the country."[29]

McCarthy commanded Aptheker to appear at a committee hearing in May 1953. "As we enter," Aptheker wrote of the experience the next month, dripping sarcasm, "we find McCarthy's circus to be a large one. The star himself is in the center of the stage, his supporting cast surrounds him, and there is his menagerie, nearly housebroken puppies, hyenas and assorted crawling things. The lights glare upon the witness, cameras grind, a dozen microphones reach out for every sound." The writer Lillian Hellman, also a target of the senator, savaged McCarthy, exceeding even Aptheker's acerbity: "It is impossible," she wrote, "to remember the drunken face of McCarthy, merry often with a kind of worldly malice, as if he were mocking those who took him seriously, and believe that he himself could take seriously anything but his boozed-up nightmares."

Cohn called Matusow to the witness table. Even now, so many years later, the transcripts of the hearings evoke in one a sense of shame. The players were, in order of appearance, Roy Cohn, chief counsel to the committee (a post Robert Kennedy had sought and failed to obtain); Harvey Matusow, paid witness against Aptheker; Sen. Joseph McCarthy, the chairman; Sen. Charles E. Potter of Michigan; Sen. Henry M. Jackson of Washington; Sen. Stewart Symington of Missouri:

> Mr. Cohn. Mr. Matusow, have you ever been a member of the Communist Party?
>
> Mr. Matusow. I have. . . . From 1947 until 1951. . . .
>
> Mr. Cohn. And when you were in the Communist movement, did you attend the Jefferson school? . . .
>
> Mr. Matusow. I did
>
> Mr. Cohn. Am I correct in assuming the members of the faculty of the Jefferson School are Communist Party members?
>
> Mr. Matusow. All members of the faculty are members of the Communist Party. . . .

Mr. Cohn. And when you studied at the Jefferson School, did you come across a man by the name of Herbert Aptheker?

Mr. Matusow. I did.

Mr. Cohn. And who was Mr. Aptheker?

Mr. Matusow. He was an instructor at the school and a lecturer. He is also an author of books which are used as the official Communist Party line in relation to the Negro question in the United States. . . .

Mr. Cohn. Was he a member of the Communist Party?

Mr. Matusow. He was.

Mr. Cohn. And an active and leading member?

Mr. Matusow. Active and leading; yes. . . .

The Chairman. . . . Mr. Cohn, may I ask: Have Mr. Aptheker's books been used in our information program?

Mr. Cohn. Yes, Mr. Chairman. Mr. Aptheker's books have been widely used in the State Department information program; in fact, the same books published by the Communist Party official publishing house and which were used in the Communist school and used by the Communist Party. . . . We know of four books—American Negro Slave Revolts; A Documentary History of the Negro in the United States; Essays in the History of the American Negro; and The Negro People in America: A Critique. . . .

The Chairman. I understand Secretary Dulles has ordered those removed from the library now.

Mr. Cohn. Secretary Dulles has ordered removed, as we understand it, books by all Communist authors, and I would assume that would certainly include books by Mr. Aptheker. I might say we have observed that one of these books on our trip abroad was located in the Information Service library in London.

Senator Potter. Are these books on the open shelf?

Mr. Cohn. All of these books are on the open shelves. . . . Mr. Chairman, I might say that . . . 31 copies of that book [*Essays in the History of the American Negro*] were purchased by the old State Department information program and have been in use, unless withdrawn under Secretary Dulles' directive.

The Chairman. In other words, the required reading in the Communist school is also required material on our bookshelves. Right?

Mr. Cohn. That appears to be the case, Mr. Chairman. . . .

Mr. Cohn. Just one last question Mr. Matusow. . . . in this Communist school, were you taught anything as to how the Communist Party was to come to power in the United States? . . .

Mr. Matusow. The Communist line is that the bourgeoisie or capitalism will not give up without a struggle; therefore we have to take arms to overthrow this bourgeoisie or capitalism.

Mr. Cohn. Now, Mr. Chairman, if we could have Mr. Matusow step aside for a few minutes, I want to call Mr. Herbert Aptheker to the stand.[30]

Roy Cohn sneered. He did not look at the witness. Roy Cohn didn't look at people, "he [looked] all around you, as thought he [wasn't] really interested in you, as though he were just testing, trying out his questions on you to see how they might fit the next guy to come up."[31] He tossed a copy of the book, *Essays in the History of the American Negro,* to the witness.

> Mr. Cohn.   Mr. Aptheker, are you the author of a book entitled "Essays in the History of the American Negro," which is in use in the State Department information program? . . .
>
> Mr. Aptheker.   You want to know whether I wrote this book? . . . Yes; I am the author.
>
> Mr. Cohn.   . . . Dr. Aptheker, when you wrote this book which has been in use in the State Department information program, were you a member of the Communist Party?
>
> Mr. Aptheker.   I will not answer such a provocative question, for the following reasons: Such a question, living in the conditions in which we do live, subjects one to the possibility of becoming an informer, than which there is nothing more dastardly. Such a question is also, in my opinion, obviously directed toward violating the first amendment of the Constitution of the United States. Such an amendment plays into the hands of guilt by association tactics, notoriously practiced by this committee.
>
>   I further refuse to answer this provocative question on the basis of the fifth amendment, which protects me against being a witness against myself. For these reasons, I will not answer this loaded question.
>
> The Chairman.   Do you tell us today that you feel that if you were to truthfully answer the question as to whether you were a member of the Communist Party at the time you wrote this book that answer might tend to incriminate you?
>
> Mr. Aptheker.   Well Senator, I think I have answered the question.
>
> The Chairman.   I will require you to answer this question. You understand that you are privileged to refuse to answer any question that you feel that a truthful answer might tend to incriminate you. You cannot refuse to answer if you feel that if you perjure yourself it would incriminate you. It is only if you feel a truthful answer to this question of whether or not you were a Communist at the time you wrote the book would tend to incriminate you that you can refuse to answer.
>
>   So, my question to you now is: Do you tell the committee, under oath, that you feel that a truthful answer to that question, as to whether you were a Communist, would tend to incriminate you? And I shall order you to answer that question.
>
> Mr. Aptheker.   I appreciate your concern, Senator. . . .
>
> The Chairman.   You said you think there is nothing more dastardly than an informer. Do you think it would be a dastardly act for you or any other American to inform of acts of espionage against the United States? Would that be a dastardly act?

Mr. Aptheker: Clearly, in my opinion, this is not my usage of "informer."

The Chairman. In other words, you think it would be proper to inform as to espionage activities?

Mr. Aptheker. If actual knowledge of espionage is held by someone, it would certainly not be dastardly or incorrect to let authorities know of such act.

The Chairman. Have you ever engaged in either espionage or sabotage?

Mr. Aptheker. Certainly not.

The Chairman. . . . Are you a member of the Communist Party as of today, as of this moment?

Mr. Aptheker. I refuse to answer that question for the reasons already stated, Senator. . . . The refusal to answer such questions is simply a hallmark of the intimidation which is prevalent in the country. People react differently to such intimidation. . . . I understand that there is no inference of guilt in refusing to answer, and that the fifth amendment was put there to protect the innocent as well as the guilty, and as a very important part of our civil rights. . . .

Senator Jackson. It cannot be on any propaganda ground. It cannot be on any philosophical ground. It has to be on that ground [that a truthful answer might tend to incriminate you] and that ground alone. That is what the constitutional amendment is there for.

Mr. Aptheker. I understand that.

Senator Jackson. So it is not fair for you to turn around and say the reasons you are not answering is that it is guilt by association or that it is a lot of other references that you might want to throw in. There is only one answer that you can give when you exercise that privilege. Otherwise you are not conscientiously abiding by the constitutional provisions.

Mr. Aptheker. I don't agree with that, either, sir. . . . Both of you gentlemen have spoken about 10 or 15 minutes. Am I to have a chance to reply?

The Chairman. No; you will have a chance to answer questions. We are not going to hear any speeches. When a witness comes before us who has been identified as a member of the Communist Party, who refuses to tell whether he is a member of the Communist Party, we are not hearing any speeches from him. . . . You can go back to your Communist school and make your speeches. Now you will only answer the questions. . . .

Senator Symington. Do you think you are a good American.

Mr. Aptheker. Yes, sir.

Senator Symington. Would you be a good American if you belonged to an organization that is dedicated to the destruction of our system of government?

Mr. Aptheker. I think I had better refuse to answer that question. Actually, I think, since you have put it in an opinion form, I would say "no" to your question.

Senator Jackson. Are there two different kinds of Communists, a philosophical communist who does not believe in espionage and sabotage, as part of the party membership, and one who does believe in espionage and sabotage as a part of the fulfillment of the membership? Can you answer that question?

Mr. Aptheker. You request my opinion on that, Senator, and I will offer my opinion. My opinion is that there are not such Communists at all; that espionage, as you put it, in relation to this, is a monstrous hoax.

Senator Jackson. Your statement is that Communist Party members do not engage in espionage or sabotage?

Mr. Aptheker. I did not mean to convey any special knowledge. You asked for an opinion. I am offering an opinion, on the basis of my knowledge, what I think I know, what my opinion is, and my reply to you is a negative one ...

Senator Symington. What did you mean by the word "informer"?

Mr. Aptheker. What did I mean by the word? ... I meant what is normally meant by it, what the dictionary meant by it, what the film, The Informer meant.

Senator Symington. I did not ask you what the dictionary says about it. I asked you what you meant by the word.... Answer what you meant by the word.

Mr. Aptheker. I answer that I am using the word in the normal dictionary sense. An informer is universally despised because he, with malice aforethought, and for reasons usually of personal gain, informs, historically always inaccurately, because that is his function, on other people....

The Chairman. Let us get down, the, to the man who informs upon his fellow members of the Communist conspiracy.

Mr. Aptheker. We can't get down to that on common ground, sir. There is no conspiracy to which you refer.

The Chairman. All right. Then let us say a man who informs on the activities of members of the Communist movement. Do you think he is committing a dastardly act?

Mr. Aptheker. Yes; I think such an informer is—

The Chairman. You may step down.

Mr. Aptheker. May I have an opportunity to read a brief statement to this committee?

The Chairman. You will have no opportunity to make any speeches to this committee, as long a you refuse to tell us whether you are engaged in the Communist conspiracy at this time. You can go outside this committee room and make all the speeches you want.

Mr. Aptheker. I have, sir, not a speech to make. I have got about 250 words. I have been brought down here from some hundreds of miles. You mean I cannot read 250 words to this committee? ...

Senator Jackson. When you make a statement to the committee, you ought to be willing to give your full background, so that the public will know just who is speaking. If you are a Communist, I suppose you are proud of it, and you ought to tell the American people you are speaking as a communist.

Mr. Aptheker. It is no question of pride. It is a question of informing....

Senator Symington. If you were once a Communist, before it became obvious that they were a great menace to the American Government and its people, why are you not perfectly willing to say that you were? Why should you be ashamed or afraid to say that you are not?

Mr. Aptheker. I am ashamed of nothing, sir. I don't know whether everybody in this room can say that. I say that I am ashamed of nothing, under oath. I have full pride in my activity.

I must again respectfully say that your question is posited on such fallacious assumptions that it is impossible to answer it reasonably, since in your question you have provided the answer which you seek and which I deny. . . .

Senator Symington. If we have a witness who comes up here under oath and says that he was a member of the Communist Party, why is it not a simple matter for you, inasmuch as we are fighting communism with all of our resources, to say, "Yes, I was a communist once, but I am no longer," if you believe you are a good American citizen.

Mr. Aptheker. Once again, the assumptions in your question are the answer that you want.

Senator Symington. Then you tell me what I would like to ask you. Phrase the question as you would like me to ask it to you.

Mr. Aptheker. Certainly. You want me to give what you think is information, names, circumstances, dates.

Senator Symington. No. That is not fair.

Senator Jackson. No one asked you the names of individuals. I asked you whether you were ever a member of the Communist Party.

Senator Symington. And if you were, why were you not proud to say that you were now a good American and not a member of the Communist Party?

Mr. Aptheker. Because such a question posits itself on the assumption that one who is a Communist cannot be a good American.

Senator Symington. I do not think so at all, if you have left the party. There is nothing illegal about being a member of the Communist Party. And if you say you were a Communist, but now that you recognize the danger of communism to America, you are not, there is nothing wrong with that. Why cannot you not say that now?

Mr. Aptheker. Because that is exactly the assumption against which I am protesting.

Senator Potter. What you are saying is that you can be a member of the Communist Party today and be a loyal American citizen?

Mr. Aptheker. That is certainly my opinion.

Senator Symington. Oh, that is your opinion, that you can be a member of the communist Party today and still be a good American.

Mr. Aptheker. Certainly that is my opinion.

Mr. Cohn. Dr. Aptheker, I want to ask you this: Do you teach at a Communist school at the present time? . . . Have you ever taught at any public university in New York? Have you ever taught at any university or college? . . .

Mr. Aptheker. One of the problems involved in that question is what you mean by "taught." I don't mean to be technical, but, for instance, if you want to know whether I have lectured in various institutions . . . I have lectured at Columbia, at Yale, at Harvard, at Brooklyn, at the University of

Chicago, at the University of North Carolina, at Allen University, at dozens of universities.

Mr. Cohn. Were you a member of the Communist Party when you delivered those lectures.

Mr. Aptheker. It must be obvious, I think, that I refuse to answer such a question. . . .

The Chairman. First, let me say the witness will be ordered to give us a list of the schools at which he has taught and lectured, under whose auspices he was brought to the various schools and universities, and the dates, as nearly as he can supply them.

You will be ordered to produce that. How much time would you want, to produce that, Dr. Aptheker?

Mr. Aptheker. Actually, the production is impossible, Senator.

The Chairman. Well, you will produce as complete a list as you can, and the names of the individuals who got you to come, and under whose sponsorship you spoke.

Mr. Aptheker. I can tell you now that that is impossible. I don't keep those things.

The Chairman. You will be ordered to produce a list as complete as you can. . . . You will be ordered to produce those. If you do not produce them, I will ask the committee to find you in contempt of the committee.

Mr. Aptheker. May I understand thoroughly what you want produced?

The Chairman. The list of all of the schools at which you taught or lectured, as nearly as you can give it; the time at which you taught or lectured in the various schools or colleges; the name of the organization or the individual under whose auspices you were brought to these various universities. And you will be ordered to produce that, and we will give you 1 week's time. That will be produced a week from today by 10 o'clock in the morning.

Mr. Aptheker. Of course, Senator, I reserve the right to invoke the fifth amendment wherever necessary in such a list, the difficulty of which is enormous.

The Chairman. We will not allow you to invoke the privilege insofar as giving us the names of the colleges at which you lectured, or the dates. If a communist organization or Communists brought you to the various schools or universities, you will be entitled to invoke the privilege insofar as not telling us who brought you there. But we will not allow the privilege insofar as the dates you spoke there. It is a matter of public record, and you will be ordered to produce that material. If you do not, I repeat, I shall ask the committee to find you in contempt. The committee may or may not go along with me. I do not know.

You may step down.[32]

And then it was over. Almost. In Brooklyn, Bettina, who was nine years old at the time, was playing at a friend's house and noticed her father on television. "I don't understand anything about the communist 'threat' or the purpose of these televised hearings," she recalled in a short memoir. "All I see is my Pop on television. I am very proud. I shout: 'Look! My daddy's on television!' There is a terrible silence in the house. My friend's parents shut off the TV. Nobody says anything. Then I go home. Then her parents say I can't play at her house anymore." The day after the hearings the *New York Times* identified Foner, the novelist Millen Brand, William Gropper, "an artist," and Aptheker as "uncooperative witnesses" and reported that McCarthy had ordered Aptheker to "produce a complete list of lectures he had given." The next week Aptheker responded to McCarthy's demand in a three-paragraph letter in which he refused to supply the names of people or groups who had invited him to speak or the schools where he had taught "on the grounds stated for my other refusals to testify, including my privilege under the Fifth Amendment." With regard to his invited lecture appearances Aptheker responded, "I have lectured . . . [at] many of the leading institutions. My memory on this matter is far from complete, but I now recall lecturing mainly on the history of the Negro people in the United States, at Columbia, Yale, Harvard, New York, the Universities of Chicago, Wisconsin, Minnesota, Michigan, North Carolina, City College in New York, Brooklyn College, Hunter College and Queens College. I have no accurate recollection at all, nor any record of the dates of those numerous engagements."[33] That he had no record was a lie.

Why did Aptheker put himself at considerable personal risk by testifying at the various trials and hearings? Nelson had asked Aptheker that very question at his state sedition trial in Pittsburgh: "Doctor, would you please tell the Jury what is your interest in this case?" "What I mean," he continued, "is some of the prosecution witnesses are getting paid for what they are saying here. What is your purpose in coming here and testifying?" Aptheker told the jury that he came to help out a friend, "to help you," he said to Nelson:

> I am here also because I am devoted to the principles of Marxism and Leninism, and to the principles of my Party, and because both principles . . . I hold, dearer than my life. I am very eager to defend these principles, the principles that have been brought into Court that have been, I believe, . . . distorted. . . . I believe that in defending him and the Party I am defending the best interests of my family . . . and my people and of my country. . . . One of my basic interests is that I wish to defend civil liberties and beliefs such as involved here, and this is another of my interests in testifying in this case. . . . The further point that I think is involved here is the struggle for the people, I believe it is for the people and the interests of my country and the American people.[34]

Aptheker ignored the risks to himself, but by the mid-1950s Fay began to worry about his personal safety. When the singer and activist Pete Seeger asked Aptheker to testify, Fay interceded for the first time. "I didn't want him to go," she told an interviewer. "I just felt that he had done so much of it that there comes a time when your luck runs out. I felt that was the time." For his part,

Aptheker felt enormous divided loyalties. "I was torn," he said. "Because how could I say no to Fay, which I hadn't done all my life. And how could I say no to Pete Seeger?" The government solved the dilemma for him when it decided not to indict Seeger. "Luckily the government dropped the indictment, probably, that's a guess on my part, that Pete was world famous. Anyway it never went to indictment." And with a sense of finality about the whole period Aptheker added, "That was the end of it."[35]

Forty-one years later Aptheker received a bizarre letter. "You will not, of course, remember me," the writer began, "although I did meet you in the far past. I am sure you must remember, however, my late husband, Louis Budenz, who died almost twenty-two years ago. . . . What I want to say to you is this: Louis always spoke of you as 'our learned theoretician.' He respected you above all of our other comrades for your scholarly understanding of Marxism. . . . Please let me extend to you my best wishes. Let us give one another the benefit of the doubt in the search for truth." In the margins of the letter Aptheker wrote, "Budenz! No reply."[36]

9   De Facto Dissolution of the Party

ALARMED BY growing government repression during the late 1940s even prior to the Smith Act trials and either unable or unwilling to analyze its own policies, the CPUSA turned in on itself. The former party member Joseph Starobin pointed out this "strange paradox: *in the name of defying the witch-hunt against them, the American Communists complemented it by engaging in a witchhunt of their own. Beleaguered from without, they went through agony from within.*"[1]

The campaign within the party to eradicate Browderism at the end of the Second World War swept away many party members and created a milieu rife with suspicion that lingered through the rest of that decade and into the next. Casting a wide net, the party adopted a new policy on homosexuals in 1948 that mirrored the federal government's so-called lavender scare persecution. It forced out openly gay members who had till then, even though "many Communists shared the prejudices of the general society" toward homosexuals, functioned without being subjected to overt hostility. Two years later Harry Hay, whom Dorothy Healey reluctantly dropped from the membership rolls in California, and several other men founded one of the first gay rights organizations, the Mattachine Society. In 1953 anticommunist gay men took control of the society's leadership and forced Hay out. Although Aptheker attempted to ameliorate party policy, the organization held to its homophobic policies for the next half century.[2]

Just as the government began its concerted assault in the late forties, the party unleashed upon itself, from within its ranks and affiliated organizations, a frenzied campaign to eradicate "white chauvinism," a term used within the party to mean antiblack. While the CPUSA could justifiably claim the mantle of a "model of racial integration" and, after the late 1920s, was never complacent about racial issues, there had been some intraparty friction ever since the decision made during the war by the leaders that "a too militant defense of black rights at home would interfere with the war effort." Some members, Aptheker among them, felt the policy went too far. The party did not support the Double V campaign during the war, but Aptheker certainly did. His opinion, expressed privately during the war and then publicly in 1946 in an article in *New Masses,* "was that . . . the implementation" of the wartime policy "left much to be desired, and that it was pushed frequently far to excess. I said so . . . and in my actions (with both Negro and white troops, in the South and in Europe) conducted myself accordingly."[3]

The immediate task, a publication of the party warned in September 1949, was to conduct "an ideological campaign against white chauvinism in every Party branch." The party in effect launched its own brand of McCarthyism: "inquisitorial type hearings and committees were set up," lamented the black communist leader Harry Haywood, who himself experienced the capricious accusations, "veteran cadres raked over the coals (often with little or no cause), censured, and many expelled." Healey, Fast, and Aptheker were all caught up in the net of the assault, although, unlike Healey and Fast, Aptheker faced accusations in mid-1949, very early in the process, and his accusers backed down.[4]

Aptheker began 1949 with a pathbreaking essay in the February issue of *M&M* titled "The Negro Woman." In the essay he proposed that the history of women in general, "the female half of humanity," had been neglected and comprised mainly "the history of coiffures and costumes and little else." The "super-neglected" history of black women arose, he said, through the triple "super-exploitation" faced by black women because of their race, class, and gender. He addressed that history in "an attempt to suggest something of the riches waiting here to be mined and that must be mined if the struggle against bourgeois history and the class it upholds is to succeed." He concentrated on presenting "highlights of the history of the mass of Negro women," drawing examples from his vast research on the documentary history of African Americans on which he was still working. He wove a tapestry of black women's voices, from the unknown slave mother whose child was sold away and the heroic Harriet Tubman and Ida B. Wells Barnett to black women who fought "heroic struggles" for workers' rights and the black women of the Communist Party. Decades before Toni Morrison found and immortalized her in *Beloved,* Aptheker wrote of Margaret Garner: "a fugitive slave, who, when trapped near Cincinnati, killed her own daughter and tried to kill herself." Aptheker called the position of black women "pivotal . . . in all democratic struggles. Appreciation of this central fact," he wrote, "should provoke the special study and special effort that it deserves." Within a few months the party leader Claudia Jones, who was born in Trinidad, published "An End to the Neglect of the Problems of the Negro Woman," an article that "relied heavily," without attribution, on Aptheker's work: she "paraphrased her discussion of black women's history (and indeed other parts of her argument as well) from Herbert Aptheker's article 'The Negro Woman.'" What Aptheker began and Claudia Jones carried forward had an enormous impact on the party. "It was rare after 1949," wrote the historian Kate Weigand, "for an issue of the *Worker* or the *Daily Worker* not to include at least one article about black women's special 'triply exploited' position in American society."[5]

Aptheker ran into trouble with the early manifestations of the white chauvinism campaign in 1949, when *Jewish Life* published his critical review of Haywood's *Negro Liberation*. Legendary in the party, Haywood "initiated the debate . . . within the [CPUSA] . . . on self-determination . . . during the 1930s . . . the theory of self-determination in the 'black belt' of the American South for the Afro-American people," a position he "vigorously fought for . . . until his expulsion [from the party] in 1959." Haywood, who had lived for several years in the Soviet Union during the late twenties, enunciated the policy embraced by the Sixth Communist International (Comintern) in 1928 and adopted by the CPUSA, which posited that "the American Negroes constituted an oppressed *nation*, . . . 'an historically developed community of people with a common language, territory, economic life and an historic tradition reflecting itself in a common culture.' " According to that theory, which called for the establishment of a separate "Negro republic," the oppressed nation existed "primarily within the limits of the 'Black Belt,' a shifting block of Southern counties that contained a majority of Negroes." The CPUSA effectively dropped the policy in 1934 with the advent of the Popular Front in the thirties.[6]

While Haywood held fast to his belief in the existence of a separate nation in the "black belt," Aptheker's examination of nationhood, expressed in June 1949 in an article in *Political Affairs,* encompassed a more internationalist view, namely, that expressed by Du Bois in the NAACP appeal to the United Nations. " 'The United Nations surely will not forget,' " Aptheker remarked, quoting Du Bois, " 'that the population of this people [the Negro people] makes it one of the considerable nations of the world. . . . In sheer number then . . . a group which has a right to be heard; and while we rejoice that other smaller nations can stand and make their wants known in the United Nations, we maintain equally that our voice should not be suppressed or ignored.' " Aptheker pointed to Du Bois's words as a confirmation of "American Communists' . . . position that the Negro question is a national question, and as marking a high point in national consciousness among American Negroes." But he scoffed at the notion that Communists had introduced the concept of the Negro people as constituting a nation. That concept, as "generally assumed," did not appear at the end of the First World War era and "was not modern at all," Aptheker claimed, but evolved historically among black Americans. "The fact is that there were many such expressions of awareness," Aptheker wrote, "sometimes reaching the stage of verbal enunciation" going back "to prerevolutionary America when the African influence was very strong . . . sometimes of attempts at formal analysis. However faulty this analysis may have been, the germ of a feeling, of a consciousness of nationality, was clearly present. . . . The concept of Negro nationality, however rudimentary or distorted the forms, has been expressed by various sections of the Negro population for well over a hundred years. Of no other people within the United States is this true, and this fact constitutes a very significant feature of Negro history."[7]

While generally positive about Haywood's book, which, Aptheker recalled, "represented the accepted party position on what was called the 'Negro Question,'" he found fault nonetheless. Aptheker acknowledged the stress Haywood placed on the import, historically, of the "special oppression of the Black population in the lack of land ownership in a then still largely rural people," but he criticized him for disregarding the "diminishing consequence . . . of this factor—given the mounting urbanization of the African-American population and its growing dispersal outside the Black belt." In ignoring the dispersal of blacks into the broader population, Haywood also, Aptheker said, "ignored the significance of a growing Black bourgeoisie and the particular challenge this represented to those fighting racism."[8]

That Aptheker's review appeared in *Jewish Life,* a magazine close to the party, and was critical of a book written by a leading black Communist and published by the party press led to denunciations of Aptheker by Haywood and several top officials of the party. The expressions of displeasure did not deter Aptheker from arguing for the truth of his analysis. "[The detractors] did not effectively refute my criticisms," he wrote in his unpublished autobiography. Within a decade the party had embraced a new interpretation and adopted an altered policy for black liberation that incorporated insights by Aptheker, Du Bois, Ben Davis, and Henry Winston. This time the party acknowledged Aptheker's observations that the two mass migrations of black people in the twentieth century out of the South to the North and West, off the land and away from an agrarian lifestyle to urban working-class existence, required a solution to racism that involved more than land and territory, more than a nation within a nation. The struggle for full social, economic, and political equality of black people still held a position of centrality in the party, but black people, most of whom were working class, constituted a strategic ally and vital component of the entire working class in the battle to achieve socialism. The move away from Haywood's "nation within a nation" analysis alienated Haywood to such an extent that he endeavored to organize a split within the party by forming the Provisional Organizing Committee for a Communist Party (POC). The POC fell almost immediately into internal "witch hunts, personal slander and character assassination," Haywood wrote, and collapsed within months. Having effectively removed himself from the party, which had, he said, "step by step, cut away at all our revolutionary principles in the name of fighting for them," Haywood was quietly expelled in 1959.[9]

Aptheker's analysis was criticized from outside the party as well. In 1949 the West Indian historian and social critic C. L. R. James published a pamphlet for the Socialist Workers Party, "The Revolutionary Answer to the Negro Problem in the USA." James reproved the party's positions for being less than revolutionary when compared to those of the Socialist Workers Party. Even more important to James, it seemed, were the origins of those positions. In the view of Andrew McIntosh, writing in *Society,* the "tendency of the Communist Party USA to turn to non-blacks (such as Herbert Aptheker) in the setting of communist policy regarding matters of the 'Negro Question' (such as self-determination for the Black Belt) outraged James." McIntosh continued, "He also viewed the use of black front men to sell white authored communist policies concerning blacks as an extension of Stalinist duplicity."[10]

While the expulsions of homosexuals and white chauvinists raged on, the party reduced its numbers further simply by not renewing memberships. In June 1951, after the Supreme Court announced its ruling that affirmed the convictions of the top leadership, the party put into action its modified "five-minutes-to-midnight" plan, thereby sending thousands of cadres into hiding in a complicated underground apparatus. Later that year, having been indicted with the second-tier leadership and awaiting his trial, V. J. Jerome, the editor of the party's theoretical journal *Political Affairs,* brought Aptheker to the magazine as associate editor. For the next five years, through his trial and three-year imprisonment, Jerome continued to be identified on the masthead as the editor of the journal, but it was Aptheker who carried out all the editorial duties. In June 1957, when Jerome left the country after being released from prison, Aptheker officially took over as editor.

Even as the party experienced what the historian Joseph Starobin called a "*de facto* dissolution" during the period from 1951 to 1956 and as many of its leaders and thousands of members went underground or were imprisoned, Aptheker emerged as a leading voice of the party. His articles appeared regularly in *M&M, Political Affairs,* and the *Worker.* In speaking engagements at colleges and universities around the country he drew crowds of four and five hundred. As he mingled with students, an experience he relished, his attention was drawn to their questions and observations about the Soviet Union. "I have heard people who were otherwise fairminded, eager to understand, and generally at least liberal in political feelings, express views concerning the USSR that were indistinguishable from those of Hitler or Hearst," he wrote in a memo to the National Administrative Committee. "On the question of the Soviet Union," he wrote, "the fact is that the enemy has succeeded in winning over the minds of the vast majority of the American people.... In my judgment, the central ideological and agitational obstacle confronting the Party today in the task of reaching out to the people is the opinion so very widely held that the Soviet Union is a backward land of terrible tyranny and brutality." He complained that the party's opposition to the dominant beliefs about the USSR had been "weak and sporadic and defensive and half-hearted." He felt the misinformation was not confined to people outside the party: even "within the Party there is very little discussion (not to speak of study) of the USSR. Many *comrades* today simply *do not know* about the USSR," he declared in 1954 in a statement whose irony became apparent less than two years later when the Soviet Union invaded Hungary. He wanted the party to move aggressively to blunt the force of anti-Soviet views. He wanted not just a defense "but pride and joy and emphasis. The marvel of this greatest event in human history should be brought forward, continuously and actively."[11]

This analysis was not a polemic directed at critics. He didn't write to the leadership of the party because he "believed for a moment, then, in charges of terrible injustice." He raised the problems he encountered among students "because [I] knew that such questions came from very decent and very progressive people and because [I] did not have persuasive replies." Rarely at a loss for words, he did not know how to respond adequately to a young black woman, "typical . . . [of] dozens of similar experiences . . . encountered by me in the past six months alone," who peppered him with questions during a ride from Swarthmore to Philadelphia. "Her views of the USSR were completely reactionary and were held with great tenacity," Aptheker wrote in his memo. "She even remarked that . . . Russia [was a] . . . tyrannical, aggressive, and threatening country!"[12]

Whatever answers Aptheker devised came from his reading of books and newspapers published between 1917 and the time he wrote his memo in 1954. In addition to the stories produced by Soviet writers and writers from other Communist parties, he read those of bourgeois reporters who wrote unfavorably about the USSR after 1917 and the refutations "by other bourgeois commentators, from Walter Lippmann to Walter Duranty to Harrison Salisbury." In November 1950 he had undertaken, in an article in *M&M,* to counter what he perceived to be "twenty-five years" of deliberate, incessant lies "about the first socialist state," lies that "the rich of the world" had used to assault and vilify the Soviet Union. He quoted *Mission to Moscow* by the former American ambassador to the USSR Joseph Davies, who wrote, "If you can picture a personality that is exactly opposite to what the most rabid anti-Stalinist anywhere could conceive, then you might picture this man [Stalin]"; W. Averill Harriman, who in a radio address of October 12, 1941, proclaimed, "We discovered that a lot of popular notions about these Russians were wrong"; Secretary of State Cordell Hull, who "informed Congress in 1943 that he had 'found in Marshal Stalin a remarkable personality, one of the great statesmen and leaders of this age'"; Under-Secretary of State Sumner Welles, who "confessed" in his *The Time for*

Decision (1944) "that official Washington in 1941 had been terribly misinformed about Russia"; and Foster Rhea Dulles of Ohio State University, who "thought it perfectly clear in his *The Road to Teheran* (1944) that '... here was striking proof that many of the ideas about the Soviet Union popularly held in this country had been founded on a total misconception of what was actually happening in Russia and of the sentiments of the Russian people.'" Aptheker praised books by reporters "who had been in the U.S.S.R. for several months or years ... from 1941 through 1944" and who wrote about "what they had themselves seen and heard and felt ... first-hand and based on prolonged observation ... James E. Brown, Erskine Caldwell, Wallace Carroll, Henry C. Cassidy, Walter Duranty, Walter Graebner, Maurice Hindus, Ralph Ingersoll, Larry Lesueur, Ralph Parker, Quentin Reynolds and Alexander Werth." While several of the works showed "distinct remnants" of anti-Soviet propaganda, he wrote, the reporters themselves, having confessed to being "victims of anti-Soviet propaganda, ... the net impression of their works contradicted such propaganda." But with the end of the Second World War and the onset of the Cold War, the tide had turned. "Today," Aptheker wrote in his article in 1950, "one picks up his morning paper and reads of the oppressed minorities of the U.S.S.R. groaning for liberation." What else could one expect, he asked, from "'the boss press' treatment of a land where workers rule and where chauvinism is a high crime?"[13]

"WHAT IS TO BE DONE?" Aptheker wrote on page 3 of his memo of 1954, echoing Lenin. He urged the leadership to acquire "actual information" in "an organized effort ... get it and keep it coming ... a systematic, organized study [to] have material available to editors, writers, speakers" and to members of the party. Get the information out to "the outfit" (his euphemism for the party), he urged. He wanted the quality and quantity of material enhanced "at once" to cover "Soviet education, science, curriculum, values. ... Novels, movies, music, scientific views ... at length in all our media." He recommended that an examination be made of bourgeois writers and of the work of writers from the USSR. To end what he called "the State Department blackout of the USSR" Aptheker outlined a "vigorous campaign" to open up the Soviet Union to examination by American eyes. "What [is the State Department] afraid of?" he asked. "We want to see for ourselves: ... Why can people—writers, teachers, workers, etc.—from almost every other country ... go to the Soviet Union ... but the State Department bars Americans?" "The main thing," he concluded, "is for a turn, for an aggressive campaign to bring the truth about the USSR to the American people and make them understand, to the best of our ability, *the impact of that truth for them.*" There is no evidence that the party leaders reacted to Aptheker's entreaties or showed any interest in his project. Most of them probably never even saw the memo: communication among the members of the National Board, most of whom were housed in different prisons, was sporadic.

Whatever ideas and advice they did offer came by letter or word of mouth from visiting relatives.[14]

During those years of the de facto dissolution, Aptheker devoted considerable attention to exposing other falsehoods that seemed to him part of the underpinning of the "big lie," that is, the caricature of the CPUSA "as an espionage agency whose members were liars, thieves and assassins in the service of the U.S.S.R." He did so in courtrooms, in testimony before the Subversive Activities Control Board and the McCarthy committee, and in books and articles. In a lengthy article for *M&M* he took special notice of *The Strange Case of Alger Hiss,* a book published in 1953 by the former lord chancellor of Great Britain, William Allen Jowitt. Aptheker criticized Jowitt for the weaknesses and omissions occasioned by "his own profound opposition to Communism," yet he found merit in Jowitt's contention that a severe miscarriage of justice had occurred through the conviction of Alger Hiss, a former New Deal State Department official convicted on charges of perjury stemming from testimony he gave to Congress when the journalist Whittaker Chambers accused him of being a Soviet spy. Aptheker's argument, however, went further than identifying merely "a miscarriage of justice." "The answer," he wrote, "is clear: *Hiss was not framed by Chambers.* Chambers was the vicious and willing tool, but *Hiss was framed by the ruling class of the United States and by its apparatus, most particularly by J. Edgar Hoover's F.B.I.*" Aptheker characterized the Hiss case as a "key strategy of McCarthyism—to identify the liberalism and mild progressivism of the New Deal with 'Communism'" and to obliterate the public's "rather idealized concept of Roosevelt and of the New Deal—of a man and a program that tried, and in considerable part succeeded, to give 'the forgotten man'—the worker, the poor farmer, the Negro people, the masses—a 'break.'"[15]

Even if the party had taken up Aptheker's call for altering the public's perception of the Soviet Union and the CPUSA, it would have been a Sisyphean struggle given the substantiation the government had at its disposal. Notably, while Aptheker called for a reappraisal, Julius and Ethel Rosenberg's trial on charges of espionage and their subsequent execution dominated the newspaper headlines throughout the country. The party, feeling that by openly endorsing the Rosenbergs' cause it would doom the couple to certain death, officially abstained from taking an active role in support of the Rosenbergs, but, like many other individual communists, Herbert and Fay worked "feverishly" in their defense. They attended demonstrations held for the Rosenbergs and signed petitions, and Herbert wrote articles. In February 1953 in an article in *M&M* published four months before the Rosenbergs' execution—in effect, a futile try to goad Sidney Hook, the NYU philosophy professor and a nemesis of Aptheker's, into an open, public debate—Aptheker said that "anti-Semitism played and plays a part in this case" but that he was convinced the Rosenbergs were innocent, that the "American ruling class . . . railroaded" them "to the chair" as part of a prowar, profascist agenda. "They are to serve," he wrote, "if they die, as object lessons of the terror to fall upon those who, like them, hate fascism and struggle for peace." As Aptheker pointed out in the article, no Jews served on the Rosenbergs' jury, but the prosecuting attorneys and the judge were Jewish. "Jewishness," wrote Nicholas von Hoffman, the biographer of the prosecutor Roy Cohn, "was a topic which ran unspoken through the Rosenberg trial."[16]

The articles, the petition drives, the demonstrations in front of the White House and in New York and those around the world did not prevent the Rosenbergs' executions. The couple was simply too potent a political symbol in a country seized by anticommunist hysteria. Their execution was a powerful symbol to Communists as well. "If two people in these United States could be so deliberately framed and put to death," wrote Fast, "then we were no longer a nation of law." The executions "steeled the resolve of some," Aptheker wrote, "even as their souls writhed in agony that Friday evening when the assembled thousands heard the cry, 'They are dead, they are dead!' " For others, he confessed, "the sheer horror of it paralyzed . . . in some cases permanently driving them out of any political activity." In the Apthekers' apartment the horror and fear manifested themselves in a conversation likely repeated in hundreds of households. Fay confided in nine-year-old Bettina, who had often joined her parents at demonstrations, including the final one on 19 June 1953. "I have something very important to tell you," Bettina recalled her mother saying in hushed tones, breathing on her daughter's cheek. "Your daddy and I are communists. You must never, ever tell anyone. Do you understand?" Later that year or perhaps the next, at Camp Wyandot, "where . . . children of communist and progressive parents [spent summers]," as the children one-upped each other over their parents' status, Bettina blurted out that her parents were Communists. "Then I freeze," she recalled. "I have betrayed the secret. I am terrified. FBI agents are lurking outside our bunkhouse. They have heard me. They will arrest my parents. . . . I fall into an exhausted, terror-filled sleep, the image of my parents dead, executed like the Rosenbergs, riding my dreams for weeks afterward."[17]

The execution of the Rosenbergs may well have been the darkest hour of repression for those Communists whom the government had not prosecuted in the early fifties. Still, less than two years later, Aptheker perceived developments that merited cautious optimism, confirming, he said, "what has been apparent all about us for the past six or eight months: the tide is turning against reaction," and there is an "abatement of the anti-Communist hysteria . . . a certain checking of McCarthyism." McCarthy's colleagues in the Senate censured him in December 1954, precipitating his slow decline until his death three years later.[18]

As he traveled around the country speaking to college and university audiences, Aptheker "half expected a barbecue," he said, "with me the pig." Instead

he found "a growing interest in what the Left has to say for itself." A few professors treated him with courtesy and in some cases genuine warmth, but often
faculty members refused either to sit on the same platform with him to debate
or, though he "explicitly urged them to do so" to engage him in question-and-
answer periods at the end of his presentations. Not so students. While he found
students to be "very distrustful of me, though personally most cordial," they were
not shy in their questioning: "The questioners were uninformed, or terribly
misinformed, but they were genuine questioners." He found the questions varied
from "the frankly friendly to the guardedly hostile," but the point for him was
that students asked about *his* views—the views of a Communist. At the University of Washington in 1955, where administrators had fired faculty members because of their actual or perceived Marxist beliefs, Aptheker "was invited to take
over a regular class . . . because [he] *was* a Marxist." At a stop in San Francisco,
the Pacifica Radio station KPFA aired an hour-long live interview with him for
its forty thousand listeners. The topic was, "What makes you a Communist and
what is it you believe?" At the end of the interview, after Aptheker expressed his
incredulity at the proposition, the station signed him to broadcast a monthly
fifteen-minute commentary for the station on a topic of his choosing, which he
proceeded to do for several years.[19]

Aptheker was right to caution against exaggerating the few bright spots that
hinted at a letup in the witch hunt. In his own case the FBI certainly didn't per-
ceive any end to the witch hunt. Agents around the country followed Aptheker's
every move. They attended his presentations and monitored the people with
whom he stayed and with whom he talked, and they observed his arrivals and
departures. In 1956 Hoover ordered his agents in New York to intensify their
investigation of Aptheker and nine other individuals "to obtain admissible evidence proving [their] current membership in the Communist Party, USA . . .
[for] prosecution . . . for failing to register under the Internal Security Act of
1950." Why the FBI and the Justice Department did not carry through on the
prosecution is unknown. Certainly Aptheker afforded them ample evidence of
his party membership through his testimony in various Smith Act trials.[20]

Perhaps the Justice Department grew more circumspect as revelations by and
about paid government informers emerged, such as that by Harvey Matusow,
who, in his sensational book *False Witness,* disavowed the testimony he had
given for so many years. Certainly the Supreme Court's reevaluations of Red
Scare legislation put a crimp in the FBI's work. When targeting Aptheker in
April 1956, Hoover noted that prosecution by the Justice Department would
go forward "provided the Supreme Court upholds the constitutionality of the
registration provisions."[21]

If cautious optimism about the lifting of McCarthyite hysteria characterized
Aptheker's state of mind at the end of 1955, his mood in January of that year was

more subdued and somber. His contact with and fondness for Elizabeth Gurley Flynn had grown during the early fifties. Her "warmth and her fierce dedication to the Socialist ideal," he wrote, "made her an admirable figure." Aptheker joined a small group of friends at Gurley Flynn's apartment the night before she surrendered to begin her three-year prison sentence. After an agreeable evening of talk about "what lay before us," Gurley Flynn accompanied the group to the stairs as they left, seemingly unconcerned about herself, looking more for assurance that her cat would be taken care of while she served her time.[22]

If Aptheker was optimistic about the gradual dissipation of McCarthyism, which he certainly was, he also found reason, paradoxically, to detect something faintly positive and inspiring even in the face of the terrorist campaign being carried out against black people in the South, exemplified by the brutal murder of fourteen-year-old Emmett Louis Till in Tallahatchie County, Mississippi. "It is of central importance to understand," he told his large KPFA radio audience in October 1955, "that the campaign of terror in Mississippi is an act of desperation on the part of the present rulers of that state, who seek thereby to crush the Negro liberation movement . . . and to undo, by force and violence, a decision of the U.S. Supreme Court [the *Brown v. Board of Education* decision of 1954, which found school segregation unconstitutional]." Aptheker rightly denounced governments and politicians at both the federal and state levels for their connivance in "the whole damnable Jim Crow system." But, he said, the murder of Till and of other southern blacks that year showed that racists in the South "are desperate because . . . they see the growing unity between Negro and white . . . they know that the Negro people are absolutely determined to have their full rights and to have them now." And black people had a growing number of allies now. The "eyes of the world . . . are on this country and on the Negro question in this country," he said, "[and] there are more white Americans, North and South, than ever before who are beginning to have some comprehension of the meaning to themselves of the continuance of Jim Crow and of abominations like lynching that bulwark Jim Crow." He reiterated the call heard throughout the century for specific actions—federal intervention, immediate implementation of the *Brown* decision, federal antilynching legislation, an end to poll taxes—that were a decade away from implementation. As 1955 drew to a close Aptheker reminded white people that the Jim Crow system directly affected their lives, diluted their representation in the House of Representatives by disenfranchising black people, corrupted their ability to participate in the political system by keeping entrenched white southern racists in positions of power in Congress; "not to speak," he concluded, "of the shame felt by any decent American of any color before the bar of world opinion in the face of such a scandal as institutionalized racism and such atrocities as the lynching of children."[23]

10   Revelations and Disputations

IN JANUARY 1956 the party, considerably weakened, emerged from the underground. It had sent hundreds of local and regional leaders into hiding and now welcomed home its top leadership, whose release on parole signaled the end of self-imposed isolation. The party had endured repression, but its members, many of whom had never understood the need for an underground movement, were happy to return to working in the open. On 20 January members gathered in Carnegie Hall and "embraced and laughed and cried" as they began an anniversary celebration for the *Daily Worker*. They eagerly awaited the evening's featured speakers, the paper's editor, John Gates, and the general secretary of the party, Eugene Dennis. Even though the party had managed to function under Foster's enforced conformity during the first half of the decade, it arose from the five-minutes-to-midnight period with half of its membership intact. The principal leaders, "who had spent time isolated from the center while in prison or underground," appeared ready to reexamine the party's policies and actions. Between the time of their release and the event at Carnegie Hall, Dennis and Gates "found many party members ready to embrace the 're-examinationist' views they had both come to hold while in jail."[1]

In his speech Dennis stunned the audience by accepting responsibility for the party's previous mistakes and committing it both to a probing examination of past policies and practices and to the adoption of a new kind of Marxism–Leninism. "We admit we have not had all the correct answers to every problem in the past," he told the hushed gathering, "nor do we have a monopoly on wisdom today. We have, like others, made not a few mistakes. Our American Communist Party . . . is going to take a new look at all problems . . . to learn from any wrong judgments, tactical mistakes or theoretical errors we may have made." A "massive, collective gasp" rushed through the audience, Peggy Dennis, Eugene's wife, recalled, and then it burst into "thunderous applause and cheers."[2]

Aptheker found Dennis's speech to be "fresh and plain and short and clear and vigorous." He assumed that Dennis meant to carry the reexamination into the realm of ideas, so a few days later he prepared a memo for the leaders outlining ways in which the party could approach the American people, "many [of whom] have the feeling that they were 'sold a bill of goods.'" He urged the leadership to "get into the debate" surrounding the meaning of McCarthyism and the "lies and slanders against the Party." He repeated, with more boldness and certainty than before, many of the themes he had iterated in his memo to the National Committee in 1954. "Aggressiveness and confidence are the two prerequisites for our getting into the battle of ideas," he asserted. He wanted the party to actively seek opportunities and face the challenges of getting its message out, to offer conciliatory proposals to religious, social, and educational groups and institutions, to publish the party's views in "fairly broad magazines and newspapers" running the gamut from specialized scholarly journals to "the *Nation, New Republic, Reporter, Harper's, Atlantic, Frontier, Progressive*" and giving special attention to "labor, Negro and farm journals and papers." Aptheker acknowledged that obstacles existed, the greatest of which "is the image of the Soviet Union which the ruling class has succeeded to a major degree in getting across to the American people." He urged the leaders to confront directly, quickly, vigorously, and consistently the "lies and slanders" directed against the Soviet Union. The paucity of truth about the Soviet Union "hurts all of our efforts at reaching the people on every other question."[3]

Exhibiting unusual magnanimity toward his adversaries, a reflection perhaps of his position as the editor of *Political Affairs,* Aptheker counseled the adoption of a stance in the party's publications that conveyed "respect for the audience and for the opponent," in a manner that "*assumes*" dedication to "certain common desires, offers the necessary respect such an assumption merits and so assumes that the same respect will be forthcoming to oneself." He had said much the same thing a year earlier in a written report of his findings as a member of a commission studying the contents of *Monthly Review* between January and October 1955. Communists paid little attention to *Monthly Review,* a magazine founded by Leo Huberman and Paul Sweezy in 1949, but it "found an audience in circles close to the Party, especially among trade unionists and academics who were by then disillusioned with the Party's leadership." In his report Aptheker criticized an essay in *Political Affairs* in 1951 written by the party's leading theoretician, Alexander Bittleman, that attacked *Monthly Review.* "An examination of the last ten issues of MR [*Monthly Review*]," Aptheker reported, "... leads me to declare that [Bittleman's] estimate was 'Leftist' when made and any such estimate today would be far out in Left field—in fact would be outside the ball park." Aptheker advised, "It is time we stopped ignoring the existence of the magazine and its editors and contributors in our own work and publications."[4]

In the memo of February 1956 Aptheker concluded with a section titled "Into the outfit," *outfit,* as noted, being a euphemism he often employed when referring to the party. "We do not have all the answers," he wrote in the report, and the party should be "listening as well as talking... offering opinion, not rules... asking questions... not always making assertions." Whatever pronouncements the party made should be "mostly suggestions." In the end he urged the leadership to promote "concerted and persistent and organized" study of ideas throughout all levels of the outfit, down into the clubs, through "comments and criticisms and discussions." He may have taken some satisfaction when, in April, it appeared that his recommendations had been heard by the leadership.[5]

In late April Dennis presided over the first open meeting of the National Committee in five years. About one hundred people attended the "enlarged meeting," as Healey recalled: members of the national leadership, district leaders, and "some prominent trade unionists." Hall, Bob Thompson, Gil Green, Winston, and Gurley Flynn were not in attendance because they were still in jail. In his report Dennis "offered . . . a daringly new concept of the Party's vanguard role," Peggy Dennis wrote, one which followed along the lines of Aptheker's assertion that the party did not have all the answers and that other Socialists and Marxists might have equally valid assumptions. Dennis said the party needed to make "a most positive approach to all honest Socialist and Marxist oriented groups and individuals" and create an atmosphere in which debate and "ideological struggle" among the various strains of Marxism "could lead eventually to the unification of all socialist-minded persons into a 'new and broader mass party of socialism.'" He "denounced 'left sectarian'" party policies, noting especially the five-minutes-to-midnight policy and the "shift to an underground existence" brought about by the party's belief (and Foster's insistence) that "domestic fascism was about to overcome all democratic resistance." Visibly angered, Foster cast the lone vote against accepting Dennis's report.[6]

Aptheker, who was not part of the leadership, and Dennis acted out of a genuine belief that the party needed a thorough reorientation. But Dennis's speech on April 28 relied on information to which many, including Aptheker, were not privy. The National Executive Committee, consisting of the top leaders in the party, had been crafting their report for the meeting since early March. After a break in the proceedings, the meeting resumed in "special session," during which the audience was "warned that no one could take notes . . . or speak about it [the special session] to anyone who was not in attendance." Then, Healey recalled, "Leon Wofsy, Dennis's political secretary, . . . started to read the text of [Nikita] Khrushchev's 'secret speech' to the Twentieth Party Congress [of the USSR] the previous February."[7] At the same time Aptheker had called on the CPUSA to make the truth about the Soviet Union known, Khrushchev did just that. He denounced Stalin's cult of personality and condemned him for presiding over a reign of terror that betrayed and perverted the Communist ideal. Khrushchev sidestepped or ignored the complicity of other party leaders, including himself, by laying all the blame on the head of the deceased Stalin. He did, however, concede that "we cannot say that these were the deeds of a giddy despot. He [Stalin] considered that this should be done in the interest of the Party, of the working masses, in the name of the defense of the revolution's gains. In this lies the whole tragedy!"[8] The litany of Stalin's crimes that Wofsy read at length—"a deliberate policy of torture and murder that lasted for decades"—is now all too familiar but at the time was unknown, and it shocked and horrified the elite of the CPUSA.[9]

Five weeks later the *New York Times* printed the text of Khrushchev's report. That day Aptheker hand-delivered a note to Dennis urging that he and as many members of the National Committee as possible write individual analyses of the Khrushchev speech—"what it means, how it was possible, what now"— that would comprise the "major part of the next issue of the magazine [*Political Affairs*]." "Would you undertake such a piece and give support to my trying to get such an issue out?" Aptheker asked Dennis. The discussion Aptheker desired did not appear in the July issue of *Political Affairs*. Instead, the National Committee as a whole, not the individual members, published an essay in *Political Affairs*. It welcomed the actions taken by Khrushchev "to end the brutalities and injustices which marred a period of Soviet life," castigated the Communist Party of the Soviet Union for not making the report public, and called on Marxists in the Soviet Union and elsewhere to investigate "how such perversions of socialist democracy, justice and internationalism were permitted to develop and continue unchecked for twenty years." The committee acknowledged that "we uncritically justified many foreign and domestic policies of the Soviet Union which are now shown to be wrong."[10]

In the same issue of *Political Affairs,* preceding the comments of the National Committee, Aptheker inserted a short commentary of his own lauding Khrushchev's actions: "It opened the book on the grievous crimes, theoretical errors and distortions of socialist life that contaminated the latter period of Stalin's regime." He gladly accepted the "new conditions," which, he wrote, "have created the need for a profound re-examination of the application of Marxist theory . . . [and] necessitate a sharp break with dogmatism [to] open up a new freedom of criticism within Communist Parties and between Communist Parties." He noted that *Political Affairs* would make its pages available to contributions by its readers "on the momentous questions now posed for solution by Marxists and supporters of Socialism in our country."[11]

Under the direction of Gates, the discussion had already begun in earnest in the *Daily Worker* and especially in *Party Voice,* the magazine of the party in New York. "With the Khrushchev report," Al Richmond, the editor of the party's West Coast paper wrote in his autobiography, "all the accumulated frustrations, discontents, doubts, grievances in and around the Communist party erupted with an elemental force." Thousands of members quietly left the party after Khrushchev's revelations, and those who remained began debating the fundamental nature of the American party just as Communists in parties around the world did. A sizable portion of the membership in the two largest state organizations, New York's and California's, in addition to the party's major publications (with the exception of *Political Affairs*), favored challenging Foster's leadership. The ensuing power struggle centered around Dennis, Foster, and Gates. Dennis held the middle ground between Foster, who supported the Soviet Party leaders unquestioningly and maintained that the CPUSA required no changes, and Gates, who called for autonomy from Soviet dictates and more internal democracy.[12] Gates advocated "a different kind of party, . . . the most democratic kind of Communist Party. . . . [He] said we must take a 'new look at the concept of democratic centralism; which seems to result in a 'semi-military type of organization'. . . . there was always a tendency for this to become transformed into 'maximum centralization and minimum democracy.' "[13]

Some of Aptheker's arguments are hard to take at face value given that the noncommunist Left had been writing about Stalin's policies for decades. Nonetheless, Aptheker immediately entered the debate, taking exception when the *Daily Worker* argued in an editorial of 7 June 1956 that American Communists, while "wholly ignorant" of Stalin's crimes, had had ample warning from reputable sources if they had only listened. "We did not want to believe these crimes could occur in a socialist state," the editorial stated, "so refused to believe." That statement, Aptheker wrote, ignored the positive reports about the Soviet Union that were voiced by people ranging from "Ambassador Davies to Stephen White of the *N.Y. Herald Tribune* . . . [to] Communist correspondents, from the United States and from other countries in the USSR who sent back full reports which were convincing." It neglected also, Aptheker emphasized, "the fact that the responsible Communist leaders of the USSR and of other countries, in the Soviet Union, gave the lie to reports which we are now told we did not believe simply because we did not want to." The charges against the Soviet Union simply did not appear to be compatible "with the actual role of the USSR in combating fascism and imperialism and war, and in building Socialism," Aptheker contended. Nonetheless, he said, "to understand our colossal errors . . . means probing much deeper than the erroneous assertion that the Left was willfully blind." The truth about the Soviet Union "was kept from Communists and from others by Communists in the Soviet Union and there is the crux of the problem." The myriad questions needing attention, from "power within a socialist state, to the problem of proletarian dictatorship and civil liberties, to the effective form for the organization of Marxist–Leninist parties in various parts of the world," should not be shunted off to the side because of "what 'should have been' and who 'should have listened to whom,'" Aptheker concluded.[14]

Joe Clark castigated Aptheker in a personal letter he wrote later that day for his continuing inattention to current developments in Eastern Europe, then protested that "you and I were not quite as innocent as you suggest." In his typewritten response three days later, Aptheker said, "I was not suggesting 'innocence' on my part, and certainly wasn't suggesting anything at all for anyone else." Clark waited a few days before replying: "I counted ten in order to avoid the asperity and bitterness I allow myself in disputes with friends, good friends," he wrote, then insisted that Aptheker write anything in *Political Affairs* and the *Daily Worker* "which will make it clear here and elsewhere that you agree with us." Readers knew, Clark avowed, that Aptheker disagreed with the *Daily Worker* in some matters, but "they don't know that your criticism of the Soviet and Czech Communists is as sharp as ours, perhaps sharper. . . . Why do you think we should carry the brunt?" Finally, Clark said,

> you [have not] accepted any responsibility for the wrongs you and I and all of us (it was quite a collective responsibility) perpetrated. Your field was history. And it was in history that the Soviet leaders perpetrated some of the worst atrocities. As a historian you must have known that Stalin's works as published by Trachty [Alexander Trachtenberg] 20 years ago, were quite different from the works you and I read in his recent collected edition. You and I knew that before the 20th congress. You and I knew that they were falsifying history. You and I bear a responsibility. We can agree that the major wrong was committed by those who actually falsified. But we were either fools or accessories. . . . And history was your field, Herb. Again, excuse the sharp tone, but I do feel an unfair burden rests on our shoulders. You should share some of it.

Aptheker seethed. On his copy of Clark's letter, in a heavy hand, he scribbled two sentences in the margin: "He tells me what I knew! Read my letter of 6/12 again."[15]

Giving himself time to cool down, Aptheker tried again, on 25 June, to clarify his position in another letter to the *Daily Worker*: "The heart of the problem . . . is, given the necessary relationship of personal and party conduct among comrades, how is one to operate when faced by deliberate falsification, and how is this to be overcome and guarded against in the future; and further, what is the nature of 'reputable evidence' for the future?" Clark again challenged Aptheker, but this time in an open letter of his own to the *Daily Worker*. He repeated many of the charges he had previously specified in his private correspondence with Aptheker. He reminded the paper's readers that Aptheker had written "authoritative and brilliant works on the Negro in American history," then asked, "Why didn't he use the same kind of scholarship in considering Soviet history?" Clark recognized the truth of Aptheker's argument in regard to "deliberate falsification" but said, "Aptheker is absolving all of us just a little too much by placing so much responsibility on 'deliberate falsification' from above." Unfortunately, Clark wrote, "Aptheker continues to blind himself to reputable evidence about current Soviet developments." Not so, Aptheker claimed in his *Daily World* rejoinder to Clark: "I suggest that Joseph Clark exercise more caution in asserting what others 'must have been aware of.' Of what he, himself, was aware, he is the best authority; as to others his testimony is not impressive." Aptheker took up Clark's challenge on his historical work. "My scholarship is in the area of American life and history," Aptheker averred, yet Clark wanted to know "why it was not equally sound in Russian history?" The question, Aptheker wrote, answered itself. He had, he said, studied several works "of those supposed to be sound in that area" and "followed with some care the writings of those in Russia whom I felt certain I could trust . . . [including] William Z. Foster . . . and Joseph Clark." Again Aptheker called for a recognition of the party's need for "real scholarship . . . in Russian life and history . . . [something] I have been calling for . . . for years."[16]

AND SO it went throughout the summer of 1956 in the party's publications. The exchanges amounted to the most freewheeling self-examination the CPUSA had ever undergone. Foster's intransigence in the face of so much energy for reform drove Gates's supporters to the barricades. Foster labeled those with whom he disagreed antiparty and anti-Soviet. Aptheker did not enter into the factional accusations that overwhelmed the discussion, but as editor of *Political Affairs* he published articles relevant to the discussion regardless of the author's position. In one article Steve Nelson called for an end to the concepts of "monolithic unity . . . and one-party rule." In essence he and Gates promoted, in the party's theoretical journal edited by Aptheker and in direct repudiation of Foster, the destruction of a "tightly organized and governed vanguard party," to be replaced by a CPUSA dedicated to a mass movement for socialism. While the Gates faction openly criticized Foster, saying the party "suffered from a 'doctrinaire acceptance and mechanical application' of many of the ideas of Marx and Lenin and had to 'free itself from deeply ingrained habits of dogmatism and doctrinairism,'" Aptheker declined to make his own position on Foster known publicly. "I do not wish here to express my own views upon . . . the position of William Z. Foster," Aptheker wrote in *Political Affairs* for November 1956, "for this is not the proper occasion." He did, however, point out that there was "overwhelming agreement . . . of the critical need for deep-going changes" in party "practices and policies, in its conduct vis-à-vis its own members and people outside its ranks." But he cautioned that the change should not entail, as some had counseled, a dissolution of the party. Revitalization would come through improving and strengthening of the party's organizations, he claimed.

Though many of his longtime friends openly opposed Foster, Aptheker seemed to some, like his comrade Junius Scales in North Carolina, "moderate and somewhat noncommittal." At one meeting of the expanded National Committee in which Foster and other "rigidly leftist Party leaders" came under attack, Scales recalled that Aptheker, speaking "very slowly and almost as if in a trance," told the meeting that "he thought that the comrades should remember that there was such a thing as befouling one's own nest; and then he sat down." Aptheker repeated those sentiments in a letter published in the *Daily Worker* in November. appealing for "comradeship and dignity and mutual respect" rather than "name-calling... insult... [and] vituperation." He urged his comrades to remember that they were all going through "an exceedingly trying period" in which "the meanings and purposes of our very lives are involved," challenges that naturally aroused "profound emotions." He encouraged disagreement and debate and change. But when the disagreement and debate ended, he wanted a viable Communist Party to survive. "Certainly, it seems to me," he wrote to comrades in Canada in December, "the place to be is inside working hard for what one believes to be right; and then, given enough changes, to stay in and keep battling. I find the alternatives... singularly unattractive and even sterile."[17]

In October, in the midst of the acrimonious debates over reforming the party, the Soviet Union, already retreating from the meager reforms that sprang from the Khrushchev disclosures, invaded Hungary. The sight of Soviet tanks opening fire on Hungarian students and workers demonstrating in the streets appalled many CPUSA members. Foster, speaking for many members, instinctively and wholeheartedly sanctioned the Soviet actions, telling one meeting of the top leaders "in his hard, arrogant way," wrote Scales, "that the Red Army would soon take care of 'this CIA revolution.'" In the pages of the *Daily Worker* Gates denounced Soviet actions that, according to the historian David Shannon, "divided the Party... more than had the debate over the Khrushchev speech or the disagreement over how serious had been the errors of the American party of the past several years." "[The] Hungarian events rocked the entire Communist world," Gates said in his memoir. "It seared the souls of Communists everywhere such as no single event had done."[18]

The arguments and recriminations within the party over the Hungarian invasion grew even more bitter and personal by the end of the year, and the party's position, finally hammered out at an intensely disputatious National Committee meeting in November, neither condemned nor condoned the invasion because, Aptheker wrote, "the Party leadership was torn and therefore impotent." The declaration made by the committee, "one of the most obviously compromised national committee statements in party history," declared that the party did not "seek to justify the use of Soviet troops... [nor] do we join in the condemnation of these actions."[19]

Aptheker felt that the party should take a public stand either for or against the Soviet invasion. "All of us are trying to get at the truth as best we know how," he wrote in the *Daily Worker* on 12 November, a week after Russian tanks had fired on Hungarian workers and students. Reiterating what he had said at every Smith Act trial, he continued, "We Communists are opposed to the use of force, from inside or outside a country, to change or impose a social system. At the same time, we Communists are not pacifists, and we do believe in resistance to force when this is used inside or outside for counter-revolutionary and reactionary purposes."[20]

Did the Soviet Union invade Hungary to put down a reactionary counter-revolution? or had the Soviet Union become "the reactionaries who despise life [and]...turn to violence?" After all, as Aptheker had written in 1948, "it is never the revolutionists who first resort to violence."[21] To answer that question, one to which he apparently already knew the answer, he began on his own and without party approval to compile information on the Hungarian uprising. Scales later warranted that Dennis had requested the research, a contention Aptheker denied. In any case, Aptheker hastily produced a book-length manuscript, but the party refused to publish it. Eventually published by Mainstream Publishers, that book, *The Truth about Hungary,* which even he admitted was immodestly titled, was arguably the most offensive and contentious of his books. To his critics at the time and for decades to come it represented the worst moment of what even some critics on the Left called Aptheker's Stalinist apologetics. *The Truth about Hungary* is singled out more often than any of his other publications and deployed by his critics to link Aptheker to Stalin, thus delegitimizing the man and tainting his entire oeuvre.[22]

Up to the time of the Khrushchev revelations, Aptheker often did praise Stalin's leadership of the Soviet Union and quoted his words approvingly. Once Khrushchev uncovered Stalin's crimes before the world, Aptheker was quick to acknowledge, in public, their essence and brutality and to take limited, if sometimes evasive, personal responsibility for his own culpability and that of the CPUSA. Nevertheless, he continued to champion the Soviet Union under Khrushchev's leadership. Decades later he continued to lament his failure to grasp the truth about Stalin until it was too late. That failure, he said repeatedly, came at a terrible price for progressive forces and the Left within the United States. "The revelations associated with Khrushchev's speech were devastating to me," he wrote in his unpublished autobiography. "Whatever were the failings and crimes in the Soviet Union, and whatever was my blindness in the face of that reality . . . it is true nevertheless, that the Left in the United States, and the Communist Party in particular, never did fully recover from the record of willful blindness in the face of the criminality of Stalin."[23]

To concentrate on unifying the American Party in advance of the 16th National Convention in February 1957, most members of the party simply ignored the Soviet invasion of Hungary once the party's ambiguous statement had been made, fearing that further discussion would exacerbate factional splits. Aptheker would not let the matter rest because, as he wrote in the introduction to *The Truth about Hungary,* he *"had* to try to understand that upheaval." In the first two-thirds of the 256-page book Aptheker probed Hungarian society under the dictatorship of Miklós Horthy prior to the Second World War, explored the impact of the war on the country, examined the political developments after the war, and discussed the difficult economic circumstances in which Hungary found itself. He blamed American imperialism, "armed with atomic weapons," for "speeding the policy of repression in the lands of Socialism" but said, in an irritating passive voice, that imperialism could not be "the basic explanation of the systematized repression which came into being." The Hungarian governmental system, he submitted, violated the law and established censorship and "crass injustices" that institutionalized "terrible violations of human rights" throughout the period from 1949 through 1953. "The actions were frightful," he wrote with genuine distress, and "were such as befitted the repressive machinery of exploitative systems. To say that they violated elementary Marxist–Leninist principles of behavior is to speak moderately; they violated elementary considerations of humanity." In that "general pattern of illegality and the inculcation of fear . . . this system of repression was a basic source of the popular discontent in Hungary . . . and did as much as any other single thing to bring the whole Party into disrepute, and to shake the faith of rank and file members in Marxism–Leninism itself." In unambiguous language he condemned the terrorism instituted by the Hungarian party against the people of Hungary. He found "the irrefutable facts concerning this terror . . . as painful to this writer, I think, as they can be to any human being—other than one whom it victimized." The appearance of that systematic terror, he wrote, "to any degree and in any form, in Socialist countries is intolerable and utterly unjustifiable—no matter what the provocation or the danger or the background."[24] He should have ended the book there, but he didn't.

Rather than condemn the brutal Soviet invasion and occupation of an independent Socialist state, Aptheker judged the chief villain in the Hungarian revolution to be an imperialist plot against Hungarian Socialism. In Aptheker's version of the events, the expropriated Hungarian ruling class, fascists, anti-Semites, Cardinal Jozsef Mindszenty, "White Terrorists," who summarily executed members of the hated secret police, and well-armed, outside counterrevolutionaries who infiltrated the leadership of the uprising and the government all conspired with American imperialists to destroy Hungarian Socialism, even though, "the [initial] motivation of the popular elements was not against Socialism, but for its refreshment." Western imperialism perverted "a peaceful mass demonstration seeking the purification of the People's Democratic system," Aptheker wrote, "into an armed assault for its overthrow," which resulted in "an exceedingly rapid turn to the extreme Right which in fact posed, in the middle of Europe, the question again of fascism and war." In that situation, he held, the Soviet Union had no choice but to invade. In Hungary, Aptheker ended, "it was not a matter of imposing Socialism by a gun; it was a question of preventing the violent overthrow of Socialism, so that in pursuit of the will of the vast majority of Hungarians, their Socialist order may be cleansed, and rejuvenated."[25]

Aptheker used few contemporaneous accounts by people who were present in Hungary, relying instead on stories published in the capitalist press, some of which appeared many months after the episode. He offered few sources for his narrative chronology of events, and in some cases used quotations for which he supplied no sources. Rather than give evidence for several of his most provocative pronouncements, he employed the passive voice and guesswork: "were being," "was accomplished," "probably," "must have," "may have been," "could have." At one point he affirmed, with the backing of evidence contrived by manipulating a source, that "batches of people were being arrested and held for subsequent mass extermination," that "scores, perhaps thousands" of those awaiting mass execution were Jews: "Anti-Semitic pogroms—hallmark of unbridled fascistic terror—were making their appearance." The source had said nothing about mass extermination or mass executions: "From time to time," the source, an eyewitness named Leslie B. Bain, wrote, "there appeared a few groups of marginal characters who gathered on street corners and started yelling 'Exterminate the Jews.'"[26] Aptheker inflated that statement into mass executions of Jews.

Except for a brief mention used to prop up another exaggeration, Aptheker ignored the firsthand account of Peter Fryer, a communist and correspondent in Budapest for the British Communist Party newspaper, the *Daily Worker*. There is no question as to why Aptheker disregarded Fryer's book, *Hungarian Tragedy*, which appeared before *The Truth about Hungary*: it refuted, on almost every point, Aptheker's own narrative and conclusions. "I was in Hungary when this happened," Fryer wrote. "I saw for myself that the uprising was neither organized nor controlled by fascists or reactionaries. . . . I saw for myself that the Soviet troops who were thrown into battle against 'counter-revolution' fought in fact not fascists or reactionaries but the common people of Hungary: workers, peasants, students and soldiers." Aptheker produced, in Fryer's words, "an apologia for the crushing of a revolution." He "slapped together every gleeful, gloating word you could find, from every conceivable reactionary source," Fryer wrote in a scathing open letter printed in the U.S. *Daily Worker*, "hailing the Hungarian events as the fulfilment of imperialist dreams" whose common interest "was to magnify to the utmost every negative and disagreeable strand" of the uprising.[27]

Discussion of Hungary in the *Daily Worker* picked up again when Aptheker's book appeared in May. The *Daily Worker* literary editor Robert Friedman exemplified the openness of the paper under Gates by publishing a review that, while friendly, criticized the book. Friedman broke "what had been standard practice," according to the historian David Shannon, of "uncritically favorable *Daily Worker* reviews for books by Communists who hewed to the party line." While

Friedman conceded that Aptheker's was a "searching examination of the Hungarian Communist government," he took issue with the author's conclusions: "I do not believe either his book, or life itself, sustains his judgement." "This was not a coup, or a palace plot, or a generals' putsch," Friedman continued. "It was a popular uprising against a Socialist government. . . . It is a sorry example of workers' rule which must rest on Soviet arms for support withheld by one's own people." Foster and others responded by attacking Friedman. Foster "praised [Aptheker's] research and 'well-organized and penetrating analysis' " and characterized the book as "a 'very effective answer to this tissue of anti-Soviet vilification and warmongering.' " Jerome wrote to Aptheker privately to declare, "What a blow for truth is your book!" He praised Aptheker's "painstaking research and objective analysis." The book brought "confirmation . . . to those whose understanding of history enabled them to cut through the distorting propaganda to the essence of the Hungarian conflict." Aptheker told Jerome that of all the books and pamphlets he had written so far, "this one on Hungary was the most challenging and, in many respects, was really excruciating. I've rarely had moments of despair while writing; rarely the feeling that I will not be able to make it, that I cannot solve it. But many were the moments with this particular book," he confessed, "and the attitude in the country and, especially, in the Party, made continued work on it sheer torture. And then, to get the Friedman 'review'!"[28]

The mainstream press ignored the book, and the reviews that appeared in the Left press were markedly subdued. Alan Max wrote in *Mainstream* that Aptheker had not adequately emphasized the failures of the Hungarian CP or "the dubious responses thereto by the leadership in the USSR." Scales, an opponent of the invasion, recalled that "whatever it was intended for, *The Truth About Hungary,* . . . a hasty, poorly documented book defending Soviet intervention in Hungary . . . damaged Herb's credibility with thousands of people who greatly respected him," among whom Scales counted himself, "as a pioneer in the field of Negro history." Scales resigned from the party in 1957 and apparently expressed some of his disappointment over the book to Aptheker, who typically overreacted by never speaking to his old friend again. In 2002, when Scales was dying, "there was an effort to get him [Herbert] to call or write to Junius," Bettina recalled, "but he refused. Rage—and the refusal to forgive *anyone, ever.*"[29]

How did Aptheker get it so fundamentally wrong? *The Truth about Hungary* was terrible history. While the first two-thirds of the book is certainly historical, it was not the kind of American history based on primary sources that Aptheker usually wrote. He strayed far beyond his field of expertise and depended fundamentally on secondary sources and Soviet propaganda. Aptheker never shied away from partisanship and never believed that a historian could or should be objective or detached. He viewed his historical work, the historian Robin D. G. Kelley wrote, "as a weapon against racism and class oppression."

"I frankly cannot understand the idea of objectivity, meaning aloofness or non-partisanship," Aptheker said in an interview with Kelley. "What do you mean by objectivity, remoteness?"

The final third of *The Truth about Hungary,* the chapters dealing with the uprising, were not history at all but political polemic, produced in haste and directed at events that transpired less than half a year earlier. Did he recall his own words? In his writing on slavery Aptheker had refuted the notion of happy, docile slaves, saying the cause of slave uprisings was slavery. Hungarians had repudiated the repressive government under which they lived, and the cause of the uprising was a repressive government. Hungary was a repressive, exploitative socialist state, and Aptheker had said as much but ignored his own observation. This episode was not a case of valiant Soviet troops bravely defending Stalingrad against a Nazi onslaught. Soviet troops in Hungary were greeted not with the joy Aptheker fantasized, "but with the white-hot patriotic fury of a people in arms." Aptheker said nothing about the thousands of Soviet troops massed along the Hungarian border. But he did say, contrary to testimony by eyewitnesses, "The Soviet Union committed mechanized armor alone; no air power was used, and apparently no or practically no infantry. The mechanized armor, basically medium tanks, fought a responsive, not an active battle." On 11 November 1956 Fryer wrote, "I have just come out of Budapest, where for six days I have watched Hungary's new-born freedom tragically destroyed by Soviet troops . . . while tank-fire rattled and jets screamed overhead. Each day the tanks patrolled the city, shelling the buildings at point-blank range. Each night they withdrew, but the heavy artillery kept up its thunder."[30]

Did Aptheker set out to deliberately falsify the record of the Hungarian revolution? Probably not. However, he defended the book for the rest of his life. His sophistic interpretation was shaped, perhaps, by his experiences during and after the Second World War. Maybe he felt that the Soviet Union, the sacred birthplace of socialism, could not survive another bout of world condemnation after Khrushchev's revelations. Whatever his reasoning or rationalization, the damage to his reputation was acute.

Aptheker said during an interview in 1999 that his close association with and profound love for Du Bois kept him from writing a biography of him, his friend and comrade. He said that to write about Du Bois and in doing so to strive for honesty and truth and steer clear of exaggeration and falsity would have been an insurmountable task under those circumstances: "I don't know how to do that if I'm writing about someone I love. . . . I'm too close. When I get to his failures, and he's human, he has failures, how shall I write about that? Some of it is so sacred." His analysis of the Hungarian revolution most likely suffered so much from the same sense of the sacred that he abandoned his belief in the role of the historian. "The cold war was frozen, the threat of war was imminent, the maniacs were in charge [in the United States], the newspapers were filled with threats," and the party's leadership had just emerged from prison, he said of the period of the late fifties. He reasoned that monopoly capitalism in its imperialistic, militarist, racist phase in the United States—a country in which he had the ability to alter that system if only he worked hard enough, he told himself—was a greater danger to the world than a corrupted Socialist system in the Soviet Union. "Is that difficult for you to understand?" he asked during an interview. "What should I do?... Well, I thought... that what I had to do was to defend the Soviet Union, and to refuse to acknowledge any blemish." He believed that people who pointed out the blemishes of the Soviet Union, "who lamented the lack of freedom in the Soviet Union," did so for propagandistic purposes only. "What the hell were they doing to Communists in the United States? What was the state of free speech in the United States at this time? We were in war," he said. "We were in combat. It's not just a theoretical discussion, an ideological counterattack, it's not that." Fay, "who was more realistic about the leadership," warned him, unsuccessfully, that human frailty was involved. But as the editor of *Political Affairs* he felt he was "one of the sources of strength in the Party, one of the main elements to combat the dissipation of the Party." He could "not give an inch," he said. "I couldn't say, 'well maybe.' No! I'd be giving them too much. So I didn't."[31]

Aptheker's friendships with Gates, Clark, Scales, and others, all of whom either quit or were expelled from the party, didn't survive the turmoil within the party in 1956–58. Ultimately, with the convergence of the dual crises and the exodus of thousands of members from the party "the American Communist movement disintegrated and those who wanted a re-examination were inevitably the chief losers," according to the former Communist Joseph Starobin. "Thousands of members had left us," Gates wrote, "and those who remained were not only few in number but were the least capable of change." With all their enthusiasm, the reformers in the party, who had the votes to carry their program, had no organizational structure. Gates did not have the desire or the capabilities or energy to coalesce a bloc around himself, and Dennis eventually accepted the easy road, repudiated his own reformist stand, and acquiesced to Foster and Moscow: Hall replaced him as general secretary of the party in 1959. Soon after the party convention of February 1957, at which Benjamin Davis had attempted, unsuccessfully, to have Aptheker elected to the leadership—"some of us had hope," he wrote to Aptheker, "... and had voted for you"—most of the dissidents began to drop out of the party. "Foster merely shrugged 'good riddance,'" according to Peggy Dennis, "and demanded punitive organization action against those who remained and did not agree with him." "Let them go, who cares?" Foster bluntly told Healey. "You must understand, Dorothy, that even if the Party goes down to only fifty members, if they are true Marxist–Leninists, staunch people, it doesn't matter. It is better to have fifty true members than fifty thousand who are not genuine Communists."[32]

Gates continued to use the *Daily Worker* to enunciate his revisionist position, but Foster engineered the destruction of the paper. By mid-February 1957 Aptheker found the *Daily Worker* under Gates's leadership marked by "Right-onesidedness, . . . tendentious to the highest degree . . . [and] the staff is stacked and is thoroughly unrepresentative of the views of that Convention [of February 1957]." He wanted balance brought back to the paper, he told Davis, but "I mean only a REDRESS of the balance, not an unbalance to the other side." When Gates threatened to resign from the party, Aptheker, who greatly admired him, wrote him a letter putting the pages of *Political Affairs* at his disposal. "You have the whole issue," Aptheker wrote, "say whatever you want. . . . you have doubts, quarrels, spread it out." Gates didn't respond. He too resigned in 1958, then sold his dissatisfaction with the party to the *New York Post* in the form of articles for which he was paid. Gurley Flynn told Aptheker that when she helped clear Gates's desk she found Aptheker's letter to him sitting on top of a stack of papers.[33]

As the party continued to suffer from high-level, prominent defections, Aptheker continued to deem the Soviet Union the foundational force for socialism in the world. When Fast left the party, Aptheker offered and Fast accepted an invitation to explain his reasoning in *Mainstream*. Aptheker then answered Fast in April 1957 in an article of his own in the same magazine. He ended it with a steadfast declaration of support for the Soviet Union: "Despite Howard Fast's disillusionment, the Soviet Union stands today, as she did when she saved the world from Hitlerism (Howard made no mention of this little fact, in recounting his decision) as the leading force in the struggle against imperialism, colonialism, racism, and war." Aptheker's uncle had opposed the old tsar; he supported the new tsars.[34]

By February 1958 the Foster faction controlled the party even though Foster remained sidelined and critically ill after suffering a stroke in 1957. The top leadership, including Dennis, Davis, Gurley Flynn (who by then was out of jail), James Jackson, and especially Robert Thompson, began to demand rigid discipline among the few remaining members, no more than three thousand and probably fewer after the party registration in the winter of 1957–58. The party had done little recruiting throughout the 1950s, and those members who remained were, like Aptheker, who was nearing fifty, middle-aged. After years of external assault, debilitating internal animosity, the Soviet invasion of Hungary, and devastating revelations about Stalinist terror, the American party was, for all intents and purposes, dead as a political force. "I hope the worst is over here, and that from now on the turn will be upward," Aptheker wrote to John Williamson in England at the end of 1957. "There is so much crying out to be done; perhaps we shall be able to make a little contribution again."[35]

11   Old Left and New

THROUGHOUT 1958 and 1959, as the party prepared for its 17th National Convention, confrontations persisted among the leadership, but on a less spectacular level than in 1956–57. Although ill and primarily confined to his bed by a stroke in October 1957, Foster remained solidly in control of the party as "chairman emeritus, an honorary title with no real authority," despite the fact that, as Foster's biographer, James R. Barrett, wrote, "there was little left to control."[1]

As the entrenched leaders of the party jockeyed for position, Dennis suggested bringing Hall, the head of the Ohio state party, to New York to install him in the leadership. He had briefly served in that capacity in 1950, when the government jailed Dennis on a conviction of contempt of HCUA. Hall, one of the Foley Square defendants, had spent eight years in federal prison: "five years on his Smith Act conviction and an additional three years for having jumped bail." He "[could] be a very charming man," Healey recalled in her autobiography, "when he [wanted] to be." He charmed party members "with declarations of support for every tendency within the Party depending on the audience." "Just lied like a bastard," Ben Dobbs, a comrade from California, recalled.[2]

As the party convention approached in 1959, Aptheker produced a manuscript titled "On the 40th Anniversary of the Communist Party of the United States of America," in which he reflected on what he called the near suicide of the party during the crisis in 1956–57. "Revisionism and outright abandonment of elementary principles of Marxism," he wrote, "became rampant." The revisionists had pushed their cause to the brink of nationalist chauvinism, or American exceptionalism, as Aptheker called it, and they coupled that perceived treason with "a strong overtone of anti-Sovietism." They denied the class struggle; they denied the Leninist critique of imperialism; they hinted that the Soviet Union might be the instigator of a new world war; and they claimed the party was no longer needed, "was discredited, was, indeed, an obstacle to progressive development in the United States and should be liquidated." Fortunately, Aptheker wrote, "a strong segment of the leadership also stood firm ... particularly ... the sterling contributions—once again—of Comrade William Z. Foster who did more than any other single individual to raise aloft and keep flying the banner of Marxism–Leninism and the sanctity of the Party."[3]

Aptheker may not have known about Hall's machinations, but his Panglossian analysis of the CPUSA National Executive Committee in his "40th Anniversary" document seems overly optimistic in retrospect: "The Party has been in the process of healing its wounds, slowly recuperating, and beginning the task of rebuilding. . . . Since the 1957 Convention . . . greater unity has been forged, and is now complete within the National Executive Committee," a development that made possible, he predicted, "the overcoming of a certain paralysis that had hobbled the Party for some months." The origin of the paralysis, revisionism, had "been routed organizationally," he claimed, "and while much still remains to be done to erase this poison ideologically, even there advances have certainly been registered since the low point of 1956–57."[4]

The convention, ignoring an attempt by Foster, Davis, and Hall to oust Dennis completely, endorsed Dennis as chairman of the party and Hall as general secretary, positions "supposed to carry coequal weight." The convention also elected Aptheker to the one-hundred-member National Committee, a position to which the party members continued to return him for the next thirty years, his only elected position in the party. When Dennis died in 1961, the party chose Gurley Flynn to replace him, the first woman to hold the position of national chair. Hall consolidated his support in the party and held on to the leadership for more than forty years until his death early in 2000.[5]

Aptheker did not like Hall and presumed the feeling was mutual. "I assume he had rather negative feelings toward me," Aptheker commented in his unpublished autobiography. The life experiences of the two men could not have been more different. After fewer than eight years of grade school education, Hall went to work in the timber industry and eventually in steel mills. Tall, barrel-chested, toned from lifting weights in prison, and supremely self-confident, Hall, as early as 1963, according to Gurley Flynn, tended to prefer a leadership style that was "cold, humorless, and prone to self-delusion." Aptheker's meetings with Hall were "always brief and formal," Aptheker recalled. "I never really felt at ease with him; I always thought that [he] was not conveying to me his actual feelings or views," Aptheker wrote. "To me he seemed always looking for his own advantage, eager for acquiescence, never really open and candid. Our meetings together were not frequent." In fact, Hall had little use for intellectuals. Gerhart Eisler, "a well-known and respected figure in the Communist movement who had lived as an exile in the United States during the 1930s and 1940s," once asked Healey why the CPUSA could not "come up with more thoughtful analyses of the problems it faced in overcoming its isolation?" "Weren't there any intellectuals in the Party leadership," he asked? "I mean *real* intellectuals. What about Herbert Aptheker?" Healey told Eisler that "whatever Aptheker's personal abilities might be, . . . inside the Party everyone knew that his opinions didn't count for much in determining policy . . . [because] the only role the Party leaders permitted intellectuals to play was that of providing a rationale for whatever the current Party line might be."[6]

But even Aptheker readily admitted that he was not a policy maker in the party and had not sought that role. Through his scholarly work and the years he spent in polemical writing at *New Masses* and *M&M* and in editing *Political Affairs,* he carved out a niche for himself in the party as an intellectual within party circles, perhaps the leading one. Aptheker's critics especially, but even some of his supporters and Aptheker himself on occasion, claimed he was a leading Communist theoretician. But Marxist theory was not his forte. "In fact his writing . . . is devoid of conjectural thinking about social phenomena that is the stock-in-trade of Marxist theory," Aptheker's colleague Mark Solomon correctly pointed out. "For example, I can't recall any speculative writing regarding the changing structure of the working class and the implications of such changes for Communist strategy and tactics; or writing . . . about theoretical problems of development in 'the socialist world,' etc. . . . there's a difference between reliance upon a materialist framework for historical study and theoretical analysis."[7]

By the late fifties the vicissitudes at *Political Affairs* involved in printing articles written by the underground leadership disappeared, but other problems continued to plague publication of the magazine. During the period when some convicted leaders had jumped bail and others had dutifully responded to the party's dictates to go underground, Aptheker often employed deceptive techniques to receive article manuscripts for publication in the magazine. "The problem was," Aptheker told one interviewer, "I . . . had to get in touch with the underground. Some of that was not too difficult because they had couriers or somebody would bring me the stuff." At other times, if he needed to contact a party leader in New York or Chicago Aptheker followed precise instructions to make a rendezvous: "I would take the subway to [a certain] station, I would get out, take a trolly," then walk to a designated corner or a bench in a park.[8]

The necessity of subterfuge disappeared as McCarthyism eased, but lack of staff support, erratic funding, and the scarcity of outlets at which to sell the magazine continued to plague Aptheker as editor. *Political Affairs* averaged sixty-four pages in each monthly edition, all of which Aptheker edited by himself, with no help from staff or assistance. "It [was] a big job," he recalled in an interview. "As the end of the month approaches," Aptheker wrote to an academic colleague in March 1959, apologizing for not responding to earlier correspondence, "the various deadlines for this magazine (the staff of which consists of one person—yours truly!) pile up and I must work at a very intensive rate to get it out."[9]

Perhaps most annoying to Aptheker was the continued blackballing of the magazine by news outlets, above all in New York City, which limited circulation of the magazine and consequently the circulation of Aptheker's ideas to relatively few people, mostly party members. After a highly exoteric comment made by his sister Minna on the nature of freedom in "our dear Democracy," Aptheker erupted in a vexatious rant over her naive notions about freedom in the United States. "Do you really know something of freedom in our America?" he inquired. "Do you know 160 of my friends were arrested in the past 5 years; and that three of them are still in jail? . . . Why do you not place a return address on your letters when you write to your own brother? And why am I careful to put no return address when I write to my sister? . . . Why is it you do not read and subscribe to the monthly magazine edited by your brother? Why is it that newsstands will not sell that magazine, though they are offered a good profit for doing so? Why is it that we cannot advertise that magazine, though we offer to pay for ads—after sweating to raise the necessary money? Do you really know what you are talking about when you speak of 'freedom' here?"[10]

Small though the number of readers of *Political* Affairs was, Aptheker covered a wide range of subjects in his monthly column, which he called "Ideas In Our Time." He devoted a sizable number of columns to criticism of U.S. foreign policy, which he viewed as the greatest danger to world peace: as early as July 1957 he foresaw that the United States and Vietnam were on a collision course. He used new books and articles in noncommunist periodicals and newspapers, especially the *New York Times,* which he denounced at every opportunity, as embarkation points when composing his columns. In his column of May 1958, devoted to examining "a widespread and rapidly growing uneasiness about U.S. foreign policy," he used as evidence articles in *Foreign Affairs,* the *Nation,* the *Atlantic, Saturday Review,* and the *New York Post,* bourgeois publications that he apparently thought validated his analysis. He cited what he called "staunch friends of capitalism" as examples that proved his Marxist critique of U.S. foreign and domestic policy. "What [were] the essential features of the foreign policy, denounced in such strong terms" by Aptheker's sources? "The Truman–Eisenhower foreign policy starts from the position that the Soviet Union is the enemy whose destruction would redound to the benefit of the United States," Aptheker asserted. Truman and Eisenhower understood, he wrote, that that goal was within the realm of possibility once the United States had developed atomic weapons. "It was to demonstrate to the Russians the invincibility of this weapon," Aptheker went on—predating the vigorous arguments put forward by revisionist historians in the 1960s that now dominate interpretation of the use of atomic weapons—"that formed an essential reason for the atrocious decision made by Truman to drop this bomb on two Japanese cities, without warning, despite the fact that he knew that Japan had started surrender negotiations in July, 1945—that is, one month before the first bomb was dropped." But since the Soviet Union's acquisition of the bomb, a stalemate had ensued, as Aptheker had written in an earlier *Political Affairs* column in which he reviewed Henry Kissinger's book *Nuclear Weapons and Foreign Policy*. "Total military victory is now meaningless—i.e., now means the annihilation of humanity," Aptheker stated in that earlier article of August 1957. By 1958 Aptheker had digested Kissinger's analysis and that of many other writers. "The masters of our country see their own concocted Cold War as plainly antecedent to, if not really part of, actual war, conducted when, how, and under the circumstances they hope they will be able to choose," he wrote with some prescience in his column of May 1958. "The war may take the form of one enormous engagement or—and there is a growing tendency towards this view—it may take the form of more or less 'limited' conflicts. . . . in any case, when projecting 'limited' warfare, they project its recurrence for an unlimited time."[11]

When ongoing crises in North Africa and the Middle East captured the attention of the world during the last half of the fifties, Aptheker devoted space in *Political Affairs* to examining the hostilities. Of the Algerian anticolonial revolution against France, Aptheker wrote in a nearly thirty-page article of the dialectical nature of imperialism: "Imperialism does not mean only victimization; . . . it means, also, resistance." Building up its forces gradually, France had five hundred thousand soldiers fighting the Algerian revolutionaries by the summer of 1958. Almost a decade before an equal number of U.S. troops engaged in the same terrorist tactics in Vietnam as France did in Algeria, Aptheker supplied the sickening details of embattled villages obliterated, villagers routinely subjected to electric shock and other forms of torture and then being slaughtered, internment camps, bribery, blackmail, assassinations, schools closed, newspapers suppressed. "Nothing whatsoever—no danger, no provocation—nothing whatsoever, can justify anything approximating the torture of one human being by another," Aptheker declared. To adopt a rationale for torture, to stoop to the level of torturers, "to move even the least bit in the direction of their methods, dignifies them, and weakens the struggle against them," he warned. The result, apart from the violence done to the victim, created an entire generation of young French men "conditioned by the abominations they are ordered to perpetrate . . . turning them into monsters."[12]

As he considered world events in his columns, Aptheker took care to examine direct or indirect American complicity in developing conflicts. In two articles analyzing events in the "Middle East or the Near East—as Europeans have named the area with their characteristic self-centeredness," Aptheker identified Western imperialism "and in the forefront American imperialism . . . more virulent and active than ever before" as having a decisive role in the turmoil, especially the Americans' unquenchable thirst for Middle East oil. Having close ties to the major oil companies since at least the administration of President Woodrow Wilson, the U.S. government had grown so open about its meddling in the affairs of nations like Iran, Iraq, Jordan, Lebanon, and Egypt during the Eisenhower administration that the CIA's involvement in overthrowing the government of Mohammad Mossadeqh in Iran in 1954 "is well known and has been openly admitted," Aptheker wrote. He expected, he said, aggressive actions by Britain, France, and the United States, such as the attempted takeover of Suez in 1956 by Britain and France and the American invasion of Lebanon in 1958. But the participation of Israel in the Suez events especially troubled him. "The further to the Right one moves in Israeli political life," he wrote, "the more fanatical does one find devotion to an aggressive foreign policy, based upon contempt for the rights and the lives of Arabs." The best way for Israel to assure its survival, he predicted, was "by action which rectifies the unforgettable atrocity of tearing one million innocent Arabic men and women from their homes and hurling them into fearful suffering." However, he warned, "should Israel continue to pursue the policy of being a tail to the kite of France or England or [U.S. Secretary of State Allen] Dulles, nothing will save it from the disaster that is manifestly imminent."[13]

That Aptheker opened the pages of *Political Affairs* to the gamut of the Left not affiliated with the party did not please Chairman Hall. "I want to lean over backwards in publishing letters," he wrote to Howard Selsam in mid-1958, "if they express at all some ideas of value."[14] Extending the list of contributors fulfilled the dual purpose of opening the pages of the magazine to a broader spectrum of Left opinion and, Aptheker hoped, increasing its legitimacy while boosting sales and exposing his ideas to a widening audience. By the early 1960s Hall's tolerance of Aptheker's editorship had reached its limits: he rejected the inclusion of contributions from nonparty leftists and decided to remove Aptheker from the magazine. FBI informants within the party reported that Hall "is of the opinion that Betty Gannett would make a good Editor of 'Political Affairs' in substitution for Aptheker. Hall added that Aptheker is not in close touch with the Party. Although Aptheker projects the correct Party line in the monthly publication of 'Political Affairs,' he never consults the Party leadership. Hall added that many people were sorry that Aptheker had been elected to the National Committee of the CP, USA."[15]

Surrounded by sycophants and "swept away by a vision of his own brilliance," Hall had little regard for the editor's position at *Political Affairs,* especially an independent editor, so he pushed Aptheker out.[16] "He had been 'removed' as editor," Bettina wrote in her memoir, *Intimate Politics,* " . . . and would not explain to me what had happened. When I asked he would grunt and snap his head in the air as if shaking off a fly. From these gestures I gathered he was removed as a result of political differences with the party leadership, but I never learned what they were." Gurley Flynn apologized profusely for the way the party's leaders treated Aptheker. "A sort of 'there's your hat—what's your hurry?' atmosphere was most uncalled for," she wrote to Aptheker. "We all deeply appreciate your very hard and difficult years with P.A. when the going was exceedingly hard."[17] Aptheker snapped his head in the air, buried his feelings, ignored (a response that became habitual) what was certainly a betrayal, and moved on.

Indicative of Aptheker's engagement with radical intellectuals outside the party was his relationship with the sociologist C. Wright Mills of Columbia University, "the thinker who did the most to define an emerging new radicalism."[18] Mills published several influential books in the 1950s, three of which, *White Collar* (1951), *The Causes of World War Three* (1958), and *The Power Elite* (1959), examined class structure in a way that Marxist critics, including Aptheker, found "more simplistic and less profound than Marx's theory of class."[19] "[To] analyze his thoughts should not be a waste of time," Aptheker wrote in his book-length examination of Mills's theories, *The World of C. Wright Mills*. "Mills controls a vivid style . . . [and] it is apparent, then, that in Mills we have a scholar of remarkable vigor and versatility," Aptheker wrote in his introduction, "with a wide range of experiences and interests and with considerable influence in and beyond the American academic community. Of the books he has so far produced, *The Power Elite* is the *magnum opus*; . . . It led Michael Harrington . . . to pronounce Mills 'the most imaginative and brilliant of all the sociologists writing from American universities,' a judgment which does not seem to me to be excessive."[20]

Aptheker and Mills had much in common. Like Aptheker, Mills "felt social criticism was prerequisite to a genuinely democratic society."[21] Both men had a "contentious intellectual style," and again, Mills, like Aptheker, "failed" or refused "to observe the noblesse oblige of sparing his colleagues in print," which "led to a deep hostility directed toward [them] and to [their] marginalization from the mainstream" of their respective disciplines.[22] Close associates of the two men spied on them and reported their findings to the FBI, and the bureau expansively monitored both. Neither could be silenced.

Carl Marzani, the head of Marzani and Munsell publishers, announced the publication of Aptheker's *The World of C. Wright Mills* sometime in late 1959 or early 1960. He sent galley proofs to Mills, and on 18 June 1960 Mills wrote to Marzani, "For some time I've been meaning to write to Mr. Aptheker since I saw the announcement of his book; . . . Now here are the galleys of his book which I am delighted to receive. This afternoon I'll read them." Mills intended to make comments that he thought Aptheker might "want to consider." "Please know," he concluded, "that I am very glad indeed about this, for reasons which a bit later during the summer I'd like to explain to Mr. Aptheker himself."[23]

Over the next two days Mills produced nineteen single-spaced typewritten pages of notes for Aptheker that he appended to the letter to Marzani. "First," he wrote, "rules and regulations: nothing that I write here should be attributed to me or included as by me in the book. To do so would, I think, make the book much less effective from every point of view. So I must make that stipulation, please." He said he did not think he and Aptheker had met, and he wanted to keep it that way: "I don't want us to until his book is beyond his reach, in the publishing works. Then of course I do very much want for us to get together, if he will, and have some big talks. . . . I need his help on several things in which I believe he will be interested!"[24] Mills and Aptheker did confer several times before Mills's untimely death in 1962. Mills continued the letter by directly addressing Aptheker:

> The end [of the introduction] isn't yet very good: but the idea is to pick it all up and throw it at them. And now I am, I really am, embarrassed. This is an obscene thing I have done, and am doing! I would offer only the following apologia: 1) if you don't like this, throw it out; but I know of course that you will. 2) I assume of course that you'll fix it up in your own style as you wish. 3) Please do not hesitate, on the other hand, to use it or as much of it in any form as you wish; don't have 'author pride' about that: 4) My aim, so far as I am aware of it, is not to puff myself etc.; to hell with that, but to make your book more interesting and influential . . . in your own terms. So don't think of me as Mills but as editor in a publishing house. . . . Any flipness of tone ought to be avoided; of course I don't mean that it shouldn't be sharp as hell. . . . I must say again: the more non-Marxists you quote and use the better: don't reverse the boycott: you be bigger than they. Your legacy is big enough for it.[25]

Aptheker responded to Mills ten days later. He accepted Mills's "generous" comments and suggestions and the manner in which he offered them. "Your editorial work certainly has made the book less weak than it would have been," Aptheker wrote. "I only wish I could acknowledge it, but I suppose this would not be possible—or proper." He lamented the difficulty he perceived Mills would have in writing a review of the book (which he evidently intended to do), even in left-wing publications; "but still," he wrote, "this is a special case I suppose and perhaps some paper will allow a maverick to have his say when a damned communist has said something about *him*. I hope so. . . . I see in the cold typing that no real hint of the appreciation I feel for your efforts and your cordiality has come through. Believe me, however, when I say I am deeply grateful."[26]

Mills sought Aptheker's help again in early April 1961 while working on his last book, *The Marxists,* as he recuperated from a heart attack. Aptheker wished him well and offered assistance with any of his colleague's efforts to obstruct "the fearfully dangerous build-up looking towards a major invasion effort against Cuba" (the Bay of Pigs invasion occurred later that month).[27] There is no further correspondence in the Aptheker papers between the two scholars, although Aptheker wrote in his unpublished autobiography that he and Mills became friends.[28] Aptheker bristled at an article that appeared in *Studies on the Left* that claimed Aptheker "came to debunk" Mills. "My work . . . was an effort to estimate his writings . . . and to analyze them from the viewpoint of Marxism–Leninism," Aptheker wrote to the editors. "We became thereafter friends and prolonged discussion continued our mutual examination of common interests and divergent approaches."[29] Mills died of a heart attack a year later at the age of forty-five. "His terribly early death is one of the great tragedies for American intellectual history," Aptheker wrote.[30]

While Mills helped lay the intellectual foundation for the New Left through the concept of participatory democracy, most of the Old Left, specifically the leadership of the Communist Party, clung to what Mills referred to as "Victorian Marxism," the theory that "the working class of the advanced capitalist societies [was] the historic agency, or even . . . the most important agency," for change.[31] The party "stood in hostile isolation from most of the new currents that grew up on the left . . . during the 1960s," Isserman wrote in his history of the party during and just after the Second World War. "Veterans of the Communist movement, defeated and dispersed, could provide neither practical leadership nor philosophical guidance to the New Left."[32] Not so Aptheker, who moved comfortably into the milieu of the New Left. He was able to contemplate and comment on Mills's transformative theory whereas many leaders in the party refused to even consider any analysis but their own. "The Party's hostile attitude toward the New Left was probably the greatest political liability we had to contend with in the 1960s," Healey claimed. "Gus regarded the New Left as a distraction or a threat to our own political prospects rather than as a fertile field for our young people to work in."[33]

The term New Left "originated in England when some Marxist intellectuals broke away from the British Communist Party." New Left Clubs appeared on British campuses, and by 1960 two New Left journals merged to form the New Left Review. In the United States, history and English graduate students at the University of Wisconsin, many of whom came out of the Young Communist League there, began publishing Studies on the Left in the fall of 1959. Aptheker accepted an offer to review Vance Packard's book The Status Seekers for the first issue. "We have been encouraged beyond expectation," Marty Sklar, the editor, wrote to Aptheker, "by the response we have received from students and professors in various parts of the country (though we could use more contacts in the South and particularly more contacts among Negro students and scholars)."[34] Aptheker too was excited by the appearance of Studies on the Left. "The views represented have one common denominator, radicalism," he wrote in Political Affairs, "otherwise the whole gamut of opinion is represented, including the Communist. . . . With such manifestoes issuing from American youth— allegedly beaten, tired, and depraved—there is every reason to turn to our work of bringing the message of peace, freedom and Socialism, and the component of

Marxism–Leninism, to our country's thought and life, with renewed enthusiasm and confidence."[35] Although most historians agree that the civil rights movement of the 1950s sparked the development of the New Left, *Studies on the Left* was, according to the historian Paul Buhl, "the first sustained intellectual journal calling for a new movement."[36]

Aptheker's connections with student radicals at the University of Wisconsin went back to the fifties. One of those students, Ron Radosh, who later renounced his radical past, completed his undergraduate work at the university in 1959, received a master's degree at the State University of Iowa, and then returned to Madison in 1961 to work on a doctorate in history.[37] Radosh, his wife, Alice, and Sol Stern formed the Iowa Socialist Discussion Club (SDC) while Radosh worked on his master's in Iowa City. "Much to our amazement," he wrote in his score-settling memoir, *Commies,* "the SDC took off. . . . [W]e . . . worked to schedule meetings and gain recruits . . . to gain understanding and support for 'the Marxist–Socialist viewpoint' on campus."[38] To help in that endeavor Radosh contacted Aptheker and invited him to speak on campus but then lamented the lack of commitment by other SDC members who worried about their prospects for academic careers should their records indicate that "they belonged to a club which sponsored a talk by you."[39] Eventually, Radosh convinced the political science faculty to sponsor Aptheker's visit, which much relieved the other, skittish doctoral candidates.

Later that year Radosh sought out Aptheker's help in getting his scholarly work published. He sent Aptheker his review of David A. Shannon's *The Decline of American Communism,* asking if he would publish it in either *Political Affairs* or *Mainstream.* But the young author exhibited the same trepidations for which he had earlier chastised his fellow SDC members: "*Make sure,*" he wrote emphatically, underlining both words, "you do not use my name on the review, but use a pseudonym, James Breese. . . . Any identification with me would finish my position at Wisconsin, and I do not even want Shannon guessing who at what school could have written this, etc." In his letter Radosh lavished praise on Aptheker for his writing: "Your analysis and arguments are the most logical and well documented to be found in any Left publication. Keep up the good work!"[40]

When students asked him for help Aptheker consistently and unselfishly assisted them whenever he could. Yet some of those students, as is evident in their correspondence over the years, continually worried about being associated with Aptheker or even having their name appear with his. Ed Moser, a graduate student in Pittsburgh who regularly corresponded with Aptheker in the early sixties, apologized for his reluctance to express his gratitude for Aptheker's help on his master's thesis. "Something troubles me," he wrote in early 1960, "and I think I should tell you about it. In my acknowledgments, I mentioned a number of people, all of whom merited mention, and I left out many . . . [but] the one to whom I should have expressed thanks most prominently was you, and I left you out altogether. Of course the reason is obvious. My career and effectiveness would not be helped by such an acknowledgment, they would be hurt. . . . Someday, of course, there will be the value placed on honest scholarship which it deserves, and everything will be different. . . . But I wanted you to know who deserves the biggest bow."[41]

Radosh, years later, devised a peculiar way of acknowledging Aptheker's contributions: in *Commies* he twice mentions Aptheker. While there is no way to verify the first incident that Radosh says occurred in one of Aptheker's classes at the Jefferson School, the second reference to Aptheker has the appearance at least of mendaciousness. In the memoir Radosh avowed that he was such a true believer that he purposely joined the Communist Party after the Soviet invasion of Hungary in 1956. By his account, four months after lavishly praising Aptheker in the letter quoted above, in January 1961 Radosh had a remarkable epiphany: although he did not say he resigned his party membership, he claimed to have abandoned communism. "We . . . were pleased that [William Appleman] Williams showed nothing but disdain for the old, sectarian, pro-Communist left wing, from which we believed ourselves to have graduated into a New Left," Radosh wrote. He maintained that Williams liked to provoke Old Leftists and that a comment made by Aptheker at a Wisconsin appearance sponsored by the Wisconsin Socialist Club had prompted a show of pique by Williams. "The next day," Radosh wrote exultantly, "when Aptheker appeared at his office for a social call, Williams met him at the door, looked him up and down, and said, 'These aren't my office hours. Come back next week.' Then he closed the door in Aptheker's face." The next week, Radosh implausibly asserts, "Aptheker actually flew back from New York to arrive for Williams' office hours. When he walked in, Williams said, 'I'm not interested in talking to you.' Aptheker turned abruptly and left."[42]

Radosh did not cite any source for the directly quoted dialogue, but beyond that there are more serious problems with this yarn. Williams and Aptheker had been in contact with each other for some years, and their relationship continued after Radosh left Wisconsin. In November 1960 Williams wrote to Aptheker praising *The World of C. Wright Mills*: "If I may presume to say so, I feel that the way you dealt with Mills is not only more powerful than, say, some of the items in [Aptheker's book from 1955] *History and Reality,* but it is also much more persuasive to those who have fences erected about their minds. I really think it would be fine if you would go back over some of those characters in the style and tone of the Mills volume, and—even more—do the same kind of thing for others."[43] Aptheker met Williams in 1963 to talk about the American Institute for Marxist Studies, which Aptheker founded. Although the meeting was cordial, in Aptheker's recollection, Williams expressed doubt that the institute could be sustained financially.[44] That Williams would have treated Aptheker with the rudeness Radosh says he did and at the time Radosh specified seems highly unlikely. "I knew Bill Williams," the historian John Bracey wrote concerning the Radosh claim. "[He] was one of the kindest gentle souls I have ever met. I can't imagine him treating Aptheker or anyone else that way. This is unbelievable!"[45]

Aptheker put his faith and trust for change in the burgeoning student population even before the emergence of the New Left and the campus uprisings of the sixties. He contemplated the same questions Mills proposed in his "Letter to the New Left": "Who is it that is getting fed up?" Mills asked. "Who is it that is getting disgusted with what Marx called 'all the old crap'? Who is it that is thinking and acting in radical ways? All over the world—in the bloc, outside the bloc and in between.?" Aptheker's actions imply that he agreed with Mills's answer: "The answer's the same," Mills determined, "it is the young intelligentsia."[46]

Exhibiting much courage, in light of the legal ramifications, Aptheker embraced a high public profile. Noticeably more pugnacious than at his McCarthy hearing almost a decade earlier, Aptheker sparred with Chief Counsel Frank S. Tavenner Jr. at an HCUA hearing in May 1961. Asked repeatedly about his membership in the party and about his affiliation with the Jefferson School, Aptheker replied defiantly, "I will answer no questions about my political affiliations or beliefs. You have in my opinion no right to ask me such a question. I find it an indecent question. . . . I have refused to answer the question under the basis of the First and the Fifth Amendments, and because of the notoriety of this Committee, which has led even the *New York Times* to urge its abolition. I will be no party to its witch-hunting processes."[47]

When the Supreme Court upheld the constitutionality of the Smith Act and the McCarran Act in 1961, Aptheker rushed into print a book titled *Dare We Be Free?* that analyzed the Court's decision by building on his columns in *Political Affairs*. "Communists would refuse to label themselves the hateful things they are called in the McCarran Act," he wrote. "They see the McCarran Act, and its registration procedure as a way-station on the well-marked road toward fascism at home and war abroad, toward cataclysmic disaster for the American People and for all humanity."[48] In *Political Affairs* Aptheker challenged the federal government to enforce provisions of the McCarran Act against him while elsewhere he taunted government agents. Reacting to one such taunt, which became in itself an accusation, an FBI agent noted that in *Political Affairs* for March 1962 Aptheker announced "specifically for the benefit of the Attorney General . . . that before he would yield to the McCarran Act requirements he would see 'his right hand wither, his tongue cleave to the roof of his mouth, and his eyes lose their sight!' "[49]

As Aptheker's notoriety grew, his audiences grew. The invitations multiplied. Via his fifteen-minute, biweekly radio broadcasts, begun in 1959 and lasting for two years—"until the effort was stopped apparently," he said, "at orders from significant financial backers of that system"—Aptheker acquired a national audience and helped ignite broader interest in his analysis of black history and contemporary issues, accomplishments that elicited even more invitations to colleges and universities.[50]

During 1960 and 1961 Aptheker traversed the country speaking on college and university campuses at the invitation of students and young faculty members eager to define and test the limits of academic freedom. College administrations during this period acted on the premise of *in loco parentis* and often treated students as parents treat their children. Many institutions had enacted bans on controversial speakers. Meg Yuckman, a student at Monmouth College in West Long Branch, New Jersey, contacted Aptheker to cancel a scheduled appearance by him in May 1961. "I regret that I must cancel the speaking date," she wrote. "The President [of the college] . . . expressed the belief there would be repercussions due to the insuing [*sic*] reasons: 1. Our nation is almost at war. 2. You, . . . are known to the F.B.I. 3. Your magazine . . . is on the House Un-American Activities list as a subversive magazine. 4. By having you speak here there would be reprecusions [*sic*] for the nation, the school, and the student body."[51] Aptheker responded three days later and closed his letter by mentioning his appearances at a number of other schools. "There were, I hope, 'repercussions' in all these institutions," he said, "but everyone of them survived my visit, and each is perhaps no worse off than before for having let me say what I wanted to and be asked what others wanted to ask me, for a few hours. Are all these colleges able to survive, but yours is not?"[52] After continued demands by students, the president at Monmouth relented, and Aptheker spoke.

Student protests at Wayne State University against a ban on outside speakers, a move designed to keep Aptheker from speaking there, forced the university president to approve a lecture by Aptheker called "The Negro in the Civil War." "'People other than students and scholars are present,' Herbert Aptheker said with wry humor, 'but I'm sure they will be no less assiduous in making notes,'" the *Detroit Free Press* reported on 17 November 1961. "'They' were a battery of reporters, photographers, FBI, State Police and Detroit police representatives and 'monitors' from such organizations as the Daughters of the American Revolution and several right-wing student groups."[53] At the University of Chicago and Roosevelt University, Aptheker addressed "the current Black liberation movement rocking the nation."[54] Altogether, more than two dozen colleges and universities hosted speeches by Aptheker in 1961.

Governmental targeting of Aptheker increased as his visibility and the audiences at his speeches as well as the people reading his written work grew. In

January 1962 the State Department revoked his passport, citing provisions of
the McCarran Act that made it illegal for Communists to travel outside the
country. He lamented the department's action in a letter to Du Bois in December. Du Bois had invited Aptheker to a conference on Du Bois's proposed *Encyclopedia Africana* to be held that month in Ghana. "I have the honor of being
one of those under the ban of the McCarran Act here in the United States," he
wrote sarcastically. "[I] am therefore legally restrained from leaving the borders
of my own country."[55]

Unable to travel outside the United States, Aptheker in 1962 again traveled
around the country supporting the right of radicals to speak, attacking the
McCarran Act, and advocating black liberation. He spoke to student audiences
at Hunter College in the Bronx, Columbia University, Amherst College, Michigan State University, the University of Pittsburgh, Brandeis University, City
College of New York, and Carleton College in Minnesota, among others. At
Carleton he shared the stage with the historian Henry Steele Commager, one of
the few prominent noncommunist historians to speak openly in favor of radicals. Aptheker expressed "deep appreciation for [Commager's defense of] the
Bill of Rights in the face of the fierce Right-wing anti-Communist and pro-war
propaganda."[56]

12   The Dangerous Enemy in Our Midst

BY APRIL 1962 the FBI had begun targeting Aptheker as part of its Counterintelligence Program (COINTELPRO), started in 1956 and supposedly ended in 1971. J. Edgar Hoover had been hunting Reds since 1919, when he wrote a "legal brief" while serving as a "Special Assistant to the Attorney General of the United States. . . . My purpose," he wrote in his frantic exposé *Masters of Deceit* is to fight "the enemy in our midst."[1] Originally conceived by Hoover as a means to destroy the Communist Party, COINTELPRO operations, which included infiltration, break-ins, surveillance, disruption, violence, and murder, eventually encompassed not only the Communist Party but also the Socialist Workers Party, the Black Panthers, the American Indian Movement, the women's movement, the Student Non-violent Coordinating Committee, gay activists, the Southern Christian Leadership Conference, Martin Luther King Jr., the African American human rights activist Malcolm X, Herbert Aptheker, and hundreds of other persons and organizations.

Aptheker's papers contain numerous letters and other documents charting his cross-country speaking engagements at colleges and universities, but these are dwarfed by the thousands of pages in Aptheker's FBI files, which contain the most complete record of his speeches, travel, attendance at party meetings, and affiliations during the 1960s. Ironically, Howard Fast wrote of himself in words that apply to Aptheker as well, the FBI documents "detailed every—or almost every—decent act I had performed in my life. If I were to seek some testament to leave to my grandchildren, proving that I had not lived a worthless existence but had done my best to help and nourish the poor and oppressed, I could not do better than to leave them this FBI report."[2]

The bureau's physical surveillance of Aptheker began in the early fifties, although on several occasions agents conducted investigations of his writing and affiliations as far back as the thirties and forties, snooping that was deemed worthy of inclusion in his file. FBI agents conducted the physical surveillance and took the photographs, but the reports reflect a sizable number of informants and agents provocateurs around the country who supplied personal information on Aptheker. He knew that the FBI had infiltrated the party, and he "was aware of being an object of FBI surveillance." Sometimes "this was deliberately made obvious," he wrote in his unpublished autobiography, "with the personnel showing themselves. Other times not visible but whether in New York City or out of town . . . the FBI followed me."[3] When the *New York Mirror* published a hysteria-laden piece warning New Yorkers about Communists living among them, including the names and addresses of the top leaders in the party, including Aptheker, he assumed the FBI had delivered the information to the *Mirror.* The story triggered an onslaught of hate mail and phone calls at Aptheker's home. In an unsigned letter from New Haven that is representative of many such missives he received, the writer said the *Mirror* story had prompted him to write: "I am writing because you are listed . . . as an important Communist & because you bear a name which sounds Jewish. . . . You are a dirty Jewish dog who is giving the rest of the decent, loyal Jews in this God-given country a black eye. . . . Drop dead all of you!"[4] Aptheker was quite surprised, though, when, in response to a Freedom of Information Act request, the FBI informed him in 1999 that its files on his activities ran to two hundred linear feet. He quipped to an interviewer who was present when the FBI phoned that he might have to add on to his house to make room for the documents when they arrived.[5] He eventually received several hundred documents dealing with COINTELPRO activities, only a small portion of the files the FBI assembled on him and Fay and a host of organizations with which Aptheker was affiliated, including the American Institute for Marxist Studies, *Studies on the Left,* the Marxist Scholars Conference, and many more.

The FBI initiated dozens of COINTELPRO operations against Aptheker. On 4 May 1962 agents in Seattle reported to FBI headquarters on a successful scheme organized to disrupt an appearance by Aptheker there. "The anti-Communist element had no difficulty seating themselves in advantageous positions," agents reported, and began an organized disruption of the talk. "Heckling and booing . . . greeted" Aptheker, then "the entire anti-Communist assembly, on a cue from one of its leaders, arose and started marching through the aisles of the hall singing patriotic songs . . . then marched out of the hall into the mezzanine where they continued their serenade despite threats from a hastily organized Communist Party 'security squad.' . . . No indication [of] FBI involvement in this matter is suspected."[6] Hoover praised the actions of his agents.[7]

Aptheker's appearance in Seattle followed engagements at Portland State University, Oregon State University, and Reed College in Portland. But the president of the University of Washington, Charles Odegaard, like many of his fellow university presidents around the country, some at the insistence of the FBI, banned Communists from speaking on campus. Aptheker pointed out the absurdity of Odegaard's actions in a letter to the *University of Washington Daily:* "In barring '[a] Communist spokesman and Communists, does President Odegaard mean to bar Picasso from lecturing on art, or [Pablo] Neruda on Poetry, or [Sean] O'Casey on playwriting, or Du Bois on history, or [John] Bernal on physics, or [John] Berger on aesthetics, or [Louis] Aragon on the novel?"[8]

The FBI attempted another COINTELPRO disruption of Aptheker's scheduled appearance at New York State University-Buffalo in October 1962. He was the fifth and last speaker in a series of lectures sponsored by the student senate. Hoover cautioned his Buffalo agents to take special precautions because "Aptheker's appearance is scheduled to be before the State University. . . . It is most important that in any action taken the Bureau's identity is fully protected so that there will be no basis for any allegations that the Bureau's investigations are interfering with academic freedom."[9] Agents in Buffalo created a mimeographed leaflet titled "Where Are Their Voices Now?" that criticized students and community members who denounced the fourth speaker in the lecture series, the prominent British fascist Sir Oswald Mosley, "but defended Aptheker as a 'historian.'" The leaflet pointed out "Aptheker's leadership position in the CPUSA and described him as the same kind of historian as one A. Hitler who wrote 'Mein Kampf.'"[10]

On the day of his appearance, as hundreds of students packed the hall, several faculty members greeted Aptheker over dinner. During the meal "word came that a court order had been obtained by a member of the State Assembly barring my talk," Aptheker recalled.[11] Early in 1963 the faculty and students at Buffalo successfully challenged the injunction barring Aptheker's speech, and later that year, as Aptheker rightly boasted, "my visit to that campus . . . resulted in an audience in the thousands rather than the hundreds [turned away on the night of the cancellation]."[12]

The FBI files reveal that the bureau was becoming increasingly alarmed at Aptheker's effectiveness on college campuses. On 2 May 1963 FBI headquarters requested "the views of the Seattle Office as to how this menace to college-level citizens can be combated."[13] Agents in Seattle responded that the best method for curtailing Aptheker's pyrotechnic oratory "is . . . wherever possible, . . . to prevent the appearance of Communist Party speakers on college campuses. Where there is no fire, there is no need for the services of a fire department."[14]

During the early 1960s Aptheker perceived another opening, "a manifest dramatic change in the country's atmosphere as compared with the previous decade, especially the developing African-American civil rights movement, the student movement and the movement against the Cold War."[15] "I have just returned from a lecture tour of Southern and Northern California and Oregon," he wrote to Corliss Lamont in November 1963. "In 25 years of this kind of effort never have I met so responsive and sincerely interested audiences and their numbers ranged from 1,900 to classes in three different universities numbering from 20 to 40 students."[16] "The best trip I've ever had—in 25 years—was the recent one to the West Coast universities," he wrote in a letter the next month.[17]

When Aptheker spoke at Reed College in April 1962 he was greeted enthusiastically by about one hundred students and faculty. He met with small groups of students for dinner and conversation later in the evening. "The youngsters wanted to know if I would be willing to teach at Reed," he reported to Fay. "I said I would. They are going to form a delegation and request this—also letters to the college paper and the administration. All this should be very educational for them," he wrote, with some evident amusement at the futility of the endeavor.[18]

Several months later the student activist Ken Margolis, whose father had worked as a lawyer on the Supreme Court appeals of the Scottsboro Boys and the Communist Party Smith Act cases, contacted Aptheker about teaching at Reed. Margolis and other students had founded a campus group called "Students For Civil Liberties [SCL] (not affiliated with ACLU), . . . to have the non-communist hireing [sic] policy discarded, and to have the Marxist point of view represented on the faculty." To achieve their goals, the SCL wanted the administration at Reed to have a letter of interest in a teaching position on file from a party member. "Since you have such a fine academic record and have expressed interest in teaching at Reed, I thought you might be willing to take such a step," Margolis wrote to Aptheker.[19] "This is the first time . . . that a permanent action group has been organised [sic] on the Reed campus," Margolis said in a second letter a few days later. "Our plans are to raise the theoretical issue first, as forcefully as possible, and then to use your application as a rallying point and, if the clause is revoked, to use your application as a test case." Margolis said the SCL felt almost certain that Richard H. Jones, the head of the History Department, would support Aptheker's appointment to the faculty.[20]

Aptheker sent his letter of application to Jones on 9 October 1962. On 17 October Margolis wrote with some excitement that their campaign had produced "some supprisingly [sic] hopeful signs—not so much for your particular case, as for some new practical hireing [sic] policies, as well as a campaign of political education for the students." Margolis related that he "threatened the President of the college with a full-scale campaign, including communications with the general public and the alumni . . . and since he has a real fear of 'bad publicity' he offered to do things quietly. For the force of the threat," he wrote, "we have you to thank." Margolis reported further that the Reed trustees, responding to agitation by faculty and students, "superceeded [sic] the earlier 'non-communist hireing [sic] clause' with a double talk resolution which reserves the same power to them, but which at least has the virtue of not being speciffically [sic] political."[21]

As Aptheker traversed the continent speaking about the civil rights movement and increasingly voicing his opposition to the incipient war against

Vietnam, the FBI moved in earnest, beginning in March 1964, to "obtain . . . additional legally admissible evidence . . . [establishing] his present Communist Party membership" in order to prosecute him "under the membership provisions" of the McCarran Act.[22]

Having prevailed in the Supreme Court in *Aptheker v. Secretary of State* on 22 June 1964, when the Court, in a six to three decision, struck down the passport provisions of the McCarran Act, Herbert and Fay left the United States for an extended "visit to the socialist world."[23] In Moscow the Apthekers visited Gurley Flynn, who was "resting in a Soviet hospital," before continuing on to Siberia. "She was her usual radiant self, witty and warm," Aptheker wrote of Gurley Flynn to comrades in the United States. "We were told that she was somewhat ill . . . and so while upset we were not alarmed."[24] When they returned to Moscow "early in September" they learned that "news about Gurley was alarming."[25] Before they could get to her bedside, she died, on 5 September. "In the Hall of Columns," or Catherine Hall, located in the Kremlin Senate, where Soviet leaders held particularly important ceremonies, "mourners passed by for eight hours. . . . robust farmers and mothers, grandparents . . . little girls in pigtails, and students from Africa, Asia, Haiti, Latin American . . . filing past by the tens of thousands."[26] "Certainly well over 25,000 must have paid their last respects," Aptheker wrote to Hy and Betty Lumer. "It was unbelievable that she lay so still—this vibrant one was so still. . . . How much colder the world is now."[27] Aptheker represented the CPUSA at the elaborate state funeral, where, according to *Time* magazine, "[Soviet Premier] Nikita [Khrushchev] himself stood solemnly in the honor guard just before the body was cremated."[28] At the funeral ceremony itself Aptheker, standing atop Lenin's mausoleum, delivered a eulogy for Flynn with Khrushchev standing at his side: "The mind rebels and the heart bleeds. . . . Comrade Elizabeth Gurley Flynn is dead. Out of the marrow of the American working class she came." "In the past two decades," Aptheker continued, "years of the Cold War, of great difficulties, of trials and imprisonment, of terror and wavering and doubt, Comrade Elizabeth stood like a tree, refreshing and holding together the Communist Party of the United States. . . . Ever green . . . will be the memory of Comrade Elizabeth Gurley Flynn."[29]

In the United States later that month FBI agents in Boston suggested that "the Bureau might wish to capitalize on the 'strange coincidences' that within the past two-year-period several notable CP leaders . . . including Elizabeth Gurley Flynn, have all died while visiting Moscow."[30] The agent wanted to plant a story with a cooperative syndicated columnist who could "cast a shadow of a doubt as to the legality of some of these deaths."[31]

While the effort to tie the Soviet Union to Gurley Flynn's death seems to have gone nowhere, in February 1965 the St. Louis FBI office proposed a COINTELPRO action against Aptheker that Hoover approved. Agents requested authority to alert a source at the *St. Louis Globe Democrat* about a speech Aptheker was scheduled to give in St. Louis.[32] The evidence implies that the agent contacted the publisher of the *Globe Democrat,* Richard Amberg, "a fierce right-wing anti-communist and foe of desegregationism [*sic*]" who "was listed . . . as one of the FBI's . . . 8,000 'correspondents' around the country." Amberg, according to an article in the *New Republic* in 1996, "eagerly loaned his paper to the bureau's cointelpro campaign."[33] Agents suggested that the *Globe Democrat* question Aptheker about the purpose of his trip to St. Louis, "including whether it concerns protests against U.S. activities in Viet Nam; whether he will speak in St. Louis; and re current status in CP."[34] The agents wanted to use their source at the "Globe Democrat, . . . [to] have reporters and photographers meet Aptheker upon his arrival to ask him questions calculated to embarrass Aptheker. Also . . . alert the local television station, an affiliate of the 'Globe Democrat,' to afford similar coverage to Aptheker. We believe it is extremely important to neutralize the propaganda efforts of Aptheker."[35]

When Aptheker's plane landed in St. Louis on 14 February, newspaper reporters and television cameras recorded his startled response. An editorial writer for the *Globe Democrat,* Patrick J. Buchanan, who later worked for Richard Nixon and ran unsuccessfully for president three times, pushed his way to the front of the pack. "Our friends at the bureau alerted us to what was up. . . . We had Dr. Aptheker's flight number, and [Denny] Walsh and I staked him out," Buchanan wrote in his autobiography.[36] Buchanan identified himself as a reporter and began to question Aptheker, using a set of questions scripted by the FBI. "How did you know I was coming here?" Aptheker asked the well-coached Buchanan.[37] Buchanan, pouncing, asked Aptheker "what his status in the communist Party [was]?" Aptheker, always vigilant where provisions of the McCarran Act were concerned, responded wryly, "I won't have any comment on that for obvious reasons."[38] Buchanan and Walsh "put a tail on Aptheker [and] . . . the middle-aged gentleman who had met Aptheker" at the airport.[39]

Thus began several days of unremitting histrionic reporting of Aptheker's visit in newspaper, television, and radio coverage. Buchanan dogged Aptheker at every step. He planted a reporter, a young Washington University graduate student, in Aptheker's audience.[40] Stories and photographs of Aptheker and Theodor Rosebury, Aptheker's host and a professor at the university, made the front page of the *Globe Democrat.* Lurid editorials cautioned, "St. Louis—Wake Up!" Buchanan camped outside Rosebury's house and banged on his door at all hours. Obviously embarrassed for Rosebury and his family by the notoriety linking their names, Aptheker approached Mrs. Rosebury and "offered to take a room in a motel. [She] vehemently protested; 'You are my invited guest and here you will remain.'"[41] Buchanan did exactly as his FBI handlers had instructed, filling the paper with anticommunist hysteria accompanied by sensational headlines, thereby provoking much delight at FBI headquarters. "As a result of this counterintelligence action," an FBI administrator wrote, "extensive publicity appeared in the St. Louis area extremely discrediting to the Communist Party.... This is an outstanding example of the service an alert press can perform in alerting Americans to the communist threat."[42] Buchanan and Amberg congratulated themselves on a job well done even though Buchanan and the *Globe Democrat* "clearly crossed the line separating journalism from clandestine support for government propaganda" and set off "a campaign of vilification against a professor [Rosebury] who had undeniably been involved in left-wing activities but against whom there was not a shred of evidence suggesting he ever did anything to undermine national security."[43] "There were bonuses all around," Buchanan wrote in his autobiography.[44]

At FBI headquarters agents seethed with contempt over unanticipated fallout from Aptheker's appearance in the St. Louis area. Five days after Aptheker spoke at Washington University, Chief Justice of the Supreme Court Earl Warren gave a speech there. In an "obvious reference to the furor caused," according to the FBI, by Aptheker's appearance, about which there would have been no supposed furor had the FBI not contrived the controversy, "[Warren] urged 'a more mature heeding of another's viewpoint,' 'compromise' and 'discussion,' and a respect for 'each other's differences.'"[45] Incensed that academic freedom actually promoted freedom of speech, agents castigated Chief Justice Warren: "It would appear [Warren] who obviously [has] an influence over the intellectual life of college students, in a misguided endeavor to define 'academic freedom' would permit CP, USA, leaders to spread lies on campuses, would encourage 'free discussion' of any point of view including that of a traitorous leader of the international communist conspiracy, and would condone, by inference, threats of subversion."[46] Groping for a way to punish Warren, Hoover authorized a COINTELPRO action against him as if he were just one more insignificant, traitorous leader. FBI agents alerted the Illinois American Legion to "the 'muddled thinking that has followed Aptheker's appearance as an identified communist functionary in Illinois, by inference, with the sanction of two universities."[47]

FACED WITH the intransigence of university officials and inspired by the free speech uprising of students at the University of California at Berkeley, in which Bettina took a prominent role among the leadership, in the fall of 1964 students across the country seized the opportunity to demand greater freedom. When the Free Speech Front (FSF) at Ohio State University (OSU) announced that Aptheker would speak there on 21 May 1965, defying a ban on outside speakers instituted by the university's president, the FBI opened a file on the group. Throughout April and May students and faculty members held rallies, sit-ins, vigils, picketing, and a teach-in, all directed at overturning the president's ban. A dozen faculty members published an open letter in the campus daily, the *Ohio State Lantern,* to the university vice president John E. Corbally on 28 April. This initiated a series of reply and response articles between the faculty and the administrators in the university paper. Some faculty members declared in a letter to the editor that they would invite Aptheker to the campus independently of student organizations: "Dr. Aptheker possesses special qualifications to present a particular interpretation and evaluation, not otherwise readily available, of the vital public issue of civil rights. . . . It is true that we believe that the present Speakers' Rule should be changed to permit lawful utterances by any speaker invited by students or faculty, without regard to any special educational contribution other than the general one of contributing to a scene of lively debate, and we hope that such a change will soon be made."[48] On 3 May 1967 additional faculty members signed another letter to the editor that urged abolishing the Speakers' Rule, adopted in 1951 by the Board of Trustees.[49] The trustee John W. Bricker had a so-called chance meeting with one of Cincinnati's FBI agents on 13 May. Bricker, a former governor of Ohio, the Republican nominee for vice president in 1944, and a two-term U.S. senator, sought and failed, through the Bricker Amendment, to change the U.S. Constitution so as to limit the president's treaty-making powers. He told the agent that "it looked like time when academic dismissals . . . might be in order."[50] Four days later Bricker phoned the FBI office in Cincinnati and relayed to them derogatory information about two faculty members who had taken part in the demonstrations against the university speakers' ban, one of whom, Harold F. Harding, was a retired major general in the U.S. Army Reserve and a former commanding general of the 83rd Infantry Division.[51] The FBI then decided to run a COINTELPRO operation against Aptheker in Cincinnati.[52]

"One significant difference between the free speech protest here [at OSU] and similar movements elsewhere is the degree of participation in it by faculty members, student leaders and top student scholars," wrote Leonard Downie Jr. in the *Providence Journal.*[53] At a demonstration held on the campus oval two thousand students—one of whom carried a sign asking, "Who's afraid of harmless Herbie?"—listened as protesters denounced the speaker ban, read telegrams and newspaper clippings supporting the FSF, and cheered the activist singer and songwriter Phil Ochs. The student leader Jeffrey Schwartz demanded that the university trustees abolish the speakers' ban at their May meeting and "stated [that] if [the] speakers' rule [was] not abolished, Aptheker will speak on campus . . . before [the] end of May. . . . Schwartz promised [that] if no immediate action by [the] board of trustees making [the] on-campus speech by Aptheker possible, FSF would bring Aptheker on-campus anyway. . . . Schwartz announced

[that] Life Magazine [was] interested in covering [the] efforts to get Aptheker on campus."[54]

Prior to the event of 21 May, Aptheker appeared in Columbus on 10 May before an overflow crowd of six hundred at an off-campus location. His aim was to help the student organizers of Students for Liberal Action, and he promised to return later that month to defy the campus speaker ban.[55] On 19 May FSF leaders decided they would proceed with their plan to bring Aptheker to campus "regardless of the possible consequences."[56]

Aptheker "eagerly welcomed" the opportunity to test the university's resolve. On the appointed day, twenty-five hundred students, "some carrying placards, gathered on the University Oval to see whether Herbert Aptheker would show up in defiance of a university rule forbidding him to speak."[57] After a series of meetings with FSF organizers, Aptheker received a standing ovation from the overflowing audience in the University Hall auditorium. When the ovation died down, Aptheker took a seat and sat mute on the stage. "He did not say a word," the *Miami Herald* reported.[58] Aptheker wrote in his unpublished autobiography that "several professors read passages . . . from some of my books," but contemporary accounts report that an FSF leader, Sanford Weinberg, "read excerpts from books authored by Aptheker" for about fifteen minutes.[59] By an agreement reached earlier that day, FSF organizers and Aptheker "decided they would ridicule the rule by having Aptheker appear silently while passages were read from his books, which students may readily obtain from the library."[60]

About fifteen minutes into the event a man who identified himself as "a veteran of World Wars I and II" called the office of the university president, Novice G. Fawcett, and announced that "he was coming to the university and would shoot Aptheker if he spoke there."[61] Alarmed university officials informed the student leaders, who, led by Schwartz, appeared on stage, surrounded Aptheker, and moved him into the wings and out of the auditorium, where other students waited in a car to whisk him off to the airport. Cincinnati FBI agents reported that "the telephoned threat could have been 'rigged' and Aptheker could have arranged it or been aware of it, with the idea in mind that it would provide a dramatic exit and excuse for Aptheker to abruptly leave the OSU campus without speaking."[62]

When asked by the *Ohio State Lantern* reporter Marci Hilt how he felt "about the dispute involved in bringing him to Columbus," Aptheker admitted that he felt "very sad about it. . . . It is sad for the country that there has to be any question at all as to whether or not somebody may speak to students and faculty on the Civil Rights movement in the United States, it's almost unbelievable." He said he "was moved by the effort to have him speak on campus . . . 'and of course, obviously, this is a matter of principles, not a matter of personalities.' "[63]

At the July meeting of OSU trustees Bricker summed up the majority opinion in rejecting a revision to the speakers' ban: "Communists, Nazis, and Fascists and members of other subversive organizations and their supporters have no right to speak at a tax-supported state university for they are not free men . . . either I am right about this—or our nation is wrong—in the prosecution of our case in Viet Nam, in our opposition to Castro and other subversive powers generally."[64]

The war in Vietnam was on Aptheker's mind, too, as he responded to a new invitation from OSU students in August. "The effort to rescind the Speaker Ban Rule . . . is an important evidence of the nation-wide revulsion now sweeping the entire academic community in the United States," Aptheker wrote to the student Ron Greene. "It is relevant in these days of the filthy war being waged in Vietnam . . . complete with napalm bombs, phosphorus shells, chemical sprays and 'beneficent' gasses—and the spreading opposition thereto, those responsible for U.S. military involvement seek the reimposition at home of McCarthyite terror." "All may be assured," Aptheker concluded, "that upon invitation I will be on that campus and will speak; nothing—except physical force—will keep me from this."[65]

In mid-September, because of continued agitation by students, "the university's Board of Trustees" announced "an elimination of the Speakers Ban Rule."[66] "This is another example of misguided individuals who believe that in order to have free speech, communist speakers must be guaranteed the right to speak to impressionable college students," aggrieved FBI agents noted.[67] At FBI headquarters, agents became more determined than ever to find a way to combat "this menace to college-level citizens."[68]

Aptheker returned to OSU under the auspices of the Students for Liberal Action on 18 October. "Every one of [the hall's] 400 seats was occupied," Aptheker recalled, "and several hundred additional students crowded into every available nook and all corridors."[69]

Beginning in January 1965, when he responded to an invitation from Michael Padwee, representing the Rutgers chapter of Students for a Democratic Society, to speak about his "On the Nature of Freedom: A Marxist View," Aptheker crisscrossed the country.[70] In February he joined Bettina for a speaking engagement at Berkeley. "The kids have won complete freedom," he wrote to Fay. "There is no longer the requirement of a faculty moderator; they may sell and do sell literature right in the lecture hall and also collect money to help meet the expenses of the lecturer."[71] Through the remainder of the school year Aptheker continued to appear on college campuses at Merritt College, Southern Illinois University, Temple University, Tuskegee Institute, City College of New York, Yale, Franconia, University of Kansas, Queens College, and Antioch, among others, taking delight in being involved in what he called "student rebellion."[72] Students at the University of Southern California invited Aptheker to test a newly revised speaker policy. "It is at this particular juncture that you . . . can be of great service to students of the University of Southern California," wrote John Sullivan, the president of Associated Students of the University of Southern California, and Greg Hill, its speakers' chairman. "Fulfillment of fundamental student rights is dependent upon your acceptance of this invitation."[73]

As his popularity among defiant students rose, the FBI continually hounded its field agents to devise a potent method for countering his effectiveness.[74] Agents in Detroit received permission in February to plant a letter to the editor in the *Detroit News* using "a fictitious name and a nonexistent address . . . which might have a disruptive effect concerning the appearance of Herbert Aptheker . . . at the Central Methodist Church." The letter questioned the motives of Methodist Church leaders who would allow an atheist a forum.[75] While his superiors cast about for exactly the right operation to discredit Aptheker, a Chicago agent came up with what the FBI considered the perfect solution.

On 27 August agents in Chicago presented Hoover with their proposed copy for a pamphlet, "to be printed . . . on good quality paper by the Bureau's Exhibits Section."[76] Urging the use of "a fictitious auspices" for the pamphlet, "the National Committee for Academic Freedom (NCAF) or some other similar type organization," the agents proposed "dissemination concurrent with or just previous to a speaking appearance on Aptheker's part," anticipating that "if used it would be provocative in the academic sense without seeming to be merely anti-communist propaganda."[77] The intent of the pamphlet was to expose Aptheker as a fraud. It began "by quoting favorable evaluations from some Black professors," the historian Julie Kailin wrote, "the reason being, presumably, to imply that *only* unqualified, incompetent Black pseudo-scholars could find worth in Aptheker's scholarship."[78] "It concluded with carefully chosen excerpts from white professors conveying the idea that as a scholar [Aptheker] left much to be desired."[79] "Any favorable citations of Aptheker's work by white scholars of such reputable stature as Richard Hofstadter, were conveniently omitted."[80] The dominant theme of the seven reviews cited in the FBI's pamphlet centers on Aptheker's lack of objectivity—both by omission of relevant historical material and by exaggerating the positive role of black people in the United States—a failing that stemmed from his Marxism.

The FBI's Exhibits Section produced an enduring piece of work. At Aptheker's various appearances for years afterward the pamphlet was handed out by carefully chosen, FBI-approved individuals to audience members as they entered auditoriums to hear Aptheker speak. Aptheker "did not then positively know . . . that this unsigned critique came from the police," but he invariably called the audience's attention to the pamphlet, noting "its nature and its anony-mous authorship."[81]

Aptheker and historians who examined the pamphlet always thought that "the best Hoover could do was to see to it that some academician who was for sale, would produce an exposé of my inadequacies as a scholar," Aptheker recalled.[82] He had good reason to hold that suspicion. The subtlety, depth of research, use of selected historians and historical journals, method of historical writing in the pamphlet, and its content, more sophisticated than the banal sub-jects of most of the FBI documents, all suggest Aptheker was correct in inferring that the FBI did indeed find a historian to write the piece. When asked about who could produce such a document, one agent readily admitted to his supe-riors, "No one in the NYO [New York Office] has been found who believes he is competent enough to prepare a document critical of Aptheker's works which would be convincing to people Aptheker comes in contact with in connection with his campus appearances."[83]

But Aptheker was wrong: an FBI agent in Chicago wrote the pamphlet as a COINTELPRO action: "Chicago relied upon reviews of Aptheker's history writing because for the kind of documented, critical comment we wanted we were limited by the way in which historians carry on their dialogue with one another." "Rarely does an historian choose as his subject matter the person of a contemporary historian except through the medium of reviews of his individual works at the time of their appearance. . . . In bringing this material together we have included both favorable and unfavorable. This is no doubt so because, op-erating as he does under a Marxist rather than an historian's discipline, he does not usually write sound, verifiable, believable history." The FBI's objective, the agent summarized, was to convey "the idea that Aptheker has played 'fast and loose' with the sources of the past. It should also raise doubts concerning the veracity of his present comments."[84]

Whoever the author was, the purpose of the pamphlet was clear, as FBI agents acknowledged in various communications. Aptheker impressed audiences. His presentations moved people and provoked discussion. His analysis altered perceptions and compelled people to think, to challenge, to act. He changed people's minds. "[His] appeal," Hoover wrote to his New York Special Agent in Charge, "to the intellectual segment of the academic community is such that his communist propaganda represents an extreme threat."[85]

Aptheker's seeming incorruptibility stymied the FBI's efforts to discredit him personally. Despite their best efforts, the New York office could find nothing to compromise his integrity.[86] "He is not known to be a woman chaser, drinker, gambler or spendthrift. Aptheker is apparently not interested in advancing him-self within the organizational structure of the Party. He spends his time writing and speaking and not as an organizer within the Party. His army record is very good, except that he was known to be a Communist."[87] Aptheker's "personal honesty and integrity," agents found, "is not known to have been questioned . . . [he] has had more campus appearances than any other CP leader and is their most able spokesman." This is one of the main reasons, Hoover wrote, "that the Bureau considers him the most dangerous Communist in the United States."[88]

13 Mission to Hanoi

CAUGHT UP in the scheme to devise a COINTELPRO operation that would finally, definitively discredit Aptheker, the FBI failed to obtain advance notice of his attendance at the World Congress on Peace held in Helsinki on 10–15 July 1965. Nor did the FBI discover the travel plans Aptheker put into action as a result of a meeting he had at that conference with delegates from North Vietnam. Aptheker was overwhelmed by the warmth of his reception in Helsinki. "Delegation after delegation head—Japan, Nepal, Italy, India, Hungary—shook my hand & hugged me," he wrote home. "Perhaps it will have a lasting impact."[1]

Delegates from North Vietnam presented Aptheker with an official invitation to visit North Vietnam to witness firsthand the destruction wrought by the United States in its ruthless war on that tiny country. Assuming, or at least suspecting, that the FBI intercepted his mail, Aptheker did not write to Fay about the invitation. The Vietnamese asked Aptheker to bring two other people with him, preferably "companions . . . whose views and politics were different from my own."[2] They asked that one of the two be a black American, to which Aptheker agreed without hesitation.

Aptheker had been writing and speaking out against American actions in Vietnam for several years; his was not a lone voice but a singular one in opposing the cacophony of support for war. Even before Kennedy's assassination in 1963, at a time when the United States had sent about seven thousand advisers to Vietnam and only some seventy American soldiers had been killed in action, Aptheker wrote a polemic in *Political Affairs* blasting the imperialist nature of America's actions in Laos, Thailand, and South Vietnam. Quoting mainstream media and noncommunist sources, Aptheker wrote a historical sketch of the three countries and then analyzed the dictatorial leadership in each country propped up by U.S. military spending.[3] Given the disastrous events in Vietnam and the failure of the U.S. foreign policy establishment over the next three decades to grasp the magnitude of that murderous fiasco, Aptheker's early, prescient analysis is illuminating.

Writing in July 1962, Aptheker charted the rise of South Vietnam's president Ngo Dinh Diem as he moved to autocratic, one-man rule in 1956. With millions of dollars in American backing, Diem packed the jails with thirty thousand people, Aptheker wrote. "No American may effectively plead ignorance as to the nature of the Diem government that the United States has bolstered today, at the cost of American lives," he asserted.[4] He quoted Chet Huntley, the prominent NBC reporter, the *Nation,* and even the *Reader's Digest* as sources of evidence that Diem's forces tortured prisoners and locked up high school students. He outlined the agreement between Vice President Lyndon Johnson and Diem that promised hundreds of millions of dollars more in economic and military aid without referring any proposed action to the United Nations or to the people of the United States:

> No treaty was submitted to Congress; no one asked the American people what they thought of these communiques and recommendations and implementa-tions. . . . Soon thereafter Defense Secretary [Robert] McNamara announced U.S. full-scale commitment to Diem's victory, and Attorney General [Robert] Kennedy stated that we were at war and that 'our' prestige was involved and that 'we' would fight until victory. Then troops poured in; now—as of June, 1962—about 6,500 military men from the U.S. are in South Vietnam, . . . and the most influential publications—the *Wall Street Journal, U.S. News & World Report,* the N.Y. *Times*—as at one command, speak of the prospects for a long-drawn-out war, lasting perhaps ten years.[5]

Robert Trumouli of the *New York Times,* Aptheker noted, reported on 1 January 1962 that the United States would spray chemical defoliant on vegeta-tion with the intent of starving the Vietnamese and begin constructing "con-centration camps" where they would forcibly relocate recalcitrant Vietnamese. "The U.S. is today doing in South Vietnam . . . what Americans did in the Philippines from 1899 to 1903," Aptheker noted. "In every case, the harvest was immense suffering and unforgettable bitterness; it brought glory to none and travail to all. Persistence in the present murderous U.S. policy in South Viet-nam," he wrote with foresight, "will have the same harvest for our Government and our people."[6]

The one bright spot Aptheker discerned in an otherwise bleak scenario was the appearance in the United States "of a bona-fide peace movement. . . . It has now enrolled tens of thousands of people in every area . . . it is growing. Its main strength lies among young people and women; it has, however, increased its influence in the Negro people's movement and in trade-union circles . . . major media and books."[7] Aptheker quoted President Kennedy's own words from 1954 on "the atrocious and hopeless character of France's colonial war in Indo-China." For the United States to continue what France had failed to accomplish, Aptheker wrote, "is a fatal course, whatever verbal assurances are offered. . . . The greatness of the United States lies in the path of liberation, of human freedom, of economic well-being, of moral purification. That is the road of true national interest. At this moment in history, this means, specifically and precisely, U.S. withdrawal from Southeast Asia, and American commitment to support there a policy of genuine neutrality, independence and democratic society."[8]

The FBI regularly monitored Aptheker's criticism of the U.S. government's Vietnam policy throughout the next few years. The first campus teach-ins and demonstrations began in 1965, when Johnson, having assumed the presidency after Kennedy's death, aggressively escalated the war. In January 1965 the United States had 23,000 troops in Vietnam; by December the number had reached 154,000. Aptheker spoke at a "get out of Vietnam" rally at Berkeley in February 1965 with "thirteen hundred students . . . in attendance."[9] He characterized the "American bombing mission into North Vietnam . . . [as] 'not retaliatory but aggressive and barbarous.'"[10] Aptheker's speech, an FBI agent wrote, "encouraged the students to picket the new federal building in San Francisco and [attempted] to excite the students to take more direct action such as picketing to make their protest known to the general public."[11] In a document Hoover sent to the Secret Service in May concerning "an individual who is believed to be covered by the agreement between the FBI and Secret Service concerning Presidential protection," Aptheker is identified as being "potentially dangerous."[12]

After returning from Helsinki, Aptheker contacted the young scholar Staughton Lynd, the first of the two people he asked to accompany him to North Vietnam. Aptheker had first met Lynd in May 1960, a few months before Lynd began teaching at Spelman, a black women's college in Atlanta. Lynd had grilled Aptheker about the early national period of U.S. history, the period that Aptheker was then, coincidentally, writing about in the third volume of his projected multivolume peoples' history of the United States.[13] Since that first meeting, Lynd had resigned from Spelman because the college administrators had fired his friend and the department head, the radical historian Howard Zinn, and in 1964 Lynd had secured a five-year appointment at Yale. The chairman of the History Department there assured "the always-controversial Staughton Lynd . . . that the department would not have asked me to Yale had it not expected to give me tenure."[14]

Lynd had "directed the freedom schools in Mississippi in 1964 . . . [and] was absorbed with the agony of Vietnam and was a major speaker at rallies and teach-ins. . . . [He] compared the Vietnamese to figures being crucified."[15] In his memoir *Reunion,* Tom Hayden, a leading member of the radical activist group Students for a Democratic Society (SDS), wrote that Aptheker's invitation prompted Lynd to worry "about the public image of traveling with a communist but there was no other practical possibility."[16] Lynd accepted Aptheker's invitation. "I would never have gone unless I trusted Herbert Aptheker as a person," Lynd said later. "Note that in this case the trust occurred between a member of the Party and a non-member. I think that Herbert felt that in the last analysis I and anyone I invited would not—at least not knowingly—exploit and betray. And I felt the same about him."[17]

Hayden said Lynd had extracted an agreement from Aptheker that Lynd would choose the third person to travel with them to Vietnam. Lynd alluded to such an agreement, although Aptheker nowhere confirms it. Regardless of who made the decision, the invitation went to "the already legendary leader of the Black revolution in progress," Bob Moses, an organizer with the Student Nonviolent Coordinating Committee (SNCC) who "proposed SNCC's most ambitious project, a massive invasion of Mississippi during the summer of 1964 by northern white student volunteers."[18] Moses visited Aptheker at his office in New York, Aptheker said, and, after a lengthy discussion, he agreed to accompany Aptheker and Lynd. Moses told Aptheker he would join them in Paris after a tour of Europe on which he was about to embark. He said he would be in contact to arrange the details.[19] Aptheker did not hear from Moses again.

Hayden speculated that "Bob couldn't or wouldn't go, perhaps reasoning that it would be too much additional pressure for SNCC to bear."[20] A year before Aptheker made his offer to Moses, Hoover claimed that "communists had infiltrated the civil right movement," and the SNCC leader John Lewis "asserted that such charges merely aided the segregationist opponents of civil rights."[21]

When they did not hear from Moses, Aptheker and Lynd approached Hayden to inquire if he had any interest in traveling with them. Hayden, as the author of the Port Huron Statement, the philosophical foundation of radical student activism, was a major force among New Left student radicals. At this point he was working in the black community of Newark with a group he had helped found, the Economic Research and Action Project. Hayden had misgivings not only about "the smear campaign that would surely be aimed at . . . SDS from the trip" but also about the questions critics would raise, particularly, "Was I an American or a traitor? . . . Being for peace was one thing, but traveling to Hanoi was quite another." Then, too, he found the invitation "almost beyond our understanding. Few, if any of us, had ever traveled outside the United States. Our involvement with the Vietnam issue was confined to reading what we could and bringing several carloads of Newark people to demonstrations in Washington."[22] As Hayden struggled to make his decision about the trip, Aptheker grew agitated at the delay. Lynd "reported . . . that Tom was hesitating; he said further that if Tom did not go he might hesitate himself." Aptheker told Lynd that although the Vietnamese wanted others to accompany him and that he preferred to go with Lynd and Hayden, he would nonetheless go alone if they refused.[23] Hayden finally decided that "the possibility of turning a corner of history outweighed the dangers."[24] He accepted Aptheker's invitation.

They were an unlikely threesome, as Newsweek pointed out in an article titled "Three Characters in Search of an Offer," published in January 1966 after they returned to the United States. The significance of their alliance, however, did not escape the *National Weekly*. "For him," they wrote of Aptheker, "the trip is already a triumph, if only by association. Never have such prominent New Leftists so openly associated themselves in a headline-grabbing affair with an old-guard Communist."[25] "We three—aged 50, 36, 26—represented three different experiences of socialist politics in America," Lynd wrote several months later in the preface to Aptheker's account of their journey, *Mission to Hanoi*. "Just as we spent hours together around tea tables attempting to understand our Vietnamese friends, so we spent other hours around breakfast and supper tables attempting to understand each other. Nor did we merely talk: *we did this thing together*."[26] They had differences, of course, Lynd admitted in a speech honoring Aptheker's fiftieth birthday. "Tom and I plagued Herbert with all the Old Left–New Left questions, and I mean all of them."[27] Aptheker valued the comradery of the two younger men. "It was not possible," he wrote later, "to visit the lands we did without learning; and it was not possible to spend hundreds of hours with those men without learning—in many ways a great deal more. We never hid our differences; on the contrary. But at no single moment in those hundreds of hours was there anything but good-will and, I believe, mutual affection. . . . Our differences were not small but our agreements were overwhelming: We despised the war in Vietnam, we hoped that our journey might make some contribution, however small, to stopping the slaughter, and we planned to give of our energies to that sacred purpose."[28]

The trio set their itinerary to coincide with the Christmas holidays in order to accommodate Lynd's teaching schedule at Yale. Because the State Department banned Americans from traveling to China and North Vietnam (as well as to Albania, Cuba, and North Korea), the three decided to acquire visas from the governments of the various countries through which they would be traveling. The maximum criminal penalty for violating the government ban was a five-thousand-dollar fine, five years' imprisonment or both. By 16 December 1965, their departure only three days away, Lynd had still not received his visa from Czechoslovakia, so Aptheker sent him to the Czechoslovak embassy in Washington with a note to the Czech ambassador, Karel Duda, requesting his assistance in expediting the process. "Once again I find myself imposing upon your good nature and requesting a particular favor. It is urgent," Aptheker wrote to Duda, "that he [Lynd] be provided with a visa for your Republic."[29] On the nineteenth, the FBI, having taken notice twice in December that Aptheker would be traveling to Prague, placed agents at Kennedy Airport in New York to monitor his movements and confirm his departure. They made note of Aptheker's departure but missed Lynd and Hayden altogether. The resultant furor within the government caused by that visit brought Aptheker as close to being arrested and put on trial as he ever came in his fifty-three years as a member of the CPUSA.

Hayden remembered that the three men "careened from plane to plane across the communist world, stopping in Prague, Moscow, and Peking [Beijing], where we were the first American travelers in many years."[30] They had brief discussions at each stop with government representatives. After spending Christmas in Beijing, the men arrived in Hanoi on 28 December 1965, a "country where," Lynd and Hayden wrote, "the Air Force has dropped more tons of destruction than during the whole Korean War."[31] They were met by a dozen representatives of their host group, the Peace Committee. Aptheker recalled that as they "walked off the plane, one of the Vietnamese friends who stayed close to me asked, 'Where is the Negro friend?' I explained the difficulty," Aptheker wrote; "he expressed chagrin."[32] They stayed in North Vietnam for ten days.

Together and separately they walked the streets of Hanoi, learned about Vietnamese cultural and social life through their guides and about Vietnamese history at the Museum of the Revolution, visited factories, spoke with veterans of the war against French colonialism, talked to workers, and had "long conversations with leaders of the Democratic Republic of Vietnam and of the National Liberation Front of South Vietnam."[33] The director at one factory, a veteran of the battle of Dien Bien Phu, which led to the French withdrawal from Vietnam, extolled the heroism of the young American Quaker Norman Morrison. At the entrance to the factory, the director pointed out, workers had "made a large poster" that celebrated Morrison's sacrifice. Morrison, the father of three and a friend of Lynd's, had "doused himself with fuel from a gallon jug" and "burned himself to death within forty feet" of McNamara's office window at the Pentagon in November.[34] The poster showed a man engulfed in flames, under which were the words, "Morrison's flames will never be extinguished."[35]

The three visitors spent most of their time in Hanoi but ventured into the countryside for a brief visit to the city of Nam Dinh, a city of ninety thousand inhabitants about a hundred miles south of Hanoi. "This is the battle-zone," Aptheker wrote in the journal he kept of the visit, "eleven times in the past, U.S. planes have roared across the city dropping bombs and strafing with rockets and machine guns."[36] The mayor of Nam Dinh welcomed them in the bomb-damaged city hall, then escorted them through a nursery school "devastated by bombs and rockets." "But as we moved through the broken bricks under those dark skies," Lynd and Hayden wrote in their memoir of the trip, "viewing the reality of the war for the first time, it was difficult to believe that anything was real: the bombing, the school, the night, our own presence on such forbidden ground."[37] They had planned to stay in Nam Dinh for two days, but on the first night, not long after their arrival, their escorts rushed them back to Hanoi because of a bombing alert.

At a meeting of the secretariat of the Vietnamese Communist Party, to which only Aptheker was invited, Aptheker found the discussion "calm and unhurried," quite unlike meetings of the CPUSA, which he thought were "rather exhausting and prolonged." A translator explained parts of the discussion to Aptheker as the meeting broke up for a "tea-time break of perhaps fifteen minutes when all might be discussed except the meeting's agenda."[38] The party chairman, Prime Minister Pham Van Dong, invited Aptheker to walk with him in an adjoining garden while they discussed matters privately, the first time he or any top Vietnamese official had met with an American. Pham, who began his political career as a student protester against French imperialism, was a founder of the Communist Party of Indochina in 1930. Pham pointed to a barred, ground-level window they passed and noted that he had spent six years in that very room as a political prisoner. "You will face difficulty, perhaps prison, when you return," Pham said, possibly thinking of his own imprisonment. "Perhaps you should stay here." Pham immediately acknowledged the absurdity of his statement, then stated unequivocally, "We will win, of course."[39]

All three of the men wanted to meet with an American prisoner. After lengthy discussions, the Vietnamese army arranged for them to meet with a captured U.S. Air Force pilot who had consented to the interview (the pilot was not identified in any of the written materials describing the meeting). Lynd and Hayden "were tense and doubtful about the propriety of the meeting. . . . Tom feared that decency compelled us to leave the man in peace and not humiliate him further. Staughton thought that there was at least a chance that we could communicate a message from the prisoner to his family."[40] With movie cameras rolling, which heightened the anxiety of all the Americans, Vietnamese army representatives ushered the American trio to their chairs in "a rather large room in which three tables—laden with [cigarettes], nuts, fruit, and tea—had been prepared. All were seated after the Americans had exchanged handshakes" with the prisoner.[41] They talked about sports, the war, the peace movement in the United States, the civil rights movement, and children. "He missed seeing his own grow up," Aptheker said of the captured pilot. "What else was there," Aptheker responded to the prisoner's concern about children, "except seeing kids grow up? All kids?" Aptheker asked. "Yes," the prisoner responded, "with some pause and almost embarrassment, of course, all kids."[42] During their conversation, the prisoner mentioned several times that he knew very little about Vietnam or the Vietnamese and said he had paid little attention to the war or the issues surrounding the war until his capture, which occurred on his first mission. "What a monstrous thing the present U.S. government had done!" Aptheker wrote in his journal: "One sees this in a direct and fearful way when he looks at the bombings. And he sees it in another way—perhaps as fearful—when he looks upon the bombardiers. . . . This was a 'good joe'—a good father, . . . knowing that there were important things that somehow he had never learned, . . . this American—well trained, vast technique at his disposal, affable, plenty of guts—and yet knowing practically nothing. And really with no ill-will in his heart, being sent by Pentagon and plutocracy to devastate a country some 10,000 miles from his home."[43]

The prisoner requested that one of the three Americans contact his wife through her brother. Lynd did so after returning to the United States and discovered that until he made contact, the family had not known whether the pilot was dead or alive.[44]

On 5 January 1966, the day before their departure from Hanoi, Pham met with all three men. "Perhaps it was his historic aura," Hayden wrote, "but he was among the most striking world leaders I have ever seen.... At sixty years, his eyes carried both the sparkle of youth and the depth of age."[45] After exchanging brief pleasantries, during which Pham expressed his preoccupation about the legal difficulties the three Americans might face on their return to the United States, he "rather quickly began talking about the urgent questions facing his—and our—country."[46] "Our greatest passion is for independence," Pham began, "this is not rhetoric, it is reality.... As long as the aggressor remains on our soil we will fight and the peoples of the world—including, I am sure, more and more American people—will support us."[47]

The United States had halted bombing of North Vietnam on 22 December 1965, the "Christmas bombing pause," as McNamara called it.[48] After Christmas, according to McNamara's account, he persuaded a skeptical President Johnson to extend the pause until the end of January 1966. "I stressed my judgment that the possibility of sparking talks that might ultimately lead to peace outweighed the military disadvantages of deferring resumption of the bombing," McNamara wrote in his memoir of the war.[49] The problem was that McNamara and Johnson, employing a Potemkin peace initiative, neglected to let the Vietnamese in on the charade. It's not clear who, but one of the three visitors asked Pham about Johnson's statement of 20 January 1965 that "he would 'knock at any door'" to achieve peace in Vietnam: "Has the United States attempted to make direct contact with the D.R.V. [Democratic Republic of Vietnam]?" "No," came Pham's abrupt reply. "Do you mean," Lynd pressed, "that no D.R.V. ambassador anywhere in the world has been contacted by the United States, as well as that there has been no direct communication with Hanoi?" "In that broader sense of the question," Pham replied, "the answer is still No." "The peace offensive is intended to deceive third parties," Pham said, "but we are not deceived."[50]

Pham requested that Lynd, Hayden, and Aptheker, should they see President Johnson, ask him to "explain exactly how the Democratic Republic of Vietnam is threatening the United States of America.... Johnson is learning that for Americans to fight a war in Asia is to court disaster.... The U.S. government must want peace. Now it does not. That is the heart of the matter. A change must come—but until it comes the problem is not going to be solved. We will fight until it comes and not one second longer."[51] Whether or not Pham's firm declaration that the United States had made no contact with the D.R.V. during the bombing pause was true—a declaration with which the presidential press secretary, Bill Moyers, took issue—"the fact that [Pham] assesses American intentions more by what we do than by what we say," Lynd and Hayden wrote, "means that whether or not the United States sent a note to North Vietnam at Christmastime, and almost regardless of that putative note's contents, no progress was possible toward peace unless the United States war effort was significantly de-escalated."[52] De-escalation was precisely what Johnson had no intention of initiating. "Johnson clearly believed that the pause had been a mistake," McNamara wrote later, "that the bombing had to be resumed."[53] In that belief Johnson had the support of the electorate. A Harris poll released on 31 January 1966 "reported that 'the vast majority of Americans would support an immediate escalation of the war—including all-out bombings of North Vietnam and increasing U.S. troop commitments to 500,000 men.'"[54] Johnson gave the American public what they wanted.

Lynd and Hayden refrained—"Maybe they were wise [to do so], I don't know," Aptheker said years later—but Aptheker agreed to broadcast a message to American troops over Radio Hanoi.[55] The *New York Daily News* quoted Aptheker: "Visiting Hanoi and its surrounding area, one may see for himself the determination of this people to be independent and the calm dedication that everywhere is apparent. . . . The movement of peace in the United States gains strength with every passing day. It is vital to the best interests of my fellow citizens that this atrocious war upon the Vietnamese people be terminated as quickly as possible."[56]

Both Aptheker and Lynd had arranged for release of statements for publication once they had left the United States in December. When news of their actions resulted in numerous newspaper accounts, pressure mounted on the federal government to prosecute the three. On 30 December a headline in the *New York Herald* blared, "3 'New Leftists' May Get Jail for Hanoi Trip," a headline which, had he seen it, surely would have amused the Old Leftist Aptheker.[57] "Three new left figures now in Hanoi on a private peace mission may find themselves in hot water when they return to the U.S. next month," the *Herald* story reported, but "legal sources noted that the government might have difficulty winning a conviction against the three, although two laws apparently prohibit their actions."[58]

On 3 January 1966, while the three men were still in Hanoi, the FBI contacted James Welden, an attorney at the Justice Department, "to determine whether the Department is actively considering prosecution when Aptheker, Lynd and Hayden return to the United States." Welden advised that "the Department is extremely interested in prosecution and has been in contact with the Department of State along this line."[59] To blunt what it perceived as Aptheker's likely coverage by the press, an agent in San Francisco proposed yet another COINTELPRO operation against him. Anticipating that Aptheker would "come to the attention of many people who have never heard of him previously," the agent wanted to send a letter to *Time* magazine that would, he hoped, discredit Aptheker.[60] Five days later, as a story about Aptheker, Lynd, and Hayden appeared in *Time,* Hoover approved the COINTELPRO scheme. Should the letter not appear in *Time,* he wrote, "you are requested to resubmit in reworded form a similar comment which the Bureau will endeavor to cause to be published."[61]

The State Department referred passport violation charges against Aptheker, Lynd, and Hayden to the Justice Department on 5 January 1966. J. Walter Yeagley, the assistant attorney general in the Internal Security Division, requested that the FBI undertake an investigation into the matter on 10 January, the day after the men arrived back in the United States.[62] The next afternoon, as the FBI prepared to begin its investigation, Yeagley called the bureau to order that certain restrictions be put on the investigation. Attorney General Nicholas Katzenbach, who served in both the Kennedy and Johnson administrations, was, said Yeagley, "concerned that the investigation might cause a furor." The *New York Times* had, on 10 January, reported, erroneously, Yeagley told the FBI, that the White House had ordered the Justice Department to refrain "from immediate prosecutive action . . . 'for fear of upsetting its current peace offensive.'" Yeagley ordered the FBI to "restrict [the] investigation to interviewing members of the press media who were known to have been at the airport when Aptheker, Lynd, and Hayden returned to the United States" and to the "customs agents in New York City," whom the FBI had already started interviewing.[63]

In addition to Helen and Robert Lynd, Staughton's parents, Fay, and the usual contingent of FBI agents, a swarm of print reporters and NBC News cameras met Aptheker, Lynd, and Hayden at Kennedy Airport when they arrived from Paris. As the television cameras rolled, Lynd and Hayden each read from a prepared press release that they later distributed to reporters, but when Aptheker stepped up to speak extemporaneously NBC "pulled the plug" on its cameras, an action that made such an impression on Aptheker that he was still miffed about it decades later. "So I was not on television," he told an interviewer in the early 1990s. "[It was] because I was a Communist."[64] According to a reporter questioned by the FBI, Aptheker said that "it was nightmarish that certain United States Senators were calling for the bombing of Hanoi and millions of women and children . . . and stated that President Johnson's policy was bringing death to Americans in Vietnam and devastation to that country, and he desired a reversal of that policy."[65] On the way home Aptheker read a copy of *Newsweek* for 10 January 1966. "It tells me," he wrote, "that BOB HOPE is in Saigon entertaining 10,000 troops with his inimical wit. The magazine says, . . . the soldiers roared and laughed when HOPE called the U.S. bombing raids on North Vietnam the best slum clearance project they ever had."[66]

On 5 January, before leaving Vietnam, and again on the twelfth, Aptheker, Lynd, and Hayden had sent telegrams to the Senate Foreign Relations Committee requesting an opportunity to testify before the committee to relate the positions of the North Vietnamese. Senators wanted nothing to do with any testimony by the three men. Sen. Frank Lausche, Democrat of Ohio and a member of the Foreign Relations Committee, took to the floor of the Senate to condemn them as criminals. He said they should not "be allowed to appear before the . . . committee . . . to give testimony and make arguments in behalf of the Communists of North Vietnam and the Ho Chi Minh Communists of South Vietnam." Rather, he went on, after a "further study of the background of these men," it would be a "grave mistake" to allow them to be "honored with the right to appear before the committee." "It seems to me," he concluded, "that the Attorney General of the United States should give vigorous attention" to their prosecution "in the furtherance of justice."[67] Senator Lausche was joined on the other side of the capitol, in the House, by Rep. O. C. Fisher of Texas. In extending his remarks for the *Congressional Record Appendix,* Fisher opined that the "three culprits, . . . these anti-American emissaries" dishonored "our troops . . . fighting and some dying in a fight against Communist aggressors." These "characters go to Hanoi," Fisher bellowed ominously, invoking the treason statute, "and give aid and comfort to the enemy." Not only were the men culprits, Fisher said, but "these three are obviously mentally, morally, and emotionally immature, they should nevertheless be made to answer for their subversive activities. Being mentally sick is in this instance not a valid excuse. After all," he went on, "who are these crackpots? Aptheker is . . . an enemy of the United States. . . . He revels in bloodletting and anarchy. Of the Negro riot in Los Angeles he was quoted last September as saying: 'of course, Watts was glorious.'" Fisher wrapped up his tirade by saying, "This motley crew are all retarded intellectuals and troublemakers. They should be made to answer for their crimes."[68]

Before Aptheker, Lynd, and Hayden went their separate ways, A. J. Muste, the indefatigable octogenarian peace activist then serving as chairman of the Fifth Avenue Peace Parade Committee, organized a symposium at the Manhattan Center on 16 January for the three men to present what was called an "Eye-Witness Report From Hanoi." Three thousand people attended to hear the activists recount their experiences in Vietnam and detail the views of North Vietnamese officials about how to end the war.[69] "The Geneva agreements of 1954 should be the basis of a negotiated peace," Aptheker said, according to an FBI agent's report. "He said the DRV is seeking to defeat American aggression on their soil" and called "the present war in Vietnam . . . atrocious, immoral and intensely unpopular."[70]

That meeting was the springboard of the decade-long efforts of all three men to press the case for ending the war in Vietnam. While each succeeded to some degree in mobilizing opposition, it took years for the majority of American citizens to turn against the war. "Initially," wrote James W. Clinton in the preface to his book of interviews with people who went to North Vietnam, *The Loyal Opposition,* "I didn't believe that the trips made by these individuals to North Vietnam had any perceptible impact on public opinion at home. Publicity associated with these trips probably reinforced preconceived pubic opinions, such as those that I once held, that their behavior was un-American, traitorous, and a disservice to the United States, particularly to servicemen fighting in Vietnam and the surviving relatives at home of those wounded, injured, or killed because of the war."[71] But, as Clinton later asserted, "The Americans who traveled to North Vietnam also were role models for those beginning to question the morality of the war, the motives of our government, and the human and economic costs incurred by both sides in the conflict."[72] "The implications of Aptheker's critique of U.S. foreign policy have become all the more important with the passing of time," the sociologist Benjamin Bowser wrote. "The most notable Aptheker foreign-policy vindication is that the war in Vietnam was exactly what he called it—unnecessary (1966). If anyone should know (and has now told), it is Robert S. McNamara, the secretary of defense who built up the Vietnam fiasco (1995). If Aptheker was right on Vietnam, he might be right about the Cold War as well."[73]

As a result of the trip, Hayden's opposition to the war deepened. He returned to Hanoi several times, most notably with the actress Jane Fonda, whom he later married. Eventually, perhaps because he needed to create a new image for himself that would attract voters in California when he ran for political office there (he served in the State Assembly in 1982–92 and in the State Senate in 1992–2000), Hayden confessed in his memoir of 1988 that he "was very wrong in certain of my judgments: time has proved me overly romantic about the Vietnamese revolution. The other side of that romanticism was a numbed sensitivity to any anguish or confusion I was causing to U.S. soldiers or to their families— the very people I was trying to save from death and deception."[74]

Lynd returned to Yale. Early press reports of the Vietnam trip usually dismissed Aptheker, after noting his communist affiliation, and focused on the Yale professor. The *Boston Traveler* on 11 January reported on students' reactions to Lynd's trip. "I believe in almost nothing he stands for," one of Lynd's former students said in the story, "but I like him as an individual very much." "I can only hope for a strong student–faculty reaction against this prime example of unjustified civil disobedience," said the senior J. Harvie Wilkinson. Another student who commented, a former chair of the Liberal Party of the Yale Political Union and later secretary of state of the United States, was John F. Kerry, who famously inquired of the Senate Foreign Relations Committee in 1971, "How do you ask a man to be the last man to die for a mistake?" Kerry said then that "while 'admiring Lynd for his personal commitment,' he felt Lynd's trip was 'tragically mistimed' in view of the Johnson Administration's peace offensive." The chair of the History Department at Yale, John Blum, "said Lynd's trip was 'his own business—not a departmental matter.' "[75] According to Lynd, the president of Yale, Kingman Brewster, "was very angry. . . . [He] termed my Christmas journey 'naive and misguided,' condemned a speech I had made in Hanoi for giving 'aid and comfort' to the enemy (a phrase from the law of treason), but implied that the university would take no punitive action."[76] By April Brewster and Blum had evidently changed their minds, and both turned against Lynd. Yale fired him.

Lynd never retreated from his radical politics and practice. He moved to Chicago, took up community organizing, earned a law degree at the University of Chicago, and then relocated to Youngstown, Ohio, where he was active in the battle to keep the city's steel mills open. For years afterward Lynd used his law practice to represent the rights of working people and prisoners and continued to agitate against the imperialist war policies of the United States.

Decades after the fact Aptheker recalled the mission to Hanoi and his two companions with fondness, although he criticized Hayden's revised account of the trip in his memoir.[77] "Overall," Aptheker wrote in his unpublished autobiography, "perhaps this 'Mission to Hanoi' did help a little in inducing Washington, finally, to terminate its atrocious war upon the Vietnamese people. Certainly, I grabbed the opportunity to speak against the war throughout the nation. Because of the notoriety . . . audiences were large, . . . [although] my own outlets were significant but minor compared to the opportunities offered Lynd and Hayden. Still, together we certainly reached millions."[78]

14 "Let My Name Forever Be Enrolled

among the Traitors"

PROPELLED BY the overwhelmingly positive reception he, Lynd, and Hayden received from the audience at the Manhattan Institute and sensing that there was broad public support at the beginning of 1966 for an anti–Vietnam War movement, Aptheker resumed his campus speaking schedule, accepting as many engagements as he could fit into his schedule. In February alone he spoke in New York, Baltimore, Detroit, San Francisco, North Carolina, and Los Angeles. In early February, the day before giving a speech at Wayne State University, Aptheker spoke to a crowd of 750 at the University of Michigan, a speech the *Detroit News* called a "scathing attack on American intervention in Vietnam." The speech prompted a motion in the Michigan State Senate by the Republican state senator Robert J. Huber that called for the Senate "to draft a letter to Wayne President William R. Keast urging him to prevent Aptheker's appearance." Lt. Gov. William G. Milliken cast a tie-breaking no vote to defeat the motion.[1] That day the *News* also reported the death of the 2,005th U.S. soldier in Vietnam.

Although Aptheker crafted his speeches as formal presentations, he didn't tie himself to the text and often extemporized. He was in his element when he was at a podium. Nothing could stop him. When he spoke, his manner was such that one friendly wag "of Protestant heritage" drolly "dubbed him 'the archbishop.'" As he usually did when speaking and writing for the general public, he quoted writers and scholars, most of whom had no connection to the party. He began his speech at the University of Michigan on 10 February 1966 with a brief history of antiwar activism in the United States in order to establish his own place in that tradition. He pointed out that if his criticism of President Johnson and the war in Vietnam made him a traitor, then he was in good company. "If this is treasonous," he said, "it has been indulged in by some strange traitors." In 1848, he told the crowd, Abraham Lincoln criticized President James Polk over the Mexican War. "Of course," he pointed out, that "was an old-fashioned war, it was declared, a declared war." Lincoln said that Polk, "[intended] to escape scrutiny by fixing the public gaze on the exceeding brightness of military glory,

181

that attractive rainbow that rises in showers of blood, that serpent's eye that charms to destroy." Such were the words of Lincoln, Aptheker said, "one of the well known traitors of the 19th century."[2]

Aptheker turned to the war in Vietnam by recounting what he had observed during his trip to Hanoi, then appended a history of American involvement in Vietnam in support of French colonialism from 1946 to 1954 and outlined the Geneva Accords that ended the French occupation of Vietnam. He tied Vietnam's quest for independence to the revolutionary heritage of the United States: "Without independence, it is passionately felt in Vietnam, that any peace can only represent surrender if peace is won without independence. Such a settlement should not be expected by anyone, least of all Americans who live in a country created in a war for independence." Vietnam, Aptheker said, was not waging war on the United States, and the Vietnamese "do not seek the destruction of our cities, let alone the capture of Washington. . . . They are seeking to defeat the American aggression upon their soil. . . . They want American troops not to be in their country." He pointed out that it was the assault on Vietnam by the United States that brought "death and maiming to thousands of Americans and ruin and devastation to Vietnam . . . [and] threatens all social progress and democratic achievement in our country."

Interjecting the issue of race into the question of the Vietnam War more than a year before Martin Luther King's renowned "Beyond Vietnam" speech at Riverside Church in New York and articulating themes similar to King's, Aptheker said, "There is impotence in the face of murder of civil rights workers in the United States and at the same time the capacity to send 200,000 American soldiers 10,000 miles from home to kill peasants and burn villages. . . . Never since the days of chattel slavery has a question of right or wrong been clearer in our country than it is today with the war in Vietnam." He mocked Johnson's assertion of American honor: "[He] speaks of our honor as a nation." "Does it honor our nation to ravage a people who have done us no harm? Does it honor our nation to spread chemical poisons upon the labor of farmers in Asia? . . . Does it honor our nation to hurl phosphorous shells and napalm bombs and beneficent gasses upon the homes and bodies of millions of men, women and children? If to shout to the heavens in denunciation of such honor be treason, please then let my name forever be enrolled among the traitors."[3]

"The war is atrocious, immoral and intensely harmful to our country and to our own every day interest," he said at the end of his speech. "I refuse to admit even the possibility of failure in this great crusade. We will not fail. We will succeed, and in succeeding we will make America a beacon of decency, justice, equality and peace."[4]

The transcript of a recording of the speech made by an FBI informant indicates that Aptheker's quips and self-deprecating remarks prompted a good deal of sympathetic applause during the question-and-answer session. The questions were overwhelmingly friendly, but not all of them were. "I admire your objectivity in your approach tonight and I [wonder] if it would be possible, that you could answer me a personal question," one male student asked. "Why is it that you haven't immigrated to the Soviet Union?" The student's question set off some commotion among the audience, but Aptheker jumped right in: "I mean, I thought that this was a very serious and perfectly straightforward question without bringing insult or injury to me," he said. "I don't know how I gave you the impression that I might want to migrate. When I'm away from here, . . . I'm very unhappy. I miss this country. In fact, I can get terribly schmaltzy about it. . . . I love it here. This is home, where I was born, my kids are here, my wife is here. I love my mother, I love my father," he quipped as the audience laughed. "I don't know how I became a RED," he said, at which point the transcript indicates "laughter and tremendous applause by audience." "I'm not talking about Russia, at all and when we have Socialism here, it will be ours. We'll have it because most American people want it, and want it passionately. Want it so passionately that it can't be held away from us. If that is not true, we'll never have Socialism here. I think it will be true in time and when we have it, it is going to be a beaut. . . . But when we have it, with our technique, our capacity, our energy, our ingenuity, and when we get rid of this festering kind of moral base of Capitalism, . . . it is going to be one hell of a country, you know it. . . . I can taste it. (Applause)."[5]

"What students appreciate in you," his friend Oliver Loud wrote to Aptheker, "—your reasonableness, your respect for their questions, your avoidance of black and white oversimplification and yet the candor and precision of your position, what you concede and what you refuse to concede in argument—is rare enough to be perhaps unrepresentative, in college teaching, in radical politics. . . . Men who do battle cannot be forever patient with those who watch."[6]

On 12 February, the day Aptheker gave his speech at Wayne State, an unidentified detective in the Michigan State Police reported to the FBI that officers had searched Kresage Science Auditorium, the building where the speech was to be given, after "an unidentified person had threatened to bomb the . . . building when Aptheker made his speech."[7] In fact, according to Dean of Student Activities J. Don Marsh, "We had many anonymous calls threatening his life . . . and we could not be responsible for his safety." While some one hundred members of Breakthrough, "a right wing organization," picketed the campus in an attempt to block Aptheker's speech, "more than 75 policemen cordoned off the campus to protect Aptheker and keep a crowd of 2,000 persons under control." Outside the auditorium several hundred students, denied entry because the audience overflowed the room's capacity, protested their exclusion.[8]

Two hours before Aptheker was to appear, the state senate passed a resolution, introduced by Majority Leader Raymond D. Dzendzel, a Democrat from

Detroit, opposing Aptheker's appearance. When William Keast, the president of Wayne State, allowed the speech to continue, Senator Dzendzel threatened consequences. He said he might "push for a provision in this year's university appropriations bill making it illegal to have communists speak on campus." State Attorney General Frank J. Kelly, "who opposed the Senate action, acknowledged his hatred for Communism but his love of free speech."[9]

The university administration had arranged for a campus reception for Aptheker after the speech, but they refused to allow him to attend after the police "told university officials that they could not be responsible for Aptheker's protection if he were allowed to roam at will."[10] Two days later Gov. George Romney of Michigan declared that if authority had rested with him, he would have stopped Aptheker's speech. "He would ban from state university campuses," the *Detroit News* reported, "speakers who directly seek to proselytize for the Communist Party. . . . I'd be inclined," the governor said, "to think that, with his record, his appearance would be for promotion of the Communist Party."[11] That same day editorial writers at the *News* castigated the state senate for trying to prevent Aptheker from speaking: "Aptheker played a cracked old record in his Michigan speeches—bitter opposition to American intervention in Vietnam. We have survived his diatribes before. We will survive his appearances here."[12]

As Aptheker prepared to leave for Hanoi in December 1965, the leaders of the new SDS chapter at the University of North Carolina (UNC) at Chapel Hill, "committed to direct confrontation with UNC authorities," narrowed down a list of speakers who the students felt would be the right choices to help them test a legislative ban on free speech. They settled on two: Frank Wilkinson, "the executive director of the national Committee to Abolish the House Un-American Activities Committee," and the "avowed communist" Herbert Aptheker.

In 1963 the North Carolina legislature passed "An Act to Regulate Visiting Speakers at State Supported Colleges and Universities," legislation that barred the use of college and university facilities to any member of the Communist Party.[13] Conceived by the North Carolina secretary of state, Thad Eure, and Rep. Ned E. Delamar, the law banning speakers was approved in what the historian William J. Billingsley called "one of the most rancorous and vitriolic" sessions of the legislature ever held. "Obsession with the specter of integration informed the varied legislative activities pursued by Assembly conservatives," Billingsley wrote, while many white North Carolinians, both inside and outside the legislature, perceived an inseparable link between Communism and black civil rights. They believed that Communists had infiltrated the colleges and universities and "sparked the Negro demonstrations." The association between Communism and demands for black civil rights "occurred with greater frequency as it became increasingly apparent that segregation, as a means of social organization, was crumbling."[14]

Two years later, in 1965, after numerous demonstrations against the speaker ban by students and faculty, the Southern Association of Schools and Colleges threatened to rescind UNC's accreditation because of the law. Gov. Dan K. Moore convinced the legislature to amend the law in a special session in November. The altered law, which quickly became known as the little speaker ban, put the "authority to regulate speaking engagements by known Communists . . . in the hands of" college and university trustees, a move that satisfied the accreditation association but did nothing to placate radical students and faculty, who thought that any ability to ban speakers compromised the intellectual and academic freedom of the university.[15]

UNC was not a hotbed of radical activism. "Despite its vaunted reputation for liberalism," the UNC campus "was mired in apathy and evinced an animosity toward any sustained critique of established authority, particularly picketing and public protest." When the SDS leaders Jim McCorkel and Chuck Schunior organized a protest against the war in October 1965, they were "vilified and Red-baited . . . [as] the most disrespected element on this campus."[16] Nonetheless, the SDS leaders sent an invitation to Aptheker in early January asking him to help them test the little speaker ban. Aptheker, who had spoken at UNC in 1950 on the topic "the roots of Negro oppression," readily agreed to speak.

"Beginning in January 1966," wrote Bob Joyce in the *Carolina Alumni Review* in spring 1984, SDS "led the University through a whirlwind three months that set the path for the destruction of the ban."[17] During the original legislative debate, proponents of the speaker ban "had singled Aptheker out as precisely the kind of speaker that should be barred from the public campuses." By January 1966 Aptheker was "already something of a cause célèbre" because of his actions in opposing speaker bans in other states. The virulence unleashed by the news of his trip to North Vietnam with Lynd and Hayden stoked the uproar when newspapers in the state reported the SDS's invitation at the end of January.[18] The General Assembly denounced the invitation and demanded that President William C. Friday block Aptheker's appearance at UNC. Privately, Friday opposed the speaker ban, but he "was alarmed and shaken" by the "indirect inference" in letters he received from legislators "that the legislature might impede or reduce its biennial appropriation to the university" if the speech went ahead.[19] On 10 February Governor Moore, an ex-officio member of the university trustees' thirteen-member Executive Committee, issued an official statement condemning the invitation, "despite warnings from faculty leaders that the ban could touch off faculty resignations and cause 'irreparable harm' to the university."[20] "Aptheker should be banned," Moore said, "because he 'is an avowed American Communist who has just returned from a visit to North Vietnam where he gave support and encouragement to the Communists there who are killing our American servicemen every day.' "[21] The next day the FBI sent twenty-five copies of the anti-Aptheker FBI pamphlet to the Charlotte Division to disseminate "in instances where effective use of the pamphlet may be anticipated."[22]

SDS leaders began a grass-roots organizing campaign by visiting every residence hall to "explain why the law had to be opposed." By early February, so overwhelmingly had student opinion crystalized in support of the Aptheker invitation that the president of the student government, Paul Dickson, an initial supporter of the speaker ban, announced at a press conference that "it was the 'unequivocal position' of the 'overwhelming majority' of the student body that Aptheker should speak." Dickson convinced the student government to sign on as cosponsors of the event.[23]

After monthlong wrangling among all the parties, the UNC acting chancellor J. Carlyle Sitterson announced on 4 March that the ban would hold. If Aptheker spoke on campus he would be arrested. On 6 March the controversy escalated when "the Carolina Forum, a student-run campus organization . . . announced that Robert Welch of the John Birch Society would be appearing on March 13." Because Welch, a UNC graduate, was not a communist, his invitation did not prompt the chancellor to invoke the speaker ban. "The invitation demonstrated the capricious and discriminatory nature of the speaker policy," Billingsly wrote. "A right-wing extremist was welcome at Chapel Hill, while anyone from the Left might be banned at the chancellor's whim."[24]

"The climax of the speaker ban crisis at Chapel Hill" occurred on 9 March 1966, "the final act of the atavistic drama that was the speaker ban," when Aptheker played his assigned role. "Aptheker had come to symbolize the kind of speaker that supporters of the law desired to ban from the public campuses." In the eyes of many citizens of North Carolina, Hoover was right: Aptheker was the most dangerous communist in the United States. "Aptheker not only was a member of the national committee of the CPUSA but also advocated the kind of black assertiveness that many white North Carolinians found threatening," Billingsly concluded. "The announced title of his planned address, 'The Negro Movement—Reform or Revolution?' could scarcely assuage the anger of UNC critics."[25]

Aptheker recalled being greeted at Chapel Hill by a national television network crew.[26] Dickson and SDS leaders accompanied him onto the campus, where two thousand students awaited him.[27] They arrived at McCorkle Place, "a spacious area . . . adorned by ancient oak trees and statuary commemorating hallowed UNC figures." Since the SDS leaders had announced their intention to bring suit if the university denied Aptheker the right to speak, they had to establish grounds for legal action, which required that Aptheker "be led onto the campus and then compelled to leave by university authorities."[28] Aptheker mounted "the base of a prominent statue of a Confederate rifleman in McCorkle Place," but before he could begin his speech the campus police chief Arthur

Beaumont interrupted. He told Dickson that if Aptheker spoke he would be breaking the law. "The chief of police also threatened to have Dickson charged with violation of UNC's honor code if Aptheker attempted to speak."[29] "I argued with him," Aptheker recalled, "an argument reaching I do not know how many via ABC, but in vain."[30] "'Can I explain this to the students?' Aptheker asked. 'If you speak you'll be breaking the law,' Mr. Beaumont said."[31] "I thought I had my rights as a citizen of the United States," Billingsley and the *New York Times* report Aptheker as saying. "'You do,' answered Beaumont. 'You have a right to obey the law.'" Dickson, acting on a prior agreement with President Friday, began to move Aptheker away from campus to avoid the spectacle of Aptheker's arrest. "Aptheker himself, for political reasons, was willing to challenge the ban and invite arrest . . . [but] not wanting to upstage the students . . . he quietly followed Dickson . . . to Franklin Street."[32] The UNC campus ended at a low stone wall on Franklin Street that students had christened Gov. Dan K. Moore's (Chapel Hill) Wall the previous week, "suggesting an obvious parallel with the Berlin Wall."[33] Standing on the sidewalk on Franklin Street, with two thousand students listening on the other side of the wall, Aptheker spoke briefly. He called the campus policy "medieval and absurd . . . [and] contended that the trustees and chief of police were violating the law by abrogating the Bill of Rights."[34] "When he finished speaking," reported the *New York Times,* "the students . . . applauded him for about one minute."[35]

Later that evening Aptheker delivered his anti–Vietnam War speech "to a standing-room-only crowd at Chapel Hill's Community Church." The SDS vice chairman Gary Waller introduced Aptheker, noting, "It is ironic that a few centuries ago, the universities had to free themselves from repressive church control. Now, we are refugees from a repressive university."[36]

Dickson carried through on his promise to sue the university. The suit, *Dickson v. Sitterson,* came before a three-judge panel on 21 February 1967, a year after Aptheker's speech. "Two of the most respected constitutional lawyers in the country," William Van Alstyne of Duke University and Danial Pollitt of UNC, represented Dickson. Deputy Attorney General Ralph Moody, a staunch anticommunist and segregationist, represented North Carolina.[37] One of the three judges, Edwin M. Stanley, owed his political position to "his zealous participation in North Carolina's most memorable McCarthy-era moment: the Smith Act trial of Junius Scales," Aptheker's estranged ex-comrade, in 1955. Stanley "had inveighed against the presence of Aptheker" in the courtroom during Scales's trial and dared "the defense to call the CP figure as a witness. Now, more than a decade later, Stanley was presiding over a trial in which the state asked the court to validate its denial of Aptheker's right to speak."[38]

On 19 February 1968 the judicial panel declared the speaker ban law null and void. Even while declaring the law unconstitutional, the judges "clearly and unequivocally endorsed the cause of anticommunism." If the law's purpose was restricting speakers who afforded students nothing of educational value, the judges reasoned, "one does not acquire an understanding of important racial problems by listening successively to a Stokeley [*sic*] Carmichael or an H. Rap Brown and an officer of the Ku Klux Klan. Countering a Herbert Aptheker with an official of the American Nazi Party may furnish excitement for young people, but it presents no rational alternatives and has but dubious value as an educational experience."[39] The trustees at UNC adopted a new speaker policy in May 1968, one that echoed the language of the voided law but did not include explicit anticommunist language.

A major unintended consequence of the controversy at UNC was the establishment of the political bona fides of Jesse Helms, a reactionary racist editorialist at the Raleigh television station WRAL. Throughout the contentious period of the speaker ban and, indeed, since 1949, when he first began a campaign of vilification against liberals at UNC, Helms ran slashing commentaries against students and university officials alike. He propelled himself into a seat in the U.S. Senate through his adroit manipulation of the battle over the ban at UNC. Nonetheless, Aptheker was instrumental at UNC, just as he was at Binghamton and Columbus and Wayne State and Berkeley, in helping to shatter prohibitions of radical speakers. "Professor Aptheker's visit to UNC played a critical role in the undoing of the speaker ban," wrote Gregg L. Michel in the *Journal of American History* in December 2001. "His travel to Chapel Hill, and his remarks to students from the campus' fringe, constituted a victory for free speech."[40]

In early March 1966 the Justice Department contacted the State Department and the CIA requesting that the agencies inquire among their operatives in "Peking or Hanoi" whether anyone had observed Aptheker, Lynd, and Hayden when they traveled abroad. The Justice Department wanted to prosecute all three men, but "the proof of their specific intent to" travel to Vietnam and China "at the time they left the United States remains the big problem."[41] Agitated by letters he received that criticized the FBI for failing to do its job, Hoover pressured his agents to close the case. Hoover's staff believed that the Justice Department seemed to be losing its appetite for prosecution. "It appears," one agent wrote, "that the Department of Justice is, in fact, 'shying away from this case' since Aptheker, Lynd, and Hayden have claimed that they were merely following the policy of the Administration to 'knock on any door' in an effort to settle the Vietnam situation." Instead of prosecuting, the Justice Department "is continuing to request additional investigation, much of which is 'farfetched.'"[42] While the FBI wanted the three men in jail, the Justice Department quietly decided to drop the investigation, although they toyed with prosecuting Aptheker under the Selective Service Act.

His opposition to the war and the obligation he felt toward the people he met in North Vietnam drove Aptheker to accept as many speaking engagements as possible. He appeared at Queens College in Flushing, Queens, two days after the UNC spectacle, and followed that lecture closely with engagements at Boston University, Brandeis, and, on 21 March, Bryn Mawr College. He spoke to nine hundred students at the University of Wisconsin later in March, and thirteen hundred people attended his lecture titled "The Negro in American History" at Harpur College in Vestal, New York, on the thirtieth.[43]

Twelve hundred students and faculty gathered to hear his antiwar speech at the University of Miami (UM) in Coral Gables, Florida, on 20 April. The *Miami News,* which had announced that Aptheker would speak at UM on 1 April, reported on an "anonymous circular" that arrived at their offices and other places around the city. It read, "Welcome Communism to the Univ. of Miami."[44] The reporter Louise Blanchard said the circular "appeared to be a protest against" Aptheker's appearance. "At first glance," she wrote, "it was designed to give the impression it was from the university . . . [but] a spokesman for the university said the announcement 'did not originate from the University of Miami, and we have no idea of the source.'" The UM spokesman thought the circular unfortunate and criticized its authors as being "rather cowardly" for not signing their names. The UM president, Henry King Stanford, assured citizens that students there were prowar. "The present student leaders 'are the same ones who were invited to the White House this spring and commended by the President for demonstrating their support for our country's policy in Viet Nam . . . I do not doubt the loyalty of our students,'" the president said, "'nor their ability to take apart the arguments of a Communist.'" Unlike his counterpart at UNC, however, President Stanford, who received numerous written protests demanding that Aptheker's speech be canceled, affirmed his adherence to academic freedom: "I am confident . . . that our students' minds will be toughened, not weakened, by this exposure and that the university will be stronger for having made it possible for ideas to be expressed, no matter how much we as loyal Americans may detest them."[45]

After two weeks of what the *Miami Herald* called a "community embroiled in controversy" over his appearance, Aptheker spoke to an overflow crowd in the union cafeteria. Two hundred or more students "were left outside," where "an elderly woman passed out American flags" and another person handed out circulars titled "Red Scum to Speak on Campus." The president of the student government, Thomas R. Spencer, introduced Aptheker, whose topic for the evening was "the American Negro movement." Spencer warned the audience that the speaker's views "might be repugnant to some people." As he began his remarks, Aptheker said, "It's interesting . . . that the young man describes my views as repugnant before I've had a chance to express my views." Notwithstanding President Stanford's contention in an interview given before the speech that "I do not doubt [the students'] ability to take apart the spurious arguments of a Communist," the best Aptheker's opponents in the audience could do was to assent when one young man shouted, "Traitor" and another "called out repeatedly 'liar, liar.'" The *Miami Herald* reported that the large crowd "listened courteously to Aptheker, with neither ovations nor widespread jeering." After the speech, two young men hanged Aptheker in effigy in front of the university. That gesture, wrote the reporters Matt Taylor and Jerry Parker, "was the most noteworthy sign of protest to develop over the speech."[46]

In May, at Indiana University in Bloomington, Aptheker spoke to a group of faculty and students at the invitation of the campus W. E. B. Du Bois Club and the Young Peoples Socialist League, a meeting that drew the ire of U.S. Rep. Richard L. Roudebush. "I had hoped I.U. officials had the backbone to tell these Communists the people of Indiana are not going to finance the forum to spread Communist poison on our university campuses," Roudebush said at a campaign appearance.[47] The FBI reported that 440 people attended the event.[48]

And so Aptheker's schedule went for the rest of 1966, then 1967, and on into the tumultuous cauldron that was 1968, as he crisscrossed the country again and again and antiwar sentiment gradually overcame the misguided policies of McNamara and Johnson: 525 people showed up here, 1,000 there, 25 at the next place, 90 at another. The size of the audience didn't matter to Aptheker. What mattered was getting the message out. "We who oppose this war must persist, must organize, must cry out, must never despair—in this crusade we dare not consider the possibility of failure," he said in Boston at a debate with I. Milton Sacks of Brandeis University. "In this crusade we must and will win."[49]

In February 1966 Aptheker met with Hall to discuss ways of generating publicity for the antiwar effort. It is uncertain who called the meeting, but later that month Hall held a press conference at party headquarters outlining the organization's desire to participate in an effort to build left-wing unity to oppose the war. He told the *New York Times* and other papers that the party was considering having Aptheker run for Congress in the 12th Congressional District, in Brooklyn, where Aptheker lived.[50] The party had not run candidates in political races for more than a decade, so over the next two months Aptheker and Hall worked to overcome the skepticism expressed by some members after Hall's press conference. In conversations with comrades Aptheker urged that any campaign he might run be seen not as that of a candidate of the party but as that of a party member running on a "platform seeking peace and combating racism[,] having non-Party people in association[,] and choosing a neutral name."[51]

On 16 May, confident now that the lingering ambivalence within the party could be overcome, Aptheker announced his candidacy at a press conference at the New Yorker Hotel. Aptheker announced to the several reporters and at least one FBI agent who attended that he was running for Congress, the sole candidate on the Peace and Freedom ticket. The FBI noted that Aptheker "stated that he would run on an independent Peace and Freedom ticket since he felt that running on a Communist ticket would hurt his chances of winning."[52] Gil Green, a CPUSA leader and writer who went underground in the fifties, wrote that the decision to run Aptheker on a Peace and Freedom ticket was a conscious effort to place Aptheker's candidacy within "a new trend toward peace candidates and toward independent political action."[53] The FBI also remarked that Aptheker said the party had pledged its "full support . . . except for funds. He expected Party members to donate money for his campaign."[54]

The FBI almost immediately began planning a COINTELPRO action against Aptheker's campaign. On 20 May an agent requested permission to use a fictitious name to call Rep. Edna Kelly, the longtime Democrat who held the seat in Brooklyn's 12th District from 1949 to 1969, and propose that she take advice on running against Aptheker from a knowledgeable source, namely, an FBI informant, a fact they would not reveal to the congresswoman.[55] Hoover authorized the call but cautioned agents to assign "a mature and experienced Special Agent" to make the call to a member of Kelly's staff.[56] All of the strategizing was preempted by Kelly herself when she contacted the FBI instead. She told agents in New York that her opponent "was Herbert Aptheker, a communist functionary." Kelly "had received information indicating that Aptheker's associates in the CP would possibly cause disturbances at the polls on election day."[57] They didn't.

The campaign was required to gather three thousand signatures to get Aptheker on the ballot. The process was onerous: "Any error in fact, in spelling, . . . the slightest technical error . . . [could] invalidate all the signatures on the sheet."[58] To overcome any possible invalidations, the campaign decided to get at least three times the required number of signatures. Herbert and Fay, students from Brooklyn College, a few members of the party, and volunteers led by the young campaign manager Blyden Jackson, a noncommunist who showed up at party headquarters to donate his time—all fanned out across the sprawling 12th District to gather signatures. By the end of the six-week period allotted by law for signing people up, the campaign turned in a list of 10,128 names to elections officials. Aptheker recruited campaign sponsors from his contacts around the country. The historians Phillip Foner and Eugene Genovese signed on, as did Lynd and Hayden, Annette Rubinstein, Green, Sidney Gluck, and Sidney Finkelstein. A. J. Muste, a tireless advocate for world peace and friend and mentor to Martin Luther King Jr., departed from his usual practice of keeping "aloof from electoral campaigns" and endorsed Aptheker. In his statement Muste pointed out that he and Aptheker did not agree on all issues, but, he said, "I share his radical stand against the Vietnam war and commend his devotion to the civil rights struggle. It is the one issue of having his name on the ballot which is decisive for me at this point and should be in my opinion for large numbers of Americans at this moment in our history."[59] The six-time Socialist Party candidate for president Norman Thomas, in a convoluted but nonetheless meaningful endorsement, said, "Of course, I support the right to sign Dr. Aptheker's petition and, since he is making a campaign against the war, I hope those petitions will be signed. I am for a candidate getting on the ballot whether or not he is of my persuasion."[60] In early June the National Coordinating Committee to End the War in Vietnam, a clearinghouse for antiwar activities across the country, with headquarters in Madison, Wisconsin, also endorsed Aptheker.[61]

Aptheker spoke "at small coffee clotches [sic] and house parties, to larger more formal meetings and symposiums, and to scores of open air rallies. He canvassed for signatures and talked to people on street corners, subway stations, shopping centers and in their homes. He appeared at two public hearings. He appeared at affairs outside his district for fund raising purposes."[62] The campaign opened two headquarters, one in Borough Park, where Aptheker had been born and grew up, and one in Bedford-Stuyvesant, a black ghetto about seven blocks from the home at 32 Ludlam Place that Herbert and Fay had purchased. "The support given this campaign," Aptheker wrote, "startled me. Money came in in satisfying quantity."[63] Green wrote in an article in *Political Affairs* in January 1967 that "in response to solicitations by mail and ads in papers, contributions began to come in from all areas of the nation. People responded to Aptheker as a man they admired and trusted."[64]

Whether Green knew the full details about how Aptheker raised funds for the campaign is not known, but Aptheker certainly did, and his comments in regard to campaign funding are, at the least, not altogether forthcoming—that is, if the FBI is to be believed. In this case, belief seems reasonable. In an FBI summary dated 16 November 1966—a document that digests Aptheker's activities between 28 September and 8 November, election day—an informant notified the FBI that, acting on instructions from Hall, he gave Hall $30,000 "for Communist Party USA, party work and for expenses incidental to the election campaign of Herbert Aptheker." The report does not say how much money went to Aptheker's campaign, although later in the report another unidentified informant substantiated the bureau's suspicion that at a meeting of the CP New York State Committee held on 9 July, a party leader stated that "the Communist Party was willing to spend $20,000 on Aptheker's campaign."[65] Hall "told Morris Childs, a leading member of the CP, USA that he was in need of substantial funds, the primary need arising from expenses of Herbert Aptheker's election campaign. Therefore, on 10/27/66, Gus Hall was furnished a total of $17,787 from CP, USA Reserve Funds by Morris Childs."[66]

The FBI documents leave several questions unanswered. That Hall received the money seems beyond doubt. But did he give Aptheker money for campaign expenses? was he asking for reimbursement for funds the party had already expended? or did he use the money for other purposes? As the historians Harvey Klehr, John Earl Haynes, and Kyrill M. Anderson elucidate in their book *The Soviet World of American Communism,* Childs and his brother Jack were for years "couriers, transferring Soviet funds to the CPUSA. Secretly, however, they were U.S. government agents," recruited by the FBI in the early 1950s. "Between 1958 and 1980," Klehr et al. wrote, "they [Morris and Jack Childs] delivered more than $28 million in Soviet subsidies to the CPUSA, reporting the while to the FBI."[67] The origin and delivery of that money were a secret closely held among a few very top leaders of the party (and government agencies) and allowed Hall to enjoy a lavish lifestyle behind the backs of party members. Aptheker maintained, after the breakup of the party in 1991, when he resigned, that he had never known about the Soviet Union's funding of the CPUSA. But he apparently received money from the party to help finance his campaign for Congress. In 1987 President Ronald Reagan awarded the Childs brothers the Presidential Medal of Freedom, making them the only spies to be decorated by the Soviet Union and the United States alike.

The FBI tracked Aptheker's campaign appearances and planted informers in both of his campaign offices to furnish their FBI overseers with the names of anyone who worked on the campaign. Agents took note of Aptheker's defeat at the polls by quoting a *New York Times* story of 10 November that recorded the final tally for the election: 2,876 votes for Aptheker; 115,348 for Congresswoman Kelly.[68] The same day the *Times* story appeared Aptheker completed a memo for Green detailing the successes and failures of the campaign. He complained that the party had been ineffective in its campaign work and furthermore had not taken "the effort SERIOUSLY." More important, he found, there was "great fear, especially in the outfit." "Fear of meeting and talking with the people, . . . [a] lack of confidence widespread."[69] "Many Party members feared 'exposure,' " Green wrote in *Political Affairs* for January 1967, " . . . some were reluctant to go out and speak to new people in behalf of a peace and freedom candidate who was a Communist. At one point, Aptheker ruefully remarked that if he were not a Communist, some Communists would be giving him greater support."[70]

About a week before the election someone set fire to Aptheker's Bedford-Stuyvesant campaign headquarters. The flames narrowly missed incinerating the occupants of the apartment above. Two days before the election, police in the Bronx staged a series of spectacular arrests of nineteen members of the Minutemen, an extremist right-wing group founded by Robert DePugh in the early 1960s. Organized in secret cells of five to fifteen members, the Minutemen stockpiled weapons and trained together to defend the country against what they deemed to be subversives. The police revealed that the men had planned to kill Aptheker and destroy three camps run by leftist groups. The raids led to the confiscation of "the biggest haul of weapons and death-dealing materials seized in this area in the memory of veteran law-enforcement officers."[71] The Bronx district attorney eventually dropped the charges against the Minutemen because the police had failed to obtain valid search warrants.

Seven months later, on 15 June 1967, a homemade pipe bomb exploded on the roof of the Allerton Community and Social Club in the Bronx, and in August the police arrested four men in connection with the explosion. The authorities seized "45 rifles, 7 shotguns, 18 sticks of dynamite, 1 antitank gun, 1 submachine gun of the type now used in Vietnam, 3 hand grenades, 1 machete, 12 hunting knives and more that a quarter-million rounds of ammunition," altogether worth more than thirty thousand dollars.[72] District Attorney Isidore Dollinger of the Bronx said the four men had rigged the device to explode during a speech by Aptheker two days prior to the actual explosion, but "police experts . . . determined that the bomb . . . had been made ineptly."[73] Dollinger charged only three of the plotters. After their conviction, Judge Arthur Markevich suspended the sentences of two of the men. He called the group's leader, Peter Psyras, who owned two restaurants in Manhattan, "nothing but a punk," compared his activities "with those of the early Nazi conspirators," and sentenced him to two years in jail.[74] How these maladroit terrorists obtained the money to buy their arsenal was never disclosed.

15   Aptheker and Du Bois

W. E. B. Du Bois died in his sleep the night of 28 August 1963 in Ghana. In Washington, D.C., wrote David Levering Lewis in his exhaustive biography *W. E. B. Du Bois: The Fight for Equality and the American Century, 1919–1963,* "250,000 of his countrymen and women began assembling along the great reflecting pool in front of the Lincoln Memorial" for the March on Washington.[1] Later that day the NAACP leader Roy Wilkins informed the gathering of Du Bois's death: "Remember that this has been a long fight. We were reminded of it by the news of the death yesterday in Africa of Dr. W. E. B. Du Bois. Now, regardless of the fact that in his later years Dr. Du Bois chose another path, it is incontrovertible that at the dawn of the twentieth century his was the voice that was calling to you to gather here today in this cause."[2]

On 1 September Aptheker, who had just returned to the United States from Europe, wrote a brief, hastily scribbled note to Du Bois's wife, Shirley: "In this century no one surpassed him. Our warmest love to you at this time of great sorrow and deep pride."[3] Graham Du Bois's letter of 2 September to Aptheker described the death of her husband and its aftermath: "My darling was given a State Burial every honor . . . accorded a Head of State. He lies now in the Castle gardens close beside the sea from which his great-great-grandfather was carried away into slavery. . . . He knew all about the Mark [march] on Washington and was the source of inspiration for the March on the U.S. Embassy here by Afro-Americans and Ghanaians which began one hour after his death. . . . This Accra March turned out to be much more militant than the Washington one."[4]

In Ghana on the day of Du Bois's death, Aptheker later wrote, "at the Doctor's State Funeral, with President [Kwame] Nkrumah of Ghana in personal attendance, the only Embassy in Ghana which was not represented—in an unprecedented insult to the African Republic—was that of the United States and . . . while all Embassies on that day flew their flags at half-mast, the Embassy of the United States did not do so. America's pariah was Africa's glory."[5] "He died in exile," Martin Luther King Jr. said, "praised sparingly and in many circles ignored . . . he was ignored by a pathetically ignorant America but not by history."[6] That history did not ignore Du Bois is, to a remarkable degree, Aptheker's fulfillment of a trust placed in him by Du Bois.

In mid-1946, as noted earlier, Aptheker, working on a Guggenheim Fellowship, agreed to help Du Bois find a publisher for his letters and other unpublished work. Aptheker regularly kept Du Bois apprised of his progress. "Let me take this opportunity to assure you that though the need to earn something approximating a livelihood has made it impossible for me recently to actively work on your letters and papers," he wrote in July 1947, "I have continued to seek financial support for that project. I am now in correspondence with Little Brown & Co. concerning this, and will keep at it until it is done."[7] Little Brown rejected the project, which prompted Aptheker to write an acerbic missive to Du Bois the next month. Noting the Little Brown rejection and his continuing correspondence with Rutgers University, Aptheker promised to send Du Bois "a detailed account of their rejection, too—pardon the bitterness. As you were good enough to remark to me at one time—I'm just beginning—and bitterness ill becomes a novice."[8] Du Bois responded with words of encouragement and made some suggestions: "What you have got to do in approaching your publishers is to let them know that you are quite aware of what their natural reaction is going to be, but that it is time for them to reappraise the situation and make some venture," he wrote. "Of course even with this argument, you are going to have a hard time to find anybody who will finance the book which you have in mind. . . . I hope you will keep trying."[9]

By 1948 "Aptheker had become indispensable to Du Bois . . . the bond familial and Du Bois would become like a grandfather to the Apthekers' precocious daughter, Bettina," Levering Lewis wrote in the second volume of his biography. "I loved Du Bois personally," Bettina wrote in her memoir, *Intimate Politics*. "I had known him all of my life. He always treated me with respect, answering my questions fully, focusing his attention on me. . . . He was affectionate, warm, funny, and very gentle. He seemed to have so much joy about him, and so much delight in life."[10] Shirley recalled that Aptheker "was not only a close friend of long standing but had proven himself a research scholar of the first order. Du Bois considered his lengthy *Documentary History of the Negro People in the United States* a work seldom equaled and certainly not excelled by any historian. And he trusted both the sincerity and the integrity of the younger man."[11]

Like Du Bois, Shirley trusted Aptheker implicitly: "In the final analysis I trust only *one white American*," she wrote of Aptheker. "White America has forced me to this position. White America will have to change before I change that decision."[12] The historian Gerald Horne wrote in his biography of Graham Du Bois that her emphatic statement in that letter "may have been referring to Herbert Aptheker"; there can be no doubt, in the context of the letter, to whom she was referring.[13]

When Aptheker published *History and Reality* (1955), a collection of his polemical essays on conservatism, liberals, reactionary American ideology, and class justice, Du Bois wrote a long note praising Aptheker, whom he now addressed as "Dear Aptheker" rather than with the more formal "Mr. Aptheker" that had characterized his earlier correspondence. "I want to thank you most sincerely for this scholarly and inspiring work," Du Bois began. "For one who like myself has spent so much of his life immersed in a small part of the vast field of the social problems, and depending on the press for a general knowledge of the world, it is easy, . . . to get an unreal story of what is happening outside his specialty." Du Bois mentioned several items of which he was ignorant, then wrote, "It is a bit frightening for one who considers himself as fairly intelligent to realize how much of the present he does not know and does not know that he does not know."[14]

Du Bois found the introductory chapter of *History and Reality* to be "of the first importance. I have read it twice."[15] In that chapter Aptheker developed what was for him the meaning of Marx's concept of historical materialism and causation in history by comparing that method of analysis to the writings of historians then current, especially Charles Beard and Arthur Schlesinger Jr. Schlesinger held, according to Aptheker, that "most important problems [are] insoluble," a position Aptheker compared to William James's pragmatism, "that philosophy of no philosophy."[16] The notion that problems were insoluble was anathema to Aptheker: "Marxists hold, then, that it is the productive activities and the experiences of the human beings responsible for those activities, that form the body of history, that constitute a history of people. They hold, also," he continued, "that the societal relationships of those human beings, particularly in terms of their condition relative to productive forces—that is, their class position—play a key role in the acting out of the drama of history." Marxists sought to understand the means of production "to understand the modes of ownership and control of these means," the class relationships, "which give rise to conflicts." The Marxist sees, then, "the resolution of those particular conflicts arising as a result of the smashing of the productive restrictions inherent in each of those modes [of production] . . . and he believes that the present conflict differs decisively, qualitatively, from all others because its resolution, . . . makes possible the elimination of class conflicts by expropriating the exploiters, by bringing into being a society consisting entirely of producers." That revolutionary change, Aptheker concluded, "will inaugurate the human epoch of history, the epoch free from man's exploitation of man, the epoch making possible the full, uninhibited and unimpeded development of mankind."[17]

"I think in general I agree with your conclusions and criticism," Du Bois wrote, commenting on that first chapter. He remarked that he had "for two years . . . studied under William James while he was developing Pragmatism. . . . The Jamesian Pragmatism as I understood it from his lips was not based on the 'usefulness' of a hypothesis, as you put it, but on its workable logic if its truth was assumed." Du Bois told Aptheker that he "assumed that human beings could alter and re-direct the course of events so as to better human conditions. I knew that this power was limited by environment, inheritance and natural law, and that from the point of view of science these occurrences must be a matter of Chance and not of Law." He didn't "rule out the possibility of some God also influencing and directing human action and natural law. However I saw no evidence of such divine guidance. I did see evidence of the decisive action of human beings."[18] Aptheker thanked Du Bois for his generosity in a letter several days later: "To have received from you—one of my revered teachers ever since I can remember thinking at all—a 'well done' is the greatest possible kind of gratification. . . . So much more work and thought must be given to these exceedingly knotty questions—especially those of the role of chance, and also, of the nature of progress. What an exhilarating thing is the search for knowledge and for comprehension. And how inspiring to us . . . to have the example of your own dedicated and fruitful and persistent search!"[19]

Several years later Du Bois sent a note to Aptheker, enclosing his response to a questionnaire the *American Scholar* had sent him. "*The American Scholar* has asked me to write one hundred words about the book which has most attracted me in the last thirty years. I am sending them the enclosed note," which read as follows:

> *A History of the American People,* in Three Volumes, By Herbert Aptheker. This work attracted me because it is the only history I know which treats the black man as an integral part of the nation rather than as an outside appendage. . . . For two centuries their unpaid labor was the foundation of American capitalism and formed the wealth of Southern planters and Northern merchants. . . . They contributed to American culture and literature. Failure to free them after the first Revolution led to a second Revolution eighty years after, which was a bloody Civil War. What other history tells this tale?[20]

The *American Scholar* did not publish Du Bois's statement.

Shortly after the federal government indicted him in February 1951, Du Bois and Shirley Graham hastily wed. The day after the wedding the couple flew to Washington, where agents of the Justice Department arrested, handcuffed, and fingerprinted the eighty-three-year-old Dubois. The government tried the eminent scholar and activist for failing to register as an agent of a foreign power. At the conclusion of the government's case the judge dismissed the charges against him. Radicals of all stripes rose to Du Bois's defense, but, as Levering Lewis notes, Du Bois "perceived a reaction to his situation that revealed a sharpening class division. His own Talented Tenth hesitated, cogitated, and then decided in the main to keep a safe distance—notwithstanding notable exceptions."[21] However, eventually there was support "from the Negroes of the nation," Du Bois wrote, "that swelled in astonishing volume as the trial neared."[22]

After the acquittal, agents of the federal government laid siege to Du Bois, harassed his friends and neighbors, opened his mail. While establishment black leaders in the civil rights movement pulled away from him, "[playing] out the hand dealt it by the national security state—uncritical patriotism in return for incremental race-relations progress," the Apthekers, among others, including figures who maintained their ties to the Communist Party and paid for their heresy with their freedom, drew closer as the inner circle around Du Bois dwindled.[23] During the years of government harassment, "the supportive presence of Shirley Graham was of course most important" in sustaining Du Bois, and "the friendship of Marxist historian Herbert Aptheker was also of particular importance to Du Bois."[24] "It was a bitter experience," Du Bois wrote, "and I bowed before the storm. But I did not break."[25]

On 15 February 1961 President Nkrumah notified Du Bois that the Ghana Academy of Learning had endorsed and voted financing for Du Bois's longtime dream, first enunciated at the beginning of the twentieth century, of compiling an *Encyclopedia Africana*.[26] The Du Boises immediately started making plans to move to Ghana sometime later that year or possibly the next. At a cocktail party in Washington, however, a lawyer whom Shirley knew very well upset their intentions by warning her that she and Du Bois "must get out of [the country] before October ninth" because on "that day the U.S. Supreme Court is going to hand down an adverse opinion on the Communist Party—and Dr. Du Bois will most certainly be one of the citizens of this country who will be prevented from traveling anywhere."[27] When Shirley related the conversation to Du Bois, "he exploded," she wrote. "Well, they shall not stop me! I'll not let them stop this work! I'll not be chained up here! We'll go—we'll go quickly!" After a brief discussion, Du Bois asked his wife to "phone Herbert, . . . ask him to come and see me in the morning. Let him know it's urgent."[28] When informed of the circumstances of Du Bois's accelerated travel schedule, Nkrumah cabled, "Come when you can. Your presence will honor Ghana."[29]

The next morning Du Bois told Aptheker he would leave the country immediately, taking with him some of his correspondence and some papers relating to Africa. "Everything else I'd like to leave here with you, Herbert, if you have room to keep them. If you can find the time, you can start their classification." Aptheker, Graham Du Bois noted, "was deeply moved. His voice was husky when he said he'd be glad to take care of the files and would consider it an honor to work on them."[30] Aptheker began transferring the files to his house the next morning. "The steel filing cabinets full of his papers ended up in our basement," Bettina wrote of the arrangement to house the more than one hundred thousand letters dating from the close of the nineteenth century, "unbelievably in the laundry room under the clothes hanging on the lines to dry."[31]

In a last act of defiance, according to Levering Lewis, one prompted by the Supreme Court decision and, according to Graham Du Bois, intended to alleviate his feeling of repugnance at "the precipitous manner of our going," Du Bois applied for membership in the CPUSA.[32] Aptheker viewed Du Bois's decision somewhat differently, as he wrote in *Political Affairs* for March 1981. Du Bois "[came] to the decision that the program and ideas of the Communist Party of the United States were nearest to his own ideas," Aptheker stated. "With the warlike policy of Washington and its policy of persecuting radicals and Communists, Du Bois decided that it might be some contribution to peace and sanity if he were not only to join the Party but to do it with a public announcement of the fact."[33] That choice represented, Aptheker wrote in another, earlier *Political Affairs* essay, "the logical culmination of his fabulous life."[34] After the public release of Du Bois's application and a story about it in the *New York Times,* Aptheker made his pleasure known to the Du Boises: "The news of the Doctor's choosing to join the Party received prominent treatment in yesterday's TIMES; and, on the whole, considering the nature of the publication, rather objective treatment. . . . Friends everywhere were offering congratulation; . . . Coming when it did, its encouraging effect was intensified."[35]

When the day arrived for the Du Boises to leave the country, Herbert, Fay, and Bettina picked them up in the Apthekers' Plymouth. Bettina recalled the couple frequently riding in the back seat of the car when her father brought them to the Apthekers' house for dinner or took them on excursions. "They would sit in the back seat . . . holding hands, giggling, sparring with each other, using my father as their straight man." At the airport, Bettina recalled, "so many friends and reporters . . . jammed into the lounge . . . with cameras flashing, champagne glasses clinking, laughter, hugs, farewells."[36] Du Bois laughed along with the rest, "one of his rare audible laughs," Aptheker recalled, "into which we all joined—with a touch of sadness, I think."[37] When John McManus, a writer at the *National Guardian,* asked Du Bois "how many volumes he projected" for the *Encyclopedia Africana* "and how long the task would be," the nonagenarian Du Bois responded, "Ten volumes, I think," then added, "with the barest suggestion of a smile, 'and about ten years per volume.' "[38]

Aptheker corresponded frequently with both Shirley and W. E. B. for the next two years. In November he wrote about breaking the speaker ban at Wayne State University. In December Du Bois responded, "I read with glee [of] your trip to Detroit. I really wonder how much America will submit to." Africa was, in that early period, "quite unreal," Du Bois averred. "I am lonesome for my few friends and news is so scarce and scrappy that I can't imagine what is going on especially in America."[39]

Almost as soon as Du Bois left the country Aptheker began to receive letters about his papers. Arna Bontemps, the well-known Harlem Renaissance writer and librarian at Fisk University, to which Du Bois had sold his library for ten thousand dollars, wrote to Aptheker telling him that the library had received requests for access to the letters. "Could you tell me what plans you have for them?" he asked.[40] Aptheker told Bontemps that he held the papers and letters for "safekeeping" at Du Bois's request. "I am simply holding them in my home in accordance with the wish expressed by him and his wife. . . . Of course, exactly what disposition is to be made of the papers at any given moment is entirely subject to the will of the Doctor and his wife."[41]

Aptheker said nothing to Bontemps about Du Bois's health, which must have been weighing on his mind after he received an alarming letter from Graham Du Bois in September 1962. Du Bois was then recovering from surgery at Vevey near Lake Geneva in Switzerland. Graham Du Bois disclosed that while Du Bois's operation had been successful his "lassitude and kind of depression . . . seems to persist." Du Bois had "[lost] confidence in himself and in the future, . . . he talks of his age as if it is an affliction." "Friends rally round to try to help," she said, but "he misses his old and tried friends. . . . He does so enjoy your letters that I know a letter from either of you [Herbert or Fay] would be a blessing."[42] When Du Bois invited Aptheker to come to Africa for a conference on the *Encyclopedia Africana* Aptheker reminded him that, since he lacked a passport, which the government had rescinded pursuant to the Supreme Court decision in the McCarran Act case, he could not travel outside the country. He did, however, make a few recommendations with regard to the *Encyclopedia*. "The momentous impact of Africa upon the Western Hemisphere, in terms of culture, language, religion, thought, science, economics merits extended study," he urged. "The two-way nature of the relationship—America-Africa and Africa-America—needs documentation and elucidation."[43]

Levering Lewis wrote that in 1963 Du Bois "was dying, slowly but lucidly."[44] His doctors attempted to maintain his lucidity with medication. Graham Du Bois swore Aptheker to absolute confidentiality in January when she reported "heartbreaking" news: Du Bois's doctors "decided that he is suffering a mental breakdown following the long months of physical strain he has been through . . . he suffers in a well of loneliness." President Nkrumah had arranged for new drugs to be "flown out from England," medicine which the doctors "believe . . . will help him."[45] Four days later Aptheker wrote to Graham Du Bois, "What you tell me breaks my heart. I cannot bear to think of him suffering in any way. Were I not a prisoner confined to the borders of this country—I was physically kept out of Canada recently—I would be on my way to Ghana."[46] By February Du Bois's condition had evidently improved, as Graham Du Bois related the events surrounding the celebration of his ninety-fifth birthday. She divulged that Aptheker's glowing, celebratory essay on Du Bois published in *Political Affairs* in February 1963 had reached them. "I'd like to give a copy to the President [Nkrumah] and of course I'll treasure it for all time. I have never read anything so moving. You, too, are a Poet!"[47] Shortly before Du Bois died he told Shirley "what he wanted me to do about the many unfinished pieces of work in his files. 'There's no reason why you and Herbert shouldn't some day publish those things which are worthwhile.' "[48]

After Du Bois's death in August the letters Aptheker received inquiring about his papers intensified. His replies always indicated that he held custodial powers only, that Graham Du Bois's desire "has been that they not be opened to other scholars." He and Fay continued to go through the papers. In October 1963 he told Graham Du Bois that "[he had] studied now about 40% with care. The richness is almost unbelievable."[49] She responded in December, "Dear, dear Herbert: . . . Obviously, you cannot throw the papers and letters open to other scholars. . . . It is my feeling that they remain for your private use alone. A lot of people are now 'in the act' of wanting to write on W.E.B.," she continued, "but as far as possible I think we should *choose* the people who write at any length about him. If there is some sincere scholar with whom you should like to share evenings reading His letters, always feel free to share them. *But this is a personal matter for you.*"[50] "No one has seen his letters, though several requests have come in," Aptheker wrote on 16 December 1963. To propel the project for the "Life and Letters" they had for years planned to publish, Aptheker asked Graham Du Bois's permission "to actively seek out support for that project. . . . For instance, I might be able to get a grant from some foundation to make it possible at least to start the effort in an organized way. Should I try that? I really don't want to do anything unless you say I should and whatever I do do, after hearing from you—I want you to know all about it at every step."[51] A few days later he reported that he had by then read through "page by page and line by line—something like 60% of the collection. It is simply fabulous and every night as I pore over these pieces of paper—sacred to me—my admiration and love and incredulity grow. Good God, there was a man! What inspiration and lessons are in those papers!"[52]

The historian John Bracey attended a speech Aptheker gave at Tuskegee Institute in the spring of 1965 on Communism as part of a series on contemporary ideologies. A professor of science from Eastern Europe challenged Aptheker on his assertion that Du Bois was a communist. "So what if Du Bois, Picasso and Einstein were favorable to Communism," Bracey recalled the professor saying, "Charles Lindbergh was a Nazi." "Aptheker went ballistic: turned bright red, grasped the podium to keep his hands from trembling and in his deepest Brooklyn accent shouted, 'you dare stand here at Tuskegee, before Black students and compare Dr. Du Bois—the scientist, the scholar of the 20th century with a goddamn stunt flyer. You owe these students an apology!" "I had never seen Herbert that mad before," Bracey wrote. "The students around me said, 'wow he really loves Du Bois doesn't he? He sounds like he wants to kick his ass.' What everyone remembered was Aptheker's blow up when he thought Du

Bois had been insulted, Bracey noted. I still see it clearly in my head after almost fifty years."[53]

In a letter to Graham Du Bois of December 1963 Aptheker reported on the planned Du Bois memorial being organized by the editors at *Freedomways,* the magazine the Du Boises had helped found. "Of course, you know all about the plans for the Carnegie Meeting on Feb 23, on which [party member] Dorothy Burnham and Esther Cooper Jackson and Ossie Davis and others are working so hard. I'm sure that will be filled to the rafters and with Ossie in charge of program it should be a thrilling evening."[54]

In January 1964 Graham Du Bois responded to Aptheker's questions as to whether he should seek support for publishing the Du Bois collection. "You are in a better position than I am to judge the *timing* of this approach," she wrote. "From where I sit I can't see the Ford, Carnegie or Rockerfeller [*sic*] Foundations giving any assistance to you on this. And it is essential *that the help be given to you* and that you have charge of the project, and do the final editing!" If he could set the plan in motion, she wrote, "you have my full and unqualified endorsement. But you must fully consider the snares and pitfalls and deceptions which you will encounter," she cautioned. "The pure in heart may see God, but they do not always see their enemies! You, along with W. E. B. are singularly pure in heart."[55]

As the Du Bois memorial began to take shape Aptheker recognized that something was amiss. He heard from friends that the organizers, Esther Cooper Jackson and Dorothy Burnham, had mailed out cards seeking sponsors for the event, but he had not received one, even though Burnham had asked for his advice on preparing the script for the evening's events, which he had provided. He wrote to Burnham requesting that he be included as a sponsor. When the committee began using its official stationery, however, Aptheker's name did not appear among those of the sponsors, who included such notable figures as James Baldwin, Arna Bontemps, Ossie Davis, John Hope Franklin, Lorraine Hansberry, Langston Hughes, Sidney Poitier, Roy Wilkins, Linus Pauling, and others. "I am completely responsible for your name being omitted from the sponsor's list," Burnham confessed to Aptheker. "I forgot to put it on a sponsor's card from your letter to us."[56] Aptheker responded the next day: "I appreciate your taking the burden of my omission from the list of Sponsors—about which people have written me and phoned me from New York to California, and I've not known what to say." He told Burnham that the issue was "deeper" than simple forgetfulness: "One might simply note the fact that I never was sent the card to be signed, which those who were would-be Sponsors did receive." The main thing, he wrote, "is that the Hall be crowded and that the presentation be worthy of its subject."[57]

The hall was indeed crowded, but Aptheker was not among the attendees. In May Graham Du Bois wrote to him asking if the text of an essay on Du Bois that she had sent for reading at the memorial had in fact been read. Hansberry had read something, but friends had told Graham Du Bois that the words were hers, not those of Du Bois. "The point is that my words merely introduced Du Bois' words. . . . If the message was not read as I sent it—WHAT WAS READ?" Along with her inquiry she enclosed the text of Du Bois's message.[58] Aptheker replied that he had not been in attendance but that Fay was, and she did not recall hearing the message Graham Du Bois had expected would be read. He then related to her the story of his not being invited to be a sponsor: "It became quite clear that it was decided that I should not participate in any way at Carnegie. . . . I left the city."[59]

Graham Du Bois was furious, as her subsequent letter to Aptheker and a vitriolic letter written a few days later to Cooper Jackson testify. To Aptheker she commented that "if Fay heard that message I sent you read at the *Memorial she would not have forgotten it!* . . . THIS IS A SERIOUS MATTER WITH ME AND I SHALL GET TO THE BOTTOM OF IT."[60] Aptheker counseled patience: "Do not be 'furious' with the folks you mention; it is not ill will in their cases so much as it is a lack of full understanding—to fully understand the Doctor—or to try to—takes great effort and concentration, as is required to understand any titan—like Shakespeare, or Beethoven or Lenin. In any case fury is for the real foe."[61] Graham Du Bois wanted nothing to do with what she perceived to be the anticommunism exhibited by the memorial committee, its attempt to whitewash her husband and placate the dominant right wing. She berated Cooper Jackson and other planners of the memorial for their "cowardice" and for attempting to "trim Du Bois down to some 'respectable' tin-type. . . . If this generation of Americans cannot accept him as he is," she wrote, "do not try to gild his image for them."[62]

In his biography of Graham Du Bois the historian Gerald Horne posits that the controversy surrounding the memorial and a special issue of *Freedomways* devoted to Du Bois's memory erupted because it involved "contending forces [seeking] to appropriate a historic icon like Du Bois. . . . A quivering trembler had erupted," he wrote, "as a result of the attempt to determine who had standing to claim the immense legacy of Du Bois." By minimizing the long-standing desires of Du Bois and by ignoring the agreements among Aptheker, Du Bois, and Graham Du Bois, Horne in essence dismissed Aptheker's designation as Du Bois's literary executor as if Aptheker was involved in a street brawl with *Freedomways*. With a simplistic, throwaway one-liner, Horne put the matter to rest: "Aptheker, who would organize Du Bois's papers, felt that this task gave him standing."[63] If Aptheker did not have standing, one wonders, who did?

Requests for access to the materials piled up into 1965. Aptheker disclosed to Bontemps, who again sought Aptheker's agreement to move the papers to Fisk University, that he and Fay had arranged the whole collection chronologically and "next will come alphabetical arrangement."[64] But events overwhelmed his work on Du Bois's papers: his trip to North Vietnam, the intense speaking schedule he maintained after that, and his run for Congress all interfered with progress on publishing Du Bois's papers. He did, however, organize the carbon copy of the manuscript of an autobiography Du Bois had completed while in Ghana. Over several months he and Fay typed out the manuscript, added notes and explanations, compiled photographs, and created a selected bibliography of Du Bois's published writings. "I am and shall follow this manuscript as though it were my own—or more so, and read and proof read and annotate in a separate section where requirement of understanding dictate," he wrote to Graham Du Bois in January 1967.[65] International Publishers, the party press, released *The Autobiography of W. E. B. Du Bois,* edited by Aptheker, early in 1968. Reading the page proofs in late 1967, Graham Du Bois praised Aptheker's work. "I have no words to thank you for all that you have done to bring forth this volume," she wrote. "I know that yours was a work of devotion and love, that your reward springs from the memory of the love and faith which W.E.B. always had in you. Any other thanks is superfluous."[66] Indeed, Aptheker received no fee for the work. He felt a keen sense of betrayal in the 1990s when Levering Lewis accused him, in the first volume of his biography, of altering Du Bois's manuscript of the autobiography. "An awful fault," Aptheker wrote in an otherwise favorable review of Levering Lewis's second volume, "for which forgiveness is very difficult."[67]

By 1968, as solicitations for permission to consult the Du Bois papers increased, Aptheker did provide information for specific requests. When a graduate student named James C. Daniel asked to work with the papers, Aptheker told him to be more specific. "It is not possible for me to have someone simply go through the entire collection—housed in my home," he wrote to Daniel. "The material is now alphabetized only through 1918 and in chronological order only by year and not yet by month and day—and all this has taken literally thousands of hours of work by my wife and me."[68] As his understanding of the content of the collection increased as he worked with the papers, Aptheker proposed a panel for the annual meeting of the American Historical Association (AHA). "Somewhat to my surprise," Aptheker told Graham Du Bois, the AHA accepted the idea, which featured papers by the historian Elliot Rudwick on Du Bois as a sociologist, Vincent Harding on Du Bois as a "Negro Nationalist," Aptheker on Du Bois as a historian, and the Yale historian C. Vann Woodward as commentator.[69]

Both the Hoover Institution at Stanford University and the Historical Society of Wisconsin expressed a desire to house the Du Bois papers that year, but Aptheker's discussions with Harvard University, where Du Bois had earned his doctorate, were the most serious. The director of Harvard University Press,

Mark Carroll, contacted Aptheker through the socialist philosopher, radical activist, and Harvard benefactor Corliss Lamont. Lamont was not a communist, but he and Aptheker had maintained a relationship over the years. Carroll asked Aptheker to submit a proposal that he could bring before the faculty advisers to the press.[70]

Aptheker envisioned two books: a one-volume, six- or seven-hundred-page compilation of Du Bois's letters and a collection of his lectures and speeches, both edited with commentary by himself.[71] The project was inadequate really, given the scope and mass of material in Du Bois's papers, but his desire to get something into print was so pressing that at that point he felt anything was better than nothing. In August he met with Ann Orlov, the editor for the behavioral sciences at Harvard, to work out the details of the proposal. He expected, he told Orlov, "that if this were undertaken it should be a definitive edition, and fully to compare with other editions done by Harvard [such] as the Theodore Roosevelt letters and that its scholarship would be as impeccable as possible."[72] Describing the meeting to Graham Du Bois, Aptheker communicated the news that "the Press is definitely interested in publishing the Papers." He wrote to her that he had told Orlov "it was the Doctor's wish that in no circumstances would anyone else here be in charge of such a project but Dr. Aptheker; that I would be happy to work with other scholars and that I would insist that black men and women have decisive roles in the production of this collection." He said he expected no royalties and instructed that all payments "be made to Mrs. Du Bois." Aptheker said he would engage in no further discussions until he had her agreement.[73]

Graham Du Bois replied that he was "right in giving [the Harvard offer] serious consideration." She reminded him of the offer Nkrumah had made at his meeting with Aptheker in Ghana in 1964: he had pledged to finance Aptheker's work on the Du Bois project by bringing both the papers and Aptheker to Ghana. That prospect was no longer available, she reminded him, because a military coup sponsored by the CIA had swept away Nkrumah's government in 1966. The "papers are valuable for the world," Graham Du Bois said, "and we would not want to keep them hid away." She thought Du Bois would approve of Harvard *under the conditions laid down by you.* She suggested that her lawyer, Bernard Jaffe, get involved in the discussions. "I'd like for you to call him in for exact legal advice," Graham Du Bois wrote. "(I trust your scholarship and integrity implicitly, but in a matter of this kind it is well to have a lawyer on hand)." The undertaking, after all, entailed a comprehensive effort and "all sorts of political considerations may arise," as Aptheker had pointed out earlier. "We want to be very sure that our interests and the interests of This Sacred Trust are well protected."[74]

In October, having received the written agreement Graham Du Bois and Aptheker had drafted, Orlov let him know that discussions "with the Harvard Board of Syndics[,] . . . the faculty committee that controls our imprint," were proceeding slowly, but they were "getting into position for at least a tentative decision."[75] By November Aptheker sensed the project was fading away. A month earlier he had told Robert S. Cohen, the physicist and philosopher, his cofounder and closest confidant at the American Institute for Marxist Studies, that Harvard seemed to be "really serious" about publishing the Du Bois papers, but "problems (mostly me) remain." Orlov, he wrote to Cohen, had been "shocked to learn that some in charge of that press said they would be happy to see the collection burn rather than have my name on a Harvard book. I told her she need not be surprised: The same sort of people burned folks like me in ovens not long ago—gentility and all. I think this shocked her a little."[76] "The Harvard matter still remains in the 'interest' stage," he apprised Graham Du Bois. "Correspondence continues and possibility remains." He imparted the news that he had also had discussions with Lippincott Publishers, which "expresses very real interest in my editing a stout volume of selections of the Doctor's letters. . . . [The] firm's interest is genuine."[77]

While Aptheker was in discussion with Harvard, the historian John Blassingame, then the chairman of the Howard University Bibliographic Workshop and the assistant editor of the Booker T. Washington Papers, contacted Aptheker with a not-so-subtle demand that he relinquish control of Du Bois's papers. "Scholars and collectors, we think [the letter was signed by two dozen representatives of colleges and universities around the country], have a moral obligation to deposit Du Bois' manuscripts in repositories where they can be safely preserved, adequately catalogued and made available for research."[78] Aptheker's rejoinder was curt: "I do think your first communication to me might better have been framed in the form of some questions rather than definite suggestions—almost directives. For instance, germane is this: what were the conditions under which my custody was undertaken?" He agreed to meet with any of the signers of the letter "so that the weighty matter you raise can be probed at some length."[79] Blassingame evidently carried a grudge over the matter and exacted his revenge several years later.

Expecting that Harvard or Lippincott or some other publisher would soon publish Du Bois's letters, Herbert and Fay worked feverishly on sorting the documents and typing out a manuscript. Aptheker updated Graham Du Bois in mid-November: "We have selected and Fay has typed—in triplicate—about 650 pages so far and this brings us mid-way into 1923. The first volume I plan to have go through 1934. . . . There may be some battles [over length] but of course I'll quite willingly fight to get the most possible in to this first one."[80] Lippincott did not publish the letters, but it did bring out Graham Du Bois's memoir of her husband, *His Day Is Marching On* in 1971. Aptheker released several books during this period, and in late 1969 he had confirmation that Harper and Row, "hard to believe," he wrote to Graham Du Bois, would publish his book *Marxism and Religion*.[81]

In October 1969, almost a year after the discussions with Harvard fell apart, Leone Stein, the director of the University of Massachusetts Press, contacted Aptheker about the Du Bois collection. After some initial telephone conversations Aptheker proposed "a stout volume" of unpublished papers, "not letters," of Du Bois, which he would edit. He said he could have the book ready by mid-1971.[82] A month later Aptheker made notes of an additional telephone conversation with Stein in which he was told there was "tremendous polarization" among members of the board of the press. Some members exhibited both fear of and hatred toward Aptheker, reactions, Stein told him, she had not expected. For the project to go forward, the board "require[d] . . . two [outside scholars] for surveillance—a word she used—over me in my editing of either the Letters or the Papers." Stein related that the board was interested in expanding Aptheker's plan to include publication of "the complete letters but with these two people over me." Aptheker "explained that I wished to be treated like any other scholar; [that] I would take lessons in honor and integrity from no one on the board of that Press. That I would be the editor and no one else; that I would welcome consultants, scholars who would HELP, who would express opinions as to where my judgment and scholarship might be faulty—etc. etc. and . . . I would be treated no differently from any other scholar associated with that Press and that I was certain both Du Bois and his widow would not agree to anything else." Stein agreed to present Aptheker's statement to the board. "She added," reads the last sentence of Aptheker's memo of the conversation, "that she was shocked to find such censorship on the board of any university press. I told her I was not."[83]

On 26 November 1969, twenty-three years after he began searching for a publisher for Du Bois's papers, Stein wrote to Aptheker that she was "delighted to report that the University of Massachusetts Press Committee has approved publication of a one or two volume selection of the unpublished papers of W. E. B. Du Bois, under your editorship." Two "mutually satisfactory scholars" would be appointed by the press to "assist you in whatever way they can, in checking matters of fact and offering their advice regarding selections." Sidney Kaplan had, she revealed, "already accepted." The letter stipulated that, with some minor modifications, royalty payments would be apportioned "10% of the list price [to] Mrs Du Bois" and the equivalent of 2½ percent to Aptheker. Stein ended the letter by indicating interest "in a more comprehensive series of publications of the writings of W. E. B. DuBois, either of the complete correspondence, and/or other unpublished material." The press "would probably have to seek a grant from NEH [National Endowment for the Humanities], which is interested, in principle. . . . I simply wish to make it clear that we do have a genuine interest, at the Press, in further publications."[84] The agreement with UMass Press proved to be solid, but the NEH interest "in principle" turned into one of those "political considerations" of which Aptheker had written Graham Du Bois.

Aptheker ended 1969 by sending a hand-delivered letter to Secretary Hall. He was outraged that one of his old collaborators and fellow party members, Phillip Foner, against whom Aptheker had earlier leveled charges of plagiarism, had announced publication, at "Merit Publishers, the Trotskyist house, no less," of two volumes of Du Bois's speeches. "In addition to the politics involved," Aptheker wrote to Hall, "Phil knows . . . I am editing his letters and other works . . . he made no effort to inform Du Bois' Estate . . . so that this was to be done without Shirley's knowledge . . . let alone any income for her. The entire matter is so awful as to be almost beyond belief."[85]

16   Publishing Du Bois

WHILE APTHEKER was embroiled in the long process of finding a publisher for the Du Bois papers and a permanent repository for Du Bois's thousands of documents, his thirty-year-long blacklisting in academia came to an end. In the spring of 1969, a month after receiving a Heritage Award from the Association for the Study of Negro Life and History—"the only white recipient of an award, . . . for pioneering and profound research in black history"—he presented a lecture at the women's liberal arts college Bryn Mawr, one of the Seven Sister colleges.[1] As part of his talk there on the distortion of truth in the writing of history he used as an example "the ways in which William Styron had stepped away from the known facts in developing the central character of his novel *The Confessions of Nat Turner.*"[2] Aptheker and Styron had a long-running feud over the book.

In March 1961 Styron wrote to Aptheker praising *American Negro Slave Revolts:* "I have made much use of it in laying the groundwork for a new novel I am writing, based on Nat Turner's revolt." He requested a copy of Aptheker's Columbia master's thesis on Turner.[3] Aptheker mailed Styron his only copy, which, Styron assured him, would be safe and returned promptly.[4] Later that month, after reading Aptheker's thesis, Styron told Aptheker he "found it a most persuasive and meaningful work, and I think it will prove to be of great value in terms of my own rendition of the man and the insurrection." Seeing the Turner rebellion as "a tremendous drama in our history," Styron added, "so far as I know you are the only person who has fully analyzed the event with respect to its ultimate effect upon the South and for that matter, the happenings of the following thirty years."[5]

There the matter rested until September 1963, when Styron published a negative review of *American Negro Slave Revolts,* which had been reissued by International Publishers. Having reinvented himself, the novelist-turned-historian-of-slavery pronounced Aptheker's book an example of "extremist revisionism." Although he "makes a good case against the theory of universal content and docility among the slaves," Styron wrote, "Aptheker fails almost completely in his attempt to prove the universality of slave rebelliousness."[6] The next year, without mentioning the negative review, Aptheker informed Styron that his Nat

Turner thesis, "after almost thirty years," would be published by International Publishers (in fact the book did not appear until 1966, published by Humanities Press). Aptheker requested Styron's permission to quote from his earlier letter praising the master's thesis.[7] Styron refused. Dripping sarcasm, he later wrote that the request showed that "Mr. Aptheker seems to have as good a nose as any bourgeois writer for the opportune plug."[8]

The Confessions of Nat Turner appeared in 1967, touching off a monumental battle among historians. Black historians especially were scathingly critical of the work. Aptheker later summed up his objections to Styron's novel when he wrote, "Whatever this book is, it is certainly not Turner as the available evidence presents him, and it is certainly not the slave society of nineteenth-century Virginia, where Turner lived and whose foundations he shook."[9] Aptheker published an exceptionally critical review in October 1967 at the request of the *Nation*. Styron's response came in two articles in the *New York Times* in February 1968 in which he said, speaking of Aptheker's writings, "They do not 'convince me or any other responsible historian,' and . . . 'neither I nor anyone else in the field of history has any respect' for Aptheker. Mr. Styron added that in criticizing the novel, 'Aptheker is grinding his ideological ax.' "[10] Aptheker and Styron battled it out in the pages of the *Nation* in an exchange in April 1968. The *Nation* cut portions of the original draft of Aptheker's half of the exchange—the angriest, most caustic bits: "The crudeness of Mr. Styron's red-baiting may be attributed to the fact that he is but an amateur at that game; one can only hope that he has sufficient character to maintain his amateur status; I might reply to Mr. Styron that neither I nor any other responsible novelist has any respect for his work."[11] Later that year a group of black writers published *William Styron's Nat Turner: Ten Black Writers Respond,* in which they ferociously denounced the novel, in many cases quoting Aptheker's research on Turner and black history. Styron was quick to blot out his early association with Aptheker. In an interview with George Plimpton published in the *New York Times Book Review* Styron wrote Aptheker out of the research phase of his work on the novel altogether, claiming the inspiration for his novel came in 1962 after he read Albert Camus's *The Stranger.*[12] Elsewhere Styron professed that "he could have consulted historical material that he was unaware of while writing the book, such as evidence that Turner had a wife." Aptheker had included that information in his Turner book, which Styron had read. "Especially important in the original Confessions," Aptheker wrote of the Turner uprising, "is the evidence of the antislavery feelings of his peers; this is not in the [Styron] novel."[13]

Aptheker had received a cool reception from radical black students at the University of Connecticut in April 1968. Jack E. Eblen noted that "some of the more militant (in their eyes, at least) of the black students seemed . . . to have been disappointed."[14] Aptheker sympathized with their feelings. "I feel something of the disappointment that the more militant of the Negro students may well have experienced," he wrote to Eblen. "I think, really, it is with *words* themselves, no matter what they say. I remember reading of Old John Brown coming to an anti-slavery convention in the late 1840s and stomping out early in the proceedings, muttering—'words, words, nothing but words.' I do not mean that the Old Man was right—at least not altogether—but surely he was understandable."[15] But at Bryn Mawr a year later, Aptheker's presentation on Turner galvanized the black students. Mindy Thompson Fullilove recalled that "he had created the potential for me to be Black at Bryn Mawr. My fellow agitators and I were determined that he would join the faculty."[16]

Throughout April 1969 black women students demanded that Bryn Mawr institute a black studies curriculum, and they wanted the school to hire Aptheker, threatening even to strike if it did not do so. At the same time students were shouting "catcalls" at the Iowa Republican House member Charles Grassley when he told them "they should have 'very little' voice in running the university because they had 'very little invested in it,'" administrators at Bryn Mawr were listening more closely to student opinion.[17] As a result of the agitation at Bryn Mawr, Arthur Dudden, the chair of the History Department there, contacted Aptheker to request an interview, which evidently went well for Aptheker. Dudden then met with the president of the college, Katharine McBride, who sent Aptheker a telegram on 28 April 1969. "Tried to call you but found you had unlisted number," McBride wrote, "wiring to offer you appointment as visiting lecturer in history for year 1969–70 should like to talk with you about the course in black history you would want to give."[18] "I have regularly sought university appointment," Aptheker had written to the historian Jesse Lemisch the previous August. "Several [history] departments have told me they desired my employment . . . no appointment has ever been made. . . . At Buffalo I received a letter from the department head—last year—stating salary terms, and urging me to accept no other appointment. I responded favorably but within ten days received a one-sentence letter from the same Head stating that the Administration did not favor the appointment and the Department did not wish to pursue the matter."[19]

The *New York Times* announced Aptheker's appointment at Bryn Mawr in mid-June in a red-baiting story headlined, "Bryn Mawr Names Aptheker a Visiting History Lecturer." "Herbert Aptheker," the story's lead sentence proclaimed, "a leader of the American Communist party, is moving to Philadelphia's Main Line in the fall."[20] The *Philadelphia Evening Bulletin* reported on the story on 1 July, quoting the Republican state senator Richard A. Tilghman, who "called on Bryn Mawr College officials to drop plans to hire Dr. Herbert Aptheker . . . an admitted Communist—stripped of his military commission and decorations by the U.S. Army because of his Communist leaning." Tilghman told President McBride "she was doing irreparable harm to the college and the student body."[21] Even in the face of political and alumni agitation against the appointment by the Bryn Mawr Civic Association, by two state representatives, and by the American Legion and the Veterans of Foreign Wars, McBride persevered. In August Mrs. Martinus H. Nickerson, the president of the Bryn Mawr Alumnae Club of Colorado, organized an Alumnae Committee in Opposition to the Aptheker Appointment. Aptheker, she pointed out in a letter to the parents of Bryn Mawr students, "is a self-professed member of the Communist Party, . . . His daughter, Bettina, was one of the originators of the so-called Free Speech Movement at Berkeley, . . . [and] he has labored to foment civil disruption. . . . We urge you," she concluded, "to make your dissent known immediately to members of the Bryn Mawr College administration."[22] McBride stood firm in her decision even though, Aptheker wrote to Lemisch, "the administration is letting out that this is costing the College a million dollars in gifts and how can they repeat that etc. etc."[23]

The press inflated the story of the appointment with giddy abandon, which no doubt delighted Aptheker. Television cameras and reporters staked out positions on campus for his first day of class and followed him into the classroom. "I have waited 31 years for this moment," the Bryn Mawr–Haverford College paper, the *News,* quoted Aptheker as saying that day as he welcomed seventy-five students to class. "History is an enormous tapestry, a whole, endless, united entity, as we Marxists say, dialectically related," he told the students, adding, "I might as well scare some of you." "[He] received hearty laughs from the students," Susan Walker reported, "though he kept a characteristically straight face."[24] Later that year Aptheker told Lemisch that "the [History] Department wants me again and so do the students. We will see."[25]

Aptheker met with the chancellor at the University of Massachusetts in the fall of 1970. Some members of the History Department and faculty in the Black Studies Department had urged the university to appoint Aptheker to teach a weekly seminar. Aptheker told the historian Alfred Young that the chancellor asked only questions dealing with his politics: "The Chancellor told me he had to ask these because the Board had told him to do so."[26] There was no appointment, although he did teach a series of nine lectures on Du Bois in 1971.[27] While warmly thanking Aptheker for giving the Du Bois lectures, Michael Thelwell, the chairman of the W. E. B. Du Bois Department of Afro-American Studies, told Aptheker that administrators denied the appointment because of his politics.[28] "Even a person hostile to your political position would have to admit that the combination of scholarship and commitment represented by your lectures was in the best tradition of Western scholarship," Thelwell wrote. "Perhaps the

simplest way to express the feelings of the department is to say that your per-
formance reached a level of excellence that was worthy of the man in whose
memory and work the lectures were dedicated."[29]

Aptheker continued to teach at Bryn Mawr through the 1972–73 school year.
Students from Haverford College, Swarthmore College, and the University of
Pennsylvania joined the women from Bryn Mawr in his classes. In 1971 Dudden
added a second course for Aptheker on the life and work of Du Bois. As part
of his agreement to teach the courses on a year-to-year basis, Aptheker insisted
that Bryn Mawr permanently add black history to the curriculum and hire a
full-time, young black scholar even if that meant he would no longer teach. His
teaching was praised by the faculty, particularly Dudden, the administration, including the newly installed president, Harris Wofford, and students. Katherine
Baxter wrote to Aptheker about her experience in his classroom: "I can only
very inadequately express my appreciation for . . . new insights and new ways of
looking at parts of American history that I had previously seen in more limited
focus. I think that even more important was the human dimension which you
brought to class each week. I have never before experienced the respect for students that you consistently evidenced. . . . You are an inspiring teacher."[30] At the
end of his first year, ninety students, of whom "about 35 [were] black," paid a
visit to Wofford "just to make sure that I was not to be unemployed," Aptheker
wrote to the historian Jeff Kaplow. "This—after 31 years of being without a 'job'
is absolutely unbelievable. But with banks burning and ships mutinying, even
my steady employment is possible!"[31]

When Bryn Mawr finally decided to appoint a permanent black historian,
President Wofford notified Aptheker. "I greatly appreciate the contributions
you have made to the College and look forward to continued association," he
wrote to Aptheker. "Permit me to say that my four years at Bryn Mawr were—for
me—thoroughly enjoyable," Aptheker responded. "I would add that Professor
Dudden was especially gracious and helpful in a situation that, certainly in its
early stages, could not have been easy for him."[32]

Even his leaving, however, was not without controversy. At Dudden's suggestion, Aptheker had provided summaries and suggestions on applicants for
the permanent position in black history. He was surprised to learn in early 1973
that the History Department had decided to hire a Nigerian scholar to teach
West African history but that the department would offer no history of blacks
in the United States in the fall. The department had "attempted to appoint
James Horton, an Afro-American historian from Brandeis University," Dudden
informed Aptheker, "but we lost him to the University of Michigan."[33] When
black students heard that no American black history would be offered, they
"demanded that a course in Afro-American history be offered in the Fall of 1973
and that either a Black scholar be hired or that I be continued at the College,"

Aptheker wrote in the *Daily World*.[34] Once again the college acquiesced to its students and promised they would hire a black historian for the fall. "I expect some pretty frantic work will be done in the next few weeks and I hope a new person can be found," Wofford told the campus community.[35] Meanwhile, the Bryn Mawr–Haverford *News* reported that Aptheker "had been under pressure to leave for some time, and one source said that he had been teaching this year without pay."[36] The Associated Press (AP) picked up the story and added some flourishes of its own: "Aptheker agreed not to push his Communist views in the classroom." That story drew a fierce response from Aptheker, who demanded a retraction. "This is false," he wrote to Executive Editor Louis D. Boccardi. "No such agreement was requested by the College and no such agreement was made by [me]."[37] The AP eventually retracted the statement.

Aptheker left Bryn Mawr to great acclaim by Chairman Dudden. "I know from being told so many times by professional historians elsewhere," Dudden wrote to Aptheker, "that their respect for Bryn Mawr College is heightened significantly by your presence here in our department." He applauded Aptheker's "typical expressions of kindness, the devotion to your scholarly discipline, and the generosity toward your students and colleagues which have characterized your years with us."[38] Aptheker, who genuinely admired Dudden, told him that despite the problems at the beginning and the end of his time at Bryn Mawr, "the fact remains that it was Bryn Mawr College and that College alone which saw fit to employ me as a teacher and it was its History Department and its Chairman in particular who helped make that experience a joyous one." The work ahead, however, was never far from Aptheker's mind: "There remains the task to assure the continuance of Afro-American history study at Bryn Mawr."[39] In April Aptheker accepted a half-time, full professorship in the Social Sciences Department at Hostos Community College in the Bronx to teach two courses each semester, beginning in the fall of 1973, one in Afro-American history and the other a seminar on Du Bois.[40]

Aptheker's teaching position at Bryn Mawr, to which he commuted from Brooklyn every Tuesday, limited his travel schedule, but he maintained an extensive agenda of guest lectures at colleges and universities, social organizations, and Communist Party functions around the country. His work on the two volumes of Du Bois's letters contracted with Lippincott proceeded as well. He worked at his office in the American Institute for Marxist Studies and at home with Fay. He "was always reading or writing, settled at the vast mahogany desk inherited from his mother with the lion heads at each of its four corners," Bettina wrote in her memoir. "He wrote by hand on a yellow pad with large, broad, confident strokes of the pen. . . . Occasionally he worked at his typewriter, set on a rickety metal table next to the desk. . . . He pecked away at it with the index finger of each hand." Millions of words in articles, book reviews, newspaper stories, editorials, letters, bibliographies, books: the output of his wide-ranging intellect and two index fingers.[41]

In February 1970 Director Leone Stein at UMass Press informed Aptheker that the press had approved the publication of the unpublished papers of Du Bois.[42] Later, when establishing the final contract, Aptheker restated his insistence, in the third person, that "all decisions as to what goes in and what does not go in are made by the Editor. He will turn to the consultants for advice and aid but he will have the decision and the power to make the decision as to what is published."[43] Together, Stein and Aptheker wrote a grant to the NEH asking for additional funding for the project, citing Aptheker as the principal investigator and Sidney Kaplan and Ernest Kaiser as consulting editors. Initially the NEH questioned Aptheker's status at UMass, so the university administrators tried to arrange for Aptheker to be given an appointment of some kind in the History Department. Stein told Aptheker in September that the appointment had gone as far as the provost but that she was "not optimistic" that the chancellor and trustees would approve of the arrangement.[44]

By mid-December the NEH had rejected Aptheker's grant request. Henry I. Tragle, assistant to the coordinator of research in the Office of the Dean of UMass Graduate School, wrote to Aptheker with suggestions for resubmitting the grant. He mentioned that the dean of the Graduate School, Mortimer Appley, had begun discussions within the university community aimed at eventually acquiring the Du Bois papers. "Although not able to suggest any practical course of action . . . ," Tragle wrote, "he [Dean Appley] is desirous of having the University become *the* center for Du Bois scholarship . . . and the possibility of the University of Massachusetts Library becoming the depository for the W. E. B. Du Bois papers." Tragle had visited William Emerson, the head of the Division of Research and Publication of the NEH in November. Emerson "was frank to indicate his own sympathy for such a publication project and almost equally frank in his reflection that some of the experts (whom he felt he could not identify by name) raised questions which pertained not so much to the desirability of publication *per se,* but rather to question if your estimate of the quantitative and qualitative value of the papers was an acceptable one." Tragle told Aptheker what his response to Emerson's remarks was: "I felt this constituted more of a reflection on [Aptheker's] integrity than a true evaluation of [his] proposed publication and I had the feeling that he agreed with me. He read me some snippets from a voluminous file, presumable [sic] the record of the review procedure."[45]

The confidential Panel Evaluation of the proposed NEH grant called the Du Bois papers "a resource of great value for Black and American history. But merits of making them available overweighed by shortcomings of PI [principal investigator] and weaknesses of plan. Should be supported only if under direction of responsible editorial board with real authority, to ensure editorial objectivity and scholarly access. Panel registered distress that materials of this value remain in possession of private individual in his house; should be deposited for safe-keeping in a university or public library."[46]

The individual reviewer's remarks, which neither Aptheker nor anyone at UMass saw, reveal a group of historians and a professor of English preoccupied with Aptheker's politics. Four of the six reviewers thought Aptheker's politics would have a negative impact on the project. Aptheker is "well known for his writing on black history . . . from a Marxist viewpoint," wrote Frank Friedel, a historian at Harvard. "Would approve," he wrote, "if PI has editorial board; otherwise would not recommend." Friedel refused to offer a numerical rating, 1–5, for the project. The Yale historian John M. Blum, who rated the project a 2, called Aptheker's approach to historical writing "particularly doctrinaire." Blyden Jackson, of Southern University in Baton Rouge, gave "no numerical rating" but feared that Aptheker "may view Du Bois solely from the Marxist angle with real hazard of project becoming too one-sided." Louis Rubin, a professor of English at UNC, gave the proposal a 3 but wrote the most critical report: Aptheker's "known . . . Marxist bias would wreak havoc with the meaning of Du Bois's life; . . . PI not capable of (any) kind of disinterested, subtle, psycho-logically-acute inquiry; editor should . . . be a black man; . . . perhaps it should be done by a team of scholars, black and white." The historian Benjamin Quarles, who gave a rating of 5, refused to be drawn into the red-baiting: "Potentially a very valuable contribution. . . . PI's qualifications for task . . . unusual and exten-sive . . . this is a major project."[47]

The Yale historian C. Vann Woodward granted a rating of 4 and appended, in retrospect, a fascinating appraisal of Aptheker's proposal. He called the value of the project "potentially very great indeed . . . of first rate importance" but then not only conveyed his misgivings about the unclear articulation of the plan in the proposal but also questioned whether Aptheker could carry out the project at home. In view of a later controversy at Yale precipitated by Wood-ward's adamant assertion that Aptheker's incompetence as a scholar precluded his teaching a seminar on Du Bois at Yale, Woodward's comments as a reviewer of Aptheker's scholarship in the NEH grant reveal a shabby duplicity on his part: "PI's competence from published work," Woodward wrote as a reviewer for the grant proposal in 1970, "is persuasive."[48] Woodward "wore the mask of a Southern gentleman scholar," Lemisch, a Yale alumnus recalled. "Woodward's reputation for liberalism was undeserved," he said. "I felt sympathy for Herbert's illusions. Aptheker felt he and Woodward were gentlemen scholars who could get along. Herbert didn't understand that rules of genteel discourse did not ap-ply to him."[49] Nonetheless, in this instance, perhaps for the last time, Woodward did not attempt to sabotage Aptheker's grant application.

Aptheker's predictable response when informed that the grant had been denied is understandable. "The National Endowment for the Humanities has rejected my application for the same reason that the University of Massachusetts has refused my appointment," he wrote to Tragle. "What bothered those 'scholars,'" he wrote in the same letter about another NEH report that divulged concerns about the unavailability of the Du Bois papers to researchers, "was the name of the person to whom Dr. Du Bois entrusted his Papers."[50] The NEH turned down two subsequent grant requests from Aptheker and UMass Press.

Aptheker had had some correspondence, albeit infrequent, with Woodward over the years. In January 1971, unaware of Woodward's role as a reviewer for his NEH grant, he wrote to Woodward, addressing him as "Professor Woodward" and asking permission to quote from a letter of 1938 that Woodward had written to Du Bois. He took the opportunity to tell Woodward that Lippincott would publish the first volume of Aptheker's selected correspondence of Du Bois, which covered the period through 1934, when Du Bois left the NAACP for the first time. He reported also that UMass Press would publish four volumes of the unpublished papers of Du Bois.[51] Woodward's response, beginning "Dear Mr. Aptheker," imparted his unease that the first volume of the letters would "go all the way down to 1934. I can not believe that this will give you adequate coverage." He reminded Aptheker that the Booker T. Washington letters would probably come to ten volumes, "and talk of a new edition of the Douglass papers is in terms of the same scope." Woodward asked, "[Can] the original manuscripts down to 1934 . . . now be made accessible to qualified research students in some good and accessible library? Have any plans been made to find such a library? May I open the question with the Yale Library?" Surely, he wrote, "you must be aware of the great need and demand among historians for free access to this material and I am sure you will want to find an appropriate solution." He asked to be kept informed about the project but said nothing about his role as a reviewer for the NEH grant.[52]

Aptheker, in a long reply addressed to "Mr. Woodward," tried to explain that Lippincott would agree only to a two-volume set of letters, "the most significant historical material." The contract allowed for the rights to publish "a full and complete edition" later. "No foundation—private or public—has been willing to help me in any way," he told Woodward. "Harvard . . . made it quite clear that it did not want my name associated with its own."[53] Woodward in turn said he was relieved, although, he wrote, "you would readily agree that, as useful as these [two volumes] are, they would not be what the scholarly community requires." Again Woodward pressed Aptheker on making the papers available to scholars: "There are many instances . . . where editors of private papers have proceeded with their editions over long periods of years while the manuscripts they are editing are made fully available to qualified scholars, for example the Booker

Washington Papers." Woodward asked, ["Couldn't you] reach some agreement with a library that would benefit both you and the other members of the scholarly community? . . . I know this must be an embarrassment to you to have a constant request for use . . . and you must regret having to reject legitimate use by others. . . . I might be of some help in finding a solution."[54] There is no record in Aptheker's papers that Woodward assisted in finding a home for the Du Bois papers, but Aptheker agreed with Woodward's admonitions while taking a swipe at the historical profession. "In view of all that the historical profession in the United States has done for me in the past thirty years," Aptheker wrote to Woodward in apparent good humor, "it would give me a special satisfaction to be able to help it in the future."[55] Woodward said he "relished the mild irony" of Aptheker's statement, reiterated his interest in taking the matter up with the library at Yale, then suggested that "perhaps the Library of Congress would be best." At that point, with Woodward assuring Aptheker that "such an arrangement would take a great burden of responsibility off your shoulders and in no way inhibit your publication plans," their correspondence breaks off without a resolution.[56]

Aptheker certainly would have welcomed a serious offer from the library at Yale to house the Du Bois papers. Why did that offer never come? Was Woodward serious about it? Given his later actions, the offer seems disingenuous at best, but other calculations may have been in play. "Woodward was capable of petty jealousy," Eugene Genovese said in an interview. "He had a very nasty side. He was jealous about Aptheker having the Du Bois papers and quite likely influenced the National Endowment for the Humanities decisions to deny Aptheker funding for the project."[57] That jealousy was not confined to Woodward. An FBI informant within the party reported in July 1972 that "blacks are envious of [Aptheker] . . . especially [name blacked out—possibly James Jackson?] because he, not [Aptheker], should be the heir of works of W. E. B. Du Bois, Black Historian." Not only that, Aptheker, according to the informant, was "criticized also for being a 'right-winger' since . . . he permits anyone who writes about Marxism, even against the CP, to have their work circulated."[58]

Aptheker delivered the finished manuscript of the Du Bois correspondence to Lippincott in December 1970. Eight months later, the editors at the firm began asking him to acquire written permission from the letters' authors to quote from them. Aptheker began sending out inquiries in September. "You can imagine the problems in terms of locating people," he wrote to Paul M. Wright at UMass Press, "(and Black people at that) who wrote letters forty or fifty or sixty years ago!" Then he heard nothing from Lippincott until February 1972, when the editor in charge of the manuscript called, "tremendously excited by the book," and told Aptheker that "it was then (only then!) going into copy-editing." Two weeks later, "after it went to the head office in [Philadelphia]," Lippincott informed Graham Du Bois's attorneys that it was "impossible to go ahead in terms of permissions!" Aptheker, visibly disgusted by the whole process, said to Wright that "what was involved here was a top-level decision by someone in Phila based on the well-known politics of the editor of the book."[59] Lippincott canceled its contract with Aptheker in March 1972. The loss of time infuriated him. Two months later UMass Press agreed to publish two volumes of Du Bois's correspondence, which Aptheker eventually expanded to three.

In 1972 Aptheker and UMass Press applied a third time for a grant from the NEH. The application included a recommendation for funding from Sen. Edward Brooke of Massachusetts. In June 1972, at a convention in New Orleans, his "sympathy" for the Du Bois project having evidently mutated, an enraged Emerson of the NEH publicly confronted Stein in a restaurant while she was having a dinner with colleagues. Ignoring her companions, he asked, "without introduction and in what can hardly be described as a friendly manner, whether I was from the press involved in the 'Ap-taker' project. . . . Then, without waiting for a response, he proclaimed that it was an 'effrontery'" that "'America's Number 1 Communist' apply to the National Endowment for a grant. Not only was it an 'effrontery,' it was 'stupidity.'" Stein reported to Aptheker, in an arresting understatement, that the prospects for funding from the NEH did not appear to be encouraging.[60] When Senator Brooke forwarded a copy of the NEH rejection, Aptheker thanked him for his help and, without mentioning Stein's name, related to him the substance of her conversation with Emerson. He told Brook, "I imagine that the radicalism of Dr. Du Bois himself did not help but I know that my own dissenting opinions certainly played a major part in the negative decision."[61]

In November, Indiana University Press contacted Aptheker asking that he publish with them on the subject of Du Bois. Naturally, he leapt at the idea, offering to prepare a biography, a project he later said he would never even attempt. "We should certainly be very much interested in such a work," Bernard Perry, the director of the press, replied.[62] "The question is not really whether or not I shall write his biography," Aptheker told Perry. "In a way my life for the past thirty, thirty-five years has been a preparation for that effort. The question is to have before me a definite commitment and a Press that has made an actual inquiry. . . . My biography will describe this fantastic life, his personality, his troubles, his courage, his practicality, his wisdom, his doubts and defeats, his victories. . . . It is true that I loved him and in this sense my biography will not be what is hilariously called 'objective' but I know too that what he valued more than life itself was Truth and when I write of him I will not forget that."[63]

Just over a month into the correspondence the prospect for the biography was dead. Perry told Aptheker that "interested as we are in the work, or I would not have written you in the first place, I, nevertheless, regret to say that the University Press Faculty Committee feels that it wants to see the complete manuscript before making a decision."[64]

After agreeing to publish the Du Bois correspondence, in March 1973 UMass Press sought out a board of "distinguished scholars, to advise Dr. Aptheker" on the project, reasoning that the existence of such a board would strengthen the odds of securing a grant from the NEH. The press contacted Woodward, Louis R. Harlan, the editor of the Booker T. Washington Papers, Kenneth B. Clark, Charles H. Wesley, and John Hope Franklin. Woodward and Harlan eventually agreed to serve; it is not clear whether Franklin ultimately served on the board, as he had indicated he would "be pleased" to do, but he did write "a strong recommendation" for a new NEH application.[65] The University of Massachusetts also reached an agreement with Graham Du Bois to purchase all of Du Bois's papers that were in Aptheker's custody. In July the university took possession of the papers, an act that generated a resolution from the Massachusetts State Department of the American Legion condemning the university for purchasing the papers of someone with left-wing tendencies.[66] Later that year the first volume of the Du Bois correspondence went on sale. "I hope you've seen Vol. I of the Correspondence by now," Aptheker wrote to Graham Du Bois in December. "Not a word—not a single word—about it in the Times or any other of the free press in the USA."[67]

Immediately upon agreeing to serve on the Advisory Board, both Woodward and Harlan began pressing Aptheker to contemplate bringing out more than the three volumes of letters UMass Press had agreed to publish. Aptheker told them that what stood in the way was money. He told Franklin that the project had received a total of only four thousand dollars as of late July 1973, two thousand each from the American Council of Learned Societies and the Rabinowitz Fund.[68] By September Aptheker told Harlan he had also privately raised about eight thousand dollars from friends. Nonetheless, the two remaining volumes would "include all the significant historical material." Having Harlan's assistance in selecting "what to include and what to omit—would be very helpful of course, as would [your] reading for accuracy, context, etc."[69] Woodward contended that he was surprised that the correspondence would not extend to ten volumes. "I had assumed when I agreed to serve on your Advisory Board," he wrote to Aptheker, "that the correspondence would be the main material included. I hope you will reconsider your plans. . . . I could not in all conscience remain on your Board in support of the present plan."[70]

Aptheker assured Woodward that the correspondence would constitute "three stout volumes of the ten being projected." Seven other volumes would consist "of his unpublished books . . . his college papers, some diaries and travel journals, . . . and quite a few unpublished essays on various subjects." Again, Aptheker reported, the problem was lack of money: "All of the above was projected when all efforts to obtain money from foundations had failed; I've never expected grants and rarely been disappointed! Of course, if a substantial grant is forthcoming, I would insist that the Press move to the publication of a fuller collection of his correspondence."[71]

In early January 1974 Woodward and Harlan, one day apart and writing in similar language (a fact that is unlikely to have been coincidental), resigned from the Advisory Board in what appears to have been an attempt to scuttle the project. "My main reason," wrote Woodward, "is that I do not agree with the editor about his policy respecting the selection and editing of the Du Bois correspondence."[72] In a series of letters written to both Woodward and Harlan over the next four months, Aptheker as well as Stein and Malcolm Call at the press sought to ascertain what specific disagreements caused the resignations. Both of the men complained about the content of the first volume of correspondence, which had appeared in October 1973. Call was puzzled by Harlan's position. "Your perusal and subsequent endorsement of the *Correspondence* galleys prior to publication" had, he thought, precluded any misunderstanding.[73] Woodward came closest to giving concrete reasons for his resignation, although he evidently pulled out of thin air his accusations that Aptheker had not done the scholarly research necessary for such an undertaking. Woodward wrote, "The first volume raised doubts about the editorial procedures and principles of selection." He continued,

> The first volume left me in considerable doubt about the thoroughness of the search for Du Bois' correspondence. . . . Among collections known to contain Du Bois' letters that were apparently not searched for this edition are the papers of R. R. Moton . . . George W. Cook . . . Ray Stannard Baker . . . Arthur B. Spingarn . . . William S. Braithwaite, . . . Charles W. Chestnut. . . . Apparently there was no attempt to use the letters of Du Bois at the American Academy of Arts and Sciences. Mr Herman Kahn of the Yale Library tells me that no use was made of a large collection of Du Bois' letters in the Manuscript Division. My fear is that the editor placed too much reliance on the personal collection kept by Du Bois himself and that much of importance has been overlooked.[74]

Aptheker responded with evident restraint to Woodward's charges of scholarly inattention. "Search for other Du Bois correspondence was very considerable," Aptheker wrote. He had visited and corresponded with all of the collections mentioned in Woodward's letter. "There is not a 'large collection' of Du Bois letters in the Yale library," he corrected Woodward. "What letters there are were examined by me and again the very few of any significance were copied by me and are now part of the collection at Amherst. I do not recall that I was ever asked—or told—about this in earlier letters," he closed, with obvious frustration. "Perhaps if Dr. Du Bois had not selected the undersigned to be responsible for the collecting and editing of his unpublished and published works a force would have been gathered and funded to make that possible. And perhaps the time will come—I think it will—when conditions will be such . . . that this will actually be undertaken."[75] Neither Woodward nor Harlan withdrew his resignation, and by July Stein had told Aptheker she had recommended to the university chancellor that, since Woodward and Harlan had resigned, the "continuation of the Board was not feasible," and it should be disbanded.[76]

In July 1975 UMass Press received an independent grant of sixty-nine thousand dollars to support the microfilming and cataloguing of the Du Bois papers, but it did not apply to the work proposed or accomplished by Aptheker. Again in 1976 the press and Aptheker applied for NEH funding. When the NEH rejection arrived, Stein and John Bracey contacted the endowment requesting an explanation. George F. Farr observed in response that the application had been "submitted to a number of scholars in the field," although he did not name them. He stated that the first volume of the *Correspondence* "has come under significant criticism for its contents; many important items have been omitted and many unimportant ones included." Farr said also that the "evaluators were concerned" about the resignations of Woodward and Harlan. He cited previous applications, averring that they had been "unsuccessful because of major questions raised about the objectivity of the editor's criteria of selection."[77]

Bracey and Stein responded with a fierce defense of Aptheker. "To fail to provide funding and then to criticize hard, but rational and objective, decisions dictated by scarce resources is patently unfair," they wrote. They brought up the subject of Harlan's positive publicity blurb for the first volume of the correspondence, which was followed by his abrupt withdrawal. "Professor Vann Woodward obviously has some very deep personal and/or political differences with Dr. Aptheker," they protested. "Professor Vann Woodward has persisted in his criticisms of Dr. Aptheker. . . . [and his criticisms] are generally agreed to have exceeded all the bounds of propriety, academic honesty, and common decency. Neither Vann Woodward nor Harlan qualify as objective evaluators of Dr. Aptheker's work." Stein and Bracey then launched into an intense criticism of their own on the funding decisions made by the NEH:

> The issue here seems to be whether or not the era of witchhunting, red-baiting, and anti-communist hysteria is over. Will the N.E.H. approve a grant to a scholar who is a communist? With two exceptions, the "scholarly reviews" [of the first volume of the Correspondence] are overwhelmingly favorable.
>
> In short, the reasons offered in your letter do not constitute a satisfactory explanation of why the grant has been rejected. Unless substantive evidence is forthcoming, and you can assure us that no conflict of interest was involved on the part of the panelists or the reviewers, we shall be forced to conclude that personal and/or political considerations determined the decision. If such is the case, we would have little choice but to raise the issue publicly. We can't shake

the conviction that if the University of Massachusetts were an elite private institution and Dr. Aptheker were not a communist, then grant support would
have been automatic. The latter point is virtually conceded in your letter.[78]

The NEH bristled at the notion that its awarding procedures had been less
than objective. Simone Reagor, the director of the Division of Research Grants,
wrote emphatically, "My review of the application file . . . yielded no suggestion
whatsoever that the Endowment's evaluations have been influenced by any consideration of Mr. Aptheker's political views."[79]

Given a copy of the letter, Aptheker thanked Stein and Bracey: "I was moved.
. . . Meanwhile, despite hell, high water and Woodwards, the work continues. . . .
I think you must be more disappointed than I with the Endowment action—
after all I've had forty years experience with academia!"[80] Meanwhile Bracey
told Aptheker that the Yale historian John Blassingame had spread a rumor that
Aptheker "had destroyed & censored . . . the Du Bois Papers. [I] asked if he could
give me names," Aptheker wrote. "[Bracey] mentioned fear; said he might in
[the] future."[81]

Despite the overwhelming agreement on the prominence of Du Bois among
scholars and staff at the NEH, Aptheker never did receive a grant to pursue his
scholarly work. "I think the reasons for the lack [of support] are the same as
those which are involved in . . . the 'censorship' of W. E. B. Du Bois and Paul
Robeson," Stein concluded. "And if Du Bois and Robeson are controversial, certainly Herbert Aptheker is. The support which we did receive, . . . was from small
foundations which have a tradition of independent thinking, and a few generous individuals, . . . otherwise, the resistance has been massive."[82] In the end,
Aptheker edited three volumes of Du Bois's correspondence and four volumes
of unpublished writings by Du Bois for UMass Press. When the third volume
of the correspondence appeared in 1978, Eric Foner reviewed it favorably in the
New York Times Book Review. "Thank you for the effort this entailed and for the
integrity it displayed," Aptheker wrote to Foner. "I did not think I'd live to see a
thoughtful and favorable review in that paper; and deeply regret that neither Du
Bois nor Shirley Du Bois lived to see that."[83] Kraus International Publications
eventually published thirty-seven volumes of the collected, published writing of
Du Bois edited by Aptheker: "It contains everything that he ever set to print,"
Aptheker said in an interview. "Everything. Every review, every letter to a newspaper, and so on . . . in 1986 it was finished." He also published a seven-hundred-
page annotated bibliography of Du Bois's writings "that annotates everything
he ever wrote," Aptheker said. "And now the world is beginning to discover
him. They buried him of course, because he was too radical . . . So now there's
an interest in him here."[84]

Graham Du Bois demanded and secured, as a condition of selling the Du Bois papers to the University of Massachusetts at Amherst, a professorship for Aptheker in the W. E. B. Du Bois Department of Afro-American Studies. "The state legislature hit the ceiling," recalled Bracey, who had known and admired Aptheker for forty years. "Herbert and August Meier," although fierce political and professional enemies, "were the most knowledgeable white scholars working in Black History," Bracey said, "two of the most important legs on which the field of Black history stands."[85] Although Aptheker had a legally signed contract for a professorship, he bargained that position away in return for a guarantee that the Du Bois Department in Afro-American Studies would build a core faculty for the study of black history. The university created five positions as a result of its agreement with Aptheker.[86] "He sacrificed . . . a political victory that would have been to his personal advantage," Bracey wrote in 1987, "for one that benefitted the larger struggle to increase the number of Black people on our campus. I have yet to see such an example of selflessness on the part of the white left of my generation."[87] Aptheker's stature, wrote Eugene and Elizabeth Fox-Genovese "as a premier American historian and as the first great white historian of the black experience needs no defense. That stature has been widely recognized throughout the black community, throughout the Left, and even throughout a bourgeois Academy that has disgraced itself by excluding him from a university professorship solely because of his courageous and inspiring political life's work."[88] "Please do not fret," Genovese wrote to Aptheker in the mid-1980s. "Your life's work stands and will stand. . . . Herbert Aptheker will fare very well indeed."[89]

In February 1996, at the dedication of the new multistory W. E. B. Du Bois Library at the University of Massachusetts Amherst, the university awarded Aptheker an honorary doctorate. That same day, as a result of pressure exerted by students, the university renamed the Tower Library, built in 1973, the W. E. B. Du Bois Library. That library "houses the world's largest collection of Du Bois works, including more than 130,000 items of correspondence, photographs, manuscripts of published and unpublished writings, audiovisual material and oral history interviews."[90]

Bracey and his colleagues—faculty, staff, and students—said in a statement at Aptheker's memorial in New York City in 2003,

> We here at the University of Massachusetts owe Herbert a priceless debt for his acts of friendship, courage and self-sacrifice that enabled our Department to establish itself on a firm foundation during its critical early years. Without his efforts, our successes surely would have been delayed or greatly diminished. We owe him for the presence in our university library of the papers of W. E. B. Du Bois. We owe him for visiting with us from time to time to encourage and

enlighten us, and to break bread, to talk and to laugh with us. We will miss him very much. There is much left to do before we live in the world that Herbert dreamed of, and that he devoted his life's work to bringing into fruition. We will continue down the paths he has charted in the study of African American peoples. We will continue the struggles that he waged against the exploitation and oppression in any way, shape or form of one human being by another.[91]

17   Yale Historians and the Challenge

to Academic Freedom

FOR FOUR months in the fall of 1975 the Church Committee of the U.S. Senate held a series of hearings devoted to the FBI's COINTELPRO operations as part of broader hearings into the outlawry of American intelligence agencies since the late 1940s. The FBI identified five threats to the United States against which it had conducted COINTELPRO operations, three of which Aptheker was associated with: the "Communist Party, USA" program (1956–71); the "Black Nationalist–Hate Group" program (1967–71); and the "New Left" program (1968–71) (the other two were the "Socialist Workers Party" program [1961–69] and the "White Hate Group" program [1964–71]). The FBI assured the Church Committee it had ceased COINTELPRO activities in 1971. The FBI had indeed curtailed some of its activities, but the lingering effects of its programs, McCarthyist blacklisting tactics, and red-baiting, while diminishing, continued to haunt radicals in the academic community. Certainly academia targeted the historians Staughton Lynd, Jesse Lemisch, Eugene Genovese, Howard Zinn, and many others, but, as Lynd wrote, "Aptheker, . . . is beyond question the American historian most discriminated against because of political belief."[1]

Early in 1975 Aptheker gave a presentation on Du Bois at the People's Center in New Haven, Connecticut. A month later the master of Davenport College, a physics professor at Yale and the leader of the college seminar program, contacted Aptheker to invite him to submit a proposal for a seminar. Several Davenport students had heard Aptheker speak the previous month and wanted him to teach a seminar.[2] Astonished, Aptheker agreed immediately. That invitation set off an explosive chain of events that ensnared Aptheker, the Yale historians C. Vann Woodward, John M. Blum, and John Blassingame, Yale University itself, dozens of other historians, the American Historical Association (AHA), and the Organization of American Historians (OAH) in a maelstrom of personal and professional animosities, charges, and countercharges that lasted into the 1990s.

Aptheker proposed a course called "The Life and Thought of Du Bois" for the once-a-week, fourteen-week seminar scheduled to begin in January 1976, and the Davenport College seminar committee agreed. Aptheker attended an interview at Davenport, answered questions from the Fellows and students, supplied recommendations, and submitted a reading list and detailed syllabus for the course. The approval process for seminars proposed by the college was usually routine. Acceptance of the course would have entailed offering Aptheker a junior faculty position at Yale: "a college seminar instructor—perhaps the most junior of all appointments." Following previous practice, Davenport College, after endorsing the seminar, sought out a sponsoring department, "a prerequisite for approval of a college seminar."[3] The college submitted its proposal to the History Department.

The chair of the History Department, John Hall, appointed a committee of three, Woodward, Blum, and Blassingame, to consider the appointment. Months went by. In early October Hall told the master of Davenport College, Jack Sandweiss, that although the department had not officially rejected the seminar, Woodward, Blum, and Blassingame were opposed, which "made it unlikely that the appointment would be approved" if Davenport College requested a formal vote.[4] At Sandweiss's request, Woodward met with the Davenport seminar committee. Woodward made it perfectly plain that he didn't find Aptheker's scholarship up to Yale's standards. "He also told the committee that he had briefly been a member of the editorial board for publication of the Du Bois correspondence, but had resigned after the first volume appeared because he 'could not endorse what Mr. Aptheker was doing.'" Woodward refused to offer any details or specifics, "explaining that it was against departmental policy to reveal information detrimental to the candidate."[5]

Undeterred, the seminar committee took the unprecedented step of requesting official sponsorship from five departments—History, American Studies, Sociology, Afro-American Studies, and Political Science. History officially rejected the proposal. "The true reason for Woodward's rejection of Aptheker is ideological," an angry student named Robert A. Blecker wrote in the *Yale Daily News*. "Woodward essentially claims that Aptheker, a Marxist, overemphasizes Du Bois' years as a Communist in editing the latter's papers."[6]

Students organized a petition in support of Aptheker's appointment and obtained more that thirteen hundred signatures within two days. The Black Student Alliance issued a statement denouncing the History Department: "Rejection of a relevant course taught by a man whose credentials are impeccable clearly reveals their true intention: to strictly bar diverging scholarly and intellectual viewpoints."[7] At one point, when the president of Yale, Kingman Brewster, refused to meet with them, seventy-five students "occupied Woodbridge Hall until he did so."[8] Woodward, Blum, Blassingame, and the History Department brushed off the students' complaints about the department's decision. In an interview with the *Yale Daily News,* Aptheker accused the department of

"McCarthyism disguised as benevolence," referring to Woodward's assertion that "we do not subject applicants to public exposure of unfavorable assessments," and several times demanded that the department divulge the basis for its rejection. "I absolutely demand that this evidence be made public," he wrote in January 1976. "However they wish to do it, I ask them to select the method but in the name of fairness and elementary decency to do it."[9] Woodward, his favorable comments as a reviewer for Aptheker's first NEH grant notwithstanding, went on to say that "Aptheker's writings 'did not measure up to the standard of scholarship desired for teachers at Yale'" and that "the real issue is a judgment of scholarly standards."[10] "I was on a routine committee to consider the proposal," Woodward said. "We considered the question and he didn't measure up. It was a question of the quality of his scholarship; we had certain standards and he didn't meet them. I knew very well that as soon as I said it it would be regarded as reactionary."[11]

The Political Science Department, in an unprecedented overruling of one department by another, sanctioned the seminar without a single dissenting vote. Aptheker said in a newspaper article that he "was told that the American studies and the philosophy departments stood ready to do the same. The single sponsorship, however, was all that was required."[12] Although the appointment had to be authorized by two additional committees, most observers assumed that at this point the battle was over.

The Junior Appointments Committee, a committee of six faculty members chaired by the deans of Yale College and the Graduate School, voted, without dissent, in favor of the seminar. The chair of the Political Science Department, Joseph LaPalombara, thinking the matter had been settled, did not attend the meeting of the final review committee, the Joint Board of Permanent Officers of Yale College and the Graduate School, whose members were tenured, full professors. The Joint Board had forty-one appointments to consider, including that of Aptheker: they approved forty and denied one, that of Aptheker. At the meeting on 8 December 1975, Woodward and Blassingame, buttressed by several other members of the History Department, mounted a "massive assault" on the appointment, what LaPalombara called "academic overkill."[13] The two professors convinced the Joint Board to kill Aptheker's seminar. "Probably no discussion of the Board's role has ever been as lively or as heated, or has raised as many important questions with the University," the *Yale Alumni Magazine* reported. "This is the first time . . . that the Board ever turned down a junior appointment."[14] Sandweiss told Aptheker that "the action was unprecedented in the history of Yale."[15]

Privately, Aptheker felt a keen sense of personal betrayal, by Woodward especially, a feeling he expressed only within the tight bounds of his family. "I know you were upset about it," Bettina wrote to her father. "However often things like this happen . . . it's something we don't ever get 'use to,' which is probably a good thing." She urged her father to contact Chairman of the CPUSA Henry Winston to inaugurate "a serious mobilization by the Party."[16] While the party did publicize the event in the *Daily World*, Aptheker chose to enlist the aid of other scholars to contest Yale's decision.

As Aptheker commented to Bettina in early February 1976, events continued "to snowball," both on the Yale campus and among radical historians who perceived a threat to the employment status of historians around the country who might be affected should "other colleges and universities . . . [follow] Yale's lead and [block] appointments and promotions of otherwise qualified candidates on political grounds."[17] Lemisch and the members of the Mid-Atlantic Radical Historians Organization (MARHO) formed the Committee for the Defense of Historians' Rights and Jobs to press for an inquiry by the AHA and the OAH into the Yale controversy. Aptheker "registered a complaint with the [AHA], citing the Statement of Professional Standards, seeking to get the reasons for his rejection." Representatives of AHA responded with a statement of interest: "If the facts are as Aptheker describes them, then there is cause for concern."[18]

Outraged students and faculty members at Yale stepped up their assault on the History Department and continued protesting into the spring. They organized a two-day event for Aptheker on the Yale campus. On the second day Aptheker presented a lecture on Du Bois that he had "originally intended" to be the first lecture in the seminar. "More than 250 students and faculty . . . gave [him] a long standing ovation."[19] Some twenty-two hundred students, "over half the undergraduates at Yale University . . . signed petitions demanding that [Aptheker] be appointed to teach" the seminar. Sandweiss, after an affirmative vote by the Davenport College seminar committee, submitted the proposal to the History Department again on 23 March. Again, according to the final draft of the Report of the Joint Committee of the American Historical Association and the Organization of American Historians (hereafter the AHA–OAH Report and the Committee, respectively) Chairman Hall rejected the appointment.[20]

As events continued to escalate, in February Woodward, worried about the effectiveness of the protest movement led by Lemisch, which he reduced to Lemisch's "Oedipal problem with his Alma Mater," sought advice from Marvin Gettleman, a radical historian who had been his student at Johns Hopkins University. Gettleman warned Woodward to take the matter seriously. "In fact a national Aptheker support committee is now taking shape that is likely to have far-reaching repercussions," Gettleman wrote to Woodward. "First," he emphasized, "this effort is not (as it might be suspected of being in certain circles) a 'Commie front operation.'" Gettleman saw solid grounds for radical scholars to take action. There had been "outrageous cases of politically-inspired dismissals, and the shunting off of radical and marxist historians into non-teaching careers, or into schools where their influence is likely to be neutralized." "In just this way," Gettleman continued, "hundreds of historians are now pondering the Aptheker case and coming around to some kind of militant support that you will be hearing of soon in New Haven."

Gettleman urged Woodward to remember that his own words had added fuel to the fire. "The single most inflammatory document that has been circulated . . . was your *Daily News* letter [questioning Aptheker's scholarly qualifications] which I plead with you to re-read with a view to understanding how it looks off the Yale Campus." He pointedly cautioned Woodward: "[Your] continued overbearing . . . haughty tone [has led] many of us [to consider] energetic protest activity." Allowing that Woodward would probably reject his candid opinion, Gettleman's aim was to "forewarn you of the coming storm."[21] Woodward feared that in the upcoming "next round" in the History Department his opponents there might prevail, he said, "with the support of other departments and if so, Aptheker may come. For his own pride and that of Marxist historians, I hope he won't. But this may well happen."[22] Woodward was correct: his critics within the department had concluded that Woodward, Blum, and Blassingame had made the decision quite outside of the History Department's "plain rules."[23]

The Aptheker matter headed Chairman Hall's agenda at the meeting of the history faculty on 19 February 1976, according to the Yale historian Ramsay MacMullen. The question was, "What shall we do if the seminar comes back to us . . . what possible action should the department take in case the Aptheker issue is reactivated?" The discussion "got nowhere," MacMullen recalled, so the group tabled the matter until the question "becomes acute," then "the chairman will call another meeting of the tenured faculty to decide on a course of action." As MacMullen said, "The point was established that, at the chairman's initiative and with our full agreement, we had taken back from him any delegated authority and would ourselves resolve the question of what to do if Aptheker should raise his head again."

During a short academic break during 5–22 March, Hall and a small group of the history faculty "disposed" of the matter, violating Hall's earlier agreement. As the events were playing out, MacMullen wrote a letter to the new chair of the department, Henry Turner, in which he said that at the meeting of the department's tenured faculty on 23 March then-Chairman Hall "ruled out our consideration of what had been done by saying the matter had been decided once and for all. How? By exercise of 'the chairman's prerogative.'" MacMullen told Turner that although Hall had "offered [the chairman's prerogative] several times, [it] struck me as very odd."[24] At least one source in the History Department told Randy Smith, a reporter for the *Yale Graduate Professional,* that "the decision was made in advance of Tuesday's departmental meeting, without consulting the department as a whole . . . [and] that several junior and tenured members of the faculty expressed concern over this procedure at the meeting."[25] At the next meeting of tenured-only faculty—and "throughout the proceedings the untenured faculty were excluded, most unhappily"—MacMullen challenged his colleagues: "No chairman at Yale has any prerogative at all in recommending a teaching appointment." MacMullen let the new chairman know about his unease over the way the department had acted in October 1976. "The seminar proposal had not been accorded due process," he said.[26]

MacMullen's letter of October 1976 and his recollections of the department's actions could have been vital to the conclusions reached in the AHA–OAH Report had the Committee had access to them, but it did not. "The truth about the resistance to the sponsorship was not brought out in subsequent inquiry by the OAH and AHA," MacMullen wrote in a letter to the *Journal of American History* in 2001.[27] In fact, what might politely be called Turner's mendacity at the time in his written responses to the Committee's questions aroused MacMullen's apprehension. "I looked at the question asked of us and your answers," MacMullen wrote to Turner in May 1977, "and I was un-relieved to find that in fact they do get into . . . the matter of how the re-submission of the seminar proposal was handled. . . . By my reading of what happened (as you know) it was not the department in any sense that responded to Jack Sandweiss, and there were indeed grounds for reconsideration."[28] MacMullen detected in Turner's letters and remarks a concern that he should not "intervene independently in the process of answering the joint committee."[29] A few years later MacMullen told the historian Charles Crowe, who had inquired into the Yale controversy, that "had proper procedures been followed, there is little doubt in my mind that Professor Aptheker would in fact have been appointed to teach."[30]

Aptheker made another appearance on the Yale campus in April 1976 at a student- and faculty-sponsored rally that drew more than three hundred people. According to the AHA–OAH Report, "The Junior and Term Appointments Committee" again voted in favor of the new proposal for the Aptheker seminar, and the new Joint Boards meeting on 23 April attracted more that ninety professors for a three-hour meeting (there is no record of their discussion). The vote was fifty-three to thirty-nine in favor of appointing Aptheker. Since the vote was only a simple majority, not the required two-thirds majority, the question was referred to the Executive Committee of the Faculty of Arts and Sciences, which eventually approved Aptheker's seminar on 26 April. The Yale Corporation added its approval on 16 May.[31]

Aptheker was surprised by the whole affair and especially by Woodward's actions. "I have some knowledge of 'what has been going on' at Yale but much of it still baffles me," he wrote to the historian Arthur Link in April prior to the meeting of the Joint Boards. "The extraordinary actions of Woodward have left me astonished and those of Blassingame flabbergasted. . . . The experience was and is most unpleasant."[32] Later he admitted knowing he and Woodward had differences, "of course, but our relationship had always been at least 'correct' and sometimes friendly."[33] "I felt sympathy for Herbert's illusions," Lemisch said in an interview.[34]

While Aptheker and Lemisch plotted a strategy for overcoming the resistance of Woodward, Blum, and Blassingame, Aptheker consulted Blassingame's book *The Slave Community* (1972), which Aptheker called "a rather careful and pedestrian effort." Aptheker wrote to Lemisch, "My *American Negro Slave Revolts* is cited more often than any other single secondary work in the volume (though I am excluded from the bibliographical essay in the book's rear). . . . All in all, there are fifteen separate footnotes to my various works, and the page references to my *American Negro Slave Revolts* cover very nearly the whole book." Aptheker found "never a reference hinting even at criticism; on the contrary, the references are those to a source that any reader will believe the author feels authoritative."[35]

Woodward had contacted Genovese after receiving Gettleman's letter with its warning about the actions to come. Genovese, a street fighter, counseled Woodward. "As an old and dear friend," Genovese wrote to Woodward, "I must break my rule about giving unsolicited advice."[36] He defended Aptheker to Woodward: "I have a good opinion of Aptheker, notwithstanding many battles; in my opinion he is a good historian who has shown enormous courage in defense of his party." Woodward ridiculed the suggestion: "Do you really think our friend Herbert is that good? I wonder what you have in mind. Certainly not his monograph on slave revolts, or the slighter things on Nat Turner or labor in the ante-bellum South. . . . [F]rankly I have to admit to my colleagues that I am unable to come up with anything that I could honestly call first rate."[37] While he may have been confident in stirring the hornet's nest, even some of Woodward's friends thought he had gone a bit too far. Arthur Schlesinger Jr., no friend of Aptheker's, "remarked to Blum that Woodward's behavior had given Aptheker 'tenure forever in the pantheon of the Left' by virtually martyring Du Bois's comrade." Even Blum assumed political motivation on Woodward's part: "Vann's a controversialist and thrives on such disputes," Blum commented, "but one still suspects . . . the extent of unspoken and perhaps even unacknowledged pleasure which he took in settling an old score with the American Communist Party for its behavior in the Angelo Herndon case in 1932." He was referring to a Georgia court that had convicted the labor organizer Herndon of violating its "insurrection law," which carried the death penalty. Woodward, who was traveling very close to the CPUSA, became chairman of the Angelo Herndon Defense Committee, an alliance that included noncommunists, socialists, and Joseph Brodsky and Alan Taub, the coordinators of the International Labor Defense, a party organization. In an unguarded moment of candor with Brodsky and Taub, Woodward claimed that Will W. Alexander, the head of the Atlanta Interracial

Commission, a member of the Defense Committee, and a frequent Woodward ally and mentor, although "a dear sweet old man," could "not be relied on" to enter into the kind of politics necessary for the Defense Committee to succeed. Brodsky and Taub, having already driven away the socialists and in an effort now to provoke a split in the noncommunist members of the Defense Committee and thereby give the party control, saw to it that Woodward's criticism made the front page of the *Daily Worker*. Woodward reconciled with Alexander but evidently, if Blum is correct, never forgave the party for its machinations in the Herndon affair. Blum's comment is intriguing given that Woodward maintained that his actions in the Aptheker controversy were not political.[38]

At the OAH annual meeting held in St. Louis in early April 1976, Lemisch presented a petition at the business meeting, signed by more than one hundred other historians, as required by the organization's constitution, to launch an investigation of the Yale–Aptheker affair. "Our struggle is raging," Lemisch and Gettleman wrote to Aptheker on a postcard from the convention, "the 'establishment' is freaked out—and we're having a swell time—wish you were here."[39] The amended constitution provided for no discussion or vote on the petition "but went directly to mail ballot."[40]

Gettleman reported to Woodward on the OAH activities. "You will have heard by now of what we consider our successful efforts in St. Louis," he wrote. The actions of the Yale Joint Board in approving Aptheker's appointment over Woodward's vocal objections had yet to occur, and Gettleman, who was genuinely fond of Woodward, hoped that "you can find some way to extricate yourself from this business."[41] Gettleman told Woodward, "The affection and high regard I have for you will not make it easy for me to fight for what I believe right in this matter, but I will do it nonetheless, hoping, perhaps against hope, that we can retain a measure of cordiality when the dust settles."[42]

The *OAH Newsletter* for July carried the discussion of the Yale-Aptheker Resolution. The resolution called on the OAH Committee for the Defense of Historians to investigate Yale's action. Since no such committee existed, OAH Executive Secretary Richard S. Kirkendall decided to refer the matter, with the agreement of the AHA, to the AHA–OAH Joint Committee on the Defense of the Rights of Historians Under the First Amendment should the Yale–Aptheker Resolution pass, which it eventually did, narrowly, by a vote of 833 in favor of an investigation and 818 against. The *Newsletter* carried a statement in support of the resolution together with an outline of events through early April; it was signed by Lemisch, Gettleman, Bracey, Martin Duberman, Michael Frisch, and Sterling Stuckey.[43] Lemisch did most of the work in putting the statement together, drafts of which passed among him, the other signers, and Aptheker.[44]

After all the maneuvering at Yale and the OAH's decision to investigate, which was finally codified when the AHA agreed to join the investigation in

December, when Aptheker's seminar at Yale in the fall of 1976 finally started, it was something of an anticlimax. No drama. No protests. Just Aptheker and fifteen or twenty students concentrating on Du Bois's life and works for twelve weeks without, Aptheker remarked, "having their minds brainwashed, their critical faculties destroyed, or their scholarly integrity compromised."[45]

The dissension over the Yale seminar kept Aptheker's name in the press, which gave the party an opening. Gus Hall convinced Aptheker to enter the U.S. Senate race in New York. His opponents were the Republican James Buckley and the Democrat Daniel Patrick Moynihan. A mere five weeks before the election, very late in the process, Aptheker announced his candidacy at a press conference at the Roosevelt Hotel in midtown Manhattan.[46]

Hastily conceived and underfunded, Aptheker's campaign rarely left Manhattan and the surrounding boroughs, although he did make a few appearances in other parts of the state. His campaign brochure looked more like an academic curriculum vitae than a political document. He outlined an aggressive program to "slash military spending, end Cold War anti-Soviet policies, outlaw racism, establish single-payer health care, and guarantee equal rights for women."[47]

In October Aptheker gave an interview to Geoffrey Stokes of the *Village Voice,* who charged in his article, among other things, that Aptheker "is also, of course, stuck with believing that homosexuality is bourgeois decadence." The story prompted John Stanley, a gay political activist who lived in Greenwich Village and a veteran of the Second World War, to contact Aptheker. "I'd like to vote for you because I'm in favor of communism," Stanley wrote, "but I'll not vote for a regime which will make me a second class citizen." Stanley asked Aptheker to refute the claim reported in the *Voice.*[48]

Stanley's letter was not the first Aptheker received from a comrade worried about the party's homophobia. Just a year earlier the party member Sarah Montgomery, with whom Aptheker corresponded from time to time, wrote to ask him "why the socialist world feels it correct to reject, even persecute, gay people."[49] Aptheker replied that he supposed "there is the reality of backwardness and prejudice which exists among Communists too. I have raised this matter—as I promised you [earlier]—at the highest level [of the party] and will continue to bring this question up because as matters stand now I personally believe the position is not a good one."[50] Reiterating that earlier position more expansively in his reply to Stanley, Aptheker denied that Stokes had even asked about homosexuality. "I stated publicly on [the radio on Wednesday, 20 October] that each village has its idiot and most have their liar but in this case that village showed it had both an idiot and a liar and that it foolishly employed him as a reporter." More to the point, Aptheker told Stanley that there was some irony in the situation "because it happens that for some years I have been proposing a re-examination of what I believe to be an erroneous position on homosexuality in much of the world-wide Communist movement. . . . I believe that sexual conduct between consenting adults is the business of these adults and nobody else's business and most certainly is not a matter subject to law and/or social condemnation. This is and has been my position; and this is by no means the first time I have stated that. You may show this to whomever you wish."[51]

Aptheker developed his position on homosexuality in the abstract, not understanding then, or perhaps ever, if Bettina is correct, just how intimately personal the issue was within his own family. At around the same time, in the summer of 1976, Bettina, also a member of the party, was agonizing over her sexual orientation. "I had been closeted for twenty years," she wrote in her memoir. "I was cautious, apprehensive, sometimes truly terrified of the consequences of my actions, and stunned by my daring to do what I had previously only imagined." Not until the late 1970s, after her divorce and her coming out, did she attempt to have a discussion with her parents about her lesbianism, and even then, she wrote in the memoir, the situation arose more by osmosis than by actual dialogue because she was not prepared to directly acknowledge her relationship with her partner, Kate Miller. "I don't know what my father understood of my relationship with Kate," she wrote in the memoir, "because we never talked about it directly."[52]

A year after the election, Aptheker and Montgomery continued their correspondence about homosexuality. The seventy-eight-year-old Montgomery, who was instrumental in founding the gay rights group Parents and Friends of Lesbians and Gays, wrote an impassioned and deeply sad letter to Aptheker in the summer of 1977 after returning from what by then had become the annual gay pride parade in New York City. Montgomery by that time had been a CPUSA member for decades. "Always," she wrote, "the Party has spoken out against oppression, lies, & denigration of human beings . . . [but] where oh where is my Party I thought as I looked over that multitude [the fifty thousand people at the parade]. . . . Is my Party so deeply homophobic that no one ever questions anything?" She told Aptheker that her forty-six-year-old son, "my child," and his forty-eight-year-old lover, who "had suffered all they could . . . they had no jobs . . . & could not start all over at their ages, . . . killed themselves." In her anguish and grief over their deaths, though her concerns were broader, she wanted to know about the fate of "20,000,000 gay people denied all their rights." The party locked her in a closet of her own, Montgomery told Aptheker, and she refused to acknowledge her membership to the people with whom she worked on gay rights. "I'll be a Communist till I die," she wrote, "but I will never never say that so long as the Party maintains this strange silence on such a large people movement. I do also admit the Party is in very strange company, . . . Anita Bryant [the homophobic pop singer] and the Catholic Church & the Religious forces plus the Klu Klux Klan [*sic*] . . . that's what makes me feel I'm on another planet."[53] "As I had promised you, there is motion on this in the

Party," Aptheker told Montgomery in his response, with, as events turned out, exceedingly premature optimism. "[There] was a meeting at a top level a short time ago and there will be more. These matters take time but once movement begins there is no doubt of the outcome."[54]

Aptheker's prediction that there would soon be movement on the party's acceptance of gay rights was off by two decades. Not until after the major split in the party in the 1990s did it address its homophobia. Even though he continued to press the leadership to alter the party's position, they refused to budge. Aptheker had basically acquiesced to "democratic centralism" by 1979, but only just. "I've had my say on the homosexual thing," he wrote to Hall in a long letter responding to his request for ideas to include in the Main Political Report at the 22nd National Convention. "I started to do [this] about 5 years ago. I still believe the Party is backward here and that sexual hangups persist that hurt us."[55]

What he did or did not say in the *Village Voice* interview had little influence on the senatorial election, which he lost by a wide margin. Although he polled a larger percentage of the vote in some precincts than the party's presidential ticket—Hall and Jarvis Tyner—the inevitable outcome matched the crushing defeat of his run for the House a decade earlier.

The race for the Senate was an interlude between the acts of the Yale–Aptheker farce, which entered its prolonged third act the month after the election. The final curtain did not fall until mid-1978. The AHA–OAH Committee moved slowly in its investigation. In February 1977 the Committee sent Aptheker a series of questions regarding the events that had transpired at Yale. In late February he responded fully and openly to the inquiries. Then, after consulting with Lynd, who had left academia to take up a career as a lawyer and preferred to keep his name out of the proceedings if possible, Aptheker sent Kirkendall a series of conditions that Lynd had proposed to ensure fairness in the investigation. Aptheker sent copies of his letter to Kirkendall to the historians Robert Wiebe, Stanley Katz and Herbert Gutman, all of whom sat on the governing boards of the two history organizations. Aptheker wanted information about what procedures the Committee would use. Further, since Aptheker had provided documents, so should Yale, including the written statements presented by Woodward and Blassingame at various hearings and other documents from interested parties. Aptheker told Kirkendall that the Committee should "hold personal interviews" with a number of people, including "Woodward, Blassingame, Blum and me."[56] Wiebe, who sat on the OAH executive board, told Aptheker that "the board's legal advisers discouraged as active an investigatory approach as you outlined" but said he was "in no position to comment on the body of your specific suggestions."[57]

Without responding to Aptheker's letter, Kirkendall and the other members of the Committee decided, when they met in Chicago in June, to ignore

Aptheker's suggestions. "We decided that the decisions that had been made about procedures were satisfactory," Kirkendall wrote to Katz at the University of Chicago Law School. "We're convinced that we have neither the experience, nor the financial resources necessary to proceed as the AAUP [American Association of University Professors] does," that is, to visit Yale and interview the participants in the conflict. Confirming the view of radical historians that historians should monitor themselves and not farm their problems out to the AAUP, Kirkendall told Katz that "historians with grievances that demand attention of that sort should take their cases to the AAUP rather than to the Joint Committee."[58] Katz subsequently told Aptheker that he was "convinced that Kirkendall has kept his word very well indeed."[59]

Lynd grew increasingly uncomfortable with the process the Committee proposed, especially when he saw Kirkendall's letter to Katz of 8 July reaffirming that the Committee would issue its final report to the OAH Executive Council in November without ever going to Yale or interviewing anyone. Lynd and Lemisch wanted to demand of the Committee that "it either investigate [all the sources and visit Yale] or permit us to do so and delay their report until we have a chance. . . . If the Committee will not come to the evidence which is at Yale, we must find a way to bring the evidence to the Committee."[60]

Having decided against going to Yale and denying Aptheker's notion that it interview the figures involved in the dispute, the Joint Committee delivered its preliminary report to the OAH executive board. On 8 November the *Yale Daily News* reported that the Joint Committee had completed its report, quoting the assurance of the president of the OAH, Kenneth Stampp, that the report would be released in January "after both the OAH and the AHA have gone through the formality of having the decision approved by their board members."[61] In a letter written jointly with Thomas Emerson of Yale Law School, a leading constitutional scholar who had agreed to represent Aptheker, Lynd protested Stampp's press statement and the Joint Committee's action, addressing his comments to the "32 people who comprise the committee of inquiry, the OAH Board, and the AHA Council."[62] Again citing the failure of the Joint Committee to visit Yale or conduct interviews, Lynd and Emerson noted that the OAH executive board balked at approving the report because the Committee had presented only "the narrative section of . . . the report," not "the report as a whole." Nonetheless the OAH board had decided to permit the report to be made public if the AHA Council agreed at its meeting in December to do so. Emerson and Lynd, on behalf of Aptheker, demanded that it not be released until the full report was approved by both the AHA and OAH governing boards. The two lawyers characterized the Joint Committee's record thus far as exhibiting "intellectual superficiality, . . . discourtesy, . . . arbitrary and undemocratic procedure, . . . [and being unfair] toward Dr. Aptheker and, for that matter, toward the Yale University history department."[63]

Lemisch felt that a whitewash by the Joint Committee was in the works even though he had not seen the report. Nonetheless, he wrote, "the friendly people I've spoken to on the OAH board characterize negatively the part of the committee report that they got to see in November."[64]

Lemisch was right to worry about a whitewash. Whereas the OAH executive board put off making a decision until a meeting of the organization in April 1978, the AHA Council, at its meeting in December 1977, adopted a resolution that accepted and endorsed the report. Both organizations released the report to their members. "There is no evidence," the Report found, "of a violation of the established procedures for considering academic appointments at Yale University, and the procedures themselves do not violate academic freedom or rights guaranteed by the First Amendment."[65] The Joint Committee accepted the Yale History Department's assertion that Woodward, Blum, and Blassingame had acted as individuals rather than as department representatives when they opposed Aptheker's appointment even after the Political Science Department had agreed the first time to sponsor the seminar: "All other acts by historians, including the presentations made at the meetings of the Joint Board, were by individuals acting for themselves."[66]

The Report simply restated the self-assessment of the History Department's responses to the Committee's questions. No independent investigation. No interviews of participants. As to the imputation of political motives in Woodward's, Blum's, and Blassingame's rejection of Aptheker, the Committee put the burden of proof on Aptheker. The Committee decided to compel Aptheker to "provide convincing evidence of improper motivation by decision makers, who, in the nature of things, decide secretly and may not fully voice their reasons even to one another."[67] Woodward was quoted in the *Yale Daily News* on 2 February 1976 as saying that "most disappointed applicants go about their business with the perfectly plausible consolation that teaching or studying at Yale is not the only possible way to pursue an honorable and rewarding career and that there are other good colleges available, even some good community colleges. A healthy response of this sort is to be encouraged."[68] Echoing Woodward's "contemptuous snarl, disguised as Ivy League witticism," as Lynd characterized it, the Report declared, "One does not normally interpret an adverse judgment in the appointment process as a challenge to an historian's integrity, or as a bill of charges that should warrant a public airing and the opportunity for a detailed refutation."[69]

Lynd summed up the Report in an essay that appeared in a Festschrift published in 1998 in honor of Aptheker: "[It revealed] a process that was not an investigation at all.... The so-called findings of the Report are nothing more than the History Department's own prior self-assessments."[70] Was a professional and political vendetta of Woodward's playing out against Aptheker? Gene Genovese surmised that the scholarly shortcomings ascribed to Aptheker had little to do with the Yale–Aptheker affair. "Woodward was capable of petty jealousy . . . he had a very nasty side," Genovese recalled in an interview. "He mentions none of his graduate students in [his memoir] *Thinking Back*. . . . He was jealous about Aptheker having the Du Bois papers. . . . Woodward lied. I had lunch with him during the Yale matter. He said his opposition to Aptheker was not political. I believed him. He told me years later that of course his opposition was political."[71] In 1993 the conservative National Association of Scholars, "funded by the right-wing John M. Olin Foundation, . . . bestowed its Sidney Hook Memorial Award on Woodward." Woodward's acceptance speech "centered around the theme that the university is not an appropriate place for political struggle, 'is not a political institution.'"[72]

Having failed to keep the Report private until the OAH membership could vote, Aptheker's defenders mobilized to have the OAH membership reject the report at its annual meeting in April 1978. Lemisch, Lynd, Mark Naison, and the radical scholars around MARHO, especially Gettleman, took the lead in devising a strategy to put in play at the meeting. They worried that Genovese, whom Gettleman called the Red Pope of Rochester and who was, they thought, as president-elect of the OAH, something of a loose cannon, would oppose any action they might bring to the meeting.[73] "You're right on Genovese," Gettleman wrote to a colleague, "don't provoke him, 'draw him in' (as you say), etc. But let's watch him carefully. As a member of the OAH council he's in it up to his ears already."[74]

Having been offered an opportunity to reply to the Report in the *OAH Newsletter* for July 1978, Aptheker drafted what Lynd called "a stunning (even witty) response to the Report."[75] Lynd wanted copies of the draft to be in the hands of the OAH Council prior to the meeting in April 1978 because he felt that while the publication in the *Newsletter* would be important, it would appear "long after the Report's initial distribution, safely after the meetings of the OAH board and the OAH membership in April, at a time when the academic world is on vacation and does not read its mail." Through the efforts of Katz the Council did receive the Report prior to the meeting.[76] In fact, the Council members Katz and Wiebe imparted their preoccupation with the Report to their fellow Council members. Especially, they said, "we are both deeply troubled by the Comments section of the report." Katz wanted the Council to comment on the Report, and he and Wiebe urged the Council to accept the conclusion of the Report but include a caveat in its resolution of acceptance that stated the following: "If substantial grounds existed for rejecting [Aptheker's] course [at Yale], none has been revealed. . . . On the basis of the available evidence, special but unstated criteria were employed in vetoing Aptheker's course, and therefore a special shadow was cast over Aptheker himself."[77] "We would both prefer a more extreme position, but fear it would result in a Phyrrhic victory," Katz told Alfred Young.[78]

Gettleman thought even that watered-down resolution was unlikely to pass. Since Aptheker and many of the other members of the group could not attend the convention in April, Gettleman accepted the task of representing the pro-Aptheker historians. He began work on a resolution for Aptheker's advocates to present. The "trial draft," which he sent around for comment stated, "WHEREAS, the OAH/AHA Joint Committee Report on Herbert Aptheker and Yale University fails to consider relevant data offered and available and accepts Yale's own rationales at face value, we reject this report as an inadequate exercise in historical analysis as well as a whitewash of Yale's disgraceful treatment of Herbert Aptheker." Gettleman reported that MARHO would provide a thousand copies of a special issue of the *Radical Historians' Newsletter* that contained a condensation of a legal brief Lynd had written on the controversy, "so that everybody at the business meeting will find it on his/her chair, and we'll have plenty for distribution."[79]

The Council met in New York on 12 April 1978. Katz had never met Aptheker. He didn't think Wiebe had either. "I'd be surprised if Bob knew Aptheker," he said in an interview. In an attempt to sway their votes, the Harvard historian Frank Friedell and Stampp invited Katz and Wiebe to have lunch "after the morning board session (and before the afternoon session at which we would vote)." Stampp "took the lead," Katz recalled, "and made the case that Vann Woodward was a good old boy (that is, a liberal who had always supported the sorts of liberal causes that he knew Bob and I supported)." Stampp and Friedell "acknowledged that Vann might have erred in the Aptheker matter but urged us to see his action as either under pressure or at any rate somehow consistent with proper academic procedure." Of primary importance to them, Katz said, "was Woodward. They loved and admired him."

After lunch, Friedell, who had mentored Katz at Harvard, spoke privately with Katz, admitting he was embarrassed "by the whole thing," yet he wanted Katz to vote with Stampp. "Bob and I politely (the whole thing was infuriatingly polite) demurred," Katz recalled, "and said that we believed Vann had behaved badly, and that it was important for the OAH to stand up for the rights of scholars and teachers, and not to give in to elite institutions and academic elites when they behaved inappropriately. Bob and I stuck to our guns in the afternoon, but as you know we were outvoted."[80] Katz and Wiebe presented their resolution, and Stampp countered with one of his own. Gutman and Genovese expressed qualms about the failure of the Committee to conduct interviews at Yale: "David Brody thought that the report was not sufficiently clear about what there was in the evidence that gave the committee confidence to say that there was no political motivation involved in Aptheker's rejection."[81]

Stampp objected vehemently. "I was very blunt about it," Stampp said in an interview. "I said, 'This is an attempt to censure C. Vann Woodward, and C. Vann Woodward has been a staunch supporter of academic freedom and civil rights and he had reasons why he did this. You all don't know what his motives are. You are going to, in effect, say that this man is an enemy of academic freedom.' And I won. We had a vote, a secret vote, and they were voted down."[82] Although Katz and Wiebe "denied that their resolutions were an attack on Woodward," after extended discussion of Stampp's resolution the Board adopted a third, compromise resolution, one that accepted the conclusion of the AHA–OAH Committee.[83] Gutman, Katz, Genovese (according to Gettleman), and one other Council member, probably Wiebe, voted against the resolution.[84] Katz recalled decades later that he left the meeting feeling absolutely certain that Genovese "had joined the other side" and had "voted against Aptheker."[85]

Stampp's relationship with Aptheker had not always been confrontational. In 1963, when Stampp chaired the History Department at Berkeley, the department had invited Aptheker to speak. About an hour before Aptheker's presentation on 18 February 1963, the university administration ordered the History Department to cancel the speech. "The History department . . . was not to pay me," Aptheker wrote about the confrontation, "and . . . it was not to sponsor me." Stampp and the department "rebelled, . . . insisted on sponsoring the talk . . . [at] Stiles Hall,—just off the campus," Aptheker recalled. At the new location Stampp introduced Aptheker. Aptheker wrote to Fay, "He also announced that while the department had been forbidden to pay me, a collection would be taken . . . a total of $45 . . . came from the audience that numbered perhaps one hundred . . . and then an ovation. Really terrific."[86]

At the OAH general membership business meeting, chaired by Genovese, Naison introduced a resolution supporting Aptheker and then turned the floor over to Gettleman.[87] Gettleman's spirited defense of Aptheker, relying primarily on Lynd's brief, focused on the inadequacy of the Committee investigation itself, which led to the whitewash of the Yale History Department and ignored the personal motives of the decision to reject the seminar. Gettleman also indicted the history profession and the professional organizations for not defending academic freedom: "In the present period of academic retrenchment it has been easy for academic departments to dismiss radicals, Marxists, women and minority teachers on questionable charges like those leveled against Herbert Aptheker—inadequate scholarship—or on no charges at all." He called for the OAH to establish a watchdog group, "the mere existence [of which] would act as a deterrent to many who would trample on academic freedom."[88] When Gettleman finished, Stampp, whose actions at the Council meeting prefigured his role at the business meeting, introduced a substitute resolution accepting the Report and codifying the Council's decision.

The Yale–Aptheker debate was the last item on the business meeting agenda. As the meeting proceeded, a sizable number of historians left. When Genovese finally called for the vote, only 115 members were still in the room. On the key vote to substitute Stampp's amendment for Naison's, 65 members voted in favor and 50 against. When Stampp's resolution became the main motion, only 100 members voted, 59 in favor to 41 against. Gettleman reported the results to the others by phone but later, in a letter, wrote that "with the exception of a droll chap named Jennings from the Newberry Library, and Paul Gates of Cornell, every male over 50 voted against us. We had women and youth, but—again it comes back to this—not enough of them stayed to 6:15 when the votes were taken."[89]

Woodward scraped the scab off an old wound a decade later when he commented on the Yale–Aptheker affair in an interview with James Green in *Radical History Review* (*RHR*). When asked about Aptheker and the seminar, Woodward again charged that Aptheker "didn't come up to our standards of scholarship" and went on to complain that the correspondence of Du Bois published by Aptheker was "pretty shallow; there are omissions, emphases, deletions," he asserted, without offering specific examples. He went further, though, revealing, perhaps inadvertently, and then covering as best he could a political motivation behind his actions in opposition to Aptheker. "Then of course [there were] his books defending Russian policy in Hungary and Czechoslovakia," Woodward said. "We didn't want to consider these two political tracts as history. It was perfectly obvious that he was following the party line, defending the invasions. But that wasn't the issue, nor was it his party connection."[90]

The interview sparked a series of outraged letters to the editors of *RHR*. Genovese, who counseled Aptheker in a personal letter to "not fret," assailed Green's interview. "The brutal attack on Herbert Aptheker in your pages in no way diminishes him," Genovese and his wife, Elizabeth, wrote to *RHR*. "It diminishes you, the more so since you and your interviewer associated yourselves, by contemptible editorial silence, with transparent red-baiting." Hugh Murray, who had worked with Aptheker at the American Institute for Marxist Studies, declared that "1970s McCarthyism should be called Woodwardism." "I was very dismayed to read C. Vann Woodward's slur against the work of Herbert Aptheker," the historian Manning Marable of Purdue University declared. "For Woodward to dismiss Dr. Aptheker's scholarship . . . is not simply outrageous, it's a slur against all progressive scholarship." "If some specific charge is being made," John Bracey wrote from the University of Massachusetts at Amherst, "I, for one, wish that Vann Woodward would make it more explicit. I am appalled that Jim Green let Vann Woodward's vague assertions and open red-baiting go unchallenged." Lemisch reminded readers that "one of the risks involved in achieving the power and deference which have come to Woodward is that no one will tell you when you have done something really awful."[91]

The radical historians who took up the defense of Aptheker, individuals like Gettleman, Lemisch, Naison, Young, Lynd, and others in addition to those at MARHO more broadly, carried forward the activism born of their struggles against the Vietnam War and the battle to counter the consensus, conservative historians who dominated the historical profession, the interpretation of history, and the two major historical associations. Woodward had said the university was not the place for politics, yet that generation of "gentlemen" historians who controlled the academy, Lemisch pointed out in his book about the profession, *On Active Service in War and Peace: Politics and Ideology in the American Historical Profession* (1975), was every bit as political as Aptheker and other radicals. The difference was that their politics were more subtly practiced, and they controlled who did and did not deserve admission to their club.[92] While Aptheker and his supporters lost the battle over the AHA–OAH Report, they essentially won the war. The controversy over Aptheker's appointment "was a significant episode in the intellectual and political history of the 1970s," Crowe remarked in a proposal for a study of the dispute. It was, he wrote, "the last major university confrontation in a decade of protest and a matrix of discussion on academic freedom, community, collegiality, standards, 'confidentiality,' historical inquiry and the nature and uses of the university."[93]

Students were at the very center of the feud at Yale; they were drawn to Aptheker, twice inviting him to present a seminar at Yale, and they defied Woodward, Blum, Blassingame as well as the History Department faculty and the university administration. "It is the Left which has spoken to them of real issues," Lemisch wrote in his book, "of pain and suffering, and of a better world which has not been seen before.... We will not go away. We exist, and people like us have existed throughout history and we will simply not allow you the luxury of continuing to call yourselves politically neutral while you exclude all of this from your history. You cannot lecture us on civility while you legitimize barbarity." Like Lemisch and other radical historians, Aptheker had simply refused to go away. For decades he had inveighed against his generation of historians, the "Laureates of Imperialism." Now Lemisch and his generation of young radicals, in their defense of Aptheker, took up the cudgel to challenge the dominance of the Woodwards, to open up the historical profession, to try to "cure it of [its] partisan and self-congratulatory fictions, [to try] to come a little closer to finding out how things actually were."[94]

18   The American Institute for Marxist Studies

BY THE early 1960s Aptheker's once-athletic build, his full chest and slim waist, had filled out, "making for a straight line, shoulders to thighs." His distinctive thick, black-rimmed glasses, which he sometimes used as a prop to emphasize a point, were set off by his crew-cut hair, which formerly had been "very short, curly, almost black" but had abruptly turned white in the summer of 1955, a physical manifestation perhaps of the inward turmoil brought on by the pressures of McCarthyism.[1] Out of the ashes of the intraparty tumult of late 1950s, Aptheker built a niche for himself as a leading intellectual in the Communist Party, though he was not part of the political staff and never sought a leadership position.

For three years, until its demise in 1963, Aptheker served on the editorial board of *Mainstream,* the party's literary publication. *Mainstream* turned into a drain on the party's finances and became a point of contention among the leaders in its last three years. When some members of the National Board criticized the magazine for a lack of orthodoxy, Aptheker defended it and urged that it continue to be funded. An FBI informant reported that during discussions of the publication's "function, role and future" a party leader "referred to Aptheker as a good general promoter and publicity man, though lacking in tactics. [He] added that Aptheker, in a bourgeois sense, is jealous and petty ... [and] believes that he is an authority on Marxism."[2] When the party shut down *Mainstream,* it did so without consulting Aptheker. "Please know that I also was not informed of [the closing of *Mainstream*] until after everything was arranged and to be done," he wrote to a friend who complained "about the manner in which that magazine's suspension was accomplished and announced." "I did not know who had been or had not been informed thereof," Aptheker said.[3] He snapped his head in the air, swallowed his anger, and moved on yet again.

Aptheker's position in the party derived from his work as a historian and public intellectual, not the most solid foundation in a party run by Hall. "I wasn't an organizational person," Aptheker recalled. "I was just an intellectual. ... My job was writing and lecturing and talking. ... I never was an organizational officer of the Party."[4] Though limited by the party leaders—and Aptheker's role may have been less limited than most—intellectuals served a specific purpose in the party:

"[To devise] a rationale for whatever the current Party line might be," according to Healey.[5] "There is truth in that," Aptheker opined, responding to Healey's observation, "but it's crude, it's one-sided, as you would expect from Dorothy. She was very bright, but she was always an organizational person. In that sense it was one-sided." "She didn't know how I functioned," Aptheker added, "she just assumed."[6] Aptheker claimed that his greatest influence on the leadership and the decisions it made came through his close relationship with the second-in-command, Henry Winston. "At his request," Aptheker said of his weekly meetings with Winston, of which he kept no record, "[we] used to meet . . . at his office. He would ask me questions in terms of the Party and the Party line and what we were doing and what the problems were. . . . In this way I directly influenced the Party, that's the point."[7] Why did Winston not discuss the closing of *Mainstream*? Aptheker didn't say, but the influence he enjoyed over Winston, as later incidents demonstrate, was probably much less than Aptheker professed or even realized at the time.

In 1959 Aptheker began discussions with other radicals to bring Left intellectuals inside and outside the party together in some kind of version of the Popular Front. As he traveled around the country speaking on college and university campuses, he engaged faculty members in conversation. He sought the support of academics for his inchoate organization, which he envisaged as a group in which radicals unaffiliated with the party could feel comfortable interacting with him and with other party intellectuals in a place where divergent opinions would be respected and where members and nonmembers alike could listen as well as talk, offer opinions instead of rules, ask questions and make suggestions rather than demands.

He took his idea to individuals within the party as well. "I was trying to make the Party change its whole attitude toward [other leftists], toward me, [toward] the whole *Monthly Review* crowd. Now their hostility was not corruption—that's the way Gus Hall put it—'they're bought.' Well, that's ridiculous," Aptheker said in an interview. "They thought differently than we did and they're quite bright, and they have great influence, so they're making sense to many people and to themselves, and we ought to listen to what they're saying, not dismiss it." He pressed for analysis of the ideas of other leftists: "I don't mean to agree with it but to explain why we don't agree with it, not to simply say he's some agent or it's nonsense. That's no refutation. What's wrong with it? Now that's what I kept hammering at in Party circles all the time." Aptheker asked his comrades why prominent radicals, Marxists, were not in the party. "Is it only [them] or is it the Party? Is it our fault also? And of course I was saying it is. And it was."[8] When Hall lashed out at *Monthly Review* and *Science & Society* at an expanded National Executive Committee (NEC) meeting in May 1963, Aptheker criticized "the sharpness of Hall's attack." Carl Winter, a member of the NEC, backed Hall's position and castigated Aptheker: "There was a need to use rough language. 'We must be sharp with these people . . . who are fighting the Party,'" Winter said. Winter especially criticized Aptheker's defense of his fellow Marxist historian Genovese, whom the party had expelled in the 1950s. Genovese had written one of the articles in *Science & Society* that Hall had found offensive. Hall accused Aptheker of not defending the party. "The attack is on the Party," he said to the NEC, "not on Herb Aptheker personally. . . . Herb must answer the attack on the Party because it is a political question."[9]

The criticisms did not endear Aptheker to Hall, and when Hall was displeased, others followed suit. "The internal power dynamics of the Communist Party at the top are more akin to feudalism than socialism," Healey recalled. "The general secretary is the lord; he surrounds himself with loyal vassals, each in charge of a minor fiefdom which is his to keep as long, and only as long, as he enjoys his lordship's continued favor." Healey and others increasingly found Hall to be susceptible to delusions of his own magnificence. "Gus was not the first person to occupy the post of general secretary of the . . . Party who was swept away by a vision of his own brilliance," she observed.[10]

Aptheker's project proposal came at an opportune time for Hall as he maneuvered to remove Aptheker as editor of *Political Affairs*. Hall told an FBI informant within the party that while Aptheker "projects the correct Party line in the monthly publication . . . he never consults the Party leadership . . . [and] was not in close touch with the Party." Hall allowed that "many people were sorry that Aptheker had been elected to the National Committee."[11]

As the concept for an organization crystallized in Aptheker's thinking, he corresponded frequently with Joseph Morray, an attorney then teaching at UC Berkeley, outlining the need he sought to address: "The demands for help in the mail—and even people stopping me in the street—how to get this, where does one find that, what are the facts about the other—prove what a service we could perform, including I think more and more through correspondence." He told Morray that part of their project should be to "develop full bibliographies, annotated, on as many subjects as possible—music, art, American literature, history, economics, anthropology, etc etc with yearly supplements." The subject of the bibliographies would be Marxism. "Could we also provide a survey—each month?—of articles and books especially important at least in the social science fields? Do you think quite a few people would be willing to subscribe to that kind of service? . . . Could we effectively sponsor symposiums and forums?" Given the multitude of different books in use at high schools and colleges around the country "explaining" Communism, Aptheker reasoned that "one of our tasks . . . would be keeping up with this and on top of it; careful analysis and critiques, and perhaps a book of our own with a challenge that it be included in the curricula of the states and schools. Outlines and texts in dozens of fields are terribly needed and with organization could be provided."[12]

Within the party Aptheker seems to have worked most closely on developing the project with Gurley Flynn, who helped him convince other party leaders of the importance of his idea. By May 1962 Aptheker felt confident enough about the scope of the endeavor, which he named the American Institute for Marxist Studies (AIMS), that he circulated a proposal within the party requesting that the party sponsor it. He envisioned an organization with offices in several cities on the East and West coasts and in the Midwest. Its purpose, he wrote, was "to legalize Marxism in the United States. To get into THE debate":

> *To give combat* to misrepresentations, distortions, slanders against, caricatures of Marxism and Communism. This would mean active polemical work, directed against press (periodicals and books) and all other media of agitation and propaganda, including organizations. Would have to be aggressive and demanding: full publicity, challenges, debates, joint appearances, etc. . . . Publication of a newsletter, by subscription; perhaps monthly to begin with. . . . Style throughout must be vigorous, dignified, useful, down-to-earth, and national. Crisp, humor, militant. . . . There are new demands and new possibilities; there is need for new forms; there is particular eagerness among youth—working and student; would help train many.[13]

By the end of the year Aptheker had convinced Hall to back his plan. Hall said that "one of the main tasks of the CPUSA during the coming year will be to set up the 'Marxist Institute,' . . . he said that this operation, although it will be most expensive, will nevertheless be 'most important.' "[14] So important, it seemed, that Hall was willing even to use party funds to help get it going. At a meeting attended by Aptheker, Hall agreed to raise money for "personnel and the maintenance of a headquarters for the institute in New York City."[15] It's not clear if Hall actually believed that AIMS was worthwhile or whether he supported it primarily to get Aptheker out of *Political Affairs,* which Hall eventually took over as editor after appointing Hyman Lumer, who served briefly after Aptheker's departure. Perhaps by funding AIMS, however minimally, Hall hoped to gain influence over Aptheker. "There are all kinds of subtle and not-so-subtle ways in which Gus has learned to reinforce his power," Healey wrote. "It's a very effective patronage system."[16] Whatever Hall's motives, on 21 January 1963 he gave "Lem Harris, a member of the CPUSA Reserve Fund operation, . . . $5,000 . . . for Herb . . . [to use] for the American Institute for Marxist Studies."[17]

Aptheker did not wait to get money from the party. Wherever he traveled he solicited organizational support and funds from friends and exponents around the country. Alexander Meiklejohn, a noted advocate of the First Amendment who in 1964 received the Presidential Medal of Freedom, agreed to become a proponent of the scheme in February 1963. "He listened with great care to the [AIMS] idea and asked many pointed questions," Herbert wrote to Fay from Berkeley, "... [for] an hour and a half ... then stated that he was for it, that what we were proposing was needed and that we could cite his name as a supporter.... The fact that he lends his name in support of the effort and empowers us to say that to others is a tremendous boost."[18] In July the writer and activist Scott Nearing, whom the party expelled in 1930, wrote to Aptheker agreeing "gladly [to] serve as one of the Institute Associates and join the Provisional Committee. Congratulations on the project."[19] When he received rejections, Aptheker replied courteously, stressing his desire to put aside differences to work for Left unity. "As to the point of working together with those of differing views," he explained to Gaylord LeRoy in November, "within the basic aim of getting a dialogue going involving the Marxist outlook, this can be done, I think.... since our work will be scholarly and will explicitly involve dialogue and discussion it should be possible to function more or less amicably. Certainly, it is worth trying," he asserted, "and no one else is; and it is overdue. I refuse to be paralyzed by the knowledge of the extreme difficulties and dangers; the thing is to try and to do the best we can and in this way, perhaps, to make a little contribution."[20]

In May 1963 he reported to an expanded meeting of party leaders that he had made real progress in recruiting AIMS adherents. He said he had uncovered a "reservoir of good will ... among wide circles of the left." Through his fund-raising efforts he had raised twenty-eight thousand dollars. "We need people who could become a part of the ... governing body, ..." he told the meeting. "No matter what these people themselves think of Marxism, good or bad, as long as they agree that Marxism is a part of our social dialogue ... we should appeal to them to join." He said AIMS needed people "who may disagree with Marxism if they only agree that it is not illegal to discuss Marxism. We will meet their objection. The important thing is to be able to discuss it." He reported that Morray, who was not a party member, would become the codirector of AIMS and that together they would solicit membership by mailing out three thousand copies of the prospectus. "The time has come for this Institute," he told the meeting, "and the effort has proven that it is a feasible project."[21]

Aptheker's hopes for AIMS proved to be attainable, despite some setbacks. By December he noted that 140 scholars from 35 universities had agreed to become members of AIMS. Late in December he wrote to Graham Du Bois to say that the "first initiating meeting" of AIMS had been held in New York. Ten scholars had accepted offers to sit on the governing board, he told her: "The prospects are exciting. I think it might make it; I'm certainly going to try."[22]

By March 1964 planning was well under way for the first AIMS symposium. Aptheker appointed himself as national director, and the board of directors, at Aptheker's urging, elected Robert S. Cohen, a physics and philosophy professor living in Boston, as chairman. Aptheker and Cohen had been friends since the early 1950s, and Cohen, a champion of free speech and an outspoken opponent of the HCUA, had written the introduction to Aptheker's collection of essays *History and Reality* in 1955. Cohen's letter of acceptance of the position appeared in the first AIMS announcement and solicitation for membership and donations. "No other democratic country so ignores the thoughts and activities of Karl Marx, and those who came after him," Cohen wrote. "I shall be glad to serve as chairman of the American Institute for Marxist Studies. . . . I have learned much from Marxism, although I am not a Marxist."[23] Cohen told members of AIMS's National Governing Council that his acceptance was based on assurances that "the Institute should maintain as broad a base as possible and should include: severe critics, neutrals, intellectuals and non-Marxists."[24]

An FBI COINTELPRO effort failed to disrupt the first AIMS symposium, "Marxism and Democracy," held at the Sheraton-Atlantic Hotel in midtown Manhattan, although Eslanda Robeson, Paul Robeson's wife, did upset the inaugural proceedings, at least in the eyes of Cohen. More than four hundred people had paid five dollars each to hear papers responding to Cohen, the evening's major presenter, who, an FBI informer wrote, "defined and traced the origins of Marxism and democracy up to the present day. Robeson spoke on Negro problems in America today," and Cohen's recollection of her talk was less than glowing.[25] "I would be foolish to conceal my distress at some of the aspects of our first symposium," he wrote. "I can find no adjective for her speech other than 'disgraceful.' You will forgive me," he appealed to Aptheker, "for finding her deliberate sneers at 'high intellectual talk' extraordinarily rude at such a meeting." Cohen was distressed as well by the "utterly partisan spirit, indeed the self-righteous partisanship, which she expressed, and of course by the fact that she glossed over the difficulties in the achievement of non-exploitive democracy."[26] Aptheker replied that reactions in New York ranged "from enthusiasm to the verdict 'colossal flop.' Both are excessive," he wrote, sidestepping Cohen's criticism of Robeson. "[I]n general, . . . a positive much more than a negative estimate is justified, I believe."[27]

At AIMS headquarters Aptheker had a small office next to the library and reading room, where a growing number of scholars conducted research. The library from the shuttered Jefferson School formed the basis of the AIMS library, which eventually grew to more than eight thousand volumes. Fay taught herself the Dewey decimal system and catalogued the burgeoning library. By June 1964 AIMS had associates at sixty-three colleges and universities and was being inundated with requests for information from faculty and students. When a request came in, Aptheker or one of the two researchers AIMS employed noted on an index card the topic of the query, the name of the correspondent, and the actions taken. If Aptheker did not have material at hand he sought the help of an

AIMS associate or sponsor. Typical was an inquiry received at the AIMS office on 14 December 1964 from a student at UCLA who was working on a history honors thesis about the shirtwaist makers' strike of 1909. On the seventeenth AIMS asked scholars affiliated with the organization for assistance in responding to the query. By the twenty-ninth Aptheker had received four bibliographies, which he copied and sent to the student.[28] He included the bibliographies in an edition of the AIMS "Newsletter" (published about every six weeks) along with bibliographies on new research in fields as varied as history, physics, literature, biology and art criticism. In its first year AIMS produced a prodigious number of scholarly works: two monographs, *Marxism and Democracy* and *The Problem of Alienation in the Modern World;* a research report, "Teaching 'About Communism' in American Public Schools"; two reprints, *Speeches Made in the United States, 1825–26* by Robert Owen and Aptheker's *David Walker's Appeal to the Colored People of the World, 1829;* bibliographic series 1, "Marxism and Economics," and series 2, "Marxism and Aesthetics"; and bibliographies of the writings of Du Bois, Foster, Daniel De Leon, Gurley Flynn, and Nearing.[29]

How much money Aptheker raised prior to the opening of AIMS is unclear, but the establishing of the office and library essentially drained his bank balance, and he was forced to try to raise funds from party organizations. That attempt upset some members of the party. Healey especially resented demands from New York for money to finance AIMS. "There is the feeling that nothing should be done until the full list of the sponsors is available," she wrote to Aptheker with some exasperation in January 1964. "This includes raising money. On that subject: we . . . need to know what your general budget is—and what you expect from here [the West Coast]. Quite frankly, we are being pressured for money on so many sides, including national projects, that everyone is building up a head of steam on the subject."[30] Healey complained at a party meeting in February that "the Los Angeles area was expected to produce . . . money [for AIMS] . . . [and] that concerning money, it was sort of a funnel-like procedure . . . in the east, they have the grandiose ideas which is the top of the funnel, and it all simmered down to the Los Angeles area where the money had to be raised."[31] A certified public accountant's report for the first nine months of operations revealed that AIMS's income for the period was $21,079 and its expenses $18,908.[32] As it turned out, the organization would operate close to the edge throughout its two decades of existence.

AIMS scheduled a second symposium for July 1964 at the 24th Annual World Fellowship Center (WFC) conference in Conway, New Hampshire. Willard Uphaus, a professor at Yale Divinity School, a longtime peace activist, and a founding sponsor of AIMS, led the WFC, which had weathered repeated state investigations into its alleged subversive nature. The FBI directorate in Washington devised a COINTELPRO operation aimed at destroying the effectiveness of both Uphaus and Aptheker.[33] FBI agents monitored and tried, unsuccessfully, to disrupt the proceedings of the conference. They also periodically reviewed the personal bank accounts of Cohen and Aptheker and the AIMS account, gaining access to them via a Chemical Bank assistant vice president. FBI documents that indicate salary payments made by AIMS showed that Aptheker received $99.55 per month for his endeavors. Most important to the bureau was its ability to register not only the names and addresses of people who wrote checks to AIMS but also the amount contributed. Given the proclivities of the agency, it's reasonable to assume that at a minimum it investigated each of those individuals, and in some cases may have ended up opening files of their own.

Through various informants and by monitoring the issues of the AIMS "Newsletter," the FBI learned in December 1964 that Aptheker had made an agreement with Paul Tillett of Rutgers University. The accord called for AIMS to conduct a major research project for the Eagleton Institute of Politics on the social costs of McCarthyism.[34] Designed by Tillett, "the project . . . [which] we feel . . . is eminently worthwhile . . . is one which seeks to discover specifically— as it were, quantitatively—just what McCarthyism cost the United States," Aptheker, in search of assistance, wrote to Robert Dunn at the Labor Research Association. "In particular, the effort seeks to ascertain what became of many of the people harassed and dismissed . . . and what became of the skills they had. . . . Anonymity may be maintained if desired," Aptheker assured Dunn, "though I have full confidence in the integrity and concern of those in charge of this inquiry."[35]

The FBI investigated Tillett and devised a COINTELPRO operation to "obtain valuable intelligence information," disrupt the Rutgers study, and "cause Rutgers University to sever its relationship with AIMS and . . . focus attention on Herbert Aptheker . . . [as well as discourage] other universities contemplating association with AIMS."[36] The operation failed, as Tillett died in 1965 before completing his study.

In early March 1965 Aptheker, making an appearance at Rutgers that was unrelated to his association with Tillett, denounced American imperialism in a speech sponsored by the Rutgers SDS and introduced by Gene Genovese. Like many of Aptheker's talks during this period, this one did not occur without controversy. In January the "Student Council Lecture Series co-chairman Frederick Borst refused to sign a voucher to provide funds for Aptheker's appearance," the Rutgers Daily Targum reported. Eventually, after considerable upheaval in the council, Borst signed the voucher.[37]

Their positions on the Vietnam War may have coincided, but Aptheker and Genovese had a complicated relationship over the years. Genovese began an on-again-off-again feud in 1963 by attacking Aptheker's American Foreign Policy *and the Cold War.* "Genovese saw Aptheker's commentaries on foreign policy as a hash of liberalism and pacifism, a weak attempt to woo the Democratic Party into alliance with the left," according to the historian Chris Phelps. " 'How pitiable,' [Genovese] sneered, 'are these impotent pleas to the liberal imperialists.' "[38] At times effusive in his praise of Aptheker's pioneering work in black history, especially of *American Negro Slave Revolts,* Genovese at other times ridiculed that same book. He didn't pull punches when in his critical phases, and both Herbert and Fay took the criticism personally. Fay urged Herbert to "have nothing to do with the man" after what she considered to be his excessive criticism of Herbert's work in *Roll, Jordan, Roll: The World the Slaves Made;* Herbert's reaction was to avoid talking to Fay about Genovese and his correspondence with him.[39] But that was Genovese's style: sharp, polemical, acerbic. Perhaps Aptheker reconciled so many times with him because he recognized something of himself in Genovese. Nonetheless, in spite of their fitful relationship, Aptheker appreciated Genovese because he seriously engaged Aptheker's scholarship, even if occasionally in a critical way.

Aptheker and Genovese both spoke out against the Vietnam War at the first Socialist Scholars Conference, held at Columbia University in September 1965. The next year, the second conference drew eight hundred Old Leftists, New Leftists, Trotskyists, and liberals to the Commodore Hotel in New York City. Genovese presented a paper titled "The Legacy of Slavery and the Roots of Black Nationalism" at a panel discussion at which Aptheker, Woodward, and Frank Kofsky, a Marxist historian at California State University, offered critical comments. Genovese opened by challenging Aptheker's conclusions in *American Negro Slave Revolts.* He argued, contrary to Aptheker's holding that "discontent and rebelliousness were not only exceedingly common, but indeed, characteristic of American Negro slaves," that blacks "did not establish a revolutionary tradition of much significance" and "far from furnishing models for rebellion, the characteristic slave leadership furnished prototypes of accommodation. Instead of examples to be followed," Genovese wrote, "they are an incubus to be exorcized, a debilitating legacy of subservience and paternalism that is to be deplored, repudiated, renounced."[40] "Slavery and its aftermath," Genovese concluded, "emasculated the black masses; they are today profoundly sick and shaking with convulsions."[41] Genovese criticized American radicals, his barb pointed at Aptheker, for having "long been imprisoned by the pernicious notion that the masses are necessarily both good and revolutionary, and by the even more pernicious notion that, if they are not, they should be."[42]

In his comment on the paper Aptheker countered Genovese's thesis, arguing that the major points he had presented in *American Negro Slave Revolts* remained valid, that in "his reading of the record . . . the annals of slavery teem with revolutionary heroes, and that their resistance to slavery provides models for present-day leaders and establishes a valid revolutionary tradition for embat-tled black America."[43] Aptheker did concede "there was—and to a large degree, there still is—an absence of a tradition of rebellion. . . . I find it remarkable his [Genovese's] failure to mention racism itself as the source of such an absence, but I think that is decisive. . . . Denial of a history on the part of racism's victim is a central element in racist ideology. This fundamentally explains, I think, the ab-sence of a tradition of rebellion among the Negro people in the United States."[44]

In a "Rejoinder" printed in *Studies on the Left* but not delivered at the confer-ence, Genovese struck personally and condescendingly at Aptheker's comment on his paper. He called portions of Aptheker's written critique "vulgar Marx-ism," what he defined elsewhere as the "superficial and opportunistic Marxism of the Communist Party."[45] "If Aptheker believes that any social system contains harmony, as well as antagonism, he may some day explain why there is hardly a line about harmony in the slave system in any of his twenty books. . . . He cannot seem to grasp that one might read his [books] and be unconvinced. . . . We share similar ideals and goals," Genovese continued, "and he knows it. We are quarrel-ing not over what should be, but over what has been, is and is becoming. . . . It is condescending, not to say pompous, to tell us that a historian needs to focus on what is becoming, for we have all had our course in Marxism."[46]

Criticism of Aptheker was not confined to Genovese. Some of Aptheker's black colleagues in the party, William Patterson, Claude Lightfoot, and, later, Henry Winston among them, whose works young black radicals read, let it be known, although not publicly, that they felt "Aptheker's views on Black people were overshadowing their own." This was "very much a part of the growing resistance to white domination in every aspect of the Party's activities as well as their increasing racial consciousness."[47]

The most vociferous criticism by a black scholar came from Harold Cruse. An ex–party member, Cruse, a black cultural nationalist who opposed integration, gained prominence just as the civil rights movement shifted into the black power era. At the time of the second Marxist Scholars Conference in 1966 he was still a year away from publishing his major work, *The Crisis of the Negro Intellectual.* Cruse proposed a paper for the conference, "Behind the Black Power Slogan," but did not present it. "Circumstances prevented me from attending this con-ference," he wrote in his book *Rebellion or Revolution* (1968). "But even before I decided I could not attend, the conference steering committee had refused to allow the paper to be presented, so I had no real motivation for attending in any event."[48] In *The Crisis of the Negro Intellectual,* which "throughout the late 60's and early 70's one could see . . . almost everywhere that young people were gathered," Cruse proposed an anti-integrationist manifesto and "urged black intellectuals and artists to establish their own institutions and reclaim black American culture from those who sought to appropriate it."[49] Cruse was always ecumenical in his criticism, but he reserved special venom for the CP and Jews, which to him were one and the same. "The Jews failed to make Marxism applicable to anything in America but their own national-group social ambitions or individual self-elevation," he wrote. "As a result, the great brainwashing of Negro radical intellectuals was not achieved by capitalism, or the capitalistic bourgeoisie, but by Jewish intellectuals in the American Communist Party."[50] Cruse made clear in his book and in the paper that went undelivered at the Marxist Scholars Conference (which he published as the last chapter of *Rebellion or Revolution*) that the chief Jewish Communist intellectual who exemplified all the others was Aptheker.

In his conference paper Genovese asserted that since "a separate economy and national territory are not serious possibilities . . . black hegemony in specific cities and districts—nationalism if you will—offers the only politically realistic hope of transcending the slave heritage . . . absorbing the nihilistic tradition into a socially constructive movement."[51] In his comment on Genovese's paper Aptheker granted the need for "enhanced power in localities" but rejected "the 'states' rights' plea of Genovese" and dismissed the notion of nationalism: "The realities of black nationalism are exaggerated by Genovese. . . . The point is that through integration one transforms," he wrote. "The effort is not simply to integrate *into* the nation; the demand is to transform a racist nation into an egalitarian one. Hence to battle for integration is to battle for basic transformation. Further integration is necessary to this nation exactly because the Negro is integral to it. . . . Genuine democratic, progressive and radical advance in this country has depended in the past, and most particularly depends in the present, upon popular mass power, united, and that means Negro-white mass power, together."[52]

In *Rebellion or Revolution* Cruse wrote witheringly, "Herbert Aptheker is one of the most un-Marxist Marxists quotable these days when it comes to heaping radical mystification on the Negro movement." His "perennial, plodding, unimaginative blindness on Negro history has led him into the inescapable swamps of theoretical obscurantism," and he "still has not grasped the basic fundamentals of Negro social development to this day." Cruse called Aptheker's Marxism "European 'book' Marxism, . . . the roots of [his] vulgar Marxian prejudices." He derided Aptheker's analysis of the triangular clash of ideologies among Booker T. Washington, Du Bois, and Marcus Garvey, in whom Cruse placed the origins of modern black thought. Furthermore, Cruse contended, Aptheker refused to understand that when Du Bois, "a younger generation radical, broke with the conservatism of Booker T. Washington on civil rights questions he did what Malcolm X was forced to do in breaking with Elijah Muhammad. . . . Aptheker is so engrossed in drooling sentimentally over his enduring love for W. E. B. Du Bois," Cruse wrote, "he loses all his historical objectivity (if he ever possessed that quality). . . . He cannot deal objectively with the black bourgeoisie as a class phenomenon in real life from a Marxist point of view. He cannot bring himself to call W. E. B. Du Bois what he really was—*a bourgeois radical intellectual* whose 'talented tenth' bourgeois elitism was nothing but a philosophy representing *his* tactic in an inner-class struggle for leadership."

Cruse continued his excoriation: "I can assure you that when some of the sons and daughters of certain of Aptheker's Communist Party leadership cronies broke with their parents' beloved Communist Party because it had grown superannuated and conservative, Herbert Aptheker did not applaud so loudly." Cruse ridiculed Aptheker's position on integration, saying that a "truly radical black program for social change in America must include the elements of *economics, politics,* and *culture* in a proper programmatic combination." It was not feasible "to follow Aptheker's mechanistic, anti-dialectical" call for integration. "Aptheker's intentions are laudable," Cruse wrote, "but his logic is anti-dialectical because it is the Negro himself who must be transformed before his self-projection can transform a racist society into something else. If after several decades of integrationism, Aptheker still cannot see that it is not transforming a racist society, then his blindness is both perverse and incurable."[53]

In his earlier work *The Crisis of the Negro Intellectual,* Cruse averred that Jewish intellectuals, "in order to ensure political and ideological power over Negroes, . . . had to master not only the cultural compulsives of their own group politics, but those of the oncoming Negro group as well." After 1929 Jews dominated the Communist Party, Cruse maintained, which "led inexorably to . . . the emergence of Herbert Aptheker and other assimilated Jewish Communists, who assumed the mantle of spokesmanship on Negro affairs, thus burying the Negro radical potential deeper and deeper in the slough of while intellectual paternalism." Aptheker "brazenly attempted to establish scholarly and theoretical dominance over Negro studies. . . . The Communist influence became a retarding, divisive, and destructive political force."[54]

Aptheker was not especially interested in Jewish concerns, although he did for some time edit the party's publication *Jewish Affairs,* in which he polemicized against "the left-progressive Jewish movement. . . . concerning the problem of anti-Semitism in the former Soviet Union and the former People's Poland. Aptheker and his party at the time denounced [people] associated with the *Jewish Currents* magazine and the Yiddish *Morgan Freiheit* for criticizing anti-Semitic publications and discrimination in those countries."[55] Aptheker was Jewish by birth, but, according to Bettina, he "rejected Judaism as religious practice in the face of the Holocaust, detesting what he saw as the acquiescence of the Jewish people in their own destruction, and the failure of any God (Jewish or otherwise) to stop such a catastrophe."[56] Socialism promised liberation for Aptheker. "When individuals have reached positions wherein God is altogether unnecessary," he wrote in *The Urgency of Marxist–Christian Dialogue,* "and when the social order reaches the stage where religious concepts will no longer be necessary, religion will evaporate if Marxism is correct."[57]

Even though he had been a special target of Cruse's vulgar anti-Semitism, Aptheker did to Cruse what he accused others of doing to him: he ignored him. He did not take Cruse's work seriously even though his book assumed a position of some authority because, according to the historian Alan Wald, "it [had] secured a niche."[58] Aptheker seems to have made only three published comments about Cruse's book. "The first was a footnote to an article of his in the April 1969 issue of *Political Affairs,* entitled, 'Anti-Semitism and Racism.'" The footnote criticized the lack of critical reaction to Cruse's anti-Semitism:

> Where anti-Semitism does appear in the writings of a Black author it is ignored if it is ensconced in sufficient anti-Communism. Thus, Harold Cruse's thoroughly poisonous book, . . . steeped in anti-Semitism of the most blatant kind and fanatically anti-Communist, has a major publisher (Morrow), gets excellent reviews, brings the author a professorship (at the University of Michigan) and is hailed for its "brilliance" by no less a "brilliant" authority than Prof. Eugene Genovese! If the American Jewish Congress, or the American Jewish Committee or any Jewish newspaper, has said a word in condemnation of Mr. Cruse's anti-Semitism it has escaped this writer.

The second reference was a cursory, one-sentence rebuke: "In a speech he delivered, Aptheker referred to 'a sickening book by Harold Cruse,'" whom he called "a renegade who is incapable of recognizing the truth and who is the author of the most blatantly anti-Semitic book to be published by a major house in the United States in fifty years."[59] Aptheker's third criticism of Cruse came in an interview of Herbert and Fay by Benjamin Bowser and Deborah Whittle in 1995: "With regard to Harold Cruse," Aptheker told the interviewers, "I have a great deal of difficulty with his work and not only because of its inaccuracy. It is in fact very inaccurate. I was once the invited guest of the Association for the Study of Negro Life and History in Washington and spoke at their breakfast meeting. . . . When I began to speak, Harold Cruse stood up and began to berate me and to criticize the association for inviting 'this jew.' The audience began to murmur against him and finally he was led out of the meeting still yelling and waving his arms. Whatever was bothering him then is certainly reflected in his work."[60]

The FBI monitored the Marxist Scholars Conference for several years but lost interest in AIMS after 1966 even though it continued to function for almost three decades. In the bureau's final Summary Report on AIMS, agents noted that in its first year of operation the organization raised $28,660 through "Contributions ($21,505) and Activities and Publications ($7,154)"; they also remarked on a celebration and fund-raising "tribute" held in Aptheker's honor.[61] Organized by Cohen, Ossie Davis, and Lynd with assistance from, among others, Genovese, Hall, Bettina, and the actor Will Geer, the event celebrated Aptheker's fiftieth birthday and drew more than seven hundred people to the decidedly bourgeois Hilton Hotel on 6th Avenue in Manhattan.[62] The FBI report observed that "Gus Hall spoke . . . and praised Aptheker for his writings, his books, and his work in the line of civil rights and peace."[63]

19   Conflict and Compromise

UNLIKE DOROTHY HEALEY, who publicly challenged the preroga-
tives Gus Hall claimed as general secretary of the party, Aptheker for far too
long found enough areas of agreement with Hall that he was able to suppress
his disagreements with him under the concepts of democratic centralism and
party unity. In April 1967 the Brooklyn real estate broker Harry Herman Kaplan
bequeathed more than a million dollars to Aptheker, Phil Foner, and Lement
Harris, a party member and agricultural expert. Kaplan wanted the money to
be used to establish a permanent daily newspaper for the party. While Foner
hesitated, Harris and Aptheker agreed to turn over to the party their portion of
the estate. In October the party announced it would resume publishing a daily
newspaper, the *Daily World*.[1] Aptheker's and Hall's agreement on what to do
with the proceeds of the Kaplan estate marked a high point in their discussions
of how to allocate the proceeds of estates left to Aptheker. In years to come
disagreements over inheritances exacerbated their growing mutual animosity.

Aptheker generally did not participate in intraparty intrigue, steering clear
of Hall and working instead through Gurley Flynn and Winston to accomplish
his goals. During the first half of the 1960s Hall consolidated his power within
the party. Because of the McCarran Act members were continually under threat
of being arrested, so the party did not hold conventions at which a program of
actions might have been drawn up. As a result, Hall was able to build an organization of one-man rule. When the Supreme Court gutted provisions of the
McCarran Act that required the party, its officers, and its members to register
with the attorney general, the party did call a convention in 1966, but by then
Hall's power base had solidified, and most of the older leaders, including Flynn,
Foster, Ben Davis, and Gene Dennis, had died. At the convention the party
issued a written program for the first time in forty-five years. A few comrades
challenged the analysis and direction presented in Hall's several-hour oral report. Aptheker made no comments about Hall in his fifteen-minute time slot
but did criticize the report's stance on "the relationship of the intellectual to
progressive developments." Focusing on his experiences over the past few years
on campuses around the country, Aptheker suggested that the draft program
recognize the "growth in . . . working-class students and faculty members of

working-class backgrounds." That growth, he said, accounted "for the maturity, imaginativeness, courage and militancy of considerable segments of the college and professional populations." But the party, he said, failed to recognize their contributions. Even worse, the party's stance "makes especially ridiculous and inappropriate the persistent remnants of a patronizing attitude towards students and professors and intellectuals; especially have the young people of the present generation earned the right of full and equal participation in social endeavors— particularly those of the Left and most particularly those of our Party. They have earned the right not only of equal participation but of earnest and careful attention; they have earned the right—in combat as it were—to be listened to most diligently."[2]

Aptheker focused his criticism on the portion of the draft report that chastised "intellectuals for what it called the 'illusion of independence.'" How did it happen, Aptheker asked, "that such intellectuals as [C. Wright] Mills and Lynd cherish this 'illusion?' They are among the best produced by any society in the past 25 years and that neither has seen fit to join us, perhaps reflects upon us as much as it does upon them." "To really cherish discussion," he continued, "to really seek mutual dialogue, to expect dignified treatment and to accord it— sincerely and really—all of us have a long way to go in this most difficult matter. That we have been sinned against does not mean we have never sinned!"[3]

Despite Aptheker's alliances with the New Left and the value and support he accorded student activism, he could not bring to an end the hostility of the party toward nonparty student organizations. "Gus regarded the New Left as a distraction or a threat to our own political prospects," Healey wrote when describing what she viewed as the party's "greatest political liability" in the 1960s.[4] Aptheker sometimes declared there was more agreement between his view of the New Left and that of the party leadership than was warranted or he simply obfuscated the party's position toward the New Left when speaking publicly while simultaneously attempting to move the leaders of the party toward his position. "The attitude of the Party towards the . . . so-called New Left is a positive one," he told an interviewer in 1968. He acknowledged the hostility toward anticommunism felt by many in the New Left, which he contended was decreasing, but he also recognized that the party was part of the problem: "Much of the suspicion against the Party is the Party's fault. It's not all the bourgeoisie and the persecution. The Party has made some terrible blunders."[5]

At the time Aptheker gave that interview, he and the party careened into yet another blunder, this one involving the military policy of the Soviet Union. According to the longtime party activist Michael Myerson, the mistake engulfed the party in a twenty-year spiral into "stagnation and exhaustion." "Of course the party is in crisis," Myerson wrote in 1990. "It is a crisis of longstanding, of over 20 years' duration, dating back at least to our full-throated approval of the armed invasion of Czechoslovakia and overthrow of its Communist leadership."[6]

The year 1968 began with the Tet Offensive, which precipitated the retreat of the United States from the Vietnam War. In February the organizers of a centennial celebration of Du Bois to be held at Carnegie Hall shunned Aptheker by not inviting him. Aptheker called the rebuff "a kind of 'injustice' otherwise known as opportunism." "But I do not feel too badly," he wrote to a comrade, "since [Ahmed Sékou] Touré and Nkrumah also were omitted."[7] Aptheker might have felt some vindication, though, because at the event, in the last major speech he gave before his assassination, Martin Luther King Jr. called for people in the United States to "cease muting the fact that Dr. Du Bois was a genius and chose to be a Communist." The "irrational obsessive anti-communism has led us into too many quagmires to be retained," King said, "as if it were a mode of scientific thinking."[8] As the year progressed, crises enveloped the United States and the world: King was murdered in April; there were urban race riots across the country; Robert Kennedy was murdered in June; for a week students occupied Columbia University; massive student protests took place in Germany and France throughout the summer; police rioted at the Democratic National Convention in Chicago; the arch-anticommunist Richard Nixon won the presidency in November, ensuring a continuation of the Cold War.

While North Vietnamese forces prepared to launch the Tet Offensive, the Communist Party in Czechoslovakia, under the leadership of Alexander Dubcek, framed its own kind of offensive. The changes began in January, and by May Day, with Dubcek installed as secretary of the Czech party, the Prague Spring, with its "torrential outpouring of popular support for the new course"— namely, partial decentralization of the economy and loosening of restrictions on the media, speech, and travel—swept Czechoslovakia. The Soviet Union and four other Warsaw Treaty countries, Bulgaria, Hungary, Poland, and the German Democratic Republic, viewed the events in Prague with alarm. In early August, after an "exchange of sharp letters" between the parties, the Soviet and Czech leaders appeared to reach an agreement at a meeting in the border town of Cierna.[9] Then, on 21 August, with the 14th Congress of the Czechoslovak Communist Party scheduled to begin in early September, at which time Dubcek's reforms would be codified, the Soviet Union, joined by its four Warsaw Pact allies, invaded Czechoslovakia.

The CPUSA broke into two factions over developments in Czechoslovakia. In California, Bettina, Healey, and Al Richmond, the editor of *People's World*, the West Coast party newspaper, supported Dubcek and the reformers. Hall and the leadership in the East used the *Daily World* to launch "a journalistic onslaught against Prague Spring, . . . promoting every lie and calumny being spread by the Soviets."[10] Prior to the Soviet invasion Healey had sought a full party debate on the developments in Czechoslovakia, but Hall refused. On 21 August Hall announced the official position of the party, declaring that the invasion "is the defense of socialism against the threat of counter-revolution. . . . an upsurge of anti-socialist elements, supported by the forces of subversion of U.S. and West German imperialism."[11] Healey, in a separate press release in California, reiterated her district's support of the Prague Spring, citing the provision in the party's draft program that called for "the complete independence and autonomy of each Communist Party."[12] The factional argument continued: Richmond and the *People's World* were critical of the invasion, and the *Daily World* offered blanket endorsement.

Over Labor Day weekend the party's one-hundred-member National Committee met in emergency session to debate the issue. Differing with the positions taken by most of the West European Communist parties, including the French, the British, and especially the independent Italian Party, the National Committee, "by a five-to-one margin," sanctioned the invasion.[13]

Bettina, who had joined the party in the early sixties, was, as noted earlier, one of the leaders of the Berkeley Free Speech and antiwar movements. By 1968 she was also a member of the National Committee, and she went to the National Committee emergency meeting as a firm supporter of the Dubcek reformers. She had been studying "the work of contemporary European Communists, including Alex Dubcek's revolutionary texts about democratizing socialism in Czechoslovakia." At the meeting, her father endorsed the takeover. "'What we must remember,' he declared, 'is that unlike the other eastern European countries, Czechoslovakia had a developed bourgeoisie.' . . . Herb also criticized the Czech Communist leaders for having praised Tomas Masaryk," Healey recalled, "the first president of the Czechoslovakian republic, despite the fact that he [Aptheker] himself, . . . has always been devoted to establishing the continuity between past American heroes like Jefferson and Lincoln and our own movement."[14]

The eventual vote in the National Committee pitted Bettina against her father. "I challenged [him] for the first time," she wrote in her memoir. "I argued privately with my father, but he remained immovable in his defense of Soviet policy. When the vote was taken, only three of us—out of 120 [?] comrades on the National Committee—opposed the invasion: Al Richmond, Dorothy Healey, and me." Bettina noted that she "thought about leaving the Communist Party" after the vote but admitted, "I couldn't do it."[15] Many others saw the party's approbation of the Soviet invasion as the final straw. Richmond left within a matter of months, while Healey held on for three more contentious years. Those who quit the party as well as many on the Left echoed the sentiments of the Marxist writer and Socialist Workers Party member Hal Draper, who remarked on radio station KPFA the day after the Soviet invasion, "We need, . . . support for Czechoslovak freedom by those Americans who have been fighting the dirty war in Vietnam right along, who have condemned American imperialism, and have been fighting for the withdrawal of American troops from that part of the world."[16]

Aptheker would have none of it though. In *Czechoslovakia and Counter-Revolution: Why the Socialist Countries Intervened,* a polemic shorter than *The Truth about Hungary* but equally damaging to Aptheker's reputation, he disputed the Vietnam analogy. Reacting to a *New York Times* advertisement placed by Stewart Meacham of the American Friends Service Committee and Dave Dellinger of the magazine *Liberation,* Aptheker wrote, "To even hint at equating Warsaw Pact troops' conduct in Czechoslovakia with that of U.S. troops in Vietnam is so fantastic an act of distortion that one is forced to excuse Meacham and Dellinger—particularly because of past services—on the basis of hysteria." To Communists who criticized the invasion, Aptheker adopted a conciliatory tone. Granting their right "to differ with the troop movement of the Warsaw Pact Powers," he reaffirmed Hall's "outstanding . . . forthright and early response" as being correct and the dissenters wrong. Those who approved of the invasion, Aptheker wrote, "did so and do so on the basis of the opinion that the continued existence of socialism in Czechoslovakia was at stake, that the continued leadership there of the Communist Party was at stake, and that this meant, also, a dire threat to the whole Warsaw Pact system and to the security of everything built with infinite labor and sacrifice, since the Bolsheviks stormed the heavens over fifty years ago." There was no good choice, Aptheker asserted. "That the troop movements were necessary is both grievous and tragic," he wrote, but ". . . the maintenance of socialism and the prevention of world war remain realizable goals rather than shattered dreams . . . an indispensable bulwark in the struggle for peace and socialism."[17]

As he had in *The Truth about Hungary,* in *Czechoslovakia and Counter-Revolution* Aptheker discounted firsthand accounts of the events in question. George Wheeler, an American Communist "who had lived in Czechoslovakia for many years," contacted Aptheker in October prior to the publication of Aptheker's booklet. "George was an agricultural economist, the only foreigner who had been accepted as an official member of the Czechoslovakian Academy of Science . . . and very knowledgeable about the real state of affairs in the country," Healey recalled.[18] "It seems to me," Wheeler wrote to Aptheker, "that scientific Marxism compels one to conclude that what happened here . . . was one of the greatest mistakes and tragedies in the history of socialism. . . . In a world of irrationality and deliberate mendacity how does one make rational interpretations?" Wheeler asked. "The worst thing for us [him and his wife, Eleanor] *personally* is that the majority of our own party refuses to believe us or even to print our short letter disassociating ourselves from the D.W. [*Daily World*] misinterpretations. . . . Practically all observers who were here . . . could find no counterrevolution. So it was fabricated, lapped up and reprinted as if already an established fact."[19]

"Having lived in the United States all my life and through the era of the Cold War I think I know what mendacity is," Aptheker responded. "We differ on the events in Czechoslovakia," Aptheker said, inexplicably, given that Wheeler had lived through them, "and your own views on this matter are very well known here and have been widely published. In fact you may be sure they will be and have been given the widest publicity by forces and organs with which your sympathies do not lie."[20] Wheeler did not take the bait in his reply but again tried to make Aptheker understand the invasion from the perspective of someone who was there. Writing after having just returned to Prague, he told Aptheker that "it was also a relief to me to find in France and England such firm support for my opinion that a great and tragic blunder has been made from *all* progressive points of view, economic, military, moral and political. This is *not* an anti-Soviet position, simply a sober analysis of the actual situation, . . . a scientific analysis of *this* situation. It is hard for those who are not here," he chided gently, "to give proper weight and perspective to different facts, to sort out the main trends, even to know truth from outright slander." Wheeler found it "almost unbelievable to read the confidence with which people thousands of miles from the scene pronounce the verdict that the Party's leaders here had underestimated the internal dangers, had lost control, etc. How do they know so much better than the leadership here . . . [these] sages who pronounce this verdict, which to their minds justifies all that was done." Sensing perhaps the stone wall that Aptheker had constructed to ward off competing opinion, Wheeler concluded, "I won't write more. . . . At this point I think that it is our duty to be critical . . . even if because our own publications refuse to share the forum, our enemies can pick up the criticism with glee. That situation was not my responsibility but that of those who refused to print on-the-spot analysis, scientific analysis of the actual situation."[21]

It took another two decades for the success of the Prague Spring to fully materialize with the collapse of the Soviet Union. Perhaps fortunately for Aptheker, aside from Woodward and a few others most people ignored his booklet.

More widely read, though still neglected, was Aptheker's book-length attempt dealing with how Marxists and religious believers might find common ground, *The Urgency of Marxist–Christian Dialogue,* published by Harper and Row in 1970.[22] During the summer of 1965 AIMS sponsored a wide-ranging series of lectures on the subject of Marxism and Christianity at the New Hampshire summer camp of Willard Uphaus's World Fellowship. Aptheker collected the lectures, including his own, "Marxism and Religion," and edited them for publication in *Marxism and Christianity,* published by Humanities Press in 1968. Before and after publication of the book, AIMS organized a series of conferences around the country that presented Marxist and Christian speakers debating the merits of cooperation between the two seemingly incompatible belief systems. The Jesuit University at Santa Clara, California, hosted the first conference, in October 1967. Aptheker observed in his speech there that "the Christian Church today is far removed from the fundamentals of Christ's teaching. . . . Marxism may win over Christianity."[23] He told an audience of more than three hundred people during the fourth session of the conference that early Christian theory, "which was 'equalitarian and communistic,'" differed remarkably from the currently weakened church, "which 'defends that system (capitalism) . . . a commitment which 'ties Christianity to a corpse.'"[24] Nonetheless, Aptheker noted, there was "a generally unrecognized similarity between the ideas of Marxists and those of liberal Christian theologians and Pope Paul VI. . . . [T]his theoretical affinity has not been emphasized. The contrary has been done—by both sides."[25] W. Richard Comstock of the University of California at Santa Barbara supported Aptheker's position: "Some people think that bringing marxism and christianity together is like mixing oil and water," he remarked during his presentation. "But there is a new spirit between the two and this conference is a sign of it."[26]

After two days of argumentative small panels in which Aptheker and Cohen represented the AIMS position on reconciliation and the speakers from Santa Clara University exhibited general skepticism that Marxism and Christianity could converge, the sixteen professors, churchmen, and philosophers gathered for the final session. They reached their broadest agreement on their desire to end racial discrimination and poverty and especially on their opposition to the war in Vietnam. James A. Pike, the former bishop of the Episcopal diocese of California, finding common cause with Aptheker, made an impassioned plea for ending the war. John Somerville, a professor of philosophy at California Western University of San Diego, called the war "absolutely illegal and . . . stupid."[27]

The conference was not without controversy and drew protesters. Several Santa Clara alumni inundated university officials with protests over Aptheker's appearance, and Catholics for Truth About Communism distributed anti-Aptheker pamphlets on campus.[28]

Not ready to abandon the subject, Aptheker spent the next two years expanding his chapter "Marxism and Religion" from *Marxism and Christianity* into book-length form while testing his ideas at various college and university speaking events and debates. While a rapprochement between Communist parties and Christians was well under way in Europe, a movement noted by Aptheker at his presentations and eventually in the book as well, his endeavors were at the leading edge in the United States.

The urgency in Aptheker's title stemmed from his belief, as exemplified in the work of AIMS to encourage dialogue among various leftists, that world peace demanded a reexamination of basic questions, "questions . . . about the nature of man, the purpose of existence, sources of alienation, and the uses of power." Marxists were ready to engage in dialogue with theologians because, as he reiterated throughout the book, there was a need to analyze the "shattering blows . . . suffered from the aberrations, crimes, and failures that have marked the course of the history of socialism; . . . the blows have been there and have required reexamination."[29] The causes of these phenomena Aptheker did not identify: certainly Hungary and Czechoslovakia were not among them. "There is repeated (and correct) reference to the crimes and errors," Bettina wrote in reference to her "central criticism" of the book, ". . . but the explanations are insufficient, and this becomes a problem in the book, if for no other reason but that an estimate of Man is (as you say) fundamental to Marxism and differs from the religious view of the 'Fall, sinfulness, etc.' Errors and Crimes—whether committed by science in nature or in society—are committed by men, and therefore pose a theoretical (at least) challenge to the estimate of man which is not met with sufficient discussion in the book—which left me vaguely irritated and frustrated."[30]

Aptheker conceded that disillusionment had alienated many Marxists from their former beliefs, but, he proposed, what bound those Marxists who had not "interpreted these failures as a total discrediting of Marxism" to the Christian tradition especially was a common militancy on behalf of the emancipation of man and against the evils of oppression, exploitation, and injustice.[31] What bound religion to Marxism? "There is a thread—a red thread, no doubt—that runs through the history and teaching of many religions and not least that of Christianity," especially early Christianity, Aptheker averred.[32] "Early Christianity," he wrote, mentioning Engels's reference to " 'notable points of resemblance between early Christianity and the working-class movement of modern history,' . . . as befits its revolutionary character . . . denounced the ruling gods and so was called atheist, excoriated the secular powers and so was called seditious, upbraided the rich and so was called deluded, pointed to private property and the accumulation of profit and its twin, covetousness, as the chief source of evil, and so was called a dangerous madness to be extirpated from the earth."[33]

In attempting to build common purpose but never gloss over Marxism's divergence from Christianity, Aptheker moved through chapters devoted to love, ethics, sex, women, death, and racism, pointing out commonalities and differences both between and among various Christians and Marxists:

> In its opposition to elitism, its insistence on mass participation and mass development, its drive toward equality, its commitment to the methods of science, its high estimate of man, and its purpose of human ennoblement, Marxism should have the capacity to overcome alienation. As for winning the kingdom

of nonviolent brotherhood without violence, the greatest doubts exist. They exist not because Marxists are enamored of violence; on the contrary, they loathe it. But those possessed of power rest their possessions upon violence; they gained what they have with violence and they do not loathe it but make of it a cult to be worshiped and call it "patriotism" or "law and order."

The source of violence lies not with the dispossessed and the insulted; it lies with those who possess and insult, among whom mercy is the most foreign of attributes. Hence, whether or not violence is required depends basically on the balance of strength among the contending forces. If those with blood on their hands and rapacity in their hearts believe that they can use violence effectively to prevent their demise they will do so. Marxists are neither pacifists nor terrorists, and not being the former, resistance will be offered where violence appears; the issue will depend upon the relationship of forces at each moment.

It is worth observing . . . a common purpose in both Marxism and Christianity: the achievement without violence of the nonviolent brotherhood of man . . . affirming that with which this Marxist agrees.[34]

As Aptheker reached out to Christians, he claimed to represent a maturing Marxist approach, a reflection of growth and change in Marxist thinking about and actions toward religion. He agreed with the leading Latin American Marxist, Roque Dalton of El Salvador, that Marxist thought had essentially overcome its "infantile disorder" of abolishing religion. Like Dalton, Aptheker emphasized that what united Communists and progressive Left Christians, "above all, are their lofty dedication to the ideal, their desire for truth and justice, their constant search for spiritual values and their common stand against the dehumanization and fetishism imposed by modern capitalism." Those points of agreement, Aptheker held, made feasible cooperation in practice.[35]

Aptheker believed that his guarded tone in the book, the subject itself, and its publication by a major mainstream publisher would ensure some media notice of *The Urgency of Marxist–Christian Dialogue*. "Even with that publisher, however, the *NY Times* maintains its splendid silence on the works of yours truly," he told the historian Pete Daniel on 9 June; "though this is his 26th book, that newspaper has yet to review one! This reassures me as to my continuing subversiveness."[36] What did he expect after all? He viewed the *Times* as the enemy, except when he wanted to be recognized by that leading capitalist newspaper. In conversation he could hardly utter the words *New York Times* unless they were preceded by *God Damn*. When Father James Conway urged his parishioners to read the book, Aptheker thanked him, although he could not keep his bitterness from creeping into the letter. "I especially appreciated you urging readers not to miss it," he wrote in late October, "[as] *Commonweal, Christian Century, Nation, New Republic,* etc. have managed not only to miss it but to ignore it. By now I should have become accustomed to such treatment by the press in this country; but let me confess I have not."[37] After reading a story by Nat Hentoff in the

Village Voice several months later expressing sympathy for authors whose books were not reviewed, Aptheker sent a short note to Hentoff. "My interest and sympathy were keen," Aptheker lamented, "not only because of general agreement but also because I think I may very well be the most prolific non-reviewed author in U.S. history!"[38]

Harper and Row came under pressure from the Church League of America for publishing the book. The house's corporate officers sent Aptheker's editor, Donald R. Cutler, a memo outlining the league's complaint. "It . . . said we merely mentioned you were a Marxist when in fact you were a Communist and the theoretician of the Communist Party, USA; and it said you had been an apologist for all the brutalities of the Soviet government," Cutler wrote to Aptheker. "And of course it is not our policy to put political affiliations on jacket copy as a regular procedure. We are not at all alarmed about this matter, but we do wish to check on inaccuracies in the Church League report. I don't in fact know whether or not you are presently a member of the Communist Party, USA . . . but it would be helpful to clarify every aspect of the report. Could you give me information on this point?"[39] Aptheker's reply to this patently naive question was short and to the point: "I am astonished that at this date any one is in doubt as to my political affiliations; nevertheless, as a matter of principle under present circumstances, I do not wish to directly reply to the question you put."[40]

Coincident with the publication of Aptheker's book by Harper and Row, the party hierarchy, specifically, the Political Committee, in the person of Helen Winter, a longtime party functionary, began a maneuver to control the work of party intellectuals, a ploy that would, in a few years, help drive Bettina from the CPUSA. "At a recent meeting," Winter wrote, ". . . there was a discussion on the need to determine guide lines for book writing authored by members of the National Committee or possibly also by any member of the Party." The Political Committee discussed, Winter told Aptheker, the need to have manuscripts "submitted to a committee before publication; that . . . the Party had a right to determine the worth of the manuscript; that in cases where the subject matter of the manuscript would affect our Party organization that such manuscripts should also be submitted to a committee." Winter and the Political Committee were of the opinion that having party members submit their writing to a committee would "help make the book a better one as an instrument in our political and ideological work," an idea that Aptheker dismissed in his reply.[41] "A committee should exist (should long since have existed) to assist," he emphasized, "in the publication work of International Publishers [the party press]." However, "in cases involving other publishers, the fact that a committee exists should be made known and comrades invited and encouraged to offer their manuscripts. . . . In such cases advice only should be present and the whole atmosphere must be one of aid," he wrote, with some restraint.[42]

In fact, Aptheker's relationship with International Publishers had deteriorated to the point that he contemplated severing his relationship with it. Earlier that year, in February 1970, he had written a series of scathing letters to Hall excoriating Jim Allen, the comrade who ran International. Aptheker angrily wrote to Hall, "What the hell is going on, and under these circumstances how can an author work with that outfit?" Allen had returned and demanded changes in the manuscript Aptheker had submitted for a new book titled *Afro-American History: The Modern Era.* Allen's directive was worded "in such rather insulting fashion that I put the whole thing aside for two weeks just to cool off," Aptheker told Hall. After Aptheker made some modifications to the manuscript, Allen decided, without mentioning it to Aptheker, although their offices were only three blocks apart, that he would not send it to the press because "certain questions he had raised I had not handled." Aptheker reminded Hall that he had other options: "I receive letters each month from publishers now asking if I have something they might see."[43]

When Allen repeatedly ignored him, Aptheker insisted several days later that he return the manuscript. Allen said he would return the manuscript but demanded that Aptheker promise "not [to] have it published elsewhere. This incensed me," Aptheker wrote in another letter to Hall. "This must be changed before I will have anything new published by International Publishers."[44] Aptheker did indeed take the book to another publisher, Citadel Press, which published *Afro-American History* in hardcover in 1971 and in a paperback edition in 1973. Many of the essays that make up the bulk of the book Aptheker drew from his periodical writings going back to 1940. His relationship with International Publishers never recovered.

Aptheker's problems with party publications were not restricted to International. He and the *Daily World,* on whose original board of directors he sat as secretary, had run afoul of each other, although the exact nature of the controversy remains elusive. When the party launched the paper in the late sixties, the editorial goals, as understood by some staff members and consistent with Aptheker's focus, "were to reach and reflect segments of the Left beyond the Party, and to reach and radicalize segments of the people beyond the Left," according to the onetime *Daily World* reporter Richard Greenleaf.[45] When he resigned from the paper in February 1970, Greenleaf complained to the party Political Committee that the paper had strayed from that mission: "If our paper is to attract people to our Party, it must show that it respects the members of its existing and its potential audience, and does not regard them as dolts to whom an inferior or meretricious product can be sold," a stance that, Greenleaf intimated, the paper continuously took.[46]

While Greenleaf and Aptheker may not have had exactly the same grievances with the paper, whose editor, Carl Winter, was the husband of Helen Winter, by late 1970 or early 1971 Aptheker was so angry he refused to write for it anymore. When confronted about his absence in the paper, Aptheker told Walter Lowenfels to write to the *Daily World:* "I merely suggest that in addition to writing me about my absence from the paper that you—as a reader—write the paper, too, saying whatever you want to say about the writer and asking about his absence."[47] Aptheker turned down a request from Phil Bronsky, another *Daily World* staffer, to write a review of a new book on the ideology of the early Republican Party by his friend Eric Foner. "Before resuming writing for the paper," Aptheker wrote dismissively to Bronsky, "I should hear from its Editors and/or Joe North."[48]

20   Black Power and the Freeing of Angela Davis

IN ITS literature the CPUSA portrayed itself throughout the 1960s and 1970s as being ready and willing to cooperate with other leftist organizations to create a unity of purpose. "We seek to make diversity most fruitful and unity most effective. . . . One compelling reason for Left unity is to maximize Left strength by the most effective fusion of new and old," the program of the party announced in 1966.[1] What the party said for general consumption and what the leaders said among themselves, however, differed dramatically, and what the party meant by unity usually meant control by the party over otherwise independent movements and groups. Party leaders "harped incessantly on the 'petit bourgeois' character and 'left adventurism' of the New Left," according to Bettina.[2] Healey blamed Hall: "We fought over the youth policy, over SDS," she told the historian Jon Wiener. "Gus's whole line was that they were a bunch of petty-bourgeois radicals. Who cares? Who needs these students?"[3]

As the various strands of Black Power emerged in the 1960s Hall and other party leaders, including prominent black leaders, reacted to them with the same hostility they held for the New Left. "On the black liberation struggle, my god," Healey said, "what battles we had on that. Front pages of the WORKER under Jim Jackson's editorship denounced Malcolm X as the most outrageous and vile individual; . . . Jackson . . . developed an absolute hatred of Malcolm X." At the party's national convention in 1966, Jackson "completely outraged our younger Black comrades and others when he . . . criticized the Lowndes County, Alabama, Black Panther Party (which was a precursor to, but separate from, the Oakland Black Panther Party established by Bobby Seale and Huey Newton)."[4]

When the Los Angeles party "organized an all-black unit, the Che–Lumumba Club," Jackson's outrage intensified: "He denounced the club at a National Committee meeting, which passed a resolution supporting his position." Healey and the Los Angeles black party leaders Charlene Mitchell (a member of the National Committee since 1957), her brothers Deacon and Franklin Alexander, and Franklin's wife, Kendra, reasoned that "the absence of a white face wasn't going to make much difference in terms of the politics represented. But it might make a huge difference in terms of our ability to recruit and hold on to Black Communists." "I doubt very much that Angela Davis . . . would have come into the Party in 1968 were it not for the Che–Lumumba Club," Healey declared.[5] Nevertheless, as Healey recalled, "there was an enormous reaction at the national meeting of the Party organization in '68 against our setting up the Che–Lumumba club, led mainly by Blacks, arguing that this was a violation of Party approaches to Marxism."[6]

The Che–Lumumba Club "allowed Black Communists to play a role within the Black community and among Black students on campuses in Los Angeles," Healey said. Many members of the club also held membership in the Black Panther Party, which did not endear them to the party leadership. "Black militants were regarded by important Party leaders as demagogic and dangerous," Healey recounted. "In the late 1960s the grievances and the language of our new recruits reflected the anger of those who were on the outside looking in, in the Black community as well as in the larger society." The Black Panther Party's early militarist posture appealed to young black people, and "guns became a symbol of revolutionary commitment. It drove many older Communists crazy to see that even our Party youth were involved in this enthusiasm for carrying guns and practicing with them," Healey asserted.[7]

Discussions of party policy with regard to black revolutionaries began and often ended in the Black Liberation Commission, of which Aptheker was a member. Aptheker thought the policy toward the Panthers was foolish, and he strongly criticized it at a meeting of the Black Liberation Commission on 4 March 1969.[8] While denouncing the "ultra nationalism" of black revolutionary groups, the party leaders also condemned any form of black violence as ultra-leftism and held that young members of the party who "were involved in this enthusiasm for carrying guns and practicing with them" should be expelled from the organization.[9] Aptheker articulated a much more nuanced approach by recognizing the appeal that the militarist posture adopted by black revolutionaries had for young black people, while at the same time he counseled against violence. "We do not think that armed insurrection by Black People in the United States is a viable method toward liberation," Aptheker told a Canadian radio interviewer in 1968. "However, such insurrections have occurred in the past [specifically he meant the Watts insurrection of 1965] and will occur in the future. When oppressed people rise up we know who's right and who's wrong." He went on, "I think that militancy of any form is certainly justified here and the uprisings are too. It's a matter now of effective strategy and the effective strategy requires struggle on all levels, on all levels it requires the merging of all Left struggles, particularly the Peace effort and the Black Liberation effort."[10]

On 10 February 1968 Aptheker gave a speech at Wayne State University in Detroit, and in response to a question about the nature of black power and militancy he told the student audience that "the docility of the Negro is a myth. Black Power is in response to the United States, which is in fact White Power.

The blacks are victimized by this predominant power, hence, the response to this power is to get out from that power. To get out from under power," he said, "you must have power. What's complicated about that?" Continuing, he told the students that oppressed black people in a racist society, if they are to effectively oppose racism, "must oppose it with power of course. So they seek power with which to stand up against the oppressor."[11]

Aptheker often claimed that party policy toward black revolutionaries was evolving, and by 1968 that became evident when two members of the Che–Lumumba Club, Angela Davis and Deacon Alexander, after protracted discussions within the club, joined the L.A. Black Panther Party. Their aim, Davis said, was to "air problems and explain and set aside past hostilities" between the party and the Panthers.[12] The next year, in response to a call from the Panthers, activists from all over the country, including several members of the party, converged in Oakland to found the United Front Against Fascism.[13] The Lumumba Party Club "forged an alliance at the top with the Black Panthers and helped them stage the . . . conference."[14]

Aptheker represented the party at the Oakland conference. Contrary to the party's program, which held that while fascism was certainly a danger the country was not yet under the control of fascists, many of the speakers at the conference contended that the United States was already in the grip of fascism, a situation that required the initiation of an armed struggle. As Aptheker ascended the platform to speak and throughout his presentation several black radicals in the hall taunted him. "The subject spoke as a representative of the CP," FBI agents noted, "and emphasized the dangers of fascism inside the United States today. He was frequently heckled by certain groups in the audience during his speech."[15] Davis deemed Aptheker's presentation to be "excellent, . . . laying out the relationship between racism today and the potential of fascism tomorrow. For me," she wrote, "it confirmed the correctness of my decision to join the Communist party almost a year ago to that date."[16]

Whatever promise the Oakland conference held out for united action dissipated quickly as soon as it ended. By September 1970 the party leaders had decided that working with the Panthers was not only counterproductive but also dangerous. The Panthers' ideas, the party leaders told each other at a Political Committee meeting, arose "from classlessness, from petty bourgeois radicalism. Most of [the] leadership in [the] Black Panther Party has [a] conscious policy that [the] Black Panther Party will replace the CPUSA. Their red-baiting is based on this. . . . We cannot allow our Party to be used."[17]

Party discussions centering on the possibility of forming a coalition with black organizations it did not control evaporated on 7 August 1970, when the seventeen-year-old Jonathan Jackson, the younger brother of the black Soledad Prison activist George Jackson, seized hostages in a courthouse in San Rafael,

California.[18] With weapons he had smuggled into the courtroom under his coat, Jackson armed the defendant, an inmate at San Quentin named James McClain, and two other San Quentin inmates scheduled to appear as witnesses, William Christmas and Ruchell Magee. The four armed men marched their hostages, the judge, the district attorney, and three jurors, to a van waiting in an adjacent parking lot. As the van prepared to leave, San Quentin prison guards, who had standing orders to shoot to kill any prisoner attempting to escape, opened fire on the van. The judge, Jackson, McClain, and Christmas died in the fusillade. The guards seriously wounded Magee, the district attorney, and one of the jurors.

A few days after the shooting the Black Panther Party staged a "revolutionary funeral" in Oakland for Jackson and Christmas. "Our comrades Jonathan Jackson and William Christmas have taught us a revolutionary lesson," Newton told a crowd of three thousand, ". . . they have intensified the struggle and placed it on a higher level. . . . They have given the revolution their lives."[19] At the same time, a nationwide search was under way for Davis, whom the State of California had charged with supplying the weapons used by Jackson.

Aptheker and his family had known Davis for more than a decade. Angela and Bettina had been members of Advance, a socialist youth club in Brooklyn organized by a group of so-called Red Diaper Babies, activist children of party members. "By designating ourselves as 'socialist,'" Bettina wrote in her memoir, "we were not officially or organizationally linked to the Communist Party."[20] Speaking to raise funds for Davis's defense after her capture, Aptheker recalled how he met her. Picketing, he remarked, was one of the activities in which Advance engaged. "Black and white little children [Angela and Bettina] used to go out—I would drive some of them out—picketing A & P and Woolworth's against racist hiring policies," Aptheker told a church audience. "Teeny [Bettina] was very frightened. My wife and I were somewhat frightened for her; but I think courage is like a muscle; I think you learn courage by displaying it."[21]

Going underground to elude the police, Davis began a two-month odyssey as she crossed the country from California to New York City. The FBI eventually captured her there. Meanwhile, the deeply divided party leaders met to decide on a course of action. Many of the comrades jailed in the 1950s feared a renewed Red Scare directed at the party because of Davis's high-profile membership and the old charges that the party advocated force and violence to overthrow the state. Some in the leadership, "although muffled in their dissent," Bettina recalled, "wanted the party to separate itself entirely from Angela, and a few actually (privately) advocated her expulsion on the grounds that she was a terrorist. . . . Many wanted Angela to disavow herself completely from Jonathan Jackson and the Soledad Brothers."[22] Those positions did not prevail, but the party did issue a statement at the end of August distancing itself from Jackson and his actions at San Rafael and intimating that since he acted alone he could be considered a terrorist. "The Communist Party has always made clear its opposition to acts of desperation or resort to gunplay on the part of individuals," Hall and Henry Winston, the national chairman, said in their statement, "no matter how awful the provocation or lofty the ideal. Communists reject the concept of revolutionary suicide or revolutionary superman-ism."[23] Aptheker, who, like Bettina, had absolute faith in Davis's innocence and viewed the situation differently from the leadership, asked to meet with Hall. "I am unhappy with that statement and wanted to put that on record," he wrote to Hall and Winston on 4 September after arriving home from a cross-country trip. "I would appreciate a few minutes to talk about this."[24]

He composed an essay taking issue with the party's position—which characterized the actions of Jackson as being desperate—and expected it to be printed in the *Daily World*. Aptheker identified white racism as the cause of what he said was an understandable act of violence. "The specific case that moved the young Black men to attempt to liberate their brother from confinement is permeated with injustice, brutal treatment and political harassment," he wrote. "Oppression breeds rebellion; an oppressed people 'have the right and the duty' (says the Declaration of Independence) to resist their oppression and this is the fundamental meaning of the Marin County liberation effort."[25]

Hall was not at all happy with Aptheker's position. He requested that Aptheker revise the essay to make it suitable for printing in the *Daily World*, and Aptheker agreed to incorporate a minor change. After his conversation with Hall, Aptheker was sure the essay would appear in the *Daily World*. "Saw Gus," he noted in the margin of a copy of his original letter to Hall and Winston outlining the essay, "with addition of one sentence, . . . affirming the Marxist–Leninist opposition to terrorism per se . . . he will speak with Editors and get it in."[26] Instead, Hall saw to it that the essay never appeared in the paper. "When I asked the Editors for an explanation," Aptheker wrote to Winston several months later, "I was told they had been told to hold it out. I have never heard further; not from Gus nor from anyone else. The last I knew was that it was to appear and not another word ever reached me; simply the failure to publish."[27]

Hall's increasing hostility to Aptheker's independent analysis and to his advising of Davis, some of which she acted on, exacerbated the already difficult situation within the party. When his essay failed to appear in the *Daily World*, Aptheker told Winston, "I have accordingly decided that—if this is proper treatment for me—apparently my writings are not desired in the paper and so I have discontinued writing for it."[28] "I will not forget," Aptheker wrote to Bettina in early January 1971, "—and probably will not forgive—the way I was dealt with in connection with that article."[29]

During September 1970, as the FBI hunted Davis in several states, Bettina and others organized a rally in Berkeley protesting the "police dragnet" and asserting her innocence. Bettina's speech at the rally, in which she stood by her father's analysis, directly contradicted the party's position and especially that of Winston. Bettina wrote of the controversy that Winston had "likened Angela's case to that of Georgi Dimitrov, . . . who was imprisoned by the Nazis," accused of setting fire to the German Reichstag in the 1930s. The fire had actually "been set by a hapless youth named Marinus van der Lubbe, who was in the employ of the Nazis." Bettina "bristled at the analogy." Jackson, Bettina asserted, "was neither hapless nor was he a police agent." Davis encouraged Bettina to circulate and publish the speech, which she did in the *National Guardian* for October 1970, thereby further angering Hall and Winston.[30] Aptheker, too, continued to push his perspective on San Rafael. At a meeting of the National Committee in November, Hall said Jackson's act amounted to terrorism and was "disruptive to the mass movement." Aptheker spoke at the meeting in opposition to that position, explaining that "political passion, by its nature, goes with social passion."[31]

When the FBI incarcerated Davis in the Women's House of Detention in Greenwich Village while awaiting extradition to California, the party recruited John Abt, a longtime party attorney, to represent her. Activists around the country organized defense committees. Those in New York, Boston, and Chicago joined the parent committee in southern California. The party's leaders wanted to control the committees. "The campaign can bring into existence an immense defense activity and create a base for the kind of defense organization we have wanted," comrades active in the New York effort told the Political Committee of the party on 20 October. "We should not see this case in isolation from the general attack on the Party."[32] The leaders proclaimed, with their usual grandiosity, that with their encouragement defense committees would be organized everywhere. They acknowledged that the fight to free Davis demanded action: "The Party can come forward much more as a Party of black and white, championing the defense of a black woman"; moreover, they reasoned, "in order to be able to fight most effectively we must preempt the field to prevent the anarchists and Trotskyites . . . [and] certain ultra-left and petty bourgeois left . . . from taking it over and narrowing it. . . . We need to explore the possibility of bringing together on a national scale some of the existing and potential defense forces on the basis of our broad policy. Any such exploration, however," the minutes of the Political Committee meeting reported, "must be done on the part of comrades only with the direction of the Political Committee and the leadership it has established for Party defense activity nationally. . . . Once the field is pre-empted by our initiatives and the policy established, concentration on broadening is needed."[33]

While the domestic movement to free Davis developed, Aptheker helped organize comrades in Europe, especially after Davis's extradition to California. When comrades in East Germany organized rallies in support of Davis in early

1971, she wrote a thank you note that Aptheker sent to his contacts. "The campaign for her that is being carried on in the DDR [Deutsche Demokratische Republik, or GDR] moved her greatly," Aptheker wrote to a Comrade Birch, "and she has written the enclosed message in her own hand while in jail and means it especially for the people of the German Democratic Republic."[34] Writing to his friend, the aged Hungarian Marxist philosopher Georg Lukács, Aptheker urged him to write an open letter to President Nixon and Gov. Ronald Reagan of California, "to be published in the press of the entire world in which you appeal for Angela."[35] Lukács declined to address Nixon: "What kind of attitude shall I adopt towards such a personality?" Lukács wrote. "I can only confront him with my marxist conviction and values and that would be utterly ridiculous." Nonetheless, Lukács contributed more than two thousand dollars to Davis's defense fund, and he organized prominent European intellectuals to join in a protest action, "though I am a very old man / to be 86 years old is quite an obstacle in organization work." He promised Aptheker that the group would send "documents of protest" to the world press and to Reagan. "If need be," he wrote to Aptheker, "we shall organize a co-ordination committee in Europe for the escalation of pressure during the trial. . . . Be assured dear comrade Aptheker," he concluded, "that I shall do everything that is within my sphere of possibility and I shall spare no efforts to free Angela Davis, to whom I send my warmest communist greetings."[36]

At her invitation, Aptheker managed to arrange several extended visits with Davis in her jail cell as he advised her in developing material for a book and helped devise a strategy for her trial. "I was in California last week for the purpose of visiting with Angela," he told Graham Du Bois in late March. "Spent two full afternoons with her and had opportunity for much work. We will help her in preparing a book. . . . Her fight for bail continues . . . her spirits are splendid and her thoughts are only of freedom—and the struggle."[37]

At about the time of that visit, Aptheker began a four-month correspondence with the "Soledad Brother" George Jackson. Aptheker, through Davis, it appears, initiated the exchange when he sent Jackson a brief note explaining that he would send several books that Jackson had requested. Soledad Prison, Davis pointed out in her autobiography, "was a household word in the Black community" in California, but the meaning of the Soledad Brothers' defense had not penetrated the ferment in which the East Coast leaders of the party operated.[38] Bettina and others "spoke again and again" at a contentious National Committee meeting in March 1971, "laying out the facts of the case, explaining the Soledad Brothers' defense and Angela's involvement."[39] In February 1970 the State of California charged the Soledad inmates Jackson, John Clutchette, and Fleeta Drumgo with the murder of a guard at the prison. Conviction carried an automatic death sentence. "The prison hierarchy," Davis wrote, "wanted to throw them into San Quentin's death chamber and triumphantly parade their gassed bodies before thousands of California prisoners, as examples of what the prison and the State did to those who refused to observe the silence of acceptance."[40] From the beginning, the black community viewed the case as a frame-up. Davis became involved with the Soledad Brothers defense early on when the Los Angeles Committee to Defend the Bill of Rights contacted the Che–Lumumba Club for assistance.[41] Through her work to build a mass movement to free the Soledad Brothers, Angela had come into the orbit of George and the Jackson family, including George's mother, Georgia, and his brother Jonathan.

George Jackson, at the age of twenty-eight, had already served ten years—ten times the minimum of a one-year-to-life prison sentence, seven and a half of them in solitary confinement—when he and Aptheker began their brief correspondence. From within the steel walls that enclosed him, Jackson had become a leading Black Panther and an adroit foe of the California prison–industrial complex. He read voraciously during his incarceration. "I met Marx, Lenin, Trotsky, Engels, and Mao when I entered prison," Jackson wrote, "and they redeemed me. . . . We attempted to transform the black criminal mentality into a black revolutionary mentality. . . . we have been transformed into an implacable army of liberation"[42] Jackson, as was his habit, jumped into his correspondence with Aptheker as if he had known the fifty-six-year-old communist for years. "I encircle the people that I dig," Jackson wrote in one of his letters; "there are only two types of people inhabiting my closet, friends and foes, the ones I accept, the ones I reject." He said to that correspondent, "I sensed from the start that we were of kindred spirits," and his letters to Aptheker, in which not a word was wasted, display that same quick sense of intimacy.[43] "We have much to discuss my friend (if possible—I hope so; I was very much impressed by both your letter and the nature of your writings)," Jackson told Aptheker in an early letter. "I know you probably are as familiar with me and what little life I've had as anyone can be, I would like to know as much about you as you would share."[44]

Throughout the four months they exchanged letters, a period brought to an end when Jackson was murdered by San Quentin prison guards on 21 August 1971, Jackson was working on the manuscript of his second book, *Blood in My Eye,* which he completed only days before his death. In all of his letters Jackson peppered Aptheker with questions surrounding the topics he addressed in his writing. In his first letter, after asking Aptheker to send him more books, he requested information on the "Protocols of the Learned Elders of Zion" in order to contest the "Nazi pseudo intellectuals all around me on the tier." He then turned abruptly to questions about the Communist Party. "Why did Gus Hall defame my brother?" he asked. "Could he have simply refrained from any comment at all if he didn't agree? Did support of Angela hinge upon a denial of my brother? If so it's alright—support Angela!! I must defend Jon tho."[45]

"Received today a most interesting letter from George Jackson; . . . raising questions about anti-Semitism and about Gus' original reaction to San Rafael," Aptheker wrote to Bettina on 21 April 1971. "I answered at length, . . . explained as best I could about Gus."[46] By "explained as best I could" Aptheker meant that in his letter to Jackson he distanced himself from Hall, put forward his own interpretation, and in the end, without ever naming him, claimed that Hall had altered his position, an assertion Aptheker surely knew was not true. "The insult to your brother to which you refer was the result of the person involved being deliberately misinformed at the time of the event," Aptheker wrote to Jackson. "I was in California then and immediately wrote an entirely different assessment recognizing the tremendous courage and historic justice of the act and placing Angela within the context of frameups and at the same time placing the whole event in terms of liberation struggles, as Nat Turner and Denmark Vesey and Gabriel Prosser, etc. But at the time, publication of that piece by me was refused; it still has not been published but I'm fighting that out myself. Meanwhile understanding has appeared and the person you mentioned in your letter takes an altogether different and correct position now."[47]

In fact, at a meeting of the National Committee just a month earlier Aptheker had forthrightly addressed the reluctance of the top leadership to alter their views on the meaning of San Rafael. "The weakness is in a place like Los Angeles among white comrades, and a place like N.Y. among white comrades," Aptheker told the committee, still pressing his interpretation of San Rafael. "At the heart . . . is the whole reality that black people are an oppressed people and the national quality of that oppression—the *national* quality of that oppression which is at the heart of San Rafael and the failure to understand that and the original statement by the Party on San Rafael affects our defense of Angela. And that must be corrected. In consciousness and expression!" Aptheker compared Davis to Frederick Douglass, who opposed the Harpers Ferry assault by John Brown, and her codefendant, Ruchell Magee, to Shields Green, who accompanied Brown on the raid and paid for the act with his life. "The analogy is not perfect," Aptheker said, "but it's clear enough to be true." Bringing his argument to a conclusion, he told the National Committee again that "black people are an oppressed people. And when they do what they did at San Rafael—we cannot— that's not gangsters. As our comrade said correctly, why isn't it gangsters? Because they are an oppressed people. We must face to that. And we did not do it at the time. And that's a hangup with us. And we've got to do it."[48]

Hall neither addressed Aptheker's remarks directly in his usual lengthy summary remarks at the end of the committee meeting nor singled him out by name, but he did include statements whose thrust could not have escaped Aptheker's attention. "[Many] of our white comrades have become highly qualified in dealing with the history, culture, poetry, music, etc. of Black Americans," Hall told the delegates. "But in a number of cases the results of the studies by our white comrades have appeared in print, often by private publishers, without any consultation, or without any contact or exchange with any of our leading Black comrades," Hall said, which certainly should have alerted Aptheker about what was yet to come. "There cannot be a situation where Black comrades are active in the struggle and are the main force in analyzing and developing policies, but where it is mainly white comrades who publish and are quoted as experts in this area."[49] How the party would address this situation Hall postponed for another meeting, but he had thrown down the gauntlet and appeared ready to openly chastise Aptheker.

Assured of Hall's change of mind, Jackson let the matter drop in his further correspondence with Aptheker. He had more pressing matters on his mind anyway. Jackson considered himself a communist, but to him, contrary to the CPUSA position that put the working class, including black workers, in the dominant position, the Black Panthers represented the vanguard that would lead a revolutionary assault on the ruling class in the United States, "giving communism a solid black face."[50] "The principal reservoir of revolutionary potential in Amerika lies in wait inside the Black Colony," Jackson wrote in *Blood in My Eye*.[51] Probing to uncover Aptheker's position on the revolutionary potential of the working class, Jackson asked in an early letter, "Just how rigid are you on the question of attacking at the productive point in the U.S.? Its entrance is fortified, and trapped in quicksand. Is a frontal assault still possible, and if so due to the difficulties wouldn't it have to be most aggressive?" Jackson proposed an indirect assault "on the productive apparatus where workers are radicalized then revolutionized in the community (commune)."[52]

Aptheker took up the point in his response while bristling at the mention of rigidity: "I don't think I am rigid . . . but then no one thinks *he* is rigid!" Aptheker acknowledged the control of state power by the bourgeoisie, then moved directly to Jackson's question: "To really change that, qualitatively, means that another and contrary class, the working class—those at the means of production and whose work is basic to what is produced—must have effective state power." That process of capturing state power, Aptheker told Jackson, worked differently according to time and place, "different in old Russia from Cuba, different in China from North Vietnam." How that process would happen in the United States was uncertain, Aptheker instructed Jackson. "To blueprint this is to be insane. . . . But at the heart must be the working class because that's where it is at. . . . And in the historic sense and the sense of socialism it is the class that is decisive. This is what I believe—in capsule—if it indicates that I am rigid, so be it—until persuaded I am wrong."[53]

"We agree on class of course," Jackson responded in his next letter. But he felt that history had "altered class antagonisms so radically" that the place to "start to making a warrior class of today's automatons" was in the community, not at the point of production. "[Is] it possible to make him see his economic interests in say a peace march," Jackson asked about working black people, "an *enforced* rent strike, a boycott on certain ... critical products, in assassination. In the death of his son at the hands of organized injustice and so on to infinity." Jackson could not wait for a revolutionizing process that proceeded from the workplace, and he did not trust the white working class to help in the process, much less to lead it. "The proletariat—the working class—is still the most revolutionary class, and still the real gravedigger of Capitalist society," he wrote in *Blood in My Eye*. "However, the notion that they alone can or must carry the revolution is too ridiculous and simplistic for any serious consideration at all. . . . The argument that centers on the ideal that all workers must be politically educated before the revolution can support a violent thrust verges on the absurd. . . . Repression is here."[54] He saw "socialism as a Black thing. But purely Black—it's necessary—anti communism is so much a part of the Black mentality that extremes must be used. And it's not just that Blacks are afraid of revolution, they really feel that it's too white."[55] "I've made many Black communist guerrillas—but in the making—every time—I was forced to emphasize that it was the Black thing to do," Jackson told Aptheker. "Later when the damaged oppressed mentality has healed somewhat we will all be able to better see that the real needs transcend [*sic*] all barriers of race and culture."[56]

Aptheker took umbrage at Jackson's assertion that anticommunism was most pronounced in the black community. "Of course I am not Black," he replied in answer to Jackson's explication of his ideology, "but I am a Communist and have been since 1939. . . . Where anti-Communism is deep is among the White population; among the Black, I think, there is a kind of latent sympathy—one underdog for another and a certain profound instance that teaches that if the oppressor hates the Communist, he can't be all bad! Besides, so many of the leading Communists have been (and are) Black." He told Jackson that propaganda accounted for some of the anticommunism among white people and acknowledged "our own failings and errors have not helped at times, too!" To Jackson's proposal that the face of Communism should be black, at least until "later when the damaged oppressed mentality has healed somewhat," Aptheker expressed his misgivings: "I worry very much though . . . I worry about the *later* and the present, too and I am not so sure about how 'damaged' the mentality has become since." He wrote, in a remarkably romanticized and incongruous formulation given Jackson's ten years in prison, "Oppression ennobles and teaches at least as much as it damages; in any case it is the brain of the oppressor which is really damaged!"[57] If Jackson felt ennobled by incarceration or oppression, he did not reveal that sentiment in either of his books. "Capture, imprisonment, is the closest to being dead that one is likely to experience in this life," he wrote to one of his editors.[58] "But nothing could mitigate the pain of confinement," he told an interviewer near the time of his correspondence with Aptheker. "Try to remember how you felt at the most depressing moment of your life, the moment of your deepest dejection. That is how I feel all the time. No matter what level my consciousness may be, asleep, awake, in between."[59]

Jackson felt that the need for revolutionary action was immediate, that fascism had already taken control of the United States. "The objective is to move people into action. I'm sure we agree on that. Once we define action," he wrote to Aptheker. "I've devoted my whole adult life to moving myself and people into action. Actions that they normally would never even consider." The problem, he pointed out, was two distinct approaches to being, "one based upon analysis of action—thought, the other thought—action and then analysis. Adoption of the latter being condemns one to his acts, the former condemns one to thought. When I consider all of the millions who have died just this century of unnatural causes resulting from monopoly capital, corporativism [sic], imperialism—society above society, I am forced to the position that perhaps we should die, act, and die if necessary, . . . ???"[60] "My pledge is to arms," he wrote in *Blood in My Eye,* "my enemies are institutions and any men with vested interests in them, even if that interest is only a wage. If revolution means civil war—I accept, and the sooner begun the sooner done."[61]

Jackson's belief that fascism had conclusively matured in the United States drove his willingness to die, to put the revolution into effect immediately, using violence if necessary. He scoffed at the party's avoidance of first use of violence. "Democratic centralism is anathema," he told Aptheker in his last letter, a month before his murder. "Angela and I have fought some pretty heated debates over the existence of a mature fascist—corporativism in this country. I say yes of course, she—and probably you say not. . . . I don't know why people who love each other and hate hierarchy also find so much to debate over. It's stimulating to a point, then it tends to retard action. The whole point of the matter. . . . I don't think there's a nice way to fight."[62]

Even though he had read *Soledad Brother,* Aptheker did not grasp Jackson's formulation of fascism. "Yes," he told Jackson in his last letter, "I have thought about fascism for some time—and read about it and fought it in Germany." The United States did not have fascism, he told Jackson. "What we have here is monopoly capitalism at an advanced state, deeply infected with racism. . . . The tendency towards fascism is highly developed here but the reality of fascism is not here." For fascism to exist, Aptheker thought, the Ku Klux Klan would have to be "openly and fully in power everywhere, without any restraint and with full power of the State and all its forces. It would be what the SS was in Germany."[63] But then, Aptheker lived a comfortable, even bourgeois, life in Brooklyn: Jackson lived in solitary confinement at Soledad Prison. "After one

concedes that . . . the definition of fascism is: a police state wherein the political ascendancy is tied into and protects the interests of the upper class—
characterized by militarism, racism, and imperialism," Jackson wrote to one of
his lawyers, " . . . we can then burn *all* of the criminology and penology libraries
and direct our attention where it will do some good."[64]

Jackson wanted cooperation, a community of action, with the Old Left but
cautioned, in *Blood in My Eye,* that "the worker's [*sic*] revolution and its vanguard parties have failed to deliver the promised changes in property relations
or any of the institutions that support them. This must be conceded without
bitterness, name-calling, or the intense rancor that is presently building." The
Old Left, he wrote, "has failed to understand the true nature of fascism." To
Jackson, the debate was settled, while "intellectuals still argue whether Amerika
is a fascist country. This concern is typical of the Amerikan left's flight from
reality, from any truly extreme position. . . . At this stage," he wrote, "how can
anyone question the existence of a fascist arrangement?"[65]

A great chasm separated the two revolutionaries, yet each strove to understand the other. In the last paragraph of his last letter to Jackson, Aptheker took
issue with Jackson's criticism of democratic centralism: "Action is the point
of the matter, but correct action. And to get the adjective means debate and
discussion. As the saying goes—without correct theory there is no proper action. There is not a nice way to fight but there is waging battle and carrying out
Mylais [massacres like that carried out by U.S. soldiers at My Lai in Vietnam];
the forces of Nixon, not Ho are guilty of the latter and that is because one seeks
to suppress human liberation and the other represented it."[66] As if to prove the
point, less than a month after Aptheker's final letter, prison guards gunned down
Jackson. California state prison authorities "never properly investigated what
happened on August 21 [1971]," Stephen Bingham, one of Jackson's lawyers, told
an interviewer. "I'm certain George was targeted," he said. Jackson's legacy is
still potent among California prison inmates. In December 2005, thirty-four
years after Jackson's death, Gov. Arnold Schwarzenegger denied clemency to
Stan Tookie Williams, a cofounder of the Crips street gang who was arrested
and convicted of a murder associated with the gang's activity. Schwarzenegger
claimed that Williams's "record of turning his life around must be a lie—because
Stan identified with Black revolutionaries of the past and present, dedicating his
autobiography to a number" of them. Schwarzenegger leveled his most damning
accusation at Williams through guilt by association: he couldn't be reformed because he had included George Jackson in the dedication of his autobiography.[67]

21 An Assault on Honor

THE PARTY leaders could not yet have read George Jackson's arguments in *Blood in My Eye* at the time of his murder, but their reaction to his rhetoric can be inferred from remarks made in reference to Huey Newton at a meeting of the Political Committee in mid-May 1971. "Newton's views are an endorsement of Mao in new garb," the minutes state. "It is part of new ways of Maoism coming to Blacks, Chicanos and many white petty-bourgeois radicals. . . . Newton speaks of the 'people' but not of the working class and monopoly. . . . Newton does not understand the stage we are in, the science of revolution, even though he speaks of being a 'revolutionary' he does not mention Marxism–Leninism."[1] Hall repudiated the Black Panthers: "We must not make the Black Panther Party out to be a Marxist revolutionary party," he told the Political Committee.[2]

The criticism of Newton's views, which had recently appeared in the *People's World,* the West Coast party paper, came during a renewed discussion of the duties and responsibilities of the party's publications, publishers, and writers that had begun a year earlier. Just prior to the meeting in May, Hall and Winston had attempted to foist upon Angela Davis and Bettina, who were putting together a collection of essays that included Aptheker's heretical unpublished essay about violence, a long piece by Winston titled "The Meaning of San Rafael." Winston's essay, later published as a pamphlet under the same title, argued for a repudiation of both Aptheker (the essay did not mention his name) and Jonathan Jackson, restating the party's original position. Davis and Bettina refused the offer. "Angela and I both made an effort to convince him [Winston]," Bettina wrote later, "that this position would be a disastrous one for the defense to take. . . . We felt it was impossible to include his essay without changing the whole tenor of our work."[3] Then, in August 1971, Herbert and Bettina published a pamphlet titled "Racism and Reaction in the United States: Two Marxian Studies." Herbert's essay was the text of the speech he had given at the National Conference for a United Front Against Fascism in 1969, and Bettina's essay was "The Social Function of Prisons in the United States." Hall expressed outrage at Bettina's essay some months later when he chastised the Political Committee for allowing the pamphlet to appear. "We must examine how it was we permitted the Bettina pamphlet," he said. "You should know it was many times worse.

It was bloody awful and as far from our position as anything can be—totally a petty-bourgeois radical concept. Danny [Rubin, a longtime party functionary] and Winnie [Winston] worked on it to bring it to some reasonable limits. But I think it was still a mistake and we should not have published it, and we should have a public criticism of that pamphlet."[4] Bettina adamantly rejected Hall's statement. "I do not know specifically to what Gus is referring," she told a correspondent, "and whatever it is he is lying about Winnie and Danny 'severely editing' whatever it was. I did not permit that kind of editing. . . . He was lying about the editing. I am certain of that."[5]

At the meeting of the Political Committee in May 1971, Hyman Lumer reported on the work of a committee set up to frame a statement on the party's publishing policy. The discussion, while perhaps coincidental, seems to have been triggered by Aptheker's essay in Davis's and Bettina's book and the position it adopted in opposition to the party line. In fact, FBI agents reported to their superiors that "for a period of many months, some members of the CPUSA leadership have been out to get Aptheker. From a Marxist–Leninist point of view, it is contended Aptheker is a 'right-winger.'"[6] The publishing policy committee, Lumer told the meeting, was unable to draft a policy statement. The reason was that Aptheker's views on the subject—namely, that comrades should be "invited and encouraged" but not required to submit their work—which he had laid out in a letter rather than give the committee credibility by meeting with it, differed from those of the committee.[7] "There is a need for collective judgement on manuscripts by leading people and those publicly looked on as expressing the Party's point of view no matter by whom published," Lumer said. He assured the Political Committee that a body set up to oversee writers would not change every sentence, "but sometimes we have to say no to publication by any publisher." In the discussion that followed, the committee members argued that "writers should welcome a collective discussion of their book when it is written and even before it is written because we believe collectivity strengthens work." The members agreed that the committee "must have the right to make decisions, not just offer 'friendly advice,' including saying that unless certain major changes are made to put a book in line with Party policy it should not be published." Any book published by "a person widely known as a Communist" would have "a big impact externally and internally," the committee determined, "and can be made use of in a major way by the enemy."[8]

The Political Committee finally adopted "Guidelines for Party Members on the Writing and Publication of Books and Pamphlets," whose contents applied to "Party members who write books and pamphlets, whether in the social sciences or in the field of creative literature." In June they mailed it out to the members, enclosing also a statement, the irony of which must have escaped the leadership, about excessive bureaucracy in the Political Committee. The guidelines are filled with CPUSA jargon about how the party expected writers to express "a Marxist–Leninist outlook . . . reflecting the principles of dialectical materialism . . . in keeping with the line and policies of the Party." Section 2 of the document outlined the duties of authors:

> All Party members, and above all those in leading Party posts or on leading Party bodies, who are looked upon as spokesmen of the Party, are required to conduct their writing activities in consultation with the appropriate Party bodies. Plans for proposed books are to be submitted in advance for discussion and recommendations, and the manuscripts, when completed, must be submitted for critical reading by comrades competent in the given field. Every manuscript must be subjected to collective judgment as to whether it is or is not in keeping with Marxist–Leninist principles and Party policy. . . . These requirements hold no matter to what publisher the work is submitted.[9]

Aptheker seethed at the absurdity of the document, then composed a letter to Hall and Winston. After sending his dismissive letter about a publishing board to Helen Winter some months earlier he had heard nothing, he told them. "If consultation is important let it be held and if it concerns functioning of comrades whose life—basically—is writing, they should be consulted with at length and with great care," he wrote. But the committee had not consulted with him; instead "this communication from the Political Committee reaches me, as an accomplished fact. But I have published 26 books and this kind of activity is of enormous consequence to me—and to others, I hope—and as for me must not be resolved by fiat." He reminded Hall and Winston that he was under contract at that very moment with four publishers for a number of books, books that had to do with Du Bois and other historical topics and that were at "various stages of production—from finished and awaiting completion of production process to outlined and in process of creation. What is it," he asked Hall and Winston, "the Political Committee envisages in this concrete case? . . . Who does what? Not what abstract body but which human being(s) and in what time length and with what powers, etc. etc." He noted the additional statement he had received the same day, which contained "sharp self-criticism of bureaucracy in the Political Committee; the above strikes me," he told the two men, "as a glaring instance of that damnable weakness." Across the top of the letter, in bold handwriting, and underlined, Aptheker wrote, "*NOT* Mailed—*too subjective but reflects aspects of thinking!*"[10] Rather than confront the leadership he just ignored the requirements.

In attempting to rein in Aptheker, Bettina, and Davis, the party sought to reassert its control over the Davis trial strategy and the interpretation of events leading up to her arrest. Above all they wanted a lawyer from the party to have a seat at the defense table, a suggestion that Davis and her chief counsel, Howard Moore, had rejected. Moore claimed, according to a report delivered by Winston at a Political Committee meeting in September, that "the Party wanted to control the trial, its strategy, its tactics, . . . If there were a Party lawyer in the case," Winston told the committee, "he [Moore] would have to retire." Winston said that his presence was needed in California "to establish once and for all our attitude in regard to the present and future of that trial," the purpose being to fix the strategy line and to develop the mass movement for her defense around it. "We cannot ignore this as the leadership of the Party," Winston said, "because, what is our primary consideration? It is the defense of the Party." The party had adopted its ideological position, Winston said, "but everyone doesn't agree with that line. In fact, the line is rejected. It is rejected, on the one hand, by Angela, and, on the other, by the chief counsel and assistant co-counsel. . . . You should know that that whole grouping up there finds themselves at variance with that line. . . . [Theirs] is a line which is influenced by petty-bourgeois radicalism, nationalism, petty-bourgeois idealism, etc."[11]

Winston directed his irritation at what he perceived to be Davis's black nationalism. Winston alleged that Davis was not focused enough on the party but was instead "becoming blacker and blacker and . . . forgetting about all of that European stuff [i.e., Marxism–Leninism]." Why, he wondered, did she continue to assume the Aptheker position, emphasizing the connections between the Davis case and "Douglass, Vesey, Turner and what-have-you[?] Why use them? Why not the Black leaders of slavery?" Winston told the Political Committee, "I read Aptheker [regarding Douglass] . . . . He [Douglass] was a consistent fighter against leftism in whatever form it took. That's why he could unite with a [figure like the abolitionist Wendell] Phillips. This same Douglass, on the other hand, opposed John Brown's tactic." Davis was no Douglass, Winston opined. She didn't disagree with the actions of Jonathan Jackson, "so, how can you say she is the Douglass of today?"

The comparison was illogical and dangerous. Winston insisted that while hitting "the system of oppression," the party needed "the labor movement. . . . Unfortunately, the working class is not mentioned once . . . not once, . . . [and] not a mumbling word to the people of the Soviet Union who play such a decisive part; you see what the Soviet Union has done, the working class there. This is the working class organized into State power." Winston demanded of the delegates accord on the notion that Davis should be made to understand the party's position: "We have to restate our position and with greater force even."[12]

Hall was even more emphatic in his presentation to the September meeting. Winston should go to California, he said, "with a sense of an appeal to last resort. . . . We must put an end to the situation where we are on the defensive. . . . We have been patient, but patience and capitulation have nothing in common." Davis had been told, Hall averred, that her attorney was deceitful: "He is a liar and he falsifies everything this Party has told him openly. He has not said an honest thing to Angela about our position. . . . Is she going to believe the Party or this lawyer who had told lies on everything. Otherwise we will not have any kind of relationship with her, unless we put it on the table and talk it out." Hall contended that Davis's politics were all wrong: "We must make it clear we are not for her defense based on the charges against her—and it is obvious she has illusions about that. . . . [O]ur interest must be, defense of this party. . . . It is not accidental that Angela has not mentioned the Soviet Union, in spite of the fact there has been a campaign like nothing in history. If she has not responded to anything from there, we should not be too surprised. That was there before the case started. Of course, she accepted Dorothy Healey's basic anti-Soviet position then and is now." Hall wanted a shift in tactics. "We have to begin to de-personalize the campaign," he said, "to de-emphasize the individual and emphasize the politics of the situation—the struggle against racism and for communism. . . . I now remember a few years ago I raised the question we must not make the Black Panther Party out to be a Marxist revolutionary party. . . . How to do it is not easy, but we must do it."[13]

The Political Committee adopted several motions after the discussion. Lumer proposed, and the committee carried, a motion to have prepared a "criticism of [the] Bettina Aptheker pamphlet." Winston agreed that Bettina's essay on prisons that appeared in the pamphlet should be censured, but he wondered why the party had not espoused a program on prisons. The committee voted to commission the writing of a book that "will deal in depth with the prison system."[14]

Winston met with Davis over two days in her cell late in September 1971. Bettina took notes. Winston declared that the party's theory of the trial had to be connected to "the alarming dangers in the country of growing reaction and fascism." He asserted that mass movements worldwide, "the growing strength of the socialist countries," and the mass struggles for black, Chicano, Puerto Rican, and women's liberation within the United States had "reached second stage." The strongest point in Davis's defense, he avowed, "is that Angela Davis is a *Communist*." Davis agreed that her defense needed to "take the offensive," but she wondered how that offensive would "translate . . . into concrete approach inside the courtroom. . . . We must make a systematic effort to defend 7th August from the perspective of the Black liberation movement," she told Winston. But that was precisely what he and the party wanted to avoid. "[The] less written about San Rafael at this juncture the better," Winston said. Davis was not deterred: "There is a need for us to place San Rafael before the people in a way different from the prosecution presentation," she maintained. She disagreed with the party response to San Rafael. "San Rafael can [not] be characterized as a terrorist act," she said. "Terrorism suggests a specific theory of revolutionary change. [We] can't be in the position of equating Jon [Jonathan Jackson] with the Weatherman." As the meeting ended, Davis voiced her trepidation about adding a party lawyer to the defense team. She "expressed her earlier concern . . . that a Communist lawyer would represent the views of the political committee in the defense . . . and the differences already aggravated around interpretation of San Rafael."[15]

Having aired his dissenting position, Winston reported to the Political Committee that he and Davis had not reached an accord on the meaning of 7 August, but they had made arrangements to continue an examination of lingering issues while the case moved forward. Davis had also agreed to the addition of a party lawyer, Doris Walker, to her defense team.[16] Not long after the meeting, "Angela wrote a 22-page letter to Winston rebutting his 'line,'" Bettina recalled, "to which Winston never responded."[17]

The conflict over the meaning of the actions that Jackson engaged in at San Rafael and their relevance to Davis's defense continued for the next few months. Sometime that fall (probably in October, although the date is not known) Davis invited Aptheker to her jail cell to discuss the issue. He wrote nine pages of notes for her, "drafted in a great hurry," outlining positive and negative factors on the meaning of San Rafael vis-à-vis her defense.[18] His "Notes to Angela" imply that, should the defense team require it, he could once again be called on as a defense expert witness on Marxism–Leninism who could testify to the meaning of the use of violence as understood by revolutionary Communists—the exact courtroom situation Davis was attempting to avoid. Building on his suppressed essay, which had by then appeared in Bettina's and Davis's book, *If They Come in the Morning,* Aptheker contended in his "Notes to Angela" that Jackson's act "fits within the historic pattern of insurrections in terms of Black history," of which he was, by his estimation, the leading expert in the field. "The effort then comes out of the continuum of Black history," he wrote, "and its essence which is resistance against oppression. In this sense to view it as simply individualistic terrorism is false."[19] Davis, Aptheker declared,

as a Communist did not and could not have had any role in the effort: . . . the act was an individualistic one and no Communist would do that. A communist functions collectively, not individually in any political effort. While the act reflected the history of Black people and the context of its times, . . . it is absolutely inconceivable that a Communist—such as Angela—would have been part of the San Rafael act . . . it is inconceivable that a Communist—a revolutionary and one who is dedicated to the liberation of the Black people (in this case her own people)—could take a condemnatory stance towards the courage and selflessness and passion which obviously motivated young Jonathan.[20]

In November the Northern California Steering Committee, which directed the movement to free Davis, circulated a memo prepared by Bettina that summarized the discussions in regard to legal strategy held among the committee members. Echoing Aptheker's "Notes for Angela" (they were attached to the memo), the committee, which by then included Walker, the party attorney, announced that the fundamental posture of the defense would be an affirmative, aggressive position relative to the events of 7 August: "It is impossible for a Communist to have advocated, organized, or participated in such an effort to free political prisoners in the United States, under prevailing conditions, and it didn't happen. Angela Davis could not have participated in the August 7th revolt because it was not a method of struggle in which she, as a Communist, could have engaged."[21]

The Steering Committee memo and Aptheker's "Notes for Angela" reignited the controversy within the party over the legal strategy to be pursued in the trial. After ruling on all of the pretrial motions, the presiding judge changed the trial venue to San Jose, and Angela disbanded "the original legal team." At that point Walker joined the trial defense team along with Leo Branton, "one of the few lawyers," Davis wrote, "courageous enough to defend Communists during the Smith Act Trials."[22] At a meeting of the party's National Angela Davis Sub-Committee on 13 January attended by Davis's four lawyers, Hall, Aptheker, and Bettina, Branton communicated his strong reservations about the defense strategy outlined by the Steering Committee. "His [Branton's] response to the present document, was that we were proposing that the main line of defense would be a defense of the Communist Party and AD [Angela Davis] as a member of the Party," according to the minutes. "His opinion was that this would play into the hands of the prosecution, that the idea that the Party was synonymous with violence, would adversely affect the jury, etc. It was his opinion that the defense should present AD as a professor, as a Black woman, etc., and should try to avoid the Communist designation." Hall, backtracking on his previous stance, in which he had advocated protecting the party as the prime objective of the defense, assured Branton that "the tactics involved in the defense would be of a broad mass character and not a narrow defense of the Party." Davis agreed with Branton, which must have exasperated Hall. Bettina told the meeting that Davis, after further conversations, "does not feel that her non-participation in Aug. 7th should be based upon, or rest upon her membership in the Party. Therefore, she doesn't like formulations e.g. 'No Communist could have ....', etc. She believes," the minutes of the meeting state, "non-participation should be based upon her own politics. BA [Bettina Aptheker] has encouraged her to develop this line of argument, and this will be very helpful in our next discussion in our efforts to unfold the details of the legal and mass strategy."[23]

Hall returned to New York, evidently infuriated at what he perceived to be Aptheker's apparent rejection of the party's position on the meaning of the actions that Jackson carried out and the influence Aptheker had over Davis, even though she had rejected the primary advice of his "Notes for Angela." Criticism of Aptheker had been building for some time among members of the Political Committee, according to FBI informants. Some members of the committee had denounced Aptheker as a right-winger because he encouraged Marxists who were not affiliated with the party to write for and publish with AIMS. The bureau's informants also reported that several leading blacks within the party were envious of Aptheker. One prominent black comrade, whose name is redacted from the FBI files but who most probably was William Patterson or James Jackson, felt that he, not Aptheker, "should be the heir of works of W. E. B. Du Bois, Black Historian."[24]

The Political Committee began a discussion of the Steering Committee's "Legal Strategy" memo after Hall's return to New York. He and Winston wanted a definitive statement, once and for all, on the meaning of 7 August and the strategy Davis should put into play at her trial. On 2 February 1972 the Political Committee arrived at a caustic final statement on the defense strategy that slashed at both the Steering Committee memo and Aptheker's "Notes for Angela." The statement acknowledged that "it was impossible for Angela, as a Communist, to have participated in the August 7 events." However, in the Steering Committee's premise that "communists abstain from participation in any action, regardless of its positive features, unless it is 'directed toward the achievement of the principal political strategy, in the most effective possible way,'" the Political Committee found "a base libel of Angela and all communists. It makes them cowards who stand on the sidelines while a 'blow for freedom' is struck and who mask their cowardice with a sanctimonious sectarian rejection of any strategy that does not fully correspond with some preconceived model of perfection." The members called the Steering Committee's statement "a travesty of Marxism." The Steering Committee had handed the prosecutors "their most potent weapon," the Political Committee professed. "It gives them the devastating argument that Angela's resort to this obvious concoction is the growing evidence of her guilt."

A winning strategy, the party held, "must start by abandoning the effort to reconcile glorification of August 7 with Angela's innocence. The contradiction is irreconcilable." Davis was right in "rejecting the formulation 'no communist could have . . . and in insisting that her defense turn on her political views—on the political views of Angela Davis, a Communist, an adherent of Marxism–Leninism." Most certainly not in Davis's interest, the party's position paper concluded, was "calling expert witnesses to testify to the teachings of the Communist Party on the subject of anarchism. It is Angela, not the Party that is on trial. . . . The prosecution would like nothing better than for us to transform the trial of Angela into a trial of the Party, a trial that they are sure of winning. . . . What are required, therefore, are witnesses who are experts, not on Marxism," the party leaders declared, in an obvious rebuke not only of their original stance but also of Aptheker, "but on Angela . . . who will testify both to her views on individual acts of violence and to her commitment to and confidence in the efficacy of *mass* struggle."[25]

Having deftly maneuvered around a direct reproach of Davis's position with regard to Jackson's act and demanding an end to the debate, Hall and Winston moved in for a direct attack on Aptheker. In a lengthy letter starting with the salutation "Dear Herb" and headed by the notice "NOT FOR PUBLICATION OR CIRCULATION FOR MEMBERS OF THE POLITICAL COMMITTY [*sic*] ONLY," Winston invited Aptheker "to participate in a political committee meeting where we could discuss problems posed in your eight and one half page document [i.e., "Notes for Angela"]." He then dove into an extraordinarily scurrilous assault on Aptheker's loyalty to the party, his scholarship, and his understanding of Marxism and implied that Aptheker's "Notes for Angela" could send her to death row. Winston went on to accuse Aptheker's work of constituting "a new phase of struggle against the Party's position on San Rafael and the Strategy required to save Angela Davis' life." Aptheker "[failed] to acknowledge the Party's deep appreciation of Jonathan Jackson's motives" and instead persisted "in referring to unnamed sources who allegedly condemn or fail to appreciate Jonathan's lofty motives and his heroism."

And who were those unidentified sources? "You have made it clear that the unnamed object of your criticism is the Party and its leaders," Winston charged, especially "by your recent unilateral intervention on the Defense strategy." Winston told Aptheker that his constant implication of insensitivity on the part of the party created "an atmosphere of antagonism to the Party and its leadership. In this atmosphere—permeated by a slanderous image of a callous and indifferent Party leadership," he proclaimed, "receptivity to the real position of the party is reduced. . . . The alleged lack of compassion by the Party for Jonathan is completely without foundation." Winston lectured Aptheker that his "posture of moral superiority and all-encompassing compassion" violated "two cardinal principles of the Party . . . democratic centralism and collective thinking and action," the consequences of which could be severe for Davis. "In violating Party decisions and the principles of democratic centralism in order to impose an alternate position on the Party, the legal defense and mass movement," he said in continuing, "you have not only obscured the true meaning of August 7th: the damage which could result from your approach jeopardizes the . . . struggle to win bail for Angela and her complete freedom."[26]

What particularly inflamed Winston was Aptheker's characterization in his "Notes to Angela" of Jackson's acts as amounting to "insurrection" and falling within "the continuum of Black history." If Davis's "life and struggles do indeed represent 'the continuum of Black history and its essence which is resistance against oppression,'" Winston wrote, "there is then not a *contradiction* between AD and San Rafael, but a *connection*. This is not only a *false,* but a provocative, a *disastrous* implication!" The posture Aptheker had assumed, Winston persisted, reveals "[you] to be deeply influenced by the ideology of petty bourgeois radicalism, which swings from right opportunism to 'left' adventurism," the charge against Aptheker that had been swirling around in the Political Committee for months. Winston drearily quoted several lengthy passages from Lenin to rebut claims made by Aptheker in his "Notes for Angela" and said Lenin's observations gave "us" a "deeper insight" into Aptheker's anti-Marxist thinking. "Your attempt to make San Rafael 'credible,'" Winston declared, "has led you to adopt a totally anti-Leninist position." Aptheker had also showed himself to hold, Winston expounded, "variable interpretations of insurrection, conspiracy, terror. In fact, you brazenly adopt the slavocracy's definition of insurrection—and thus play into the hands of today's ruling class. . . . In other words, for you it is the ruling class—not the principles of Marxism–Leninism—which defines terrorism, insurrection, etc. You unfortunately follow in the wake of the racist oppressors." In closing, Winston qualified Aptheker's scholarship as "careless . . . regrettable . . . and impermissible." Then he was finished. "I would like to stop at this point. I have faith in the collective wisdom of all of us in drawing the right conclusions from Leninism, which after all, is the only Marxism which guides not only our Party, but the World Communist Movement. I am sure that we will find the proper answer to this question when we meet." He signed the acerbic letter, "As ever, Winnie."[27]

William Patterson, a member of the Political Committee and a leading black member of the party, sycophantically applauded Winston's letter to Aptheker but went further by accusing Aptheker of racism. "I accept Comrade Winston's letter in toto," he wrote to other members of the Political Committee, urging them to publicly support Winston's scourging of Aptheker. "I deem Comrade Winston's letter to Comrade Herbert Aptheker to be of such vital significance to . . . the struggle against all and any form of white chauvinism, conscious or unconscious, that political committee members should I believe express their position in regards to it."[28]

The personal and professional character assassination in Winston's letter stunned Aptheker. Winston was his closest confidant in the leadership. He compiled handwritten notes covering most of the allegations, then composed a response to Winston of which only the first page survives. He described Winston's letter as "extraordinary." "The nine-page memo drafted in a great hurry at the request of Angela—and I went there at her request—was supplemented by a 14 page statement also done in one sitting and at her request," he wrote. "The ad hominem and absolutely assaulting character of your letter is astonishing to me."[29] What else he wrote is not clear, but it provoked Winston to respond promptly. "I was taken aback by your letter of yesterday," Winston wrote, with a noticeable lack of credulity. "I believe that you completely misunderstood the content of my letter." Winston invited Aptheker to attend a meeting of the Political Committee to discuss the charges. "My frank opinion, Herb, is that your presence is necessary and will be very valuable. I do hope you will reconsider your conclusions."[30] But Aptheker wanted nothing to do with a Star Chamber proceeding. "I have re-read the letter to the Political Committee members concerning me signed by you which I received yesterday," Aptheker wrote. "It is not possible for me to participate in a collective discussion where I have been characterized in those terms in that letter. Nobody—and that includes even Henry Winston—I repeat, NOBODY can impugn my honor as a scholar and then simply invite me to participate in a discussion." If the charges in the letter were accurate, "why want me at a discussion?" he asked Winston. "What else do I have? Nothing. When I am able to discuss this with you and with no one else we will meet and talk; otherwise just in terms of my blood-pressure alone—which is very high doctors tell me—I would not chance being in such a discussion as you request while people have read that letter about me."[31]

APTHEKER SHOULD have had some inkling that a personal rebuke was in the works after Winston published his pamphlet, "The meaning of San Rafael," which appeared in August 1971. In the pamphlet, Winston, having equated Jackson's act to terrorism, launched into an assault in a section titled "The Dangers of False Analogies." "Some people," he wrote, skirting Aptheker's name, "create inapplicable analogies between the past and present, pointing to the deeds of Nat Turner or of John Brown and his Black comrade-in-arms. They advance the mistaken view that San Rafael is an example of a revolutionary act today." No such comparison should be applied: "In the fight for correct tactics, it is essential to understand that analogies often limp and are certainly inadequate." Winston, predating Patterson's remarks, found racism in the anonymous writers who identified such dangerous affinities. When white radicals advanced "interpretations of San Rafael as a revolutionary act . . . it has the added implication of white chauvinism. In doing this, they are not carrying out their special responsibility of involving white workers in the fight against racist oppression, but are instead standing on the sidelines awarding medals to dead Black heroes." In fact, Winston wrote toward the end of the pamphlet, "those Black and white radicals who would like to see the Communist Party retreat from its Leninist position on San Rafael are playing into the hands of those who promote racist provocation and disruption . . . the same chauvinist manifestations that have plagued the New Left since its inception." Likely not by accident Winston singled out Tom Hayden, Aptheker's companion in Vietnam, for special scorn. "Hayden," he wrote, "is oblivious to the most fundamental of

Marxist principles. . . . [He] confuses taking the lead against racism with giving leadership to the Black liberation movement. . . . It is unfortunate," he concluded, in a veiled swipe at Aptheker, "that certain white radicals—who would surely condemn the crudely obvious white chauvinism revealed in Hayden's advocacy of this suicidal 'strategy' for Black liberation fighters—fail to recognize that their own interpretation of San Rafael as a revolutionary act is, at the very least, affected by the same concepts of 'strategy' and by the same chauvinist influences."[32]

Early in March 1972 Aptheker did appear at a meeting of the Political Committee "to defend his position relative to the shootout at San Rafael," according to an FBI report. The informant noted, cryptically, that Aptheker's "position was that the incident at San Rafael was an 'insurrection.' Gus Hall . . . opposed Aptheker's position." The informant went on to observe that the struggle within the Political Committee over Aptheker's position was "not merely a struggle over doctrine or theory. What is involved is a struggle between black and white as well. Ever since communist blacks have regained a certain racial and historical consciousness they have been envious of Aptheker. An example of this being the close association Aptheker had with W. E. B. Du Bois. . . . Du Bois left Aptheker a legacy of writings and contracts," the informer noted (only partially accurately because Du Bois left no contracts for Aptheker), "regarding the editing and publishing of his collected works." One party member, the agent stated, "has been complaining for years that he is the rightful heir to the works of Du Bois and, therefore, . . . has been jealous of Aptheker."[33] That member's name is blacked out in the FBI report, but, again, it's probably Jackson's or Patterson's.

While it appears that Aptheker reestablished working relationships with all of his comrades on the Political Committee, the thought lingers that the attack on his reputation and scholarship created a rupture between Aptheker and the party leadership that never really healed and, like a subduction fault, built up stress for the next two decades. Nonetheless, he was a party man! Aptheker undoubtedly understood that the personal onslaught reflected the great emphasis the party placed on centralism and the small degree to which it relied on democracy. On the other hand, some of the leaders kept up a low-grade needling of Aptheker and a full-blown campaign of vilification of Bettina that eventually drove her from the party.

In the end, the San Jose jury believed Davis, who took Branton's advice on legal strategy, and acquitted her. In late June 1972 the party staged a victory rally in Madison Square Garden in New York. Fifteen thousand people, mostly blacks, attended. The party leaders arranged to fly all the members of the National United Committee to Free Angela Davis from the West Coast for the rally. All, that is, except Bettina, whom they did not invite. At a reception given by the party before the event Louise Patterson, William Patterson's wife, whom Bettina had known since childhood, publicly thanked all the members of the National United Committee by name. All, that is, except Bettina. Davis's mother twice shouted over the crowd, "Louise! What about Bettina?" Bettina recalled that at that moment, facing such public repudiation and in spite of being Aptheker's daughter, she was "no longer a trusted comrade, no longer a part of the inner circle."[34]

Four years later the party removed Bettina from the National Committee, recently renamed the Central Committee. When she asked her father why she had been removed, "he cleared his throat," which enraged her, she recalled. "For the first time," she wrote in her memoir, "I felt a surge of real fury at my father, followed by fear. What I had always thought [turned out to be] true: I was expendable to him. I could be jettisoned if the party required this of him." Even though Davis and Bettina and her father had held the same position on the meaning of 7 August, Bettina felt the party had betrayed her. "I was taking the fall for Angela (through no fault of her own) and for my father," she wrote, "both of whom were too important and too famous to be renounced or rebuked."[35]

22   Party Control

"THE COMMUNIST PARTY wanted control of the American Institute for Marxist Studies [AIMS]," recalled Robert Cohen, the chairman of AIMS throughout its twenty-five-year existence.[1] "He [Herbert] had to fight to keep it broad," Fay said in an interview. "The Party wanted to take it over." "Yes," Aptheker chimed in during the same interview. "Who is Cohen?" the leaders asked. "They [the party leaders] are rather narrow people. They are not intellectual people. I mean Hall was a steelworker. He didn't know what the hell was going on in this kind of world, just as I don't know what's going on in his world. He didn't fully appreciate."[2] Aptheker and Cohen, who, at considerable personal risk, had testified for the defense at the Smith Act trial of Junius Scales in North Carolina and against the closing of the Jefferson School in 1956 before a New York state legislative committee, fought just as vigorously to keep AIMS independent. Yet from rank-and-file insurgent union movements to the defense of Angela Davis, the leaders rejected autonomous "united front" organizations like AIMS and attempted to rein in such independent operations.

By 1973, after nine years of independence from the party, Cohen worried that Aptheker had strayed from the founding credo of AIMS, namely, inclusion of all strains of Marxist thought, and had adopted a lopsided focus on party orthodoxy in the AIMS "Newsletter." Cohen told Aptheker of his concern and also that of other Marxists who were not affiliated with the party but were interested in AIMS. He noted "their increasing disturbance at what appears to them to be polemical usage of the AIMS 'Newsletter,' mainly through biased samplings of radical and progressive and Marxist periodicals or books. . . . You can imagine some of the areas of dispute," Cohen wrote in a letter to Aptheker. The neglect in coverage of "Chinese Marxist affairs and commentaries . . . [and] Maoist groups" headed Cohen's examples. "Another," he mentioned, "is the allegedly far more complete listing of articles from U.S. CP Jewish sources than from those progressive Jewish sources in the U.S. which the American CP criticizes." Cohen called the criticism "a sensitive matter of policy which cannot be ignored."[3]

Aptheker, who at that very moment, in June 1973, was engaged in an effort to fend off the party's interference in AIMS, responded defensively, without revealing the delicate balancing act he had to conduct with the party. He said the criticisms were "sniping" and were "bound to appear as the political struggle intensified and especially as concerted efforts . . . are going forward to destroy the communist Party." Aptheker reminded Cohen that "without the Party, of course, AIMS would never have come into being." Both he and the party "saw AIMS as a non-Party effort," Aptheker asserted. AIMS, he wrote, apologizing for the "heat in this letter," had kept to that bargain, "and the 'Newsletter' is assembled by me with this in mind and has been for ten years. And has grown from 400 to 3,550 circulation with letters coming in all the time affirming its preciousness."[4]

What Aptheker likwise did not tell Cohen was that he was at that time occupied in a heated controversy with Hyman Lumer and other party leaders that had begun the previous month over charges of racism and the party's attempt to divest AIMS of its autonomy. Someone not identified in the documents reported to the leaders that in a speech Aptheker had referred to black people as "colored." "I confess that 'Negro' rolls off my tongue more easily and with greater comfort than 'Black,'" Aptheker wrote to his longtime comrade Lloyd Brown as the controversy swirled around him. "[In] some ways Afro-American may be more exact. I tend to take Du Bois' attitude on this and use all interchangeably and think the whole matter is far less important than a million other matters."[5] As to the charges of racism for his having used the word *colored,* Aptheker dismissed the matter out of hand, telling Lumer that the accusation "is in error in all respects; . . . I used it in terms of NAACP; in terms of Du Bois' usage and his vision of the unity of the colored peoples of the world and this as a part of the further unity of the oppressed of the earth."[6]

Of greater worry to Aptheker were his interactions with a delegation of Los Angeles party members who had appeared at the AIMS offices in early May. One comrade had called for an appointment, but four people appeared for a discussion. "I was somewhat startled," he told Lumer, "to learn from the four comrades that it had been decided to establish a Los Angeles Institute for Marxist Studies—the first I had heard of this." When his visitors asked him to "explain the functioning of AIMS," Aptheker offered the delegation a curt, abbreviated description of his work. Evidently miffed at his attitude, the Los Angeles comrades reported to party leaders that Aptheker was rude to them. "[It] is therefore possible . . . more than possible," Aptheker reported to Lumer, "that I conveyed a sense of haste and this may have been viewed as rudeness." The charge of rudeness Aptheker brushed off, but he found "somewhat startling the information that my behavior was discussed by many comrades in a party school apparently for some time with charges of racism involved and that my presence at this discussion did not seem to be necessary to anyone. . . . If I were in Alaska this might be understandable but since I am usually in mid-Manhattan I find this extraordinary and bureaucratic."[7]

As if to prove the truth of Aptheker's jibe at bureaucracy, Lumer sent Aptheker's letter to the Political Committee. Three days before Cohen registered his unease about the "Newsletter," the Political Committee delegated Lumer to ask Aptheker to attend a meeting of the Administrative Committee to take up the charges against him.[8] Aptheker replied the next day in a succinct note to Lumer: "Will you please let me know, in writing, the specific purpose of the projected meeting and the personnel that is to constitute the entire body of such a meeting."[9] Lumer waited almost three weeks to get back to him with the news that the committee would consist of himself, Jim Jackson, Sylvia Newcomb, and Tony Monteiro, and the purpose of the meeting was "to discuss with you the questions raised in the documents of which you have received copies."[10] By then Aptheker had had enough, so he put an end to the memo wars. "For me to attend that meeting, with the personnel you indicate and the subject you state," he wrote to Lumer, "would be to give approval to the method followed in connection with me. I will not do that." He called the actions of Lumer and others those of a kangaroo court: "My alleged behavior was discussed by many people without any notice to me and without my participation. This occurred now months ago. The results of that discussion . . . were a finding of 'guilty' and now seems to be public property. Just the other day I heard reference to this finding and this in my presence; I can imagine what is being said outside my presence. This conduct was wrong; it is that conduct which is to be investigated, in my opinion."[11]

While Aptheker could easily brush off incoherent charges of racism, maintaining the autonomy of AIMS against the continual probing of Hall took considerably more effort. The party offered no additional financial assistance to AIMS even as it grew tremendously, and Hall's animosity toward Aptheker's independence at the institute added stress to the continual financial difficulty Aptheker encountered in keeping AIMS afloat. Even though Aptheker was teaching regularly during this period, he did not hold a full-time, tenured position, so AIMS was his lifeline to academia.

The accomplishments of AIMS were impressive. As Aptheker observed in his letter to Cohen, the "Newsletter" circulation had grown from four hundred in 1964 to about thirty-five hundred in 1973, and research libraries in every state subscribed to it. The "Newsletter" provided information about AIMS publications, conferences of interest to scholars, and, most important, lengthy bibliographies in each issue that furnished citations to recently published periodical articles, dissertations, and books. AIMS had sponsored seven symposia that attracted more than twenty-five hundred attendees. "It [AIMS] inspired and assisted in the creation of similar institutes in half a dozen countries, from India to Chile," Aptheker said with pride in a fund-raising letter. It had published "thirty-two monographs, papers and bibliographies," and its library, used by hundreds of researchers, especially students and professors, held eight thousand volumes. Fay often spent time overseeing the library collections, and three other people worked "part-time for the Institute at salaries so low" Aptheker felt "ashamed to mention them." He himself received no salary for the singular, time-consuming effort that was required of him to assemble and edit all the content of the dense, four- to six-page publication.

Yet expenses continually mounted—postage doubled in ten years, a 35 percent increase in rent, rises in telephone, electricity, and printing costs—necessitating constant entreaties for donations. "At this moment of greatest service and significant growth," Aptheker wrote in 1973, "AIMS also faces its most severe economic difficulties." He appealed for money and suggestions that would help in "overcoming the stifling money problems."[12] Salvation came in the form of an estate left to Aptheker by Anna J. Bernstein in early 1975. That bequest of $53,470, which Hall thought should go to the party but which Aptheker kept to bolster the financial security of AIMS, proved to be a respite for a few years from the constant quest for funding. Keeping the money did not endear Aptheker to Hall.

Hall's criticism of Aptheker's autonomy may have affected some editorial decisions Aptheker made at the "Newsletter." Cohen continued to press Aptheker to broaden the bibliographic coverage. "I am still pained at the low level of the periodical coverage in the Newsletter," he wrote in February 1975, "especially since an increasing proportion of the listings now come from the CP or related cluster of magazines . . . and many of them on examination are hardly outstanding, relative to the mass that are not listed from other radical-Marxist-socialist sources. Indeed much of the material is simple polemic, with little thought or scholarship." Cohen, who understood that the party wanted to exert more control over AIMS, sidestepped that issue by suggesting that together they should find some way to preserve Aptheker's "personal approach to this task while easing the task itself." In uncharacteristically harsh language, Cohen concluded his letter by declaring, "As it is now, the Newsletter is not a useful tool for most Marxist intellectual activists in any field of activity."[13] Aptheker bristled at the criticism: "I dissent vigorously . . . from your judgement that 'the Newsletter is not a useful tool for most Marxist intellectual activists in any field of activity'; I think it is and is very useful indeed."[14]

Even though the top leadership held him suspect, Aptheker's status with the rank-and-file membership in the party remained secure. Party members nationwide knew and respected his work as a historian, speaker, and polemicist, and this high repute allowed him room to maneuver. To him, the movement, the party, was everything: every time he was rebuked he cloaked himself in denial and carried on. Evidently the leadership decided they couldn't touch Aptheker, but they could, and did, reach out to his daughter.

IN SEPTEMBER 1971 Hall had, as we have seen, told the Political Committee emphatically that the party should publicly criticize Bettina's essay called "The Social Function of Prisons in the United States," which also appeared in the book she coedited with Davis, *If They Come in the Morning: Voices of Resistance* (1972). He allowed the euphoria of Davis's acquittal to subside before carrying through on his promise. When the West Coast party newspaper, *People's World,* published a critical, though not unfavorable, review of Bettina's and Angela's book in early 1974, the time seemed right. Two scathing reviews appeared in *Political Affairs* and the *Daily World,* and although Hall did not sign his name to them, this hatchet job had all the earmarks of a Hall operation. When the first review appeared in *Political Affairs* for February 1974, Aptheker sent a quick note to Bettina: "I read . . . the so-called review of your book. . . . It is disgraceful. I note also its insulting failure to comment at all on Angela's essay—a failure as cowardly as it is insulting." He told Bettina not to worry about the review and mentioned that he had given the same advice to Fay, but he went on, "I could not do it and so I called P.A. and Hy [Lumer] was out so I exploded to Barry Cohen and hung up on him. . . . I don't know what else I'll do but the crassness of this—on the part of the editors I mean—is astonishing."[15]

He acted quickly. Three days later at party headquarters, after being told that Hall was unavailable, Aptheker met with Winston for half an hour to register a complaint. Winston, who had supported the recommendation to publicly criticize Bettina in 1971, pleaded ignorance: "He had not read the reviews and did not know about them," he maintained, but he told Aptheker that "Bettina's book was done an injustice and therefore the Party was." Winston signaled more trouble ahead for Bettina when he observed, "The youngster will take this and much more—she has in the past and no doubt, things being what they are, will have to in the future."[16] Aptheker did not let the matter rest there, although he told Bettina after his meeting with Winston, "Now I feel a little better."[17] He sent brief letters to the editors of both *Political Affairs* and the *Daily World.* "I write to register my vigorous objection to the 'review' . . . the word review is placed in quotation marks because the contents bore slight resemblance to the book being devastated. It even seems to question the propriety of Bettina's being a member of the Party's National council." He questioned the motives of the writers, considering that the name of the coeditor of the book, Angela Davis, "was not even so much as mentioned by the reviewers. Why [Davis's name is missing] is clear to any one reading the review and the introduction—but not to readers of the newspaper. The review hurts the Party," he concluded.[18]

By 1976, in the face of the charges of scholarly incompetence leveled by Woodward and dutifully repeated by the "God-damned" *New York Times* swirling about him and with rumors circulating within the historical profession that he was acting unethically by withholding access to the Du Bois papers, unsubstantiated political charges by comrades in the party aroused Aptheker's ire. Lumer, the *Political Affairs* editor, was once again at the center of the controversy. AIMS had sponsored a well-attended, successful conference that centered on the bicentennial of the United States. A few days after the conference Lumer wrote a letter to Aptheker: "It has come to my attention that among the speakers at the bicentennial conference was Morris Schappes. I simply want you to know that I regard the invitation of such a person as utterly inexcusable."[19] Schappes, whom Aptheker knew well, spent thirteen months in jail when he perjured himself to protect comrades at the Rapp–Coudert Committee hearings, a New York state investigation of City College in the 1930s. He earned the enmity of the party some years later when he left it and became the editor of *Jewish Currents,* a magazine associated with the CPUSA until it broke away in 1956. The party, which claimed that Jews were not persecuted in the Soviet Union, warned in 1969 that "*Jewish Currents* was slipping into 'a blind alley of Jewish nationalism.'" Schappes countered by voicing his "fear that there might be an 'eventual and inevitable total disappearance and obliteration of Jewish life in the Soviet Union.'"[20] Aptheker, who had faithfully followed the party's established dictate and cut off contact with anyone who had abandoned the party, responded to Lumer immediately. "I am surprised and chagrined that you would write me the kind of letter you did . . . without inquiry. Of course Morris Schappes was not 'among the speakers'; did you not see the program?" he asked. "And why not ask me first before assuming the truth of these kinds of malicious rumors and half-baked gossip?" He told Lumer that Schappes had bought a ticket to the conference and attended a panel discussion examining the Rapp–Coudert hearings "for which he went to jail." Schappes had spoken from the audience during the comment period, Aptheker told Lumer: "Henry Klein spoke about the same incident; so did I and so did many others." "How this kind of thing can be spread and then taken seriously and assumed to be accurate without even the courtesy of an inquiry from me is really astonishing," Aptheker concluded.[21]

Twice that year Fay, who was now seventy-one years old, had been mugged while shopping in the neighborhood around home. "She had yelled and fought back and run after her assailants," Bettina wrote of her mother.[22] Then, in October, during his campaign for the U.S. Senate, Aptheker was walking up the street a few doors from his home in Brooklyn when a "tall black man, very young with a club or a blackjack," mugged him. The sixty-two-year-old Aptheker fought back, his youthful training as a boxer giving him unreasonable confidence, but to no avail. His assailant "never uttered a word," Aptheker recalled in an interview, "just kept hitting me." He then opened a switchblade and began to slash Aptheker. "I thought maybe he was going to kill me," Aptheker said. When a neighbor appeared on the street and shouted at the man, "Leave the doctor alone, leave the doctor alone," the attacker grabbed a letter Aptheker had in his pocket "from Shirley Graham, I think for evidence that he had done what he was supposed to do. Why else?" grab the letter, he asked. "And he ran away. . . . But he was put up to it I don't know by what maniac."[23]

Bettina talked to her parents about moving, urging them to relocate to California: "[Mother] was ready; my father wasn't." Fay, a determined, persuasive woman, "had made up her mind" and told Bettina to "go ahead with plans to find them a house in San Jose."[24] Fay and Bettina began to work on Herbert, although his comrade Barry Cohen thinks Aptheker needed less convincing than the two women in his life might have thought. "Herbert may have wanted to distance himself from party controversy by the '76 move," Cohen said in an interview. "He may have wanted to isolate himself from all the pressure."[25]

Bettina encouraged her father to move even as she and Fay had evidently already made the decision. In April she wrote to Herbert alerting him to the changing nature of the city in which he had lived his whole life: you know that "the City has become unbearably oppressive." "She fears not so much for herself," Bettina said of her mother, "as for you." The mugging attack on Herbert had a tremendous effect on Fay. "While her imagination of potential dangers may at times be excessive," Bettina wrote, "there can be little doubt that it reflects a pervasive reality; and, more, an (unspoken) anguish she feels of what it would be like for you should you ever be alone." In addition to citing the personal reasons for moving, but without directly addressing the party controversies, Bettina implied that her father's work would benefit if he were at a remove from the party center: "Your work—already done, and that which you have as yet to complete—is of such moment, of such consequence—that your ability to fulfill what history commands, must be guaranteed, to the extent that we are capable of doing so."[26] Aptheker agreed. "I think and hope that in terms of book production I will be able to do more—and more easily—in California than here," he told Bettina as he and Fay, inveterate New Yorkers, made final preparations for their move.[27]

Whatever the reason—probably a combination of factors—Fay and Herbert moved to San Jose in the summer of 1977. They sold their house in Brooklyn, and Aptheker made arrangements for AIMS, which would from then on function on both coasts, thereby increasing costs and creating a logistical nightmare for its publications. He initially put the administrative and library work in the hands of Arthur Zipser and Henry Klein, but over the next eight years volunteers in the New York AIMS office arrived and departed regularly. Eventually, Danny Rubin, who held a number of positions in the leadership, assumed most of the major responsibilities for seeing that the New York office functioned if not efficiently at least with some semblance of normality. Aptheker officially opened a West Coast AIMS branch in downtown San Jose, rented office space, and relocated his personal library there but left the volumes in the AIMS reading room in place. He viewed the move optimistically, as an expansion of AIMS. As he settled in on the West Coast he kept in touch with the AIMS chairman, Robert Cohen. "This move was a difficult one physically and psychologically for me," he wrote in August. "It was necessary for Fay, however, and so we have done it."[28] He told Corliss Lamont in December that he was "well settled." He mentioned the panoramic view from his office overlooking San Jose, something certainly not available in the canyons of New York City, and he noted, with evident pleasure, "I actually am able to walk to work for the first time in my life!"[29]

Almost immediately academic opportunities opened for Aptheker. He began preliminary negotiations for conducting seminars at nearby Santa Clara University, a Catholic school. At dinner one evening with Fania Davis, Angela's sister, who at the time was working on a degree at Boalt Hall, the UC Berkeley law school, Davis asked Aptheker if he "would like to teach there and if so what." When he realized she was asking in all seriousness, he suggested a course on racism and American law.[30] Davis went to work organizing a campaign to have Aptheker appointed a visiting lecturer. When he wrote to Cohen in August that "there is some effort being made now to have me teach a course on Racism and the Law in the U.C. Berkeley law school," he did not hold out much hope of acquiring a teaching position at a university that had once had him thrown off campus. "Several professors and students want it but the administration, of course does not. Perhaps another Yale is in the offing," he quipped. Much to his surprise, however, Davis and her fellow students prevailed in their endeavor, and by November Robert H. Cole of Boalt Hall wrote to confirm the details of Aptheker's appointment. "I think that I've now done all the administratively relevant things I can do to insure that you will be able to offer your course here next semester," he told Aptheker. "So far as I can tell, there should be no obstacle to your doing so, and I certainly expect that you will be giving the course."[31] He taught the first class in 1978. Boalt Hall paid him one thousand dollars for a class that met one day a week for ninety minutes. In 1979 he added another class to his schedule, "Labor and the Law," and he taught both classes for the next twelve years, earning about six thousand dollars per year by the time he decided to quit teaching. "Students have been first-rate," he told a correspondent after the first year, "and I've learned much teaching this."[32]

By the latter half of the 1970s the worst ravages of the McCarthyite Red Scare were over, although remnants lingered. The House of Representatives abolished the HCUA in 1975, and in the wake of the Vietnam War and Watergate the Church Committee in the Senate exposed COINTELPRO and ostensibly curbed the actions of the FBI. The surveillance of the Aptheker family ended, as did that of AIMS and other organizations in which Herbert was involved. Aptheker never did see more than several dozen of the thousands of pages in his FBI file, but in 1977 he received the first disclosures from the U.S. Department of

Justice Office of Professional Responsibility when it began to notify the targets of COINTELPRO about the operations conducted against them.

Ken Lawrence, the director of the American Friends Service Committee Mississippi Surveillance Project, contacted Aptheker in 1978 concerning COINTELPRO operations against him. "I presume you have seen the FBI's pamphlet attacking your integrity as an historian," he wrote. "Did you know, or presume, that the FBI authored and distributed it?"[33] Aptheker acknowledged having seen the pamphlet at several meetings and told Lawrence that the Department of Justice had notified him of only one COINTELPRO operation. "People distributed them but I never dignified them by any comment," he told Lawrence. "Again I assumed they were written and distributed by the FBI but this proof is appreciated."[34]

Aptheker's teaching at Berkeley and the growing attention and approbation given to his historical writing, especially *American Negro Slave Revolts,* by young members of the historical profession awakened in Aptheker a sense that a decidedly positive shift was taking place in academia and among the Left in general: but then he always confused personal vindication, a softening view of himself within academia, with a change in the public's perception of the party. "There is a change on the Left and it is towards us [the Communist Party]," he told Si Gerson in April 1979 in relating his satisfaction with events at a recent meeting of the Organization of American Historians at which Genovese had paid tribute to the pioneering work of Marxists, "including the undersigned by name."[35]

A YEAR earlier, in February 1978, answering what she said was "an insistent internal voice that grew louder with each passing year" beckoning her to "live true to myself—my lesbian identity, my interests in a new teaching career, and my dedication to immersing myself in a feminist life," Bettina had divorced her husband, Jack Kurzweil. To build a new life and "breakout from old structures," she began to extricate herself from her position as chair of the Santa Clara County Party club and from her service on party committees. Then, in 1979, she renewed an acquaintance and fell in love with Kate Miller, one of her former students who was now teaching U.S. women's history at Monterey Peninsula College. This development precipitated her public coming out and her decision to live openly as a lesbian after having "been closeted for twenty years."[36]

While Bettina was apprehensive about how Herbert and Fay would react to her new "lifestyle," she wanted them to share in her happiness and to meet Kate, even though she was "not prepared to directly acknowledge" their relationship.[37] Bettina was unaware that her father had pressured Hall and other party leaders for almost a decade to repudiate the party's systemic homophobia. She conceded in her memoir that she didn't know what her father understood of her relationship with Kate "because we never talked about it directly" and went on to say, in a fleeting reference to an anecdote depicting his aversion toward homosexuals, that he was "very homophobic toward gay men."[38] Yet quietly over the years Aptheker had made great strides to overcome his homophobia. Although it's not clear which event occurred first, the very month Bettina brought Kate to her parents' home for dinner Aptheker made yet another appeal, in response to a letter from Hall requesting help in the preparation of the Main Political Report for the 22nd National Convention, for ending the party's homophobia.[39] Toward the end of his recommendations about the report, under "other thoughts," Aptheker told Hall, as he had Winston and James Jackson in earlier communications, that the party needed to focus attention on the "great significance of the women's movement" and on gay and lesbian liberation. "I've had my say on the homosexual thing—this I started to do about 5 years ago," he wrote. "I still believe the Party is backward here and that sexual hang-ups persist that hurt us. The inhumanity of the profit system makes imperative the end of that system. That is why there is a Communist Party. That is the bottom line—literally!"[40]

Bettina had agitated since the late sixties to alter the party's stance on women workers and to begin to accept the feminist movement, a battle she and some other party women continually lost. "The Party never put even a fraction of its very small political weight towards organizing women workers," she recalled. "Most women in Party leadership, especially at the national level, were the wives of Party functionaries . . . [who] held various and lesser staff positions."[41] Yet by the mid-1970s the message had reached some of the leaders. In 1975 Lou Diskin, the head of International Publishers, asked Bettina to write a book on women. She consented and over the next four years produced an outline and conducted research on the topic. In 1979 Diskin and Bettina signed a publishing contract for the book, which was to be titled *Woman's Legacy: Essays on Race, Sex and Class in American History.*

Diskin told Bettina he admired the manuscript and reminded her that they would have to get party approval for publication. Although Bettina "bristled at the idea of [seeking] party approval," she agreed to send the manuscript to Alva Buxenbaum, the head of the party's national women's commission. When Bettina told Diskin there would likely be controversy over a chapter "on domestic labor because of the way it discussed women's unpaid labor in the home," he attempted to reassure her about her writing. He contended that party approval "in this case was just a formality," but Bettina was wary: "Having been burned before," she wrote in her memoir, remembering the controversy over the book she coauthored with Davis almost a decade earlier, "I knew differently."[42]

Holding tight to "orthodox formulations of Marxism," the party leaders protested, after reading Bettina on domestic labor, that "the only people who were exploited under capitalism were workers *at the point of production.*" Women who stayed at home, who worked for no pay in the home "caring for children, the sick, the elderly" did so, according to party theory, as a "labor of love," labor that had trivial economic meaning.[43] In the manuscript Bettina challenged that formulation. She moved beyond class "as the principal or only instrument of oppression upon which all others rested" to examine domination based on her conviction that race, sex, and class were "interdependent and interlocking." The chapter on domestic labor "was where these ideas were most evident," she wrote. "It was precisely here that one could see most vividly the connections because black women, embodying the collision of race, sex and class, had been employed as domestic servants in such overwhelming numbers especially between the 1930s and the 1960s." She gained insight into the plight of domestic workers too by recounting her childhood experiences, her "unease with the way my parents employed, and I felt, exploited" the black women they engaged for household work.[44] "My parents also employed women—all African American—to clean our house," she wrote in her memoir. "I was confused, trying to reconcile Dora [one of their housekeepers] cleaning our house for what I thought was very low pay for the hard, hard physical labor she did, with my father writing and giving lectures on African American history, and excoriating those who oppressed black people and continued to deny them true equality."[45]

Bettina knew perfectly well the consequences inherent in deviating from what the party leaders decided was orthodox. Her father, too, understood those ramifications, yet he persisted in rationalizing and avoiding them. Alan Wolfe, the political scientist and sociologist who earlier in his career was a member of the collective that put out the Marxist-oriented journal *Kapitalistate,* pointed out the party's intolerance of heresy in a letter written to Aptheker in late December 1979. "Many of us who were active in the New Left saw ourselves rejecting . . . the establishment of the kind of politics that had failed the previous generation of radicals," he wrote. "My own experience with the CP was not the one you describe," he said. "I found party members to be intolerant of our deviations from orthodox theory, doctrinaire, and given to lecturing us on our mistakes. . . . But let me repeat, it was not the criticism itself but the holier than thou way in which it was delivered that upset me."[46] Aptheker answered candidly: "I do not doubt for a moment some of the unpleasant experiences you describe," he wrote. "These subjective encounters exist in all organizations (and human relationships) and I'm sure you will believe me when I state that they have not missed me in the over 40 years of my own Party membership! They must be evaluated for what they are, however, I think; such episodes and encounters should not determine one's own collective efforts and associations."[47]

The party leaders heard the same kind of complaints from comrades outside the rarified precincts of party headquarters. They responded early in January

1980 with a resolution prepared by the Political Bureau titled "Making A Turn In Its Work," in which, among other things, they purported to be seeking ways to overcome the "cadre crises" within the party. The convoluted, jargony language could hardly have inspired confidence among "cadre." The leaders promised to "strengthen a comradely, considerate Leninist style of relations with co-workers and comrades on lower levels by overcoming bureaucratic, commandist, rude, agitational and subjectivist relations: Improve the atmosphere still more for comrades to be able to ask questions and express differences without concern that an over-all and lasting negative judgment and characterization of them will be made or that the very act of posing a difference means they are challenging the Party or its leadership."[48] The leaders' intention to carry out these reforms, if it existed at all, evaporated quickly, yet the rhetoric persisted for the next decade.

Not long after International Publishers sent out its catalogue in spring 1980 listing its new books, among which, scheduled for publication in July, was Bettina's *Woman's Legacy,* Diskin informed her in May, by letter, that the "national party chair Henry Winston [and] two members of the national women's commission had [all] read the manuscript and had 'lodged the most serious complaints.'" Confirming the judgment of heresy, Bettina received a letter from one of the women on the commission who objected that Bettina's analysis was "the opposite of Marxism" and cautioned her to clearly indicate when speaking publicly that she did not represent the position of the party. The party leaders, through Buxenbaum, also sent an extraordinary edict to the California party leaders decreeing that they should not allow Bettina to teach a "cadre training class" that summer in San Francisco called "The Struggle for Women's Equality" because she "was no longer ideologically fit to teach for the party."[49]

Encouraged by her father to fight the leadership, Bettina met with Diskin and members of the women's commission in Diskin's office at International. The interrogation and attempted censorship outraged Bettina. Throughout the conversation the criticisms were couched as purely general ideological statements with no specifics, and no one proposed any particular revisions; one of the women had not even bothered to read the manuscript. Bettina did agree to have the manuscript reviewed by other comrades who had a more academic background, which made her more confident that she could deal with specifics. Bettina's partner, Kate, seems to have had a correct analysis of the party's position: "She said the party had no intention of allowing the book to be published because I was living as a lesbian; they were just going through the motions."[50]

Diskin strung Bettina along throughout the summer as she revised the manuscript. In October, after consenting to Bettina's proposal for what revisions should be made, Diskin sent her the original manuscript, "unrevised, copy edited, [and] many pages with blue tags for queries to the author" but otherwise with no comment. By November Bettina faced the inevitable: "In my estimate," she wrote to her father after receiving notice from Winston of a proposed meeting to discuss the book, "there is no intention of a discussion about *Woman's Legacy*. Rather, the purpose of the meeting will be to insure necessary adjustments in procedure and attitude so that you will continue to write for International. . . . But this issue—'The Woman question'—will have to be dealt with sooner or later."[51] "I believed at the time (and still do)," Bettina wrote in her memoir, "that someone very high in the party leadership had ordered that this book not be published under any circumstances."[52]

However sanguine Aptheker had been in January with respect to one's duty to overcome "subjective encounters" and to continue "collective efforts and associations," Diskin's treatment of Bettina caused him to sever his forty-year relationship with International. "My own view is that Bettina's effort represents a very important and pioneering effort to apply dialectical materialism to aspects of the history of women in the United States," he wrote to Diskin, Winston, and Buxenbaum. "It is the first such effort and those who come later may well add and amend and improve; this is the natural and inevitable process of science. But Bettina's effort is a first and a very serious, stimulating and helpful probing of a most complex subject." But beyond Diskin's and Buxenbaum's estimation that the manuscript was anti-Marxian, Aptheker was appalled at how the party treated Bettina. "If I did not have first-hand knowledge of the brusqueness, discourtesy and bureaucratic arrogance displayed in this instance I would find it incredible. I have had some examples of this myself . . . [but] I never experienced the like of what Bettina did. . . . The result has been International's loss of the writing of a young, tested and talented comrade who should have about 35 or 40 more years of productivity. That it also has persuaded the old comrade who writes this letter that International is not for him is a minor consideration since, if he is still to be productive that is a matter of only a few more years at best."[53]

It wasn't just International but the party as well that lost Bettina. UMass Press eventually published *Woman's Legacy* in 1982 to broad, favorable reviews by scholarly, feminist, and black presses. As Bettina pondered the controversy surrounding the publication of her manuscript, she found a void where once she had a "willingness to fight for [the party] when my work and activities were severely criticized." She could no longer find anything to say when asked to encourage people to join the party.[54] Bettina resigned from the party on 12 October 1981.

Once he had severed his relationship with International, Aptheker, as he had done for the past decade, consigned the actions of the party's leaders to whatever place he kept open for filing incidents that might cause him to question his own continued collective efforts within the party. When Bettina showed him her resignation letter prior to sending it to the leaders, his first thought, according to her, went to the adverse publicity it would bring to the party. "You must not send this," he told Bettina. "What if the *New York Times* got hold of it and printed it?" Then, Bettina recalled, the confrontation turned into a shouting match that required Fay to put a stop to.[55]

Resignation from the party had always been the ultimate betrayal in Aptheker's judgment. He had shunned even intimate old friends like Scales, Fast, and others who had resigned from the party as unredeemable enemies. But not his daughter: "He was not prepared to renounce me," Bettina wrote, "he was not prepared to lose me." Aptheker seldom drank, but after the yelling stopped he produced a bottle of wine, poured a glass for Fay and Bettina and himself, and proposed a toast "To the family." Aptheker never again talked to Bettina about her resignation, she said, and gradually her parents also "stopped talking about the party in my presence, except to tell me about the death of one or another comrade."[56]

23   Renewal and Endings

IN EARLY November 1977 the thirty-fifth anniversary of the publication of *American Negro Slave Revolts* approached. Aptheker raised the idea among his younger colleagues, who were now moving into positions of leadership in the professional historical organizations, that the American Historical Association (AHA) or the Organization of American Historians (OAH) might want to take notice of his book. "A thought has occurred to me," he wrote to the historian Sterling Stuckey. "Sessions have been held in the last few years by various historical organizations devoted to particular books—Phillips', Gutman, Fogel & Engerman, Elkins and others. My American Negro Slave Revolts . . . has so far managed to escape such a session. I think I know why but the reason has nothing to do with scholarship." Aptheker wanted Stuckey to suggest to the AHA or the OAH that such a session be held for his volume.[1]

That eventuality failed to materialize, but a year or so later an invitation gave Aptheker reason to hope that sentiment within the historical organizations vis-à-vis his major work on slavery was changing. He was asked by the organizers of the OAH convention in 1979, to be held in New Orleans, to chair a session titled "Marxism and Afro-American History." Genovese, the outgoing president of the OAH and the first Marxist historian to hold that position, paid tribute in his presidential address to "the pioneering work of Marxists," including Aptheker. Genovese used the opportunity of the meeting to heal old wounds by inviting Aptheker to breakfast in the "presidential suite," where they had a conversation that Aptheker characterized as one of "rapprochement mixed with apology."[2]

Aptheker was not as quick as Genovese appeared to be in New Orleans to leave the old polemical battles behind. In a cordial, although pointed, letter written in 1979 he urged Genovese to explain and publish an apology for remarks he had made in "Marxian Interpretations of the Slave South," an eleven-year-old essay that Aptheker had taken as a personal attack. "I have come upon that section of your published writings that were most offensive and which were in my mind when I referred to your charge of 'cowardice' as helping explain adherence to the Communist Party, USA," Aptheker wrote. "Since this essay is entitled 'Marxian Interpretations of the Slave South' and since it is sprinkled with references to (a very limited) portion of my work, I think I may be forgiven for construing this as having personal reference."[3]

In his reply Genovese exhibited a solicitous attitude toward Aptheker's slighted feelings. "Ah so!" he wrote. "That wretched article on Marxian interpretations of the Slave South. Where do I begin? First, no, I never had you in mind with a charge of cowardice—how could I when at the very moment I was loudly saying the opposite? Whom did I mean? God knows. One of these polemical thrusts against god-knows whom, which look good as factional fireworks and then you want to eat." He had, he wrote, "always—always—spoken with the highest respect for your courageous defense of the party and the movement."[4] "In truth," Genovese wrote in a later letter, "it was a bad year for political cheap shots, and that is one article I wish I had written differently, not to mention not republished without revision in *In Red & Black*."[5] Moreover, sometime later Genovese, in thanking Aptheker for writing a review of his *From Rebellion to Revolution: Afro-American Slave Revolts in the Making of the New World*, said he admired Aptheker's own ability when it came to polemic. "Your criticism at its best," he wrote. "I only wish I had had the benefit of the criticism before publication. I think you are unnecessarily touchy at some points, but it is a free country(!) Besides, you are so good at polemical thrusts that I confess to enjoying them even when I am the victim and I think you are off-base. I flatter myself that I am pretty good myself on that terrain, and I cannot resist the professional admiration."[6]

After their breakfast meeting in New Orleans in 1979 Aptheker was of the opinion that Genovese would arrange a session on *American Negro Slave Revolts* for the OAH meeting in 1980. He told Genovese that "[although] my understanding was after our meeting that you would undertake some effort [to arrange the session, John] Bracey told me about ten days ago that he had heard the panel was not to be undertaken this coming April; that there is to be a session on Du Bois's RECONSTRUCTION instead."[7] Aptheker said he hoped a session could be arranged for 1981.

Genovese laid the blame on Bracey, whom Aptheker truly admired. "Bracey was to follow up on the session on your book," Genovese wrote. "He made it a matter of principle. I should have known better. He is an exceptionally bright fellow—but responsible he is not."[8] "Expect nothing worthwhile from Bracey," he said acidly in another letter. "He looked like a brilliant rising star ten years ago but has turned into an academic hustler, so far as I can tell. Still, he always had a fine mind, and maybe, just maybe, he will get himself together and rise to the occasion."[9] "I have no recollection of this," Bracey asserted in annotating this passage. "I wasn't even speaking to Genovese at this point."[10] Genovese promised to contact Warren Susman, the head of the OAH Program Committee for 1981. "This time I shall make sure of it myself—if it can be done."[11]

Over the next few months, some of which Aptheker, at the invitation of the East German government, spent as Distinguished Visiting Professor of History at Humboldt University in East Berlin, Genovese and Aptheker made arrangements for the presentation at the OAH session in 1981. Genovese thought that in addition to a paper by Aptheker, Stuckey might present one, and Nathan Huggins could be asked to chair the session. Vincent Harding or Peter Wood might be considered as backups, he speculated.[12] Aptheker thought Stuckey a "fine choice" but said he didn't "think very highly of the work of Huggins" and rejected him. He thought John Hope Franklin would be the best choice to chair the panel: "Our outlooks differ of course but my regard for him and his work is high and I think this is mutual."[13] Genovese wasn't so sure about Franklin. "I shall be amazed if he accepts," he told Aptheker. "He is a decent man, and I like him. But I wonder if you have any idea how deeply reactionary he is—and how hostile to Marxists of any kind. Still, we shall try."[14] "I know that John Hope is conservative," Aptheker wrote in return. "He always was—and also devout.... But he is a fine man and on the whole his books have been good—especially when the time of appearance is kept in mind. Maybe he will accept."[15]

Franklin in fact did accept the invitation to chair the session, and Genovese, Stuckey, Joshua Leslie, and Aptheker were to present papers. When Aptheker received the OAH program for the meeting in February 1981, however, he saw that it contained no mention of their session. He lamented the omission in a letter to his AIMS colleague Robert Cohen, hoping "this was not a Cold War act and nothing otherwise sinister."[16] His obvious regret appeared in a letter to Genovese: "I hope this does not reflect impact of a revived anti-Communism or anything at all sinister." "Still, I must confess that I permitted myself to expect that this would take place," he said, with evident bitterness, "thus violating a long-standing rule by which I have learned to conduct my life: have no positive expectations and endure no significant disappointments."[17]

Genovese voiced genuine outrage. He called Susman, he said, "to find out what happened." According to Genovese, Susman acknowledged that he and Genovese had made the arrangements for the session. "There was no question of some 'breakdown in communications,' 'misunderstanding,'" Genovese wrote to Aptheker, Stuckey, Leslie, Franklin, and Richard Kirkendall. Relating his conversation with Susman to Franz Kafka's *The Castle* or *The Trial,* Genovese recounted for the other historians his recollection of it:

Genovese: Warren, what on earth happened?
Susman: I don't know.
G: What the hell do you mean, you don't know? Don't you think I deserve some explanation?
S: I have nothing to say. Talk to someone else on the committee.

G: I already did that and was told that he never heard of the panel and referred me back to you.

S: That's not true.

G: Then it did go to the committee?

S: Yes.

G: Well, what was said? What was the disposition? Why did I not even get the courtesy, extended to anyone else, of a formal, if mimeographed rejection?

S: I don't know. I can't recall. I'll have to check.

G: Check what? Why was it turned down after you assured me that it had been okayed and that it had your personal and indeed warm endorsement?

S: I don't have anything to say.

G: But you will no doubt assure me that it was not political.

S: It was not political. You know me better than that.

G: No, I don't know you better than that! If it was not political, then tell me what it was.

S: I don't know.

G: It has nothing to do with the Aptheker case at Yale? Nothing to do with what happened to me at Harvard and Maryland? Nothing to do with the packing of the program with ideological and political cronies who have it in for both Herbert and me? Nothing to do with anything political?

S: That's right.

G: But you can't tell me what it does have to do with?

S: No.

G: Goodbye, Warren.[18]

Aptheker reported to Genovese that Stuckey received an altogether different response from Susman. When Stuckey called him, Susman blamed the cancellation of the session on Genovese's poor health. Aptheker considered attending the OAH meeting in Detroit anyway to present the sequence of events at the OAH open business meeting, but Genovese counseled against the idea. "Susman will simply deny everything," he told Aptheker. "Since I never insisted that Susman give me assurances in writing, it will be my word against his." He noted that "people inside the OAH tell me that the program was fouled up in a manner altogether unprecedented. Still," he continued, "there are too many political payoffs on that program for me to swallow easily." They let the matter drop but not before Aptheker told Genovese he was "continually astonished at this kind of extraordinary behavior—I suppose the point is that it is not extraordinary but I cannot reconcile myself to that."[19] "Do not allow yourself to 'burn,'" Aptheker advised Genovese at the end of March, "the bastards are not worth it and it is possible to burn oneself out."[20]

Genovese talked to Manning Marable about the situation, and together they developed a totally different notion, namely, finding a university to sponsor an entire conference devoted to *American Negro Slave Revolts*. They had to put that idea aside, however, because "various universities and foundations are so tight for money that we are not sanguine about financing a conference." In the end they submitted to Aptheker the idea of developing "a volume of essays around your slave revolt book."[21] Aptheker responded favorably: "The idea of a kind of festschrift around the slave revolt book pleases me very much indeed. 1983 is its 40th anniversary.... I will co-operate with this effort in every possible way." He proposed that at least Charles Wesley, Rayford Logan, and Franklin be asked to contribute if they were up to the effort.[22]

In 1983 International Publishers, which held the rights to the book, issued a fortieth-anniversary edition of *American Negro Slave Revolts* with an introduction by Bracey. In its various editions, the book had, by that time, sold about thirty-five thousand copies. That year, too, the OAH held an outwardly uncontroversial session devoted to the book, one in whose planning and execution Genovese did not participate. Herbert Shapiro, a historian at the University of Cincinnati, organized the session, and Harding chaired. Shapiro's paper dealt directly with *American Negro Slave Revolts,* Peter Wood presented a talk on the 1780s inspired by the slave revolts book, and Aptheker and Leslie commented on the two papers.

Two Festschrifts devoted to Aptheker eventually appeared in the last two decades of the twentieth century along with a fiftieth-anniversary edition of *American Negro Slave Revolts.* Gary Okihiro edited the first series of essays, *In Resistance: Studies in African, Caribbean, and Afro-American History,* published by UMass Press in 1986. The book originated in a conference held at Stanford University in the spring of 1983 that brought together historians of Africa, the Caribbean, Latin America, and the United States to celebrate the fortieth anniversary of *American Negro Slave Revolts.* In addition to a bibliographical comment by Bettina and chapters by Wood, Shapiro, and Aptheker, the volume contained a glowing essay contributed by Genovese on Aptheker's career and influence.[23]

Aptheker first met with Okihiro, a professor at the Catholic-sponsored Santa Clara University in California, over lunch in May 1982. Okihiro, the chair of the ethnic studies program, offered Aptheker a teaching position as resident scholar at Santa Clara. Aptheker readily accepted the one-year appointment to teach one two-hour class every week. Okihiro granted him a private office, stationery, a typist, a researcher, and the opportunity to make recommendations to help the Santa Clara ethnic studies program.[24] Aptheker wrote to Lynd that one of Santa Clara's vice presidents, a priest unhappy over Aptheker's appointment, told Okihiro that he hoped Aptheker "would be forgotten and not get the minimum registration of 15 [students]." But enrollment in Aptheker's class, as it had at Berkeley, increased every term, from thirty students in the fall of 1982 to forty-five that winter and to sixty in the spring. Nonetheless, in May 1983 Okihiro told Aptheker his teaching contract would not be renewed. "Why, I asked," Aptheker wrote to Lynd. "Because this Vice President (a priest, of course) told [Okihiro] that a corporation, learning that I was teaching had withdrawn a grant of $70,000, so that was that. I asked if he would be willing to fight; he said, alas, no. But he did ask me to be again resident scholar . . . of course I accepted."[25] Later in the year, after officials at Santa Clara had invited him to present a paper titled "Marx and Christianity: 100 Years Later" at a conference, Aptheker was abruptly disinvited. "The University of Santa Clara is embarrassed by my presence on campus," Aptheker wrote to the philosophy professor James W. Felt, "[and] this is why I was asked not to teach there again this year. After 45 years I am still a little surprised at this treatment in the free world, especially when it [the conference] seeks to discuss 'Marxism.' "[26]

The second Festschrift, *African American History and Radical Historiography: Essays in Honor of Herbert Aptheker,* edited by Shapiro, appeared a dozen years later, in 1998.[27] This volume alluded only indirectly to Aptheker's political life, emphasizing his scholarship instead, and contained essays by the sociologists and historians Mark Solomon, Stuckey, Foner, Lemisch, Marable, Lynd, and Shapiro, among others. "The essays published here reflect the wide influence that Herbert Aptheker has exerted and continues to exert on U.S. scholars," Shapiro wrote in his introduction. "Aptheker's career," he continued, "reminds us of the political conformism of the Right and Far Right that did not stop at dispute but sought to destroy careers and altogether exclude radicals from the marketplace of ideas."[28]

Throughout the seventies, even after his move to San Jose, Aptheker had steadfastly rebuffed the efforts of the party's leaders to take control of AIMS, but by 1983 the financial pressure under which the institute had operated for half a dozen years finally forced him to capitulate. Aptheker continued to produce the bimonthly newsletter in San Jose, but he shipped it off to New York, where Danny Rubin and his two part-time assistants took charge of printing and mailing. Cohen, still acting as AIMS's chairman, urged Aptheker to cut expenses in late 1982 by closing the New York library and office. "I believe that a drastically reduced scale of operations is no serious defeat for you or for AIMS," he assured Aptheker, "unless you found it impossible to continue the Newsletter. All the rest is second to that."[29] Aptheker was not unaware that AIMS was in desperate financial straits. "As of this moment," he wrote to Rubin in November, "it is doubtful—highly doubtful—that AIMS can maintain itself financially." He asked Rubin to request money from the party to keep the organization running for a few months while he appealed to newsletter subscribers for money. He recommended also that the New York office be closed and the office equipment moved to party headquarters. He said he would cover the costs incurred by the

San Jose office himself: "With real effort at least the Newsletter can be saved and with that AIMS as an entity."[30]

Aptheker appealed directly to Winston for financial assistance, but his request produced only limited financial aid in the form of several hundred dollars.[31] The New York AIMS office did close in 1983 but instead of moving it to party headquarters, Rubin found a tiny corner in the dilapidated Ukrainian Hall on East 4th Street where he could operate for fifty dollars a month. The party allowed workers at the *Daily World* to compose and print the newsletter but only on a volunteer basis, the work to be done during lunch breaks or after hours. Producing the newsletter under those chaotic conditions and with little help, Rubin sometimes took almost a month to finish it.[32]

In return for the financial aid it did provide, the party assumed control of AIMS. The leaders decided, evidently with Aptheker's acquiescence, that he would continue to edit the newsletter, but they would find a new director for the institute (presumably someone more pliable), make Aptheker director emeritus, and sponsor a banquet announcing his retirement as director. After discussions with Rubin in which they set the date of the banquet for 26 February 1984, Winston solicited ideas from Aptheker about "how to make up the kind of event that it should be."[33] Aptheker's sense was that the program should concentrate on the past and future of AIMS, "especially the latter," as the main political purpose of the event—including an announcement that Aptheker would retire as director and assume the title of director emeritus—and should include "some note of the work of the Director for the past twenty years." He pushed Winston and the party to come to some decision by the time of the banquet about what would happen next at AIMS: "[It] should be clear by that time who (or what collective group, with some of its personnel) are to function as Director," he told Winston. Aptheker made a list of some potential speakers for the banquet.[34] Noticeably absent from it was Cohen, who had served as AIMS board chairman for most of its twenty years of existence. Aptheker did not explain the oversight, if that's what it was; perhaps he simply wanted to save himself and Cohen the embarrassment of acknowledging the party's fait accompli.

Most of the people whom Aptheker put forward did indeed become official sponsors of the event. It was called "An Afro-American History Month Celebration: For Equality and the Defeat of Reaganism A Dinner Honoring Dr. Herbert Aptheker" and took place, as planned, on 26 February 1984 at the Martin Luther King, Jr. Labor Center on West 43rd Street. In addition to Aptheker, the speakers included Winston; Ernest DeMaio, the UN Representative of the World Federation of Trade Unions; Leith Mullings, an anthropology professor at City College and Marable's wife; and Johnnetta Cole, an anthropology professor at Hunter College. Their breach evidently healed,

Aptheker must have been pleased with Winston's remarks as he heaped praise on Aptheker's contributions to "the fight for equality and freedom."[35]

Three days after the banquet Aptheker congratulated Rubin for his efforts in making the dinner "eminently successful" but displayed some irritation, reflecting his precarious position as AIMS director emeritus, over the comments of DeMaio and Mullings. "I did think Ernie's remarks about 'semi-retirement' were insensitive—as well as inaccurate. And I did not quite understand the remark by Leith that I would continue to edit the Newsletter 'for a while.' What does that mean?"[36]

Cole's remarks that afternoon came back to haunt her years later when President-elect Bill Clinton, in 1992, contemplated nominating her for the position of secretary of education in his cabinet. The *Daily World* writer Geoffrey Jacques reported that Cole, in her speech, "called Aptheker's dedication to combating racism 'the central theme' of his work. His work, she said, showed how important it is to develop quality scholarship in opposition to the ideas put forth against the people's movements. 'Today as never before,' she said, scholarship 'must be put to use' for the people."[37] When Clinton appointed Cole to his transition team, she was president of Spelman College, the prestigious school for black women in Atlanta. The appointment touched off a firestorm of anticommunist hysteria reminiscent of the McCarthy era in the pages of the Jewish weekly *Forward, Commentary,* the *New York Times* editorial pages, and the syndicated column by Rowland Evans and Robert Novak. David Twersky fired the first shot in *Forward,* then followed that story with one in *Commentary* repeating his denunciation from the previous article. Twersky charged that Cole's "past association with such organizations as the pro-Castro Venceremos Brigades and the pro-Soviet U.S. Peace Council . . . [and] an out-and-out supporter of the Communist side in that war [Vietnam]" made her unfit to serve in the Clinton administration. But her heresy went even further, said Twersky, who quoted Jacques's article from the *Daily World:* "Cole's pro-Castro activities extended up to the mid-80s, and it was not 40 but only eight years ago that she made a speech praising Herbert Aptheker, the veteran Communist-party theoretician, for '[developing] quality scholarship in opposition to the ideas put forward against the peoples' movement.'"[38] A. M. Rosenthal joined in on the pummeling of Cole, writing on 15 December 1992, "I think her appointment [to the Clinton transition team] was a mistake that should be explained. I hope she does not hang around government much longer. Propagandists for dictatorships don't suit my particular nose."[39] Cole did not serve as secretary of education: like Lani Guinier, another black woman considered for an administration position whom the right wing vilified, Cole was left by President Clinton slowly twisting in the wind.

Cohen, who, as noted, served for nineteen years as the chair of the AIMS board before resigning that position in 1983, was anything but pleased by the decision to turn AIMS over to the party. "I was astonished to receive a form letter inviting me to join in sponsoring a dinner honoring you at the time of your retirement," Cohen wrote on 4 April 1984, two months after the event. "Whatever may be the political purpose of this event, I find it astonishing that I was not asked to join this initiating group of sponsors early in the planning. Indeed no one who has been active in AIMS seems to have participated in planning the occasion. . . . I have no objection to those who signed the invitation letter, but they are not to be said as noted for support of AIMS in the past, at any rate not with observable action." Cohen wanted to know how Aptheker had made the decision to retire: "How can you have decided to retire . . . to take the title and position of Director Emeritus, and have made no attempt to clear this entire transition with your Board? And in view of the conception of AIMS as a partnership in Marxist scholarship and education among Communists and Christians and non-Communist scholars with humane and socialist interests, and all the rest, why would you make this change without consulting the rest of us?"[40]

Aptheker attempted to soothe Cohen's anger and disbelief. "At [the] last Board meeting, very scantily attended (as was true of previous one)," Aptheker wrote, "you had resigned as Chair and remained on Board only on belated suggestion of Allen [possibly Charles R. Allen Jr., a journalist who was a "founding sponsor" of AIMS]—whose contribution there as always was a long speech and promises and nothing done then or at any other time. . . . We could not continue in the old way and if AIMS was to continue in any form drastic action was needed at once. . . . I continue putting out NEWSLETTER and we'll see if we can make it. We will try."[41] When the last AIMS "Newsletter" appeared, Cohen wrote to Aptheker, "I usually do not grieve at a memorial service or a funeral but rather celebrate happy or creative or just plain human times, and the same with your valiant AIMS. . . . Congratulations for what you tried to do, and what you did do, and all your heartfelt intelligent motives and works."[42]

Aptheker did try, and AIMS limped along for two more years, surviving for the first several months on the five thousand dollars raised at the dinner and then on income from property and cash left to Aptheker in legacy wills. The party did not name a new director, and the board slowly drifted away. By September 1985 Aptheker had completely lost control of AIMS.

The final issue of the "Newsletter," volume 22, number 6, appeared in December 1985. "With extreme regret," Aptheker wrote in the opening paragraph, "the Director is compelled to declare that it is no longer possible—for financial reasons—to continue AIMS." He then listed the institute's major accomplishments: "Thirty-five symposia; published eleven books in the Historical Series; four books in its Monograph Series, thirty-six in our Occasional Papers Series and sixteen in our Bibliographical Series." "The interest in Marxism has never been more intense," he continued, "but the sad fact is that funds to support AIMS have not been forthcoming. . . . So, this is *aufwiedersehn*."[43] To Rubin, Aptheker tersely wrote in mid-November, "Apparently this closes out this particular effort."[44]

Rebuffed by the party, Aptheker contacted David Laibman at *Science & Society* (*S&S*) and proposed the idea of continuing the newsletter in some form at that Marxist quarterly. Through Rubin he kept the party abreast of what he was doing because he anticipated disapproval by the leaders based on "past unhappy experiences," old animosities and wounds unhealed among the party, and the radicals surrounding *S&S*.

Laibman urged that he and Aptheker move carefully.[45] The problem for his colleagues, Laibman noted, had to do with the section of the AIMS "Newsletter" called "From the World of Magazines." Echoing complaints that Cohen had lodged years earlier about material selected for inclusion, Laibman acknowledged that coverage in the "Newsletter" reflected "an entirely legitimate political perspective" that prompted "a certain imbalance." He insisted that "*S&S* must be shaped as a forum in which the various tendencies can be debated." To accomplish this, he told Aptheker, "it must not seem that publications which are influenced by contrary tendencies have been excluded from consideration *a priori*."[46]

What Laibman proposed was that in each issue of *S&S* incorporating the AIMS "Newsletter" it "be announced as under your editorship; that we agree that coverage will be widened as indicated above, in exchange for your 'editorial autonomy'; and finally that we contract (so to speak) for one year (four issues), after which the Board will vote again on whether to make the arrangement permanent." If Aptheker agreed, Laibman wrote, "that [arrangement] stands a good chance of winning approval of our colleagues."[47]

Aptheker again approached the party through Rubin with the proposal.[48] "We have criticisms," Rubin said, representing the leaders of the party, but he presented a different option. He, Winston, Hall, and others had met with the physicist and Marxist philosopher Erwin Marquit of the University of Minnesota, the principal founder of the Marxist Educational Press (MEP). Marquit approached the party with an idea for a new quarterly journal. Rubin wrote to Aptheker that "[Marquit] would very much like to see the [Aptheker] bibliography in that Journal without such a 'broadening.'. . . [We] lean toward the MEP journal. . . . for Herb Aptheker to cite sources that are related to centers of the phony left that we seek to avoid relations with would cause confusion as to Party policy."[49] "I never cited 'phony left,'" Aptheker shot back at Rubin, "though once in a great while I did cite something held to be of merit in MR [*Monthly Review*].

But I would not change my ways & of course did not plan to do so with *S&S*. I think the MEP arrangement would be much better."[50] Marquit announced the inclusion of the newsletter bibliography in the new MEP journal, *Nature, Society and Thought*. "We are very pleased that Herbert Aptheker has expressed his willingness to continue the bibliography he had prepared for AIMS in the issues of the journal," he told Aptheker. "This should be of great help to us for obtaining initial subscriptions."[51] In the end, the bibliography did not appear, but Aptheker published a column called "Books and Ideas" in *Nature, Society and Thought* until shortly before his death.

Even the demise of AIMS did not dampen Aptheker's ebullient spirits that year. When Woodward made a "gratuitous and stupid attack" on Aptheker's life and work in an interview in *Radical History Review,* letters of support flooded his mailbox.[52] Eugene and Betsey Genovese, who had been close friends with Woodward for a long time, severed their relationship with him. "This much I can tell you," Genovese wrote to Aptheker. "Many, many people, including Woodward's students, are enraged. I feel sorry for those students. For years they have offered him loyalty, love, protection on a scale perhaps unprecedented. He is now old and cranky, and they are having a hard time in attacking him. . . . [We] know how they feel. I think they should just fall silent. What else can they do? But for myself, I have had enough and want no more to do with him." Genovese and other historians deluged *Radical History Review* with letters condemnatory of Woodward. "Still," he assured Aptheker, "the evidence of the respect and admiration that people all over the Left, and not only the Left, have for you is pouring in on all sides. That much you have to know. Please treat the rest with the contempt it deserves."[53]

Then, too, earlier that year, in September 1986, Kraus International Publishers and UMass Press sponsored a gala event at the Schomburg Center for Research in Black Culture in New York City to celebrate the completion of Aptheker's four-decade labor of love: preparing the writings of Du Bois for publication. "The final two volumes in his Collected Writings are due any day," he informed Graham Du Bois's son, David Du Bois, in early May. "The Kraus–Thomson volumes, plus the posthumous Autobiography (1968) and the six volumes I edited for Univ. of Mass. Press make a total of 44 books—a precious legacy indeed."[54] "Historians will always be in your debt for making Du Bois readily accessible," Arthur P. Dudden, the chair of the History Department at Bryn Mawr wrote with "heartfelt congratulations."[55] At the ceremony David Du Bois paid tribute to both Herbert and Fay for the dedication they showed in seeing the project to its completion. "I know," he told the audience,

> perhaps as well as anyone, certainly better than most what confidence Dr. DuBois had in Dr. Herbert Aptheker. This confidence was shared by my

mother and I witnessed the repeated and forceful demonstration of her confidence following Dr. DuBois' death, much to the consternation and frustration of those who in the interest of expediency or out of fear dared to challenge Dr. Aptheker's role as Literary Editor. . . . As is now demonstrated by the finished work, it was a confidence well placed. We are all deeply indebted to Dr. Herbert Aptheker for his long-time devotion to Dr. DuBois, as scholar, activist, sage and poet.[56]

Winston, Aptheker's lifeline to the party leadership, attended the event at the Schomburg Center, and that was the last time Aptheker saw him: he died in the Soviet Union in December 1986 while seeking medical treatment. Aptheker and others assumed that a black or Latino comrade would assume the post of party chair, but Hall, after waiting several months, announced that "Winnie was one of a kind, he cannot be replaced." Hall left the chair position empty for a short while, then assumed it himself, becoming both general secretary and chair.[57]

Many party members, viewing Hall's maneuver as a slap in the face to black and Latino members, leveled charges of racism at him and the party. Why, the members wondered, was Mikhail Gorbachev promoting *glasnost,* or openness, in the Soviet Union while Hall was suppressing democracy and openness within the CPUSA with an iron first? Hall's power grab inflamed the turbulent mood within the party, a mood that would tear it apart at the end of the decade.

24   Rebellion in a Haunted House

THE CRISIS that ripped the party apart in 1991 didn't erupt into open conflict until the late eighties, yet dissatisfaction with the organization's focus, decision making, structure, and leadership had been brewing just beneath the surface for two decades. Membership steadily dwindled: by 1991 the party had fewer than three thousand members, if that. At times Aptheker seemed aware of the party's weaknesses, urging Hall and Winston to adapt the focus to changing circumstances, especially to change the party policy on feminism and homosexuality and to cooperate more closely with other groups on the Left. At other times Aptheker adamantly brushed aside any suggestions, especially when made by people who were not party members, that the party was less than perfect. "The Communist Party USA is the leading force on the Left in the present time," he told Rona Mendelsohn of *U.S. News & World Report* in 1980. "Its morale is high; its unity is exemplary. It is growing. . . . It spearheads efforts for peace, against racism, for working-class consciousness and organization, for a mass, labor and Black people's based political party."[1] What he founded these extravagant claims on is not clear; certainly not on evidence or analysis. His personal willingness to unite with others on the Left he confused as a willingness of the party to follow suit, seemingly oblivious to the persistent hostility of the leadership toward other leftist individuals and organizations. When Aptheker published a piece in the AIMS "Newsletter" "by someone Gus viewed as hostile to the Party," Danny Rubin commented, "he would be critical of Herbert as being a 'liberal'. . . . In such instances, if Gus said anything to Herbert about it, and I doubt he ever did, Herbert would say the AIMS Board of party and non-Party people make the decisions. . . . Gus felt Herbert could have done something about such publications but did not. . . . Herbert may not know that Gus expressed such views to a number of us."[2]

Perhaps Aptheker believed that if he kept repeating the word *unity* enough it would become a reality. "There is a change on the Left and it is towards us," he asserted to Si Gerson, who had asked Aptheker's opinion about publishing an essay in Genovese's short-lived journal *Marxist Perspectives.* Gerson understood that the party leaders were suspicious of Genovese and *Marxist Perspectives,* although Aptheker had listed several articles published in it in AIMS bibliographies. As "evidence of positive change," Aptheker recounted meeting with Genovese "in his presidential suite" at his inauguration as the first Marxist president of the Organization of American Historians. Genovese "paid tribute to the pioneering work of Marxists" in his presidential address, Aptheker told Gerson, "including the undersigned by name," as if mentioning *Aptheker* equated to Genovese accepting the party that had expelled him "for having zigged when [he] was supposed to zag."[3] Genovese may have praised Aptheker, but he had no use for the party.

When preparing for the 22nd National Convention in 1979, Hall asked Aptheker for help in writing the Party Program. "I would like to get your thinking," Hall wrote, "on how to most effectively raise the deal with such questions as: the struggle for democracy and democratic institutions and your ideas about how to relate the present day struggles to the struggles of our people throughout U.S. history. Generally I agree with you that we must increasingly claim some of the heritage and make the connection between today and yesterday." Aptheker urged Hall, as he had Winston and others, to consider gay rights and the "great significance of [the] women's movement," and he recommended that the party "should be in [the] leadership of efforts on behalf of the handicapped."[4] Had Hall taken seriously the suggestions of Aptheker and others, including Bettina, who quit the party not long after Aptheker wrote his letter to Hall, the party might have averted its decade-long slow-motion suicide. As it was, at that point in the early 1980s, the "male-dominated, . . . male-*centered*, . . . fiercely anti-feminist and homophobic" organization led by Hall resisted all efforts to institute an authentic new program for the CPUSA.[5]

While Hall failed to institute meaningful changes in the party's direction and focus, he did acknowledge, at least rhetorically, the apprehensions being raised around him. The party's Political Bureau, led by Hall and Winston, who was, according to Bettina, "more prone to listen," adopted a resolution in January 1980 focusing on "the main weaknesses" of the Political Bureau "and how to begin the process of overcoming them."[6] Even though Hall delivered the report on which the Political Bureau based the resolution, it was an exercise in futility: it was all form and no substance or follow-up. The meeting conformed to the usual procedure: Comrade Hall made his pronouncements, then the Political Bureau responded, "unanimously," to his dictates. What had developed, Michael Myerson said, was that the "highest body of the Party is the general secretary, who in turn selects the political bureau or national board, which in turn selects the national committee. . . . Those who questioned the leadership on even the smallest thing were considered 'anti-Party' and were ostracized and isolated. Toadyism, loyalty to the top, was encouraged. . . . Our very structure [was] built around an all-knowing general secretary at the top. . . . It is essential that the general secretary surround himself in his most intimate circle with mediocrities."[7]

Aptheker tried again in November 1981 to impress on Hall the importance of the women's movement to the future of the organization. As his own thinking had evolved—earlier in the year he had told Bettina that "the movement of women is of absolutely top consequence and its relative absence from dominant Marxian writing and practice is perhaps its greatest current failing"—Aptheker's sense of how urgent the need for change was in the party's emphasis increased, although his tone was restrained. "What the Party as such publishes and says on the women's movement is not yet sufficient," he told Hall, and "still tends to deal with this as simply a matter of equal pay or questions of working conditions, etc. All this is very important but the movement encompasses the whole question of male supremacy, in home, marriage, personal relations, propaganda, 'jokes' and every other damn thing. The Party as such does not yet reflect the depths of this movement and its great consequence."[8]

Far more worrisome to Aptheker and many other prominent members than the party's backward position on feminism and its virulent homophobia, especially after Winston's death in 1986, was the appearance of overt racism within the party and Hall's retreat on the organization's most cherished and meaningful accomplishment, the fight against racism. In 1981, when the party held what it called an Extraordinary Conference to discuss the "changing nature of the working class," Hall attempted "to bring about a major policy shift within the CP to move away from an emphasis on blacks."[9] Aptheker and Hall took opposing positions on the subject. "Herbert, as usual, wanted to maintain the Party focus on Blacks and the South as a special area of the country," the former party leader Charlene Mitchell recalled, "and Herbert's analysis of the nature of the working class always began and ended with the importance, the central place, black workers should have. Gus, however, lost interest in an emphasis on black people." At party meetings and conferences Aptheker "attempted to keep the focus on the meaning of the South and black folks," Mitchell said. "Herbert made very forceful speeches . . . to put forward his position but he did not push for a conflict between himself and other Party leaders. He tried to bring people to his position."[10]

According to Rubin, who for thirty-one years served in top leadership positions, as early as 1969 Hall sowed confusion within the party when he moved to reorient "the Party's theoretical approach and practice" on black liberation from a focus on the struggle as a national question to one of class.[11] Myerson thought it "nothing short of disastrous" for Hall "to eliminate the national question and subjugate the question of racial oppression to that of class oppression."[12] Hall had refused to "acknowledge the changing nature of the working class, and to act on it," Myerson claimed, much as Aptheker had noted in 1979 in his counsel as to what the party's central objectives and stances should be. Hall's stress on "industrial concentration in the gutted steel industry" made sense vis-à-vis the party's future only if one were Rip Van Winkle aroused from slumber after fifty years, Myerson wrote.[13] The "stupidity" carried over into politics as well, in Myerson's and Rubin's view. "Gus and main Party leaders felt there were petty bourgeois influences coming into the Party" after the sixties, Rubin said, "students and Black Panthers especially." The party "refused to support" Jesse Jackson's presidential bids in 1984 and 1988 "because he was a bourgeois preacher."[14]

Ensconced on the eighth floor of party headquarters on 23rd Street, what Myerson called "something of a haunted house . . . a fortress," Hall handily rebuffed all appeals to reorient the organization's priorities.[15] He used cash, money stuffed in envelopes—"Gus Hall does what he wants . . . envelopes go all over"—handed out by his secretary "to centralize power" in his hands. "In this way," the longtime party insider Barry Cohen, who was the editor of *People's Weekly World* until the purge of 1991, remarked, "Gus maintained his cult of personality."[16] "Gus used the money he had control over in the Party as a plum for members who went along with him and did his bidding," Mitchell remembered. "He decided who got it, and he never said where it came from."[17] Aptheker too didn't pay attention to or ask about where the money came from. "Herbert didn't have his eye on money, or even give it a thought," Mitchell said, "because he was concerned about actions the Party took and he simply didn't ask." Like many others, Mitchell said, Aptheker maintained a "willful blindness."[18] The source of significant party funds was such a tightly held secret that even Organizational Secretary Rubin, who "was supposed to have control over the day to day and other finances of the Party," didn't know the origin of the money held in "secret accounts" by Hall. "I came to disbelieve Gus," Rubin said in an interview, when he said that "large donors" who wished to remain anonymous were the source of the funds.[19]

The money in fact came from the Soviet Union, millions of dollars—$28 million between 1958 and 1980, "particularly large . . . subsidies . . . throughout the 1980s," perhaps as much as $2 million per year, culminating in a $3-million subsidy in 1988, which the historians Harvey Klehr, John Earl Haynes, and Kyrill M. Anderson documented in their book *The Soviet World of American Communism*.[20]

The rationale for Hall's "autocratic centralism" was "invariably that 'the enemy' is at work, is watching for signs of disunity," Myerson told party members in 1990. "All violations of democratic procedure, even of common decency and civil behavior, are explained away as if we are forced to operate under clandestine circumstances."[21] But Hall's hold on power began to slip away when Mikhail Gorbachev, whom Aptheker called "the foremost personality in the globe today," emerged as general secretary of the Soviet Union in 1985.[22] In "a politically stagnant and economically decrepit country," Gorbachev moved boldly by introducing, as noted earlier, *glasnost,* "or openness, which gave the press, and Soviet citizens, unprecedented freedom to criticize the Kremlin; and *Perestroika,* market reforms and democratization of the political process, until then dominated by the Communist Party."[23] Gorbachev's move toward democratization in the Soviet Union exacerbated the struggle for control within the CPUSA. Gorbachev called for a reexamination of the past in the USSR and encouraged communists in other countries to do the same. "Moscow's new 'orders' were that national parties should not take orders," David McReynolds reported in the *Socialist* magazine.[24]

Expressing an opinion diametrically opposed to that of Hall, Aptheker deemed perestroika to be a profound turnabout, but he misread the mood in the Soviet Union decisively when he said that it did "not represent the abandonment of communism. It represents an effort at purification, renovation in light of the colossal scientific and technological revolutions that we are just beginning to grasp. . . . They will not give up state ownership."[25] Nonetheless, he praised the "renovations in the Soviet Union . . . under the leadership of Mikhail Gorbachev." The idea that Gorbachev's changes projected, as he remarked in a speech at the UN in December 1988, "the primacy of universal human values" gave Aptheker great comfort.[26] To Aptheker, Gorbachev's reforms meant a move away from rigidity toward policies adapted to a changing world. Gorbachev's reforms held out the possibility of disarmament, Aptheker stated, and a refocusing of the world's energies, led by a revived Marxism in the Soviet Union; in Gorbachev's words, the future promised "life over death, peace over war, sufficiency over privation, literacy over illiteracy, health over disease, equality over elitism, [and] racism . . . such values must become universal if the Earth is to survive."[27] "Today," Aptheker remarked in an article, "the U.S.S.R., in pressing for disarmament and for an end to war, again is leading humanity towards salvation."[28]

By the late 1980s Aptheker still had not confronted Hall and the leadership openly, although he did voice oblique criticisms of them both vocally and in print. In 1989, in a speech presented at the annual dinner of the party publication *Jewish Affairs* celebrating the seventieth anniversary of the organization, he itemized the accomplishments of the movement: the fight against racism, capitalism, war, unemployment, colonialism; the battle to promote decent housing, quality education, good health care for all, civil liberties, civil rights, dignified living, clean air and water, and "a clean society." Then he turned to the party's darker moments. It had made mistakes, he told the audience: "Sometimes [it was] rigid and narrow, sometimes opportunist and minimizing class reality; sometimes acting too late or even not at all; . . . in its response to the ten percent of our people whose sexual orientation differs from most, to the special and continuing indignities and inequalities heaped upon women; in its failure to heed in time this or that criticism, to become in time aware of this or that blindness. These have marred the past and some mar the present."[29]

Others in the party were not so reluctant to challenge Hall, and these confrontations led to a momentous factional split in 1991, coinciding with an attempt by Communist Party hardliners in the Soviet Union to oust Gorbachev in a coup. Party members were outraged when they learned that Hall and other members of the leadership suppressed the results of a party discussion on democratic centralism. Party clubs around the country "developed position papers," expecting that the organization would publish the results, but the papers, Myerson avowed, "disappeared down a rat hole."[30] The party's leaders decided to treat the 140 written papers "eyes only," that is, allowing exclusive access only to a specially designated subcommittee of the National Board. Responding to Hall's actions and sensing perhaps his weakening grip on power, "many of the authors of these papers . . . circulated them informally to other comrades." Hall cried foul, telling the National Committee at a meeting in January 1990 that those "covert" and "factional" papers opened the party up to the FBI. "How can we separate such letters from letters the enemy circulates among our members?" Hall asked the leaders.[31] When Hall canceled a meeting of the National Committee planned for June 1990, a meeting at which Myerson intended to distribute his paper on democratic centralism, Myerson began circulating the paper through the mail. "To help distinguish this from the work of the FBI," Myerson wrote in a footnote, "let me indicate that I have been a member of the Party for most of my adult life."[32] Ironically, most FBI informants within the party could boast of the same longevity, a fact that did not escape Myerson's notice. "With all the charges of FBI infiltration floating around," he told the National Committee in August 1990, "it would seem imperative that a review commission would investigate particularly the classic and most obvious way enemy agents have traditionally penetrated Communist party leadership, i.e. through currying favor and blind loyalty to top-down leadership, adulation of those in a position to advance careers, silence in the face of leadership errors, etc."[33]

At a contentious joint meeting of the National Committee and the National Council held on 4 and 5 August 1990 many party members were in open rebellion. Mitchell, "a leading African American member of the National Board . . . over the objections of the majority of the 23-member National Board, . . . reported on 'differences that have existed over a long period and have had less and less opportunity to be expressed.' Mitchell criticized Hall's outright rejection of discussions and Hall personally: the party "has not seen fit to deal with these racist influences in our Party and its leadership," she told the meeting.[34]

The National Committee set up a "special committee of the national board" to investigate "racism within the leadership" and directed it to deliver a report to the National Committee meeting in January. The special committee chair, Sam Webb, did not call a meeting of the committee until 21 January, four days before the National Committee meeting. Webb apologized at the January meeting and asked the National Committee for more time to conduct the investigation, which set off a firestorm of outrage among dissidents, especially African American comrades, on the National Committee.[35]

Hall and other leaders put together a draft of the main resolution for the party's 25th National Convention that they began circulating soon after the combative meeting of the National Committee in January 1991. By May differences over the positions taken in the draft had resulted in the appearance of two openly rival camps. One, headed by Hall, barricaded itself in party headquarters, adamantly refusing to examine or alter in the least their positions. "That's when they started looking in people's wastebaskets and monitoring people's speeches," Carl Bloice, the associate editor of *People's Weekly World,* said in an interview. "That's when they started deciding they were going to rig the delegations" for the convention.[36] The other faction, dissidents led by Mitchell and including Aptheker and most of the prominent black members of the party, began working on a resolution of its own.

In August, when hardliners within the Communist Party in the Soviet Union attempted a coup to oust Gorbachev from power, Hall sided with the coup plotters. He sent a tape recording to party clubs around the country in which he unilaterally endorsed the coup as party policy. "Much of the party was absolutely outraged," David McReynolds of the *Guardian* reported, "and in the first stages the anti-Hall forces seemed a majority, especially in the Party's two largest districts, New York and Northern California," where Aptheker lived.[37] On 26 August Hall hastily called for an emergency meeting of the National Committee to convene on 1 September to discuss the issue. Aptheker thought the meeting premature and precipitate. "I think this haste is highly ill-advised," he wrote in a fax to 23rd Street. "I cannot be present and I imagine many others would find this impossible. Urge a later date so that a fuller attendance might be achieved with extended debate and discussion."[38] Nonetheless, after a seven-day postponement the meeting went ahead, disastrously for Hall. The National Committee "voted 33 to 30 to denounce the coup. More important, nearly a third of the NC refused to vote in favor of the concept of a democratic centralist Marxist–Leninist party."[39]

In October Mitchell's faction issued a document drafted by, among others, Angela Davis and Barry Cohen, "An Initiative to Unite and Renew the Party." By December it had garnered more than nine hundred signatures, including Aptheker's. The initiative "demanded that the leaders of the Party should stop falsifying reality." It called for an accounting of finances and publication of membership figures. It charged Hall with "propagating a cult of the individual around himself" and criticized him "for surrounding himself with toadies, . . . for not presenting his reports to the National Committee meetings for collective discussion, . . . for reducing Party theoretical literature on the situation in the United States and abroad largely to his own speeches, and for his general anti-intellectualism."[40] "The Initiative was an effort—and it was organized, nobody makes any secret about that, . . . to break through this wall that was being put up between those people who had things to say, and the membership," Bloice told Max Elbaum of the *Guardian*.[41] Aptheker didn't say explicitly why he signed the initiative, although he welcomed the challenge to what had become the party's "theory, policies and practice" under Hall. The initiative's demands for authentic democracy within the party and its pinpointing of the failure of the leadership to address positions for which Aptheker had pushed for years must have satisfied him: among other things the initiative criticized the leaders for their failure to recognize the crisis in world socialism, "[downgrading] . . . attention to the struggle for African American equality, an area in which . . . [it had] historically made some of . . . [its] proudest contributions," and ignoring the movements centered on women, gays, and lesbians as well as peace and the environment.[42]

Reacting to the appearance of the initiative, Hall and his forces moved ruthlessly to discredit those who had signed it and to rig the upcoming convention. Party headquarters deluged local clubs with memos and reports. The National Committee adopted a resolution at its November meeting denouncing the signers, condemning "the conspiracy" and demanding an "immediate end to the factional activity."[43]

Where sympathizers of Hall controlled party organizations, Hall purged the initiative supporters from the roll of credentialed delegates to the convention and replaced them with his own backers. "Some thirty percent of the delegates, all supporters of the Initiative, were denied their seats on spurious technical grounds," Erwin Marquit wrote later in his analysis of the events.[44] Hall organized security squads and contracted with the Cleveland police force to keep uncredentialed party members off the convention floor in order "to 'protect' this leadership from the membership of the Party," the party member Jay Schaffner wrote.[45] Just before leaving for Cleveland, obviously paranoid by this time, Hall "had the locks changed at the National Office and the fuses removed from the fuse boxes so that no one could use the computers."[46]

Hall held most of the cards as the 25th National Convention assembled in Cleveland on 6 December 1991. One attendee, Margy Wilkerson, described the convention center as "an armed camp. Armed Cleveland cops. Many, many security people. . . . Everyone was tense."[47] On the first day, Hall dominated events with his presentation of a three-hour report. "It was amazing," Wilkerson wrote. "Void of political content and full of invective and lies—all directed at discrediting the 'signers of the initiative'—the factionalists."[48] "It is clear," Hall said toward the end of his harangue, "that the more extreme elements in the factional situation have reached such a level that it is difficult to separate or distinguish their activities from those of enemy agents. That's just a fact of life."[49] Hall then left the convention for the rest of the day, a signal that the subsequent discussion of the report meant nothing to him.

On the second day, Aptheker attempted to gain recognition to speak from the floor, but the chair ignored him. Despite his fifty-two years of fierce loyalty and unyielding belief in the CPUSA, when he affixed his signature to the initiative he became persona non grata. As he persisted in his attempt to be recognized, a comrade sitting behind him shouted, "Sit down!" and, according to one observer, she may have added, "old man." "Who do you think you are?" the woman jeered. The diminutive, seventy-six-year-old scholar whirled around "to face her and slammed his fist into the table" so hard that "blood spurted from his arm. Blood vessels burst through his skin, soaking his sleeve and splattering the blouse of a woman nearby."[50] At that moment, he later told Bettina, he locked eyes with Hall. "Gus was laughing," Aptheker told Bettina later. "He was laughing at me! The son of a bitch!"[51] Aptheker's display of temper exemplified the polarized mood in the grand ballroom of the Cleveland Sheraton City Center as the two opposing factions battled for the heart of the minuscule U.S. Communist Party.

Although the leadership, controlled by Hall, had allowed Aptheker and some other dissidents access to the floor of the convention, most of them designated as nonvoting delegates, the party leaders had locked out scores of elected delegates and employed the off-duty police officers to verify the credentials of everyone who attempted to gain access to the ballroom. But Hall's forces were not able to keep track of all the initiative signers, and the day after his speech, when the convention reconvened to discuss its content, the chair recognized Robert Chacanaca. Chacanaca called attention to his Native American heritage, then set off pandemonium when he announced, "In honor of our tradition of respecting our elders, which I am sure you understand, . . . I would like to cede my time to Herbert Aptheker." When the shouting died down, the chair refused to allow Chacanaca to relinquish his time "but indicated," after a lengthy debate, "that Herbert would get to speak."[52]

It's not clear what tipped Aptheker into open confrontation with Hall and the leadership, although the void left by Winston's death and Hall's subsequent actions surely contributed. Hall's approval of the foiled coup in the Soviet Union may have been a deciding factor. This wasn't the first time Aptheker had come into conflict with Hall and others in the party leadership nor was it the first factional crisis within the party in which Aptheker had participated. His alienation from Hall and the party grew incrementally for three decades, although until the convention he had not directly confronted Hall or his own growing estrangement. For fifty-two years Aptheker had maintained his loyalty to the CPUSA, to the Soviet Union as the birthplace of socialism, and to a worldwide socialist revolution based on Marxist–Leninist principles. At every crucial point in his five decades as a member, when conflict racked the party, when factions developed, when scores of thousands of comrades left the party or were expelled, Aptheker swallowed his resentments, brushed aside the personal and professional insults, remained, persisted, and promoted his version of an American Marxist–Leninist revolution. The party was everything to Aptheker. His conviction was that one simply could not be effective acting alone: only through unity and collective action within the Communist movement could one bring about the revolution.

But alienation and crisis were on Aptheker's mind as he strode across the floor making his way to the speaker's podium. Hall allowed Aptheker alone, of all the dissidents at the convention, time to speak. Hall denied the editor of *Political Affairs*, Leonard Levenson, "a comrade with decades of service, wounded in fighting fascism in Spain," delegate status and labeled him a guest. Jim Jackson, "an African American comrade of over sixty years' valiant service, repeatedly jailed for fighting Jim Crow, one who was underground for over five years during McCarthyism, was denied five minutes to voice his opinion."[53] "I'll never forget . . . Jim Jackson," Aptheker later told an interviewer, "[he] who had given his life to the party, was forbidden to speak. . . . When he went to the microphone it was shut off. . . . He left. . . . It was one of the most tragic moments I ever saw in my life."[54]

Many delegates called Aptheker's taking the floor "the most dramatic single moment of the official convention proceedings."[55] "Most of the people from Northern California were in tears," Aptheker's former son-in-law, Jack Kurzweil, recalled. "When he finished, people from our delegation, and New York and other districts—we had been seated on the edges of the hall—just stood up and cheered, chanting 'CPUSA, CPUSA.' But the people in the middle, many with eyes downcast, just sat. In effect, when that happened, the convention was over. After that, there's nothing more."[56]

"The crisis in the world-wide revolutionary movement is most profound," Aptheker began, reading from prepared notes. Directing the audience's attention to the collapse of the Soviet Union and other Communist regimes, Aptheker asked them to think dialectically. "Marxism holds that circumstances make human beings and human beings make circumstances," he reminded them. "To speak of a systemic source of the crisis and collapse in the USSR . . . is to insist that the nature of the governing parties . . . was the basic source of the crisis. And what was that nature—it was authoritarian, domineering, brutal and guilty of colossal crimes—not only suppressions but also massive human extermination." He warned comrades not to euphemize the reality of Soviet brutality by using such terms as "mistakes . . . as Comrade Sam Webb did recently" or to put in quotation marks Khrushchev's thirty-five-year-old revelations. "No quotation marks are needed for those revelations," he said. "And what did they reveal?" he asked. "Monstrous crimes which had been engaged in for years, involving mass murder; and these revelations also showed that comrades of other countries had been systematically deceived. . . . [M]any of us were easily deceived; we were credulous because we felt we had to be. Hence the revelations were stunning; . . . first the stunning reality and this compounded by the fact that we had consistently denied that reality."[57] "Our honesty is decisively questioned," Aptheker told the delegates, "[as] for a revolutionary nothing replaces honesty. Without integrity revolutionary commitment is impossible." He prided himself on his honesty. "I've always . . . strived to be honest and truthful, to the point," he said in an interview, "not to exaggerate, not to falsify, not to do anything wrong."[58]

Aptheker chose his words carefully and kept his eye on the clock, for Hall had allowed him only five minutes. "He stopped us from speaking," Aptheker recalled later, "but he couldn't stop Aptheker from speaking, that would have been too scandalous—even for Gus."[59] Having cultivated a facility with words and ideas all his adult life as a scholar and revolutionary, Aptheker meant to impress upon the delegates the urgency he felt and to use his skills as the party's leading intellectual to bring the convention around to his dissident point of view. "Integrity is central for a revolutionary," he said, because his own integrity was, he felt, in tatters. Hall and other top organizational leaders in the party, including Bill Foster and Gene Dennis, had arranged that also. Weighing most heavily on his mind were recent revelations offering proof that the Soviet Union had, since the 1930s, secretly transferred tens of millions of dollars to finance CPUSA operations. "What we had continually denied, and denied under oath, and I had denied as a witness for the party many times, is that we were financed by Moscow," he said several years after the convention.[60] Even that night in Cleveland, though, he knew that the accusations were true.[61] As he said later in an interview,

> That [the secret Soviet financing of the CPUSA] was outrageous. I had spent much of my life denying it, and denying it under oath, in defense of the party, with the party leadership there, listening to my testimony, and the party leadership knowing that what I was saying was not true and that what the government was saying *was* true. But we didn't know that. We denied it. . . . But it came out that *Gus* knew it, and *Gus* supported it, and *Gus* was paid for it. *Gus* was on Moscow's payroll while I was swearing under oath that this was untrue. And I was the party's chief witness in case after case after case in which the government insisted that we were a paid agent of Moscow and I *swore* that this was not true. And the government chose not to prove it for their own reasons. They could have, I suppose, proven it. I suppose they could have proven it—

I'm sure they could have. People like Angela Davis and Aptheker had *sworn* in public that this [was] ridiculous and part of imperialist propaganda. Well, it wasn't. We were wrong. And Gus knew we were wrong and played us for suckers. That's despicable.[62]

Aptheker ended his remarks in Cleveland with a call for renewal in the party: "It is that authoritarianism, anti-democratic, and eventually anti-humanistic distortion" that characterized the USSR and East European Communist parties that must be combated, he said. "Our Party must learn these lessons, must give up denial, must transform its character so that it becomes the democratic, energetic coming together of men and women differing in many characteristics but united in irrevocable commitment to equality, to peace, to freedom, to an end to racism, male chauvinism, anti-Semitism, to an end to unemployment, slums and impoverishment, to socialism."[63]

Kurzweil was right: at the conclusion of Aptheker's remarks the convention was over for the signers of the initiative. They moved across the street from the convention hall to meet in a room that Jay Schaffner had reserved in November prior to the convention so dissidents and noncredentialed party members would have a place to gather. When Hall discovered that Schaffner had rented the room, he and the National Committee sent a "Dear Comrades" letter to party members condemning Schaffner and the initiative signers for seeking to "split our Party."[64] At the rented hall Aptheker, after several people had spoken, took the floor. He did not realize yet that his five-decade association with the Communist Party was over. "In a historic sense," he told the other dissidents, "we're not leaving a Communist Party. A split or disruption is not the point. . . . We must give as little ammunition as possible . . . to the forces around Gus Hall." He urged grace in defeat: "There is a need for modesty, for listening," he told his comrades. "The difficulty is to remember that at times we were wrong and others were right. Humility is part of a humane approach." He looked to a future in the wilderness as members of the opposition: "If there is any new form that is set up, we must stress education, and take up difficult questions like psychology and the problems of power. I am with you all. When we have socialism in the U.S. it will be because the mass of American people want it so badly it cannot be kept from them."[65]

25   Comrades of a Different Sort

HALL UNDERSTOOD what the signers of the initiative did not: that to maintain his power and position of leadership he would purge as many members of the party as was necessary. By the time Aptheker and the two hundred or so other dissidents met across the street from the convention in Room 211, that process was well under way. Aptheker recalled that he "was shocked to find myself designated a 'non-voting Delegate' [at the convention]—after having been designated by my club and having been a member of the National Committee without interruption for 34 years."[1] When he entered Room 211 he was no longer a member of the National Committee, as Hall's preferred election list for the new committee carried the day. The preferred list "was to include Comrades Charlene Mitchell, Angela Davis, Herbert Aptheker, Kendra Alexander and a number of others," the National Committee informed party members in a memo not long after the convention, but "the Presiding Committee . . . decided unanimously that the proposed list for the new National Committee could not include any of those who have been organizing factionally against the Party."[2] "All signers of the Initiative were excluded," Carl Bloice wrote in the *People's Weekly World* shortly after the convention. "Gone from the new 125-member National Committee are such well-known figures as Angela Davis, James Jackson, Charlene Mitchell, Daniel Rubin, Barry Cohen, Carl Bloice, Kendra Alexander, Ishmael Flory, Herbert Aptheker and Gil Green."[3] Max Elbaum, who witnessed the events at the convention and published his observations in *Cross-roads* and the *Nation,* recalled that "it was searing to see the tyrannical side of communism on display, and to be reminded that at one time or another almost all of us who have participated in the communist movement have committed or supported similar abuses."[4] Aptheker too found the atmosphere dark and malevolent: "The Cleveland event demonstrated organization bankruptcy, . . . the atmosphere repressive," he wrote candidly a few days after the convention. "Had that leadership held state power, past history suggests that those signers [of the initiative] would now be dead."[5]

Initially, many people in the room, including Aptheker, did not intend to split from the party. "The dissidents did not feel like a faction, as was claimed by Gus and the hardliners," Mitchell said. "The idea was not for the dissidents to break away from the CP but to provide some kind of mechanism for the dissidents to keep in touch, to debate and comment on issues." Eventually the group decided by consensus that in order to carry forward a collective endeavor they would have to form some kind of organization. Aptheker said (although at least one other person claimed ownership of the suggestion) that he proposed, and the group adopted, the name Committees of Correspondence after the shadow-government groups set up to coordinate agitation against the British during the American Revolution. "He explained the revolutionary aspect of the name," Mitchell said during an interview, "connecting it to the founding fathers as a way for them to keep in touch."[6]

At some point during the discussions the group unanimously endorsed two policy resolutions, one of which Aptheker had long urged on the party. The first, which the Northern California District approved in October, called on the party to "issue a comprehensive apology" to the people of Japanese descent who had been interned by the United States during the Second World War. The second resolution, which Aptheker supported, was almost as long in coming as the first: it openly addressed gay and lesbian issues. "In the past our Party has been slow to actively support the rights of Gays, Lesbians and Bisexuals," the resolution began. "We now have to improve our active level of support." It continued, "The CPUSA, now remembering with deep regret the earlier homophobia that brought it to expel its gay and lesbian members, now offers its long overdue but sincere apologies to the victimized comrades we lost, and extends its hopeful invitation for their return."[7]

Even though the initiative signers tried, in Mitchell's words, "to save our party—that's what we did, regardless of the lies," after the convention they found themselves to be "Communists without a Party," according to Davis.[8] "A profound sense of sadness overcomes me," Davis wrote just prior to the convention, "when I ask myself, when was the last time I could in good faith invite a fervent and spirited young activist—as I was when I joined the party—to consider becoming a member of my party."[9]

Hall and his forces had firm control of the party's assets. He controlled the fortress on 23rd Street, which he locked down even tighter after the convention. He controlled the party presses. He alone managed the several million dollars in cash on hand, estimated by one writer at between $3 million and $6 million, although only Hall knew for certain.[10] Hall, "who liked to stuff his wallet with bills of large denominations," had also amassed a trove of personal holdings. "He owns and lives in a big mansion, with sauna, expensive and original art and an underground garage in an affluent section of a New York suburb," the right-wing columnist Arnold Beichman crowed in the reactionary *Washington Times,* quoting Michael Myerson. "He flies first-class and stays at first-class hotels,"

Beichman continued, ". . . has a chauffeur-driven limousine . . . [and] an estate and power-boat out on Long Island in chic Hampton Bays."[11]

Hall purged all the members who had signed the initiative from party organizations. He started with the press, at first censoring articles by and then firing the two top staff people at the *People's Weekly World* (*PWW*), Barry Cohen and Bloice. Len Levenson, a signer of the initiative, was out as editor of *Political Affairs*. Hall then fired party staff members and refused to give them severance pay even though their wages were "dirt-level." "These are comrades who have given their lives to this party," the *PWW* writer Jack Zylman said in a letter to the new editor of the paper "who are being scrapped like junk, not with thanks but with spittle."[12]

By the middle of January Aptheker was finished as the editor of *Jewish Affairs,* not, however, because he was fired but because he resigned. "This action is taken," he told the National Board in a handwritten letter, "because, as one of the several hundred comrades who issued the Initiative, . . . I have been insulted by the characterizations of this group in Comrade Hall's report to the XXV Convention. This action is taken also to emphasize my rejection of the legality (not to speak of decency) of that Convention." To emphasize his disgust with the treatment he had received he listed for the National Board what he felt were his accomplishments and service to the party during his "52 years" as a member: a contributor to all of the party publications and the editor of several; the founder and director of AIMS; a witness for the party at Smith Act and McCarran Board and state sedition trials; "breaking speaking bans against Communists at scores of colleges and universities"; peace and antiwar efforts and the trip to Vietnam. "In the face of this dastardly behavior meted out to me and hundreds of devoted comrades," he wrote in closing, "and deeply opposed as I am to the devious acts of an ossified, bureaucratic clique, it is necessary for me to publicly terminate my position as Editor of *Jewish Affairs*." In a conciliatory gesture, he told the National Board that he would "assist in producing the January–February 1992 issue and with that my resignation takes effect."[13]

When Jim West, who handled correspondence for the National Board, urged him to reconsider his resignation, Aptheker remained firm: "My resignation stands," he told West. "Overcome *denial* in yourself, James West. Look at yourself before asking me to re-think resignation from the editorship of *Jewish Affairs*."[14] Aptheker did put together the January–February issue, including in it the statement of resignation he had tendered to the National Board and the resignation letter of the associate editor, Al Kutzik. When Hall saw an advance copy of the magazine with those letters included, he confiscated the entire run and removed Aptheker's and Kutzik's statements. Aptheker and Kutzik then proceeded to send a letter to the magazine's subscribers explaining their resignations and

Hall's actions. They encouraged readers to send in their names and addresses "if you want a xerox copy of all 24 pages of the confiscated January/February issue which is probably the last *Jewish Affairs* that will ever appear, and certainly a collector's item."[15]

The Committees of Correspondence moved ahead with its organizing efforts, using the names of Aptheker, Davis, and others in a press release announcing the formation of the group: "Leading Communists who participated in launching the Committees argue that the overriding political task of the moment in which the left should participate is to create a broad front against reaction and militarism, for expanded democracy, equality, jobs, economic security, peace and solidarity, and radical social reforms."[16]

As planning went ahead for a conference of the Committees to be held in June, Aptheker insisted that the organizers focus on the "movement toward a *national united Left.*" To accomplish that end, which he had championed unsuccessfully for years within the party, Aptheker suggested creating "the *Coalition of a Democratic Left* (CODL)." He envisioned an organization that "would seek to unite *all* who consider themselves of the Left with an orientation toward, a commitment for, a Socialist United States of America as its strategic goal." The foundational issues, he said, would be "the centrality of the attack upon racism . . . a rejection of elitism, anti-Semitism, [and] sexism . . . . The struggle against these scourges must be militant, principled and unequivocal. . . . The need is great; the time is now."[17]

Throughout December and January, members in the Northern California District, which represented all members north of Fresno, debated whether or not to secede from the party. The district passed a resolution on 29 January that presented them with two options: "(1) to stay in the CPUSA but disassociate from the National Center politically and financially, and (2) to break with the CPUSA and form the ICC [Independent Communists of California]." Hall's supporters within the district rejected both options and called instead for the heretics to return to the fold.[18] Bettina's former husband, Jack Kurzweil, weighed in against Hall's advocates and in favor of secession. At an "extraordinary membership meeting" of the Northern California District on 9 February 1992 attended by two-thirds of its 325 members, Aptheker made his position clear: he was finished with the party. "It is desperate leadership,—. . . bankrupt . . . bureaucratic, arrogant, unfeeling which has driven the Party to its weakest position in history—. . . wherefore it is shamelessly begging some of us upon whom it has spat, to forgive it and to come back," he told the meeting. "To what? To paranoia." He put forward his idea for "a Coalition of the Democratic Left to which all, including members of the C.P. who favor the kind of socialism I have suggested, are urged to join." He told the membership that he moved away from the party without reservation. "I am in no hurry about leaving the C.P.," he said, "which I have served to the best of my ability for fifty-two years. What problems this may present to me I will face as they appear. I am less distressed than the chair-warmers at 23rd Street."[19]

Four days later, Kendra Alexander, the chair of the Northern California District, issued a press release with the results of the vote at the meeting: "At an extraordinary meeting, the membership of the Northern California District of the Communist Party voted . . . by a nearly five-to-one majority . . . to disaffiliate from the Communist Party–USA, its parent organization. . . . The organization voted to affiliate with a national network of present and former Party members and others called 'Committees of Correspondence' established by the reform movement at the conclusion of the Cleveland Convention."[20] On 5 March, the New York Communist Party followed suit and declared itself "independent of the CPUSA."[21]

Despite the all-consuming nature of the battle within the party, Aptheker found time for other, more pleasant pursuits. In late February 1992 he spoke to a gathering at Harvard University on his favorite topic, the life and work of W. E. B. Du Bois.[22] In March his groundbreaking book *Anti-Racism in U.S. History,* almost two decades in the making, was published. His final original scholarly contribution to the study of African American history, the work was an examination of white antiracism up to the start of the Civil War. Aptheker had begun assembling research on this unexamined topic in the 1970s, when a young black boy asked him, after a lecture he had given on John Brown, "Did I hear you right? Did you say that John Brown was white? . . . 'God,' the child exclaimed, 'that blows my mind!' "[23] The sense of wonder expressed by that black youth at the notion that white people not only fought racism but also sacrificed their lives to the cause continues to be felt even today: in February 2012 a forty-year-old black man incarcerated at a prison in Washington state asked a history professor, after reading Aptheker's book, "Why didn't I know this? Why was I not taught this in school? My life might have been different!"[24] That "neglect and obfuscation of white anti-racism have encouraged the despairing notion that racism was not only pervasive in United States history," the historian Mark Solomon wrote in a review of Aptheker's book, "but virtually innate, immutable, and unchallenged."[25]

As was the case with respect to any work by Aptheker that challenged received interpretations, reviewers of the book, whom Herbert Shapiro in the *Journal of American History* characterized as "often frankly polemical," both praised and criticized the book.[26] Most contentious, even to Aptheker's old friend Lynd, writing in the *William and Mary Quarterly,* were Aptheker's assertions that "(1) anti-racism is more common among so-called lower classes than among the so-called upper class; (2) anti-racism especially appears among white people who have had significant experiences with people of African origin; and

(3) anti-racism seems to be more common among women than men."[27] Most of the reviewers found the book to be provocative, likely to stimulate further research and writing, and "another readjustment of our intellectual and moral sights," as the historian Winthrop D. Jordan wrote.[28] In *Science & Society* Solomon applauded the book for being "important and wise." It "resonates with impressive scholarship," he wrote, "and an impassioned affirmation that racism can be fought and eradicated, that black and white unity can be battled for and won. . . . The questions and reservations provoked by Aptheker's study do not undermine his basic thesis; they encourage further study, harder thinking, and a greater appreciation of the persistence of racism and the wisdom and virtue of the anti-racists who understood the centrality of racial equality for the progress of the entire society."[29]

In 1994 Aptheker released the last two volumes of his *A Documentary History of the Negro People in the United States*, which brought the number of volumes in the collection to seven. The two books met with universal acclaim in the scholarly community. "He was one of the openers in the movement to unearth Afro-American history and present it to the general public," Franklin said in an interview. "It [the *Documentary History*] fueled the modern civil rights movement. It provided the kind of information the movement needed when it got going."[30] Aptheker must have welcomed and probably expected complimentary reactions by Franklin and other scholars, but comments about himself and the *Documentary History* emanating from another quarter took him quite by surprise. The talk show host Arsenio Hall, on his nationally syndicated television program, asked the popular, well-known comedian Bill Cosby, "Who's the most amazing person you have ever met? Miles Davis? Groucho Marx?" After a long pause Cosby responded, "I would say . . . the most amazing person is a fellow who lives in San Jose. His name is Herbert Aptheker." While the baffled Hall listened, Cosby "extolled the virtues of a 78-year-old historian and lifelong radical whose name has largely faded from public memory. Hall may not have gotten it, but in the powerful black celebrity's unexpected tribute there was a modest righting of some cosmic scales." "Forget the communism," Cosby said. "Forget the past. It's Herbert's present that's probably the reason why no one has decided to take him on. . . . Suppose you were a scholar teaching American history and these volumes come along that state you've left out a good 25 percent . . . it makes you look very bad."[31]

On April 1, less than a month after *Anti-Racism in U.S. History* appeared, Aptheker suffered a stroke. "He lost much of his capacity for short-term memory, and his right leg was permanently impaired," Bettina recalled.[32] He spent weeks first in a hospital and then in a rehabilitation center. The stroke affected Aptheker's memory, but "his historical memory remained intact." Gradually, with the help of therapists, "he improved but he never recovered his full mental acuity, and his health deteriorated" during the last decade of his life.[33] Over the next few years he experienced a series of lesser strokes, "like the after-shocks from an earthquake," Bettina remembered, "affecting one or another part of his body."[34] Encouraged by his therapist to keep a "stroke notebook," Aptheker, beginning on 28 April and continuing for the next two months, re-corded the recovery of his short-term memory, commented on events in the news—"President's [George H. W. Bush] speech was especially insipid, vapid, & essentially police is the future," he wrote in one entry—recalled the names of friends, and, when the therapist's assignments asked him to write about his past, began resurrecting memories that eventually became the manuscript of his unpublished autobiography.[35]

The autobiography went unpublished despite Aptheker's efforts to place it with a publisher. He worked on the first of what he envisioned as a two-volume memoir for three years and then, in 1995, sent it for consideration to his friend Bruce Wilcox, the director of UMass Press. He hoped that Angela Davis might write an introduction for the work. Wilcox read the manuscript, found it to be "a fascinating document," and sent it to two outside readers for comment. Wilcox told Aptheker it might need "some editorial pruning" because readers might be "overwhelmed by the sheer number of names that are mentioned."[36] Late in January 1996 Wilcox reported on the first of the two outside reviews. "I am sure you will be as disappointed as I am," Wilcox wrote, "to read such a criti-cal assessment."[37] The reader, in a harshly critical report, conceded that Aptheker "has a story to tell" but went on to point out at some length the problems with it, among other things that "he is not able to tell his own story without massive revisions, cuts and further probing. Aptheker writes with a directness border-ing on naivety . . . short on emotion and analysis and long on biblio babble, lists of names, books and lectures dates . . . his tedious tour of his 20 years of date books. . . . He lightly brushes on so much paint that he fails to explain his ideas, contributions, or paint a portrait. He misses the forest and counts every tree. . . . The book needs re-organization and re-writing."[38] Irascible as ever despite his deteriorating health, Aptheker responded to Wilcox's letter by writing in long-hand a plainspoken rejoinder that a friend who managed his correspondence then typed: "What I wrote is what is to be used—period. Corrections, yes—changes no. . . . What you have—with some corrections, deletions etc. is what I want published. . . . I repeat—what I sent you is, substantially, what is to be associated with my name as author. . . . If U. Mass. is unable or unwilling to do that, so be it, but it will be published substantially in present form."[39]

Early the next month the other reader, Ernest Allen Jr., a professor of Afro-American studies at the University of Massachusetts, also told Wilcox, albeit in obviously sympathetic terms, that he did "not recommend publication of the manuscript in its present form."[40] Allen praised portions of the manuscript, as had the other reader: "What I regard to be genuinely interesting, highly infor-mative, and well-written sections [are] those bearing on his wartime experiences and his activities around the founding of the American Institute for Marxist Studies." Reiterating some of the first reader's criticisms but probing much deeper into the manuscript, Allen exposed the central conundrum of the work:

> First, there is simply too much information concerning what appears to be every single speech, article, and book that Dr. Aptheker ever made or wrote.... Second—and this matter is much more acute because it strikes a personal note: Dr. Aptheker's acute defensiveness, which bleeds forth from almost every page, negatively affects the quality of his MS. How can I best put this? Dr. Aptheker made a decision in his life to become a Communist. As a result of his political convictions, neither the dominant newspapers or academic journals have been willing to give him his due.... This lack of recognition has nothing to do with Dr. Aptheker's ability, but with his political convictions, which are reviled by the institutions in question. To me, all of this seems very clear. My sense, how-ever, is that Dr. Aptheker wishes to maintain the anti-capitalist political con-victions to which he is entitled, while receiving proper recognition from domi-nant, pro-capitalist institutions which he himself views as the enemy. Since the recognition which he truly deserves has not occurred, he appears to seek some sort of vindication which comes out, quite frankly, in tortuous ways. How else to interpret his numerous statements (which I take to be lamentations) that "such and such a newspaper or journal never reviewed my book or never men-tioned me"? Well, should such institutions really be expected to support those who seek their demise—at least in their given form? The point is that Herbert Aptheker has nothing at all to apologize for.... Proclamations to the contrary, the Cold War is not yet buried in this land. I do not wish to appear excessively harsh, but if Dr. Aptheker were to accept the cruel possibility that he just might never receive all the proper acclaim that is due him in his lifetime as a result of his politics, perhaps he would not try so hard to "vindicate" himself in his autobiography. Incidentally, the autobiography would be infinitely more read-able as well. Herbert Aptheker is in no need of vindication, and one hopes that someday soon he, too, will get the message.[41]

Finally, Allen was baffled by the almost total lack of "thoughtfulness" in Aptheker's manuscript vis-à-vis the Communist Party. Indeed, the manuscript is virtually devoid of any analysis that would shed light on Aptheker and the party. "What *was* the Communist Party? Why did Aptheker join it?" Allen asked. How did the party decide that Aptheker would edit *Political Affairs*? "What were the debates that raged within the CPUSA at various times, the nature of the purges which took place of people who did not agree with the official Party position at a given moment?" Aptheker simply did not delve into any of the details that would illuminate the inner workings of the party. Yes, "the

CPUSA is essentially portrayed as a victim . . . but the Communist Party was not a knitting circle. . . . Thus it really confounds me," Allen concluded, "that he actually has very little to say about the internal as well as external politics of the CPUSA. . . . His immense historiographical skills simply have not carried over into the art of autobiography."[42]

By April Aptheker had agreed to work with Allen as an editor, but Allen had to bow out because of previous commitments. "Although I would be greatly honored to work closely with you as an editor on your autobiography, that is just not possible at the moment," he told Aptheker.[43] "I . . . felt that his autobiography would take up far more time than I had to give," Allen recalled. "I admit to having been concerned with his seeming reluctance (in his manuscript) to discuss much of substance involving the internal life of the CPUSA over time. It seemed to me that it was going to take a person of uncommon intellectual endurance to extract from Dr. Aptheker the compelling kinds of details about his personal and political life that would assuredly make for highly interesting reading, and I did not think that I was the person to successfully assist in that venture."[44] Aptheker succeeded in publishing sections of the autobiography in several journals, notably the material dealing with the Second World War, which both UMass reviewers had praised.[45] He then forced Wilcox to make a final decision on publishing the unedited manuscript. "You said that unless we made a commitment to going forward without further delay, you would take the project elsewhere," Wilcox reminded Aptheker in a letter. "I am sorry to report that I cannot make such a commitment. . . . Under the circumstances, I think you should take the manuscript to another publisher."[46] Aptheker was never able to find that publisher.

Anti-Racism in U.S. History and the last two volumes of the *Documentary History,* unlike any publication of Aptheker's over five decades, went unmentioned in the Communist Party press. The reason was clear: beginning in the summer of 1992 and continuing until the death of Hall in 2000, even as the octogenarian Aptheker grew more feeble and housebound, the party sought, with unmitigated relentlessness, to make a fatal thrust against him in the party press and in the courts. The onslaught began in the pages of *Political Affairs* for June–July 1992 with a long, vituperative denunciation of Aptheker's speech of December 1991 at the 25th National Convention. Written by Victor Perlo, a member of the National Board, the article stated, "Having aligned himself with the right opportunist faction, his indecision represents a certain stage in the process of ideological decline and dissolution as he struggles to embrace the inevitable social democratic conclusions of classless 'new thinking'. . . . Aptheker should not forget the implications and consequences of his actions and statements. Surely he would not now become part of and join forces with the new anti-communist crusade?"[47] When his friend Clarence Kailin sent Aptheker a copy of a response to Perlo's article, Aptheker wrote in the margins, "Thanked— I don't read P.A. & did not read Perlo—poor guy."[48]

Aptheker's convention speech had irritated Hall, but his actions with regard to the inheritances he received via the wills of party members after his resignation from the party enraged Hall to such a degree that he sought restitution in the capitalist judicial system. "Gus was apoplectic that Aptheker refused to turn over money left to him in wills," Barry Cohen said in an interview.[49] The party filed suit against Aptheker, Danny Rubin, Emil Shaw, and even Bernice Linton, who had worked in the party's offices for more than thirty years, to recover money left to them in the will of one Rachel Friedenberg, who was not a party member. Friedenberg, unbeknownst to them, had named Aptheker and Rubin as her heirs. Each received eighteen thousand dollars after legal expenses. The party had long encouraged its members to include the party in their wills, but because "the CPUSA was unincorporated" and could therefore not legally be named in a will any bequests had to go to "trustworthy rank and file people" as conduits.[50] In the past, before his split with the party, Aptheker had turned over to the party some of the money he inherited—in one instance to keep the *Daily World* afloat—but he often retained a portion of the proceeds, especially to keep AIMS going. "Gus said that the money should go to the Party but Aptheker said no," Cohen asserted. "People know me and my work," Cohen recalled Aptheker saying, "and intended for the money to advance that work."[51]

Aptheker and Rubin vigorously defended their position in response to the party's suit. "Our theory," Rubin told Aptheker in laying out the case, "is we question whether the money was intended just simply for the CPUSA rather than for our judgement as to how to use it for the general progressive purposes indicated in her will."[52] Neither Aptheker nor Rubin had talked to Friedenberg about the bequest, which expressed her confidence that "the money would be used 'in support of organizations and institutions devoted to the public welfare and good of the people of this country.' "[53] Neither of them had authorized the party to "pass on our names to Friedenberg," Rubin reminded Aptheker. "We were not asked and did not agree with CPUSA to be named in Friedenberg will. Aptheker was not asked and did not agree and did not turn over money to the CPUSA from any will or in general," Rubin posited, perhaps unaware that Aptheker had indeed previously done just that. As the lawsuit played out, Rubin and Aptheker weighed the alternatives available for presenting evidence to refute the party's claims. One tactic they pursued was to call on "all those in the present leadership who have been involved with wills and the procedures around them" for depositions. Rubin warned Aptheker that their calling of Hall and his secretary, Carole Marks (a tactic he felt sure the party would resist), would be portrayed by the leadership as being anticommunist and a "fingering" of Hall.

They would thus open themselves up for attack in the party press. More troubling, to Rubin at any rate, was the possibility that a trial might result in criminal charges. "There are no accusations of crimes by them involved[,] though a few questions they might be asked come close to sensitive areas," Rubin wrote. "I believe there were criminal offenses they were involved with in relation to finances. I'm sure we agree we should not be involved in exposing them to prosecution and I have a personal added reason in that as the person nominally in charge of finances from 1965–1976 I might become involved as a co-conspirator."[54]

Even at that late date Aptheker and Rubin were worried about exposing the party to criminal charges, but Hall and the National Board, in their zeal to destroy prominent former members, went recklessly on their way. In the course of a civil suit "over control of some Bay Area property . . . , [the party] stated their intention . . . to call . . . Kendra Alexander, until 1992 the Northern California Party leader, into court to demand she answer a new version of the infamous question about some of her associates—are they now or have they ever been members of the Communist Party." The party filed a grotesque Motion for Order Compelling Answers in State Superior Court that "would require Alexander to name names in a deposition." The party argued that Alexander had "refused to give testimony or produce documents that might identify present or former members of the Communist Party."[55] The party's actions left the former members in California seething, while others were simply baffled. When Hall told the *New York Times* that the CPUSA "was the fastest growing political organization in the USA," Aptheker's old friend and colleague Lloyd Brown reasoned that Hall "has become delusional. It is sad," he wrote in a short note to Aptheker, "that a once important and vital organization has become not only irrelevant but ridiculous. Something dead but not buried."[56]

As the party's suit against Aptheker and Rubin ground its way through the courts, Hall used the pages of the party press to assault the two men. In a published report he said they "have stolen money willed to the Party and the paper," and then, in *Political Affairs* for March 1994, Hall said that not only Aptheker and Rubin but also the entire Committees of Correspondence was implicated: "Their almost sole activity is their continuing efforts to steal Party assets and Party wills. . . . [The Committees of Correspondence] was a scheme to gather together all the totally discredited opportunists, the unprincipled fakers and out-and-out scoundrels, mixed in with a sprinkling of FBI agents."[57] Aptheker gave an interview to WMUA in Boston while he was in Massachusetts to participate in a ceremony in Amherst to rename the main campus library at the University of Massachusetts after Du Bois. He said, in part, that "he left the Communist Party because 'of the relationship of the CPUSA with the CP of the Soviet Union' of which he said 'we knew nothing. . . . And I certainly was not a foreign Agent! I can tell you that.'" Hall lashed out in the *People's Weekly World*. Writing in the guise of the party's "African American Equality Commission," Hall boldly accused Aptheker of making statements that "went beyond disagreeing with the Party and can only be described as blatant anti-communism. . . . Aptheker has made slanderous attacks against our party before. In fact, anti-communism is becoming a basic part of his politics today. . . . The question must be asked, however, why is Herbert Aptheker redbaiting the Party? Why is he swimming in the cesspool of McCarthyism when most Americans have rejected this slander?"[58] Aptheker judged Hall's statement to be pitiful: "Gus had his glory days when helping organize the CIO[,] and the USSR had its glorious moment when it withstood Hitlerism. But both Hall & the leadership of the USSR became corrupt. As a result, Socialism has been dealt a terrible blow, but not a fatal one. . . . [We] must persist in the effort to create a decent social order whose name will be socialism. That is the fundamental reply to Gus Hall's slander."[59]

Late in 1996 Rubin made a settlement with the party that ended its suit against him and Aptheker. Another will, that of Rosalind Trachtenberg, the widow of Alexander Trachtenberg, had named Rubin and another person as her heirs. The party sued Rubin over that bequest also. In settling the Trachtenberg will, the party demanded that Rubin "give them money from this will to also settle their claim" in the ongoing suit against Rubin and Aptheker. Rubin agreed to give the party half of the Friedenberg estate. He also paid the legal expenses he and Aptheker had incurred, over five thousand dollars. "As a result," Rubin wrote to Aptheker, "there is no longer anything hanging over your, Bernice's or my head."[60] Yet the party, in the person of Hall, could not resist taking one final parting shot, even though it had agreed in the settlement with Rubin "to avoid and refrain from any recrimination, vituperation or pejorative comments."[61] In a statement released to the *People's Weekly World* and published on 2 November 1996, the party announced the settlement with Aptheker and Rubin. Even though the party recognized "the class nature of the judicial system" and its "reactionary judges," it had filed suit against Aptheker, Rubin, and the others because "their efforts can only be described as theft, . . . motivated by a despicable combination of anti-communism, lack of integrity, corruption and personal greed. . . . [They] dishonored their trust . . . [and] as a result, the Party was forced to spend thousands of dollars to take legal action. . . . The Party considers it shameful and reprehensible that a few ex-communists have become so anti-communist that they have stooped to stealing Party money."[62]

In 2000, shortly before his death, Hall resigned the post of party chairman in favor of Sam Webb. The party then named Hall its honorary chairman. He died on 13 October 2000. Characteristic of his actions throughout the 1990s was a statement he gave to the news media in 1991 as the Soviet Union crumbled: "Mr. Hall conducted a news conference at the party's Manhattan office, warning of a new wave of witch hunts and McCarthyism, but this time in the Soviet

Union, which he had visited only a few months earlier," Sam Tanenhaus wrote in his obituary of Hall in the *New York Times*. "Asked if he had plans to visit again in the near future, he said no. Instead, he pointed to the world's last bastion of Stalinism. 'The world should see what North Korea has done,' Mr. Hall said. 'In some ways it's a miracle. If you want to take a nice vacation, take it in North Korea.'"[63]

26   Now It's Your Turn

As he often did in his published books, Herbert wrote an acknowledgment to Fay in *Anti-Racism in U.S. History:* "Fay P. Aptheker again read
every word, raised important questions, and gently corrected errors. This has
been true for over fifty years," he wrote. "The passage of time has intensified
the indebtedness."[1] Fay was ten years older than Herbert and more politically
sophisticated, and he credited her with helping his own political development.
But Fay was practical, too, and connected him to the world. "Your father . . .
can't even screw in a light bulb!" Bettina recalled her mother saying.[2] Fay pulled
Herbert out of the world of the mind, forced him to appreciate, as he wrote in
his unpublished autobiography, "elements of reality including the artistic and
aesthetic which had been outside my consciousness. . . . This relationship—
reaching sixty years as these words are written—was basic to my life; that life
is unthinkable without Fay."[3] So unthinkable, he told the audience after par-
ticipating on a conference panel in 1983, that he "selfishly" wanted to go first,
before his comrade and friend, wife, and lover. "Your closing remarks on Fay
deeply moved—and chilled—me," Genovese told him. "I knew exactly what you
meant . . . I get physically ill at the thought that I might survive her [his own
wife, Betsey]," which he did.[4]

By the mid-1990s both Fay and Herbert had serious medical issues, including
vision problems and difficulty maintaining their balance. Herbert continued to
experience a series of lesser strokes after the major one he had in 1992, and Fay
"lost most of her vision due to macular degeneration . . . though . . . she was still
able to read the newspaper and do her crossword puzzle every morning, with a
magnifying glass and a powerful reading lamp."[5] Herbert had some memory im-
pairment from the stroke, but both he and Fay remained mentally sharp. They
qualified for the San Jose Meals on Wheels program, which supplied them with
their midday meal.[6]

The aging couple welcomed an almost constant stream of scholars, documentary filmmakers, students, and journalists at the house, people who were seeking
to interview Herbert for various projects and obtain biographical information.
Fay always "sat nearby and didn't hesitate to interrupt with corrections or elabo-

rations: 'No, Herbert, it wasn't that way at all!' she would interject. He almost always deferred to her memory. She dazzled visitors," Bettina recalled.[7]

But the unthinkable did indeed happen: in June 1999 Fay collapsed and was rushed to the hospital. She had developed sepsis, an infection throughout her body caused by gallstones blocking the digestive tract to the liver. When Herbert and Bettina arrived at the hospital, Fay was in critical condition. According to Bettina's memory of the episode, Herbert, denying the terminal prognosis pronounced by her doctor, lied to Fay, telling her the "prognosis is very good." Bettina, who thought her mother "needed to know she was dying," contradicted Herbert. "No, it's not! . . . That's not what the doctor said," she told Fay and then explained to her the critical nature of her illness.[8]

Herbert wanted the doctors to do everything to save Fay. Reluctantly, after consulting with Fay and Herbert, Bettina signed the "permission forms authorizing intubation and surgery to remove the gallstones and drain the poison from her system."[9] Fay underwent surgery but never regained consciousness. As the doctors planned to perform an additional surgery to remove her gallbladder Herbert and Bettina had a conversation that settled the matter. "I remembered a conversation Mom and I had," Bettina remembered Herbert saying. "She didn't want this. We were joking, you know, but we said to each other not to do this, with all the tubes and the respirator. We agreed. We wouldn't do this." Herbert decided to remove the life support system. "You're the lucky one," he told the unconscious Fay as the medical staff prepared to disconnect the life support. "You get to go first. You were always the lucky one." When the machine was unplugged, Fay took "only four widely spaced spasmodic breaths on her own" before dying. Herbert "stood and walked slowly out of the room."[10]

Although Bettina tried to convince Herbert to move into an assisted living apartment, he steadfastly refused to leave his San Jose home for the next three years. Although the unthinkable had happened, Herbert attempted to fill the void by returning to familiar pursuits. He continued to submit reviews for his column "Books and Ideas" in *Nature, Society and Thought.* Frustrated by the lack of additional venues for his writing, and even at that late date having never really given up reestablishing the AIMS "Newsletter," Aptheker had written Marquit in 1997 suggesting that Marxist Educational Press, which Marquit ran, publish a new Aptheker newsletter. "What I would very much like is to be able to review and comment upon books and developments with regularity—the sort of thing I did for some years for P.A. [*Political Affairs*] & M & M [*Masses & Mainstream*]," Aptheker told Marquit. He suggested "6 or 8 pages," for which "subscribers would pay a minimum—enough to cover postage & paper. . . . If I could have that newsletter I could do it," he told Marquit. "Fay & I easily compiled a list of several score people who would want this & tell their friends about it, etc."[11] Marquit evidently preferred a regular column in *Nature, Society and Thought* instead because by the end of July 1997 Aptheker was reviewing the page proofs for the first column.[12]

Once a week, at the invitation of the historian Clayborne Carson, the project's director, Aptheker commuted from his home in San Jose to work at the library of the Martin Luther King, Jr. Papers Project housed at Stanford University. "The work helped to keep Dad alive," Bettina said.[13] Carson also worked with Aptheker on the preparation of an eighth volume of the *Documentary History* to bring that work up to date.

Aptheker continued his public speaking sporadically. Three months after Fay's death, he addressed students at San Jose State University about the history of race. "I'm approaching the end," he told them, "so I still want to do what I can." When asked by the students what practical things they could do to fight racism, Aptheker told them, "One can be careful. . . . One should study and learn of the African American people—of their history and their struggle. It will make you better people if you do that. . . . Your duty is to acquaint yourself and learn about racism, and how it exists today. If you do that, you will participate, black and white together, in the struggle against this monstrosity. . . . [N]ow it's your turn."[14]

Students at Santa Clara University, led by Aldo Billingslea, organized a program they called "A Celebration Honoring Dr. Herbert Aptheker" in February 2000. The speakers lauded Aptheker's contribution to the history of black people and the struggle against racism. Tributes came in from across the country. "I have thought of you so many times these last few months," John Hope Franklin wrote to Aptheker and the organizers of the event. "You and I, the survivors[,] are in the same boat. I hope that you are bearing up well. After all, there is yet much to be done."[15] Manning Marable hailed Aptheker as "one of the most important American historians of the twentieth century . . . informed by a passionate commitment to social justice," and Sterling Stuckey paid tribute to Aptheker's invaluable work with Du Bois, then closed with a personal note: "While I am sure there are other, perhaps many who have this quality, Herbert is the one 'white' man in whose presence I have never felt the press of race, which is undoubtedly a factor in both his character and scholarship."[16] In his written remarks for the celebration, Eric Foner, the DeWitt Clinton Professor of History at Columbia University, implied that Dorothy Parker probably had it right with her modern rendition of the old universal proverb about revenge being a dish best served cold: "Herbert is one of the few historians to enjoy the satisfaction of seeing scholarship, dismissed when first published as outside the mainstream of historical interpretation, come to define that very mainstream for another generation. . . . Herbert today has the compensation of knowing that his writings . . . are admired, cited, and (the highest praise of all) rebutted by teachers and students alike. . . . So long as the issues central to Aptheker's writings—racial injustice, class inequality, political mobilization—remain unresolved in American society generations of historians will continue to learn from his writings."[17]

A few months later, in June 2000, the *Journal of American History* published "An Autobiographical Note" by Aptheker, a vignette describing the revocation of his commission in the U.S. Army, accompanied by an interview of Aptheker and an afterword by Robin D. G. Kelley. The publication of Aptheker's and Kelley's pieces set off a fierce polemical battle in successive issues of the letters section of the journal in December 2000 and September 2001. It is obvious in his reply to two letters that voiced the most vehement criticism of him that Aptheker's state of health had not dimmed the power of his pen. He said a letter sent by Michael Merrill was "full of venom" and his "sophomoric efforts at sarcasm, embroidered with invented quotation marks, are juvenile."[18]

After Hall stepped down from the leadership, some of Aptheker's old comrades gradually began to rejoin the Communist Party. Marquit expressed his regrets to Aptheker when he rejoined. "I must apologize to you for rejoining the Party," Marquit wrote, "because you were the victim of some of the most egregious acts by the Gus Hall gang. Not only that, you had so much more time and sacrifice in the Party than I, so more was robbed from you than me."[19] When Rubin received an invitation from the new party leadership to rejoin, he sent Aptheker a copy of the letter. "They also gave Jim Jackson and Lou Diskin similar letters," Rubin reported. Rubin praised the rhetoric issuing from 23rd Street, pointing out that Sam Webb, the new party chairman, gave a keynote speech at the party's convention in 2001 that departed "from Gus Hall's knownothingism. They [party leaders] have said in public documents that they have been much too harsh in treating people with whom they had differences and that in the 1992 split they were not all right and we all wrong."[20] Mentioning nothing about the catastrophic events occurring in New York City that day (perhaps he had not yet turned on his television), Aptheker responded on 11 September 2001: "Best of luck to you in rejoining," he told Rubin. "I find it very interesting that Jackson, Diskin & you received the letter; I did not."[21] At the end of July 2002, after reading Webb's latest report to the party, sent to him by Rubin, Aptheker told Rubin that "the Webb report was good." Nonetheless, he offered Webb advice: "Even more emphasis on war danger. More on women. More on the *corruption* of rulers. More emotion—more sense of the danger. Suggesting unity of Left and near Left. Openness; seeking; of help; terrible direction of present *usurper* of power."[22]

As Aptheker's health continued its slow decline, he "had more and more difficulty walking and fell frequently." He eventually sold his house and moved into an assisted living apartment. Bettina said he sometimes asked her "to help him to die." She refused. In the late summer of 2002 he contracted pneumonia, "and then he suffered a heart attack. He lost the ability to write," Bettina reported, "but he kept on reading."[23]

In September the National Board of the CPUSA, ready to reconcile even with Aptheker but unaware of his physical condition, prepared a letter inviting him to "come home." Before the letter went out, news of Aptheker's heart attack reached the board members, prompting them to reconsider sending it. Rubin called Aptheker to tell him of the letter's existence and explained that the leadership had thought it inappropriate to send the letter just then because their motives might be suspect. As Rubin recollected, Aptheker told him that "he understood the reasons why it had not been sent after he became so seriously ill, but he asked me to have it sent so that he could seriously consider it and talk it over with others before responding one way or the other."[24] In the letter the party acknowledged Aptheker's illness and offered "our comradely best wishes for an improvement in your health." Several comrades had "renewed their membership in the party,... [including] Danny Rubin, Dorothy Burnham, Lou and Bernice Diskin and recently Ishmael Flory," the National Board reported, and "we are very happy that we now also have a very positive working relationship with Jim Jackson and other formerly active comrades." The letter continued,

> You have played an outstanding role in the life of our Party over many decades. Your contribution has had a profound influence on all of our lives. It's our feeling that our Party would not be complete without your joining the list of distinguished party leaders who are politically coming home. . . . We think it is time to reactivate your membership. In fact as we see it, the time for you to come home to your party is long overdue. . . . We want you to know that we are self-critical and think the way The Peoples Weekly World treated you in the past was a big mistake on our part. We sincerely apologize to you for that. . . . We await your reply.[25]

Aptheker did not rejoin the party. He told Jarvis Tyner that "his health was not good and he did not want to rejoin but he wanted to work on building left unity."[26]

Aptheker spent the last few weeks of his life in a private home in Mountain View, California, with twenty-four-hour-a-day care. On a "beautiful sunny Monday, St. Patrick's Day," 17 March 2003, two days before the United States launched its preventive war against Iraq, Herbert died. Bettina and Kate were at his bedside.[27]

Sixteen days later Gloria L. Young, the clerk of the board, informed Bettina that the San Francisco Board of Supervisors "adjourned its regular meeting . . . out of respect to the memory of Herbert Aptheker. . . . The members of the Board, with a profound sense of civic and personal loss, are conscious of the many fine qualities of heart and mind which distinguished and brought justifiable appreciation to Mr. Aptheker."[28]

Aptheker's comrades and friends on the West Coast held a memorial service at Stanford University at the end of the month. In October the Committees of Correspondence, the Communist Party, and other leftist groups organized a memorial service at Saint Peter's Church in New York City. The masters of ceremony were Ossie Davis, Ruby Dee, and Mary Louise Patterson. Hundreds of family members, friends, comrades, and colleagues filled the auditorium to pay tribute to Herbert and Fay. Davis opened the service by reading a passionate denunciation of slavery from one of Aptheker's books. Eric Foner then paid tribute to Aptheker's contribution to the study of black history. Johnnetta Cole, Robin Kelly, Aptheker's comrades Charlene Mitchell, Barry Cohen, and the new executive vice chair of the CPUSA, Jarvis Tyner, all offered remembrances of Herbert and Fay. Then Bettina delivered a moving, often humorous and loving eulogy to her parents.

Bettina received testimonials from all over the country. "Herb Aptheker was one of the great scholars of the 20th Century," Pete Seeger declared, "it was an honor to know him."[29] John Hope Franklin, who outlived Aptheker by six years, told Bettina of his great distress upon reading his obituary in the *New York Times:* "Your father was one of the great warriors whom I greatly admired. In times such as this we are in need of his spirit and his voice." In the statement by Franklin read at the memorial service he vowed to continue the struggle: "We never gave up, Fay until her end, and Herbert until his later end. I am as resolved as they were to carry on this fight for justice and equality until my own end, sooner or later, and in every step of the way I shall affectionately remember Fay and Herbert, not only for their commitment and dedication but also for their warm and unselfish humanity, their marvelous wit, and sense of humor."[30] Aptheker's colleague and former chair of the History Department at Bryn Mawr, Arthur Power Dudden, recalled Aptheker's impact: Herbert's appointment, he said, "substantially strengthened our department, not only while he taught here but for years afterward."[31] Ben Jealous, then the director of the U.S. Domestic Human Rights Program at Amnesty International and later the head of the NAACP, told Bettina that her father had had a profound influence on his life. "I speak of him whenever a young person asks me about books and authors that have shaped my thinking," Jealous said.[32] "[I was] moved by his passion for justice and his unrelenting hatred for racism," Aptheker's fellow historian and friend Herbert Shapiro wrote. "He utilized his formidable talents to powerfully challenge the racist myths that have corrupted American society and served to rationalize class, racial and gender exploitation."[33]

Aptheker was at the forefront of the social and political movements that roiled the United States from the 1930s to the 1990s, including the Popular

Front, the Second World War, the civil rights and black liberation movements, the Red Scare and McCarthyism, the Cold War and the Vietnam War, free speech, student protest and the New Left, and opposition to nuclear weapons, which he once called "portable crematoria." In articles, pamphlets, and books and in hundreds of public presentations, disregarding threats to his personal freedom and assault by government agencies, terrorists, and fellow historians, he pursued a fervent quest for human fulfillment and human liberation of mind, body, and spirit for all who suffered from bigotry and exploitation. For decades and despite the opposition of both black historians (who thought they should be the caretakers) and white he discharged the sacred trust placed in him to preserve the legacy of W. E. B. Du Bois, whom, like Aptheker himself, the historical profession wrote out of the canon of U.S. history. They each found a home and sanctuary in the Communist Party. His shunning by the mainstream profession notwithstanding, Aptheker changed forever the way historians look at the experience of black people in slavery; as Eugene Genovese said, there is before Herbert and there is after Herbert. Few historians achieve the distinction of altering historiography in the way Aptheker did. More than a Communist intellectual, he was an American intellectual who wrote, with remarkable prescience, multiple analyses of an imperialist U.S. foreign policy that was heading for a doctrine of preventive war decades before President George W. Bush assured that doctrine as official U.S. policy.

And yet, for all his accomplishments, there was a terrible flaw in Aptheker. On the one hand, as the historian Chris Phelps wrote in the *Chronicle of Higher Education,* "the extent to which Herbert Aptheker could symbolize intellectual freedom, however, was profoundly limited by his habitual excusing of repression by single-party regimes cast in the Soviet mold. This moral double standard was tragic, not only for American Communism but for the whole of the American left" and for Aptheker himself.[34] Then, too, members of the CPUSA around the country looked up to Aptheker. They expected that the champion of black rights and the rights of political dissidents who spoke truth to power in the government of the United States was also speaking truth to those in power in the party as well. They were wrong. He didn't. His failure to challenge Gus Hall, that is, to challenge the Stalinization of the American Party, was a tragic disservice to the fight for socialism, to his comrades and the Left more broadly, and to his family. Especially when the party assaulted Bettina, his actions were inexplicable and bordered on the cowardly. When it came to challenging the leadership of the party, especially Hall, he equivocated and rationalized for far too long. He indulged in private rages, but his public silence was a profound lie that diminished him and helped to destroy his party.

As a country the United States is still struggling with the questions that mobilized Aptheker through eight decades: What is patriotism? What is the place of dissent in a free society? What are the limits of free speech? What does it mean to be an American? Should college professors be fired or not hired because of their political beliefs? Should historians mix activism with scholarship? Should civil liberties be sacrificed for security? Why is racism still a potent force in the United States, and how do we end it? How do we restore republican self-government and end war?

Aptheker's life and work, his accomplishments and his faults, widen the vista for understanding the contribution and importance of black people in the United States, the battle against racism, the role of the Communist Party in the history of radicalism in the United States, the role of anticommunism in suppressing domestic radicalism, and the struggle of one man, acting with others, to demand that the reality of democracy in the United States match the rhetorical flourishes that flaunt it.

When asked how he had managed to produce such an enormous oeuvre during his lifetime, Aptheker responded quietly but resolutely, "I work hard."[35]

Afterword

I FIRST met Gary Murrell at my parents' home when he began extensive interviews with my father for a proposed biography. My mother had recently died, and my father was in a terrible way, swamped with grief and clearly unable to fully fend for himself in their San Jose home. I think working with Gary was important to him, providing purpose and structure in his life. Gary extended a warm hand of friendship, good humor, and a professional ambience that encouraged my father's memory of his experiences and people and events, and to tell his stories, many of which he had repeated for decades. Interviewing elders, especially one like my father who was used to audiences in both public and private settings, is exceptionally challenging. For example, as Gary observes in his introduction, the repetition of stories, almost word for word, meant that the story itself became the memory, rather than the events ostensibly recalled. In addition, Gary observed that when he discussed the policies and practices of the Communist Party, and especially its leadership, he did so by rote and was unable or unwilling to summon emotion. That was for Gary. In my experience my father displayed fierce emotion in relation to the party and its defense that, at times, bordered on fanaticism.

I have two particular memories to illustrate this, one personal and the other political. In September 1981, having made the decision to leave the Communist Party, I went to see my parents at their home in San Jose. I had typed a letter of resignation to the chair of the Communist Party in Northern California. Although I had struggled with my continued membership for years, my resignation was precipitated by the party's rejection of my book *Woman's Legacy* for being "too feminist." My father read the letter and immediately informed me that I could not send it, and when I said my mind was made up, he began shouting at me, becoming almost hysterical. My mother, ever the voice of reason, intervened, and told Herbert to stop. She said it sharply, decisively, and then said, "She's made up her mind. That's enough." He stopped immediately. Then after a moment's silence, he said to me, "All right. But you must not send this letter." Astonished, I asked, "Why not?" And he said, "Because the *New York Times* might get hold of it and publish it." I was so nonplussed by such an absurdity that I was completely silent. Then I said, "All right, I won't send *this* letter, but I am resigning from the Party." He got up and left the living room and went into the kitchen. He returned with three glasses. I think he brought in some wine, but it might have been juice, and he filled our glasses. Then he offered a toast, "To the family," he said. And we drank.

The second memory I have that speaks to my father's attitude about the party is in relation to the Soviet Union's air-to-ground missile that shot down a South Korean passenger plane, flight 007, on September 1, 1983, killing all on board. I was absolutely appalled. Having breakfast with my parents one morning shortly after this horrific event, I said something about how terrible it was. To my astonishment my father roared his defense of the Soviet Union. It was a spy plane, he said, deliberately flying over a sensitive military site. Soviet military had no alternative but to shoot it down, no matter the civilian casualties. He began citing articles he had read in the *Nation* and even, he said, in the *New York Times*. My mother, usually more temperate, said the same, although she was not shouting and, indeed, seemed very saddened by "the necessity." I said there could be no justification whatsoever for killing 269 men, women, and children, to which my father growled to my mother (referring to me in the third person as though I was not in the room), "You can't talk to her. She's a fanatic pacifist!"

Although these stories took place when I was an adult, they were typical of both our family dynamic and my father's attitudes toward the party, and toward those issues allied with the party that he considered sacred. Consider what it would be like to be the only child in such a family during the height of the McCarthy repression of the 1950s and you can have some sense of the emotional and psychological contours of my childhood. Of course, I fervently believed that unless I adhered to the party's line I would be cast out along with the other party renegades against whom my father thundered.

These are aspects of my father's personality and psychology that a biographer could not know or fully appreciate from the outside. Yet Gary is sensitive enough, having culled through thousands of letters and documents and conducted hundreds of hours of interviews, to hint at these dynamics, to sense the near-fanatic attachment to the Communist Party. It was, therefore, very moving to consider Gary's account of my father's refusal to rejoin the party near the end of his life, after Gus Hall was long gone, and more than a decade after the debacle of the party's 25th National Convention in Cleveland when so many had left the party, including my father, driven out finally by its utter bankruptcy and corruption. Gary portrays the anguish of my father's refusal to rejoin with great sensitivity.

In contrast to this aspect of his life in the party, my father could manifest considerable courage. His repeated appearances at the Smith Act trials, his defiance of McCarthy at the Senate hearings, his indefatigable appearances on campus after campus contesting the Communist speakers' bans are a testament

Herbert, Bettina, and Fay Aptheker, San Jose, California, summer 1990.

to this, and in all of these moments he touched the lives of thousands of people and, I expect, gave courage to more than a few faced with their own persecutions and fears. Gary's accounts of these events are extensive, dramatic, and well documented.

Likewise, as Gary shows, my father's historical scholarship was impeccable. Gifted with tenacity and patience, he persevered in efforts to compile the first two volumes of *A Documentary History of the Negro People,* published in 1951. I cite these volumes in particular because they presented the most challenging archival work. At a time when southern white-run libraries sometimes refused him access (and African American janitors let him in at midnight!) and when there were no Xerox machines so that he had to copy documents by hand (he once told me he had transcribed something like 250,000 words in those first years), the completion of the *Documentary History* was a gift to both the African American community and the historical profession. His writings on slave revolts, on maroon encampments, on African Americans in the Civil War, and so much else in essays and books were pioneering, echoing the works of W. E. B. Du Bois and other African American scholars while also breaking new ground and providing new evidence. Likewise, his almost single-handed production of the forty volumes of Du Bois's collected works, his editing of four volumes of Du Bois's letters and unpublished papers, and his six-hundred-page annotated bibliography of Du Bois's published work provide wonderful resources for generations of researchers.

Gary's biography provides a candid and balanced narrative of my father's life. I helped him in all ways that I could because I believed in his sincerity, his integrity as a historian, and his commitment to the project over more than a decade, and because I believed my father's life and work was worthy of a book-length biography. I am gratified that he carried this project through to completion. That said, important parts of the story are missing. Most significant is that there is not nearly enough said about my mother, Fay P. Aptheker. Since Gary started his work after her death, he had never personally known her. Using my descriptions of her in my memoir, interviews she had given, and her own account of her life in the book she compiled, *The Aptheker Family,* Gary provides us with a summary of her childhood and first marriage. However, insofar as she is present in the biography, it is almost entirely as an accessory to Herbert, the one to whom he wrote, his confidant, and his editor. She was all of those things. But she was also her own person with her own life. My mother, who was born into great poverty in a Russian-Jewish immigrant family, was orphaned at the age of four. She and her two older sisters were raised by their maternal grandmother. She went to work in the garment industry as a young teen, while managing to finish high school at night. Determined to continue her education, my mother enrolled in Hunter College, and although she did not graduate, she majored in English literature, and was a voracious and critically astute reader throughout her life. She particularly enjoyed fiction, mysteries, and biography, and I can remember her reverence for Simone de Beauvoir and de Beauvoir's books lining her shelves. (Father had a huge library of thousands of books in our home, and my mother kept her own books in two separate bookcases in their bedroom.) Ten years older than my father, Mother joined the Communist Party in 1929, a decade before he did. She was a union organizer and traveled to Europe as a young woman with her radical cohorts. She also was a fine musician, an accomplished pianist, modern dancer, and singer. She was forty when she married my father and had lived a full, cultured, and adventurous life. (I should add here, as Gary also notes, that my parents lived together for seven years because his family disapproved of their relationship.)

Once with Herbert, and especially after their marriage, my mother devoted herself to my father *to make his life possible.* This is the crucial point. He could not have functioned without her. I mean that literally. She was his ballast, without which his emotional, psychological, and physical ship would have sunk. My mother was much stronger than my father, much clearer, much more realistic, and much sturdier emotionally. She had the reputation in the family for anger— and she could fly off the handle, that's true. But it was my father's rage, especially I think as a result of the war, which needed to be controlled. As Herbert's wife my mother certainly expected her "due," and she could be exacting and exasperating in her sense of entitlement. Her unquestioned and unquestionable loyalty to my father could also blind her politically and personally. Yet she also read virtually everything that Herbert wrote before it was published, and gave him critical feedback. She typed many of his handwritten manuscripts. My mother was a passionately intelligent woman and possessed of extraordinary stamina. She worked full-time as a travel agent (and despite the efforts of the FBI in the 1950s to get her fired). It was her salary that supported our family.

One of the most difficult challenges for Gary in writing this biography came with the publication of my memoir, *Intimate Politics,* in November 2006, and its disclosure of the sexual abuse I experienced at the hands of my father. I realize that while that loomed largest for Gary in his reading of the memoir, it was only a part of my story. I wrote the memoir to share stories of the movements for social justice that I had participated in, and to "split open" a woman's life with feminist purpose in order to weld together the political and the personal. Incest was a part of that story. In his introduction to Herbert's biography Gary's approach to the disclosure of incest is to weigh the truth of my telling. I found this very disappointing, though this is almost *always* the response to disclosures about sexual violence. He summarizes a debate that took place online just after the book's publication about whether or not I was telling the truth, yet he leaves out a letter from the labor historian Ruth Needleman, herself an incest survivor, which made me wonder if he considered her testimony untrustworthy. Gary also cites letters from my father to my mother during the war in which Herbert described the condition of the war-traumatized children he encountered. Herbert's anguish is clear, and Gary suggests that given his feelings for children it is impossible to imagine him as an abuser. That Gary thinks one has much to do with the other reveals a common lack of understanding about the nature of incest. Be that as it may, Herbert's use of the word "fondle" in one of those letters to Fay sent a cold chill down my spine. I pray this was the careless use of a word and not a literal description of his interactions with those children.

Incest is universally condemned on the one hand, and furiously denied on the other, not only by most perpetrators, but often also by others in the same family, and among friends, and colleagues. Discussion of incest, then, almost always turns on whether or not the survivor is telling the truth. Whether the alleged absence of truth is based on the repression of memory, or the freshest of memories, it always pivots on the victim and her or his account. Even in the case of the Catholic Church and the terrible evidence of child sexual abuse by priests, there was continual cover-up and denial for years until the evidence was simply overwhelming. In a profound sense, the paradox for anyone revealing incest and child sexual abuse is that the taboo is so strong, and the stereotypes about its "monstrous" perpetrators so impenetrable, that the disclosure itself becomes, in fact, "unspeakable."

Since my memoir was published I have received hundreds of letters from people all over the country thanking me for it, and for its disclosures. Most of these letters, many sent as e-mails, are from women; some are from men; most are from folks in and around the Communist Party and the Left more generally. They are from people of all races and ethnicities. The letter writers reveal dozens of cases of child sexual abuse, rape, domestic violence, and like traumas to themselves or within their families, and the silences to which they were condemned. Others wrote to express solidarity, or simply to share stories from their own lives.

I told the story of incest because the memoir, intertwining the personal and the political, and the political *as* personal, could not be told without it. For those who have read the memoir, they know that my father did not deny it; on the contrary, he apologized for it with overwhelming anguish. Later, he told me he could not remember it, but he never accused me of lying. Rather he said he could not live with the truth of it, and therefore we would have two realities: his and mine.

THERE IS a photograph of my parents on the occasion of my mother's ninetieth birthday party, held at a restaurant in San Jose. Fifty or so people came, and it was a festive occasion, my mother dressed to the nines, as she so loved to do. In the photograph they are both laughing, I mean *really* laughing, and it is a charming picture, so full of life and humor that anyone viewing it would themselves break into a broad grin. For all of the gravitas that seems so much a part of Gary's portrait of my father, both my parents could be funny and playful and very loving. I would like people to remember that about them, that great swell of humanness in the midst of all else.

Bettina Aptheker
Santa Cruz, California

Herbert and Fay Aptheker, San Jose, California, February 1990.

Notes

Abbreviations

AP   Herbert Aptheker Papers, M1032, Dept. of Special Collections, Stanford University Libraries, Stanford, Calif.

TL   Tamiment Library and Robert F. Wagner Labor Archives, New York University, New York City.

"Unrepentent Rebel"   Herbert Aptheker, "An Unrepentent [*sic*] Rebel," manuscript of an unpublished autobiography. In the author's possession. On the title, see chapter 1, note 15.

Fischer interview I   Herbert Aptheker, interview by Jack Fischer, San Jose, Calif., October 1993, typescript, box 120, folders 23, 24, 25, Herbert Aptheker Papers, Department of Special Collections and University Archives, Stanford University Libraries.

Fischer interview II   Herbert Aptheker, interview by Jack Fischer, no date or place; probably in San Jose, Calif., after Fischer interview I. In the author's possession.

McCarthy interview   Herbert Aptheker, interview by Tim McCarthy, typescript, New York City, 10 September 1994. In the author's possession.

Murrell interview   Herbert Aptheker, interview by the author, audio and video recording, San Jose, Calif., 21–30 August 1999.

1. An Immigrant Family's New York

1. Irving Howe, *World of Our Fathers* (New York: Harcourt Brace Jovanovich, 1976), 5.

2. Fay Aptheker, *The Aptheker Family* (San Jose, Calif.: privately published, 1990), 1. Some members of the Aptheker family recall that Abraham "was 'a kind of mayor'— another was told by her mother that he was a Notary Public and a semi-official dignitary of the shtetl." Howe, *World of Our Fathers,* 10.

3. Aptheker, *The Aptheker Family,* 7. It appears that most of Abraham's and Hannah's children eventually emigrated to the United States, but no one in the Aptheker family knows for sure what happened to Abraham and Hannah. Some members of the family say they emigrated to the United States while others refute that claim. Howe, *World of Our Fathers,* 27, 28, 32.

4. Aptheker, *The Aptheker Family,* 7–8.

5. Ibid., 44–45.

6. Fischer interview I, 8–15; McCarthy interview, 1–2.

7. Fischer interview I, 11.

8. Ibid., 7.

9. Ibid., 6.

10. Bettina Aptheker, "Eulogy" for her father, 16 October 2003, in the author's possession.

11. Fischer interview I, 443.

12. Ibid., 13–14.

13. Ibid., 37–38.

14. Aptheker, "Eulogy."

15. "Unrepentent Rebel," 11. The misspelling of "Unrepentent" is Aptheker's. It's impossible to know if he misspelled the word on purpose for some reason. In all of my research of his writings it is the only misspelling I encountered. He wrote the manuscript after his major stroke in 1992, so perhaps that has some bearing.

16. McCarthy interview, 3; "Unrepentent Rebel," 9–11.

17. "Unrepentent Rebel," 10; McCarthy interview, 3.

18. Fischer interview I, 43.

19. "Unrepentent Rebel," 15.

20. Isaac Asimov, *I. Asimov* (New York: Doubleday, 1994), 53–55; HA's Columbia University transcripts, box 78, folder 9, AP; "Unrepentent Rebel," 16.

21. Murrell interview.

22. Robert W. Iverson, *The Communists and the Schools* (New York: Harcourt, Brace, 1959), 125–26; HA to Julie Kailen, 16 March 1979, box 57, folder 16, AP.

23. Harold P. Perkall to HA, 18 July 1942, box 1, folder 10, AP; *New York Daily News,* 3 October 1935, 6; Penny M. Von Eschen, "African American Anticolonialism," in Mari Jo Buhle, Paul Buhle, and Dan Georgakas, *Encyclopedia of the American Left* (New York: Oxford University Press, 1998), 6–8; Iverson, *The Communists and the Schools,* 130–31.

24. Fay Aptheker in Fischer interview I, 80.

25. Aptheker, *The Aptheker Family,* 8–11.

26. Ibid., 27–29.

27. Bettina Aptheker, "The Weight of Inheritance," in *Red Diapers: Growing Up in the Communist Left,* ed. Judy Kaplan and Linn Shapiro (Urbana: University of Illinois Press, 1998), 279.

28. Aptheker, *The Aptheker Family,* 30–32.

29. HA and Fay Aptheker in Fischer interview I, 80–82, 150.

30. HA and Fay Aptheker in Fischer interview I, 123–25; Aptheker, *The Aptheker Family,* 32.

2. The Red Decade

1. The Workers School, opened by the CPUSA in 1923, adopted a curriculum "to give workers that knowledge of revolutionary theory and tactics, and labor history, which is essential for militant activity in the struggle against capitalism." Course work at the Workers School prepared students for "the protracted and many-sided struggle to contest

bourgeois cultural hegemony . . . so that the proletariat may prepare itself for its destined role as the ruling class under socialism." The curriculum "was militant industrial trade unionism, workers' improvement, anti-imperialism, the attainment of racial equality and the defense of the Soviet Union and its policies." As the historian Marvin Gettleman has pointed out, the Workers School "did not dispense grades or grant academic degrees." The school "agenda [was] defined by the Leninist principle of the unity of theory and action," enabling students to study Marxist principles in the classroom and then join their fellow students and faculty members at the next May Day celebration or anti-imperialist march in the streets. The Workers School, serving "a largely proletarian student body," attracted first hundreds, then thousands of "mainly foreign-born adult student workers . . . by the 1930s." Their study of black history led students to demonstrate against lynching and support efforts to defend the Scottsboro Boys, young black men charged with raping white women in Scottsboro, Alabama. Marvin Gettleman, "Workers Schools," in Mari Jo Buhle, Paul Buhle, Dan Georgakas, *Encyclopedia of the American Left* (New York: Oxford University Press, 1998), 902–3; Marvin Gettleman, "Engaged Pedagogy: Curriculum and Politics at U.S. Communist Labor Schools 1923–1957," manuscript, in the author's possession; Gettleman, "The Lost World of Communist Labor Schools in the United States, 1923–1957," manuscript, in the author's possession; Marvin Gettleman, "The New York Workers School, 1923–1944: Communist Education in American Society," in *New Studies in the Politics and Culture of U.S. Communism,* ed. Michael E. Brown, Randy Martin, Frank Rosengarten, and George Snedeker (New York: Monthly Review Press, 1993), 265, 270.

2. Gettleman, "Workers Schools," 903.

3. Fischer interview I, 60, 99.

4. Janet Lee, "Hutchins, Grace," and "Rochester, Anna," in Buhle, Buhle, and Georgakas, *Encyclopedia,* 343–45, 701–2; Murrell interview. On Dunn's secret party membership, see Harvey Klehr, *The Heyday of American Communism: The Depression Decade* (New York: Basic Books, 1984), 373n476.

5. "Unrepentent Rebel," 20; Bill Moseley to Robert W. Dunn, 2 January 1936, Labor Research Association Papers, box 5, folder "Southern Differential Aptheker 1935–36," Tamiment Library and Robert F. Wagner Labor Archives, New York University; HA, "The Southern Differential," typescript, Labor Research Association Papers, box 5, folder "Southern Differential Aptheker 1935–36," Tamiment Library, New York University.

6. HA to Julie Kailin, 18 March 1979, box 57, folder 16, AP.

7. "Unrepentent Rebel," 43; Fischer interview I, 59.

8. Samuel E. Morison and Henry S. Commager, *The Growth of the American Republic,* vol. 1, 3rd ed. (New York: Oxford University Press, 1942), 537–39. Several years later, as a member of a delegation sponsored by the NAACP, Aptheker confronted Morison, a Harvard historian, on his use of the term "Sambo" in *The Growth of the American Republic.* Morison claimed not to understand all the fuss. After all, he told Aptheker, "my own friends . . . call me Sambo," Fischer interview I, 89.

9. Fischer interview I, 89.

10. Ibid., 90. Carter G. Woodson to HA, 3 November 1936, box 1, folder 1, AP.

11. Bettina Aptheker, "Biographical Comment," in *In Resistance: Studies in African,*

Caribbean, and Afro-American History, ed. Gary Y. Okihiro (Amherst: University of Massachusetts Press, 1986), 211–13; Fischer interview I, 88–89; HA, *Nat Turner's Slave Rebellion* (New York: Humanities Press, 1966), i, 3.

12. Fischer interview I, 90–91.

13. Ibid., 121–22, 133–34; HA, "American Negro Slave Revolts," Part 1, *Science & Society* 1 (Summer 1937): 512–38, and Part 2, *Science & Society* 2 (Summer 1938): 386–92.

14. David Peck, "New Masses," in Buhle, Buhle, and Georgakas, *Encyclopedia,* 554–55. "Unrepentent Rebel," 30; Jim Williams, "International Publishers," in Buhle, Buhle, and Georgakas, *Encyclopedia,* 375; Clarence L. Mohr, "Southern Blacks in the Civil War: A Century of Historiography," *Journal of Negro History* 59, no. 2 (April 1974): 187. "In a similar manner," Mohr wrote, "the recent historiography of the Reconstruction and 'New South' eras lends some support to Aptheker's class hypothesis while rejecting his terminology. . . . Nearly all of the most recent revisionist monographs on Reconstruction recognize the importance of both racial and economic class divisions. This theme is especially obvious in C. Vann Woodward's groundbreaking study *The Origins of the New South* (Baton Rouge: LSU Press, 1950)." Fischer interview I, 101.

15. "Unrepentent Rebel," 43–44; Fischer interview I, 72–75; McCarthy interview, 15–17; Murrell interview.

16. Murrell interview; "Unrepentent Rebel," 67; HA, "Ideas on Trial: The Intellectual Leadership of V. J. Jerome," *Political Affairs,* March 1952, 1–11.

17. Bettina Aptheker to the author, 26 August 2009.

18. Irving Howe and Lewis Coser, *The American Communist Party: A Critical History* (New York: Praeger, 1962), 205, 206, 211.

19. Fischer interview I, 75.

20. Gerald Horne, "The Red and the Black: The Communist Party and African-Americans in Historical Perspective," in *New Studies in the Politics and Culture of U.S. Communism,* 205; Mark Naison, "Revisiting American Communism: An Exchange," *New York Review,* 15 August 1985, 42.

21. Maurice Isserman, *If I Had a Hammer: The Death of the Old Left and the Birth of the New Left* (New York: Basic Books, 1987), 12; Dorothy Ray Healey and Maurice Isserman, *California Red: A Life in the American Communist Party* (1990; reprint, Urbana: University of Illinois Press, 1993), 82; Klehr, *Heyday,* 178; George Charney, *A Long Journey* (Chicago: Quadrangle Books, 1968), 59; James G. Ryan, *Earl Browder: The Failure of American Communism* (Tuscaloosa: University of Alabama Press, 1997), 127.

22. Charney, *A Long Journey,* 60, 75; Klehr, *Heyday,* 207–8; Healey and Isserman, *California Red,* 59, 69.

23. Michael Jabara Carley, *1939: The Alliance That Never Was and the Coming of World War II* (Chicago: Ivan R. Dee, 1999), xiv, xvii.

24. HA, interview by Debby Cohen, April 1976, Tamiment Oral Series II, box 1, Tamiment Library, New York University; Cooper Thompson, Emmett Schaeffer, and Harry Brod, eds., *White Men Challenging Racism: 35 Personal Stories* (Durham: Duke University Press, 2003), 19.

25. Carley, *1939,* xviii, xix, 62.

26. "Unrepentent Rebel," 67; McCarthy interview, 13–24; Murrell interview.

27. Healey and Isserman, *California Red,* 81; Melech Epstein, quoted in Maurice Isserman, *Which Side Were You On? The American Communist Party during the Second World War* (Urbana: University of Illinois Press, 1993), 33; Al Richmond, *A Long View from the Left: Memoirs of an American Revolutionary* (New York: Delta, 1972), 284.

28. Isserman, *Which Side?* 45; Charney, *A Long Journey,* 127.

29. Murrell interview; Ryan, *Earl Browder,* 170.

30. Ryan, *Earl Browder,* 168; "Unrepentent Rebel," 67; HA, "Negroes in Wartime," *New Masses* 34, no. 5 (22 April 1941): 13–16.

31. Klehr, *Heyday,* 390.

32. Annette Rubinstein, "Hitler–Stalin Pact," in Buhle, Buhle, and Georgakas, *Encyclopedia,* 321; Healey and Isserman, *California Red,* 82; Richmond, *A Long View,* 284; McCarthy interview, 14; Murrell interview. In this connection see also Carley, *1939.*

33. McCarthy interview, 14; HA, *Daily Worker,* 2 November 1939, 1; A. B. Magil, *New Masses* 34 (2 January 1941): 9.

34. Paul Buhle and Dan Georgakas, "Communist Party, USA," in Buhle, Buhle, and Georgakas, *Encyclopedia,* 151.

35. William Henry Huff, quoted in Pete Daniel, *The Shadow of Slavery: Peonage in the South, 1901–1969* (Chicago: University of Illinois Press, 1972), 175, 176; unidentified escapee to HA, in HA, "America Has Her Peon, Too," *New Masses* 35, no. 10 (28 May 1940): 11; Fischer interview I, 105–11; Fischer interview II, 1–7; Murrell interview; "Unrepentent Rebel," 52–57.

36. Daniel, *The Shadow of Slavery,* x; Thomas R. Frazier, ed., *Readings in African-American History,* 3rd ed. (New York: Wadsworth, 2001), 182; HA, "America Has Her Peon, Too," 9, 10. Pete Daniel to HA, 9 March 1970, papers of Pete Daniel, in the author's possession; Daniel, *The Shadow of Slavery,* 174.

37. M. V. Holmes, Chairman of the International Workers Order Education Committee, to HA, 2 August 1937, box 1, folder 2, AP; Elaine Woo, "Louise T. Patterson; Last Survivor of Harlem Renaissance," *Los Angeles Times,* 19 September 1999; Robin D. G. Kelley, "Patterson, Louise Thompson," in Buhle, Buhle, and Georgakas, *Encyclopedia,* 590–91; Martin Duberman, *Paul Robeson: A Biography* (New York: Alfred A. Knopf, 1989), 250.

38. Charles H. Martin, "International Labor Defense," and Maurice Jackson, "Patterson, William L.," in Buhle, Buhle, and Georgakas, *Encyclopedia,* 368–70, 591–92.

39. "Unrepentent Rebel," 52, 53; Fischer interview I, 106; Fischer interview II, 3; Daniel, *The Shadow of Slavery,* 176.

40. Fischer interview II, 4; Fischer interview I, 106–7; Daniel, *The Shadow of Slavery,* 176; "Unrepentent Rebel," 53; Henrietta Buckmaster, *Let My People Go* (New York: Harper & Brothers, 1941), xii.

41. J. Edgar Hoover to Colonel William Henry Huff, 10 February 1940, reprinted in HA, "America Has Her Peon, Too," 11.

42. Fischer interview I, 107–9; Fischer interview II, 4–7; HA to Pete Daniel, 2 March 1970, papers of Pete Daniel, in the author's possession. See also Daniel, *The Shadow of Slavery,* 176–77.

43. Daniel, *The Shadow of Slavery,* 178, 179.

44. "Unrepentent Rebel," 35, 36.

45. Kate Weigand, *Red Feminism* (Baltimore: Johns Hopkins University Press, 2001), 28, 37, 38, 40; Mary Inman to HA, 24 August 1941, 17 September 1941, 30 September 1941, and HA to Mary Inman, [20 or 25] October, 1941, box 1, folder 8, AP.

46. Howard Selsam to HA, 19 November 1941, box 1, folder 7, AP; Dorothy K. Funn to HA, 28 February 1940, box 1, folder 5, AP. On this letter Aptheker has noted in the margin "it turned out later that she was an FBI informant." Fischer interview I, 126, 127.

3. "Double V"

1. Al Richmond, *A Long View from the Left: Memoirs of an American Revolutionary* (New York: Dell, 1972), 283, 285; "Unrepentent [*sic*] Rebel," 68.

2. Maurice Isserman, *Which Side Were You On? The American Communist Party during the Second World War* (Urbana: University of Illinois Press, 1993), 180.

3. The information is derived from Aptheker's military record, which is not complete. The army informed Aptheker's attorneys in 1989 that much of his military record was destroyed by a fire in 1973 that, the army claimed, destroyed most of the Second World War files. David [no last name] to HA, 16 May 1989, Rabinowitz, Boudin, Standard, Krinsky & Lieberman, Attorneys at Law, 740 Broadway, New York, New York. Copies of the letter and the military records were provided to the author by Aptheker.

4. HA to Fay Aptheker, 24 February 1942, box 155, folder 3; HA to Fay Aptheker, 11 April 1942, 8 May 1942, box 155, folder 6, AP; Fischer interview I, 143–44.

5. L. D. Reddick, "The Negro Policy of the United States Army, 1775–1945," *Journal of Negro History* 5, no. 35 (1949): 24, 25, 27; Stephen Ambrose, *Citizen Soldiers* (New York: Simon and Schuster, 1997), 345; E. Franklin Frazier, quoted in, Richard M. Dalfiume, "The 'Forgotten Years' of the Negro Revolution," in *The Negro in Depression and War*, ed. Bernard Sternsher (Chicago: Quadrangle Books, 1969), 299; HA to Fay Aptheker, 1 June 1942, box 155, folder 9, AP; Seymour J. Schoenfeld, *The Negro in the Armed Forces: His Value and Status—Past, Present, and Potential* (Washington, D.C.: Associated Publishers, 1945), 50; "Unrepentent Rebel," 78.

6. HA to Min[na] [Artson], 5 October 1942, box 1, folder 10, AP; Fay Aptheker, *The Aptheker Family* (San Jose, Calif.: privately published, 1990), 32.

7. Robert W. Mullen, *Blacks in America's Wars* (New York: Monad Press, 1973), 54; unidentified author, "The Mystery of the 364th," www.bestofneworleans.com.archives; Irving Howe and Lewis Coser, *The American Communist Party: A Critical History* (New York: Praeger, 1962), 415; Wilson Record, *The Negro and the Communist Party* (New York: Atheneum, 1971), 222–23; Congress, House of Representatives, Representative John Rankin, speaking for maintaining a segregated blood supply by the American Red Cross, 77th Cong., 2nd sess., *Congressional Record* 88 (28 May 1942): A1985.

8. Ulysses Lee, *United States Army in World War II: The Employment of Negro Troops* (Washington, D.C.: Center of Military History United States Army, 1965), 349, 350, 356; "The Mystery of the 364th"; "Unrepentent Rebel," 79; HA, "A Few Battles against Racism," *Black Scholar* 26 (Summer 1996): 3.

9. Fischer interview I, 147, 148; "Unrepentent Rebel," 81, 82.

10. Ibid., 156–58; Fischer interview II, 14; Murrell interview; "Unrepentent Rebel," 83–84.

11. Fischer interview I, 157–58; "Unrepentent Rebel," 83–84.

12. Fischer interview I, 161; Fischer interview II, 12; "Unrepentent Rebel," 89; HA, "A Few Battles against Racism," 6–7.

13. "Unrepentent Rebel," 98–99, 103.

14. Bettina Drew, *Nelson Algren: A Life on the Wild Side* (Austin: University of Texas Press, 1989), 158–59; "Unrepentent Rebel," 97; Fischer interview I, 164–66.

15. HA's military records, as cited in note 3 above; Army of the United States, "Separation Qualification Record," in the author's possession.

16. Isserman, *Which Side?* 181, 182; "Unrepentent Rebel," 103, 104.

17. HA to Fay Aptheker, [probably very early] April 1943, box 156, folder 2, AP.

18. Isserman, *Which Side?* 239; E. E. Conroy, Special Agent in Charge (hereafter SAC) to J. Edgar Hoover, 4 January 1945. Through the Freedom of Information Act I have in my possession several thousand pages of Aptheker's FBI records. Of those documents in my possession the letter of 4 January is the earliest FBI document mentioning Aptheker. All FBI documents referred to hereafter are in the author's possession.

19. J. Edgar Hoover to Assistant Chief of Staff, G-2, War Department, 16 January 1945.

20. Stephen Ambrose called the Battle of the Bulge "the greatest battle the U.S. Army has ever fought." Ambrose, *Citizen Soldiers,* 186.

21. Ambrose, *Citizen Soldiers,* 229; HA to Fay Aptheker, 30 January 1945, box 156, folder 5; 29 March 1945, box 156, folder 8; 27 April 1945, box 156, folder 9, AP.

22. Ambrose, *Citizen Soldiers,* 207, 348, 349; Mullen, *Blacks in America's Wars,* 59; Reddick, "The Negro Policy," 28; HA to Fay Aptheker, 27 January 1945, box 156, folder 5; 20 March 1945, 21 March 1945, box 156, folder 8; AP; HA, "Integration Among Combat Troops in World War II," an essay first published in *New Masses,* 12 February 1946, in HA, *Afro-American History: The Modern Era* (New York: Carol, 1992), 214.

23. "Unrepentent Rebel," 112, 113.

24. U.S. Army, "Separation Qualification Record"; HA to Fay Aptheker, 17 April 1945, box 156, folder 9, AP; "Unrepentent Rebel," 114, 115; HA to Fay Aptheker, 10 June 1945, box 156, folder 12, AP.

25. HA to Fay Aptheker, 18 May 1945, box 156, folder 10; 10 June 1945, box 156, folder 12, AP.

26. HA to Fay Aptheker, 27 April 1945, box 156, folder 9; 4 May 1945, box 156, folder 10, AP.

27. Martin Gilbert, *The Day the War Ended* (New York: Henry Holt, 1995), 62, 374; Laura June Hilton, "Prisoners of Peace: Rebuilding Community, Identity and Nationality in Displaced Persons Camps in Germany, 1945–1952" (PhD diss., Ohio State University, 2001), 70, 74, 75, 86; U.S. Army, "Separation Qualification Record"; HA to Fay Aptheker, 20 and 26 April 1945, box 156, folder 9, AP.

28. "Unrepentent Rebel," 116–17; Fischer interview I, 192–93.

29. Gilbert, *The Day,* 374; HA to Fay Aptheker, 21 May 1945, box 156, folder 11, AP; Gilbert, *The Day,* 243; Hilton, "Prisoners of Peace," 80; "Unrepentent Rebel," 117–18; Fischer interview I, 195; Bettina Aptheker to the author, 20 March 2013.

30. HA to Fay Aptheker, 20 April 1945, 28 April 1945, box 156, folder 9, AP.

31. HA to Fay Aptheker, 1 May 1945, box 156, folder 9, AP; "Unrepentent Rebel," 120.

32. Gilbert, *The Day,* 215; HA to Fay Aptheker, 8 May 1945, box 156, folder 10; 7 June 1945, box 156, folder 12, AP.

33. HA to Fay Aptheker, 19 June 1945, box 156, folder 13, AP; James V. Sanden and C. W. Wilmore, "Efficiency Report" on Capt. Herbert Aptheker, in the author's possession.

34. HA to Fay Aptheker, 22 June 1945, box 156, folder 13, AP.

35. HA to The Editor, *Field Artillery Journal,* Washington, D.C., 19 February 1944, box 85, folder 15, AP; HA, *American Foreign Policy and the Cold War* (New York: New Century, 1962), 86.

36. H. Bruce Franklin, "Antiwar and Proud of It," *The Nation,* 11 December 2000, 6.

4. The Aptheker Thesis

1. Robin D. G. Kelley, "'But a Local Phase of a World Problem': Black History's Global Vision, 1883–1950," *Journal of American History* 86, no. 3 (December 1999): 1074; August Meier and Elliott Rudwick, *Black History and the Historical Profession, 1915–1980* (Chicago: University of Illinois Press, 1986), 1, 2, 94; HA, *Toward Negro Freedom* (New York: New Century, 1956), 7.

2. Meier and Rudwick, *Black History,* 94–95.

3. Ibid., 3, 4; HA, *American Negro Slave Revolts,* 50th Anniversary Edition (New York: International, 1993), 13; HA, "Resistance and Afro-American History: Some Notes on Contemporary Historiography and Suggestions for Further Research," in *In Resistance,* ed. Gary Okihiro (Amherst: University of Massachusetts Press, 1986), 11; Eugene Genovese, foreword to Ulrich Bonnell Phillips, *American Negro Slavery* (Baton Rouge: Louisiana State University Press, 1966), viii, xix.

4. Kelley, "Local Phase of a World Problem," 1074; HA, *Nat Turner's Slave Rebellion* (New York: Humanities Press, 1966), 5, 35. The American Institute for Marxist Studies (AIMS) published Aptheker's master's thesis (1936) through Humanities Press in 1966.

5. HA, *American Negro Slave Revolts,* 11, 13; McCarthy interview, 43; HA, "American Negro Slave Revolts," *Science & Society* 1 (Summer, 1937): 512; Herbert Shapiro, "The Impact of the Aptheker Thesis: A Retrospective View of *American Negro Slave Revolts,*" *Science & Society* 48 (1984): 55.

6. HA, "American Negro Slave Revolts," 513.

7. HA, "Maroons within the Present Limits of the United States," *Journal of Negro History* 24 (April 1939): 167, 168, 176, 183. Aptheker waited in vain throughout the remainder of his life for the dictionary to catch up to his research, but it never did. Dictionaries still define *Maroon* as a fugitive black slave in the West Indies in the seventeenth and eighteenth centuries. Eugene Genovese, *From Rebellion to Revolution* (New York: Vintage, 1979), 73; Sylviane A. Diouf, *Slavery's Exiles: The Story of the American Maroons*

(New York: New York University Press, 2014); Robert Paquette, telephone interview by the author, 11 April 2003.

8. HA [written under the pseudonym Herbert Biel], "Class conflicts in the South—1850–1860," *Communist*, February 1939, 170; HA, "Class Conflicts in the South, Part II," *Communist,* March 1939, 278–79; HA, "The Negro in the Civil War," in HA, *Essays in the History of the American Negro* (New York: International, 1945), 167. This volume pulled together three pamphlets by Aptheker that International had published: "The Negro in the American Revolution (1940)"; "The Negro in the Abolitionist Movement (1941)"; "The Negro in the Civil War (1938)." John Hope Franklin, "Introduction," in HA, *To Be Free* (New York: Carol, 1991), 5.

9. Eugene Genovese, *The Southern Front* (Columbia: University of Missouri Press, 1995), 206.

10. Ibid., 206–7.

11. Franklin, "Introduction," 5; Charles S. Sydnor, "The Negro in the Civil War," *Mississippi Valley Historical Review* 26 (1939): 94; B. I. Wiley, "The Negro in the Civil War," *American Historical Review* 45 (1939): 244; Julie Kailin, "Toward Nonracist Historiography," in *African American History and Radical Historiography: Essays in Honor of Herbert Aptheker,* ed. Herbert Shapiro (Minneapolis: MEP Publications, 1998), 26; Aptheker, "The Negro in the Civil War," in Aptheker, *Essays in the History of the American Negro* (New York: International, 1945), 205.

12. August Meier and Elliot Rudwick, *From Plantation to Ghetto,* 3rd ed. (New York: Farrar, Straus and Giroux, 1989), 68–69; Mark Solomon, "Herbert Aptheker's Contributions to African American History," in Shapiro, *African American History,* 5.

13. Fay Aptheker in Fischer interview I, 151; Frank Tannenbaum to HA, 28 October 1942, box 1, folder 11, AP.

14. HA to Julie Kailin, 18 March 1979, box 57, folder 16, AP.

15. HA, *American Negro Slave Revolts,* 368, 18, 369, 78, 132, 139.

16. Ibid., 162–63, 374; Murrell interview.

17. E. Franklin Frazier, "American Negro Slave Revolts," *American Journal of Sociology* (January 1944): 374–75; Ellis O. Knox, "The Sub-human Myth," *Journal of Negro Education* 14 (1945): 206–9; Malcolm Cowley, "Review of *American Negro Slave Revolts,*" *New Republic,* 13 March 1944, 352.

18. J. G. de Rouhac Hamilton, "Review of *American Negro Slave Revolts,*" *American Historical Review* 49 (April 1944): 504–6.

19. McCarthy interview, 48; Kenneth W. Porter, quoted in Shapiro, "The Impact of the Aptheker Thesis," 60–61.

20. Meier and Rudwick, *From Plantation to Ghetto,* 240; Eric Foner in Gary Murrell, "On Herbert Aptheker and His Side of History: An Interview with Eric Foner," *Radical History Review* 78 (2000): 11, 13; David Brion Davis, "Slavery and the Post–World War II Historians," *Daedalus* 103, no. 1 (Winter 1974): 2.

21. Robin D. G. Kelley, "Afterword," *Journal of American History* 87, no. 1 (June 2000): 169.

22. Eric Foner in Murrell, "On Herbert Aptheker," 12–13; HA, "The American Historical Profession," in *The Unfolding Drama,* ed. Bettina Aptheker (New York:

International, 1979), 152; Staughton Lynd, "The Bulldog Whitewashed: A Critique of the Investigation of Herbert Aptheker's Nonappointment at Yale University," in Shapiro, *African American History,* 119.

23. Kenneth M. Stampp, "The Historian and Southern Negro Slavery," *American Historical Review* (April 1952): 613–24, quoted in Shapiro, "The Impact of the Aptheker Thesis," 61; Kenneth Stampp, *The Peculiar Institution* (New York: Vintage, 1956), 134.

24. William Styron, "Overcome," *New York Review of Books,* 26 September 1963, 18.

25. HA, *American Negro Slave Revolts,* viii; Edmund S. Morgan, "The Big American Crime," *New York Review of Books,* 3 December 1998, 14–18; and "Plantation Blues," *New York Review of Books,* 10 June 1999, 30–33.

26. Tony Horwitz, "Untrue Confessions," *New Yorker,* 13 December 1999, 80–89 (emphasis added).

27. Genovese, *The Southern Front,* 204, 205.

28. John Bracey, "Foreword, 40th Anniversary Edition," in HA, *American Negro Slave Revolts,* 50th Anniversary Edition, 3.

29. Eric Foner in Murrell, "On Herbert Aptheker," 10.

5. Into the Fires

1. HA to Fay Aptheker, 23 October 1945, box 157, folder 3, AP.

2. Willard Edwards, "House Names 13 Army Officers Listed as Reds," *Chicago Daily Tribune,* in "Correlation Summary," FBI, 16 February 1965, FBI files; "The Pentagon Facts & Figures," www.defenselink.mil; HA to Fay Aptheker, 7 December 1945, box 157, folder 7, AP.

3. "Unrepentent Rebel," 126, 127, 128; HA to Fay Aptheker, 12 December 1945, box 157, folder 8, AP; HA to Julie Kailen, 18 March 1979, box 57, file 16, AP. Repeated attempts to locate Aptheker's study of ground forces have proved unsuccessful. Aptheker said in an interview with Robin D. G. Kelly that the study "was printed as *History of the Armed Ground Forces of World War II.* I never got a copy," he said. "But it went to each member of Congress, probably for appropriations." See Robin D. G. Kelley, "Interview of Herbert Aptheker," *Journal of American History* 87, no. 1 (June 2000): 151–67.

4. Fischer interview I, 138; "Unrepentent Rebel," 74.

5. Bettina Aptheker to the author, 26 August 2009.

6. "Unrepentent Rebel," 123.

7. Bettina Aptheker to the author, 26 August 2009.

8. "Unrepentent Rebel," 123.

9. On post-traumatic stress disorder (PTSD) symptoms, see www.mayoclinic.com.

10. Bettina Aptheker to the author, 26 August 2009.

11. Bettina Aptheker, "Eulogy," at a memorial service for her parents, New York City, 16 October 2003, in the author's possession.

12. Bettina Aptheker to the author, 26 August 2009.

13. Murrell interview.

14. McCarthy interview, 14.

15. Murrell interview.

16. Ellen Schrecker, *No Ivory Tower* (New York: Oxford University Press, 1986), 30.

17. Eric Foner in Gary Murrell, "On Herbert Aptheker and His Side of History: An Interview with Eric Foner," *Radical History Review* 78 (2000): 14, 15, 16; HA to Kailen, 18 March 1979; unidentified author, "Phillip S. Foner," a brief biography of Foner's Communist activities, 25 August 1950, folder 14-0-1097, Counterattack Papers, Tamiment Library, New York University; HA to Fay Aptheker, 28 May 1945, box 156, folder 11, AP; HA, interview by Fred Zimring, 5 July 1977, Dunham-Zimring Collection, Temple University, 2.

18. "Unrepentent Rebel," 130; Fischer interview I, 227; Foner in Murrell, "On Herbert Aptheker," 15; Schrecker, *No Ivory Tower,* 265, 266.

19. HA to Kailen, 18 March 1979; Henry Allen Moe to HA, 10 April 1946, box 2, folder 5, AP; "1945 U.S. and Canadian Fellows," http://www.gf.org. In 2003 the Guggenheim Foundation awarded 184 United States and Canadian Fellowships, a total of $6,750,000 (an average grant of $36,685). There were 3,282 applicants.

20. "Unrepentent Rebel," 134.

21. Manning Marable, *W. E. B. Du Bois: Black Radical Democrat* (Boston: Twayne, 1986), 144; David Levering Lewis, *W. E. B. Du Bois: The Fight for Equality and the American Century, 1919–1963* (New York: Henry Holt, 2000), 494; Gerald Horne, *Black and Red: W. E. B. Du Bois and the Afro-American Response to the Cold War, 1944–1963* (Albany: State University of New York Press, 1986), 24.

22. W. E. B. Du Bois, *The Autobiography of W. E. B. Du Bois,* ed. HA (New York: International, 1968), 328, 329; Levering Lewis, *W. E. B. Du Bois,* 520.

23. Fischer interview I, 232; "Unrepentent Rebel," 134, 135.

24. Anson Phelps Stokes to W. E. B. Du Bois, 20 December 1946; W. E. B. Du Bois to Anson Phelps Stokes, 31 December 1946, in *The Correspondence of W. E. B. Du Bois,* ed. HA, paperback ed. (Amherst: University of Massachusetts Press, 1997), 3:130, 131.

25. HA, editorial comment in *Correspondence of W. E. B. Du Bois,* 175; HA to W. E. B. Du Bois, 5 January 1948; W. E. B. Du Bois to HA, 8 January 1948, in *Correspondence of W. E. B. Du Bois,* 3:176, 177.

26. HA to Fay and Bettina Aptheker, 14 November 1946, box 157, folder 14, AP.

27. John Baxter Streater Jr., "The National Negro Congress, 1936–1947" (PhD diss., University of Cincinnati, 1981), 329–30, 331; "Unrepentent Rebel," 135; Fischer interview I, 232, 233; National Negro Congress, "First Petition to United Nations from the African-American People (1946)," in *A Documentary History of the Negro People in the United States,* ed. HA (New York: Carol, 1993), 5:136, 137; HA, *Afro-American History: The Modern Era* (New York: Citadel, 1992), 301–11.

28. HA, *Documentary History,* 5:135; "Unrepentent Rebel," 135–36; FBI, Summary Report, 25 April 1949.

29. Levering Lewis, *W. E. B. Du Bois,* 521, 531, 534.

30. "Unrepentent Rebel," 150; Fischer interview I, 240–41, 242; Levering Lewis, *W. E. B. Du Bois,* 522; Bettina Aptheker to the author, 26 August 2009.

31. Lloyd L. Brown, "Aptheker and Myrdal's Dilemma," in *African American History and Radical Historiography: Essays in Honor of Herbert Aptheker,* ed. Herbert Shapiro (Minneapolis: MEP, 1998), 112, 113.

32. HA to Fay Aptheker, 10 January 1946, box 157, folder 10, AP; HA, *The Negro People in America: A Critique of Gunnar Myrdal's "An American Dilemma"* (New York: International, 1946), 18, 19.

33. Maurice Isserman, e-mail to the author, 9 May 2014.

34. HA, *The Negro People in America,* 19, 20, 21, 22, 66, 67.

6. Prelude to McCarthyism

1. Maurice Isserman, *Which Side Were You On? The American Communist Party during the Second World War* (Urbana: University of Illinois Press, 1993), 184.

2. Irving Howe and Lewis Coser, *The American Communist Party* (New York: Praeger, 1962), 425–26.

3. Isserman, *Which Side Were You On?,* 242, 37; Joseph R. Starobin, *American Communism in Crisis, 1943–1957* (Berkeley: University of California Press, 1975), 79; James G. Ryan, *Earl Browder: The Failure of American Communism* (Tuscaloosa: University of Alabama Press, 1997), 247.

4. Ryan, *Earl Browder,* 276; Isserman, *Which Side Were You On?,* 242.

5. Bettina Aptheker to the author, 26 August 2009.

6. John Gates, *The Story of an American Communist* (New York: Thomas Nelson & Sons, 1958), 105; Isserman, *Which Side Were You On?,* 240.

7. David Peck, "New Masses," in *Encyclopedia of the American Left,* ed. Mari Jo Buhle, Paul Buhle, and Dan Georgakas (New York: Oxford University Press, 1998), 554–55; Annette Rubenstein, "Mainstream," in Buhle, Buhle, and Georgakas, *Encyclopedia,* 469–70.

8. Henrietta Buckmaster to HA, 26 March 1948, box 2, folder 10, AP; David Cuate, *The Great Fear: The Anti-Communist Purge under Truman and Eisenhower* (New York: Simon and Schuster, 1978), 26.

9. Caute, *The Great Fear,* 26, 29, 30, 27, 28; Michal R. Belknap, *Cold War Political Justice: The Smith Act, the Communist Party, and American Civil Liberties* (Westport, Conn.: Greenwood, 1977), 42; Joel Kovel, *Red Hunting in the Promised Land* (New York: Basic Books, 1994), 129.

10. HA, "Task Force A. D. A.," *Masses & Mainstream* 1, no. 4 (June 1948): 28, 29; HA, "The Face of the Lesser Evil," *Masses & Mainstream* 1, no. 1 (March 1948): 36.

11. Belknap, *Cold War Political Justice,* 46, 48.

12. Ibid., 51.

13. HA to Fay Aptheker, 21 July 1948, box 158, folder 5, AP.

14. "Summary Report," FBI New York Field Office, 25 April 1949. There is no indication in the thousands of pages of Aptheker's FBI files to account for the FBI's misidentification of Aptheker. This "Summary Report," like many others completed over the next thirty years, included a bibliography of Aptheker's writings. Until the late 1980s, when the independent scholar John Moore began a systematic compilation of Aptheker's written work, the FBI kept the most complete bibliography.

15. HA, "Communism and Chaos," *Masses & Mainstream* 1, no. 7 (September 1948): 19, 18, 28, 29.

16. "Communist Leader Stabbed on Street near Queens Home," *New York Times,* 22 September 1948, 1.

17. Manning Marable, *W. E. B. Du Bois: Black Radical Democrat* (Boston: Twayne, 1986), 173, 174; Arthur M. Schlesinger Jr., "The U.S. Communist Party," *Life,* 19 July 1946, 90.

18. David Levering Lewis, *W. E. B. Du Bois: The Fight for Equality and the American Century, 1919–1963* (New York: Henry Holt, 2000), 527, 536; HA, in an introduction to correspondence in *The Correspondence of W. E. B. Du Bois,* ed. HA, paperback ed. (Amherst: University of Massachusetts Press, 1997), 3:255.

19. Lloyd Brown, interview by the author, New York City, 11 May 2001; "Unrepentent Rebel," 166.

20. Brown, interview by the author.

21. "Unrepentent Rebel," 176.

22. Levering Lewis, *W. E. B. Du Bois,* 540; Marable, *W. E. B. Du Bois,* 180, quoting Du Bois; W. E. B. Du Bois to HA, 19 September 1950, box 3, folder 5, AP; "Unrepentent Rebel," 219, 193; Howard Fast, *Being Red* (Armonk, N.Y.: M. E. Sharpe, 1990), 299.

23. W. E. B. Du Bois to HA and Shirley Graham, 9 June 1950; Shirley Graham to HA, 10 June 1950; C. F. Kellogg to HA, 12 June 1950, box 3, folder 5, AP.

24. HA, in an introduction to correspondence in *Correspondence of W. E. B. Du Bois,* 261; W. E. B. Du Bois to HA, 11 April 1949, box 3, folder 6, AP. The letter also appears in *Correspondence,* 3:261–62.

25. John Gates, *The Story of an American Communist* (New York: Thomas Nelson & Sons, 1958), 121–22 (emphasis added); Belknap, *Cold War Political Justice,* 81.

26. James R. Barrett, *William Z. Foster and the Tragedy of American Radicalism* (Chicago: University of Illinois Press, 1999), 237; Belknap, *Cold War Political Justice,* 59, 68, 89; Michael Steven Smith, "Smith Act Trials, 1949," in Buhle, Buhle, and Georgakas, *Encyclopedia,* 755.

27. Belknap, *Cold War Political Justice,* 83, 85; HA, *Dare We Be Free? The Meaning of the Attempt to Outlaw the Communist Party* (New York: Citizens' Committee for Constitutional Liberties, 1961), 13; Dorothy Ray Healey and Maurice Isserman, *California Red: A Life in the American Communist Party* (1990; reprint, Urbana: University of Illinois Press, 1993), 115–16, 140.

28. Ellen Schrecker, *Many Are the Crimes* (Boston: Little, Brown, 1998), 196, 197; Belknap, *Cold War Political Justice,* 92.

29. SAC New York to J. Edgar Hoover, 24 August 1949, redacted trial digest, beginning on page 12,818 of the trial transcript, FBI documents.

30. Schrecker, *Many Are the Crimes,* 199; Belknap, *Cold War Political Justice,* 114.

31. HA, *Why Defend the Rights of Communists?* (New York: New Century Publishers, 1949), 6–7, 9, 12, 14, 15; Barrett, *William Z. Foster,* 229–30; [writer's name blacked out] to J. Edgar Hoover, 24 September 1951; J. Edgar Hoover to [recipient's name blacked out], 1 October 1951, FBI documents.

32. Belknap, *Cold War Political Justice,* 134.

33. Chief Justice Vinson, in Gerald Gunther, *Constitutional Law,* 11th ed. (Mineola, N.Y.: Foundation Press, 1985), 1020, 1018.

34. William O. Douglas, in ibid., 1024.

35. Belknap, *Cold War Political Justice,* 122.

36. Brown, interview by the author.

7. The Time of the Toad

1. HA, *Laureates of Imperialism* (New York: Masses & Mainstream, 1954), 16, 15; HA, in an essay first published in October 1949 titled "The Schlesinger Fraud," in *History and Reality* (New York: Cameron Associates, 1955), 115; "Unrepentent Rebel," 184; Lloyd Brown, interview by the author, New York City, 11 May 2001.

2. Jesse Lemisch, *On Active Service in War and Peace: Politics and Ideology in the American Historical Profession* (Toronto: New Hogtown Press, 1975), 82; Arthur Schlesinger Jr., *The Vital Center,* rev. ed. (Cambridge: Riverside Press, 1962), 38, 174, 209, 204, 102, 104–5, 212, 213.

3. HA, *History and Reality,* 116–19, 121, 120, 129.

4. Albert Feuerwerker to HA, 13 October 1949; HA to Albert Feuerwerker, no date; Albert Feuerwerker to HA, 25 November 1949; HA to Howard Fast, 23 November 1949; box 3, folder 2, AP.

5. "Unrepentent Rebel," 185; Fischer interview I, 219.

6. Murrell interview; Paul Chevigny, e-mail to the author, 2 June 2003; Peter Filardo, interview by the author, New York City, 16 May 2001; Chevigny to the author, 2 June 2003.

7. Arthur Schlesinger Jr. to the author, 30 August 2000. There is no record of a second Schlesinger–Aptheker debate.

8. HA, "Marx and American Scholarship," in *History and Reality,* 217.

9. Sidney Hook, "Should Communists Be Permitted to Teach?" *New York Times Magazine,* 27 February 1949, 26, 28; Hook, "What Shall We Do About Communist Teachers?" *Saturday Evening Post,* 10 September 1949, 164; HA, "Communism and Truth: A Reply to Sidney Hook," in *History and Reality,* 89, 90, 102–3. Hook's letter could not be found in Aptheker's papers.

10. Lemisch, *On Active Service,* 52. "What part are we as historians to play in what everybody is calling education for democracy?" President Conyers Read of the American Historical Association (AHA) asked in his Presidential Address in 1949. Read admonished historians to "fight an enemy whose value system is deliberately simplified in order to achieve quick decisions. . . . Total war, whether it be hot or cold, enlists everyone and calls upon everyone to assume his part. The historian is no freer from this obligation than the physicist." Historians had to "recognize certain fundamental values as beyond dispute," Read said. "We must carry back into our scrutiny of the past the same faith in the validity of our democratic assumption which, let us say, the astronomer has in the validity of the Copernican theory." To Read, if a historian's research uncovered evidence that questioned "fundamental values" that information should be suppressed. "We must realize that not everything which takes place in the laboratory is appropriate for broadcasting at the street corners. And we must recognize the pathological for what it is and

not discuss with equal indifference the diseased and the healthy organism. . . . One can afford to be dull, if one has good friends at court, but one cannot afford to be unorthodox, at least not when the merits of democracy are in question. This sounds like the advocacy of one form of social control as against another," he concluded. "In short, it is." Conyers Read, "The Social Responsibilities of the Historian," *American Historical Review* 60, no. 2 (January 1950): 281, 283, 284, 282; HA, *Laureates of Imperialism,* 29, 15–16.

11. Lemisch, *On Active Service,* 69; Nevins, quoted in Lemisch, *On Active Service,* 69.

12. Eric Foner, "The Historical Scholarship of Herbert Aptheker," in *African American History and Radical Historiography: Essays in Honor of Herbert Aptheker,* ed. Herbert Shapiro (Minneapolis: MEP, 1998), 77; HA, *Laureates of Imperialism,* 36, 38–39, 39–40, 18–19.

13. Lemisch, *On Active Service,* 52; Ellen Schrecker, *No Ivory Tower: McCarthyism and the Universities* (New York: Oxford University Press, 1986), 341.

14. Eluhu S. Hicks, "City College Text Slanders Negroes," *The Worker,* 26 March 1959, 8; HA, *Laureates of Imperialism,* 42, 43.

15. Murrell interview; Sterling Stuckey, "From the Bottom Up: Herbert Aptheker's *American Negro Slave Revolts* and *A Documentary History of the Negro People in the United States,*" in Shapiro, *African American History,* 48; Fischer interview I, 209, 210, 212; *A Documentary History of the Negro People in the United States,* ed. HA (New York: Citadel Press, 1979), 1:82, 1–2.

16. HA, "History and Reality," an essay that first appeared in the fall of 1947 in *History and Reality,* 41, 42.

17. HA, "Introduction," *Documentary History* (emphasis added).

18. W. E. B. Du Bois, "Preface," in HA, *Documentary History.*

19. L. D. Reddick and Harvey Wish, quoted in Julie Kailin, "Toward Nonracist Historiography: The Early Work of Herbert Aptheker," in Shapiro, *African American History,* 34; John Hope Franklin, "Review of *A Documentary History,*" *Journal of Southern History* 18, no. 2 (May 1952): 267, 268; John Hope Franklin, interview by the author, 8 January 2000.

20. Lloyd Brown quoting Saunders Redding in "Racism and the Reviewers," *Masses & Mainstream* 5, no. 5 (May, 1952): 53; Brown quoting the New Orleans *Christian Advocate,* 54; Brown quoting J. A. Rogers in the *Pittsburgh Courier,* 54.

21. W. E. B. Du Bois, quoted in Brown, "Racism and the Reviewers," 54.

22. Brown, "Racism and the Reviewers," 53, 54.

23. Stuckey, "From the Bottom Up," 47, 48.

24. Manning Marable, "The Historical Scholarship of Herbert Aptheker," in Shapiro, *African American History,* 69, 70.

25. Ibid., 73.

26. Gwen Patton, e-mail to the author, 9 June 2003.

27. Marable, "Historical Scholarship," 73.

28. Stuckey, "From the Bottom Up," 47–48; Fischer interview I, 216.

29. Karl Marx and Friedrich Engels, *The Communist Manifesto,* ed. Frederic L. Bender (New York: Norton, 1988), 73; Karl Marx in *The Marx–Engels Reader,* ed. Robert C. Tucker, 2nd ed. (New York: Norton, 1978), 174, 145.

8. Are You Now or Have You Ever Been?

1. Fay Aptheker in Fischer interview II, 2, 51, 50; HA to Hans Freistadt, 24 October 1949, box 3, folder 6; HA to Fay Aptheker, 8 February 1949, box 158, folder 7, AP.

2. Manning Marable, in *African American History and Radical Historiography: Essays in Honor of Herbert Aptheker,* ed. Herbert Shapiro (Minneapolis: MEP, 1998), 73.

3. FBI Correlation Summary, 10 December 1965, 13, 19. The informer reported on a "housewarming party of the Westside Branch of the California Labor School in Los Angeles" held on 8 October 1949.

4. SAC, New York to Director, FBI, 12 June 1950. Budenz identification of Du Bois is found in "Synopsis of Facts," prepared by SAC New York, 25 May 1954, 11, a report made for the Philadelphia FBI office; Ellen Schrecker, *Many Are the Crimes* (New York: Little, Brown, 1998), 208.

5. Adjutant General C. A. Beall, Jr., to Major Herbert Aptheker, 28 November 1950 and 28 December 1950, Aptheker's military records, in the author's possession; "Unrepentant Rebel," 156–60; HA to The Editor, *New York Post,* 29 December 1959, box 6, folder 27, AP.

6. John Abt, transcribed oral history, 71–72, Reference Center for Marxist Studies at Communist Party headquarters, Manhattan (hereafter cited as Abt Oral History). The transcribed interview does not indicate where, when, or by whom the series of interviews were conducted.

7. Ibid., 75; David Caute, *The Great Fear* (New York: Simon and Schuster, 1978), 171.

8. Abt Oral History, 78.

9. Ibid., 78, 83.

10. Ibid., 82.

11. John Gates, *The Story of an American Communist* (New York: Thomas Nelson & Sons, 1958), 144, 142, 146; Abt Oral History, 88; HA to Fay Aptheker, 12 June 1952, box 158, folder 10, AP; HA, "Taking the Stand," *Masses & Mainstream* 5, no. 8 (August 1952): 22.

12. Abt Oral History, 88; HA, "Taking the Stand," 23–24; "Unrepentent Rebel," 235.

13. HA, "Taking the Stand," 24–25.

14. Ibid., 27; *New York Times,* 2 July 1952, 2.

15. Caute, *The Great Fear,* 171, 172, 581; Abt Oral History, 78, 132, 134.

16. Michal R. Belknap, *Cold War Political Justice: The Smith Act, the Communist Party, and American Civil Liberties* (Westport, Conn.: Greenwood, 1977), 152. The exact number of those prosecuted is hard to pin down. Belknap claims there were 126, James Barrett says 134. James Barrett, *William Z. Foster and the Tragedy of American Radicalism* (Chicago: University of Illinois Press, 1999), 239.

17. Barrett, *William Z. Foster,* 239; Belknap, *Cold War Political Justice,* 158; Fischer interview I, 373, 374.

18. George Charney, *A Long Journey* (Chicago: Quadrangle, 1968), 206; SAC, Philadelphia to Director, FBI, 5 May 1954, 35; HA to Elizabeth Gurley Flynn, 16 October 1953, box 4, folder 6, AP.

19. Elizabeth Gurley Flynn to HA, 6 October 1953, box 4, folder 6, AP.

20. HA to Elizabeth Gurley Flynn, 9 October 1953, box 4, folder 6, AP.

21. Belknap, *Cold War Political Justice,* 157; Steve Nelson to HA, 16 June 1955, box 4, folder 14, AP.

22. James R. Barrett and Rob Ruck, "Introduction," in Steve Nelson, James R. Barrett, and Rob Ruck, *Steve Nelson, American Radical* (Pittsburgh: University of Pittsburgh Press, 1981), xi, 325, 330; Steve Nelson, *The 13th Juror* (New York: Masses & Mainstream, 1955), 189.

23. "Unrepentent Rebel," 264; Nelson, *The 13th Juror,* 187; SAC Hallford to Director and New York, 16 January 1952; SAC New York to Director, FBI, 29 January 1952; Communications Section to SAC's Baltimore, New York, Washington Field Office, 24 March 1952; Mr. Ladd to A. H. Belmont, 24 March 1952; SAC New York to Director, FBI, 28 April 1952; "Correlation Summary," 10 December 1965.

24. Nelson, *The 13th Juror,* 187, 189, 192; HA, "Taking The Stand," 22; Nelson, Barrett, and Ruck, *Steve Nelson,* 336, 337.

25. "Unrepentent Rebel," 265.

26. Volumes 1 and 2, Transcript of Record, Supreme Court, October Term 1955, Number 10, Commonwealth of Pennsylvania, *Petitioner* vs. *Steve Nelson,* Certiorari granted October 14, 1954, 350 U.S. 497; (1955 Term Docket #10), 962–63 (hereafter cited as Nelson Trial Transcript). Note that this record of the state trial comes from the Supreme Court case and is part of that record. In the original court transcripts Aptheker's testimony occurs on pages 1827–2252.

27. Nelson, *The 13th Juror,* 192.

28. Schrecker, *Many Are the Crimes,* 256, 262, 257; Nicholas von Hoffman, *Citizen Cohn* (New York: Doubleday, 1988), 145; Milton Bracker, "Books of 40 Authors Banned by U.S. in Overseas Libraries," *New York Times,* 22 June 1953, 1; David M. Oshinsky, *A Conspiracy So Immense* (New York: Free Press, 1983), 279.

29. Frederic Frommer, "Closed-Door McCarthy Transcripts Unsealed," Associated Press, 5 May 2003; R. R. Palmer, "Presidential Address," *American Historical Review* 76, no. 1 (February 1971): 1–15.

30. HA, "Subpoena No. 235," *Masses & Mainstream* 6, no. 6 (June 1953): 1; Hearings before the Permanent Subcommittee on Investigations of the Committee on Government Operations United States Senate, Eight-Third Congress, First Session, 6 May and 14 May, 1953: 367–73 (hereafter cited as McCarthy Committee Hearing).

31. Theodore Kaghan, quoted in von Hoffman, *Citizen Cohn,* 149.

32. McCarthy Committee Hearing, 373–85.

33. Bettina Aptheker, "The Weight of Inheritance," in *Red Diapers: Growing Up in the Communist Left,* ed. Judy Kaplan and Linn Shapiro (Urbana: University of Illinois Press, 1998), 283; C. P. Trussell, "McCarthy Asks List of Reds on Papers," *New York Times,* 7 May 1953, A16; HA to Senator Joseph R. McCarthy, 11 May 1953, box 3, folder 15, AP.

34. Nelson Trial Transcript, 1062–64.

35. Fay Aptheker and HA in Fischer interview I, 387.

36. Margaret Rogers Budenz to HA, 23 February 1994, box 79, folder 20, AP.

9. De Facto Dissolution of the Party

1. Joseph R. Starobin, *American Communism in Crisis, 1943–1957* (Berkeley: University of California Press, 1972), 198.

2. David K. Johnson, *The Lavender Scare: The Cold War Persecution of Gays and Lesbians in the Federal Government* (Chicago: University of Chicago Press, 2004); Dorothy Ray Healey and Maurice Isserman, *California Red: A Life in the American Communist Party* (1990; reprint, Urbana: University of Illinois Press, 1993), 129, 130.

3. Healey and Isserman, *California Red*, 125; Maurice Isserman, *Which Side Were You On? The American Communist Party during the Second World War* (Urbana: University of Illinois Press, 1993), 119; HA and Horace R. Cayton, "Whose Dilemma?" *New Masses,* 23 July 1946, 12.

4. National Education Department, Communist Party, *The Struggle against White Chauvinism: Outline for Discussion and Study Guide for Schools, Classes, Study Groups* [no publisher listed], September 1949, 15, 19; Healey and Isserman, *California Red*, 126. Starobin, *American Communism,* 199–200; Harry Haywood, *Black Bolshevik: Autobiography of an Afro-American Communist* (Chicago: Liberator, 1978), 588.

5. HA, "The Negro Woman," *Masses & Mainstream* 2, no 2 (February 1949): 10, 12, 17; Kate Weigand, *Red Feminism* (Baltimore: Johns Hopkins University Press, 2001), 185, 108.

6. William Eric Perkins, "Haywood, Harry," in *Encyclopedia of the American Left,* 2nd ed., ed. Mari Jo Buhle, Paul Buhle, and Dan Georgakas (New York: Oxford University Press, 1998), 297; Irving Howe and Lewis Coser, *The American Communist Party: A Critical History* (New York: Praeger, 1962), 206.

7. HA, "The Road to Negro Liberation," *Jewish Life,* February 1949, 29–30; W. E. B. Du Bois, quoted in HA, "Consciousness of Negro Nationality: An Historical Survey," *Political Affairs* 28, no. 6 (June 1949): 89, 95.

8. HA, "Consciousness of Afro-American Nationality to 1900," in *Afro-American History: The Modern Era* (New York: Carol, 1992), 110. The essay is a revised version of the 1949 *Political Affairs* essay.

9. "Unrepentent Rebel," 188, 189; Haywood, *Black Bolshevik,* 622, 623. On the development of a refined position on black liberation, see HA to Benjamin Davis, 3 July 1956 and Benjamin Davis to HA, 5 July 1956, box 4, folder 27, AP.

10. Andrew McIntosh, "Profile: C. L. R. James and the Black Jacobins Revisited," *Society,* May/June 2003, 70–71.

11. Starobin, *American Communism,* 220; HA to National Administrative Committee, November, 1954, box 86, folder 6, AP.

12. HA, "Disagrees with Editorial," *Daily Worker,* 12 June 1956, 4; HA to National Administrative Committee, November, 1954.

13. HA, "Disagrees with Editorial," 4; HA, "Reading Between the Lies: The Anti-Soviet Experts," *Masses & Mainstream* 3, no. 11 (November 1950): 48, 49–50, 51, 60.

14. HA to National Administrative Committee, November 1954.

15. HA, "Behind the Hiss Frameup," *Masses & Mainstream* 6, no. 10 (October 1953): 3, 8, 12, 13; William Allen Jowitt, *The Strange Case of Alger Hiss* (New York: Doubleday, 1953).

16. "Unrepentent Rebel," 241; HA, "Communism and Truth: A Reply to Sidney Hook," *Masses & Mainstream,* 6, no 2 (February 1953), reprinted in HA, *History and Reality* (New York: Cameron, 1955), 101, 102; HA, "New Light on the Rosenberg–Sobell Case," *Masses & Mainstream* 8, no. 6 (June 1955): 33; Nicholas von Hoffman, *Citizen Cohn* (New York: Doubleday, 1988), 109, 108.

17. Howard Fast, *Being Red* (Armonk, N.Y.: M. E. Sharpe, 1994), 283; "Unrepentent Rebel," 244; Bettina Aptheker, "The Weight of Inheritance," in *Red Diapers: Growing Up in the Communist Left,* ed. Judy Kaplan and Linn Shapiro (Urbana: University of Illinois Press, 1998), 283, 284.

18. HA, "West Coast Impressions," *Masses & Mainstream* 8, no. 8 (August 1955): 41, 42.

19. HA, "New Light on the Rosenberg–Sobell Case," 33; HA, "The Campus Asks Questions," *Masses & Mainstream* 8, no. 3 (April 1955): 9, 8, 11.

20. SAC, New York to J. Edgar Hoover, 31 July 1954, FBI Memorandum; F. J. Baumgardner to A. H. Belmont, 19 October 1954, FBI Memorandum; Report created by Seattle FBI office, 27 September 1955; Director, FBI to SAC, New York, 6 April 1956.

21. Harvey Matusow, *False Witness* (New York: Cameron and Kahn, 1955); Director, FBI to SAC, New York, 6 April 1956; Helen Camp, *Iron in Her Soul: Elizabeth Gurley Flynn and the American Left* (Pullman, Wash.: Washington State University Press, 1995), 250, 251.

22. "Unrepentent Rebel," 287.

23. HA, "The Lynching of a Child," in HA, *Toward Negro Freedom* (New York: New Century, 1956), 175, 176, 177.

10. Revelations and Disputations

1. Peggy Dennis, *The Autobiography of an American Communist* (Westport, Conn.: Lawrence Hill, 1977), 221; Joseph Starobin, *American Communism in Crisis, 1943–1957* (Berkeley: University of California Press, 1975), 223; James R. Barrett, *William Z. Foster and the Tragedy of American Radicalism* (Urbana: University of Illinois Press, 1999), 253; Maurice Isserman, *Which Side Were You On? The American Communist Party during the Second World War* (Urbana: University of Illinois Press, 1993), 249.

2. Dennis, *Autobiography,* 222.

3. HA, memo outlining actions the party could take to "get into the debate, uphold our position in the debate, and get the message across to Party members," February 1956, box 86, folder 34, AP.

4. HA, "Get into the debate" memo; Starobin, *American Communism,* 205; HA, "Preliminary Report on 'The Monthly Review'—January, 1955—October 1955," box 86, folder 11, AP.

5. HA, "Get into the debate" memo.

6. Dorothy Ray Healey and Maurice Isserman, *California Red: A Life in the American Communist Party* (1990; reprint, Urbana: University of Illinois Press, 1993), 151, 152; Dennis, *Autobiography,* 223.

7. Healey and Isserman, *California Red,* 152.

8. John Gates, *The Story of an American Communist* (New York: Thomas Nelson and Sons, 1958), 168.

9. Healey and Isserman, *California Red,* 152, 155.

10. HA to Eugene Dennis, 6 June 1956, box 4, folder 27, AP; "Statement of the National Committee, C.P.U.S.A.," *Political Affairs* 35, no. 7 (July 1956): 34–35, 36.

11. HA, "On Party Relations and the Khrushchev Report," *Political Affairs* 35, no. 7 (July 1956): 33.

12. Al Richmond, *A Long View from the Left* (New York: Dell, 1972), 369; Editorial, *Daily Worker,* 6 June 1956, 1.

13. Gates, *The Story,* 176–77.

14. HA, "Disagrees with Editorial," *Daily Worker,* 12 June 1956, 4.

15. Joe Clark to HA, 12 June 1956; HA to Joe Clark, 15 June 1956; Joe Clark to HA, 21 June 1956, box 4, folder 26, AP.

16. HA to The Editor, *Daily Worker,* 25 June 1956; Joseph Clark to The Editor, *Daily Worker,* no date of publication (sometime between 25 June and 4 July 1956, when Aptheker's response appeared in the paper); HA to The Editor, *Daily Worker,* 4 July 1956, box 4, folder 27, AP.

17. Dennis, *Autobiography,* 228. John Gates, "Time for a Change," *Political Affairs* 35, no. 11 (November 1956): 45–46; Steve Nelson, "On a New United Party of Socialism," *Political Affairs* 35, no 11 (November 1956): 57–59; Barrett, *William Z. Foster,* 257; Gates, quoting a Draft Resolution of September 1956, *The Story,* 170; HA, "A Discussion with Critics," *Political Affairs* 35, no. 11 (November 1956): 57–59; Junius Irving Scales and Richard Nickson, *Cause at Heart: A Former Communist Remembers* (Athens: University of Georgia Press, 1987), 308; HA to The Editor, *Daily Worker,* 7 November 1956, box 4, folder 27, AP; HA to Will and Mona Allister, 10 December 1956, box 4, folder 24, AP.

18. Scales and Nickson, *Cause at Heart,* 308; David A. Shannon, *The Decline of American Communism* (New York: Harcourt, Brace, 1959), 315, 316; Gates, *The Story,* 177, 179.

19. "Unrepentent Rebel," 279.

20. HA, "Question of Fascism," *Daily Worker,* 12 November 1956, 4.

21. HA, "Communism and Chaos," *Masses & Mainstream* 1, no. 7 (September 1948): 29.

22. Scales and Nickson, *Cause at Heart,* 313.

23. "Unrepentent Rebel," 277–78.

24. HA, *The Truth about Hungary* (New York: Mainstream, 1957), 10, 148, 149, 150.

25. Ibid., 198, 233, 255.

26. Ibid., 220, 221.

27. Peter Fryer, *Hungarian Tragedy* (1957; reprint, London: Index, 1997), 11; Peter Fryer, "Fryer Writes to Aptheker on the Truth about Hungary," *Daily Worker,* 15 July 1957, 1.

28. Shannon, *The Decline,* 342; Robert Friedman, "Aptheker's 'Truth about Hungary,'" *Daily Worker,* 19 June 1957, 6, 7; Foster, quoted in Shannon, *The Decline,* 343; V. J. Jerome to HA, 30 June 1957; HA to V. J. Jerome, 2 July 1957, V. J. Jerome Papers, Yale University.

29. Alan Max, "Hungary," *Masses & Mainstream* 9, no. 9 (1957): 54–60; Scales and Nickson, *Cause at Heart,* 313–14; Bettina Aptheker to the author, 26 August 2009.

30. Robin D. G. Kelley, "Afterword," *Journal of American History* 87, no. 1 (June 2000): 170; HA in Robin D. G. Kelley, "Interview of Herbert Aptheker," *Journal of American History* 87, no. 1 (June 2000): 155; Fryer, *Hungarian Tragedy,* 75; HA, *The Truth about Hungary,* 242; Fryer, *Hungarian Tragedy,* 80.

31. Murrell interview; Bettina Aptheker, unpublished "Eulogy," delivered at Saint Peter's Church, New York City, 16 October 2003, copy in the author's possession.

32. Starobin, *American Communism,* 227; Gates, *The Story,* 181; Benjamin J. Davis, Jr. to HA, 14 February 1957, box 5, folder 9, AP; Dennis, *Autobiography,* 232; Healey and Isserman, *California Red,* 164.

33. HA to Benjamin Davis, 13 February 1957, Benjamin Davis Papers, Manuscripts, Archives and Rare Books Division, Schomburg Center for Research in Black Culture, New York Public Library; Murrell interview. For Aptheker's opinion on Gates, see HA, *History and Reality* (New York: Cameron, 1955), 238, 245.

34. HA, "More Comments on Howard Fast," *Masses & Mainstream* 9, no. 4 (April 1957): 42.

35. HA to John Williamson, 30 October 1957, box 5, folder 23, AP.

11. Old Left and New

1. James R. Barrett, *William Z. Foster and the Tragedy of American Radicalism* (Urbana: University of Illinois Press, 1999), 266.

2. Dorothy Rae Healey and Maurice Isserman, *California Red: A Life in the American Communist Party* (1990; reprint, Urbana: University of Illinois Press, 1993), 172, 173; Peggy Dennis, *The Autobiography of an American Communist* (Berkeley: Lawrence Hill, 1977), 237; Ben Dobbs, quoted in Healey and Isserman, *California Red,* 173.

3. HA, "On the 40th Anniversary of the Communist Party of the United States of America." Manuscript, date uncertain although probably close to September 1959, box 7, folder 11, AP.

4. Ibid.

5. Healey and Isserman, *California Red,* 173; Dennis, *Autobiography,* 237–38.

6. "Unrepentent Rebel," 290; Helen C. Camp, *Iron in Her Soul: Elizabeth Gurley Flynn and the American Left* (Pullman: Washington State University Press, 1995), 289; Healey and Isserman, *California Red,* 224.

7. Mark Solomon, e-mail to the author, 27 November 2004.

8. Fischer interview I, 354–55, 356.

9. Ibid., 354; HA to Professor Christian Bay, 31 March 1959, box 6, folder 7, AP.

10. Minna Artson to HA, 13 June 1959; HA to Minna Artson, 16 June 1959, box 6, folder 6, AP.

11. The writers are quoted in HA, "Ideas in Our Time," *Political Affairs* 37, no. 5 (May 1958): 47–48, 49, 50; HA, "Ideas in Our Time," *Political Affairs* 36, no. 8 (August 1957): 5.

12. HA, "Algeria, France and Freedom," *Political Affairs* 37, no. 7 (July 1958): 11, 12, 16.

13. HA, "The Mid-East: Peace or War? (Part I)," *Political Affairs* 37, no. 8 (August 1958): 53, 55; HA, "The Mid-East: Peace or War (Part II)," *Political Affairs* 37, no. 9 (September 1958): 40, 54, 55.

14. HA to Howard Selsam, 14 July 1958, box 6, folder 1, AP.

15. New York FBI Field Office report, 30 October 1962.

16. Healey and Isserman, *California Red,* 175, 178.

17. Elizabeth Gurley Flynn to HA, 24 March 1963, box 9, folder 18, AP.

18. Irwin Unger, *The Movement: A History of the American New Left 1959–1972* (New York: Dodd, Mead, 1974), 19.

19. Tom Bottomore, "Mills, Charles Wright (1916–1962)," in *Encyclopedia of the American Left,* ed. Mari Jo Buhle, Paul Buhle, Dan Georgakas, 2nd ed. (New York: Oxford University Press, 1998), 497.

20. HA, *The World of C. Wright Mills* (New York: Marzani and Munsell, 1960), 8, 9.

21. Mike Forrest Keen, *Stalking the Sociological Imagination: J. Edgar Hoover's FBI Surveillance of American Sociology* (Westport, Conn.: Greenwood, 1999), 171.

22. Ibid. In this sentence "contentious intellectual style" and "to observe the noblesse oblige of sparing his colleagues in print" are quotations taken by Keen from Irving Louis Horowitz, *C. Wright Mills: An American Utopian* (New York: Free Press, 1983), 83, a critical biography of Mills.

23. C. Wright Mills to Carl Marzani, 18 June 1960, box 7, folder 12, AP.

24. Ibid.

25. Ibid.

26. HA to C. Wright Mills, 28 June 1960, box 7, folder 12, AP.

27. HA to C. Wright Mills, 7 April 1961, box 8, folder 7, AP.

28. "Unrepentent Rebel," 301.

29. HA to The Editors, *Studies on the Left,* 11 May 1962, box 9, folder 6, AP.

30. Ibid.

31. C. Wright Mills, "Letter to the New Left," *New Left Review,* no. 5 (September–October 1960): 18–23.

32. Maurice Isserman, *Which Side Were You On? The American Communist Party during the Second World War* (Urbana: University of Illinois Press, 1993), 255.

33. Healey and Isserman, *California Red,* 185.

34. Marty Sklar to HA, box 6, folder 33, AP.

35. HA, "Signs of a Change," *Political Affairs,* January 1960, 61–65.

36. Paul Buhl, "New Left," in Buhl, Buhl, and Georgakis, *Encyclopedia,* 546.

37. Ron Radosh, *Commies: A Journey Through the Old Left, the New Left and the Leftover Left* (San Francisco: Encounter, 2001), 66, 67.

38. Ibid.

39. Ronald Radosh to HA, 3 March 1960, box 7, folder 16, AP.

40. Ronald Radosh to HA, 27 September 1960, box 7, folder 16, AP.

41. Ed Moser to HA, 14 May 1960, box 7, folder 12, AP.

42. Radosh, *Commies,* 72.

43. William Appleman Williams to HA, November 1960, box 7, folder 19, AP.

44. "Unrepentent Rebel," 392.

45. John Bracey to the author, margin notes on an earlier draft of this chapter, May 2013.

46. Mills, "Letter to the New Left."

47. Transcript of a House Committee on Un-American Activities Committee hearing, 31 May 1961, box 88, folder 15, AP, 355–58, 361–62.

48. HA, *To Be Free* (New York: Citizens' Committee for Constitutional Liberties, 1961), 57.

49. Director, FBI to SAC, Buffalo, 3 October 1962.

50. "Unrepentent Rebel," 336, 352–54.

51. Meg Yuckman to HA, 6 May 1961, box 7, folder 12, AP.

52. HA to Meg Yuckman, 9 May 1961, box 7, folder 12, AP.

53. Untitled article, *Detroit Free Press,* 17 November 1961, 5, box 88, folder 2, AP.

54. Ibid.

55. HA to W. E. B. Du Bois, 12 December 1962, box 8, folder 20, AP.

56. "Unrepentent Rebel," 366.

12. The Dangerous Enemy in Our Midst

1. Nelson Blackstock, *COINTELPRO: The FBI's Secret War on Political Freedom* (New York: Vintage, 1975), vii; J. Edgar Hoover, *Masters of Deceit: The Story of Communism in America and How to Fight It* (New York: Henry Holt, 1958), v, viii.

2. Howard Fast, *Being Red: A Memoir* (New York: M. E. Sharp, 1994), 166–67.

3. "Unrepentent Rebel," 349.

4. Unsigned letter to HA, undated, box 88, folder 16, AP.

5. Murrell interview. The FBI called Aptheker just before one of our sessions began.

6. SAC, Seattle to Director, FBI, 4 May 1962.

7. Director FBI to SAC Seattle, FBI Memorandum, 14 May 1962.

8. HA to The Editor, *University of Washington Daily,* 26 April 1962, box 9, folder 3, AP.

9. Director, FBI to SAC, Buffalo, 3 October 1962.

10. F. J. Baumgardner to W. C. Sullivan, FBI Memorandum, 17 October 1962.

11. "Unrepentent Rebel," 366–67.

12. Ibid., 367

13. SAC, Seattle to Director, FBI, FBI Memorandum, 29 May 1963.

14. Ibid.

15. "Unrepentent Rebel," 375.

16. HA to Corliss Lamont, 4 November 1963, box 10, folder 1, AP.

17. HA to Robert Cohen, 11 December 1963, box 9, folder 14, AP.

18. HA to Fay Aptheker, 25 April 1962, box 158, folder 14, AP.

19. Ken Margolis to HA, 27 September 1962, box 8, folder 29, AP.

20. Margolis to HA, 5 October 1962, box 8, folder 29, AP.

21. Margolis to HA, 17 October 1962, box 8, folder 29, AP.

22. SAC, New York to Director, FBI, 13 March 1964.

23. "Unrepentent Rebel," 424.

24. HA to Hy and Betty Lumer, 7 September 1964, Microfilm roll 4221, Elizabeth Gurley Flynn Papers, Tamiment Library, New York University.

25. Ibid.

26. Art and Ester Shields, "Thousands at Funeral in Red Square Bid Farewell to Elizabeth Gurley Flynn," *The Worker,* 13 September 1964, 1, 10.

27. HA to Hy and Betty Lumer, 7 September 1964.

28. "End of the Rebel Girl," *Time,* 18 September 1964, 41–42.

29. HA quoted in, Helen Camp, *Iron in Her Soul: Elizabeth Gurley Flynn and the American Left* (Pullman: Washington State University Press, 1995), 322; "Unrepentent Rebel," 424A–425.

30. SAC, Boston to Director, FBI, FBI Memorandum, 14 September 1964.

31. FBI Memorandum, 14 September 1964.

32. SAC, St. Louis to Director, FBI, 11 February 1965.

33. Charles Lane, "Daddy's Boy: The Roots of Pat Buchanan's Authoritarianism," *New Republic,* 22 January 1996.

34. SAC, St. Louis, 11 February 1965.

35. F. J. Baumgardner to W. C. Sullivan, FBI Memorandum, 12 February 1965.

36. Patrick J. Buchanan, *Right from the Beginning* (Washington, D.C.: Regnery, 1990), 295.

37. Patrick J. Buchanan and Denny Walsh, "Top Commie Talks at Meeting Here," *St. Louis Globe Democrat,* 15 February 1965, A, 1.

38. Ibid.

39. Buchanan, *Right from the Beginning,* 295.

40. Ibid., 296.

41. "Unrepentent Rebel," 456–57.

42. F. J. Baumgardner to Mr. Sullivan, FBI Memorandum, 24 February 1965.

43. Lane, "Daddy's Boy."

44. Buchanan, *Right from the Beginning,* 296.

45. F. J. Baumgardner to Mr. Sullivan, FBI Memorandum, 17 March 1965.

46. Ibid.

47. Ibid.

48. Letter to the editor signed by ten faculty members, *Ohio State Lantern,* 28 April 1965, copied in an FBI file.

49. Letter to the editor signed by sixty-seven faculty members, *Ohio State Lantern,* 3 May 1965, copied in an FBI file.

50. Cincinnati FBI office to Director, FBI, 13 May 1965.

51. Edmund D. Mason, SAC Cincinnati to Director, FBI, 17 May 1965.

52. W. C. Sullivan to F. J. Baumgardner, FBI memorandum, 20 May 1965.

53. Leonard Downie Jr., "Ohio Campus to Protest Ban on Free Speech," *Providence Journal,* 6 May 1965, box 91, folder 24, AP.

54. SAC Cincinnati to Director FBI, 7 May 1965, "Free Speech Front Demonstration at Ohio University," FBI File on the Ohio Free Speech Movement. The file supplied to the author by the FBI on the Ohio Free Speech Movement runs to about two hundred pages.

55. FBI Memorandum, 14 May 1965.

56. FBI Memorandum, 20 May 1965; F. J. Baumgardner to W. C. Sullivan, FBI Memorandum, 20 May 1965.

57. "Attempt to Defy Ohio State Rule on Speakers Ends in a Reading," *New York Times,* 24 May 1965, 34.

58. "Defiant Ohio State Students Offer (silent) Banned Guest," *Miami Herald,* 25 May 1965, Counter Attack Papers, Tamiment Library, New York University.

59. "Unrepentent Rebel," 444; FBI Memorandum, 25 May 1965.

60. "Defiant Ohio State," 25 May 1965.

61. FBI Memorandum, 25 May 1965.

62. SAC, Cincinnati to Director, FBI, 21 May 1965.

63. Marci Hilt, "Aptheker Calls Dispute 'Sad,'" *Ohio State Lantern,* 11 May 1965, 1.

64. "OSU Trustees to Meet Faculty Panel on Rule," *Columbus Evening Dispatch,* 7 July 1965, 1.

65. HA to Mr. Ron Greene, 20 August 1965, box 91, folder 26, AP.

66. "Unrepentent Rebel," 444.

67. F. J. Baumgardner to W. C. Sullivan, FBI Memorandum, 20 September 1965.

68. SAC, Seattle to Director, FBI, 29 May 1963.

69. "Unrepentent Rebel," 444.

70. Michael Padwee to HA, 6 January 1965, folder 16, Padwee Collection, Tamiment Library, New York University.

71. HA to Fay Aptheker, 9 February 1965, box 158, folder 17, AP.

72. "Unrepentent Rebel," 439.

73. John Sullivan and Greg Hill to HA, 1 October 1965, box 14, folder 26, AP.

74. SAC, Boston to Director, FBI, FBI Memorandum, 14 July 1965.

75. SAC, Detroit to Director, FBI, 10 February 1965.

76. SAC, Chicago to Director, FBI, FBI Memorandum, 27 August 1965.

77. FBI Memorandum, 27 August 1965.

78. Julie Kailin, "The Communist Scholar in the United States: A Case Study of Herbert Aptheker," manuscript, 69, in the author's possession.

79. "Unrepentent Rebel," 453.

80. Kailin, "The Communist Scholar in the United States," 70.

81. "Unrepentent Rebel," 453.

82. Ibid.

83. SAC, New York to Director, FBI, FBI Memorandum, 21 September 1965.

84. SAC, Chicago to Director, FBI, FBI Memorandum, 7 October 1965.

85. Director FBI to SAC, New York, 10 August 1965.

86. SAC, New York to Director, FBI, FBI Memorandum, 21 September 1965.

87. Ibid.

88. Director FBI to SAC, New York, 10 August 1965.

13. Mission to Hanoi

1. HA to Fay Aptheker, 12 July 1965, box 158, folder 17, AP.

2. HA, *Mission to Hanoi* (New York: International, 1966), 12.

3. HA, "Southeast Asia and the United States," *Political Affairs* 41, no. 7 (July 1962): 21–35.

4. Ibid., 26.

5. Ibid., 28.

6. Ibid., 28, 29.

7. Ibid., 33.

8. Ibid., 34, 35.

9. FBI, Memorandum, San Francisco, 17 March 1965.

10. Ibid.

11. FBI, Memorandum, New York, 17 March 1965.

12. J. Edgar Hoover to United States Secret Service, 21 May 1965.

13. International Publishers issued the first volume of Aptheker's projected multi-volume work, *A History of the American People: The Colonial Era,* in 1959. The second volume, *A History of the American People: The American Revolution 1763–1783,* appeared in 1960, but he did not finish the third, and ultimately the final volume, *A History of the American People: The Early Years of the Republic,* until 1976. All three were published by International Publishers.

14. Staughton Lynd, "Academic Freedom Your Story and Mine," *Columbia University Forum,* Fall 1967, 24, 25.

15. Tom Hayden, *Reunion: A Memoir* (New York: Random House, 1988), 176, 177.

16. Ibid., 176.

17. Staughton Lynd, "Aptheker at Fifty: Remarks at a Birthday Dinner," *Liberation,* July 1966, 37.

18. "Unrepentent Rebel," 441; Clayborne Carson, *In Struggle: SNCC and the Black Awakening of the 1960s* (Cambridge: Harvard University Press, 1981), 96.

19. "Unrepentent Rebel," 441. Aptheker's account is the only one available. There is no contemporaneous document to back up this claim. Neither Lynd nor Hayden mentions any meeting between Aptheker and Moses. My attempt to contact Bob Moses to discuss the issue elicited no response.

20. Hayden, *Reunion,* 176.

21. Carson, *In Struggle,* 107.

22. Hayden, *Reunion,* 176.

23. "Unrepentent Rebel," 442.

24. Hayden, *Reunion,* 176.

25. Clipping, 10 January 1966, attached to an FBI Memorandum, SAC, Boston to Director, FBI, 12 January 1966.

26. Staughton Lynd, "Preface," in HA, *Mission to Hanoi,* 10.

27. Lynd, "Aptheker at Fifty," 37.

28. HA, *Mission to Hanoi,* 15–16.

29. HA to Dr. K. Duda, 16 December 1965, box 15, folder 15, AP.

30. Hayden, *Reunion,* 181.

31. Staughton Lynd and Thomas Hayden, *The Other Side* (New York: Signet, 1967), 57.

32. "Unrepentent Rebel," 447.

33. HA, *Mission to Hanoi,* 13.

34. Robert Strange McNamara, *In Retrospect: The Tragedy and Lessons of Vietnam* (New York: Vintage, 1996), 216.

35. HA, *Mission to Hanoi*, 23; Hayden, *Reunion*, 185.

36. HA, *Mission to Hanoi*, 43.

37. Lynd and Hayden, *The Other Side*, 73.

38. "Unrepentent Rebel," 449.

39. Ibid., 450.

40. Lynd and Hayden, *The Other Side*, 98.

41. HA, *Mission to Hanoi*, 50.

42. Ibid., 52.

43. Ibid., 53.

44. Lynd and Hayden, *The Other Side*, 101.

45. Hayden, *Reunion*, 191.

46. HA, *Mission to Hanoi*, 60.

47. Ibid., 61.

48. McNamara, *In Retrospect*, 207–31.

49. Ibid., 226.

50. Lynd and Hayden, *The Other Side*, 117–18.

51. HA, *Mission to Hanoi*, 63.

52. Lynd and Hayden, *The Other Side*, 124–25.

53. McNamara, *In Retrospect*, 229.

54. Ibid.

55. HA, quoted in James W. Clinton, *The Loyal Opposition: Americans in North Vietnam, 1965–1972* (Denver: University Press of Colorado, 1995), 19.

56. "GIs Hear Sour Quote of U.S. Red," *New York Daily News*, 9 January 1966, 6.

57. "3 'New Leftists' May Get Jail for Hanoi Trip," *New York Herald*, 30 December 1965, box 8, folder 9-1326, Counter Attack Papers, Tamiment Library.

58. Ibid.

59. F. J. Baumgardner to W. C. Sullivan, FBI Memorandum, 3 January 1966.

60. SAC, WFO [Washington Field Office] to Director, FBI, 2 January 1966.

61. Director, FBI to SAC, WFO, 7 January 1966.

62. J. Walter Yeagley to Director, FBI, Justice Department Memorandum, 10 January 1966.

63. F. J. Baumgardner to W. C. Sullivan, FBI Memorandum, 11 January 1966.

64. HA, quoted in Clinton, *Loyal Opposition*, 19.

65. New York FBI Office, fifty-eight-page report on the investigation of Aptheker, Lynd, and Hayden, 25 January 1966.

66. HA, transcript of a recording of a speech delivered on 10 February 1966, page 4, recorded by an FBI source, transcribed and forwarded to headquarters by SAC, Detroit to Director, FBI, 7 April 1966.

67. Sen. Frank Lausche, *Congressional Record–Senate*, 20 January 1966, 674.

68. Rep. O. C. Fisher, Congressional Record-Appendix, 10 January 1966, A21.

69. FBI, New York to Director, FBI, 16 January 1966.

70. FBI report of investigation, 25 January 1966.

71. Clinton, *Loyal Opposition,* xxiii.
72. Ibid.
73. Benjamin P. Bowser, "The Sociology of Herbert Aptheker," in *African American History and Radical Historiography: Essays in Honor of Herbert Aptheker,* ed. Herbert Shapiro (Minneapolis: MEP, 1998), 98.
74. Hayden, *Reunion,* 243.
75. Don Meikly, "Students Rap, Praise Lynd," *Boston Traveler,* 11 January 1966, 1.
76. Lynd, "Academic Freedom Your Story and Mine," 25.
77. HA, quoted in Clinton, *Loyal Opposition,* 18.
78. "Unrepentent Rebel," 452, 53.

14. "Let My Name Forever Be Enrolled among the Traitors"

1. "One hour of 'heated debate' over Herbert Aptheker scheduled appearance at Wayne State University in State Senate," *Detroit News,* 11 February 1966, B-7.
2. William Mandel to Gary Murrell, e-mail, 12 August 2001; HA, "Speech of Herbert Aptheker at Ann Arbor, Michigan," FBI transcript of a speech delivered by Aptheker, February 1966, 1–2.
3. Ibid., 8, 9, 10.
4. Ibid., 11.
5. Ibid., 37.
6. Oliver Loud to HA, 3 December 1959, box 6, folder 23, AP.
7. FBI Supplementary Correlation Summary, 17 August 1967.
8. Untitled article, *Detroit News,* 12 February 1966, A-3.
9. Ibid.
10. Ibid.
11. Untitled article, *Detroit News,* 14 February 1966, A-1, 7.
12. Untitled editorial, *Detroit News,* 14 February 1966, A-24.
13. William J. Billingsley, *Communists on Campus: Race, Politics, and the Public University in Sixties North Carolina* (Athens: University of Georgia Press, 1999), 173, 3.
14. Ibid., 65, 83.
15. Bob Joyce, "Reds on Campus: The Speaker Ban Controversy," *Carolina Alumni Review,* Spring 1984, 9.
16. Billingsley, *Communists on Campus,* 178, 177.
17. Joyce, "Reds on Campus," 10.
18. Billingsley, *Communists on Campus,* 181.
19. Ibid., 186.
20. "Aptheker Speech Barred in Carolina," *New York Times,* 8 February 1966.
21. Billingsley, *Communists on Campus,* 188.
22. SAC, New York to Director, FBI, 11 February 1966; Billingsley, *Communists on Campus,* 187, 183.
23. Billingsley, *Communists on Campus,* 190.
24. Ibid., 204.
25. Ibid., 199.

26. "Unrepentent Rebel," 454.

27. "University Stops Talk by Aptheker," *New York Times,* 10 March 1966, A-8.

28. Billingsley, *Communists on Campus,* 198, 199.

29. Ibid., 202–3.

30. "Unrepentent Rebel," 454.

31. "University Stops Talk," *New York Times.*

32. Billingsley, *Communists on Campus,* 203.

33. Ibid., 198–99.

34. Ibid., 203.

35. "University Stops Talk," *New York Times.*

36. Billingsley, *Communists on Campus,* 203.

37. Ibid., 211.

38. Ibid., 216, 217.

39. Ibid., 218, 219.

40. Gregg L. Michel, "Letters to the Editor," *Journal of American History* 88, no. 3 (December 2001): 1228.

41. W. C. Sullivan to F. J. Baumgardner, FBI Memorandum 15 March 1996.

42. F. J. Baumgardner to W. C. Sullivan, FBI Memorandum, 21 March 1966.

43. FBI, thirty-three-page Summary Report on Aptheker's activities for the period 1 April 1966 to 1 June 1966, 6 June 1966. Aptheker did not keep a detailed record of all his speeches, but the FBI surveillance of his movements led agents to keep records of his speeches, which at various times they summarized. The summary includes the place of the speeches, the date, the number of people who attended, and often the title of the presentation.

44. "Top Communist to Talk at U-M," *Miami News,* 1 April 1966. A-20; Louise Blanchard, "Mystery Circular Raps Red's Speech at U-M," *Miami News,* 11 April 1966.

45. Blanchard, "Mystery Circular," *Miami News.*

46. Matt Taylor and Jerry Parker, "Red Packs UM Hall; Student Protest Scanty," *Miami Herald,* 21 April 1966, A-1; "Reasonably Polite U-M Crowd Packs Hall to Hear Red," *Miami News,* 21 April 1966.

47. "Roudebush Raps I.U. for Letting Red Talk," *Indianapolis Star,* 2 May 1966, A-27.

48. FBI Summary Report, 6 June 1966, 20.

49. HA, "The U.S. in Vietnam: An Appraisal," text of Aptheker's remarks at a debate in Boston, 11 December 1966, in *Political Affairs* 46, no. 1 (January 1967): 34–41.

50. FBI Summary Report, 6 June 1966, 20.

51. "Unrepentent Rebel," 462.

52. FBI Summary Report, 6 June 1966, 21.

53. Gil Green, "The Aptheker Campaign," *Political Affairs* 46, no. 1 (January 1967): 26.

54. FBI Summary Report, 6 June 1966, 21.

55. SAC, New York to Director, FBI, 1 June 1966.

56. Director, FBI to SAC, New York, 14 June 1966.

57. SAC, NY to FBI Headquarters, "Correlation Summary," 17 August 1967.

58. Green, "The Aptheker Campaign," 24.

59. Campaign flyer, "Statement by A. J. Muste," box 94, folder 2, AP; "Thomas and Muste Speak Up on Aptheker," *The Aptheker Advocate* 1, Issue 1, August 1966, box 119, folder 14, AP.

60. Campaign flyer, "Thomas and Muste Speak Up on Aptheker."

61. Paul Hofmann, "New Liberal–Radical Coalition Maps 'Good Society' Platform," *New York Times,* 11 June 1966, A-12.

62. Green, "The Aptheker Campaign," 26.

63. "Unrepentent Rebel," 465.

64. Green, "The Aptheker Campaign," 29–30.

65. FBI Summary Report on Aptheker's activities between 28 September and 8 November 1966, 16 November 1966.

66. FBI Summary Report on Aptheker's activities between 9 November 1966 to 9 February 1967, 16 February 1967.

67. Harvey Klehr, John Earl Haynes, and Kyrill M. Anderson, *The Soviet World of American Communism* (New Haven: Yale University Press, 1998), 148.

68. FBI Report on Aptheker's Run for Congress, forty-seven pages, 16 November 1966.

69. HA, "comments on election, prepared for Gil," 10 November 1966, box 94, folder 1, AP.

70. Green, "The Aptheker Campaign," 30.

71. Unidentified newspaper clipping, box 94, folder 5, AP.

72. Al Sostchen and Bill Burrus, "Arsenal Seized in Bronx," *New York Post,* 23 August 1967, 3.

73. Murray Schumach, "Arsenal Uncovered by Raids in Bronx; 4 Suspects Seized," *New York Times,* 23 August 1967, A-1, 41.

74. Edward C. Burkes, "Anti-Red Bomb Plotter Gets Two Years," *New York Times,* 6 February 1968.

15. Aptheker and Du Bois

1. David Levering Lewis, *W. E. B. Du Bois* (New York: Henry Holt, 2000), 570.

2. Roy Wilkins, quoted in Manning Marable, *W. E. B. Du Bois: Black Radical Democrat* (Boston: Twayne, 1986), 214.

3. HA to Shirley Graham Du Bois, 1 September 1963, box 9, folder 15, AP.

4. Shirley Graham Dubois to HA and Fay Aptheker, 2 September 1963, box 9, folder 15, AP.

5. HA to The Editor, *Michigan Chronicle,* date uncertain but probably January or February 1964, box 10, folder 13, AP.

6. Martin Luther King Jr., "Honoring Dr. Du Bois," *Freedomways,* Spring 1968, 105.

7. HA to W. E. B. Du Bois, 19 July 1947, box 2, folder 7, AP.

8. HA to W. E. B. Du Bois, 5 August 1947, box 2, folder 8, AP.

9. W. E. B. Du Bois to HA, 12 August 1947, in *The Correspondence of W. E. B. Du Bois,* ed. HA, paperback ed. (Amherst: University of Massachusetts Press, 1997), 3:176.

10. Bettina Aptheker, *Intimate Politics: How I Grew Up Red, Fought for Free Speech, and Became a Feminist Rebel* [bound galleys] (Emeryville, Calif.: Seal Press, 2006), 70.

11. Shirley Graham Du Bois, *His Day Is Marching On* (New York: Lippincott, 1971), 324.

12. Shirley Graham to HA, 10 June 1950, box 3, folder 5, AP.

13. Gerald Horne, *Race Woman: The Lives of Shirley Graham Du Bois* (New York: New York University Press, 2000), 140.

14. W. E. B. Du Bois to HA, 10 January 1956, box 83, folder 13, AP.

15. Ibid.

16. HA, *History and Reality* (New York: Cameron, 1955), 30.

17. Ibid., 35–36.

18. W. E. B. Du Bois to HA, 10 January 1956.

19. HA to W. E. B. Du Bois, 20 January 1956, box 83, folder 13, AP.

20. W. E. B. Du Bois to HA, 25 August 1961, box 7, folder 4, AP.

21. Levering Lewis, *W. E. B. Du Bois,* 550.

22. W. E. B. Du Bois, in *The Autobiography of W. E. B. Du Bois,* ed. HA (New York: International, 1968), 391.

23. Levering Lewis, *W. E. B. Du Bois,* 556.

24. Marable, *W. E. B. Du Bois,* 196.

25. Du Bois, *Autobiography,* 395.

26. Levering Lewis, *W. E. B. Du Bois,* 566.

27. Graham Du Bois, *His Day,* 323.

28. Ibid., 324.

29. "Unrepentent Rebel," 383.

30. Graham Du Bois, *His Day,* 324–25.

31. Aptheker, *Intimate Politics,* 69.

32. Levering Lewis, *W. E. B. Du Bois,* 567; Graham Du Bois, *His Day,* 325.

33. HA, "W. E. B. Du Bois and Africa," *Political Affairs* 40, no. 3 (March 1961): 19–29.

34. HA, "Dr. Du Bois and Communism," ibid., 13–20.

35. HA to W. E. B. and Shirley Graham Du Bois, 24 November 1961, box 7, folder 26, AP.

36. Aptheker, *Intimate Politics,* 72–73.

37. "Unrepentent Rebel," 385.

38. HA, "Ideas in Our Time," *Political Affairs* 42, no. 2 (February 1963): 36.

39. W. E. B. Du Bois to HA, 12 December 1961, in *Correspondence* 3:436.

40. Arna Bontemps to HA, 20 December 1962, box 8, folder 18, AP.

41. HA to Arna Bontemps, 26 December 1962, box 8, folder 18, AP.

42. Shirley Graham Du Bois to HA and Fay Aptheker, 10 September 1962, box 8, folder 20, AP.

43. HA to W. E. B. Du Bois, 12 December 1962, box 8, folder 20, AP.

44. Levering Lewis, *W. E. B. Du Bois,* 569.

45. Shirley Graham Du Bois to Herbert and Fay Aptheker, 20 January 1963, box 9, folder 15, AP.

46. HA to Shirley Graham Du Bois, 24 January 1963, box 9, folder 15, AP.

47. Shirley Graham Du Bois to HA, 25 February 1963, box 9, folder 15, AP.

48. Graham Du Bois, *His Day,* 363.

49. HA to Shirley Graham Du Bois, 18 October 1963, box 9, folder 15, AP.

50. Shirley Graham Du Bois to HA, 9 December 1963, box 9, folder 15, AP.

51. HA to Shirley Graham Du Bois, 16 December 1963, box 9, folder 15, AP.

52. HA to Shirley Graham Du Bois, 27 December 1963, box 9, folder 15, AP.

53. John Bracey to the author, margin notes in an earlier draft of this chapter, May 2013.

54. HA to Shirley Graham Du Bois, 16 December 1963.

55. Shirley Graham Du Bois to HA, 5 January 1964, box 10, folder 15, AP.

56. Dorothy Burnham to HA, 17 February 1964, box 10, folder 15, AP.

57. HA to Dorothy Burnham, 18 February 1964, box 10, folder 15, AP.

58. Shirley Graham Du Bois to HA, 17 May 1964, box 11, folder 15, AP.

59. HA to Shirley Graham Du Bois, 22 May 1964, box 11, folder 15, AP.

60. Shirley Graham Du Bois to HA, 26 May 1964, box 10, folder 15, AP.

61. HA to Shirley Graham Du Bois, 2 June 1964, box 10, folder 15, AP.

62. Shirley Graham Du Bois to Esther Cooper Jackson, 31 May 1964, box 10, folder 15, AP.

63. Horne, *Race Woman,* 218, 220.

64. HA to Arna Bontemps, 24 August 1965, box 15, folder 3, AP.

65. HA to Shirley Graham Du Bois, 19 January 1967, box 26, folder 20, AP.

66. Shirley Graham Du Bois to HA, 19 December 1967, box 26, folder 20, AP.

67. HA, "More on a great life," *Nature, Society, and Thought* 13, no. 3 (2000): 385.

68. HA to James C. Daniel, 24 June 1968, box 26, folder 20, AP.

69. HA to Shirley Graham Du Bois, 14 November 1968, box 28, folder 14, AP.

70. Mark Carroll to HA, 21 May 1968, box 28, folder 6, AP.

71. HA to Mark Carroll, 22 May 1968, box 28, folder 6, AP.

72. HA to Ann Orlov, 2 October 1968, box 28, folder 14, AP.

73. HA to Shirley Graham Du Bois, 23 August 1968, box 28, folder 14, AP.

74. Shirley Graham Du Bois to HA, 11 September 1968, box 28, folder 14, AP.

75. Ann Orlov to HA, 7 August and 21 October 1968, box 26, folder 14, AP.

76. HA to Robert Cohen, 8 October 1968, box 28, folder 13, AP.

77. HA to Shirley Graham Du Bois, 14 November 1968, box 28, folder 14, AP.

78. John W. Blassingame to HA, 31 July 1968, box 28, folder 11, AP.

79. HA to "Ladies and Gentlemen," 5 August 1968, box 28, folder 11, AP.

80. HA to Shirley Graham Du Bois, 14 November 1969, box 31, folder 5, AP.

81. Ibid.

82. HA to Leone Stein, 27 October 1969, box 31, folder 13, AP.

83. HA, memo of a phone conversation, 10 November 1969, box 31, folder 13, AP.

84. Leone Stein to HA, 26 November 1969, box 31, folder 13, AP.

85. HA to Gus Hall, 17 December 1969, box 31, folder 8, AP.

16. Publishing Du Bois

1. *New York Times,* 16 February 1969, S-25.

2. Mindy Thompson Fullilove, "Texts, Contexts, and Subtexts: Herbert Aptheker and the Human Spirit," in *African American History and Radical Historiography: Essays in Honor of Herbert Aptheker,* ed. Herbert Shapiro (Minneapolis: MEP, 1998), 155.

3. Styron, quoted in "Unrepentent Rebel," 469.

4. William Styron to HA, 18 March 1961, box 52, folder 12, AP.

5. William Styron to HA, 27 March 1961, box 52, folder 12, AP.

6. William Styron, "Overcome," *New York Review of Books,* 26 September 1963, 18–19.

7. HA to William Styron, 5 August 1964, box 52, folder 12, AP.

8. William Styron, "William Styron Replies," *Nation,* 22 April 1968, 544.

9. HA, *Afro-American History: The Modern Era* (Secaucus, N.J: Citadel, 1973), 85.

10. William Styron, quoted in HA, "Truth & Nat Turner: An Exchange," *Nation,* 22 April 1968, 543.

11. HA, "Styron's Turner—Again," edited draft of an article that appeared in the *Nation,* box 52, folder 12, AP.

12. George Plimpton, "William Styron: A Shared Ordeal," *New York Review of Books,* 8 October 1967, 1.

13. HA, *Afro-American History,* 85.

14. Jack E. Eblen to HA, 17 May 1968, box 26, folder 3, AP.

15. HA to Jack E. Eblen, 20 May 1968, box 26, folder 3, AP.

16. Fullilove, "Texts, Contexts," 156.

17. Jack Hovelson, "Legislator, U.N.I. Students Clash on Campus Speakers," *Des Moines Register,* March, 1969, A-1, box 99, folder 31, AP.

18. Katharine McBride, telegram, 28 April 1969, box 29, folder 23, AP.

19. HA to Robert Ross and Jesse Lemisch, 29 August 1968, box 29, folder 9, AP.

20. "Bryn Mawr Names Aptheker a Visiting History Lecturer," *New York Times,* 17 June 1969, box 97, folder 12, AP.

21. Untitled article, *Evening Bulletin,* 1 July 1969, A-10.

22. Mrs. Martinus H. Nickerson to Dear Parents of Bryn Mawr Students, 25 August 1969, box 29, folder 23, AP.

23. HA to Jesse Lemisch, 28 November 1969, box 31, folder 12, AP.

24. Susan Walker, "Aptheker Holds First College Course; A Gentle Man," *The News,* 19 September 1969, 1.

25. HA to Jesse Lemisch, 28 November 1969, box 31, folder 12, AP.

26. HA to Alfred Young, 10 July 1972, box 41, folder 11, AP.

27. HA to Louis Ruchames, 31 December 1970, box 35, folder 12, AP.

28. HA to Alfred Young, 10 July 1972, box 41, folder 11, AP.

29. Michael Thelwell to HA, 23 May 1972, box 41, folder 6, AP.

30. Katherine Baxter to HA, 1 June 1970, box 33, folder 5, AP.

31. HA to Jeff Kaplow, 18 March 1970, box 34, folder 13, AP.

32. Harris Wofford to HA, 14 December 1972; HA to Harris Wofford, 27 December 1972, box 39, folder 7, AP.

33. Arthur Dudden to HA, 17 April 1973, box 41, folder 15, AP.

34. HA, "Wire service stirs anti-Communist smut against Aptheker," *Daily World,* 11 May 1973, 8.

35. Andrew Silk, "Afro-American History Post in Doubt; Blacks Issue New Statement," *The News,* 30 March 1973, 1, 4.

36. Ibid., 4.

37. HA to Louis D. Boccardi, 18 April 1973, box 41, folder 13, AP.

38. Arthur Dudden to HA, 17 April 1973, box 41, folder 15, AP.

39. HA to Arthur Dudden, 18 April 1973, box 41, folder 15, AP.

40. Patricia Oldham to HA, 20 April 1973, box 41, folder 15, AP.

41. Bettina Aptheker, *Intimate Politics: How I Grew Up Red, Fought for Free Speech, and Became a Feminist Rebel* [bound galleys] (Emeryville, Calif.: Seal Press, 2006), 14–15.

42. Leone Stein to HA, 12 February 1970, with handwritten notations by Aptheker, box 35, folder 1, AP.

43. HA to Leone Stein, 9 December 1970, box 35, folder 1, AP.

44. Leone Stein to HA, 9 September 1970, box 35, folder 1, AP.

45. Henry Tragle to HA, 16 December 1970, box 36, folder 1, AP.

46. "Application Summary," National Endowment for the Humanities (NEH), application H-7708, October 1970, received through a Freedom of Information Act request, in the author's possession. The NEH said in response to a Freedom of Information Act request that all of the other applications and reviewers' comments had been destroyed.

47. Ibid.

48. Ibid. (emphasis added).

49. Jesse Lemisch, interview by the author, 28 March 2001.

50. HA to Henry I. Tragle, 28 December 1970 box 36, folder 1, AP; "Grant Report from The Association of American University Presses," Grant Number H67-0-111, National Endowment for the Humanities, box 36, folder 1, AP.

51. HA to C. Vann Woodward, 15 January 1971, box 39, folder 3, AP.

52. C. Vann Woodward to HA, 26 January 1971, box 39, folder 3, AP.

53. HA to C. Vann Woodward, 1 February 1971, box 39, folder 3, AP.

54. C. Vann Woodward to HA, 16 February 1971, box 39, folder 3, AP.

55. HA to C. Vann Woodward, 25 February 1971, box 39, folder 3, AP.

56. C. Vann Woodward to HA, 17 March 1971, box 37, folder 12, AP.

57. Eugene Genovese, telephone interview by the author, 29 September 2001.

58. New York, FBI, Memorandum, 26 July 1972, report on Communist Party Central Committee meeting.

59. HA to Paul M. Wright, 17 April 1972, box 40, folder 11, AP.

60. Leone Stein, e-mail to the author, 5 June 2014; Leone Stein to Alfred Young, 12 December 1972, box 39, folder 7, AP.

61. HA to Edward Brooke, 4 December 1972, box 39, folder 7, AP.

62. Bernard Perry to HA, 21 November 1972, box 40, folder 3, AP.

63. HA to Bernard Perry, 13 December 1972, box 40, folder 3, AP.

64. Bernard Perry to HA, 22 December 1972, box 40, folder 3, AP.

65. John Hope Franklin to Malcolm Call, 15 March 1973, box 43, folder 9; John Hope Franklin to HA, 30 July 1973, box 43, folder 7, AP.

66. Untitled article, *Springfield Sunday Republican,* 15 July 1973, 1, 12.

67. HA to Shirley Graham Du Bois, 5 December 1973, box 43, folder 6, AP.

68. HA to John Hope Franklin, 1 August 1973, box 43, folder 7, AP.

69. HA to Louis R. Harlan 25 September 1973, box 43, folder 10, AP.

70. C. Vann Woodward to HA, 21 August 1973, box 44, folder 8, AP.

71. HA to C. Vann Woodward, 28 August 1973, box 44, folder 8, AP.

72. C. Vann Woodward to Leone Stein, 28 January 1974, box 46, folder unidentified, probably 11 or 12, AP.

73. Malcolm Call to Louis R. Harlan, 15 February 1974, box 46, folder unidentified, probably 11 or 12, AP.

74. C. Vann Woodward to HA, 27 February 1974, box 46, folder unidentified, probably 11 or 12, AP.

75. HA to C. Vann Woodward, 1 March 1974, box 46, folder unidentified, probably 11 or 12, AP.

76. Leone Stein to HA, 31 July 1974, box 46, folder 13, AP.

77. George F. Farr to Leone Stein and John Bracey, 30 June 1976, box 51, folder 3, AP.

78. Leone Stein and John Bracey to George F. Farr, 12 July 1976, box 51, folder 3, AP.

79. Simone Reagor to Leone Stein and John Bracey, 6 August 1976, box 51, folder 7, AP.

80. HA to Leone Stein, 21 July 1976, box 51, folder 3, AP.

81. HA, memo to himself, 7 June 1976, box 49, folder 25, AP.

82. Leone Stein to Bud Salk, 30 August 1977, box 54, folder 14, AP.

83. HA to Eric Foner, 5 January 1979, box 57, folder 10, AP.

84. HA, interview by James W. Clinton, 14 November 1990, San Jose, Calif., box 76, folder 7, AP.

85. John Bracey, interview by the author, Boston, 26 March 2004.

86. Ibid.

87. John Bracey to Editors, *Radical History Review* 1987, no. 37 (9 February 1987), box 70, folder 20, AP.

88. Eugene Genovese and Elizabeth Fox-Genovese to Editors, *Radical History Review* 1986, no. 36 (15 December 1986), box 70, folder 1, AP.

89. Eugene Genovese to HA, 10 December 1986, box 70, folder 1, AP.

90. Beth Goldstein, "W. E. B. Du Bois Remembered: Library Formally Dedicated," University of Massachusetts *Chronicle,* 29 February 1996.

91. John Bracey, "Statement for Herbert Aptheker's Memorial Service," 30 March 2003, provided to the author by Bettina Aptheker. In the author's possession.

17. Yale Historians and the Challenge to Academic Freedom

1. Staughton Lynd, "The Bulldog Whitewashed: A Critique of the Investigation of Herbert Aptheker's Nonappointment at Yale University," in *African American History and Radical Historiography: Essays in Honor of Herbert Aptheker,* ed. Herbert Shapiro (Minneapolis: MEP, 1998), 119.

2. Jack and Letha Sandweiss to HA, 10 March 1975, box 49, folder 9, AP.

3. Fred Strebeigh, "The Aptheker Case: 'Massive Attack on a Minor Appointment,'" *Yale Alumni Magazine* 39, no. 5 (February 1976): 29.

4. Ibid., 30.

5. Ibid.

6. Ibid.

7. HA, "Challenge to integrity: Worst attack for a scholar," *Daily World,* 29 January 1976, 6.

8. Robert A. Blecker, "Aptheker and Power," *Yale Daily News,* 4 February 1977, 2, 11.

9. HA, "Challenge to integrity," 6.

10. C. Vann Woodward, quoted in Jesse Lemisch, "If Howard Cossell can teach at Yale, why can't Herbert Aptheker?," pamphlet distributed on the Yale campus and at the AHA meeting, April 1976, papers of Marvin Gettleman, in the author's possession; C. Vann Woodward, letter to the editor, "Aptheker," *Yale Daily News,* 2 February 1976; Strebeigh, "The Aptheker Case," 30. All items cited from the Gettleman papers in this chapter are in the author's possession. The historian Paul Buhle wrote that the radical historians working on the Aptheker defense had as a "first idea for a Defense Committee . . . a slogan like 'Defend the Butcher of Budapest,'" but they "had to settle for the levity of asking whether Yale could consider Aptheker qualified after they had hired Howard Cosell for the same job." Paul Buhle to Professor Hoglund, summer 1976, Paul Buhle Papers, Tamiment Library, New York University.

11. C. Vann Woodward, "An Interview Between Comer Vann Woodward and John Herbert Roper," 4–5 November 1982, Memphis, Tennessee, John Herbert Roper Papers #4235, Southern Historical Collection, Wilson Library, University of North Carolina at Chapel Hill.

12. HA, "Aptheker hired by Yale, fired by 'ad hoc' group," *Daily World,* 18 December 1975, 4.

13. Joseph LaPalombara, "Aptheker: Academic Overkill," *Yale Daily News,* 17 December 1975, 1.

14. Strebeigh, "The Aptheker Case," 29.

15. HA, "Challenge to Integrity," 6.

16. Bettina Aptheker to HA, 11 December 1975, box 49, folder 22, AP.

17. HA to Bettina Aptheker, 2 February 1976, box 49, folder 22, AP. Lemisch, "If Howard Cossell Can Teach," pamphlet.

18. Lemisch, "If Howard Cossell Can Teach," pamphlet.

19. "Dr. Aptheker Cheered by 250 at Yale Lecture," *Daily World,* 24 February 1976.

20. "Yale University and Dr. Herbert Aptheker," A Report of the Joint AHA–OAH Committee on the Defense of the Rights of Historians Under the First Amendment, final draft, 6 December 1977, 11 (hereafter cited as AHA–OAH Draft Report.) In the author's possession.

21. Marvin Gettleman to C. Vann Woodward, 4 March 1976, Gettleman papers.

22. C. Vann Woodward to Marvin Gettleman, 15 March 1976, Gettleman papers.

23. Ramsay MacMullen to Henry Turner, 28 October 1976, papers of Ramsay MacMullen. All items from the MacMullen papers cited in this chapter are in the author's possession

24. Ibid.

25. Randy Smith, "Profs Question 2nd Aptheker Veto," *Yale Graduate Professional* 5, no. 19 ½ (25 March 1976): 1.

26. Ramsay MacMullen, e-mail to the author, 29 May 2014; MacMullen to Turner, 28 October 1976.

27. Ramsay MacMullen to the Editor, *Journal of American History* 87, no. 4 (March 2001): 1600.

28. Ramsay MacMullen to Henry [Turner], 10 May 1977, MacMullen papers.

29. Ramsay MacMullen to Mrs. Hanna Gray, 26 May 1977, MacMullen papers.

30. Ramsay MacMullen to Charles Crowe, 7 December 1983, MacMullen papers.

31. AHA–OAH Draft Report, 11–13.

32. HA to Arthur S. Link, 15 April 1976, box 51, folder 2, AP.

33. HA, quoted in John Herbert Roper, *C. Vann Woodward, Southerner* (Athens: University of Georgia Press, 1987), 283.

34. Jesse Lemisch, interview by the author, 28 March 2001.

35. HA to Jesse Lemisch, 6 February 1975 [misdated], box 107, folder 39, AP.

36. Eugene Genovese to C. Vann Woodward, 7 April 1976, Gettleman papers.

37. Ibid.; C. Vann Woodward to Eugene Genovese, 23 February 1976, box 50, folder 8, AP.

38. Arthur Schlesinger Jr. and John M. Blum, cited in Roper, *C. Vann Woodward,* 284, 57, 58.

39. Jesse Lemisch and Marvin Gettleman to HA, date obscured [early April 1976], box 51, folder 1, AP. Lemisch says that the wording on the card is "totally Marv and not at all Jesse" so Gettleman may have written the card and signed both their names. Jesse Lemisch, e-mail to the author, 23 June 2014.

40. AHA–OAH Draft Report, 15.

41. Marvin Gettleman to C. Vann Woodward, 14 April 1976, Gettleman papers.

42. Marvin Gettleman to C. Vann Woodward, 7 April 1976, Gettleman papers.

43. Jesse Lemisch to Mike Wallace et al., 24 February 1976, Paul Buhle Papers, Tamiment Library, New York University.

44. "The Yale–Aptheker Resolution," *OAH Newsletter,* July 1976, 3–6.

45. Robert A. Blecker, "Aptheker and Power," *Yale Daily News,* 4 February 1977, 2.

46. "Statement of Dr. Herbert Aptheker Communist Candidate for U.S. Senator from New York," 22 September 1976, papers of Tony Flood, in the author's possession.

47. Campaign brochure, "Dr. Herbert Aptheker for the U.S. Senate," box 109, folder 33, AP.

48. John Stanley to HA, 20 October 1976, box 52, folder 2, AP.

49. Sarah Montgomery to HA, 13 September 1975, box 48, folder 11, AP.

50. HA to Sarah Montgomery, 16 September 1975, box 48, folder 11, AP.

51. HA to John Stanley, 22 October 1976, box 52, folder 2, AP.

52. Bettina Aptheker, *Intimate Politics: How I Grew Up Red, Fought for Free Speech, and Became a Feminist Rebel* [bound galleys] (Emeryville, Calif.: Seal, 2006), 326, 329–30.

53. Sarah Montgomery to HA, 30 July 1977, box 53, folder 6, AP.

54. HA to Sarah Montgomery, 1 August 1977 [misdated as 1 July 1977], box 53, folder 6, AP.

55. HA to Gus Hall, 25 June 1979, box 59, folder 3, AP.

56. HA to Richard W. Leopold and Charles Gibson, 25 February 1977; HA to Richard Kirkendall, 24 March 1977, box 53, folder 4, AP.

57. Robert Wiebe to HA, 7 June 1977, box 53, folder 17, AP.

58. Richard Kirkendall to Stanley Katz, 8 July 1977, box 54, folder 12, AP.

59. Stanley Katz to Staughton Lynd, with a copy to HA and Jesse Lemisch, 14 July 1977, box 54, folder 12, AP.

60. Staughton Lynd to Tom Emerson, 30 July 1977, box 54, folder 13, AP.

61. Kenneth Stampp, quoted in Thomas Emerson and Staughton Lynd to AHA–OAH Joint Committee, 4 December 1977, box 53, folder 13, AP.

62. Staughton Lynd to HA, 4 December 1977, box 54, folder 13, AP.

63. Emerson and Lynd to AHA–OAH Joint Committee, 4 December 1977.

64. Jesse Lemisch to Alden Whitman (with copies to Staughton Lynd and HA), 16 December 1977, box 54, folder 13, AP.

65. "Findings," AHA–OAH Report.

66. Ibid.

67. Lynd, "The Bulldog Whitewashed," 148.

68. C. Vann Woodward, quoted in ibid., 149.

69. AHA–OAH Report.

70. Lynd, "The Bulldog Whitewashed," 150–51.

71. Eugene Genovese, telephone interview by the author, 29 September 2001.

72. Herbert Shapiro, " 'Political Correctness' and the U.S. Historical Profession," in Shapiro, *African American History,* 327.

73. Marvin Gettleman to "Friends and Comrades," [Jesse Lemisch, Staughton Lynd, Mark Naison, and others] 23 February 1978, box 55, folder 18, AP. "In what way or ways should our strategy in this matter take account of the fact that Brother Genovese is president-elect of the OAH this year, and is sure to oppose any action?" Gettleman wrote to the rest of the group.

74. Marvin Gettleman to Charles Crowe, 8 December 1983, Gettleman papers; Marvin Gettleman to Jim [O'Brien?], 11 March 1978, Gettleman papers.

75. Staughton Lynd to Marvin Gettleman, 27 February 1978, box 55, folder 18, AP.

76. Lynd, "The Bulldog Whitewashed," 138.

77. Stanley N. Katz and Robert H. Wiebe to Executive Board Colleague, 10 March 1978, Gettleman papers.

78. Stanley N. Katz to Alfred Young, 27 March 1978, Gettleman papers.

79. Marvin Gettleman to Staughton, Herb, Jesse and Al [Young?], 5 April 1978, Gettleman papers.

80. Stanley N. Katz, telephone interview by the author, 22 June 2014; Stanley N. Katz, e-mail to the author, 22 June 2014; Katz, interview by author; Katz to the author, 22 June 2014.

81. "Executive Board Discussion of the Report," *OAH Newsletter,* July 1978.

82. Kenneth Stampp, http://texts.cdlib.org, 253.

83. "Executive Board Discussion of the Report," *OAH Newsletter,* July 1978.

84. Marvin Gettleman to Herb, Staughton, Al, 17 April 1978, Gettleman papers.

85. Katz, interview by author.

86. HA to Fay Aptheker, 19 February 1963, box 158, folder 15, AP.

87. "The Business Meeting," *OAH Newsletter,* July 1978.

88. Marvin Gettleman, "Statement in Response to the OAH/AHA Report on Herbert Aptheker and Yale University," 14 April 1978, Gettleman papers. Gettleman's remarks are faithfully transcribed in the *OAH Newsletter,* July, 1978.

89. Gettleman to Herb, Staughton, Al, 17 April 1978.

90. C. Vann Woodward, interview by James Green, *Radical History Review,* no. 36 (1986): 80–100.

91. Eugene D. and Elizabeth Fox-Genovese; Hugh Murray; Manning Marable; John Bracey; Jesse Lemisch, letters to The Editors, *Radical History Review,* no. 38 (1987): 144–46.

92. Lemisch, *On Active Service* (Toronto: New Hogtown Press, 1975), 117.

93. Charles Crowe, "An Historical Inquiry into the Herbert Aptheker Controversy," a proposal for research, 29 November 1983, attached to a letter to Marvin Gettleman, Gettleman papers.

94. Lemisch, *On Active Service,* 117.

18. The American Institute for Marxist Studies

1. Bettina Aptheker, "The Weight of Inheritance," in *Red Diapers: Growing Up in the Communist Left,* ed. Judy Kaplan and Linn Shapiro (Urbana: University of Illinois Press, 1998), 282.

2. FBI Summary Report, 14 December 1961.

3. HA to Anton [unknown], 14 October 1963, box 10, folder 6, AP.

4. Murrell interview.

5. Dorothy Healey and Maurice Isserman, *California Red: A Life in the American Communist Party* (1990; reprint, Urbana: University of Illinois Press, 1993), 224.

6. Murrell interview.

7. Ibid.

8. Ibid.

9. FBI report on meeting of National Executive Committee, 27–28 May 1963. The report appears to be compiled either from detailed notes by one or more informers who attended the meeting or from a tape recording of the meeting.

10. Healey and Isserman, *California Red,* 175, 176.

11. FBI Summary Report, 30 October 1962.

12. HA to Joseph Morray, 27 December 1962, box 8, folder 29, AP.

13. HA, Proposal to establish the American Institute for Marxist Studies, 29 May 1962, as an attachment to SAC, New York to Director, FBI, 20 June 1962.

14. SAC, New York to Director, FBI, 11 December 1962.

15. SAC, New York to Director, FBI, 20 December 1962. The informer, from information in this and subsequent FBI documents, seems to be one of the Childs brothers, probably Morris. For more, see Harvey Klehr, John Earl Haynes, and Kyrill M. Anderson, *The Soviet World of American Communism* (New Haven: Yale University Press, 1998), 148.

16. Healey and Isserman, *California Red,* 176.

17. SAC, New York to Director, FBI, 21 January 1963.

18. HA to Fay Aptheker, 20 February 1963, box 158, folder 15, AP.

19. Scott Nearing to HA, 16 July 1963, box 9, folder 7, AP.

20. HA to Gaylord LeRoy, 3 November 1963, box 10, folder 1, AP.

21. FBI report on meeting of National Executive Committee, 27–28 May 1963.

22. HA to Shirley Graham Du Bois, 27 December 1963, box 9, folder 15, AP.

23. Robert S. Cohen, in an AIMS advertising brochure, late March or early April 1964, papers of Danny Rubin. All items from the Rubin papers cited in this chapter are in the author's possession.

24. Robert Cohen, quoted in "Minutes of National Governing Council," 24 October 1964, box 1, folder, "Aptheker, Herbert (1959–74)," Labor Research Association Papers, Tamiment Library, New York University.

25. FBI Memorandum prepared by the New York FBI office, 24 April 1964.

26. Robert Cohen to HA, 29 April 1964, box 10, folder 14, AP.

27. HA to Robert Cohen, 2 May 1964, box 10, folder 14, AP.

28. Five-by-eight-inch file card, box 15, folder 16, AP.

29. Minutes of AIMS National Governing Council, 24 October 1964, Rubin papers.

30. Dorothy Healey to HA, 22 January 1964, box 11, folder 1, AP.

31. Dorothy Healey, quoted in FBI Summary Report, 29 June 1964.

32. Minutes of AIMS National Governing Council, 24 October 1964.

33. SAC, Philadelphia to Director, FBI, December 1965.

34. F. J Baumgardner to W. C. Sullivan, FBI Memorandum, 17 May 1965.

35. HA to Robert Dunn, 13 January 1965, box 1, folder, Aptheker, Herbert (1959–74), Labor Research Association Papers, Tamiment Library, New York University. A copy of a letter containing the exact same language appears in Aptheker's FBI file. It is unclear whether it is this letter, in which case the FBI had an informer in Dunn's organization, or perhaps Aptheker sent the same letter to several people on the same day.

36. SAC, New York, to Director, FBI, 8 February 1965.

37. "Aptheker to Speak Tomorrow at Scott," *Rutgers Daily Targum,* 9 March 1965; Steve Houff, "Aptheker Blasts Imperialism, Attacks 'Illusionary Freedom,'" *Rutgers Daily Targum,* 11 March 1965.

38. Chris Phelps, "Herbert Aptheker: The Contradictions of History," *Chronicle of Higher Education* 53, no. 7 (6 October 2006): B12–13.

39. Bettina Aptheker, *Intimate Politics: How I Grew Up Red, Fought for Free Speech, and Became a Feminist Rebel* [bound galleys] (Emeryville, Calif.: Seal Press, 2006), 57.

40. C. Vann Woodward, "Comment," *Studies on the Left* 6, no. 6 (1966): 36, 37.

41. Eugene Genovese, "The Legacy of Slavery and the Roots of Black Nationalism," *Studies on the Left* 6, no. 6 (1966): 19.

42. Ibid., 3.

43. C. Vann Woodward, "Comment," 36.

44. HA, "Comment," *Studies on the Left* 6, no. 6 (1966): 30.

45. Eugene Genovese, *In Red and Black: Marxian Explorations in Southern and Afro-American History* (New York: Vintage, 1971), 197.

46. Eugene Genovese, "Rejoinder," *Studies on the Left* 6, no. 6 (1966): 57–58, 58–59, 60.

47. John Bracey, e-mail to Bruce Wilcox, 13 June 2013, copy in the author's possession.

48. Harold Cruse, *Rebellion or Revolution?* (New York: William Morrow, 1968), 25.

49. Stanley Crouch, "Introduction," in Harold Cruse, *The Crisis of the Negro Intellectual* (New York: New York Review of Books, 2005), vii; Rachel Donadio, "The Cultural Revolutionary," *New York Times,* 29 May 2005.

50. Harold Cruse, *The Crisis of the Negro Intellectual* (New York: Quill, 1984), 158.

51. Genovese, "The Legacy," 22.

52. HA, "Comment," 34.

53. Cruse, *Rebellion or Revolution?*, 203, 204, 205, 210, 212, 223, 224, 242, 246.

54. Cruse, *The Crisis of the Negro Intellectual*, 147, 163, 226–27.

55. Sid Resnick, "Harold Cruse's Attack on Jewish Communists: Comment," *Science & Society* 64, no. 4 (Winter 2000–2001): 395, 399.

56. Aptheker, *Intimate Politics,* 50.

57. HA, *The Urgency of Marxist–Christian Dialogue* (New York: Harper and Row, 1970), 7.

58. Alan Wald, "Narrating Nationalisms: Black Marxism and Jewish Communists Through the Eyes of Harold Cruse," *Science & Society* 64, no. 4 (Winter 2000–2001): 415.

59. Resnick, "Harold Cruse's Attack," 398–99.

60. HA, interview by Benjamin Bowser and Deborah Whittle, 5 June and 4 August 1995, reprinted in *Herbert Aptheker on Race and Democracy: A Reader,* ed. Eric Foner and Manning Marable (Urbana: University of Illinois Press, 2006), 241.

61. New York, FBI Agent Herbert P. Larson, FBI Summary Report, 6 July 1966.

62. Invitation to a tribute to HA, box 1, folder, Aptheker, Herbert (1959–74), Labor Research Association Papers, Tamiment Library, New York University.

63. FBI Summary Report, 6 July 1966.

19. Conflict and Compromise

1. FBI New York, Summary Report, 25 October 1967 to 29 January 1968. New York FBI agents reported in February 1968 that while the probate of the will was "proceeding smoothly," Phil Foner had told party officials that "he wants no part of his inheritance and would like to 'get out of it' using the excuse that it may jeopardize his new appointment as an instructor at Lincoln University." Agents reported that Foner had "attempted to get a 'chunk' of the money" for himself rather than turning it over to the party but the party's attorneys and Gus Hall had convinced him otherwise. FBI informers claimed that Foner decided to "give his legacy to" Aptheker and Harris.

2. HA, typescript of remarks at the 18th National Convention CPUSA, 24 June 1966, box 93, folder 27, AP.

3. HA, remarks at the 18th Convention.

4. Dorothy Healey and Maurice Isserman, *California Red: A Life in the American Communist Party* (1990; reprint Urbana: University of Illinois Press, 1993), 185.

5. HA, "Aptheker," an interview in *Confrontation* 1, no. 1 (1968): 8.

6. Michael Myerson, "On the Crisis in the Party," June 1990, papers of Danny Rubin.

7. HA to Otto H. Olsen, 5 February 1968, box 28, folder 6, AP.

8. Martin Luther King Jr., "Honoring Dr. Du Bois," *Freedomways,* Spring 1968, 109.

9. Al Richmond, *A Long View from the Left* (New York: Dell, 1972), 412.

10. Healey and Isserman, *California Red,* 229.

11. Gus Hall, press release of 21 August 1968, quoted in Healey and Isserman, *California Red,* 230.

12. Healey and Isserman, *California Red,* 231–32.

13. Ibid., 233. "Under Gus's leadership," Healey later wrote, "the American CP had

picked up the dubious distinction of being the chief ideological sheepdog in the international Communist movement, barking on command when any of the other lambs threaten to stray from the fold. The Soviet leaders would contact Gus and tell him what they wanted him to say, he would say it." Healey thought the Soviet Union had supplied the facts, if not the entire report itself, in Hall's report to the National Committee.

14. Ibid.

15. Bettina Aptheker, *Intimate Politics: How I Grew Up Red, Fought for Free Speech, and Became a Feminist Rebel* [bound galleys] (Emeryville, Calif.: Seal Press, 2006), 183.

16. Hal Draper, "The Russian Invasion of Czechoslovakia," transcript of a KPFA commentary, 22 August 1968, in the author's possession.

17. HA, *Czechoslovakia and Counter-Revolution: Why the Socialist Countries Intervened* (New York: New Outlook, 1969), 5, 6, 7, 8.

18. Healey and Isserman, *California Red*, 229; see also Richmond, *A Long View*, 411, 412.

19. George Wheeler to HA, 7 October 1968, box 29, folder 16, AP.

20. HA to George Wheeler, 14 October 1968, box 29, folder 16, AP.

21. George Wheeler to HA, 9 December 1968, box 29, folder 16, AP.

22. HA, *The Urgency of Marxist–Christian Dialogue* (New York: Harper and Row, 1970).

23. FBI San Francisco, Memorandum, "Participation of Herbert Aptheker in Christian–Marxist Dialogue," University of Santa Clara, Santa Clara, California, October 17–19, 1967, 2 November 1967.

24. Dick Flood, "Marxist–Christian Affinity," *San Jose News*, 19 October 1967, 19.

25. John Dart, "Aptheker Cites Marxist, Christian Similarities," *Los Angeles Times*, 19 October 1967, B-11.

26. Don Cox, "World Relationships Changing," *San Francisco Monitor*, 26 October 1967, 1.

27. Flood, "Marxist–Christian Affinity," 23.

28. Dart, "Aptheker Cites Similarities," B-11.

29. HA, *The Urgency of Marxist–Christian Dialogue*, 139.

30. Bettina Aptheker to HA, 26 May 1970, box 33, folder 4, AP.

31. HA, *The Urgency of Marxist–Christian Dialogue*, 29, 30.

32. Ibid., 139.

33. Ibid., 134.

34. Ibid., 44–45.

35. Roque Dalton, "Catholics and Communists in Latin America," *World Marxist Review*, January 1968, 82–90, quoted in HA, *The Urgency of Marxist–Christian Dialogue*, 173–74.

36. HA to Pete Daniel, 9 June 1970, box 33, folder 12, AP.

37. HA to James Conway, C. S. P., 29 October 1970, box 33, folder 12, AP.

38. HA to Nat Hentoff, 8 March 1971, box 38, folder 3, AP.

39. Donald R. Cutler to HA, 31 December 1970, box 38, folder 2, AP.

40. HA to Donald R. Cutler, 12 January 1971, box 38, folder 2, AP.

41. Helen Winter to HA, 14 September 1970, box 36, folder 6, AP.

42. HA to Helen Winter, 16 September 1970, box 36, folder 6, AP.

43. HA to Gus Hall, 25 February 1970, box 34, folder 8, AP.

44. HA to Gus Hall, 27 February 1970, box 34, folder 8, AP.

45. Richard Greenleaf, "Memorandum to the Political Committee," date uncertain although probably late February 1970, Rubin papers.

46. Ibid.

47. HA to Walter Lowenfels, 21 June 1971, box 37, folder 1, AP.

48. HA to Phil Bronsky, 12 January 1971, box 37, folder 16, AP.

20. Black Power and the Freeing of Angela Davis

1. *New Program of the Communist Party U.S.A.* (New York: Political Affairs Publishers, 1966), 112, 116.

2. Bettina Aptheker, "Red Feminism: A Personal and Historical Reflection," *Science & Society* 66, no. 4 (Winter 2002–3): 521.

3. Dorothy Healey in Jon Wiener, "The Communist Party Today and Yesterday: An Interview with Dorothy Healey," *Radical America,* May–June 1976, 41.

4. Ibid.; Dorothy Healey and Maurice Isserman, *California Red: A Life in the American Communist Party* (1990; reprint, Urbana: University of Illinois Press, 1993), 208.

5. Healey and Isserman, *California Red,* 209.

6. Healey in Wiener, "Interview," 29.

7. Healey and Isserman, *California Red,* 208, 209, 210, 212.

8. FBI informers' report (agents NY T-5 and NY T-13) contained in a periodic update to Aptheker's FBI file, covering most of 1969, December 1969, or early 1970.

9. Healey and Isserman, *California Red,* 212.

10. HA, transcript of an interview conducted in Edmonton, Alberta, 15 January 1968. The transcript was provided by the FBI, but the two interviewers' names are blacked out.

11. HA, report of the Detroit, Michigan, FBI, 29 February 1968 concerning two speeches presented by Aptheker on 10 February 1968 in Detroit, one at the Park Sheraton Hotel in the evening and an afternoon presentation at Wayne State University. Aptheker's remarks appear in a transcript provided by a source to the FBI. The source, one of three present at the event, appears to have transcribed Aptheker's remarks from a tape recording.

12. Angela Davis, *An Autobiography* (New York: International, 1988), 191.

13. Ibid., 198.

14. Healey and Isserman, *California Red,* 208.

15. Comments from FBI informers, December 1969 or early 1970.

16. Davis, *An Autobiography,* 199.

17. Political Committee meeting minutes, 1 September 1970, papers of Danny Rubin.

18. Ibid. Charlene Mitchell reported on planning for the Constitutional Convention called by the Black Panther Party for 5–7 September 1970. She reported that the CP had been "led to believe that there would be [a] truly united front type of organization, but actually what developed was a Black Panther Party front organization." She commented that while the CP and the Panthers agreed on certain issues, "a main question is that the Black Panther Party does not deal with the working class as the basic class in society."

Revising the U.S. Constitution could be democratized at "certain points," she told the committee, "but it is not the Constitution that will make the revolution, but rather the working class." During discussion the party leaders agreed that a fight over the Constitution would be a diversion that arose from "classlessness, from petty bourgeois radicalism. Most of the leadership in Black Panther Party has conscious policy that Black Panther Party will replace the CPUSA. Their red-baiting is based on this. Any concession to this is liquidationism. We cannot allow our Party to be used."

19. Sol Stern, "The Campaign to Free Angela Davis and Ruchell Magee," *New York Times,* 27 June 1971.

20. Bettina Aptheker, *Intimate Politics: How I Grew Up Red, Fought for Free Speech, and Became a Feminist Rebel* [bound galleys] (Emeryville, Calif.: Seal Press, 2006), 59.

21. HA, speech sponsored by the Women's International League for Peace, 5 May 1971, box 37, folder 5, AP.

22. Aptheker, *Intimate Politics,* 212–13.

23. Henry Winston and Gus Hall, "Communists View Tragedy of San Rafael," *Daily World,* 29 August 1970.

24. HA to Gus Hall and Henry Winston, 4 September 1970, box 34, folder 8, AP.

25. HA, "America's Most Wanted Criminal," in Angela Davis, *If They Come in the Morning* (New York: Joseph Okpaku, 1971), 258.

26. Margin notes to carbon copy of HA to Hall and Winston, 4 September, 1970; HA to Henry Winston, 21 June 1971, box 37, folder 12, AP.

27. HA to Henry Winston, 15 June 1971, box 37, folder 12, AP.

28. Ibid.

29. HA to Bettina Aptheker, 13 January 1971, box 37, folder 14, AP.

30. Aptheker, *Intimate Politics,* 213, 214.

31. FBI Compilation Report for 1972.

32. Political Committee meeting minutes, 20 October 1970, Rubin papers.

33. Ibid.

34. HA to Comrade Birch, 8 April 1971, box 36, folder 13, AP.

35. HA to Georg Lukács, 4 December 1970, box 34, folder 18, AP.

36. Georg Lukács to HA, 23 December 1970, box 34, folder 18, AP.

37. HA to Shirley Graham Du Bois, 29 March 1971, box 36, folder 17, AP.

38. Davis, *An Autobiography,* 250.

39. Aptheker, *Intimate Politics,* 214.

40. Davis, *An Autobiography,* 253.

41. Ibid., 251.

42. George Jackson, *Soledad Brother: The Prison Letters of George Jackson* (Chicago: Lawrence Hill, 1994), 16, 26.

43. Ibid., 215, 216.

44. George Jackson to HA, 25 April 1971, box 38, folder 6, AP. Jonathan Jackson, when giving me permission to quote from the letters, requested that the first citation to a letter contain the following statement: "Reproduced with the permission of Jonathan Jackson Jr."

45. George Jackson to HA, 15 April 1971, box 38, folder 6, AP.

46. HA to Bettina Aptheker, 21 April 1971, box 36, folder 12, AP.

47. HA to George Jackson, 21 April 1971, box 38, folder 6, AP.

48. HA, remarks at a National Committee meeting, 14 March 1971, Rubin papers.

49. Gus Hall, "Racism: The Nation's Most Dangerous Pollutant," presented to the National Committee, 14 March 1971, Rubin papers.

50. Jackson to HA, 25 April 1971.

51. George Jackson, *Blood In My Eye* (New York: Bantam, 1972), 9.

52. Jackson to HA, 25 April 1971.

53. HA to George Jackson, 29 April 1971, box 38, folder 6, AP.

54. Jackson, *Blood In My Eye,* 38, 39.

55. George Jackson to HA, 4 May 1971, box 38, folder 6, AP.

56. Ibid.

57. HA to George Jackson, 7 May 1971, box 38, folder 6, AP.

58. Jackson, *Soledad Brother,* 14.

59. Gregory Armstrong, "Preface" to Jackson, *Blood In My Eye,* xv.

60. George Jackson to HA, 11 June 1971, box 38, folder 6, AP.

61. Jackson, *Blood In My Eye,* 88.

62. George Jackson to HA, 22 July 1971, box 38, folder 6, AP.

63. HA to George Jackson, 26 July 1971, box 38, folder 6, AP.

64. Jackson, *Soledad Brother,* 18.

65. Jackson, *Blood in My Eye,* 103, 104.

66. HA to Jackson, 26 July 1971.

67. Joe Allen, "An Interview with His Lawyer, Stephen Bingham: The Murder of George Jackson," *Counterpunch,* 2 March 2006.

21. An Assault on Honor

1. Minutes of Political Committee meeting, 13 May 1971, papers of Danny Rubin.

2. Gus Hall, "Remarks" at Political Committee meeting, 20 September 1971, Rubin papers.

3. Bettina Aptheker, *Intimate Politics: How I Grew Up Red, Fought for Free Speech, and Became a Feminist Rebel* [bound galleys] (Emeryville, Calif.: Seal, 2006), 220.

4. Hall, "Remarks," 20 September 1971.

5. Bettina Aptheker, e-mail to the author, 9 August 2010.

6. FBI report on Herbert Aptheker, 26 July 1972.

7. HA to Helen Winter, 16 September 1970, box 36, folder 6, AP.

8. Minutes of Political Committee Meeting, 13 May 1971.

9. "Guidelines for Party Members on the Writing and Publication of Books and Pamphlets," adopted by the Political Committee, 8 June 1971, box 36, folder 21, AP.

10. HA to Gus Hall and Henry Winston, 25 June 1971, box 36, folder 21, AP.

11. Henry Winston, "Report by Comrade Winston," 20 September 1971, Rubin papers.

12. Ibid.

13. Hall, "Remarks," 20 September 1971.

14. "Motions made on Report by Comr. Winston," 20 September 1971, Rubin papers.

15. Bettina Aptheker, "Notes of Discussion," compiled by Bettina Aptheker, 23 September 1971, Rubin papers.

16. Political Committee meeting minutes, 29 September 1971, Rubin papers.

17. Bettina Aptheker to the author, 9 August 2010.

18. HA to Henry Winston, 9 February 1972, box 41, folder 9, AP.

19. HA, "Notes for Angela—San Rafael, attitude towards," Fall 1971, Rubin papers.

20. Ibid.

21. Northern California Steering Committee, "Legal Strategy," November 1971, Rubin papers.

22. Angela Davis, *An Autobiography* (New York: International, 1988), 328.

23. Minutes of the National Angela Davis Sub-Committee, 13 January 1972, Rubin papers.

24. FBI New York, periodic report on Herbert Aptheker, 26 July 1972. Given later actions, the redacted name could be Henry Winston, although I think that James Jackson or William Patterson is the more likely candidate.

25. "On Legal Strategy," approved by Political Committee, 2 February 1972, box 41, folder 9, AP.

26. Henry Winston to HA, 7 or 8 February 1972, box 41, folder 9, AP.

27. Ibid.

28. William Patterson to members of the Political Committee, date uncertain but probably sometime in February 1972, Rubin papers.

29. HA to Henry Winston, 9 February 1972, box 41, folder 9, AP.

30. Henry Winston to HA, 10 February 1972, box 41, folder 9, AP.

31. HA to Henry Winston, 11 February 1972, box 41, folder 9, AP.

32. Henry Winston, *The Meaning of San Rafael* (New York: New Outlook, 1971), 5, 8, 15, 18.

33. FBI New York, periodic report on Herbert Aptheker, 26 July 1972. Again, it seems likely that the person mentioned is either James Jackson or William Patterson.

34. Aptheker, *Intimate Politics*, 243, 244.

35. Ibid., 245.

22. Party Control

1. Robert Cohen, telephone interview by the author, December 2002.

2. Fay Aptheker and HA in Fischer interview I, 440, 441.

3. Robert Cohen to HA, 18 June 1973, box 43, folder 2, AP.

4. HA to Robert Cohen, 20 June 1973, box 43, folder 2, AP.

5. HA to Lloyd Brown, 25 June 1973, box 42, folder 20, AP.

6. HA to Hy Lumer, 11 May 1973, box 43, folder 16, AP.

7. Ibid.

8. Hy Lumer to HA, 13 June 1973, box 43, folder 16, AP.

9. HA to Hy Lumer, 14 June 1973, box 43, folder 16, AP.

10. Hy Lumer to HA, 9 July 1973, box 43, folder 16, AP.

11. HA to Hy Lumer, 10 July 1973, box 43, folder 16, AP.

12. Fund-raising letter addressed to "All Friends of AIMS," no date, although in the text it refers to AIMS's "ninth year of functioning," which places it in 1973. In the author's possession.

13. Robert Cohen to HA, 14 February 1975, box 47, folder 6, AP.

14. HA to Robert Cohen, 21 February 1975, box 47, folder 6, AP.

15. HA to Bettina Aptheker, 21 March 1974, box 44, folder 10, AP.

16. HA to Bettina Aptheker, 25 March 1974, box 44, folder 10, AP.

17. Ibid.

18. HA to The Editor, *Daily World,* 25 March 1974, box 44, folder 18, AP.

19. Hy Lumer to HA, 12 May 1976, box 51, folder 2, AP.

20. Douglas Martin, "Morris Schappes Dies at 97; Marxist and Jewish Scholar," *New York Times,* 9 June 2004.

21. HA to Hy Lumer, 14 May 1976, box 51, folder 2, AP.

22. Bettina Aptheker, *Intimate Politics: How I Grew Up Red, Fought for Free Speech, and Became a Feminist Rebel* [bound galleys] (Emeryville, Calif.: Seal, 2006), 285.

23. Fischer interview II.

24. Aptheker, *Intimate Politics,* 286.

25. Barry Cohen, interview by the author, New York City, 29 May 2001.

26. Bettina Aptheker to HA, 15 April 1977, box 52, folder 13, AP.

27. HA to Bettina Aptheker, 17 May 1977, box 52, folder 13, AP.

28. HA to Robert Cohen, 30 August 1977, box 54, folder 3, AP.

29. HA to Corliss Lamont, 12 December 1977, box 54, folder 13, AP.

30. HA to Julie Kailin, 21 March 1979, box 57, folder 16, AP.

31. Robert H. Cole to HA, 4 November 1977, box 54, folder 4, AP.

32. HA to Kailin, 21 March 1979, box 57, folder 16, AP.

33. Ken Lawrence to HA, 13 September 1978, box 56, folder 3, AP.

34. HA to Ken Lawrence, 19 September 1978, box 56, folder 3, AP.

35. HA to Si Gerson, 20 April 1979, box 57, folder 11, AP.

36. Aptheker, *Intimate Politics,* 292, 295, 297, 311, 326.

37. Ibid., 329.

38. Ibid., 330.

39. Gus Hall to HA, 15 June 1979, box 59, folder 3, AP.

40. HA to Gus Hall, 25 June 1979, box 59, folder 3, AP.

41. Bettina Aptheker, "Red Feminism: A Personal and Historical Reflection," *Science & Society* 66, no. 4 (Winter 2002–3): 524.

42. Aptheker, *Intimate Politics,* 302, 303.

43. Ibid., 304.

44. Ibid., 303.

45. Ibid., 52–53.

46. Alan Wolfe to HA, 30 December 1979, box 61, folder 14, AP.

47. HA to Alan Wolfe, 3 January 1980, box 61, folder 14, AP.

48. "Resolution of the PB on Making a Turn in Its Work," Unanimously Adopted, 15 January 1980, papers of Danny Rubin.

49. Aptheker, *Intimate Politics,* 339, 340.

50. Ibid., 340, 341.

51. Bettina Aptheker to HA, 21 November 1980, box 60, folder 1, AP.

52. Aptheker, *Intimate Politics,* 348.

53. HA to Lou Diskin, Alva Buxenbaum, and Henry Winston, 6 November 1980, box 60, folder 1, AP.

54. Aptheker, *Intimate Politics,* 354.

55. Ibid., 352, 353.

56. Ibid., 353.

23. Renewal and Endings

1. HA to Sterling Stuckey, 2 November 1977, box 55, folder 2, AP.

2. HA to Si Gerson, 20 April 1979, box 57, folder 11, AP.

3. HA to Eugene Genovese, 10 July 1979, box 59, folder 2, AP.

4. Eugene Genovese to HA, 20 September 1979, box 59, folder 2, AP.

5. Eugene Genovese to HA, 6 October 1979, box 59, folder 2, AP.

6. Eugene Genovese to HA, 14 March 1980, box 60, folder 8, AP.

7. HA to Eugene Genovese, 23 October 1979, box 59, folder 2, AP.

8. Eugene Genovese to HA, 3 November 1979, box 59, folder 2, AP.

9. Eugene Genovese to HA, 28 September 1981, box 62, folder 11, AP.

10. John Bracey to the author, margin notes on an early draft of this chapter, 13 June 2013.

11. Genovese to HA, 3 November 1979, box 59, folder 2, AP.

12. Eugene Genovese to HA, 27 January 1980, box 60, folder 8, AP.

13. HA to Eugene Genovese, 24 February 1980, box 60, folder 8, AP.

14. Genovese to HA, 14 March 1980, box 60, folder 8, AP.

15. HA to Eugene Genovese, 8 April 1980, box 60, folder 8, AP.

16. HA to Robert Cohen, 27 February 1981, box 62, folder 4, AP.

17. HA to Eugene Genovese, 24 February 1981, box 62, folder 11, AP.

18. Eugene Genovese to HA, Sterling Stuckey, Joshua Leslie, John Hope Franklin, and Richard Kirkendall, 27 February 1981, box 62, folder 11, AP.

19. HA to Eugene Genovese, 8 March 1981, and Eugene Genovese to HA, 16 March 1981, box 62, folder 11, AP.

20. HA to Eugene Genovese, 19 March 1981, box 62, folder 11, AP.

21. Eugene Genovese to HA, 28 September 1981, box 62, folder 11, AP.

22. HA to Eugene Genovese, undated [probably sometime during October 1981], box 62, folder 11, AP.

23. Gary Okihiro, ed., *In Resistance: Studies in African, Caribbean, and Afro-American History* (Amherst: University of Massachusetts Press, 1986).

24. HA, "Memo to self," 10 May 1982, box 65, folder 1, AP.

25. HA to Staughton Lynd, 28 July 1983, box 66, folder 6, AP.

26. HA to Professor James W. Felt, S. J., 19 October 1983, box 65, folder 14, AP.

27. Herbert Shapiro, ed., *African American History and Radical Historiography: Essays in Honor of Herbert Aptheker* (Minneapolis: MEP, 1998).

28. Ibid., xi.

29. Robert Cohen to HA, 23 September 1982, box 64, folder 6, AP.

30. HA to Danny Rubin, 24 November 1982, papers of Danny Rubin.

31. HA to Henry Winston, 10 January 1983, Rubin papers.

32. Lillian Gicherman to HA, 23 and 30 November 1983, Rubin papers.

33. Henry Winston to HA, 1 December 1983, box 66, folder 15, AP.

34. HA to Henry Winston, 6 December 1983, box 66, folder 15, AP.

35. Geoffrey Jacques, "Tribute to Herbert Aptheker in N.Y.," *Daily World,* photocopy with no date, Rubin papers.

36. HA to Danny Rubin, 29 February 1984, box 67, folder 5, AP.

37. Jacques, "Tribute to Herbert Aptheker in N.Y."

38. David Twersky, "A New Kind of Democrat," *Commentary* 95, no. 2 (February 1993): 51, 52.

39. A. M. Rosenthal, "On My Mind; The Special Interests," *New York Times,* 15 December 1992.

40. Robert Cohen to HA, 4 April 1984, box 67, folder 2, AP.

41. HA to Robert Cohen, 10 April 1984, box 67, folder 2, AP.

42. Robert Cohen to HA, 17 January 1986, box 69, folder 20, AP.

43. HA, ed., "AIMS Newsletter" 22, no. 6 (November–December 1985), in the author's possession.

44. HA to Danny Rubin, 13 November 1985, Rubin papers.

45. David Laibman to HA, 26 March 1986, box 70, folder 6, AP.

46. Ibid.

47. Ibid.

48. HA to Danny Rubin, 10 April 1986, Rubin papers.

49. Danny Rubin to HA, 21 April 1986, box 70, folder 10, AP.

50. HA to Danny Rubin, 25 April 1986, Rubin papers.

51. Erwin Marquit to HA, 11 May 1986, box 69, folder 7, AP.

52. John Bracey to Editors and Jim Green, *Radical History Review,* 9 February 1987, box 70, folder 20, AP.

53. Eugene Genovese to HA, 15 December 1986, box 69, folder 4, AP.

54. HA to David Du Bois, 5 May 1986, box 69, folder 21, AP.

55. Arthur P. Dudden to HA, 6 October 1986, box 69, folder 21, AP.

56. David Du Bois to Paul L. Kranz, 2 October 1986, "Remarks at the Kraus International/U. Mass Press affair for Dr. Herbert Aptheker," box 69, folder 21, AP.

57. David McReynolds, "Democracy Currents Challenge Communist Party U.S.A.," *Socialist,* January–February, 1992.

24. Rebellion in a Haunted House

1. HA to Rona Mendelsohn, 23 June 1980, box 61, folder 1, AP. Mendelsohn had written to Aptheker with a list of questions concerning a book *U.S. News & World Report Books* was planning, a "comprehensive study of our involvement in Vietnam." Mendelsohn

phoned Aptheker, then wrote to him stating her questions. "I'm certain," she began, "this is the first time an organization such as *U.S. News* has asked for your opinion on world affairs." Rona Mendelsohn to HA, 20 June 1980, box 61, folder 1, AP.

2. Danny Rubin to the author, 6 November 2001.

3. HA to Si Gerson, 20 April 1979, box 57, folder 11, AP. On Genovese, see Peter Novick, *That Noble Dream: The 'Objectivity Question' and the American Historical Profession* (New York: Cambridge University Press, 1988), 412.

4. HA to Gus Hall, 25 June 1979, papers of Danny Rubin.

5. Bettina Aptheker, "Red Feminism: A Personal and Historical Recollection," *Science & Society* 66, no. 4 (Winter 2002–3): 521, 522, 523.

6. Ibid., 521; "Resolution of the PB on Making a Turn in Its Work," 15 January 1980, Rubin papers.

7. Michael Myerson, "On the Crisis in the Party," June 1990, 5, 6, Rubin papers.

8. HA to Gus Hall, 17 November 1981, box 63, folder 21, AP.

9. Charlene Mitchell, interview by the author, New York City, 22 May 2001.

10. Ibid.

11. Danny Rubin, interview by the author, Brooklyn, New York, 2 July 2002.

12. Myerson, "On the Crisis," 8.

13. Ibid.

14. Rubin, interview by author.

15. Myerson, "On the Crisis," 10.

16. Gil Green, "Interview with Gil Green," by Anders Stephanson, in *New Studies in the Politics and Culture of U.S. Communism,* ed. Michael E. Brown, Randy Martin, Frank Rosengarten, and George Snedeker (New York: Monthly Review Press, 1993), 32; Barry Cohen, interview by the author, New York City, 29 May 2001.

17. Mitchell, interview by author.

18. Ibid.

19. Rubin, interview by author.

20. Harvey Klehr, John Earl Haynes, and Kyrill M. Anderson, *The Soviet World of American Communism* (New Haven: Yale University Press, 1998), 147–59.

21. Myerson, "On the Crisis," 11.

22. HA, in Jack Fischer, "Why Communism Isn't Dead: A Marxist Scholar Assesses the Dramatic Changes Taking Place in the East and Offers His Views on What Shape Communism Will Take in the Future," an interview with HA, *San Jose Mercury News,* 17 January 1990.

23. Amy Knight, "The Mysterious End of the Soviet Union," *New York Review of Books,* 5 April 2012, 74.

24. David McReynolds, "Democracy Currents Challenge Communist Party U.S.A. Hardliners," *Socialist,* January–February 1992.

25. HA in Fischer, "Why Communism Isn't Dead."

26. HA, "To Make the World Anew: Gorbachev's UN Address," *Jewish Affairs,* January/February 1989, 4.

27. Ibid.

28. HA, "On The 70th Anniversary of the Communist Party, U.S.A.," *Jewish Affairs,* November/December 1989, 6.

29. Ibid.

30. Myerson, "On the Crisis," 1.

31. Ibid.

32. Ibid.

33. Michael Myerson, transcribed notes of remarks made at the National Committee–National Council meeting, 4–5 August 1990, Rubin papers.

34. Erwin Marquit, "Organizational Crisis of Marxism-Leninism in the USA," 2 October 1992, posted at pnnews@igc.apc.org, 2. In the author's possession.

35. Sandy Patrinos, report of the January 1991 meeting of the National Committee, Rubin papers.

36. Carl Bloice, in Max Elbaum, "The Convention Was a Quasi-Purge," *Guardian,* 8 December 1991.

37. McReynolds, "Democracy Currents."

38. HA to CP headquarters, 26 August 1991, box 119, folder 50, AP.

39. McReynolds, "Democracy Currents."

40. Marquit, "Organizational Crisis," 6.

41. Bloice in Elbaum, "The Convention Was a Quasi-Purge."

42. Kendra Alexander, Charlene Mitchell, Daniel Rubin, Carl Bloice et al., "An Initiative to Unite and Renew the Party," accompanying a letter addressed to "Dear Comrades," 21 October 1991. In the author's possession.

43. Resolution of the National Committee, CPUSA, 16, 17 November 1991, Committees of Correspondence Papers, Tamiment Library, New York University.

44. Marquit, "Organizational Crisis," 7.

45. Jay Schaffner to Mom and Dad, 22 December 1991, http://garnet.berkeley.edu (no longer available).

46. McReynolds, "Democracy Currents."

47. Margy Wilkerson, "Margy Wilkerson's Very Personal Account of the 25th Convention of the Communist Party, USA," http://garnet.berkeley.edu (no longer available).

48. Ibid.

49. Gus Hall, "Forge Unity Through Struggle," report to the 25th National Convention of the Communist Party, USA, Cleveland, Ohio, December 5–8, 1991, 45, in the author's possession.

50. Wilkerson, "Margy Wilderson's Personal Account"; Bettina Aptheker, *Intimate Politics: How I Grew Up Red, Fought for Free Speech, and Became a Feminist Rebel* [bound galleys] (Emeryville, Calif.: Seal, 2006), 427.

51. Aptheker, *Intimate Politics,* 427.

52. Wilkerson, "Margy Wilkerson's Personal Account."

53. HA, "Aptheker's Comments to the Extraordinary Membership Meeting, Northern California Communist Party, February 9, 1992," http://garnet.berkeley.edu (no longer available).

54. McCarthy interview, 32.

55. Max Elbaum, "Upheaval in the CPUSA: Death and Rebirth," *Crossroads,* January 1992, 17, 10.

56. Jack Kurzweil, quoted in ibid., 10.

57. HA, "Comments at XXV convention," in the author's possession.

58. Ibid.

59. Murrell interview.

60. Ibid.

61. With the collapse of the Soviet Union, as noted previously, the contents of secret KGB files came pouring out. Among the revelations which surfaced were proof that the Soviet Union had always had a hand in the direction of CPUSA policy and had provided tens of millions of dollars to finance CPUSA operations. These connections were known only to a few of the top leaders of the party, among whom Aptheker was not one. In this regard, see Klehr, Haynes, Anderson, *The Soviet World of American Communism* and Christopher Andrew and Vasili Mitrokhin, *The Sword and the Shield* (New York: Basic Books, 1999).

62. Murrell interview.

63. HA, "Comments at XXV convention."

64. CP National Committee to "Dear Comrades," "An appeal to stand for the unity of our Party to the signers of the 'Initiative,'" November 1991, in the author's possession.

65. HA, "Comments by Dr. Aptheker in Room 211 at the Close of Discussion," in Elbaum, "Upheaval in the CPUSA," 12.

25. Comrades of a Different Sort

1. HA, "Remarks, S. F.," 14 December 1991, box 119, folder 37, AP.

2. CPUSA memo, "The 25th National Convention Made History," in the author's possession.

3. Carl Bloice, "A Critical Movement, A Crucial Convention," *People's Weekly World,* Special Supplement, 21 December 1991, 9.

4. Max Elbaum, "Upheaval in the CPUSA: Death and Rebirth?" *Crossroads,* January 1992, 5; Max Elbaum, "De-Stalinizing the Old Guard," *Nation,* 10 February 1992, 158–62.

5. HA, "Remarks, S.F."

6. Charlene Mitchell, interview by the author, New York City, 22 May 2001.

7. "The Spirit of Room 211," resolutions originating in the Northern California District, *Crossroads,* January 1992, 19.

8. Charlene Mitchell, interview by Max Elbaum, in Max Elbaum, "Eleven delegates talk about their personal experiences, the crisis in the CPUSA and where the Committees of Correspondence may go from here," *Crossroads,* January 1991, 12; Angela Davis, quoted in Erwin Marquit, "Organizational Crisis of Marxism–Leninism in the USA," 3 October 1992, in the author's possession.

9. Angela Davis to "Dear Comrades," 5 December 1991, Committees of Correspondence Papers, Tamiment Library, New York University.

10. David McReynolds, "Democracy Currents Challenge Communist Party U.S.A.," *The Socialist,* January-February 1992.

11. Arnold Beichman, "Comrade Pooh-bah Charges It," *Washington Times,* 6 March 1992, F3.

12. Jack Zylman to The Editor, *People's Weekly World,* 4 February 1992, in the author's possession.

13. HA to National Board CPUSA, 16 January 1992, box 77, folder 19, AP.

14. James West to HA, 23 January 1992; HA to James West, 30 January 1992, box 78, folder 5, AP.

15. HA and Alfred J. Kutzik to Dear *Jewish Affairs* Readers, 18 March 1992, in the author's possession.

16. Committees of Correspondence, Press Release, 23 December 1991, in the author's possession.

17. HA to [unintelligible], 22 January 1992, box 78, folder 6, AP.

18. Aaron Cohen and nine others to All Members Northern California CPUSA, 3 February 1992, box 77, folder 14, AP.

19. HA, "Remarks by Herbert Aptheker Extraordinary membership meeting Communist Party of Northern California," 9 February 1992, in the author's possession.

20. Kendra Alexander, Press Release, 13 February 1992, in the author's possession.

21. Barry Cohen to "All and sundry," 9 March 1992, in the author's possession.

22. HA, "W. E. B. Du Bois His Life & Work," speech at Harvard University, 25 February 1992. Original handwritten draft of the speech, in the author's possession.

23. HA, *Anti-Racism in U.S. History: The First Two Hundred Years* (Westport, Conn.: Praeger, 1993), xiii.

24. Gary Murrell. The remark came during discussion in a class I teach at the Stafford Creek Corrections Center in Aberdeen, Washington, and represented a sentiment widespread in class, which was composed entirely of African Americans.

25. Mark Solomon, "Racism and Anti-Racism in U.S. History," *Science & Society* 57, no. 1 (Spring 1993): 74.

26. Herbert Shapiro, review of *Anti-Racism in U.S. History,* in *Journal of American History* 79, no. 4 (March 1993): 1575.

27. Staughton Lynd, "Tear sheet" review of *Anti-Racism in U.S. History, William and Mary Quarterly* (July 1993): 631–34; HA, *Anti-Racism in U.S. History,* xiv.

28. Winthrop D. Jordan, review of *Anti-Racism in U.S. History,* in *American Historical Review,* February 1993, 226; Shapiro, "review," 1575.

29. Solomon, "review," 78.

30. John Hope Franklin, quoted in Jack Fischer, "One Man Who Changed History: Scholar and Lifelong Leftist Hailed for Contributions to Black Studies," *San Jose Mercury News,* 20 February 1994, A-1.

31. Bill Cosby, quoted ibid.

32. Bettina Aptheker, *Intimate Politics: How I Grew Up Red, Fought for Free Speech, and Became a Feminist Rebel* [bound galleys] (Emeryville, Calif.: Seal, 2006), 427.

33. Ibid., 427.

34. Ibid., 442.

35. HA, "Stroke Notebook," 2 May 1992, copy in the author's possession.

36. Bruce Wilcox to HA, 11 October 1995, box 80, folder 19, AP. Aptheker's autobiographical manuscript ends, oddly, in the 1960s.

37. Bruce Wilcox to HA, 23 January 1996, box 80, folder 8, AP.

38. "Reader A," enclosed with Wilcox to HA, 23 January 1996.

39. HA to Bruce Wilcox, handwritten response on the Wilcox letter of 23 January 1996.

40. Bruce Wilcox to HA, 5 February 1996, box 80, folder 8, AP.

41. Ernest Allen Jr., "Reader B," to Bruce Wilcox, 2 February 1996, box 80, folder 8, AP.

42. Ibid.

43. Ernest Allen Jr., to HA, 17 April 1996, box 80, folder 29, AP.

44. Ernest Allen Jr., e-mail to the author, 25 June 2014.

45. HA, "A Few Battles Against Racism," *Black Scholar* 26, no. 2 (Summer 1996): 2–9; HA, "An Autobiographical Note," *Journal of American History* 87, no. 1 (June 2000): 147–50.

46. Bruce Wilcox to HA, 7 August 1996, box 80, folder 8, AP.

47. Victor Perlo, "A Reply to Herbert Aptheker," *Political Affairs,* June/July 1992, 27.

48. Aptheker's handwritten margin comments that probably were typed by an assistant as a response to Clarence Kailin to HA, 1 August 1992, box 77, folder 20, AP.

49. Barry Cohen, interview by the author, New York City, 29 May 2001.

50. Danny Rubin to HA, 3 November 1993, box 78, folder 22, AP; Danny Rubin to HA, 19 November 1994, papers of Danny Rubin.

51. Cohen, interview by author.

52. Rubin to HA, 3 November 1993.

53. Alva Buxenbaum, Lou Diskin, Sig Eisenscher, Mollie Gold to Dear Friend, January 1995, box 80, folder 23, AP.

54. Rubin to HA, 3 November 1993.

55. Press Release, Ad Hoc Committee against Naming Names, 10 May 1993, in the author's possession.

56. Lloyd Brown to HA, 23 December 1994, box 79, folder 4, AP.

57. Gus Hall, quoted in Buxenbaum et al., January 1995.

58. Gus Hall, "The Du Bois Legacy vs. the Cesspool of Anti-communism," *People's Weekly World,* 30 March 1996, 17.

59. HA to *People's Weekly World,* 11 April, 1996, box 81, folder 3, AP.

60. Danny Rubin to HA, 23 November 1996, box 81, folder 11, AP.

61. Leon Quat [attorney for Daniel Rubin] to Communist Party USA, 14 November 1996, Rubin papers.

62. Statement issued by the CPUSA, *People's Weekly World,* 2 November 1996, 4.

63. Sam Tanenhaus, "Gus Hall, Unreconstructed American Communist of 7 Decades, Dies at 90," *New York Times,* 17 October 2000.

26. Now It's Your Turn

1. HA, *Anti-Racism in U.S. History* (Westport, Conn.: Praeger, 1993), ix.

2. Bettina Aptheker, *Intimate Politics: How I Grew Up Red, Fought for Free Speech, and Became a Feminist Rebel* [bound galleys] (Emeryville, Calif.: Seal, 2006), 440.

3. "Unrepentent Rebel," 69.

4. Eugene Genovese to HA, 20 June 1983, box 65, folder 15, AP.

5. Aptheker, *Intimate Politics,* 439.

6. Tracey Kaplan, "Meals on Wheels Alters Course Plan to Offer Frozen Food, Not Hot Lunches, Gets Chilly Reception," *San Jose Mercury News,* 16 January 1998, 1A.

7. Aptheker, *Intimate Politics,* 439.

8. Ibid., 443.

9. Ibid., 445.

10. Ibid., 447, 448.

11. HA to Doris and Erwin Marquit, 31 May 1997, box 82, folder 9, AP.

12. Doris Marquit to HA, 17 July 1997, box 82, folder 9, AP.

13. Aptheker, *Intimate Politics,* 461.

14. Mindy Leigh Griser, "Aptheker Speaks to Students about Eradicating Racism," *Spartan Daily,* September 1999, San Jose State University.

15. John Hope Franklin to HA, 23 December 1999, in the author's possession.

16. Manning Marable to Aldo Billingsley, no date, in the author's possession; Sterling Stuckey, "In tribute to Herbert Aptheker," 4 February 2000, in the author's possession.

17. Eric Foner to Aldo Billingslea, no date, in the author's possession.

18. HA, Letters, *Journal of American History* 87, no. 3 (December 2000).

19. Erwin Marquit to HA, 22 August 2000, in the author's possession.

20. Danny Rubin to HA, 2 September 2001, papers of Danny Rubin.

21. HA to Danny Rubin, 11 September 2001, Rubin papers.

22. HA to Danny Rubin, 31 July 2002, Rubin papers.

23. Aptheker, *Intimate Politics,* 461, 62.

24. Danny Rubin to the author, 24 September 2002.

25. Sam Webb, Jarvis Tyner, Elena Mora to HA, copied in Jarvis Tyner, e-mail to the author, 17 December 2003.

26. Jarvis Tyner, in a speech at Aptheker's memorial in New York City on 16 October 2003. Jarvis Tyner, e-mail to the author, 11 December 2003.

27. Aptheker, *Intimate Politics,* 462.

28. Gloria L. Young to Bettina Aptheker, 2 April 2003, in the author's possession.

29. Pete Seeger to Bettina Aptheker, 25 March 2003, in the author's possession.

30. John Hope Franklin to Bettina Aptheker, 20 March 2003, and John Hope Franklin, "Remembering Herbert and Fay Aptheker," no date, in the author's possession.

31. Arthur Power Dudden to Bettina Aptheker, 20 March 2003, in the author's possession.

32. Ben Jealous, e-mail to Bettina Aptheker, 29 March 2003, copy in the author's possession.

33. Herbert and Judith Shapiro, e-mail to Bettina Aptheker, 26 March 2003, copy in the author's possession.

34. Christopher Phelps, "The Author Replies," *Chronicle of Higher Education,* 11 October 2006, B-18.

35. Mark Solomon to Bettina Aptheker, 22 March 2003, in the author's possession.

Index

Belknap, Michal, 71, 78, 99, 101
Berger, John, 157
Bernal, John, 157
Bernstein, Anna J., 300
"Beyond Vietnam," 182
Big-Business historians, 87
Bilbo, Theodore, 13; and sending black people
  back to Africa, 13
Billingslea, Aldo, 350
Billingsley, William J., 184–88
Bingham, Stephen, 283
Bittleman, Alexander, 71, 127
Black, Hugo, 81
Black Belt theory, 117–19
black bourgeoisie, 118
black Communists, 271–72
The Black Family in Slavery and Freedom,
  1750–1925, 54
Black Folk Then and Now, 23
Black Liberation Commission of the CPUSA,
  and Black Panther Party, 272
black liberation movement, 55, 92, 153, 272–72,
  288, 295, 325
blacklisting, 227
Black Nationalism, 56, 253–56, 287
Black Panther Party, 271, 280, 284, 288, 326; and
  COINTELPRO, 155
black power, 254; CPUSA hostility toward, 271
Black Reconstruction, 52
black revolutionaries, 272–73
black scholars, and reviews of *American Negro
  Slave Revolts,* 50
black soldiers in World War II: and Double V
  campaign, 28; and integrated officer candidate
  schools, 28; and integration in front-line units,
  34–35; and Jim Crow policies, 27–28; and
  lack of discrimination, 27; and Lee Street riot,
  29–30; and segregated training camps, 29–30
Black Student Alliance, Yale University, 228
black student radicals, 91; disappointment with
  Aptheker, 211–12
black students, 211–12, 272; demand colleges hire
  Aptheker, 60, 212
black–white unity, 44, 49, 125, 340
black women, and special oppression of, 23–25
black women's history, and CPUSA, 115–16
Blaine, Anita McCormick, 74
Blanchard, Louise, 189
Blassingame, John, 54; and demand that Aptheker
  release the papers of Du Bois, 207; and rumor
  that Aptheker destroyed and censored the
  papers of Du Bois, 224; and Yale–Aptheker
  affair, 227–28, 232–33, 237, 239, 244

Blecker, Robert A., 228
Bloice, Carl, 329–30, 335, 337
Blood in My Eye, 278, 280–83, 284
Bloor, Ella Reeve (Mother), 24
blue-hair Reds, 84
Blue Heron Press, 76
Blum, John M.: and Aptheker's NEH grant
  application, 217; and C. Vann Woodward's
  political motivations, 233–34; and Yale–
  Aptheker affair, 227–28, 233, 237, 239, 244
Boalt Hall Law School, 304
Boas, Franz, 23
Boccardi, Louis, D., 215
Bolshevik Revolution, 1
Bontemps, Arna, 200–201, 204
Boorstin, Daniel, 106
Borough Park, Brooklyn, 3–4
Borst, Frederick, 252
Boston Traveler, 179
Boston University, 189
bourgeois democracy, 103
bourgeois historians, 90
bourgeois history, 116
bourgeois ideology, 86
bourgeoisie, 82, 84, 86, 107
bourgeois intellectual, 83
bourgeois property, 103
bourgeois reporters, 120
bourgeois writers, 121
Bowser, Benjamin, 179, 257
Bracey, John, xiv, 55–56, 202–3, 234, 312, 315; and
  Aptheker's legacy, 225–26; and Aptheker's
  appointment at University of Massachusetts,
  225–26; and red-baiting of Aptheker at the
  NEH, 223–24; and William Appleman
  Williams, 152; and C. Vann Woodward, 243
Bracker, Milton, 105
Braithwaite, William S., 222
Brand, Millen, 113
Brandeis University, 190, 214
Branton, Leo, 290
Breakthrough (right-wing organization), and
  picket of Aptheker at Wayne State University,
  183
Brewster, Kingman, 228; and firing of Staughton
  Lynd, 180
Bricker, John W., and speaker ban at Ohio State
  University, 162–64
Bricker Amendment, 162
British imperialism, 18
Brodsky, Joseph, 233–34
Brody, David, 241
Bronsky, Phil, 270